The Hymnal 1982

Contents

Indexes

Preface

In the past several decades, the renewal of the spiritual life of the Church has created a pressing need for new hymnody and liturgical music. This has served as a catalyst for a world-wide outburst of creative liturgical and musical activity of a magnitude perhaps unparalleled since the Reformation. *The Hymnal 1982*, the culmination of more than a decade of work by the Standing Commission on Church Music, incorporates many of the riches of this contemporary renaissance. This hymnal is a response to the challenge of the Church's mission to spread the Good News of Jesus Christ to a changed and changing world.

The Hymnal 1982 is a revision of *The Hymnal 1940*, and as such stands on the foundation laid by The Joint Commission on Revision of the Hymnal. The precepts guiding that commission led to a comprehensive book of unusual appeal and excellence which served as a model for a number of hymnals produced since the middle of the twentieth century.

As an initial step in its revision process, the Standing Commission on Church Music developed a philosophical statement expressing the Commission's commitment to maintain and enhance the rich repertoire which constitutes the singing tradition of the people of God. This commitment led to the development of the following objectives:
- to prepare a body of texts which presents the Christian faith with clarity and integrity;
- to restore music which has lost some of its melodic, rhythmic, or harmonic vitality through prior revision;
- to reflect the nature of today's Church by including the works of contemporary artists and works representing many cultures;
- to strengthen ecumenical relationships through the inclusion of texts and tunes used by other Christian traditions;
- to create a hymnal embodying both practicality and esthetic excellence.

The Hymnal 1982 retains the best of the past and sets forth many riches of our own time. The Commission looked for theological orthodoxy, poetic beauty, and integrity of meaning. At the same time the Commission was especially concerned that the hymnody affirm "the participation of all in the Body of Christ the Church, while recognizing our diverse natures as children of God." This work has resulted in the sensitive alteration of texts which "could be interpreted as either pejorative or discriminatory," while preserving the artistic quality and intent of the originals. Language deemed "obscure or so changed in the contemporary usage as to have a different meaning"* has been clarified. Texts and music which reflect the pluralistic nature of the Church have been included, affording the use of Native American, Afro-American, Hispanic, and Asian material. Study and research into historic hymnody have led to the inclusion of chant tunes in rhythmic forms, of early settings of chorales and Psalter tunes, and of tunes whose roots lie deep in the treasury of American folk hymnody.

Often, consistency of style and practice seemed a less important goal than a representation of the wonderful variety of materials that are available. The recent renaissance of hymn-writing imparts rich benefits to *The Hymnal 1982*. The Commission drew many new hymns from the wealth of available material and commissioned authors and composers to write hymns on themes for which nothing suitable could be found. Here we must record gratitude for the work of the late F. Bland Tucker, a poet and priest whose wisdom and skills enhanced the work of the commissions which produced both this book and *The Hymnal 1940*.

In designing *The Hymnal 1982*, the Commission sought to create a book which is comprehensive and musically practical. Most tunes which are used more than once appear in different keys or harmonizations. Further variety in the performance of hymns is facilitated by descants and alternative accompaniments. The use of instruments in addition to the organ is encouraged through the inclusion, where appropriate, of guitar chords and bell and percussion parts. Details on notation and performance appear in the general performance notes in the Accompaniment Edition and with some individual hymns.

The Commission gave serious thought to the evaluation of texts for theological and literary merit by consultants representing congregations across the country before reaching final decisions on the contents of the book. In addition, the testing of new tunes in liturgical settings over an extended period of time determined their appropriateness for congregational singing.

The Commission gratefully acknowledges the contributions of Carl P. Daw, Jr., Georgia M. Joyner, Marilyn J. Keiser, Anne K. Le Croy, J. Waring McCrady, James McGregor, Bruce Neswick, Charles P. Price, McNeil Robinson II, F. Bland Tucker†, and John E. Williams, Jr.

The Hymnal 1982 is truly a book of and for the people, reflecting their involvement in its creation and responding to their desire for new songs with which to praise God. May God prosper this handiwork!

Geoffrey Butcher	Marion J. Hatchett
Charles J. Child, Jr.	David J. Hurd, Jr.
Robert H. Cochrane	Roy F. Kehl
Elizabeth Morris Downie	James H. Litton
Carol Morey Foster	Richard T. Proulx
Raymond F. Glover	Arthur Rhea
Jerry D. Godwin	Walter C. Righter
Eric S. Greenwood	Russell Schulz-Widmar
William M. Hale	Frederic P. Williams
	Alec Wyton

* Report of the Standing Commission on Church Music to the 1982 General Convention of the Episcopal Church.

† Deceased

Service Music

The Daily Office

Daily Morning Prayer I
Preces

S 1

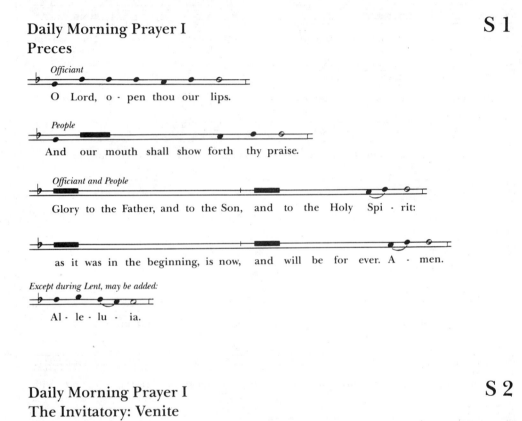

Officiant

O Lord, o - pen thou our lips.

People

And our mouth shall show forth thy praise.

Officiant and People

Glory to the Father, and to the Son, and to the Holy Spi - rit:

as it was in the beginning, is now, and will be for ever. A - men.

Except during Lent, may be added:

Al - le - lu - ia.

Daily Morning Prayer I
The Invitatory: Venite

S 2

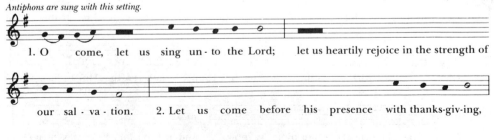

Antiphons are sung with this setting.

1. O come, let us sing un - to the Lord; let us heartily rejoice in the strength of

our sal - va - tion. 2. Let us come before his presence with thanks-giv-ing,

and show ourselves glad in him with psalms. [Ant.] 3. For the Lord is a great God,

and a great King a-bove all gods. 4. In his hand are all the cor-ners

of the earth, and the strength of the hills is his al-so. 5. The sea is

his and he made it, and his hands pre-pared the dry land. [Ant.] 6. O come,

let us wor-ship and fall down and kneel before the Lord our Ma-ker.

7. For he is the Lord our God, and we are the people of his pasture

and the sheep of his hand. [Ant.] 8. O wor-ship the Lord in the

beau-ty of ho-li-ness; let the whole earth stand in awe of him.

9. For he cometh, for he com-eth to judge the earth, and with

righteousness to judge the world and the peo-ples with his truth. [Ant.]

(Gloria Patri may be added)

Glo-ry to the Fa-ther, and to the Son, and to the Ho-ly Spi-rit:

As it was in the be-gin-ning, is now, and will be for ev-er. A-men. [Ant.]

Setting: Plainsong, Tone 7; adapt. **Bruce E. Ford (b. 1947)**

Daily Morning Prayer I
The Invitatory: Venite

An antiphon may be sung before and after this setting.

1. O come, let us sing unto the Lord; let us heartily rejoice in the strength of our sal - va - tion.

2. Let us come before his presence with thanks - giv - ing, and show ourselves glad in him with psalms.

3. For the Lord is a great God, and a great King a - bove all gods.

4. In his hand are all the corners of the earth, and the strength of the hills is his al - so.

5. The sea is his and he made it, and his hands prepared the dry land.

6. O come, let us worship and fall down and kneel before the Lord our Ma - ker.

7. For he is the Lord our God, and we are the people of his pasture and the sheep of his hand.

8. O worship the Lord in the beauty of ho - li - ness; let the whole earth stand in awe of him.

9. For he cometh, for he cometh to judge the earth, and with righteousness to judge the world and the peo - ples with his truth.

(Gloria Patri may be added)

Glory to the Father, and to the Son, and to the Ho - ly Spi - rit: As it was in the beginning, is now, and will be for ev - er. A - men.

Setting: Plainsong, Tone 2; adapt. The Standing Commission on Church Music, 1979, alt.

The Invitatory: Venite

S 4 — Edwin George Monk (1819-1900)

S 5 — John Naylor (1838-1897)

S 6 — C. Teesdale (1782-1855)

S 7 — Thomas Attwood Walmisley (1814-1856)

Antiphons may be sung with these chants.

1 O come, let us ⌐sing unto the⌐ Lord; *

   let us heartily rejoice in the ⌐strength of⌐ our sal⌐vation.

2 Let us come before his ⌐presence with thanks⌐giving, *

   and show ourselves ⌐glad in ⌐him with ⌐psalms.   [Ant.]

3   For the Lord is a ' great ' God, *
      and a great ' King a ' bove all ' gods.

4   In his hand are all the ' corners of the ' earth, *
      and the strength of the ' hills is ' his ' also.

†5   The sea is ' his and he ' made it, *
      and his hands pre ' pared the ' dry ' land. [Ant.]

6   O come, let us worship and ' fall ' down *
      and ' kneel before the ' Lord our ' Maker.

7   For he is the ' Lord our ' God, *
      and we are the people of his ' pasture
      and the ' sheep of his ' hand. [Ant.]

8   O worship the Lord in the ' beauty of ' holiness; *
      let the ' whole earth ' stand in ' awe of him.

9   For he cometh, for he cometh to ' judge the ' earth, *
      and with righteousness to judge the world
      and the ' peoples ' with his ' truth. [Ant.]

(Gloria Patri may be added)
    Glory to the Father, and ' to the ' Son, *
      and ' to the ' Holy ' Spirit:
    As it was in the be ' ginning, is ' now, *
      and ' will be for ' ever. A ' men. [Ant.]

†*Second half of double chant.*

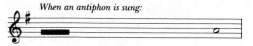

When an antiphon is sung:

When no antiphon is sung:

1. O come, let us sing unto the Lord;

1. O come, let us sing unto the Lord;

let us heartily rejoice in the strength of our sal-va-tion.   2. Let us come before his

presence with thanks-giv-ing,   and show ourselves glad in him with psalms.[Ant.]

3. For the Lord is a great God,   and   a   great   King a-bove all gods.

4. In his hand are all the corners of the earth,   and the strength of the hills is

his al-so.   5.   The sea is his and he made it,   and   his   hands   prepared

the dry land. [Ant.] 6. O come, let us worship and fall down   and kneel before the

The Invitatory: Psalm 95

S 9

George S. Talbot
(1875-1918)

S 10

Maurice Green
(1695-1755)

Antiphons may be sung with these chants.

1   O come, let us ⌐sing unto the⌐Lord; *

     let us heartily rejoice in the⌐strength of⌐our sal⌐vation.

2   Let us come before his⌐presence with thanks⌐giving, *

     and show ourselves⌐glad in⌐him with⌐psalms. [Ant.]

3   For the Lord is a⌐great⌐God, *

     and a great⌐King a⌐bove all⌐gods.

4   In his hand are all the⌐corners of the⌐earth, *

     and the strength of the⌐hills is⌐his⌐also.

†5   The sea is⌐his and he⌐made it, *

     and his hands pre⌐pared the⌐dry⌐land. [Ant.]

6   O come, let us worship and⌐fall⌐down *

     and⌐kneel before the⌐Lord our⌐Maker.

7   For he is the⌐Lord our⌐God, *

     and we are the people of his⌐pasture

     and the⌐sheep of his⌐hand. [Ant.]

†*Second half of double chant.*

Lord our Ma-ker. 7. For he is the Lord our God, and we are the people

of his pasture and the sheep of his hand. [Ant.] 8. Today if ye will hear

his voice, harden not your hearts as in the provocation, and as in the day

of temptation in the wil-der-ness; 9. When your fathers tempt-ed me, proved me,

and saw my works. 10. Forty years long was I grieved with this generation, and said,

It is a people that do err in their hearts, for they have not known my ways;

11. Unto whom I sware in my wrath, that they should not enter in - to my rest. [Ant.]

(Gloria Patri may be added)

Glory to the Father, and to the Son, and to the Ho - ly Spi - rit:

As it was in the beginning, is now, and will be for ev - er. A-men. [Ant.]

Setting: Plainsong, Tone 2; adapt. The Standing Commission on Church Music, 1979, alt.

8   Today if ye will hear his voice,ˌharden not yourˌhearts *
        as in the provocation,
        and as in theˌday of tempˌtation in theˌwilderness;

9   When yourˌfathersˌtempted me, *
        —ˌproved me, andˌsaw myˌworks.   [Ant.]

10   Forty years long was I grieved with this generˌation, andˌsaid, *
        It is a people that do err in their hearts,
        forˌthey have notˌknown myˌways;

11   Unto whom Iˌsware in myˌwrath, *
        that they should notˌenterˌinto myˌrest.   [Ant.]

(Gloria Patri may be added)

Glory to the Father, andˌto theˌSon, *
    andˌto theˌHolyˌSpirit:
As it was in the beˌginning, isˌnow, *
    andˌwill be forˌever. Aˌmen.   [Ant.]

Daily Morning Prayer I
The Invitatory: Jubilate

S 11

Antiphons are sung with this setting.

1. O   be   joyful   in   the   Lord   all   ye   lands;   serve   the   Lord   with   gladness

and   come   before   his   pres - ence   with   a   song. [Ant.] 2. Be   ye

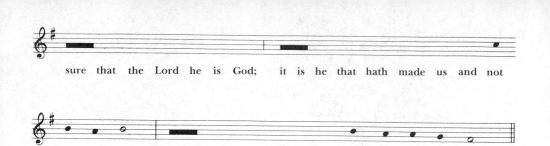

sure that the Lord he is God; it is he that hath made us and not

we our-selves; we are his people and the sheep of his pas-ture. [Ant.]

3. O go your way into his gates with thanksgiving and in-to

his courts with praise; be thankful unto him and speak good of his Name. [Ant.]

4. For the Lord is gracious; his mercy is ev-er-last-ing;

and his truth endureth from generation to gen-er-a-tion. [Ant.]

(Gloria Patri may be added)

Glo-ry to the Fa-ther, and to the Son, and to the Ho-ly Spi-rit:

As it was in the be-gin-ning, is now, and will be for ev-er. A-men. [Ant.]

Setting: Plainsong, Tone 7; adapt. Bruce E. Ford (b. 1947)

Daily Morning Prayer I
The Invitatory: Jubilate

S 12 — Edward John Hopkins (1818-1901)

S 13 — Henry Aldrich (1647-1710)

S 14 — Thomas Kelway (1695-1749)

S 15 — Christopher Gibbons (1615-1676)

Antiphons may be sung with these chants.

1   O be joyful in the ˈLord all ye ˈlands; *
    serve the Lord with gladness
    and come before his ˈpresence ˈwith a ˈsong.   [Ant.]

2   Be ye sure that the Lord he is God;
    it is he that hath made us and not ˈwe our ˈselves; *
    we are his ˈpeople and the ˈsheep of his ˈpasture.   [Ant.]

3   O go your way into his gates with thanksgiving
    and into his ˈcourts with ˈpraise; *
    be thankful unto ˈhim and speak ˈgood of his ˈName.   [Ant.]

4   For the Lord is gracious;
    his mercy is ˈever ˈlasting; *
    and his truth endureth from gener ˈation to ˈgener ˈation.   [Ant.]

(Gloria Patri may be added)

Glory to the Father, and ˈto the ˈSon, *
    and ˈto the ˈHoly ˈSpirit:
As it was in the be ˈginning, is ˈnow, *
    and ˈwill be for ˈever. A ˈmen.   [Ant.]

Christ our Passover *Pascha nostrum*

Al - le - lu - ia,   al - le - lu - ia,   al - le - lu - ia.

1. Christ our Passover is sac - ri - ficed for us,   therefore let us keep the feast,

2. Not with old leaven, neither with the leaven of mal - ice and wick - ed - ness,

but with the unleavened bread of sin - cer - i - ty and truth. [Ant.] 3. Christ   be - ing

raised from the dead di - eth no more;   death hath no more do - min - ion o - ver him.

4. For in that he died, he died un - to sin once;   but in that he liveth, he liv - eth un - to God.

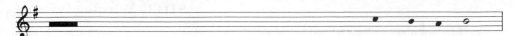

5. Likewise reckon ye also yourselves to be dead in-deed un-to sin,

but alive unto God through Je-sus Christ our Lord. [Ant.] 6. Christ is ris-en

from the dead, and become the first fruits of them that slept. 7. For since by

man came death, by man came also the resur - rec-tion of the dead.

8. For as in Ad-am all die, even so in Christ shall all be made a-live. [Ant.]

(Gloria Patri may be added)

Glo - ry to the Fa-ther, and to the Son, and to the Ho-ly Spi-rit:

As it was in the be - gin-ning, is now, and will be for ev-er. A-men. [Ant.]

Setting: Plainsong, Tone 7; adapt. Bruce E. Ford (b. 1947)

Christ our Passover *Pascha nostrum*

S 17 — Richard Woodward (1744-1777)

S 18 — John Stainer (1840-1901)

S 19 — R. Tomlinson (18th cent.)

S 20 — James Nares (1715-1783)

1   Alleluia, ꞋalleꞋluia. *
    AlleꞋluia, ꞋalleꞋluia.

2   Christ our Passover is Ꞌsacrificed forꞋus, *
    thereforeꞋlet usꞋkeep theꞋfeast,

3   Not with old leaven,
    neither with the leaven ofꞋmalice andꞋwickedness, *
    but with the unleavenedꞋbread of sinꞋcerity andꞋtruth.

4   Alleluia, ꞋalleꞋluia. *
    AlleꞋluia, ꞋalleꞋluia.

5   Christ being raised from the deadꞋdieth noꞋmore; *
    death hathꞋno more doꞋminionꞋover him.

6   For in that he died, he died untoꞋsinꞋonce; *
    but in that he liveth, heꞋlivethꞋuntoꞋGod.

7   Likewise reckon ye also yourselves to be dead inꞋdeed untoꞋsin, *
    but alive unto God throughꞋJesusꞋChrist ourꞋLord.

8   Alleluia, ꞋalleꞋluia. *
    AlleꞋluia, ꞋalleꞋluia.

9 Christ is ˈrisen from the ˈdead, *
   and become the ˈfirst fruits of ˈthem that ˈslept.

10 For since by ˈman came ˈdeath, *
   by man came also the resurˈrection ˈof the ˈdead.

11 For as in ˈAdam all ˈdie, *
   even so in Christ shall ˈall be ˈmade aˈlive.

12 Alleluia, ˈalleˈluia. *
   Alleˈluia, ˈalleˈluia.

   (Gloria Patri may be added)

   Glory to the Father, and ˈto the ˈSon, *
   and ˈto the ˈHoly ˈSpirit:

   As it was in the beˈginning, is ˈnow, *
   and ˈwill be for ˈever. Aˈmen.

   Alleluia, ˈalleˈluia. *
   Alleˈluia, ˈalleˈluia.

Daily Morning Prayer I
Salutation and The Lord's Prayer

S 21

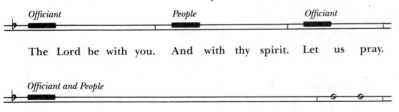

Officiant   *People*   *Officiant*

The Lord be with you.   And with thy spirit.   Let us pray.

Officiant and People

Our Father, who art . . . . for ever and ever. A · men.

Suffrages A

Cantor or Officiant

V. O Lord, show thy mercy upon us;

People

R. And grant us thy salva - tion.

V. Endue thy ministers with right - eous - ness;

R. And make thy chosen people joy - ful.

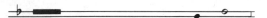

V. Give peace, O Lord, in all the world;

R. For only in thee can we live in safe - ty.

V. Lord, keep this nation un - der thy care;

R. And guide us in the way of jus - tice and truth.

V. Let thy way be known up - on earth;

R. Thy saving health among all na - tions.

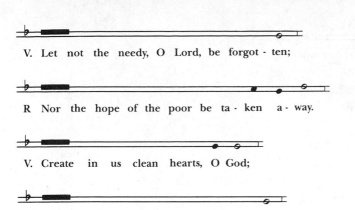

V. Let not the needy, O Lord, be forgot - ten;

R Nor the hope of the poor be ta - ken a - way.

V. Create in us clean hearts, O God;

R. And sustain us with thy Holy Spi - rit.

Daily Morning Prayer I
Suffrages B

S 23

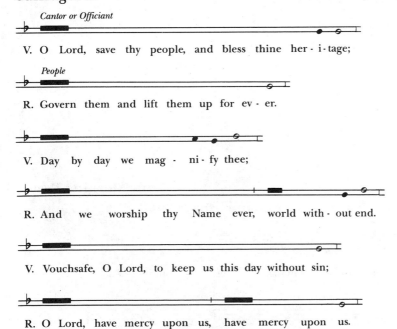

Cantor or Officiant

V. O Lord, save thy people, and bless thine her - i - tage;

People

R. Govern them and lift them up for ev - er.

V. Day by day we mag - ni - fy thee;

R. And we worship thy Name ever, world with - out end.

V. Vouchsafe, O Lord, to keep us this day without sin;

R. O Lord, have mercy upon us, have mercy upon us.

V. O Lord, let thy mercy be upon us;

R. As our trust is in thee.

V. O Lord, in thee have I trust - ed;

R. Let me never be confound - ed.

Concluding Versicle and Response

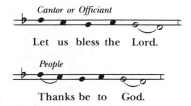

Cantor or Officiant

Let us bless the Lord.

People

Thanks be to God.

Concluding Versicle and Response in Easter Season

Cantor or Officiant

Let us bless the Lord, al - le - lu - ia, al - le - lu - ia.

People

Thanks be to God, al - le - lu - ia, al - le - lu - ia.

Daily Evening Prayer I
Preces

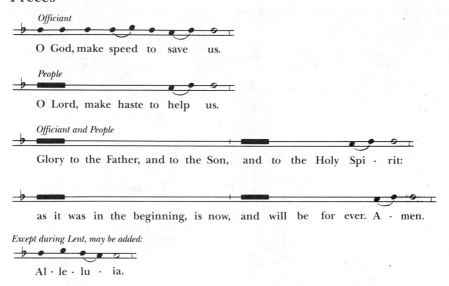

Officiant

O God, make speed to save us.

People

O Lord, make haste to help us.

Officiant and People

Glory to the Father, and to the Son, and to the Holy Spi - rit:

as it was in the beginning, is now, and will be for ever. A - men.

Except during Lent, may be added:

Al - le - lu - ia.

Daily Evening Prayer I
O Gracious Light   *Phos hilaron*

1. O gra - cious Light, pure brightness of the everliving Father in hea - ven, O Jesus Christ, ho - ly and bless - ed! 2. Now as we come to the setting of the sun, and our eyes behold the ves - per light, we sing thy praises, O God: Father, Son, and Ho - ly Spi - rit.

3. Thou art worthy at all times to be praised by happy voic - es, O Son of God,

O Giv - er of Life, and to be glo - ri - fied through all the worlds.

Setting: Victor Judson Schramm (1944-1984)

S 28
Salutation and The Lord's Prayer

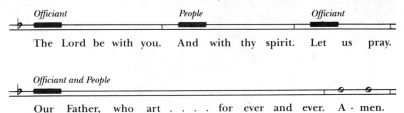

Officiant ... *People* ... *Officiant*

The Lord be with you. And with thy spirit. Let us pray.

Officiant and People

Our Father, who art . . . . for ever and ever. A - men.

For Suffrages A, see S 22.

S 29
Suffrages B, Tone I

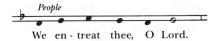

Cantor or Officiant

That this evening may be holy, good, and peace - ful,

People

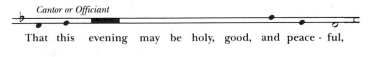

We en - treat thee, O Lord.

(This response is sung after each of the following petitions)

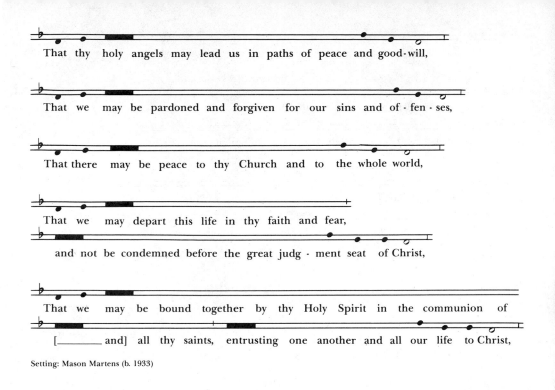

That thy holy angels may lead us in paths of peace and good-will,

That we may be pardoned and forgiven for our sins and of-fen-ses,

That there may be peace to thy Church and to the whole world,

That we may depart this life in thy faith and fear,

and not be condemned before the great judg-ment seat of Christ,

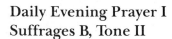

That we may be bound together by thy Holy Spirit in the communion of

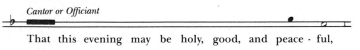

[_____ and] all thy saints, entrusting one another and all our life to Christ,

Setting: Mason Martens (b. 1933)

Daily Evening Prayer I
Suffrages B, Tone II

S 30

Cantor or Officiant

That this evening may be holy, good, and peace-ful,

People

We en-treat thee, O Lord.

(This response is sung after each of the following petitions)

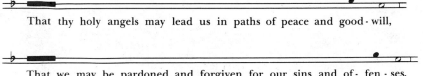

That thy holy angels may lead us in paths of peace and good-will,

That we may be pardoned and forgiven for our sins and of-fen-ses,

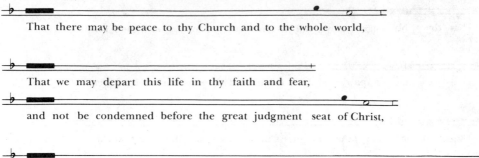

That there may be peace to thy Church and to the whole world,

That we may depart this life in thy faith and fear,

and not be condemned before the great judgment seat of Christ,

That we may be bound together by thy Holy Spirit in the communion of

[_____ and] all thy saints, entrusting one another and all our life to Christ,

Setting: From the Litany of the Saints; adapt. Mason Martens (b. 1933)

S 31

Daily Evening Prayer I

Concluding Versicle and Response

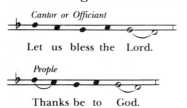

Cantor or Officiant

Let us bless the Lord.

People

Thanks be to God.

S 32

Daily Evening Prayer I

Concluding Versicle and Response in Easter Season

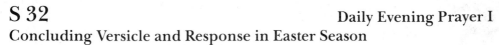

Cantor or Officiant

Let us bless the Lord, al-le-lu-ia, al-le - lu - ia.

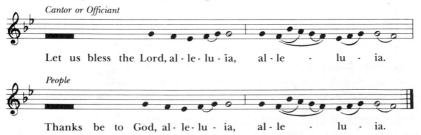

People

Thanks be to God, al-le-lu-ia, al-le - lu - ia.

Daily Morning Prayer II
Preces

Officiant

Lord, o‑pen our lips.

People

And our mouth shall pro‑claim your praise.

Officiant and People

Glory to the Father, and to the Son, and to the Holy Spi ‑ rit:

as it was in the beginning, is now, and will be for ever. A ‑ men.

Except in Lent, add:

Al ‑ le ‑ lu ‑ ia.

Daily Morning Prayer II
The Invitatory: Venite/Psalm 95

Antiphons are sung with this setting.

1. Come, let us sing to the Lord; let us shout for joy to the Rock of our

sal ‑ va ‑ tion. 2. Let us come before his presence with thanks‑giv ‑ ing

and raise a loud shout to him with psalms. [Ant.] 3. For the Lord is a

great God, and a great King a - bove all gods. 4. In his hand are

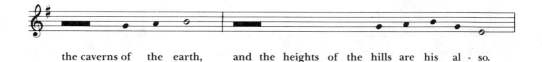

the caverns of the earth, and the heights of the hills are his al - so.

5. The sea is his, for he made it, and his hands have mold- ed the dry land. [Ant.]

6. Come, let us bow down, and bend the knee, and kneel before the Lord

our Ma - ker. 7. For he is our God, and we are the people of his pasture

and the sheep of his hand. Oh, that today you would heark - en to his voice! [Ant.]

Venite ends here.

(Gloria Patri may be added)

Psalm 95 continues:

8. Hard - en   not your hearts, as your   forebears did in   the   wil - der - ness,

at Meribah, and on that day at Mas - sah, when they tempt - ed   me.

9. They   put   me   to   the   test,   though they   had   seen   my works. [Ant.]

10. For - ty   years long I detested that genera - tion and said,

"This people are wayward in their hearts; they   do   not know my ways."

11. So I swore in   my wrath,   "They shall not en - ter in - to   my rest." [Ant.]

(Gloria Patri may be added)

Glo - ry   to the Father, and to the Son,   and to the Ho - ly Spi - rit:

as it was in the begin - ning, is now,   and will be for ev - er. A - men. [Ant.]

Setting: Plainsong, Tone 4; adapt Bruce E. Ford (b. 1947)

The Invitatory: Venite

1. Come, let us sing to the

Lord; _____ let us shout for joy to the Rock of our sal -

va - tion. _____ 2. Let us come be - fore his pres - ence with thanks - giv - ing, _____

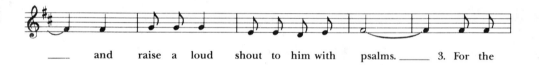

_____ and raise a loud shout to him with psalms. _____ 3. For the

Lord is a great God, _____ and a great King a - bove all

gods. _____ 4. In his hand are the cav - erns of the earth, _____

and the heights of the hills are his al - so. _____ 5. The

sea is his, for he made it, _____ and his hands have

mold - ed the dry land. ___ 6. Come, let us bow down, and bend the

knee, _____ and kneel be - fore the Lord our Ma - ker. ____ 7. For

he is our God, _____ and we are the peo - ple of his

pas - ture _____ and the sheep of his hand. _____

_____ Oh, that to - day you would heark-en to his voice!_____

Setting: Jack Noble White (b. 1938)

Antiphons may be sung with these chants.

1   Come, let us ˈsing to the ˈLord; *

     let us shout for joy to the ˈRock of ˈour salˈvation.

2   Let us come before his ˈpresence with thanksˈgiving *

     and raise a loud ˈshout to ˈhim with ˈpsalms. [Ant.]

3   For the Lord is a'grëat'God, *

     and a great'King a'bove all'gods.

4   In his hand are the'caverns of the'earth, *

     and the heights of the'hills are'hïs'also.

†5   The sea is'his, for he'made it, *

     and his hands have'molded the'drÿ'land. [Ant.]

6   Come, let us bow down, and'bend the'knee, *

     and'kneel before the'Lord our'Maker.

7   For he is our God,

     and we are the people of his pasture and the'sheep of his'hand. *

     Oh, that to'day you would'hearken to his'voice! [Ant.]

Venite ends here.
(Gloria Patri may be added)

Psalm 95 continues:

8   Harden not your hearts,

     as your forebears'did in the'wilderness, *

     at Méribah, and on that day at'Massah,'when they'tempted me.

9   They'put me to the'test, *

     —'though they had'seen my'works. [Ant.]

10   Forty years long I detested that gener'ation and'said, *

     "This people are wayward in their hearts;

     'they do not'know my'ways."

11   So I'swore in my'wrath, *

     "They shall not'enter'into my'rest." [Ant.]

(Gloria Patri may be added)

Glory to the Father, and'to the'Son, *

     and'to the'Holy'Spirit:

As it was in the be'ginning, is'now, *

     and'will be for'ever. A'men. [Ant.]

† *Second half of double chant.*

The Invitatory: Jubilate

Antiphons are sung with this setting.

1. Be joy - ful in the Lord, all you lands; serve the Lord with gladness

and come before his pres - ence with a song. [Ant.] 2. Know this:

The Lord him - self is God; he himself has made us, and we are his;

we are his people and the sheep of his pas - ture. [Ant.] 3. En - ter his gates

with thanksgiving; go in - to his courts with praise; give thanks to him

and call up - on his Name. [Ant.] 4. For the Lord is good; his mercy is

ev - er - last - ing; and his faithfulness en - dures from age to age. [Ant.]

(Gloria Patri may be added)

Glo - ry to the Father, and to the Son, and to the Ho - ly Spi - rit:

As it was in the begin - ning, is now, and will be for ev - er. A - men. [Ant.]

Setting: Plainsong, Tone 4; adapt. Bruce E. Ford (b. 1947)

Daily Morning Prayer II
The Invitatory: Jubilate

S 42 — Peter Hurford (b. 1930)

S 43 — Richard Woodward (1744-1777)

S 44 — James Nares (1715-1783)

S 45 — Henry Walford Davies (1869-1941)

Antiphons may be sung with these chants.

1 Be joyful in the ¦ Lord, all you ¦ lands; *
  serve the Lord with gladness
  and come before his ¦ presence ¦ with a ¦ song. [Ant.]

2 Know this: The Lord him ¦ self is ¦ God; *
  he himself has made us, and we are his;
  we are his ¦ people and the ¦ sheep of his ¦ pasture. [Ant.]

3 Enter his gates with thanksgiving;
  go into his ¦ courts with ¦ praise; *
  give thanks to ¦ him and ¦ call upon his ¦ Name. [Ant.]

4 For the Lord is good;
  his mercy is ¦ ever ¦ lasting; *
  and his faithfulness en ¦ dures from ¦ age to ¦ age. [Ant.]

(Gloria Patri may be added)
Glory to the Father, and ¦ to the ¦ Son, *
  and ¦ to the ¦ Holy ¦ Spirit:
As it was in the be ¦ ginning, is ¦ now, *
  and ¦ will be for ¦ ever. A ¦ men. [Ant.]

Christ our Passover *Pascha nostrum*

1. Al - le - lu - ia. Christ our Passover has been sac - ri - ficed for us; there - fore let us keep the feast, 2. Not with the old leaven, the leaven of mal - ice and e - vil, but with the unleavened bread of sincerity and truth. Al - le - lu - ia.

3. Christ be - ing raised from the dead will nev - er die a - gain; death no longer has do - min - ion o - ver him. 4. The death that he died, he died to sin, once for all; but the life he lives, he lives to God.

5. So al - so consider yourselves dead to sin, and a - live to God

in Jesus Christ our Lord. Al - le - lu - ia.

6. Christ has been raised from the dead, the first fruits of those who have fal - len a - sleep. 7. For since by a man came death, by a man has come also the resur - rec - tion of the dead. 8. For as in Ad - am all die, so al - so in Christ shall all be made a - live. Al - le - lu - ia.

(Gloria Patri may be added)

Glo - ry to the Father, and to the Son, and to the Ho - ly Spi - rit: As it was in the be - gin - ning, is now, and will be for ever. A - men. Al - le - lu - ia.

Setting: Plainsong, Tone 1, Introit Form; adapt. Norman Mealy (b. 1923), alt.

Christ our Passover   *Pascha nostrum*

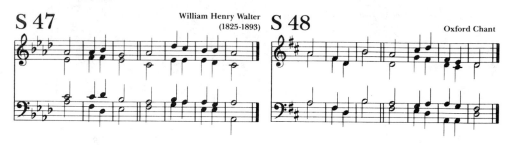

S 47 — William Henry Walter (1825-1893)

S 48 — Oxford Chant

S 49 — John Hindle (1761-1796)

S 50 — Tonus Peregrinus; adapt. David Hurd (b. 1950)

1   Alleluia, ꞌalleꞌluia. *
     Alleꞌluia, ꞌalleꞌluia.

2   Christ our Passover has been ꞌsacrificed for ꞌus; *
     therefore ꞌlet us ꞌkeep the ꞌfeast,

3   Not with the old leaven, the leaven of ꞌmalice and ꞌevil, *
     but with the unleavened ꞌbread of sin ꞌcerity and ꞌtruth.

4   Alleluia, ꞌalleꞌluia. *
     Alleꞌluia, ꞌalleꞌluia.

5   Christ being raised from the dead will ꞌnever die a ꞌgain; *
     death no ꞌlonger has do ꞌminion ꞌover him.

6   The death that he died, he died to sin, ꞌonce for ꞌall; *
     but the life he ꞌlives, he ꞌlives to ꞌGod.

7 So also consider yourselves'dead to'sin, *

    and alive to God in'Jesus'Christ our'Lord.

8 Alleluia,'alle'luia. *

    Alle'luia,'alle'luia.

9 Christ has been'raised from the'dead, *

    the first fruits of'those who have'fallen a'sleep.

10 For since by a'man came'death, *

    by a man has come also the resur'rection'of the'dead.

11 For as in'Adam all'die, *

    so also in Christ shall'all be'made a'live.

12 Alleluia,'alle'luia. *

    Alle'luia,'alle'luia.

(Gloria Patri may be added)

Glory to the Father, and'to the'Son, *

    and'to the'Holy'Spirit:

As it was in the be'ginning, is'now, *

    and'will be for'ever. A'men.

Alleluia,'alle'luia. *

    Alle'luia,'alle'luia.

Daily Morning Prayer II
Salutation and The Lord's Prayer

Officiant   *People*   *Officiant*

The Lord be with you.   And also with you.   Let us pray.

Officiant and People

Our Father in heaven . . . ever.   A - men.

or

Our Father, who art in heaven . . . ever.   A - men.

Suffrages A

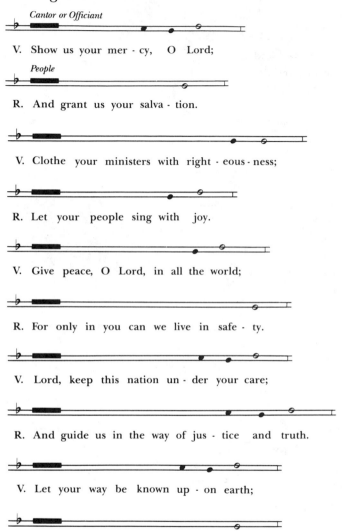

Cantor or Officiant

V. Show us your mer - cy, O Lord;

People

R. And grant us your salva - tion.

V. Clothe your ministers with right - eous - ness;

R. Let your people sing with joy.

V. Give peace, O Lord, in all the world;

R. For only in you can we live in safe - ty.

V. Lord, keep this nation un - der your care;

R. And guide us in the way of jus - tice and truth.

V. Let your way be known up - on earth;

R. Your saving health among all na - tions.

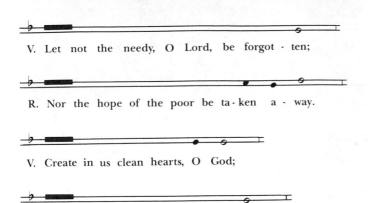

V. Let not the needy, O Lord, be forgot - ten;

R. Nor the hope of the poor be ta - ken a - way.

V. Create in us clean hearts, O God;

R. And sustain us with your Holy Spi - rit.

Daily Morning Prayer II
Suffrages B

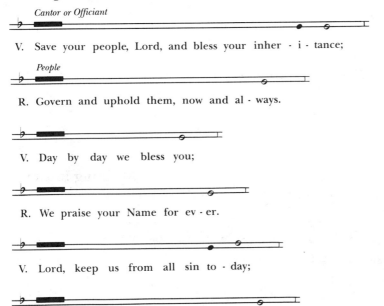

Cantor or Officiant

V. Save your people, Lord, and bless your inher - i - tance;

People

R. Govern and uphold them, now and al - ways.

V. Day by day we bless you;

R. We praise your Name for ev - er.

V. Lord, keep us from all sin to - day;

R. Have mercy on us, Lord, have mer - cy.

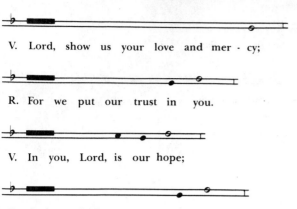

V. Lord, show us your love and mer - cy;

R. For we put our trust in you.

V. In you, Lord, is our hope;

R. And we shall never hope in vain.

S 54
Concluding Versicle and Response

Cantor or Officiant

Let us bless the Lord.

People

Thanks be to God.

S 55
Concluding Versicle and Response in Easter Season

Cantor or Officiant

Let us bless the Lord, al - le - lu - ia, al - le - lu - ia.

People

Thanks be to God, al - le - lu - ia, al - le - lu - ia.

An Order of Worship for the Evening
Greeting: Tone I

Officiant ... *People*

Light and peace, in Jesus Christ our Lord. Thanks be to God.

In Lent and in Easter Season, the Opening Acclamations S 78–S 83 are used instead.

Setting: Ambrosian chant; adapt. Mason Martens (b. 1933)

An Order of Worship for the Evening
Greeting: Tone II

Officiant ... *People*

Light and peace, in Je - sus Christ our Lord. Thanks be to God.

In Lent and in Easter Season, the Opening Acclamations S 78–S 83 are used instead.

Daily Evening Prayer II
Preces

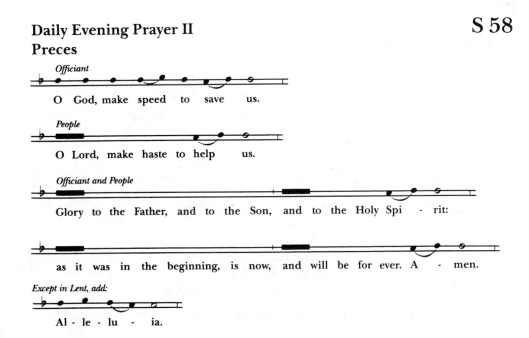

Officiant

O God, make speed to save us.

People

O Lord, make haste to help us.

Officiant and People

Glory to the Father, and to the Son, and to the Holy Spi - rit:

as it was in the beginning, is now, and will be for ever. A - men.

Except in Lent, add:

Al - le - lu - ia.

O Gracious Light   *Phos hilaron*

1. O gra-cious Light, pure bright-ness of the ev-er-liv-ing

Fa-ther in hea-ven, O Je-sus Christ, ho-ly and bless-ed!

2. Now as we come to the set-ting of the sun, and our

eyes be-hold the ves-per light, we sing your prais-es, O God:

Fa-ther, Son, and Ho-ly Spi-rit. 3. You are wor-thy at all times

to be praised by hap-py voic-es, O Son of God, O Giv-er

of life, and to be glo-ri-fied through all the worlds.

Setting: Mode 2 melody, centonized Bruce E. Ford (b. 1947) and James McGregor (b. 1930)

Daily Evening Prayer II
O Gracious Light   *Phos hilaron*

1. O gra-cious Light, pure bright-ness of the ev-er-liv-ing Fa-ther in hea-ven, O Je-sus Christ, ho-ly and bless-ed!

2. Now as we come to the set-ting of the sun, and our eyes be-hold the ves-per light, we sing your prais-es, O God: Fa-ther, Son, and Ho-ly Spi-rit.

3. You are wor-thy at all times to be praised by hap-py voic-es, O Son of God, O Giv-er of life, and to be glo-ri-fied through all the worlds.

Setting: Ronald Arnatt (b. 1930)

O Gracious Light   *Phos hilaron*

1. O gra-cious Light, pure bright-ness of the ev-er-liv-ing

Fa - ther in heaven, O Je-sus Christ, ho - ly and

bless - ed!   2. Now   as   we   come   to   the   set-ting   of   the

sun, and our eyes be-hold the ves-per light, we sing your

prais - es, O God: Fa-ther, Son, and Ho-ly Spi - rit.

3. You   are   wor-thy   at   all   times   to   be   praised by   hap - py

voic - es, _____ O Son of God, O Giv - er of

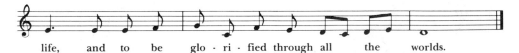

life,   and   to   be   glo - ri - fied through all   the   worlds.

Setting: McNeil Robinson II (b. 1943)

Officiant *People* *Officiant*

The Lord be with you.   And also with you.   Let us pray.

Officiant and People

Our   Father   in   heaven . . . ever.   A - men.
or
Our Father, who art in heaven . . . ever.   A - men.

For Suffrages A, see S 52.

Cantor or Officiant

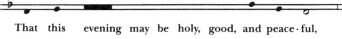

That this   evening may be holy, good, and peace - ful,

People

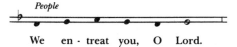

We   en - treat you,   O   Lord.

(This response is sung after each petition)

That your   holy angels may lead us in paths of peace and good - will,

That we   may be pardoned and forgiven for our sins and of - fen - ses,

That there   may be peace to your Church and to the whole world,

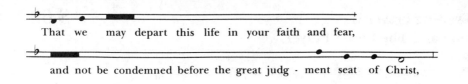

That we may depart this life in your faith and fear,

and not be condemned before the great judg - ment seat of Christ,

That we may be bound together by your Holy Spirit in the communion of

[____ and] all your saints, entrusting one another and all our life to Christ,

Setting: Mason Martens (b. 1933)

S 64

Daily Evening Prayer II

Suffrages B, Tone II

Cantor or Officiant

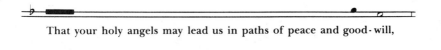

That this evening may be holy, good, and peace-ful,

People

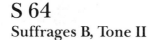

We en - treat you, O Lord.

(This response is sung after each petition)

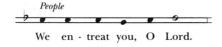

That your holy angels may lead us in paths of peace and good - will,

That we may be pardoned and forgiven for our sins and of - fen - ses,

That there may be peace to your Church and to the whole world,

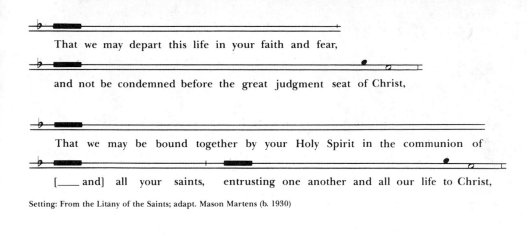

That we may depart this life in your faith and fear,

and not be condemned before the great judgment seat of Christ,

That we may be bound together by your Holy Spirit in the communion of

[____ and] all your saints, entrusting one another and all our life to Christ,

Setting: From the Litany of the Saints; adapt. Mason Martens (b. 1930)

Daily Evening Prayer II
Concluding Versicle and Response

S 65

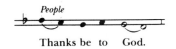

Cantor or Officiant

Let us bless the Lord.

People

Thanks be to God.

Daily Evening Prayer II
Concluding Versicle and Response in Easter Season

S 66

Cantor or Officiant

Let us bless the Lord, al‑le‑lu‑ia, al‑le‑lu‑ia.

People

Thanks be to God, al‑le‑lu‑ia, al‑le‑lu‑ia.

The Great Litany

S 67

The Great Litany

The Officiant at the Litany may be a lay cantor.

Officiant — O God the Father, Creator of heaven and earth, **People** — Have mer‑cy up‑on us.

Officiant — O God the Son, Redeemer of the world, **People** — Have mer‑cy up‑on us.

Officiant — O God the Holy Ghost, Sanctifier of the faith‑ful, **People** — Have mer‑cy up‑on us.

Officiant — O holy, blessed, and glorious Trinity, one God, **People** — Have mer‑cy up‑on us.

Officiant — Remember not, Lord Christ, our offenses, nor the offenses of our forefathers; neither reward us according to our sins. Spare us, good Lord, spare thy people, whom thou hast redeemed with thy most precious blood, and by thy mercy preserve us for ev‑er. **People** — Spare us, good Lord.

Officiant — From all evil and wickedness; from sin; from the crafts and assaults of the devil; and from everlast‑ing dam‑na‑tion,

People — Good Lord, de‑liv‑er us.

(This same response is sung after the petitions that follow)

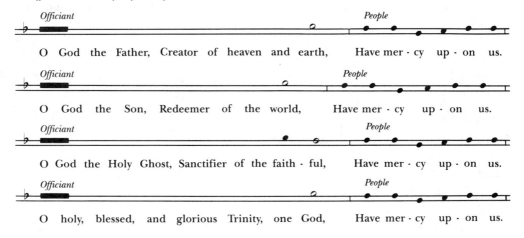

We sinners do beseech thee to hear us, O Lord God; and that it may please thee to rule and govern thy holy Church Universal in the right way,

People

We beseech thee to hear us, good Lord.

(This same response is sung after the petitions that follow)

Officiant Son of God, we beseech thee to hear us.
People Son of God, we beseech thee to hear us.

O Lamb of God, that takest away the sins of the world, Have mer‑cy up‑on us.
O Lamb of God, that takest away the sins of the world, Have mer‑cy up‑on us.

O Lamb of God, that takest away the sins of the world, Grant us thy peace.

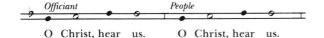

O Christ, hear us. O Christ, hear us.

When the Litany is sung immediately before the Eucharist, the Litany concludes with the Kyries (which may be sung to any setting), and the Eucharist begins with the Salutation and the Collect of the day.

On all other occasions, the Litany continues as follows:

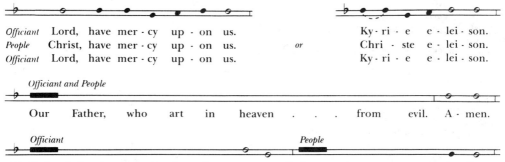

Officiant Lord, have mer‑cy up‑on us.
People Christ, have mer‑cy up‑on us.
Officiant Lord, have mer‑cy up‑on us.

or

Ky‑ri‑e e‑lei‑son.
Chri‑ste e‑lei‑son.
Ky‑ri‑e e‑lei‑son.

Officiant and People

Our Father, who art in heaven . . . from evil. A‑men.

Officiant   *People*

V. O Lord, let thy mercy be showed up‑on us. R. As we do put our trust in thee.

The Officiant sings the concluding Collect.

Setting: John Merbecke (1510?‑1585?), alt.

Proper Liturgies for Special Days

For Palm Sunday, see Hymns 153-157

S 68

The Great Vigil of Easter

Versicle and Response: "The Light of Christ"

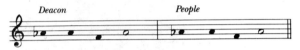

The light of Christ.   Thanks be   to God.

At the second and third pause, the Versicle and Response is sung successively a step higher.

S 69

The Great Vigil of Easter

The Exsultet: Responses

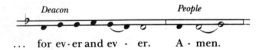

... for ev-er and ev - er.   A - men.

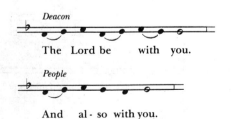

The Lord be   with you.

And   al - so with you.

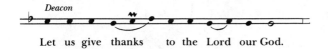

Deacon

Let us give thanks to the Lord our God.

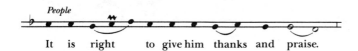

People

It is right to give him thanks and praise.

Deacon   *People*

... for ev - er and ev - er. A · men.

The Great Vigil of Easter
Great Alleluia

S 70

After the Epistle, this Alleluia is traditionally sung three times by the Celebrant or by a Cantor, at successively higher pitches (one whole tone each time), the Congregation repeating it each time.

Al·le - - - lu - ia.

Holy Baptism

S 71
Opening Acclamation

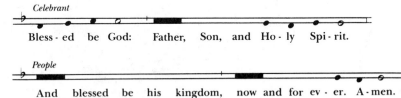

Celebrant

Bless - ed be God: Father, Son, and Ho - ly Spi - rit.

People

And blessed be his kingdom, now and for ev - er. A - men.

Setting: Ambrosian chant; adapt. Mason Martens (b. 1933)

S 72
Opening Acclamation in Easter Season

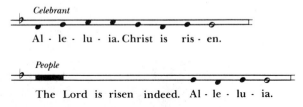

Celebrant

Al - le - lu - ia. Christ is ris - en.

People

The Lord is risen indeed. Al - le - lu - ia.

Setting: Ambrosian chant; adapt. Mason Martens (b. 1933)

S 73
Opening Acclamation in Lent

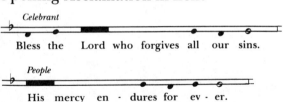

Celebrant

Bless the Lord who forgives all our sins.

People

His mercy en - dures for ev - er.

Setting: Ambrosian chant; adapt. Mason Martens (b. 1933)

Holy Baptism
Versicles

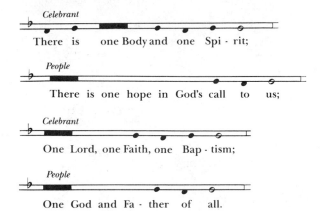

Celebrant

There is one Body and one Spi - rit;

People

There is one hope in God's call to us;

Celebrant

One Lord, one Faith, one Bap - tism;

People

One God and Fa - ther of all.

Setting: Ambrosian chant; adapt. *Hymnal 1982*

Holy Baptism
Litany and Thanksgiving over the Water

People's response

Lord, hear our prayer.

The Amen after the Collect is monotoned.

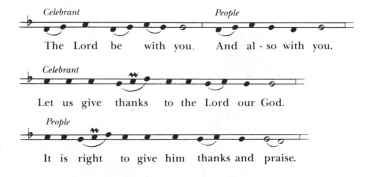

Celebrant   *People*

The Lord be with you. And al - so with you.

Celebrant

Let us give thanks to the Lord our God.

People

It is right to give him thanks and praise.

Conclusion

Celebrant   *People*

A - men.

The Holy Eucharist

S 76
Opening Acclamation

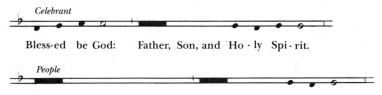

Bless-ed be God: Father, Son, and Ho - ly Spi - rit.

And blessed be his kingdom, now and for ev - er. A - men.

Setting: Ambrosian chant; adapt. Mason Martens (b. 1933)

S 77
Opening Acclamation

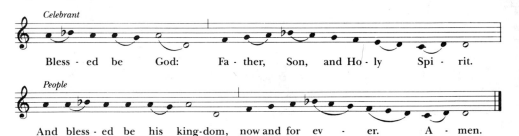

Bless - ed be   God: Fa - ther,   Son,   and Ho - ly   Spi - rit.

And bless - ed be his king-dom, now and for ev - er.   A - men.

Setting: From *Missa orbis factor*; arr. David Hurd (b. 1950)

The Holy Eucharist

Opening Acclamation for Easter Day through the Day of Pentecost

S 78

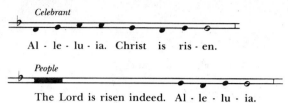

Celebrant

Al - le - lu - ia. Christ is ris - en.

People

The Lord is risen indeed. Al - le - lu - ia.

Setting: Ambrosian chant; adapt. Mason Martens (b. 1933)

The Holy Eucharist

Opening Acclamation for Easter Day through the Day of Pentecost

S 79

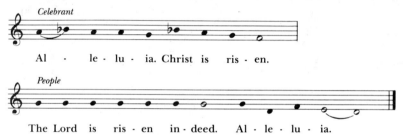

Celebrant

Al - le - lu - ia. Christ is ris - en.

People

The Lord is ris - en in - deed. Al - le - lu - ia.

Setting: From *Missa orbis factor*; arr. David Hurd (b. 1950)

The Holy Eucharist I

Opening Acclamation in Lent

S 80

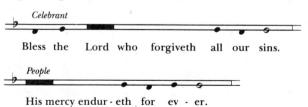

Celebrant

Bless the Lord who forgiveth all our sins.

People

His mercy endur - eth for ev - er.

Setting: Ambrosian chant; adapt. Mason Martens (b. 1933)

S 81

The Holy Eucharist I

Opening Acclamation in Lent

Celebrant

Bless the Lord who for‑giv‑eth all our sins.

People

His mer‑cy en‑dur‑eth for ev‑er.

Setting: From *Missa orbis factor*; arr. David Hurd (b. 1950)

S 82

The Holy Eucharist II

Opening Acclamation in Lent

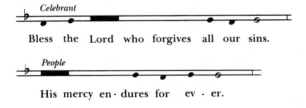

Celebrant

Bless the Lord who forgives all our sins.

People

His mercy en‑dures for ev‑er.

Setting: Ambrosian chant; adapt. Mason Martens (b. 1933)

S 83

The Holy Eucharist II

Opening Acclamation in Lent

Celebrant

Bless the Lord who for‑gives all our sins.

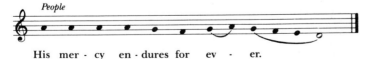

People

His mer‑cy en‑dures for ev‑er.

Setting: From *Missa orbis factor*; arr. David Hurd (b. 1950)

For settings of Gloria in excelsis, *see S 201–S 204 and S 272–S 281.*

Kyrie eleison

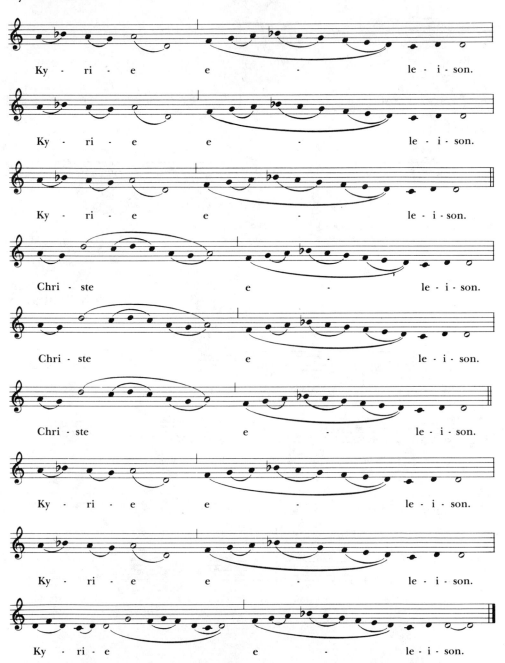

Setting: Plainsong, Mode 1; Mass 11, "Orbis factor;" arr. David Hurd (b. 1950)

S 85
Kyrie eleison

Ky - ri - e e - le - i - son. Ky - ri - e e - le - i - son.

Chri - ste e - le - i - son. Chri - ste e - le - i - son.

Ky - ri - e e - le - i - son. Ky - ri - e e - le - i - son.

Setting: Plainsong, Mode 3; Mass 16; adapt. Schola Antiqua, 1983
Melody rhythmic version © 1984, Schola Antiqua Inc. Used by permission.

S 86
Kyrie eleison

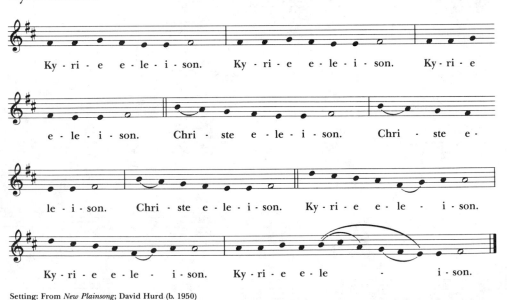

Ky - ri - e e - le - i - son. Ky - ri - e e - le - i - son. Ky - ri - e

e - le - i - son. Chri - ste e - le - i - son. Chri - ste e -

le - i - son. Chri - ste e - le - i - son. Ky - ri - e e - le - i - son.

Ky - ri - e e - le - i - son. Ky - ri - e e - le - i - son.

Setting: From *New Plainsong*; David Hurd (b. 1950)

The Holy Eucharist
Kyrie eleison

Setting: From *Corpus Christi Mass*; Jackson Hill (b. 1941)

S 88

Kyrie eleison

Ky - ri - e   e - le - i - son._____

Ky - ri - e   e - le - i - son._____

Chri - ste   e - le - i - son._____

Chri - ste   e - le - i - son._____

Ky - ri - e   e - le - i - son._____   Ky - ri -

e   e - le - i - son._____

Setting: McNeil Robinson II (b. 1943)

Kyrie eleison

Setting: James McGregor (b. 1930), after *Verbum caro factum est*, Hans Leo Hassler (1564–1612)

S 90

Lord, have mercy upon us   *Kyrie*

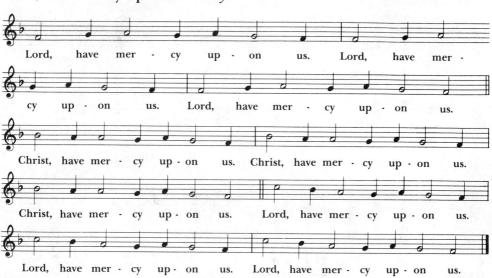

Setting: John Merbecke (1510?-1585?); adapt. *Hymnal 1982*

S 91

Lord, have mercy upon us   *Kyrie*

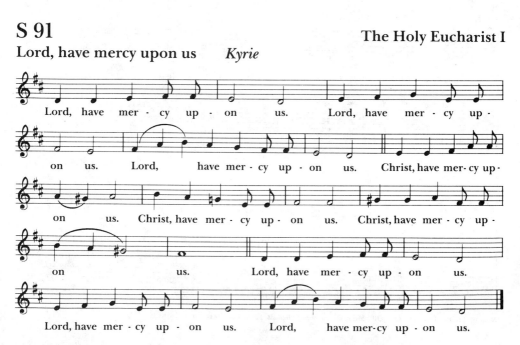

Setting: From *Missa de Sancta Maria Magdalena*, Healey Willan (1880-1968)

The Holy Eucharist I
Lord, have mercy upon us *Kyrie*

Setting: From *Missa Marialis*; **Plainsong, Mode 1**; Mass 9, "Cum jubilo"; adapt. Charles Winfred Douglas (1867-1944)

Lord, have mercy upon us   *Kyrie*

Lord, _____ have mer - cy up - on us.

Lord, _____ have mer - cy up - on us.

Lord, have mer - cy up - on us.

Christ, _____ have mer - cy up - on us.

Christ, _____ have mer - cy up - on us.

Christ, have mer - cy up - on us.

Lord, _____ have mer - cy up - on us.

Lord, _____ have mer - cy up - on us.

Lord, _____ have mer - cy up - on us.

Setting: Leo Sowerby (1895–1968)

The Holy Eucharist II
Lord, have mercy   *Kyrie*

Cantor or Choir   *All*

Lord,   have   mer - cy.   Lord,   have   mer - cy.

Cantor or Choir   *All*

Christ,   have   mer - cy.   Christ,   have   mer - cy.

Cantor or Choir   *All*

Lord,   have mer - cy. Lord,   have   mer - cy.

Setting: Plainsong, Mode 4; Mass 18; adapt. Mason Martens (b. 1933)

The Holy Eucharist II
Lord, have mercy   *Kyrie*

Cantor or Choir   *All*   *Cantor or Choir*

Lord, have   mer - cy.   Lord, have mer - cy.   Christ, have   mer - cy.

All   *Cantor or Choir*   *All*

Christ, have   mer - cy.   Lord, have   mer - cy.   Lord, have   mer - cy.

Setting: From the Litany of the Saints; adapt. Richard Proulx (b. 1937)

Lord, have mercy *Kyrie*

Lord, have mer - cy. Lord, have mer - cy.
Lord, ___

Lord, have mer - cy. Lord, have mer - cy.

Christ, have mer - cy. Christ, have mer - cy.
Christ, ___ Christ, Lord, ___

Christ have mer - cy. Christ, have mer - cy.

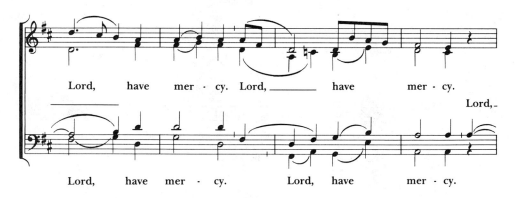

Lord, have mer - cy. Lord, ___ have mer - cy.

Lord, ___

Lord, have mer - cy. Lord, have mer - cy.

Setting: From *Deutsche Messe*; Franz Peter Schubert (1797-1828); arr. Richard Proulx (b. 1937)

The Holy Eucharist II
Lord, have mercy   *Kyrie*

S 97

Lord, have mer - cy.   Lord, have mer - cy.   Lord, have mer - cy.

Christ, have mer - cy.   Christ, have mer - cy.   Christ, have mer - cy.

Lord, have mer - cy.   Lord, have mer - cy.   Lord, have mer - cy. _____

Setting: Richard Felciano (b. 1930)

Lord, have mercy *Kyrie*

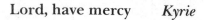

Lord, have mer - cy.

Lord, have mer - cy. Lord, have mer - cy.

Christ, have mer - cy. Christ, have mer - cy. Christ, have mer - cy.

Lord, have mer - cy. Lord, have mer - cy. Lord, have mer - cy.

Setting: William Mathias (b. 1934)

Holy God *Trisagion*

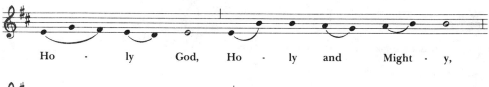

Ho - ly God, Ho - ly and Might - y,

Ho - ly Im - mor - tal One, Have mer - cy up - on us.

Ho - ly God, Ho - ly and Might - y,

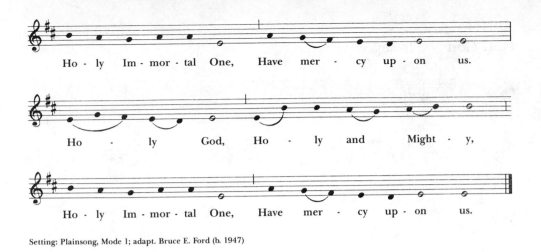

Setting: Plainsong, Mode 1; adapt. Bruce E. Ford (b. 1947)

The Holy Eucharist

Holy God   *Trisagion*

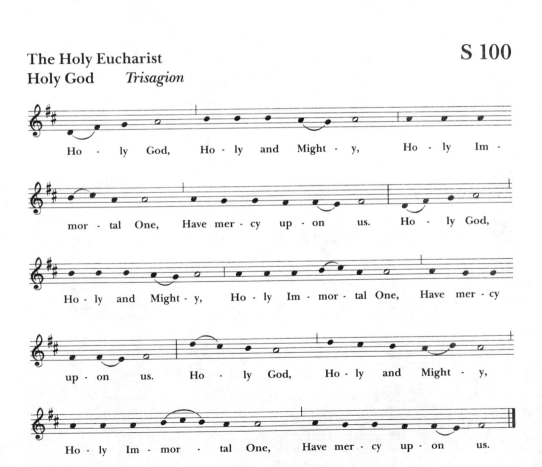

Setting: From *New Plainsong*; David Hurd (b. 1950)

S 101
Holy God *Trisagion*

Ho-ly God, Ho-ly and Might-y, Ho-ly Im-mor-tal One, Have mer-cy up-on us. Ho-ly God, Ho-ly and Might-y, Ho-ly Im-mor-tal One, Have mer-cy up-on us. Ho-ly God, Ho-ly and Might-y, Ho-ly Im-mor-tal One, Have mer-cy up-on us.

Setting: John Rutter (b. 1945)

S 102
Holy God *Trisagion*

Ho-ly God, Ho-ly and Might-y, Ho-ly Im-mor-tal One, Have mer-cy up-on us.

Setting: Ver. *Hymnal 1982*, after Alexander Archangelsky (1846-1924)

The Holy Eucharist I
The Nicene Creed (Traditional)

I be-lieve in one God, the Fa-ther Al-might-y, ma-ker of heav-en and earth, and of all things vis-i-ble and in-vis-i-ble; And in one Lord Je-sus Christ, the on-ly-be-got-ten Son of God, be-got-ten of his Fa-ther be-fore all worlds, God of God, Light of Light, ve-ry God of ve-ry God, be-got-ten, not made, be-ing of one sub-stance with the Fa-ther; by whom all things were made; who for us men and for our sal-va-tion came down from hea-ven, and was in-car-nate by the Ho-ly Ghost of the Vir-gin Ma-ry, and was made man; and was cru-ci-fied al-so for us un-der Pon-tius Pi-late; he suf-fered and was bur-ied; and the third day he rose a-gain

according to the Scriptures, and ascended into heaven, and sitteth on the right hand of the Father; and he shall come again, with glory, to judge both the quick and the dead; whose kingdom shall have no end. And I believe in the Holy Ghost the Lord, and Giver of Life, who proceedeth from the Father and the Son; who with the Father and the Son together is worshiped and glorified; who spake by the Prophets. And I believe one holy Catholic and Apostolic Church; I acknowledge one Baptism for the remission of sins; and I look for the resurrection of the dead, and the life of the world to come. Amen.

Setting: Plainsong, Mode 4; Credo I; adapt. Charles Winfred Douglas (1867–1944), alt.

We be-lieve in one God, the Fa-ther, the Al-might-y, ma-ker of

hea-ven and earth, of all that is, seen and un-seen. We be-lieve

in one Lord, Je-sus Christ, the on-ly Son of God, e-ter-nal-ly

be-got-ten of the Fa-ther, God from God, Light from Light, true God

from true God, be-got-ten, not made, of one Be-ing with the Fa-ther.

Through him all things were made. For us and for our sal-va-tion

he came down from hea-ven: by the pow-er of the Ho-ly Spi-rit

he be-came in-car-nate from the Vir-gin Ma-ry, and was made man.

For our sake he was cru-ci-fied un-der Pon-tius Pi-late;

he suf-fered death and was bur-ied. On the third day he rose a-gain

in ac·cord·ance with the Scrip-tures; he a-scend-ed in-to hea-ven

and is seat·ed at the right hand of the Fa·ther. He will come a-

gain in glo·ry to judge the liv·ing and the dead, and his king·dom

will have no end. We be·lieve in the Ho·ly Spi·rit, the Lord,

the giv·er of life, who pro·ceeds from the Fa·ther and the Son.

With the Fa·ther and the Son he is wor·shiped and glo·ri·fied.

He has spo·ken through the Pro·phets. We be·lieve in one ho·ly

cath·o·lic and a·po·sto·lic Church. We ac·know·ledge one bap·tism

for the for·give·ness of sins. We look for the re·sur·rec·tion of the dead,

and the life of the world to come. A - men.

Setting: Plainsong, Mode 4; Credo I; adapt. Mason Martens (b. 1933)

The Nicene Creed (Contemporary)

Introduction

We be-lieve in one God, the

Fa - ther, the Al - might - y, ma - ker of hea - ven and

earth, of all that is, seen and un - seen. We be-lieve in

one Lord, Je - sus Christ, the on - ly Son of God, e - ter - nal - ly be -

got - ten of the Fa - ther, God from God, Light from Light, true God from

true God, be - got - ten, not made, of one Be - ing with the Fa - ther.

Through him all things were made. For us and for our sal - va - tion

he came down from hea - ven: by the pow - er of the Ho - ly Spi - rit

he be - came in - car-nate from the Vir - gin Ma - ry, and was made man.

For our sake he was cru - ci - fied un - der Pon - tius Pi - late;

he suf - fered death ___ and was bur - ied. On the third day he

rose a-gain in ac-cord-ance with the Scrip-tures; he a-scend-ed

in-to hea-ven and is seat-ed at the right hand of the Fa-ther.

He will come a-gain in glo-ry to judge the liv-ing and the

dead, and his king-dom will have no end. We be-lieve in the

Ho-ly Spi-rit, the Lord, the giv-er of life, who pro-ceeds from the

Fa-ther and the Son. With the Fa-ther and the Son he is wor-shiped and

glo-ri-fied. He has spo-ken through the Pro-phets. We be-lieve in

one ho-ly cath-o-lic and a-po-sto-lic Church.

We ac-know-ledge one bap-tism for the for-give-ness of sins.

We look for the re-sur-rec-tion of the dead,____

and the life of the world to come. A-men. A-men.____

Setting: Calvin Hampton (1938-1984)

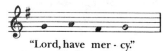

Deacon or Cantor

With all our heart and with all our mind, let us pray to the Lord, say-ing

"Lord, have mer - cy."

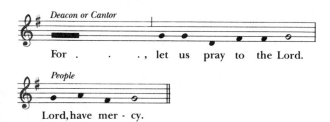

Deacon or Cantor

For . . ., let us pray to the Lord.

People

Lord, have mer - cy.

(This response is sung after each petition)

Deacon or Cantor concludes

In the communion of [_____ and of all the] saints, let us commend

ourselves, and one an - o - ther, and all our life, to Christ our God.

People

To thee, you, O Lord our God.

Silence

The Celebrant adds a concluding Collect which may be monotoned or sung to Collect Tone II found in the Musical Appendix to the Altar Edition of the Holy Eucharist.

The responses may be sung in harmony, as follows:

Lord, have mer - cy.   To thee, you, O Lord our God.   A - men.

S 107

The Prayers of the People: Form III

Deacon or Cantor   *People*

Fa - ther, we pray for your holy Cath - o - lic Church; That we all may be one.

Deacon or Cantor

Grant that every member of the Church may truly and hum - bly serve you;

People

That your Name may be glorified by all peo - ple.

Deacon or Cantor

We pray for all bishops, priests, and dea - cons;

People

That they may be faithful ministers of your word and sac - ra - ments.

Deacon or Cantor

We pray for all who govern and hold authority in the nations of the world;

People

That there may be jus - tice and peace on earth.

Deacon or Cantor

Give us grace to do your will in all that we un - der - take;

People

That our works may find fa - vor in your sight.

Deacon or Cantor

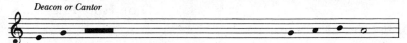

Have com - passion on those who suffer from any grief or trou -ble;

People

That they may be deliv - ered from their dis - tress.

Deacon or Cantor

Give to   the depart - ed   e - ter - nal rest;

People

Let   light   perpetual   shine up - on   them.

Deacon or Cantor

We praise   you for your saints who have entered in - to   joy;

People

May we also come to share in your hea - ven - ly king -dom.

Deacon or Cantor

Let   us   pray for our own needs, and the needs of   o - thers.

Silence

The People may add their own petitions.

The Celebrant adds a concluding Collect which may be sung in monotone.

Setting: Anaphoral chant; adapt. Bruce E. Ford (b. 1947)

S 108

The Prayers of the People: Form IV

Deacon or Cantor

Let us pray for the Church and for the world.

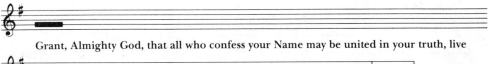

Grant, Almighty God, that all who confess your Name may be united in your truth, live

together in your love, and reveal your glory / in the wórld. *Silence*

Deacon or Cantor   *People (unison or harmony)*

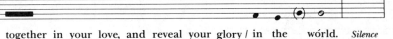

Lord, in your mer - cy   Hear our prayer.

Guide the people of this land, and of all the nations, in the ways of justice and peace; that we may honor one another and serve the / common góod.

Silence

Lord, in your mercy
Hear our prayer.

Give us all a reverence for the earth as your own creation, that we may use its resources rightly in the service of others and to your hon- / or and glóry.

Silence

Lord, in your mercy
Hear our prayer.

Bless all whose lives are closely linked with ours, and grant that we may serve Christ in them, and love one another as / he loves ús.

Silence

Lord, in your mercy
Hear our prayer.

Comfort and heal all those who suffer in body, mind, or spirit; give them courage and hope in their troubles, and bring them the joy of / your salvátion.

Silence

Lord, in your mercy
Hear our prayer.

We commend to your mercy all who have died, that your will for them may be fulfilled; and we pray that we may share with all your saints in your e- / ter-nal kíngdom.

Silence

Lord, in your mercy
Hear our prayer.

The Celebrant adds a concluding Collect which may be monotoned or sung to Collect Tone II found in the Musical Appendix to the Altar Edition of the Holy Eucharist.

After the Collect

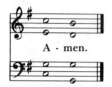

A - men.

The following alternative harmonizations may be sung:

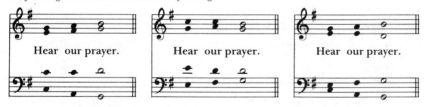

Hear our prayer. Hear our prayer. Hear our prayer.

Setting: David Hurd (b. 1950)

The Prayers of the People: Form V

Deacon or Cantor

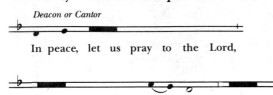

In peace, let us pray to the Lord,

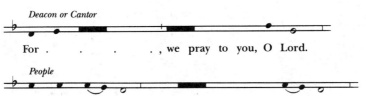

saying, "Lord, have mer - cy." *or* "Ky - ri - e e - lei - son."

Deacon or Cantor

For . . . ., we pray to you, O Lord.

People

Lord, have mer - cy. *or* Ky - ri - e e - lei - son.

(This response is sung after each petition)

Deacon or Cantor concludes

Re - joic - ing in the fellowship of [the ever-blessed Virgin Mary, (blessed N.) and] all

the saints, let us commend ourselves, and one another, and all our life to Christ

People

our God. To you, O Lord our God.

Silence

The Celebrant adds a concluding Collect which may be monotoned or sung to Collect Tone I found in the Musical Appendix to the Altar Edition of the Holy Eucharist.

Alternatively, the Celebrant may conclude with the following Doxology:

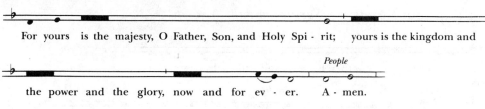

For yours is the majesty, O Father, Son, and Holy Spi - rit; yours is the kingdom and

People

the power and the glory, now and for ev - er. A - men.

Setting: Mason Martens (b. 1933)

The Holy Eucharist I
The Peace

S 110

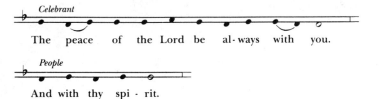

Celebrant

The peace of the Lord be al- ways with you.

People

And with thy spi - rit.

The Holy Eucharist II
The Peace

S 111

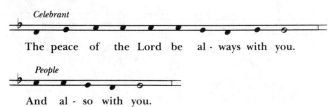

Celebrant

The peace of the Lord be al - ways with you.

People

And al - so with you.

Setting: Ambrosian chant; adapt. Mason Martens (b. 1933)

S 112

Lift up your hearts   *Sursum corda*

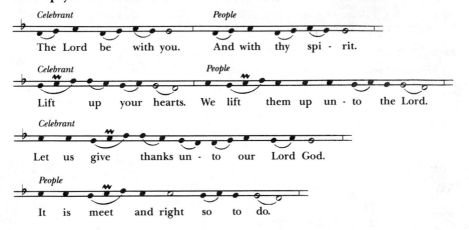

Celebrant The Lord be with you. *People* And with thy spi - rit.

Celebrant Lift up your hearts. *People* We lift them up un - to the Lord.

Celebrant Let us give thanks un - to our Lord God.

People It is meet and right so to do.

S 113

Holy, holy, holy   *Sanctus*

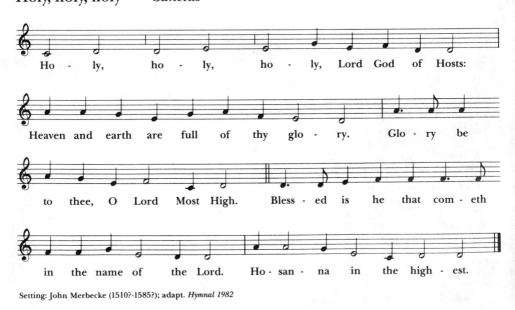

Ho - ly, ho - ly, ho - ly, Lord God of Hosts:

Heaven and earth are full of thy glo - ry. Glo - ry be

to thee, O Lord Most High. Bless - ed is he that com - eth

in the name of the Lord. Ho - san - na in the high - est.

Setting: John Merbecke (1510?-1585?); adapt. *Hymnal 1982*

The Holy Eucharist I
Holy, holy, holy *Sanctus*

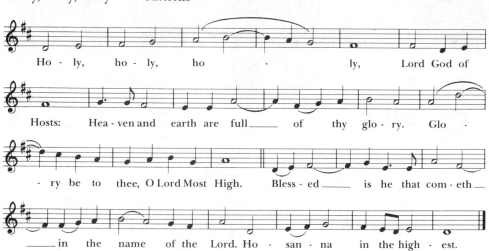

Ho - ly, ho - ly, ho - ly, Lord God of Hosts: Hea - ven and earth are full ____ of thy glo - ry. Glo - ry be to thee, O Lord Most High. Bless - ed ____ is he that com - eth ____ in the name of the Lord. Ho - san - na in the high - est.

Setting: From *Missa de Sancta Maria Magdalena*, Healey Willan (1880-1968)

The Holy Eucharist I
Holy, holy, holy *Sanctus*

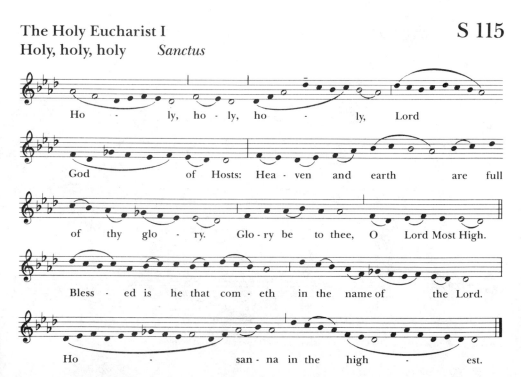

Ho - ly, ho - ly, ho - ly, Lord God of Hosts: Hea - ven and earth are full of thy glo - ry. Glo - ry be to thee, O Lord Most High. Bless - ed is he that com - eth in the name of the Lord. Ho - san - na in the high - est.

Setting: From *Missa Marialis*; Plainsong, Mode 5; Mass 9; adapt. Charles Winfred Douglas (1867-1944) and Bruce E. Ford (b. 1947)

Holy, holy, holy *Sanctus*

Ho - ly, ho - ly, ho - ly,

Lord God

of Hosts: Hea - ven and earth are full

of thy glo - ry. Glo - ry be to thee, O

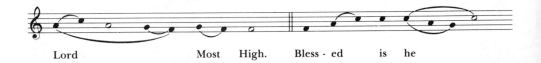

Lord Most High. Bless - ed is he

that com - eth in the name of the Lord.

Ho - san - na in the high - est.

Setting: From *Missa de Angelis*; Mode 5; Mass 8; adapt. Charles Winfred Douglas (1867-1944)

The Holy Eucharist I
Holy, holy, holy   *Sanctus*

S 117

Unison or harmony

Ho - ly, ho - ly, ho - ly,___ Lord God of Hosts: Heaven and

earth are full of thy glo - ry. Glo- ry be to thee, O Lord Most High.

Bless - ed is he that com - eth in the name of the

Lord. Ho - san - na in the high - est.

Setting: James McGregor (b. 1930), after *Verbum caro factum est*, Hans Leo Hassler (1564-1612)

S 118

Conclusion of Eucharistic Prayer and Amen

Celebrant ... *People*

A - men.

S 119

The Lord's Prayer (Traditional)

Our Fa - ther, who art in hea - ven, hal - low - ed

be thy Name, thy king - dom come, thy will be done,

on earth as it is in hea - ven. Give us this day our

dai - ly bread. And for - give us our tres - pas - ses,

as we for - give those who tres - pass a - gainst us. And lead

us not in - to temp - ta - tion, but de - liv - er us

from e - vil. For thine is the king - dom, and the power,

and the glo - ry, for ev - er and ev - er. A - men.

Setting: Plainsong; adapt. Charles Winfred Douglas (1867-1944)

The Holy Eucharist II
Lift up your hearts   *Sursum corda*

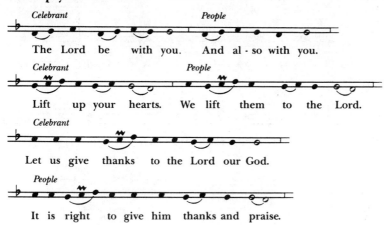

Celebrant — *People*

The Lord be with you. And al-so with you.

Celebrant — *People*

Lift up your hearts. We lift them to the Lord.

Celebrant

Let us give thanks to the Lord our God.

People

It is right to give him thanks and praise.

The Holy Eucharist II
Holy, holy, holy Lord   *Sanctus*

Ho - ly, ho - ly, ho - ly Lord,

God of power and might, heaven and earth are full of your glo - ry.

Ho - san - na in the high - est. Bless - ed is he who comes

in the name of the Lord. Ho - san - na in the high - est.

Setting: Plainsong, Te Deum Tone; adapt. James McGregor (b. 1930)

S 122

Holy, holy, holy Lord *Sanctus*

Ho - ly,   ho - ly,   ho - ly   Lord,   God   of

power   and   might,   hea - ven   and   earth   are   full   of   your   glo - ry.

Ho - san - na   in   the   high - est.   Bless - ed   is   he   who   comes

in   the   name   of   the   Lord.   Ho - san - na   in   the   high - est.

Setting: Plainsong; Mass 18; adapt. Mason Martens (b. 1933)

S 123

Holy, holy, holy Lord *Sanctus*

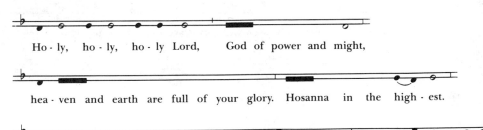

Ho - ly,   ho - ly,   ho - ly   Lord,   God   of   power   and   might,

hea - ven   and   earth   are   full   of   your   glory.   Hosanna   in   the   high - est.

Bless - ed   is   he   who   comes   in   the   name   of   the   Lord.   Ho - san - na   in   the   high - est.

Setting: Mozarabic chant, ca. 8th cent.; adapt. Howard E. Galley (b. 1929)

The Holy Eucharist II
Holy, holy, holy Lord   *Sanctus*

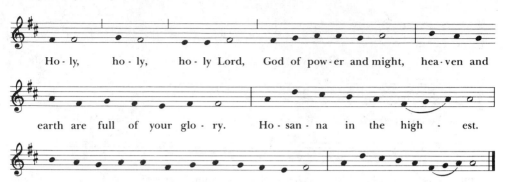

Ho - ly, ho - ly, ho - ly Lord, God of pow-er and might, hea - ven and earth are full of your glo - ry. Ho - san - na in the high - est. Bless - ed is he who comes in the name of the Lord. Ho-san - na in the high - est.

Setting: From *New Plainsong*; David Hurd (b. 1950)

The Holy Eucharist II
Holy, holy, holy Lord   *Sanctus*

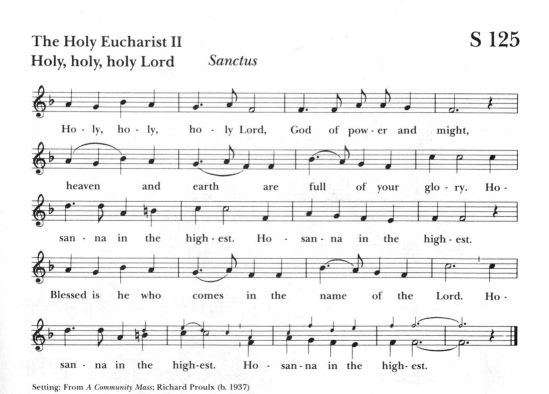

Ho - ly, ho - ly, ho - ly Lord, God of pow-er and might, heaven and earth are full of your glo - ry. Ho - san - na in the high - est. Ho - san - na in the high - est. Blessed is he who comes in the name of the Lord. Ho - san - na in the high - est. Ho - san - na in the high - est.

Setting: From *A Community Mass*; Richard Proulx (b. 1937)

S 126

Holy, holy, holy Lord   *Sanctus*

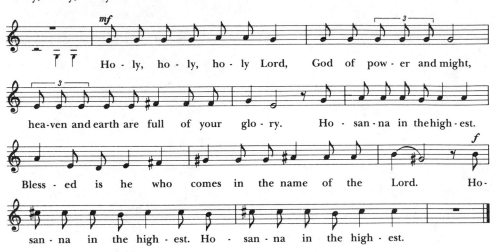

Holy, holy, holy Lord, God of pow-er and might, hea-ven and earth are full of your glo-ry. Ho-san-na in the high-est. Bless-ed is he who comes in the name of the Lord. Ho-san-na in the high-est. Ho-san-na in the high-est.

Setting: Richard Felciano (b. 1930)

S 127

Holy, holy, holy Lord   *Sanctus*

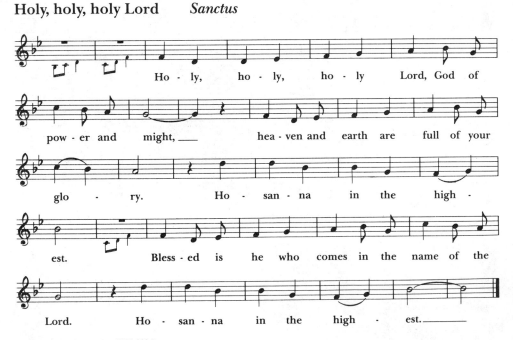

Ho-ly, ho-ly, ho-ly Lord, God of pow-er and might, hea-ven and earth are full of your glo-ry. Ho-san-na in the high-est. Bless-ed is he who comes in the name of the Lord. Ho-san-na in the high-est.

Setting: Calvin Hampton (1938-1984)

The Holy Eucharist II
Holy, holy, holy Lord *Sanctus*

S 128

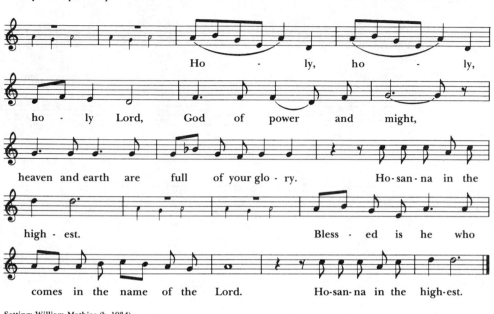

Setting: William Mathias (b. 1934)

The Holy Eucharist II
Holy, holy, holy Lord *Sanctus*

S 129

Setting: Robert Powell (b. 1932)

S 130

Holy, holy, holy Lord   *Sanctus*

Setting: From *Deutsche Messe*, Franz Peter Schubert (1797-1828); arr. Richard Proulx (b. 1937)

S 131

The Holy Eucharist II

Holy, holy, holy Lord   *Sanctus*

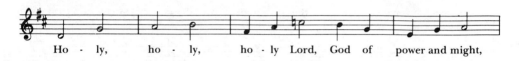

Ho - ly, ho - ly, ho - ly Lord, God of power and might,

heaven and earth are full of your glo - ry. Ho -

san - na in the high - est. Bless - ed is he who comes in the

name of the Lord. Ho - san - na in the high - est.

Setting: Gerald R. Near (b. 1942)

S 132

The Holy Eucharist II

Memorial Acclamation: Prayer A

Christ has died. Christ is ris - en. Christ will come a - gain.

Setting: Antiphon tone; adapt. Bruce E. Ford (b. 1947)

The Holy Eucharist II
Memorial Acclamation: Prayer A

S 133

Celebrant

There - fore we pro - claim the mys - ter - y of faith:

Celebrant and People

Christ has died. Christ is ris - en. Christ will come a - gain.

Setting: Ambrosian chant; adapt. Mason Martens (b. 1933)

The Holy Eucharist II
Memorial Acclamation: Prayer A

S 134

Christ has died. Christ is ris - en. Christ will come a - gain.

Setting: Plainsong, Te Deum Tone; adapt. Richard Proulx (b. 1937)

The Holy Eucharist II
Memorial Acclamation: Prayer A

S 135

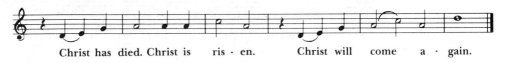

Christ has died. Christ is ris - en. Christ will come a - gain.

Setting: Jackson Hill (b. 1941)

S 136

The Holy Eucharist II

Memorial Acclamation: Prayer B

Celebrant

There - fore, ac - cord - ing to his com - mand, O Fa - ther,

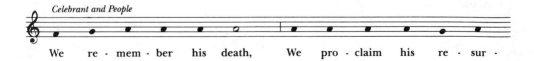

Celebrant and People

We re - mem - ber his death, We pro - claim his re - sur -

rec - tion, We a - wait his com - ing in glo - ry.

Setting: Ambrosian anaphora chant; adapt. Mason Martens (b. 1933)

S 137

The Holy Eucharist II

Memorial Acclamation: Prayer B

Celebrant

There - fore, ac - cord - ing to his com - mand, O Fa - ther,

Celebrant and People

We re - mem - ber his death, We pro - claim his re - sur -

rec - tion, We a - wait his com - ing in glo - ry.

Setting: Plainsong, Te Deum Tone; adapt. Mason Martens (b. 1933)

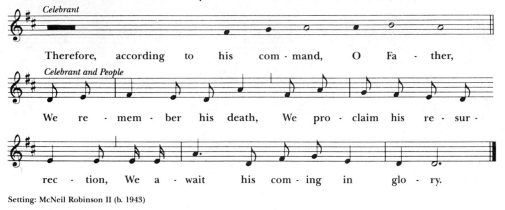

Celebrant

Therefore, according to his com-mand, O Fa-ther,

Celebrant and People

We re-mem-ber his death, We pro-claim his re-sur-

rec-tion, We a-wait his com-ing in glo-ry.

Setting: McNeil Robinson II (b. 1943)

The Holy Eucharist II
Memorial Acclamation: Prayer D

S 139

Celebrant

. . . we praise you and we bless you.

Celebrant and People

We praise you, we bless you, we give

thanks to you, and we pray to you, Lord our God.

Setting: Plainsong, Te Deum Tone; adapt. Mason Martens (b. 1933)

S 140

Memorial Acclamation: Prayer D

We praise you, we bless you, we give thanks

to you, and we pray to you, Lord our God.

Setting: Ambrosian chant; adapt. Richard Proulx (b. 1937)

S 141

Memorial Acclamation: Prayer D

Celebrant ... we praise you and we bless you. *All* We

praise you, we bless you, we give thanks to

you, and we pray to you, Lord our God.

Setting: McNeil Robinson II (b. 1943)

S 142

Conclusion of Eucharistic Prayer and Amen

Celebrant *People* A - men.

The Holy Eucharist
Amen

S 143

A - men.   A - men.   A - men.

Setting: From *Missa de Angelis*; Plainsong, Mode 6; adapt. Mason Martens (b. 1933)

The Holy Eucharist
Amen

S 144

A - men.   A - men.

Setting: Henri Dumont (1610-1684); adapt. Mason Martens (b. 1933)

The Holy Eucharist
Amen

S 145

A - men.   A - men.

Setting: Henri Dumont (1610-1684); adapt. Mason Martens (b. 1933)

The Holy Eucharist
Amen

S 146

A - men.   A - men.   A - men.

Setting: McNeil Robinson II (b. 1943)

S 147
Amen

A - men.   A - men.   A - men.

Setting: McNeil Robinson II (b. 1943)

S 148
The Lord's Prayer (Contemporary)

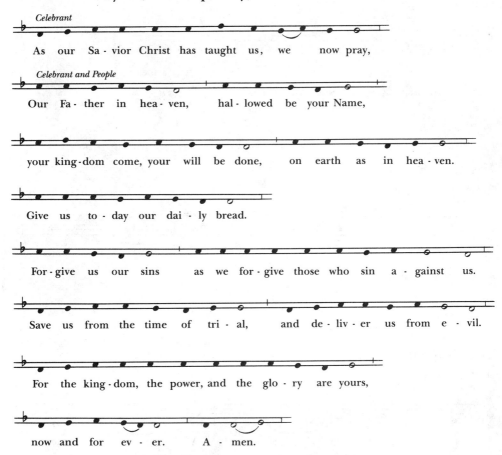

Celebrant

As our Sa - vior Christ has taught us, we now pray,

Celebrant and People

Our Fa - ther in hea - ven, hal - lowed be your Name,

your king - dom come, your will be done, on earth as in hea - ven.

Give us to - day our dai - ly bread.

For - give us our sins as we for - give those who sin a - gainst us.

Save us from the time of tri - al, and de - liv - er us from e - vil.

For the king - dom, the power, and the glo - ry are yours,

now and for ev - er. A - men.

Setting: Ambrosian chant; adapt. Mason Martens (b. 1933)

The Holy Eucharist II
The Lord's Prayer (Contemporary)

Our Fa-ther in hea-ven, hal-lowed be your Name,

your king-dom come, your will be done, on earth as in

hea-ven. Give us to-day our dai-ly bread.

For-give us our sins as we for-give those who

sin a-gainst us. Save us from the time of trial,

and de-liv-er us from e-vil. For the king-dom, the pow-er,

and the glo-ry are yours, now and for ev-er. A-men.

Setting: McNeil Robinson II (b. 1943)

The Lord's Prayer (Contemporary)

Unison or harmony

Our Fa-ther in hea-ven, hal-lowed be your Name, your king-dom come, your will be done, on earth as in heaven. Give us to-day our dai-ly bread. For-give us our sins as we for-give those who sin a-gainst us. Save us from the time of trial, and de-liv-er us from e-vil. For the king-dom, the power, and the glo-ry are yours, now and for ev-er. A-men.

Slightly faster

Setting: From *Intercession Mass*; David Hurd (b. 1950)

Fraction Anthem: Christ our Passover

This setting is not used in Lent.

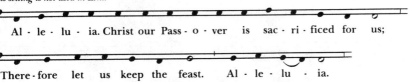

Setting: From *Missa orbis factor*; Plainsong, Tonus Peregrinus; arr. David Hurd (b. 1950)

The Holy Eucharist

S 152

Fraction Anthem: Christ our Passover

This setting is not used in Lent.

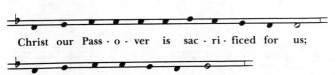

This setting may be sung full by all, or by the choir, or as a versicle and response.

Setting: Ambrosian chant; adapt. Mason Martens (b. 1933)

The Holy Eucharist

S 153

Fraction Anthem: Christ our Passover

This setting may be sung full by all, or by the choir, or as a versicle and response.

Setting: Ambrosian chant; adapt. Mason Martens (b. 1933)

S 154

Fraction Anthem: Christ our Passover

This setting is not used in Lent.

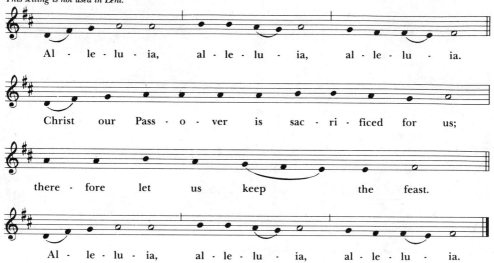

Setting: From *New Plainsong*; David Hurd (b. 1950)

S 155

Fraction Anthem: Christ our Passover

This setting is not used in Lent.

Setting: Gerald R. Near (b. 1942)

The Holy Eucharist
Fraction Anthem: Christ our Passover

Christ our Pass-o-ver is sac-ri-ficed for us; there-fore let us keep the feast.

Setting: Gerald R. Near (b. 1942)

The Holy Eucharist I
Fraction Anthem: O Lamb of God   *Agnus Dei*

O Lamb of God, that ta-kest a-way the sins of the world, have mer-cy up-on us.

O Lamb of God, that ta-kest a-way the sins of the world, have mer-cy up-on us.

O Lamb of God, that ta-kest a-way the sins of the world, grant us thy peace.

Setting: John Merbecke (1518?-1585?); adapt. *Hymnal 1982*

S 158

Fraction Anthem: O Lamb of God *Agnus Dei*

O Lamb of God, that ta-kest a-way the sins of the world, have mer-cy up-on us. O Lamb of God, that ta-kest a-way the sins of the world, have mer-cy up-on us. O Lamb of God, that ta-kest a-way the sins of the world, grant_____ us thy peace.

Setting: From *Missa de Sancta Maria Magdalena*, Healey Willan (1880-1968)

O   Lamb   of God,   that   ta -   kest a - way

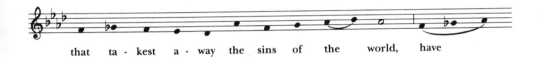

the   sins   of   the   world, have   mer -   cy

up - on   us.   O   Lamb   of   God,

that   ta - kest a - way the sins of   the   world,   have

mer - cy   up - on   us.   O   Lamb   of

God,   that   ta -   kest a - way the sins   of

the   world,   grant   us   thy   peace.

Setting: From *Missa Marialis*; Plainsong, Mode 5; Mass 9; adapt. Charles Winfred Douglas (1867-1944)

S 160

Fraction Anthem: Lamb of God *Agnus Dei*

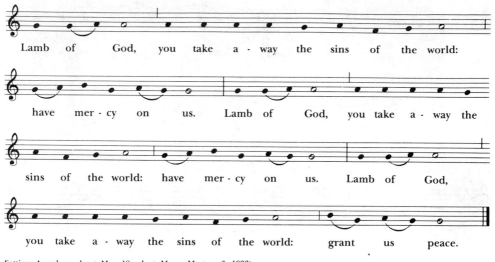

Lamb of God, you take a-way the sins of the world: have mer-cy on us. Lamb of God, you take a-way the sins of the world: have mer-cy on us. Lamb of God, you take a-way the sins of the world: grant us peace.

Setting: Anaphora chant; Mass 18; adapt. Mason Martens (b. 1933)

S 161

Fraction Anthem: Lamb of God *Agnus Dei*

Lamb of God, you take a-way the sins of the world: have mer-cy on us. Lamb of God, you take a-way the sins of the world: have mer-cy on us. Lamb of God, you take a-way the sins of the world: grant us peace.

Setting: From *New Plainsong*; David Hurd (b. 1950)

The Holy Eucharist II
Fraction Anthem: Lamb of God *Agnus Dei*

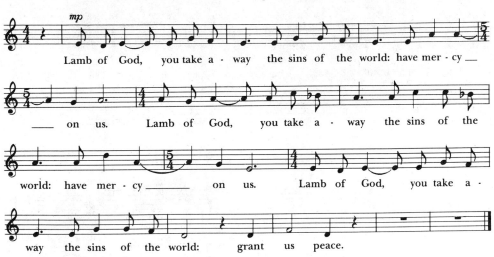

Lamb of God, you take a-way the sins of the world: have mer-cy ___ ___ on us. Lamb of God, you take a-way the sins of the world: have mer-cy ___ on us. Lamb of God, you take a-way the sins of the world: grant us peace.

Setting: Richard Felciano (b. 1930)

The Holy Eucharist II
Fraction Anthem: Lamb of God *Agnus Dei*

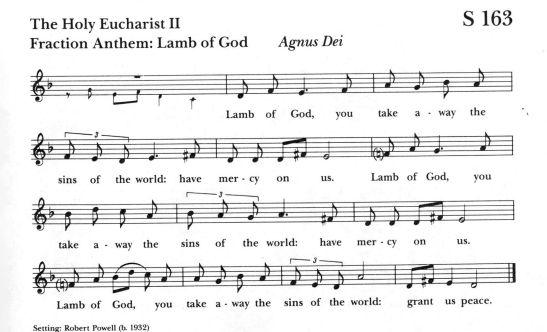

Lamb of God, you take a-way the sins of the world: have mer-cy on us. Lamb of God, you take a-way the sins of the world: have mer-cy on us. Lamb of God, you take a-way the sins of the world: grant us peace.

Setting: Robert Powell (b. 1932)

S 164

Fraction Anthem: Jesus, Lamb of God *Agnus Dei*

Je - sus, Lamb of God: have mer - cy on us.

Je - sus, bear - er of our sins: have mer - cy on us.

Je - sus, re - deem - er, re - deem - er of the world:

give us your peace, give us your peace.

Setting: From *Deutsche Messe*; Franz Peter Schubert (1797-1828); arr. Richard Proulx (b. 1937)

The Holy Eucharist
Fraction Anthem: Jesus, Lamb of God   *Agnus Dei*

Je - sus, Lamb of God: have mer - cy

on us.   Je - sus, bear - er of our sins: have mer - cy

on us.   Je - sus, re - deem - er of the world: give us your peace.

Setting: William Matthias (b. 1934)

The Holy Eucharist
Fraction Anthem: Jesus, Lamb of God   *Agnus Dei*

Je - sus, Lamb of God: have mer - cy on

us.   Je - sus, bear - er of our sins: have mer - cy on us.

Je - sus, re - deem - er of the world: give us your peace.

Setting: Gerald R. Near (b. 1942)

S 167

Fraction Anthem: The disciples knew the Lord Jesus

This setting is not used in Lent.

Antiphon
Cantor; then All

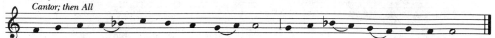

The dis-ci-ples knew the Lord Je-sus in the break-ing of the bread.

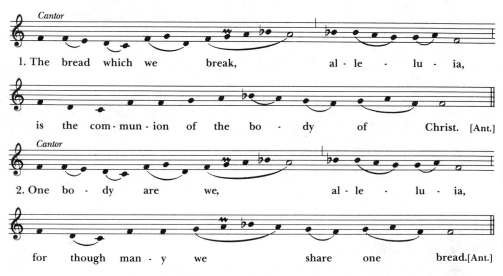

Cantor

1. The bread which we break, al-le-lu-ia,

is the com-mun-ion of the bo-dy of Christ. [Ant.]

Cantor

2. One bo-dy are we, al-le-lu-ia,

for though man-y we share one bread.[Ant.]

Setting: Mode 6 melody; adapt. Mason Martens (b. 1933)

S 168

Fraction Anthem: My flesh is food indeed

Antiphon
Cantor; then All

My flesh is food in-deed, and my blood is drink in-deed, says the Lord.

Cantor

Those who eat my flesh and drink my blood dwell in me and I in them. [Ant.]

Setting: Ambrosian chant; adapt. Mason Martens (b. 1933)

Fraction Anthem: My flesh is food indeed

Cantor or Choir

My flesh is food in - deed, and my blood is drink in -

deed, says the Lord. My Lord. Those who eat my

flesh and drink my blood dwell in me, and I in them. My

flesh is food in - deed, and my blood is drink in - deed, says the Lord.

Setting: Ray W. Urwin (b. 1950)

Fraction Anthem: Whoever eats this bread

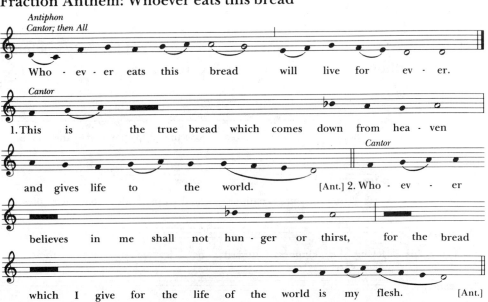

Antiphon
Cantor; then All

Who - ev - er eats this bread will live for ev - er.

Cantor

1. This is the true bread which comes down from hea - ven

and gives life to the world. [Ant.] 2. Who - ev - er

believes in me shall not hun - ger or thirst, for the bread

which I give for the life of the world is my flesh. [Ant.]

Setting: Mode 1 melody; adapt. Mason Martens (b. 1933)

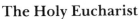

S 171

Fraction Anthem: Be known to us

This setting is not used in Lent.

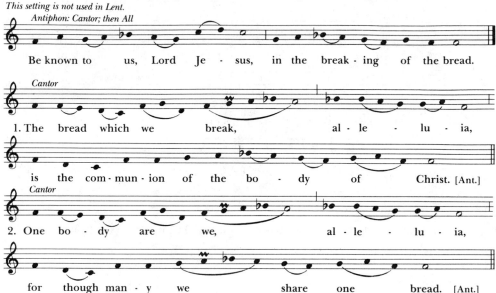

Antiphon: Cantor; then All

Be known to us, Lord Je - sus, in the break - ing of the bread.

Cantor

1. The bread which we break, al - le - lu - ia,

is the com - mun - ion of the bo - dy of Christ. [Ant.]

Cantor

2. One bo - dy are we, al - le - lu - ia,

for though man - y we share one bread. [Ant.]

Setting: Mode 6 melody; adapt. Mason Martens (b. 1933)

S 172

Fraction Anthem: Blessed are those who are called

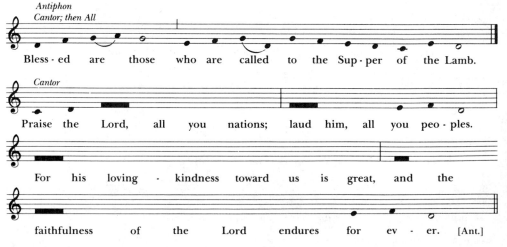

Antiphon
Cantor; then All

Bless - ed are those who are called to the Sup - per of the Lamb.

Cantor

Praise the Lord, all you nations; laud him, all you peo - ples.

For his loving - kindness toward us is great, and the

faithfulness of the Lord endures for ev - er. [Ant.]

Setting: Ambrosian chant; adapt. Mason Martens (b. 1933)

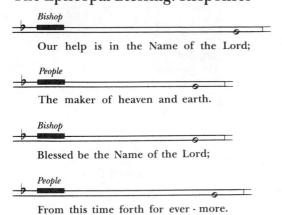

Bishop

Our help is in the Name of the Lord;

People

The maker of heaven and earth.

Bishop

Blessed be the Name of the Lord;

People

From this time forth for ever - more.

The Bishop sings the blessing.

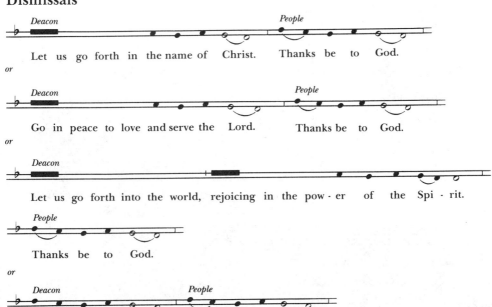

Deacon　　　　　　　　　　*People*

Let us go forth in the name of Christ.　Thanks be to God.

or

Deacon　　　　　　　　　　*People*

Go in peace to love and serve the Lord.　Thanks be to God.

or

Deacon

Let us go forth into the world, rejoicing in the pow - er of the Spi - rit.

People

Thanks be to God.

or

Deacon　　　　　　　　*People*

Let us bless the Lord.　Thanks be to God.

S 175

Dismissals in Easter Season

Deacon

Let us go forth in the name of Christ, al·le·lu·ia, al·le — lu — ia.

People

Thanks be to God, al·le·lu·ia, al·le — lu — ia.

or

Deacon

Go in peace to love and serve the Lord, al·le·lu·ia, al·le — lu — ia.

People

Thanks be to God, al·le·lu·ia, al·le — lu — ia.

or

Deacon

Let us go forth into the world, rejoicing in the power of the Spi·rit, al·le·lu·ia, al·le — lu — ia.

People

Thanks be to God, al·le·lu·ia, al·le — lu — ia.

or the following

Let us bless the Lord, al - le - lu - ia, al - le - lu - ia.

Thanks be to God, al - le - lu - ia, al - le - lu - ia.

The Holy Eucharist
Dismissals in Easter Season

S 176

Let us go forth in the name of Christ, al - le - lu - ia, al - le - lu - ia.

Thanks be to God, al - le - lu - ia, al - le - lu - ia.

or

Go in peace to love and serve the Lord, al - le - lu - ia, al - le - lu - ia.

Thanks be to God, al - le - lu - ia, al - le - lu - ia.

or the following

Deacon

Let us go forth into the world, rejoicing in the pow-er of the Spi-rit, al-le-lu-ia, al-le-lu-ia.

People

Thanks be to God, al-le-lu-ia, al-le-lu-ia.

or

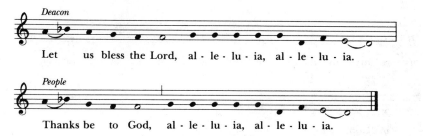

Deacon

Let us bless the Lord, al-le-lu-ia, al-le-lu-ia.

People

Thanks be to God, al-le-lu-ia, al-le-lu-ia.

Setting: From *Missa orbis factor*; Plainsong, Tonus Peregrinus; adapt. David Hurd (b. 1950)

Canticles

Canticle 1

A Song of Creation   *Benedicite, omnia opera Domini*

This Canticle may be shortened by omitting section II or III.

I Invocation

1. O all ye works of the Lord, bless ye the Lord; praise him and magnify him for ev - er. 2. O ye angels of the Lord, bless ye the Lord; praise him and magnify him for ev - er.

II The Cosmic Order

3. O ye heavens, bless ye the Lord; O ye waters that be above the firmament, bless ye the Lord; 4. O all ye powers of the Lord, bless ye the Lord; praise him and magnify him for ev - er.

5. O ye sun and moon, bless ye the Lord; O ye stars of heaven,

bless ye the Lord; 6. O ye showers and dew, bless ye the Lord;

praise him and magnify him for ev - er. 7. O ye winds of God,

bless ye the Lord; O ye fire and heat, bless ye the Lord;

8. O ye winter and summer, bless ye the Lord; praise him and magnify

him for ev - er. 9. O ye dews and frosts, bless ye the Lord;

O ye frost and cold, bless ye the Lord; 10. O ye ice and snow,

bless ye the Lord; praise him and magnify him for ev - er.

11. O ye nights and days, bless ye the Lord; O ye light and darkness,

bless ye the Lord; 12. O ye lightnings and clouds,

bless ye the Lord; praise him and magnify him for ev - er.

III The Earth and its Creatures

13. O let the earth bless the Lord; O ye mountains and hills,

bless ye the Lord; 14. O all ye green things upon the earth,

bless ye the Lord; praise him and magnify him for ev - er.

15. O ye wells, bless ye the Lord; O ye seas and floods, bless ye the Lord;

16. O ye whales and all that move in the waters, bless ye the Lord;

praise him and magnify him for ev - er. 17. O all ye fowls of the air,

bless ye the Lord; O all ye beasts and cattle, bless ye the Lord;

18. O ye children of men, bless ye the Lord; praise him and magnify him for ev - er.

IV The People of God

19. O ye people of God, bless ye the Lord; O ye priests of the Lord,

bless ye the Lord; 20. O ye servants of the Lord, bless ye the Lord;

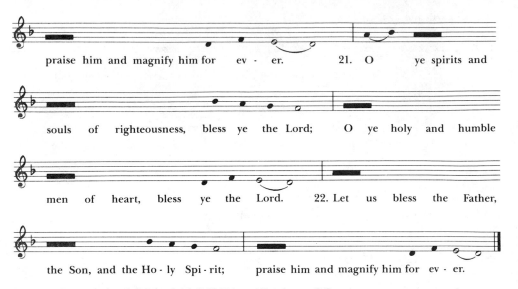

praise him and magnify him for ev - er. 21. O ye spirits and

souls of righteousness, bless ye the Lord; O ye holy and humble

men of heart, bless ye the Lord. 22. Let us bless the Father,

the Son, and the Ho - ly Spi - rit; praise him and magnify him for ev - er.

Setting: Plainsong, Tonus Peregrinus, verses 1-2, 19-22; Plainsong, Tone 1, verses 3-18;
  adapt. The Standing Commission on Church Music, 1979

Canticle 1

A Song of Creation *Benedicite, omnia opera Domini*

S 178 — Stephen Elvey (1805-1860)

S 179 — John F. Burrows (19th. cent.)

This Canticle may be shortened by omitting section II or III. The entire Canticle, or section I with section II or III and section IV, may be sung to a double chant.

I Invocation

1 O all ye works of the Lord,ˈbless ye theˈLord; *
      praise him andˈmagnifyˈhim forˈever.

2 O ye angels of the Lord,ˈbless ye theˈLord; *
      praise him andˈmagnifyˈhim forˈever.

S 178

John Robinson
(1682-1762)

S 179

Jonathan Battishill
(1738-1801)

II   The Cosmic Order

3   O ye heavens, 'bless ye the 'Lord; *
     O ye waters that be above the 'firmament, 'bless ye the 'Lord;

4   O all ye powers of the Lord, 'bless ye the 'Lord; *
     praise him and 'magnify 'him for 'ever.

5   O ye sun and moon, 'bless ye the 'Lord; *
     O ye stars of 'heaven, 'bless ye the 'Lord;

6   O ye showers and dew, 'bless ye the 'Lord; *
     praise him and 'magnify 'him for 'ever.

7   O ye winds of God, 'bless ye the 'Lord; *
     O ye fire and 'heat, 'bless ye the 'Lord;

8   O ye winter and summer, 'bless ye the 'Lord; *
     praise him and 'magnify 'him for 'ever.

9   O ye dews and frosts, 'bless ye the 'Lord; *
     O ye frost and 'cold, 'bless ye the 'Lord;

10 O ye ice and snow, 'bless ye the 'Lord; *
     praise him and 'magnify 'him for 'ever.

11 O ye nights and days, 'bless ye the 'Lord; *
     O ye light and 'darkness, 'bless ye the 'Lord;

12 O ye lightnings and clouds, 'bless ye the 'Lord; *
     praise him and 'magnify 'him for 'ever.

James Turle
(1802-1882)

Jonathan Battishill
(1738-1801)

III   The Earth and its Creatures

13   O let the earth ˈbless the ˈLord; *

O ye mountains and ˈhills, ˈbless ye the ˈLord;

14   O all ye green things upon the earth, ˈbless ye the ˈLord; *

praise him and ˈmagnify ˈhim for ˈever.

15   O ye wells, ˈbless ye the ˈLord; *

O ye seas and ˈfloods, ˈbless ye the ˈLord;

16   O ye whales and all that move in the waters, ˈbless ye the ˈLord; *

praise him and ˈmagnify ˈhim for ˈever.

17   O all ye fowls of the air, ˈbless ye the ˈLord; *

O all ye beasts and ˈcattle, ˈbless ye the ˈLord;

18   O ye children of men, ˈbless ye the ˈLord; *

praise him and ˈmagnify ˈhim for ˈever.

S 178 Stephen Elvey
(1805-1860)

S 179 John F. Burrows
(19th cent.)

IV   The People of God

19   O ye people of God,ˈbless ye theˈLord; *

O ye priests of theˈLörd,ˈbless ye theˈLord;

20   O ye servants of the Lord,ˈbless ye theˈLord; *

praise him andˈmagnifyˈhim forˈever.

21   O ye spirits and souls of the righteous,ˈbless ye theˈLord; *

O ye holy and humble men ofˈhëart,ˈbless ye theˈLord.

22   Let us bless the Father, the Son, and theˈHolyˈSpirit; *

praise him andˈmagnifyˈhim forˈever.

A Song of Praise — *Benedictus es, Domine*

Antiphon

Pro - claim the great-ness of the Lord our God: he is the Ho - ly One.

1. Bless - ed art thou, O Lord God of our fa - thers; praised and exalted above all for ev - er.

2. Blessed art thou for the Name of thy Maj - es - ty; praised and exalted above all for ev - er.

3. Blessed art thou in the temple of thy ho - li - ness; praised and exalted above all for ev - er.

4. Blessed art thou that beholdest the depths, and dwellest between the Cher - u - bim; praised and exalted above all for ev - er.

5. Blessed art thou on the glorious throne of thy king - dom; praised and exalted above all for ev - er.

6. Blessed art thou in the firmament of hea - ven, praised and exalted above all for ev - er.

7. Blessed art thou, O Father, Son, and Holy Spi - rit; praised and exalted above all for ev - er. [Ant.]

Setting: Plainsong, Tone 8; adapt. Bruce E. Ford (b. 1947)

Canticle 2
A Song of Praise   *Benedictus es, Domine*

S 181 George A. MacFarren (1813-1887)

S 182 John Jones (1728-1796)

S 183 J. Soaper (1743-1794)

S 184 John Goss (1800-1880)

1 Blessèd art thou, O Lord ˈGod of our ˈfathers; *
   praised and exalted aˈböve ˈall for ˈever.

2 Blessèd art thou for the ˈName of thy ˈMajesty; *
   praised and exalted aˈböve ˈall for ˈever.

3 Blessèd art thou in the ˈtemple of thy ˈholiness; *
   praised and exalted aˈböve ˈall for ˈever.

4 Blessèd art thou that beholdest the depths,
   and dwellest beˈtween the ˈCherubim; *
   praised and exalted aˈböve ˈall for ˈever.

5 Blessèd art thou on the glorious ˈthrone of thy ˈkingdom; *
   praised and exalted aˈböve ˈall for ˈever.

6 Blessèd art thou in the ˈfirmament of ˈheaven; *
   praised and exalted aˈböve ˈall for ˈever.

†7 Blessèd art thou, O Father, Son, and ˈHoly ˈSpirit; *
   praised and exalted aˈböve ˈall for ˈever.

† *Second half of double chant.*

S 185

The Song of Mary *Magnificat*

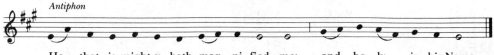

Antiphon

He that is might-y hath mag-ni-fied me: and ho-ly is his Name.

1. My soul doth mag-ni-fy the Lord, and my spi-rit

hath rejoiced in God my Sav-ior. 2. For he hath re-gard-ed

the low-li-ness of his hand-maid-en. 3. For be-hold from hence-forth

all gen-er-a-tions shall call me bless-ed. 4. For he that is

might-y hath mag-ni-fied me, and ho-ly is his Name.

5. And his mer-cy is on them that fear him through-out all gen-er-a-tions.

6. He hath showed strength with his arm; he hath scat-tered the

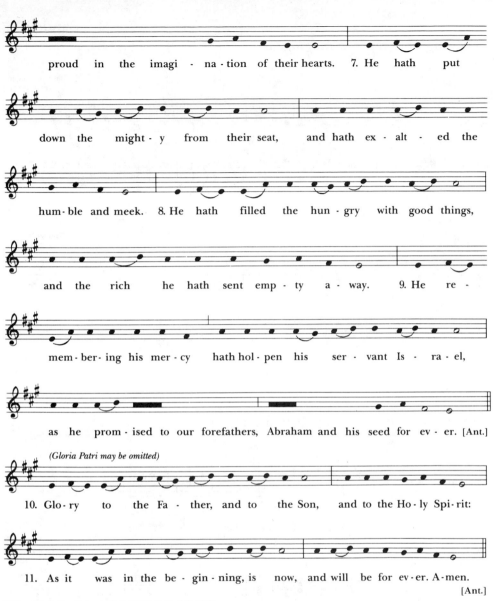

proud in the imagi - na - tion of their hearts. 7. He hath put

down the might - y from their seat, and hath ex - alt - ed the

hum - ble and meek. 8. He hath filled the hun - gry with good things,

and the rich he hath sent emp - ty a - way. 9. He re -

mem - ber - ing his mer - cy hath hol - pen his ser - vant Is - ra - el,

as he prom - ised to our forefathers, Abraham and his seed for ev - er. [Ant.]

(Gloria Patri may be omitted)

10. Glo - ry to the Fa - ther, and to the Son, and to the Ho - ly Spi - rit:

11. As it was in the be - gin - ning, is now, and will be for ev - er. A - men.

[Ant.]

Setting: Mode 8 antiphon; adapt. Bruce E. Ford (b. 1947).
  Plainsong, Tone 8 (Solemn); adapt. Charles Winfred Douglas (1867-1944), alt.

The Song of Mary   *Magnificat*

S 186

William Crotch
(1775-1847)

S 187

Samuel Wesley
(1766-1837)

S 188

Henry Walford Davies
(1869-1941)

S 189

Benjamin Hutto
(b. 1947)

1 My soul doth ' magnify the ' Lord, *
    and my spirit hath re'joiced in ' God my ' Savior.

2 For ' he hath re'garded *
    the ' lowliness ' of his ' handmaiden.

3 For be'hold from ' henceforth *
    all gener'ations shall ' call me ' blessed.

4 For he that is mighty hath ' magnified ' me, *
    and ' holy ' is his ' Name.

†5 And his mercy is on ' them that ' fear him *
    throughout ' all ' gener'ations.

6 He hath showed ' strength with his ' arm; *
    he hath scattered the proud in the imagi'nation ' of their ' hearts.

7 He hath put down the ' mighty from their ' seat, *
    and hath ex'alted the ' humble and ' meek.

8 He hath filled the ' hungry with ' good things, *
    and the rich he hath ' sent ' empty a'way.

9 He remembering his mercy hath holpen his ' servant ' Israel, *
    as he promised to our forefathers, '
    Abraham and his ' seed for ' ever.

(Gloria Patri may be omitted)

Glory to the Father, and ' to the ' Son, *
    and ' to the ' Holy ' Spirit:
As it was in the be'ginning, is ' now, *
    and ' will be for ' ever. A'men.

†*Second half of double chant.*

S 190

The Song of Zechariah *Benedictus Dominus Deus*

7. That we being delivered out of the hand of our en-e-mies

might serve him with-out fear, 8. In holiness and right-eous-ness be-

fore him, all the days of our life. 9. And thou, child, shalt be called the pro-

phet of the High-est, for thou shalt go before the face of the Lord to

pre-pare his ways; 10. To give knowledge of salvation un-to

his peo-ple for the remis-sion of their sins, 11. Through the tend-er

mer-cy of our God, whereby the dayspring from on high hath vis-

it-ed us; 12. To give light to them that sit in darkness and in the

shad-ow of death, and to guide our feet into the way of peace. [Ant.]

(Gloria Patri may be omitted)

13. Glo-ry to the Fa-ther, and to the Son, and to the Ho-ly Spi-rit:

14. As it was in the be-gin-ning, is now, and will be for ev-er. A-men.

[Ant.]

Setting: Plainsong, Tonus Peregrinus; adapt. Bruce E. Ford (b. 1947)

The Song of Zechariah   *Benedictus Dominus Deus*

S 191

Edward John Hopkins
(1818-1901)

S 192

Thomas Attwood
(1765?-1838)

S 193

George Mursell Garrett
(1834-1897)

S 194

Richard Lloyd
(b. 1933)

S 195

William Morley
(1680-1731)

1   Blessèd be the Lord 'God of 'Israel, *

    for he hath 'visited and re'deemed his 'people;

2   And hath raised up a mighty sal'vation 'for us *

    in the 'house of his 'servant 'David,

3   As he spake by the mouth of his 'holy 'prophets, *

    which have 'been since the 'world be'gan:

4   That we should be 'saved from our 'enemies, *

    and from the 'hand of 'all that 'hate us;

5   To perform the mercy 'promised to our 'forefathers, *

    and to re'member his 'holy 'covenant;

6   To perform the oath which he sware to our 'forefather 'Abraham, *

    that 'he would 'give 'us,

7   That we being delivered out of the 'hand of our 'enemies *

    might 'serve him with 'out 'fear,

8   In holiness and 'righteousness be'fore him, *

    — 'all the 'days of our 'life.

9   And thou, child, shalt be called the 'prophet of the 'Highest, *

    for thou shalt go before the face of the 'Lord to pre'pare his 'ways;

10   To give knowledge of salvation 'unto his 'people *

    for the re'mission 'of their 'sins,

11   Through the tender 'mercy of our 'God, *

    whereby the dayspring from on 'high hath 'visited 'us;

12   To give light to them that sit in darkness

  and in the 'shadow of 'death, *

    and to guide our 'feet into the 'way of 'peace.

(Gloria Patri may be omitted)

Glory to the Father, and 'to the 'Son, *

    and 'to the 'Holy 'Spirit:

As it was in the be'ginning, is 'now, *

    and 'will be for'ever. A'men.

S 196

The Song of Simeon   *Nunc dimittis*

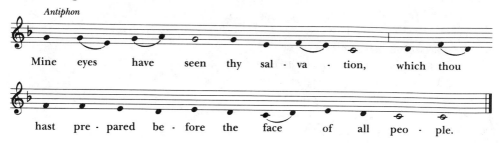

Antiphon

Mine eyes have seen thy sal-va-tion, which thou

hast pre-pared be-fore the face of all peo-ple.

1. Lord, now lettest thou thy ser-vant de-part in peace, ac-cord-ing

to thy word;   2. For mine eyes have seen thy sal-va-tion,

which thou hast prepared before the face of all peo-ple,

3. To be a light to light-en the Gen-tiles,

and to be the glory of thy peo-ple Is-ra-el.   [Ant.]

(Gloria Patri may be omitted)

4. Glo-ry to the Fa-ther, and to the Son,   and to the Ho-ly Spi-rit:

5. As it was in the be-gin-ning, is now,   and will be for ev-er. A-men.

[Ant.]

Setting: Mode 7 antiphon; adapt. Bruce E. Ford (b. 1947). Plainsong, Tone 7;
 adapt. The Standing Commission on Church Music, 1979

Canticle 5
The Song of Simeon   *Nunc dimittis*

S 197 — John Naylor (1838-1897)

S 198 — Frederick A. Gore Ouseley (1825-1909)

S 199 — John Blow (1649?-1708)

S 200 — Michael Wise (1648?-1687)

1 Lord, now lettest thou thy servant de'part in 'peace, *
   ac'cording 'to thy 'word;

2 for mine eyes have 'seen thy sal'vation, *
   which thou hast prepared before the 'face of 'all 'people,

3 To be a light to 'lighten the 'Gentiles, *
   and to be the 'glory of thy 'people 'Israel.

(Gloria Patri may be omitted)

Glory to the Father, and 'to the 'Son, *
   and 'to the 'Holy 'Spirit:

As it was in the be'ginning, is 'now, *
   and 'will be for'ever. A'men.

S 201

Canticle 6

Glory be to God *Gloria in excelsis*

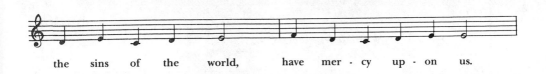

the sins of the world, have mer - cy up - on us.

6. Thou that ta - kest a - way the sins of the world,

re - ceive our prayer. 7. Thou that sit - test at the right hand

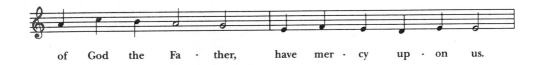

of God the Fa - ther, have mer - cy up - on us.

8. For thou on - ly art ho - ly; thou on - ly art the Lord;

9. thou on - ly, O Christ, with the Ho - ly Ghost, art most

high in the glo - ry of God the Fa - ther. A - men.

Setting: John Merbecke (1510?-1585?); adapt. *Hymnal 1982*

S 202

Glory be to God *Gloria in excelsis*

Canticle 6

1. Glo-ry be to God on high, and on earth peace,

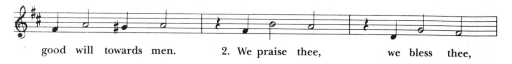

good will towards men. 2. We praise thee, we bless thee,

we wor-ship thee, we glo-ri-fy thee, we give

thanks to thee for thy great glo-ry, 3. O Lord God, heaven-ly

King, God ___ the Fa-ther Al-might - - - y. ___

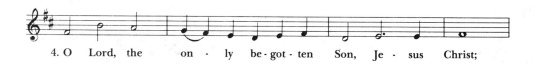

4. O Lord, the on-ly be-got-ten Son, Je-sus Christ;

5. O Lord God, Lamb of God, Son of the Fa-ther, that

ta - kest a - way the sins of the world, have mer - cy up -
on us. 6. Thou that ta - kest a - way the sins of the
world, re - ceive our prayer. 7. Thou that sit - test at the
right hand of God the Fa - ther, have mer - cy up - on us.
8. For thou on - ly art ho - ly; thou on - ly art the Lord; 9. thou
on - ly, O Christ, with the Ho - ly Ghost, art most
high in the glo - ry of God the Fa - ther. ___
A - - - - - - - men.

Setting: From *Missa de Sancta Maria Magdalena*, Healey Willan (1880-1968)

Glory be to God   *Gloria in excelsis*

1. Glo - ry be to God on high, and on earth peace, good will to - wards men. 2. We praise thee, we bless thee, we wor - ship thee, we glo - ri - fy thee, we give thanks to thee for thy great glo - ry, 3. O Lord God, hea - ven - ly King, God the Fa - ther Al - might - y. 4. O Lord, the on - ly be - got - ten Son, Je - sus Christ; 5. O Lord God, Lamb of God, Son of the Fa - ther, that ta - kest a - way the

sins of the world, have mer-cy up-on us.

6. Thou that ta-kest a-way the sins of the world,

re-ceive our prayer. 7. Thou that sit-test at the

right hand of God the Fa-ther, have mer-cy up-on us.

8. For thou on-ly art ho-ly; thou on-ly art the

Lord; thou on-ly, O Christ, with the Ho-ly

Ghost, art most high in the glo-ry of God the

Fa-ther. A-men.

Setting: From *Missa Marialis*; Plainsong, Mode 8; Mass 9; adapt. Charles Winfred Douglas (1867-1944)

Glory be to God   *Gloria in excelsis*

1. Glory be to God on high, and on earth peace, good will towards men.

2. We praise thee, we bless thee, we wor-ship thee, we glorify thee, we give thanks

to thee for thy great glo - ry, 3. O Lord God, heaven - ly King,

God the Father Al - might - y. 4. O Lord, the only - begotten Son, Je - sus Christ;

O Lord God, Lamb of God, Son of the Fa - ther,

5. that takest away the sins of the world, have mercy up - on us.

6. Thou that takest away the sins of the world, re - ceive our prayer.

7. Thou that sittest at the right hand of God the Fa - ther, have mercy up - on us.

8. For thou on - ly art ho - ly; thou on - ly art the Lord; 9. Thou only, O Christ,

with the Ho - ly Ghost, art most high in the glory of God the Fa - ther. A - men.

Setting: *Old Scottish Chant*, from *Chants or Tunes for Particular Hymns*, 1763?, alt.

S 205

We Praise Thee *Te Deum laudamus*

Optional Introduction

1. We praise thee, O God; we acknowledge thee to be the Lord.

All the earth doth worship thee, the Father ev - er - last - ing.

2. To thee all Angels cry aloud, the Heavens and all the Powers there - in.

To thee Cherubim and Seraphim con - tin - ual - ly do cry:

3. Holy, holy, holy, Lord God of Sa - ba - oth;

Heaven and earth are full of the majesty of thy glo - ry.

4. The glorious company of the apostles praise thee. The goodly

fellowship of the pro - phets praise thee. 5. The noble army of

martyrs praise thee. The holy Church throughout all the world

doth ac - know - ledge thee, 6. the Father, of an infinite majesty,

thine adorable, true, and on - ly Son, also the Holy Ghost the Com - fort - er.

7. Thou art the King of glo - ry, O Christ. Thou art the everlasting

Son of the Fa - ther. 8. When thou tookest upon thee to de - liv - er man,

thou didst humble thyself to be born of a Vir - gin.

9. When thou hadst overcome the sharp - ness of death,

thou didst open the kingdom of heaven to all be - liev - ers.

10. Thou sittest at the right hand of God, in the glory of the Fa - ther.

We believe that thou shalt come to be our judge. 11. We therefore pray thee,

help thy ser - vants, whom thou hast redeemed with thy pre - cious blood.

12. Make them to be numbered with thy saints, in glory ev - er - last - ing.

Setting: Plainsong, Tone 8; adapt. Alastair Cassels-Brown (b. 1927)

We Praise Thee *Te Deum laudamus*

S 206
Stephen Elvey
(1805-1860)

S 207
T. Norris
(1741-1790)

The entire Canticle may be sung to one double chant.

1   We praise thee, O God; we acknowledge ' thee to be the ' Lord. *
      All the earth doth worship ' thee, the ' Father ever ' lasting.

2   To thee all ' Angels cry a ' loud, *
      the Heavens and ' all the ' Powers there ' in.

3   To thee Cherubim and ' Sera ' phim *
      con ' tinual ' ly do ' cry:

4   Holy, holy, holy, Lord ' God of ' Sabaoth; *
      Heaven and earth are full of the ' majesty ' of thy ' glory.

5   The glorious company of the a ' postles ' praise thee. *
      The goodly ' fellowship of the ' prophets ' praise thee.

6   The noble army of ' martyrs ' praise thee. *
      The holy Church throughout all the ' world doth ac ' knowledge ' thee,

†7   the Father, of an ' infinite ' majesty, *
      thine adorable, true, and only Son,
      also the ' Holy ' Ghost the ' Comforter.

†Second half of double chant.

S 206
Richard Farrant
(1525?-1580)

S 207

William Henry Havergal
(1793-1870)

8 Thou art the King of ʹglory, O ʹChrist. *
    Thou art the everʹlasting ʹSon of the ʹFather.

9 When thou tookest upon thee to deʹliver ʹman, *
    thou didst humble thyʹself to be ʹborn of a ʹVirgin.

10 When thou hadst overcome the ʹsharpness of ʹdeath, *
    thou didst open the kingdom of ʹheaven to ʹall beʹlievers.

11 Thou sittest at the right hand of God, in the ʹglory of the ʹFather. *
    We believe that thou shalt ʹcome to ʹbe our ʹjudge.

S 206

Stephen Elvey
(1805-1860)

S 207

T. Norris
(1741-1790)

12 We therefore pray thee, ʹhelp thy ʹservants, *
    whom thou hast reʹdeemed with thy ʹprecious ʹblood.

13 Make them to be ʹnumbered with thy ʹsaints, *
    in ʹglory ʹever ʹlasting.

The Song of Moses *Cantemus Domino*

Antiphon

Al - le - lu - ia, al - le - lu - ia, al - le - lu - ia.

Antiphon in Lent and at the Easter Vigil (♭)

I will sing to the Lord for he has ris - en up in might.

Antiphon in Easter Season (♭)

I will sing to the Lord for he has ris - en up in might, al - le - lu - ia.

1. I will sing to the Lord, for he is lofty and up - lift - ed; the horse and its rider has he hurled in - to the sea. 2. The Lord is my strength and my re - fuge; the Lord has be - come my Sa - vior. 3. This is my God and I will praise him, the God of my people and I will ex - alt him. 4. The Lord is a might - y war - rior; Yah - weh is his Name. 5. The chariots of Pharaoh and his army has he hurled in - to the sea; the finest of those who bear armor have been drowned in the Red Sea. 6. The fathomless deep has o - ver - whelmed them; they sank into the depths like a stone. 7. Your right hand, O Lord, is glor - ious

in might; your right hand, O Lord, has overthrown the en - e - my.

8. Who can be compared with you, O Lord, a - mong the gods? Who is like you,

glorious in holiness, awesome in renown, and worker of won - ders?

9. You stretched forth your right hand; the earth swal - lowed them up.

10. With your constant love you led the peo - ple you re - deemed;

with your might you brought them in safety to your ho - ly dwell - ing.

11. You will bring them in and plant them on the mount of your pos -

ses - sion, 12. The resting - place you have made for your - self, O Lord,

the sanctuary, O Lord, that your hand has es - tab - lished.

13. The Lord shall reign for ever and for ev - er. [Ant.]

(Gloria Patri may be omitted)

14. Glo - ry to the Fa - ther, and to the Son, and to the Ho - ly Spi - rit:

15. As it was in the be - gin - ning, is now, and will be for ev - er. A - men. [Ant.]

Setting: Mode 1 antiphons, adapt. Bruce E. Ford (b. 1947). **Plainsong, Tone 1,** verses 1-3, 10-15; Plainsong, Tonus Peregrinus, verses 4-9; adapt. Norman Mealy (b. 1923)

1　I will sing to the Lord, for he is ˈlofty and upˈlifted; *

　　the horse and its rider has he ˈhurled ˈinto the ˈsea.

2　The Lord is my ˈstrength and my ˈrefuge; *

　　the ˈLord has beˈcome my ˈSavior.

3　This is my God and ˈI will ˈpraise him, *

　　the God of my ˈpeople and ˈI will exˈalt him.

4　The Lord is a ˈmighty ˈwarrior; *

　　— ˈYahweh ˈis his ˈName.

5　The chariots of Pharaoh and his army has he ˈhurled into the ˈsea; *

　　the finest of those who bear armor have been

　　　ˈdrowned in the ˈRed ˈSea.

6　The fathomless ˈdeep has overˈwhelmed them; *

　　they ˈsank into the ˈdepths like a ˈstone.

7　Your right hand, O Lord, is ˈglorious in ˈmight; *

　　your right hand, O Lord, has ˈoverˈthrown the ˈenemy.

8　Who can be compared with you, O Lord, aˈmong the ˈgods? *

　　who is like you, glorious in holiness,

　　awesome in reˈnown, and ˈworker of ˈwonders?

9　You stretched forth your ˈright ˈhand; *

　　the ˈearth ˈswallowed them ˈup.

10　With your constant love you led the ˈpeople you reˈdeemed; *

　　with your might you brought them in

　　　ˈsafety to your ˈholy ˈdwelling.

11　You will bring them ˈin and ˈplant them *

　　on the ˈmount of ˈyour posˈsession,

12　The resting-place you have made for yourˈself, O ˈLord, *

　　the sanctuary, O ˈLord, that your ˈhand has esˈtablished.

†13　The ˈLord shall ˈreign *

　　for ˈever ˈand for ˈever.

(Gloria Patri may be omitted)

Glory to the Father, and ˈto the ˈSon, *

　　and ˈto the ˈHoly ˈSpirit:

As it was in the beˈginning, is ˈnow, *

　　and ˈwill be for ˈever. Aˈmen.

†*Second half of double chant; for the triple chant, verse 13 and the Gloria Patri are sung to the entire* **chant.**

S 213

Canticle 9

The First Song of Isaiah   *Ecce, Deus*

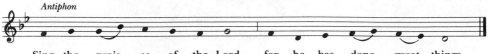

Sing the prais - es of the Lord, for he has done great things.

1. Sure - ly, it is God who saves me; I will trust in him and not

be a - fraid. 2. For the Lord is my stronghold and my sure de - fense,

and he will be my Sa - vior. 3. Therefore you shall draw water

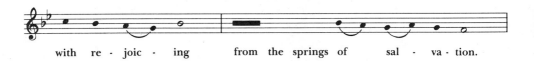

with re - joic - ing from the springs of sal - va - tion.

4. And on that day you shall say, Give thanks to the Lord and call

up - on his Name; 5. Make his deeds known a - mong the peo - ples;

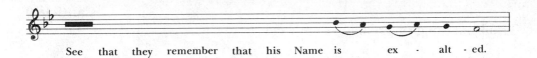

See that they remember that his Name is ex - alt - ed.

6. Sing the praises of the Lord, for he has done great things,

and this is known in all the world. 7. Cry aloud, inhabitants of

Zi - on, ring out your joy, for the great one in the

midst of you is the Holy One of Is - ra - el. [Ant.]

(Gloria Patri may be omitted)

Glory to the Fa - ther, and to the Son, and to the Ho - ly Spi - rit:

As it was in the be - gin - ning, is now, and will be for ev - er. A - men.

[Ant.]

Setting: Plainsong, Tone 3; adapt. Bruce E. Ford (b. 1947)

The First Song of Isaiah   *Ecce, Deus*

S 214 — Ray Francis Brown (1897–1965)

S 215 — Robert Bremner (1720–1789)

S 216 — David Hurd (b. 1950)

1. Surely, it is ' God who ' saves me; *
   I will trust in ' him and ' not be a ' fraid.

2. For the Lord is my stronghold and my ' sure de ' fense, *
   and ' he will ' be my ' Savior.

3. Therefore you shall draw ' water with re ' joicing *
   — ' from the ' springs of sal ' vation.

4. And on that ' day you shall ' say, *
   Give thanks to the ' Lord and ' call upon his ' Name;

†5. Make his deeds known a ' mong the ' peoples; *
   see that they re ' member that his ' Name is ex ' alted.

6. Sing the praises of the Lord, for ' he has done ' great things, *
   and this is ' known in ' all the ' world.

7. Cry aloud, inhabitants of Zion, ' ring out your ' joy, *
   for the great one in the midst of you is the ' Holy ' One of ' Israel.

   (Gloria Patri may be omitted)

   Glory to the Father, and ' to the ' Son, *
   and ' to the ' Holy ' Spirit: *

   As it was in the be ' ginning, is ' now, *
   and ' will be for ' ever. A ' men.

† *Second half of double chant.*

1. Seek the Lord while he wills to be found;   call upon him when he draws near.

2. Let the wicked for - sake their ways   and the e - vil ones their thoughts;

3. And let them turn to the Lord, and he will have com - pas - sion, and to our God, for he will rich - ly par - don. 4. For my thoughts are not your thoughts,

nor your ways my ways, says the Lord.   5. For as the heavens are higher than the earth,

so are my ways higher than your ways, and my thoughts than your thoughts.

6. For as rain and snow fall from the hea-vens   and return not again, but wa - ter the earth,

7. Bringing forth life and giv - ing growth,   seed for sowing and bread for eat - ing,

8. So is my word that goes forth from my mouth;   it will not return to me emp - ty;

9. But it will accomplish that which I have pur - posed,   and prosper in that for which

(Gloria Patri may be omitted)

I sent it.   10. Glory to the Father, and to the Son,   and to the Ho - ly Spi - rit:

11. As it was in the beginning, is now,   and will be for ev - er.   A - men.

Setting: Plainsong, Tone 2; adapt. The Standing Commission on Church Music, 1979, alt.

The Second Song of Isaiah   *Quaerite Dominum*

S 218

John Goss
(1800-1880)

S 219

Richard Clark
(1786-1856)

S 220

Ned Rorem
(b. 1923)

S 221

Henry Purcell (1659-1695)
arr. James Turle (1802-1882)

1 Seek the Lord while he ˈwills to be ˈfound; *
   call upˈon him when ˈhe draws ˈnear.

2 Let the wicked forˈsake their ˈways *
   and the ˈevil ˈones their ˈthoughts;

3 And let them turn to the Lord, and he will ˈhave comˈpassion, *
   and to our God, for ˈhe will ˈrichly ˈpardon.

4 For my thoughts ˈare not ˈyour thoughts, *
   nor your ways ˈmy ways, ˈsays the ˈLord.

5 For as the heavens are ˈhigher than the ˈearth, *
   so are my ways higher than your ways,
   and ˈmy ˈthoughts than ˈyour thoughts.

6 For as rain and snow ˈfall from the ˈheavens *
   and return not aˈgain, but ˈwater the ˈearth,

†7 Bringing forth life and ˈgiving ˈgrowth, *
   seed for ˈsowing and ˈbread for ˈeating,

8 So is my word that goes ˈforth from my ˈmouth; *
   it will ˈnot reˈturn to me ˈempty;

9 But it will accomplish that which ˈI have ˈpurposed, *
   and prosper in ˈthat for ˈwhich I ˈsent it.

(Gloria Patri may be omitted)

Glory to the Father, and ˈto the ˈSon, *
   and ˈto the ˈHoly ˈSpirit:

As it was in the beˈginning, is ˈnow, *
   and ˈwill be for ˈever. Aˈmen.

† *Second half of double chant.*

Canticle 10
The Second Song of Isaiah   *Quaerite Dominum*

S 222

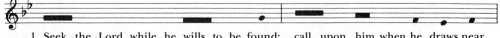

1. Seek the Lord while he wills to be found; call upon him when he draws near.

2. Let the wicked for - sake their ways   and the evil ones their thoughts;

3. And let them turn to the Lord, and he will have com - passion,

and to our God, for he will richly pardon. 4. For my thoughts are not

your thoughts, nor your ways my ways, says the Lord. 5. For as the heavens are

higher than the earth, so are my ways higher than your ways, and my

thoughts than your thoughts. 6. For as rain and snow fall from the heavens

and return not again, but water the earth, 7. Bringing forth life and

giv - ing growth, seed for sowing and bread for eating, 8. So is my word that goes

forth from my mouth; it will not re - turn to me empty; 9. But it will

accomplish that which I have purposed, and prosper in that for which I sent it.

Setting: Norman Mealy (b. 1923)

S 223   Canticle 11
The Third Song of Isaiah   *Surge, illuminare*

1. A - rise, shine, for your light has come, and the glory of the Lord has dawned up - on

you. 2. For behold, darkness covers the land; deep gloom en - shrouds the peo - ples.

3. But over you the Lord will rise, and his glory will ap-pear up-on you. 4. Nations will

stream to your light, and kings to the brightness of your dawn - ing. 5. Your gates will

always be o - pen; by day or night they will nev-er be shut. 6. They will call you,

The City of the Lord, The Zion of the Holy One of Is - ra - el. 7. Violence will

no more be heard in your land, ruin or destruction with - in your bor - ders.

8. You will call your walls, Sal - va - tion, and all your por - tals, Praise. 9. The sun will no

more be your light by day; by night you will not need the bright-ness of the moon.

10. The Lord will be your everlasting light, and your God will be your glo - ry.

(Gloria Patri may be omitted)

11. Glory to the Father, and to the Son, and to the Ho - ly Spi - rit:

12. As it was in the beginning, is now, and will be for ev - er. A - men.

Setting: Plainsong, Tone 5, adapt. The Standing Commission on Church Music, 1979, alt.

The Third Song of Isaiah *Surge, illuminare*

S 224

Cambridge Chant

S 225

Herbert S. Oakeley
(1830-1903)

S 226

W. H. Longhurst
(1819-1904)

S 227

J. Marcus Ritchie
(b. 1946)

1   Arise, shine, for your'light has'come, *
       and the glory of the'Lord has'dawned up'on you.

2   For behold, darkness'covers the'land; *
       deep'gloom en'shrouds the'peoples.

3   But over you the'Lord will'rise, *
       and his'glory will ap'pear up'on you.

4   Nations will'stream to your'light, *
       and kings to the'brightness'of your'dawning.

5   Your gates will'always be'open; *
       by day or'night they will'never be'shut.

6   They will call you, The'City of the'Lord, *
       The Zion of the'Holy'One of'Israel.

7   Violence will no more be'heard in your'land, *
       ruin or de'struction with'in your'borders.

8   You will call your'walls, Sal'vation, *
       and'all your'portals,'Praise.

9   The sun will no more be your'light by'day; *
       by night you will not'need the'brightness of the'moon.

10   The Lord will be your ever'lasting'light, *
       and your'God will'be your'glory.

(Gloria Patri may be omitted)

Glory to the Father, and'to the'Son, *
       and'to the'Holy'Spirit:
As it was in the be'ginning, is'now, *
       and'will be for'ever. A'men.

Gloria Patri must be used with chant S 225.

S 228

A Song of Creation   *Benedicite, omnia opera Domini*

One or more sections of this Canticle may be used. Whatever the selection, it begins with the Invocation and concludes with the Doxology.

Invocation

1. Glo - rify the Lord, all you works of the Lord, praise him and highly

exalt him for ev - er.   2. In the firmament of his pow - er,

glo - ri - fy the Lord, praise him and highly exalt him for ev - er.

I The Cosmic Order

3. Glo - ri - fy the Lord, you angels and all pow - ers of the Lord,

O heavens and all waters a - bove the hea - vens.   4. Sun and moon and

stars of the sky, glo - ri - fy the Lord,   praise him and highly exalt him for ev-

er.   5. Glo - ri - fy the Lord, every shower of rain and fall of dew,

all winds and fire and heat.   6. Winter and summer, glo - ri - fy the Lord,

praise him and highly exalt him for ev - er. 7. Glo - ri - fy the Lord,

O chill and cold, drops of dew and flakes of snow. 8. Frost and cold,

ice and sleet, glo - ri - fy the Lord, praise him and highly exalt him

for ev - er. 9. Glo - ri - fy the Lord, O nights and days,

O shining light and en - fold - ing dark. 10. Storm clouds and thunderbolts,

glo - ri - fy the Lord, praise him and highly exalt him for ev - er.

II The Earth and its Creatures

11. Let the earth glori - fy the Lord, praise him and highly ex - alt him for ev - er.

12. Glorify the Lord, O mountains and hills, and all that grows up - on the earth,

praise him and highly ex - alt him for ev - er. 13. Glorify the Lord, O springs

of water, seas, and streams, O whales and all that move in the wa - ters.

14. All birds of the air, glori‐fy the Lord, praise him and highly ex‐alt him for ev‐er. 15. Glorify the Lord, O beasts of the wild, and all you flocks and herds. 16. O men and women everywhere, glori‐fy the Lord, praise him and highly ex‐alt him for ev‐er.

III The People of God

17. Let the people of God glo‐ri‐fy the Lord, praise him and highly ex‐alt him for ev‐er. 18. Glorify the Lord, O priests and ser‐vants of the Lord, praise him and highly ex‐alt him for ev‐er. 19. Glorify the Lord, O spirits and souls of the right‐eous, praise him and highly ex‐alt him for ev‐er. 20. You that are holy and humble of heart, glo‐ri‐fy the Lord, praise him and highly ex‐alt him for ev‐er.

Doxology

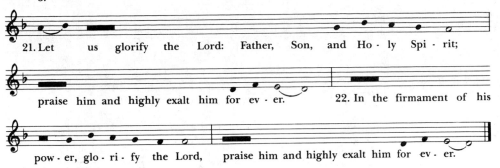

21. Let us glorify the Lord: Father, Son, and Ho-ly Spi-rit;

praise him and highly exalt him for ev-er.   22. In the firmament of his

pow-er, glo-ri-fy the Lord,   praise him and highly exalt him for ev-er.

Setting: Plainsong, Tonus Peregrinus, verses 1-2, 21-22; Plainsong, Tone 1, verses 3-10; Plainsong, Tone 4; verses 11-16;
    Plainsong, Tone 7, verses 17-20; adapt. The Standing Commission on Church Music, 1979, alt.

Canticle 12
A Song of Creation   *Benedicite, omnia opera Domini*

S 229
R. Goodson
(1655-1719)

S 230
Edwin George Monk
(1819-1909)

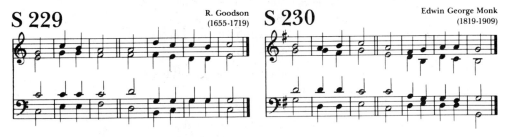

One or more sections of this Canticle may be used. Whatever the selection, it begins with the Invocation and concludes with the Doxology. The entire Canticle, or the Invocation with one or more sections and the Doxology, may be sung to one double chant.

Invocation

1   Glorify the Lord, all you 'works of the 'Lord, *
        praise him and 'highly ex'alt him for 'ever.

2   In the firmament of his power, 'glorify the 'Lord, *
        praise him and 'highly ex'alt him for 'ever.

S 229

William Crotch
(1775-1847)

S 230

Thomas Attwood
(1765?-1838)

I   The Cosmic Order

3   Glorify the Lord, you angels and all 'powers of the 'Lord, *
    O heavens and all 'waters a'bove the 'heavens.

4   Sun and moon and stars of the sky, 'glorify the 'Lord, *
    praise him and 'highly ex'alt him for 'ever.

5   Glorify the Lord, every shower of rain and 'fall of 'dew, *
    all 'winds and 'fire and 'heat.

6   Winter and summer, 'glorify the 'Lord, *
    praise him and 'highly ex'alt him for 'ever.

7   Glorify the Lord, O 'chill and 'cold, *
    drops of 'dew and 'flakes of 'snow.

8   Frost and cold, ice and sleet, 'glorify the 'Lord, *
    praise him and 'highly ex'alt him for 'ever.

9   Glorify the Lord, O 'nights and 'days, *
    O shining 'light and en'folding 'dark.

10 Storm clouds and thunderbolts, 'glorify the 'Lord, *
    praise him and 'highly ex'alt him for 'ever.

S 229

William Boyce
(1711-1779)

S 230

John Goss
(1800-1880)

II   The Earth and its Creatures

11   Let the earth glorify the Lord, *
  praise him and highly ex alt him for ever.

12   Glorify the Lord, O mountains and hills,
  and all that grows upon the earth, *
  praise him and highly ex alt him for ever.

13   Glorify the Lord, O springs of water, seas, and streams, *
  O whales and all that move in the waters.

14   All birds of the air, glorify the Lord, *
  praise him and highly ex alt him for ever.

15   Glorify the Lord, O beasts of the wild, *
  and all you flocks and herds.

16   O men and women everywhere, glorify the Lord, *
  praise him and highly ex alt him for ever.

S 229

William Crotch
(1775-1847)

S 230

Thomas Attwood
(1765?-1838)

III   The People of God

17   Let the people of God glorify the Lord, *
     praise him and highly ex alt him for ever.

18   Glorify the Lord, O priests and servants of the Lord, *
     praise him and highly ex alt him for ever.

19   Glorify the Lord, O spirits and souls of the righteous, *
     praise him and highly ex alt him for ever.

20   You that are holy and humble of heart, glorify the Lord, *
     praise him and highly ex alt him for ever.

S 229

R. Goodson
(1655-1719)

S 230

Edwin George Monk
(1819-1909)

Doxology

21   Let us glorify the Lord: Father, Son, and Holy Spirit; *
     praise him and highly ex alt him for ever.

22   In the firmament of his power, glorify the Lord, *
     praise him and highly ex alt him for ever.

Canticle 13
A Song of Praise   *Benedictus es, Domine*

S 231

1. Glo - ry to you, Lord God of our fa - thers; you are worthy of praise; glo - ry to you. 2. Glory to you for the radiance of your ho - ly Name; we will praise you and highly exalt you for ev - er. 3. Glory to you in the splendor of your tem - ple; on the throne of your majesty, glo - ry to you. 4. Glory to you, seated between the Cher - u - bim; we will praise you and highly exalt you for ev - er. 5. Glory to you, beholding the depths; in the high vault of heaven, glo - ry to you. 6. Glory to you, Father, Son, and Holy Spi - rit; we will praise you and highly exalt you for ev - er.

Setting: Plainsong, Tone 8; adapt. The Standing Commission on Church Music, 1979, alt.

A Song of Praise   *Benedictus es, Domine*

S 232 — R. Tomlinson (18th cent.)   **S 233** — The Imperial Tune (ca. 1630)

S 234 — Thomas Attwood (1765?-1838)

S 235 — David Koehring (b. 1940)

1 Glory to you, Lord ' God of our ' fathers; *
   you are worthy of ' praise; ' glory to ' you.

2 Glory to you for the radiance of your ' holy ' Name; *
   we will praise you and ' highly ex ' alt you for ' ever.

3 Glory to you in the ' splendor of your ' temple; *
   on the throne of your ' majesty, ' glory to ' you.

4 Glory to you, seated be ' tween the ' Cherubim; *
   we will praise you and ' highly ex ' alt you for ' ever.

5 Glory to you, be ' holding the ' depths; *
   in the high vault of ' heaven, ' glory to ' you.

6 Glory to you, Father, Son, and ' Holy ' Spirit; *
   we will praise you and ' highly ex ' alt you for ' ever.

Canticle 13
A Song of Praise   *Benedictus es, Domine*

1. Glo - ry to you, _____ Lord God of our fa - thers; _____ you are wor - thy of praise; glo - ry to you. _____

2. Glo - ry to you _____ for the ra - di - ance of your ho - ly Name; ___ we will praise you and high - ly ex - alt you for ev - er. _____

3. Glo - ry to you _____ in the splen - dor of your tem - ple; _____ on the throne of your ma - jes - ty, glo - ry to you. _____

4. Glo - ry to you, seat - ed be - tween the Cher - u - bim; _____ we will praise you and high - ly ex - alt you for ev - er. _____

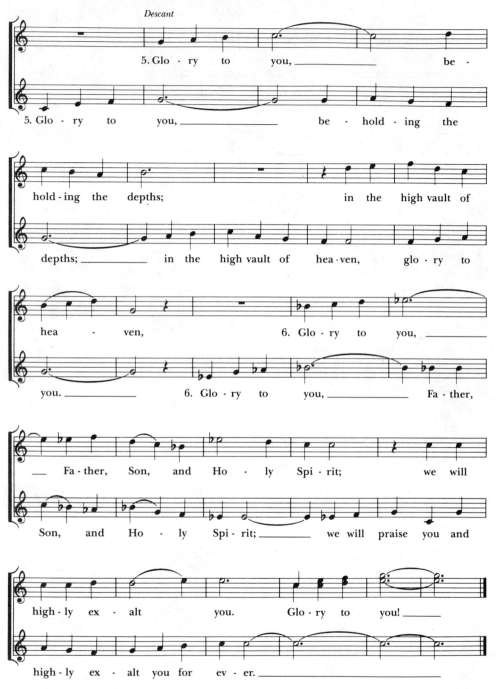

Descant

5. Glo - ry to you, _____ be -
hold - ing the depths; in the high vault of
hea - ven, 6. Glo - ry to you, _____
_ Fa - ther, Son, and Ho - ly Spi - rit; we will
high - ly ex - alt you. Glo - ry to you! _____

5. Glo - ry to you, _____ be - hold - ing the
depths; _____ in the high vault of hea - ven, glo - ry to
you. _____ 6. Glo - ry to you, _____ Fa - ther,
Son, and Ho - ly Spi - rit; _____ we will praise you and
high - ly ex - alt you for ev - er. _____

Setting: John Rutter (b. 1945)

Canticle 14

S 237

A Song of Penitence   *Kyrie Pantokrator*

Antiphon

Your mer - ci - ful prom - ise is be - yond all mea - sure;

it sur - pas - ses all that our minds can fath - om.

1. O Lord and Ruler of the hosts of hea - ven, God of Abraham,

Isaac, and Jacob, and of all their right - eous off - spring:

2. You made the heavens and the earth, with all their vast ar - ray.

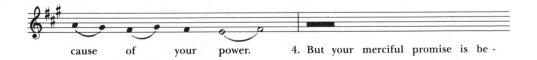

3. All things quake with fear at your pres - ence; they tremble be -

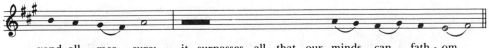

cause of your power. 4. But your merciful promise is be -

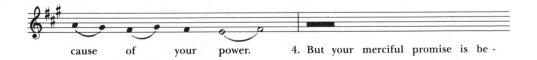

yond all mea - sure; it surpasses all that our minds can fath - om.

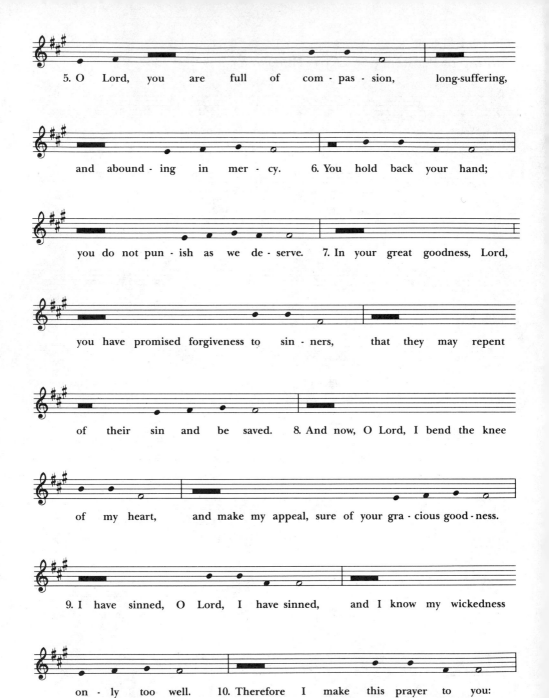

5. O Lord, you are full of com‑pas‑sion, long-suffering,

and abound‑ing in mer‑cy. 6. You hold back your hand;

you do not pun‑ish as we de‑serve. 7. In your great goodness, Lord,

you have promised forgiveness to sin‑ners, that they may repent

of their sin and be saved. 8. And now, O Lord, I bend the knee

of my heart, and make my appeal, sure of your gra‑cious good‑ness.

9. I have sinned, O Lord, I have sinned, and I know my wickedness

on‑ly too well. 10. Therefore I make this prayer to you:

Forgive me, Lord, for-give me. 11. Do not let me per-ish

in my sin, nor condemn me to the depths of the earth.

12. For you, O Lord, are the God of those who re-pent,

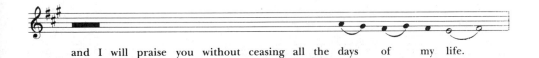

and in me you will show forth your good-ness. 13. Unworthy as I am,

you will save me, in accordance with your great mer-cy,

and I will praise you without ceasing all the days of my life.

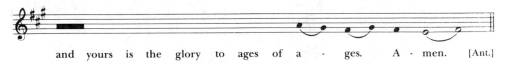

14. For all the powers of heaven sing your prais-es,

and yours is the glory to ages of a - ges. A-men. [Ant.]

Setting: Mode 3 antiphon, adapt. Bruce E. Ford (b. 1947). Plainsong, Tone 3, verses 1-4, 12-14; Plainsong, Irregular Tone, verses 5-11; adapt. The Standing Commission on Church Music, 1979

A Song of Penitence   *Kyrie Pantokrator*

S 238 Verses 1-11

Matthew Camidge
(1758-1844)

Verses 12-14

S 239

Allison's Psalms, 1599;
arr. Luke Flintoff (1678-1727)

S 240

Ned Rorem
(b. 1923)

S 241

Samuel Wesley
(1766-1837)

1   O Lord and Ruler of the[']hosts of[']heaven, *

O Lord and Ruler of the ' hosts of ' heaven, *
    God of Abraham, Isaac, and Jacob,
    and of ' all their ' righteous ' offspring:

2   You made the ' heavens and the ' earth, *
    with ' all their ' vast ar ' ray.

3   All things quake with ' fear at your ' presence; *
    they ' tremble be ' cause of your ' power.

4   But your merciful promise is be ' yond all ' measure; *
    it surpasses ' all that our ' minds can ' fathom.

5   O Lord, you are ' full of com ' passion, *
    long-' suffering, and a ' bounding in ' mercy.

6   You hold ' back your ' hand; *
    you do not ' punish as ' we de ' serve.

7   In your great goodness, Lord, you have promised for ' giveness to ' sinners, *
    that they may re ' pent of their ' sin and be ' saved.

8   And now, O Lord, I bend the ' knee of my ' heart, *
    and make my appeal, ' sure of your ' gracious ' goodness.

9   I have sinned, O ' Lord, I have ' sinned, *
    and I know my ' wickedness ' only too ' well.

10   Therefore I ' make this ' prayer to you: *
    For ' give me, ' Lord, for ' give me.

†11   Do not let me ' perish in my ' sin, *
    nor condemn me to the ' depths ' of the ' earth.

12   For you, O Lord, are the God of ' those who re ' pent, *
    and in me ' you will show ' forth your ' goodness.

13   Unworthy as I am, you will save me,
    in accordance with your ' great ' mercy, *
    and I will praise you without ' ceasing all the ' days of my ' life.

†14   For all the powers of heaven ' sing your ' praises, *
    and yours is the glory to ' ages of ' ages. A ' men.

†*Second half of double chant if the Camidge tunes, S 238, are used together.*

The Song of Mary   *Magnificat*

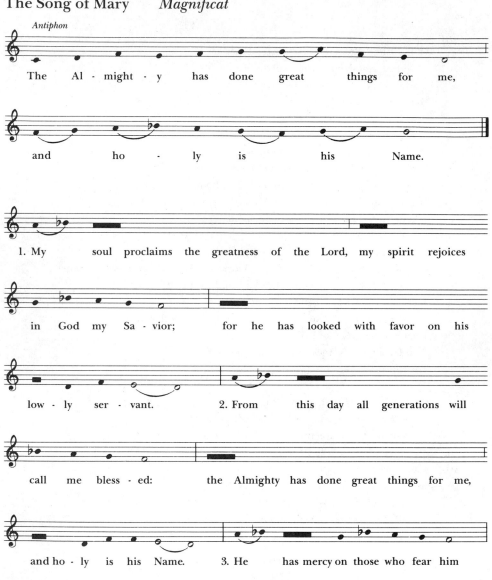

Antiphon

The Al - might - y has done great things for me,

and ho - ly is his Name.

1. My soul proclaims the greatness of the Lord, my spirit rejoices

in God my Sa - vior; for he has looked with favor on his

low - ly ser - vant. 2. From this day all generations will

call me bless - ed: the Almighty has done great things for me,

and ho - ly is his Name. 3. He has mercy on those who fear him

in every gen - er - a - tion. 4. He has shown the strength of his arm,

he has scattered the proud in their con - ceit. 5. He has cast down

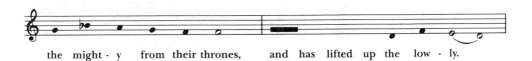

the might - y from their thrones, and has lifted up the low - ly.

6. He has filled the hun-gry with good things, and the rich he has sent a - way

emp - ty. 7. He has come to the help of his ser - vant Is - ra - el,

for he has remembered his promise of mer - cy, 8. The promise he

made to our fa - thers, to Abraham and his children for ev - er. [Ant.]

(Gloria Patri may be omitted)

9. Glo - ry to the Fa - ther, and to the Son, and to the Ho - ly Spi - rit:

10. As it was in the be - gin-ning, is now, and will be for ev - er. A - men.

[Ant.]

Setting: Plainsong, Tonus Peregrinus; adapt. Bruce E. Ford (b. 1947)

The Song of Mary *Magnificat*

S 243

William Henry Havergal
(1793-1870)

S 244

George Mursell Garrett
(1834-1897)

S 245

Benjamin Hutto
(b. 1947)

S 246

W. Lawes (1596-1662);
arr. Joseph Corfe (1790-1820)

1   My soul proclaims the greatness of the Lord,
        my spirit rejoices in ' God my ' Savior; *
           for he has looked with ' favor on his ' lowly ' servant.

2   From this day all generations will ' call me ' blessed: *
           the Almighty has done great things for me,
           and ' holy ' is his ' Name.

3   He has mercy on ' those who ' fear him *
           in ' every ' gener ' ation.

4   He has shown the ' strength of his ' arm, *
           he has scattered the ' proud in ' their con ' ceit.

5   He has cast down the ' mighty from their ' thrones, *
           and has ' lifted ' up the ' lowly.

6   He has filled the ' hungry with ' good things, *
           and the ' rich he has ' sent away ' empty.

7   He has come to the help of his ' servant ' Israel, *
           for he has re ' membered his ' promise of ' mercy,

8   The promise he ' made to our ' fathers, *
           to ' Abraham and his ' children for ' ever.

(Gloria Patri may be omitted)

Glory to the Father, and ' to the ' Son, *
           and ' to the ' Holy ' Spirit:
As it was in the be ' ginning, is ' now, *
           and ' will be for ' ever. A ' men.

S 247

Canticle 15

The Song of Mary   *Magnificat*

Antiphon
Unison or harmony

1. My soul pro - claims the great - ness

1. My soul pro -

of the Lord, my spi - rit re - joic - es in

claims the great - ness of the Lord, my

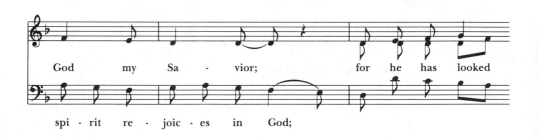

God my Sa - vior; for he has looked

spi - rit re - joic - es in God;

with fa - vor on his low - ly ser - vant.

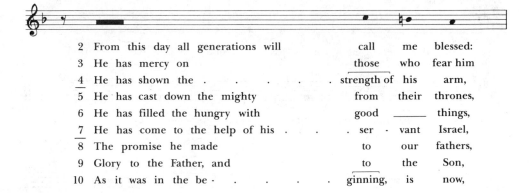

2 From this day all generations will   call   me   blessed:
3 He has mercy on   those   who   fear him
4 He has shown the .   .   .   . . strength of   his   arm,
5 He has cast down the mighty   from   their   thrones,
6 He has filled the hungry with   good _____   things,
7 He has come to the help of his .   .   . ser - vant   Israel,
8 The promise he made   to   our   fathers,
9 Glory to the Father, and   to   the   Son,
10 As it was in the be - .   .   .   . ginning,   is   now,

2 the Almighty has done great things for me, and holy   is   his Name.
3 in   every   gen - er - ation. [Ant.]
4 he has scattered the .   .   .   . . proud in their   con - ceit.
5 and has   lifted   up   the lowly. [Ant.]
6 and the rich he has   sent   a - way empty.
7 for he has remembered his .   .   .   prom - ise   of mercy,
8 to Abraham and his   chil - dren for ever. [Ant.]
9 and   to the Ho - ly Spirit:
10 and will be for .   .   .   .   . ev - er.   A - men. [Ant.]

The Antiphon may be sung in unison, with the counter-melody played by an instrument, or it may be sung in three parts.

Setting: *Cathedral of the Isles*, Betty Carr Pulkingham (b. 1928)

S 248

Canticle 16

The Song of Zechariah *Benedictus Dominus Deus*

Antiphon

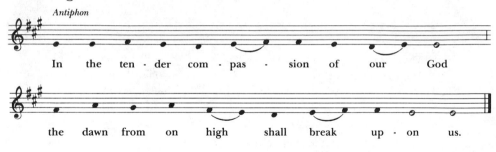

In the ten-der com-pas-sion of our God

the dawn from on high shall break up-on us.

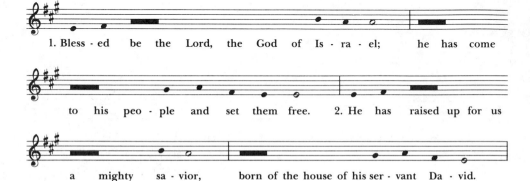

1. Bless-ed be the Lord, the God of Is-ra-el; he has come

to his peo-ple and set them free. 2. He has raised up for us

a mighty sa-vior, born of the house of his ser-vant Da-vid.

3. Through his holy prophets he promised of old, that he would save us

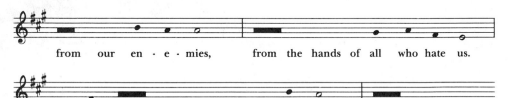

from our en-e-mies, from the hands of all who hate us.

4. He prom-ised to show mercy to our fa-thers and to remember his

ho-ly cov-e-nant. 5. This was the oath he swore to our father

A - bra - ham,   to set us free from the hands of   our   en - e - mies,

6. Free to   worship him with - out fear,   holy and righteous in his sight all the

days of   our life.   7. You, my   child, shall be called the prophet of the Most High,

for you will go before   the Lord to   pre - pare his way,   8. To give

his people knowledge of sal - va - tion   by the for - give - ness of their sins.

9. In   the   tender compassion of our God   the dawn from on high shall

break up - on us,   10. To shine on those who dwell in darkness and the

shadow of death,   and to guide our feet in - to   the way of peace. [Ant.]

(Gloria Patri may be omitted)

11. Glo - ry   to the Father, and to   the Son,   and to the Ho - ly Spi - rit:

12. As it was in the beginning, is now,   and will be for ev - er. A - men. [Ant.]

Setting: Plainsong, Tone 8; adapt. Bruce E. Ford (b. 1947)

The Song of Zechariah *Benedictus Dominus Deus*

S 249

Thomas Attwood Walmisley
(1814-1856)

S 250

John Fenstermaker, Jr.
(b. 1942)

S 251

Samuel Sebastian Wesley
(1810-1876)

S 252

Anon.

1 Blessèd be the Lord, the|God of|Israel; *
   he has come to his|people and|set them|free.

2 He has raised up for us a|mighty|savior, *
   born of the|house of his|servant|David.

3 Through his holy prophets he promised of old,
   that he would|save us from our|enemies, *
   from the|hands of|all who|hate us.

4 He promised to show|mercy to our|fathers *
   and to re|member his|holy|covenant.

5 This was the oath he swore to our|father|Abraham, *
   to set us|free from the|hands of our|enemies,

6 Free to worship him with|out|fear, *
   holy and righteous in his|sight all the|days of our|life.

7 You, my child, shall be called the prophet of the|Most|High, *
   for you will go before the|Lord to pre|pare his|way,

8 To give his people|knowledge of sal|vation *
   by the for|giveness|of their|sins.

9 In the tender com|passion of our|God *
   the dawn from on|high shall|break up|on us,

10 To shine on those who dwell in darkness and the
   |shadow of|death, *
   and to guide our|feet into the|way of|peace.

(Gloria Patri may be omitted)

Glory to the Father, and|to the|Son, *
   and|to the|Holy|Spirit:
As it was in the be|ginning, is|now, *
   and|will be for|ever. A|men.

S 253

The Song of Simeon   *Nunc dimittis*

1. Lord, you now have set your ser-vant free to go in peace as

you have prom-ised; 2. For these eyes of mine have seen the Sa-vior,

whom you have prepared for all the world to see: 3. A Light to en-

lighten the na-tions, and the glory of your peo-ple Is-ra-el.

(Gloria Patri may be omitted)

4. Glo-ry to the Father, and to the Son, and to the Ho-ly Spi-rit:

5. As it was in the begin-ning, is now, and will be for ev-er. A-men.

Setting: Plainsong, Irregular Tone; adapt. The Standing Commission on Church Music, 1979

Canticle 17

The Song of Simeon   *Nunc dimittis*

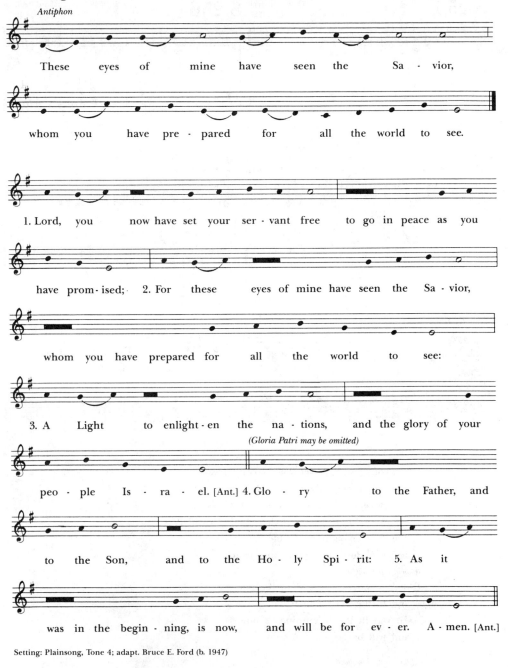

Antiphon

These eyes of mine have seen the Sa - vior,

whom you have pre - pared for all the world to see.

1. Lord, you now have set your ser - vant free to go in peace as you

have prom - ised; 2. For these eyes of mine have seen the Sa - vior,

whom you have prepared for all the world to see:

3. A Light to enlight - en the na - tions, and the glory of your

(Gloria Patri may be omitted)

peo - ple Is - ra - el. [Ant.] 4. Glo - ry to the Father, and

to the Son, and to the Ho - ly Spi - rit: 5. As it

was in the begin - ning, is now, and will be for ev - er. A - men. [Ant.]

Setting: Plainsong, Tone 4; adapt. Bruce E. Ford (b. 1947)

The Song of Simeon   *Nunc dimittis*

S 255 — Thomas Purcell (d. 1682?)

S 256 — William Richard Bexfield (1824-1853)

S 257 — Henry G. Ley (1887-1962)

S 258 — Thomas Dupuis (1733-1796)

S 259 — Charles Fisk (1925-1983)

1 Lord, you now have set your | servant | free *
    to go in | peace as | you have | promised;

2 For these eyes of mine have | seen the | Savior, *
    whom you have prepared for | all the | world to | see:

†3 A Light to en | lighten the | nations, *
    and the | glory of your | people | Israel.

(Gloria Patri may be omitted)

Glory to the Father, and | to the | Son, *
    and | to the | Holy | Spirit:

As it was in the be | ginning, is | now, *
    and | will be for | ever. A | men.

† *Second half of double chant.*

Canticle 17
The Song of Simeon *Nunc dimittis*

S 260

1. Lord, you now have set your ser-vant

free to go in peace as you have prom-ised; 2. For these

eyes of mine have seen the Sa - vior, whom you have pre-pared for all the

world to see: 3. A Light to en - light - en the na - tions, and the

glo - ry of your peo - ple Is - ra - el. 4. Glo - ry to the

Fa - ther, and to the Son, and to the Ho - ly Spi - rit: 5. As it

was in the be - gin - ning, is now, and will be for ev - er. A - men.

Setting: Ronald Arnatt (b. 1930)

S 261

A Song to the Lamb   *Dignus es*

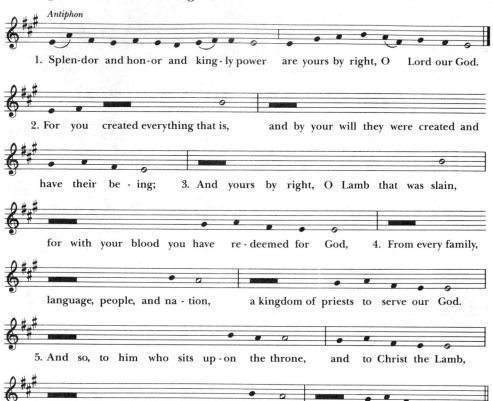

Antiphon

1. Splen-dor and hon-or and king-ly power   are yours by right, O   Lord our God.

2. For   you   created everything that is,   and by your will they were created and

have their be - ing;   3. And yours   by right, O Lamb that was slain,

for with your blood you have   re - deemed for   God,   4. From every family,

language, people, and na - tion,   a kingdom of priests to serve our God.

5. And so, to   him   who   sits up - on   the throne,   and   to Christ the Lamb,

6. Be worship and praise, dominion and splen - dor,   for ever and for ev-er - more.[Ant.]

When the Antiphon is not sung, this setting of the first two verses is used.

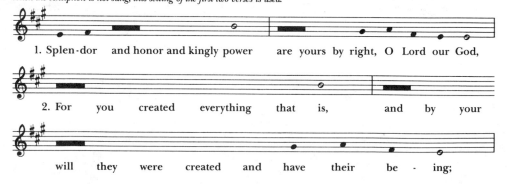

1. Splen-dor   and honor and kingly power   are yours by right, O Lord our God,

2. For   you   created   everything   that   is,   and   by   your

will   they   were   created   and   have   their   be - ing;

Setting: Plainsong, Tone 8; adapt. Bruce E. Ford (b. 1947)

Canticle 18
A Song to the Lamb *Dignus es*

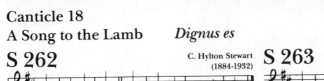

S 262 C. Hylton Stewart (1884-1932)

S 263 E. Stanley Roper (1878-1953)

S 264 Richard Woodward (1744-1777)

S 265 Daniel Pinkham (b. 1923)

1 Splendor and honor and 'kingly 'power *
  are yours by 'right, O 'Lord our 'God,

2 For you created 'everything that 'is, *
  and by your will they were cre'ated and 'have their 'being;

3 And yours by right, O 'Lamb that was 'slain, *
  for with your 'blood you have re'deemed for 'God,

4 From every family, language, 'people, and 'nation, *
  a kingdom of 'priests to 'serve our 'God.

5 And so, to him who sits up 'on the 'throne, *
  — 'and to 'Christ the 'Lamb,

6 Be worship and praise, do'minion and 'splendor, *
  for 'ever and for 'ever 'more.

S 266

A Song to the Lamb   *Dignus es*

Setting: Calvin Hampton (1938-1984)

Canticle 19

The Song of the Redeemed   *Magna et mirabilia*

Antiphon

All na-tions will draw near and fall down be-fore you, be-cause your just and ho-ly works have been re-vealed.

1. O ru-ler of the universe, Lord God, great deeds are they that you have done, surpassing human un-der-stand-ing.

2. Your ways are ways of right-eous-ness and truth, O King of all the a-ges.

3. Who can fail to do you homage, Lord, and sing the prais-es of your Name? for you only are the Ho-ly One.

4. All nations will draw near and fall down be-fore you, because your just and holy works have been re-vealed. [Ant.]

(Gloria Patri may be omitted)

5. Glory to the Fa-ther, and to the Son, and to the Ho-ly Spi-rit:

6. As it was in the be-gin-ning, is now, and will be for ev-er. A-men. [Ant.]

Setting: Plainsong, Tone 1; adapt. Bruce E. Ford (b. 1947)

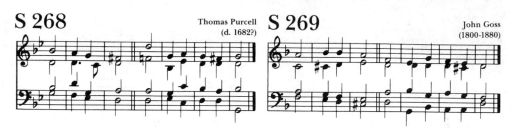

The Song of the Redeemed   *Magna et mirabilia*

S 268   Thomas Purcell (d. 1682?)

S 269   John Goss (1800-1880)

S 270   Henry Smart (1813-1879)

S 271   Maurice Greene (1695-1755)

1   O ruler of the universe, Lord God,
    great deeds are they that[']you have[']done, *
    surpassing[']human[']under[']standing.

2   Your ways are ways of[']righteousness and[']truth, *
    O[']King of[']all the[']ages.

3   Who can fail to do you homage, Lord,
    and sing the[']praises of your[']Name? *
    for you[']only[']are the[']Holy One.

4   All nations will draw near and fall[']down be[']fore you, *
    because your just and holy[']works have[']been re[']vealed.

(Gloria Patri may be omitted)

Glory to the Father, and[']to the[']Son, *
and[']to the[']Holy[']Spirit:
As it was in the be[']ginning, is[']now, *
and[']will be for[']ever. A[']men.

Canticle 20

Glory to God   *Gloria in excelsis*

S 272

1. Glo - ry to God in the highest, and peace to his peo - ple on earth.

2. Lord God, hea - ven - ly King, almighty God and Fa - ther,

we worship you, we give you thanks, we praise you for your glo - ry.

3. Lord Jesus Christ, only Son of the Fa - ther, Lord God, Lamb of God,

4. you take away the sin of the world: have mer - cy on us;

5. you are seated at the right hand of the Fa - ther: re - ceive our prayer.

6. For you alone are the Ho - ly One, you alone are the Lord,

7. you alone are the Most High, Jesus Christ, with the Ho - ly Spi - rit,

in the glory of God the Fa - ther. A - men.

Setting: Mozarabic chant (15th cent.); adapt. David Warren Steel (b. 1947), alt.

S 273
Glory to God   *Gloria in excelsis*

Canticle 20

Setting: Plainsong, Mode 7; Mass 13 (12th cent.); adapt. Mason Martens (b. 1933)

Canticle 20

Glory to God   *Gloria in excelsis*

S 274

Glo - ry to God in the high - est, and peace to his peo - ple on earth.

Lord God, hea - ven - ly King, al - might - y God and Fa - ther, we

wor - ship you, we give you thanks, we praise you for your glo - ry.

Lord Je - sus Christ, on - ly Son of the Fa - ther, Lord God, Lamb

of God, you take a - way the sin of the world: have mer - cy on us;

you are seat - ed at the right hand of the Fa - ther: re - ceive our prayer.

For you a - lone are the Ho - ly One, you a - lone are the Lord, you a -

lone are the Most High, Je - sus Christ, with the Ho - ly Spi - rit,

in the glo - ry of God the Fa - ther. A - men.

Setting: Plainsong, Mode 4; Mass 15; adapt. Schola Antiqua, 1983
Melody rhythmic version © 1984, Schola Antiqua Inc. Used by permission.

Glory to God   *Gloria in excelsis*

1   Glory to ꞏGod in the ꞏhighest, *
        and ꞏpeace to his ꞏpeople on ꞏearth.
2   Lord God, heavenly King,
    almighty ꞏGod and ꞏFather, *
        we worship you, we give you thanks,
        we ꞏpraise you ꞏfor your ꞏglory.

3   Lord Jesus Christ, only ꞏSon of the ꞏFather, *
        Lord ꞏGöd, ꞏLamb of ꞏGod,
4   you take away the sin of the world; have ꞏmercy ꞏon us; *
        you are seated at the right hand of the ꞏFather; re ꞏceive our ꞏprayer.

5   For you a ꞏlone are the ꞏHoly One, *
        you a ꞏlöne ꞏare the ꞏLord,
6   you alone are the ꞏMöst ꞏHigh, *
        Jesus Christ, with the Holy Spirit,
        in the glory of ꞏGod the ꞏFather. A ꞏmen.

Glory to God *Gloria in excelsis*

1. Glo - ry to God in the high - est, and peace to his peo - ple on earth.

2. Lord God, hea - ven - ly King, al - might - y God and Fa - ther, we wor - ship you,

we give you thanks, we praise you for your glo - ry. 3. Lord Je - sus Christ,

on - ly Son of the Fa - ther, Lord God, Lamb of God,

4. you take a - way the sin of the world: have mer - cy on us;

5. you are seat - ed at the right hand of the Fa - ther: re - ceive our prayer.

6. For you a - lone are the Ho - ly One, you a - lone are the Lord,

7. You a - lone are the Most High, Je - sus Christ, with the Ho - ly Spi - rit,

in the glo - ry of God the Fa - ther. A - men.

Setting: From *New Plainsong*; David Hurd (b. 1950)

Glory to God *Gloria in excelsis*

1. Glo - ry to God in the high - est, and peace to his peo - ple on earth. 2. Lord God, heaven - ly King, al - might - y God and Fa - ther, we wor - ship you, we give you thanks, we praise you for your glo - ry. 3. Lord Je - sus Christ, on - ly Son of the Fa - ther, Lord God, Lamb of God, 4. you take a - way the sin of the world: have mer - cy on us; 5. you are seat - ed at the right hand of the Fa - ther: re - ceive our prayer. 6. For you a - lone are the Ho - ly One, you a - lone are the Lord, 7. you a - lone are the Most High, Je - sus Christ, with the Ho - ly Spi - rit, in the glo - ry of God the Fa - ther. A - - men.

Setting: William Mathias (b. 1934)

Canticle 20
Glory to God *Gloria in excelsis*

S 279

Setting: Gerald R. Near (b. 1942)

S 280

Glory to God *Gloria in excelsis*

Canticle 20

1. Glo-ry to God in the high-est, and peace to his peo-ple on earth. 2. Lord God, heaven-ly King, al-might-y God and Fa-ther, we wor-ship you, we give you thanks, we praise you for your glo-ry. 3. Lord Je-sus Christ, on-ly Son of the Fa-ther, Lord God, Lamb of God, 4. you take a-way the sin of the world: have mer-cy on us; 5. you are seat-ed at the right hand of the Fa-ther: re-ceive our prayer. 6. For you a-lone are the Ho-ly One, you a-lone are the Lord, 7. you a-lone are the Most High, Je-sus Christ, with the Ho-ly Spi-rit, in the glo-ry of God the Fa-ther. A-men.

Setting: Robert Powell (b. 1932)

Canticle 20
Glory to God   *Gloria in excelsis*

S 281

1. Glo-ry to God in the high-est, and peace to his peo-ple on earth. 2. Lord God, heaven-ly King, al-might-y God and Fa-ther, we wor-ship you, we give you thanks, we praise you for your glo-ry. 3. Lord Je-sus, Lord Je-sus, Lord Je-sus Christ, on-ly Son of the Fa-ther, Lord God, Lamb of God, 4. you take a-way the sin of the world: have mer-cy on us; you take a-way the sin of the world: have mer-cy on us; 5. you are seat-ed at the right hand of the Fa-ther: re-ceive our prayer. 6. For you a-lone are the Ho-ly One, you a-lone are the Lord, 7. you a-lone are the Most High, Je-sus Christ, with the Ho-ly Spi-rit, in the glo-ry of God the Fa-ther. A-men.

Setting: Richard Felciano (b. 1930)

You are God   *Te Deum laudamus*

1. You are God: we praise you; You are the Lord: we ac-
claim you; 2. You are the e-ter-nal Fa-ther: All cre-a-
tion wor-ships you. 3. To you all an-gels, all the powers
of hea-ven, Cher-u-bim and Ser-a-phim, sing in end-
less praise: 4. Ho-ly, ho-ly, ho-
ly Lord, God of power and might, heaven and earth
are full of your glo-ry. 5. The glo-rious com-pan-y
of a-pos-tles praise you. The no-ble fel-low-ship
of pro-phets praise you. The white-robed ar-my
of mar-tyrs praise you. 6. Through-out the world

the ho · ly Church ac · claims you; Fa · ther, of ma · jes · ty
un · bound · ed, your true and on · ly Son, wor · thy of all wor · ship,
and the Ho · ly Spi · rit, ad · vo · cate and guide.

7. You, Christ, are the king of glo · ry, the e · ter · nal Son of the Fa · ther.

8. When you be · came man to set us free you did not shun
the Vir · gin's womb. 9. You o · ver · came the sting of death
and o · pened the king · dom of hea · ven to all be · liev · ers.

10. You are seat · ed at God's right hand in glo · ry.
We be · lieve that you will come and be our judge.

11. Come then, Lord, and help your peo · ple, bought with the price of your
own blood, 12. and bring us with your saints to glo · ry ev · er · last · ing.

Setting: Plainsong, Te Deum Tone (Solemn); adapt. Bruce E. Ford (b. 1947)

You are God *Te Deum laudamus*

S 283
Arr. after Martin Luther
(1483-1546)

S 284
Thomas Attwood
(1765?-1838)

S 285
Benjamin Hutto
(b. 1947)

S 286 Verses 1-8; 13-14
Jonathan Battishill
(1738-1801)

Verses 9-12

S 287 Verses 1-2; 13-14

Richard Wayne Dirksen
(b. 1921)

Verses 3-12

1   You are 'God: we 'praise you; *
     You are the 'Lord: 'we ac'claim you;

2   You are the e'ternal 'Father: *
     All cre'ation 'worships 'you.

3   To you all angels, all the 'powers of 'heaven, *
     Cherubim and Seraphim, 'sing in 'endless 'praise:

4   Holy, holy, holy Lord, God of 'power and 'might, *
     heaven and 'earth are 'full of your 'glory.

5   The glorious company of a'postles 'praise you. *
     The noble 'fellowship of 'prophets 'praise you.

6   The white-robed army of 'martyrs 'praise you. *
     Throughout the world the 'holy 'Church ac'claims you;

7   Father, of 'majesty un'bounded, *
     your true and only Son, 'worthy 'of all 'worship,

8   And the 'Holy 'Spirit, *
     — 'advo'cate and 'guide.

9   You, Christ, are the 'king of 'glory, *
     the e'ternal 'Son of the 'Father.

10   When you became man to 'set us 'free *
     you did not 'shun the 'Virgin's 'womb.

11   You overcame the 'sting of 'death *
     and opened the kingdom of 'heaven to 'all be'lievers.

12   You are seated at God's right 'hand in 'glory. *
     We believe that you will 'come and 'be our 'judge.

13   Come then, Lord, and 'help your 'people, *
     bought with the 'price of 'your own 'blood,

14   And bring us 'with your 'saints *
     to 'glory 'ever 'lasting.

You are God *Te Deum laudamus*

Unison or harmony

1. You are God: we praise you; You are the Lord: we ac-

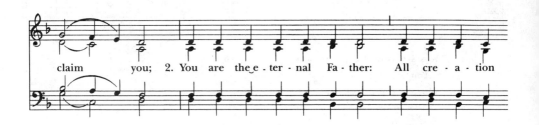

claim you; 2. You are the e- ter- nal Fa- ther: All cre- a- tion

wor- ships you. 3. To you all an- gels, all the powers of hea-

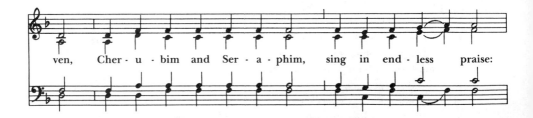

ven, Cher- u- bim and Ser- a- phim, sing in end- less praise:

of death and o-pened the king-dom of hea-ven to all be-liev-ers. 10. You are seat-ed at God's right hand in glo-ry. We be-lieve that you will come and be our judge. 11. Come then, Lord, and help your peo-ple, bought with the price of your own blood, 12. and bring us with your saints to glo-ry ev-er-last-ing.

This pitch for unison singing and for men's voices in harmony; for singing in harmony by mixed voices, a whole tone or minor third higher.

Setting: Slavonic chant; adapt. and harm. Mason Martens (b. 1933)

Hymns

Hymns

1 Fa - ther, we praise thee, now the night is
2 Mon - arch of all things, fit us for thy
3 All ho - ly Fa - ther, Son, and e - qual

o - ver, ac - tive and watch - ful, stand we all be -
man - sions; ban - ish our weak - ness, health and whole-ness
Spi - rit, Trin - i - ty bless - ed, send us thy sal -

fore thee; sing - ing we of - fer prayer and med - i -
send - ing; bring us to hea - ven, where thy saints u -
va - tion; thine is the glo - ry, gleam - ing and re -

ta - tion: thus we a - dore thee.
nit - ed joy with - out end - ing.
sound - ing through all cre - a - tion.

Words: Latin, 10th cent.; tr. Percy Dearmer (1867-1936)
Music: *Christe sanctorum*, melody from *Antiphoner*, 1681

11 11. 11 5

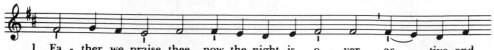

1 Fa - ther, we praise thee, now the night is o - ver, ac - tive and
2 Mon - arch of all things, fit us for thy man - sions; ban - ish our
3 All ho - ly Fa - ther, Son, and e - qual Spi - rit, Trin - i - ty

watch - ful, stand we all be - fore thee; sing - ing we of - fer
weak - ness, health and whole-ness send - ing; bring us to hea - ven,
bless - ed, send us thy sal - va - tion; thine is the glo - ry,

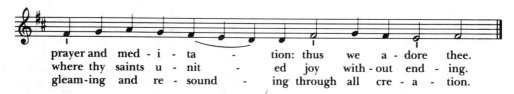

prayer and med - i - ta - tion: thus we a - dore thee.
where thy saints u - nit - ed joy with - out end - ing.
gleam-ing and re - sound - ing through all cre - a - tion.

Words: Latin, 10th cent.; tr. Percy Dearmer (1867-1936)
Music: *Nocte surgentes*, plainsong, Mode 3, Nevers MS., 13th cent.;
     ver. Schola Antiqua, 1983
Music: Melody rhythmic version © 1984, Schola Antiqua Inc. Used by permission.

11 11. 11 5

1 Now that the day - light fills the sky, we
2 Our hearts and lips may he re - strain; keep
3 From e - vil may he guard our eyes, our
4 that we, when this new day is gone, and
5 To God the Fa - ther, heaven - ly Light, to

1 lift our hearts to God on high, that he, in all we
2 us from caus - ing o - thers pain, that we may see and
3 ears from emp - ty praise and lies; from self - ish - ness our
4 night in turn is draw - ing on, with con - science free from
5 Christ, re - vealed in earth - ly night, to God the Ho - ly

1 do	or	say,	would	keep	us	free	from	harm this day:
2 serve	his	Son,	and	grow	in	love	for	ev - ery - one.
3 hearts re -	lease,	that	we	may	serve,	and	know his	peace;
4 sin	and	blame,	may	praise	and	bless	his	ho - ly	Name.
5 Ghost	we	raise	our	e -	qual	and	un -	ceas - ing praise.

Words: Latin, 6th cent.; st. 1, tr. John Mason Neale (1818-1866); sts. 2-4, tr. Peter Scagnelli (b. 1949).
    St. 5, Charles Coffin (1676-1749); tr. John Chandler (1806-1876)
Music: *Herr Jesu Christ*, melody from *Cantionale Germanicum*, 1628   LM

Morning   4

1 Now	that	the	day - light	fills	the	sky,	we	lift	our
2 Our	hearts	and	lips	may	he	re - strain;	keep	us	from
3 From	e - vil	may	he	guard	our	eyes,	our	ears	from
4 that	we,	when	this	new	day	is	gone,	and	night	in
5 To	God	the	Fa - ther,	heaven - ly	Light,	to	Christ,	re -

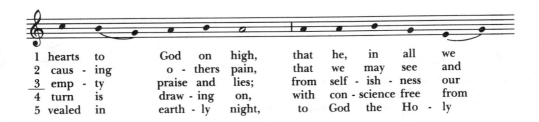

1 hearts	to	God	on	high,	that	he,	in	all	we
2 caus - ing	o - thers	pain,	that	we	may	see	and
3 emp - ty	praise and	lies;	from	self - ish - ness	our
4 turn	is	draw - ing	on,	with	con - science	free	from
5 vealed	in	earth - ly	night,	to	God	the	Ho - ly

1 do	or	say,	would	keep	us	free	from	harm this day:
2 serve	his	Son,	and	grow	in	love	for	ev - ery - one.
3 hearts re -	lease,	that	we	may	serve,	and	know his	peace;
4 sin	and	blame,	may	praise	and	bless	his	ho - ly	Name.
5 Ghost	we	raise	our	e -	qual	and	un -	ceas - ing praise.

Words: Latin, 6th cent.; st. 1, tr. John Mason Neale (1818-1866); sts. 2-4, tr. Peter Scagnelli (b. 1949).
    St. 5, Charles Coffin (1676-1749); tr. John Chandler (1806-1876)
Music: *Verbum supernum prodiens*, plainsong, Mode 2, Nevers MS., 13th cent.   LM

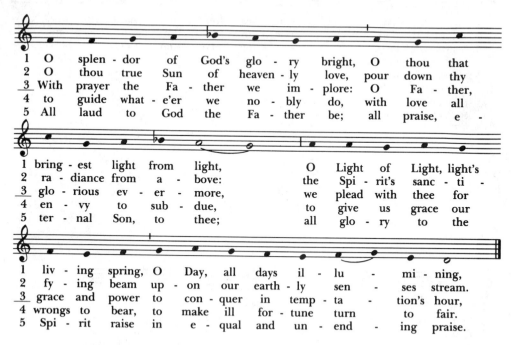

1 O splen - dor of God's glo - ry bright, O thou that
2 O thou true Sun of heaven - ly love, pour down thy
3 With prayer the Fa - ther we im - plore: O Fa - ther,
4 to guide what - e'er we no - bly do, with love all
5 All laud to God the Fa - ther be; all praise, e -

1 bring - est light from light, O Light of Light, light's
2 ra - diance from a - bove: the Spi - rit's sanc - ti -
3 glo - rious ev - er - more, we plead with thee for
4 en - vy to sub - due, to give us grace our
5 ter - nal Son, to thee; all glo - ry to the

1 liv - ing spring, O Day, all days il - lu - mi - ning,
2 fy - ing beam up - on our earth - ly sen - ses stream.
3 grace and power to con - quer in temp - ta - tion's hour,
4 wrongs to bear, to make ill for - tune turn to fair.
5 Spi - rit raise in e - qual and un - end - ing praise.

Words: Ambrose of Milan (340-397); tr. Robert Seymour Bridges (1844-1930), alt.
Music: *Splendor paternae gloriae*, plainsong, Mode 1, Worcester MS., 13th cent.

LM

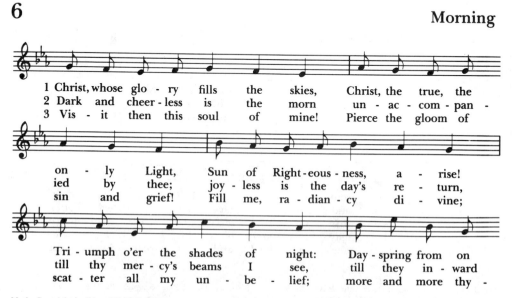

1 Christ, whose glo - ry fills the skies, Christ, the true, the
2 Dark and cheer - less is the morn un - ac - com - pan -
3 Vis - it then this soul of mine! Pierce the gloom of

on - ly Light, Sun of Right - eous - ness, a - rise!
ied by thee; joy - less is the day's re - turn,
sin and grief! Fill me, ra - dian - cy di - vine;

Tri - umph o'er the shades of night: Day - spring from on
till thy mer - cy's beams I see, till they in - ward
scat - ter all my un - be - lief; more and more thy -

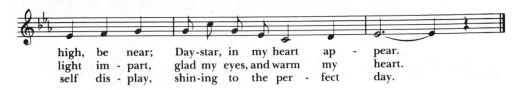

high,   be   near;   Day-star, in my heart   ap -   pear.
light im - part,   glad my eyes, and warm   my   heart.
self   dis - play,   shin-ing to the per - fect   day.

Words: Charles Wesley (1707-1788)
Music: *Christ Whose Glory*, Malcolm Williamson (b. 1931)

77. 77. 77

Morning

7

1 Christ, whose glo - ry   fills the skies, Christ the true, the   on - ly Light,
2 Dark and cheer-less   is the morn   un - ac - com - pan - ied by thee;
3 Vis - it then this   soul of mine! Pierce the gloom of   sin and grief!

Sun of Right-eous - ness, a - rise!   Tri-umph o'er the   shades of night:
joy - less is the   day's re - turn,   till thy mer - cy's   beams I see,
Fill me, ra - dian - cy di - vine;   scat - ter all my   un - be - lief;

Day-spring from on   high, be   near;   Day-star, in my   heart ap - pear.
till they in - ward light im - part,   glad my eyes, and   warm my heart.
more and more thy - self dis - play,   shin-ing to the   per - fect day.

Words: Charles Wesley (1707-1788)
Music: *Ratisbon*, melody from *Geystliche gesangk Buchleyn*, 1524; adapt. att. William Henry Havergal
(1793-1870); harm. William Henry Havergal (1793-1870), alt.

77. 77. 77

Unison or harmony

1 Morn-ing has bro - ken like the first morn - ing,
2 Sweet the rain's new fall sun - lit from hea - ven,
3 Mine is the sun - light! Mine is the morn - ing

black-bird has spo - ken like the first bird.____
like the first dew - fall on the first grass.____
born of the one light E - den saw play!____

Praise for the sing - ing! Praise for the morn - ing!
Praise for the sweet - ness of the wet gar - den,
Praise with e - la - tion, praise ev - ery morn - ing,

Praise for them, spring - ing fresh from the Word!____
sprung in com - plete - ness where his feet pass.____
God's re - cre - a - tion of the new day!____

Words: Eleanor Farjeon (1881-1965), alt.
Music: *Bunessan*, Gaelic melody; harm. Alec Wyton (b. 1921)

55. 54. D

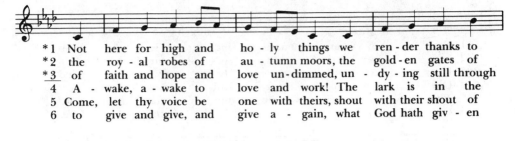

*1	Not	here for high and	ho - ly	things we	ren - der thanks to
*2	the	roy - al robes of	au - tumn moors, the	gold - en gates of
*3	of	faith and hope and	love un - dimmed, un -	dy - ing still through
4	A - wake, a - wake to	love and work! The	lark is in the
5	Come, let thy voice be	one with theirs, shout	with their shout of
6	to	give and give, and	give a - gain, what	God hath giv - en

1	thee,	but	for the	com - mon	things of	earth, the
2	spring,	the	vel - vet	of soft	sum - mer	nights, the
3	death,	the	re - sur - rec - tion	of the	world, what
4	sky,	the	fields are	wet with	dia - mond	dew, the
5	praise;	see	how the	gi - ant	sun soars	up, great
6	thee;	to	spend thy - self	nor	count the	cost; to

1	pur - ple	pa - gean - try	of	dawn - ing	and of
2	sil - ver	glis - ter - ing	of	all the	mil - lion
3	time there	comes the	breath of	dawn that	rus - tles
4	worlds a - wake	to cry	their	bless - ings	on the
5	lord of	years and	days! So	let the	love of
6	serve right	glo - rious - ly	the	God who	gave all

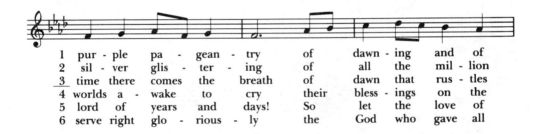

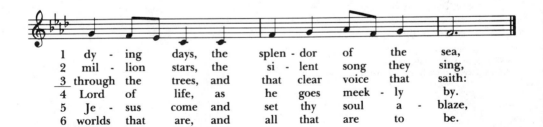

1	dy - ing	days, the	splen - dor	of the	sea,
2	mil - lion	stars, the	si - lent	song they	sing,
3	through the	trees, and	that clear	voice that	saith:
4	Lord of	life, as	he goes	meek - ly	by.
5	Je - sus	come and	set thy	soul a -	blaze,
6	worlds that	are, and	all that	are to	be.

Words: Geoffrey Anketel Studdert-Kennedy (1883-1929)
Music: *Morning Song*, melody att. Elkanah Kelsay Dare (1782-1826)

86. 86. 86

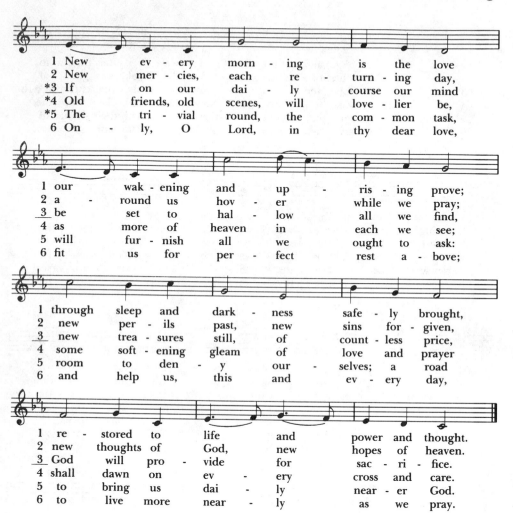

1 New every morn - ing is the love
2 New mer - cies, each re - turn - ing day,
*3 If on our dai - ly course our mind
*4 Old friends, old scenes, will love - lier be,
*5 The tri - vial round, the com - mon task,
6 On - ly, O Lord, in thy dear love,

1 our wak - ening and up - ris - ing prove;
2 a - round us hov - er while we pray;
3 be set to hal - low all we find,
4 as more of heaven in each we see;
5 will fur - nish all we ought to ask:
6 fit us for per - fect rest a - bove;

1 through sleep and dark - ness safe - ly brought,
2 new per - ils past, new sins for - given,
3 new trea - sures still, of count - less price,
4 some soft - ening gleam of love and prayer
5 room to den - y our - selves; a road
6 and help us, this and ev - ery day,

1 re - stored to life and power and thought.
2 new thoughts of God, and new hopes of heaven.
3 God will pro - vide for sac - ri - fice.
4 shall dawn on ev - ery cross and care.
5 to bring us dai - ly near - er God.
6 to live more near - ly as we pray.

Words: John Keble (1792-1866)
Music: *Kedron*, melody att. Elkanah Kelsay Dare (1782-1826)

LM

Morning

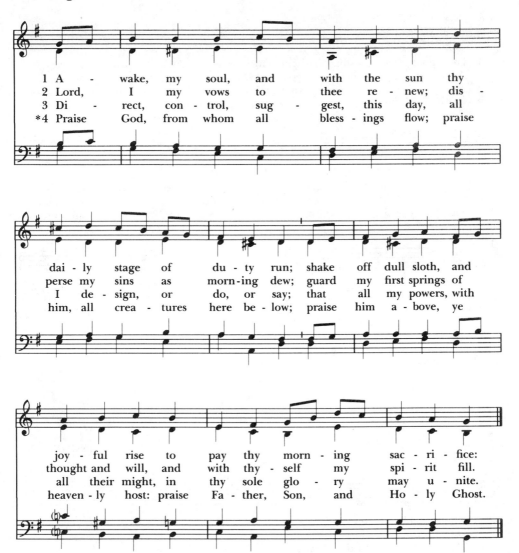

1 A - wake, my soul, and with the sun thy
2 Lord, I my vows to thee re - new; dis -
3 Di - rect, con - trol, sug - gest, this day, all
*4 Praise God, from whom all bless - ings flow; praise

dai - ly stage of du - ty run; shake off dull sloth, and
perse my sins as morn-ing dew; guard my first springs of
I de - sign, or do, or say; that all my powers, with
him, all crea - tures here be - low; praise him a - bove, ye

joy - ful rise to pay thy morn - ing sac - ri - fice:
thought and will, and with thy - self my spi - rit fill.
all their might, in thy sole glo - ry may u - nite.
heaven - ly host: praise Fa - ther, Son, and Ho - ly Ghost.

Words: Thomas Ken (1637-1711), alt.
Music: *Morning Hymn*, melody François Hippolyte Barthélémon (1741-1808);
  harm. *The Church Hymnal for the Church Year*, 1917

LM

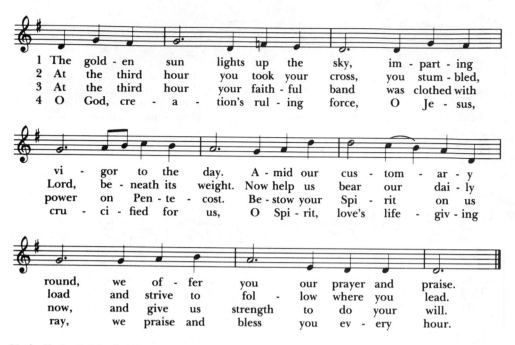

1 The gold-en sun lights up the sky, im-part-ing
2 At the third hour you took your cross, you stum-bled,
3 At the third hour your faith-ful band was clothed with
4 O God, cre - a - tion's rul-ing force, O Je - sus,

vi - gor to the day. A - mid our cus - tom - ar - y
Lord, be - neath its weight. Now help us bear our dai - ly
power on Pen - te - cost. Be - stow your Spi - rit on us
cru - ci - fied for us, O Spi - rit, love's life - giv - ing

round, we of - fer you our prayer and praise.
load and strive to fol - low where you lead.
now, and give us strength to do your will.
ray, we praise and bless you ev - ery hour.

Words: Charles P. Price (b. 1920)
Music: *Danby*, English melody; adapt. Ralph Vaughan Williams (1872-1958)

LM

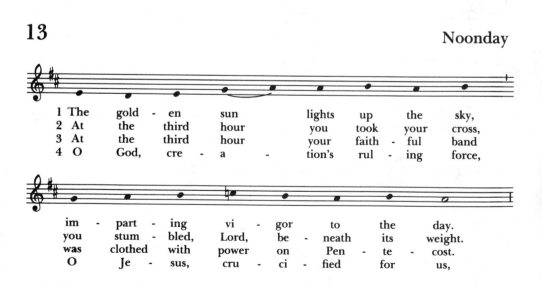

1 The gold - en sun lights up the sky,
2 At the third hour you took your cross,
3 At the third hour your faith - ful band
4 O God, cre - a - tion's rul - ing force,

im - part - ing vi - gor to the day.
you stum - bled, Lord, be - neath its weight.
was clothed with power on Pen - te - cost.
O Je - sus, cru - ci - fied for us,

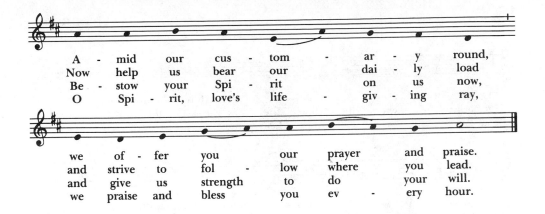

A - mid our cus - tom - ar - y round,
Now help us bear our dai - ly load
Be - stow your Spi - rit on us now,
O Spi - rit, love's life - giv - ing ray,

we of - fer you our prayer and praise.
and strive to fol - low where you lead.
and give us strength to do your will.
we praise and bless you ev - er - y hour.

Words: Charles P. Price (b. 1920)
Music: *Verbum supernum prodiens*, plainsong, Mode 8, Einsiedeln MS., 13th cent.

LM

Noonday

14

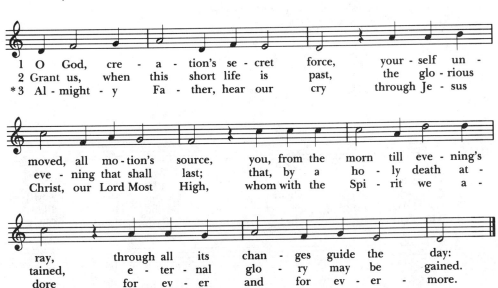

1 O God, cre - a - tion's se - cret force, your - self un -
2 Grant us, when this short life is past, the glo - rious
*3 Al - might - y Fa - ther, hear our cry through Je - sus

moved, all mo - tion's source, you, from the morn till eve - ning's
eve - ning that shall last; that, by a ho - ly death at -
Christ, our Lord Most High, whom with the Spi - rit we a -

ray, through all its chan - ges guide the day:
tained, e - ter - nal glo - ry may be gained.
dore for ev - er and for ev - er - more.

Words: Ambrose of Milan (340-397); tr. John Mason Neale (1818-1866), alt.
St. 3, James Waring McCrady (b. 1938)
Music: *O Heiland, reiss*, melody from *Rheinfelsisches Deutsches Catholisches Gesangbuch*, 1666

LM

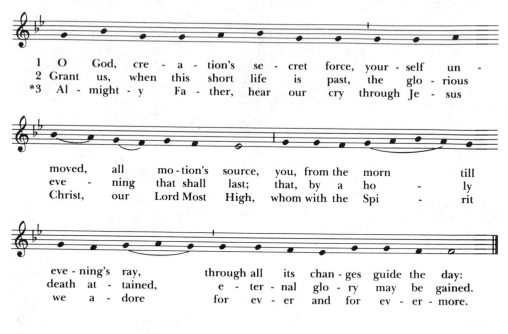

1 O God, cre - a - tion's se - cret force, your - self un -
2 Grant us, when this short life is past, the glo - rious
*3 Al - might - y Fa - ther, hear our cry through Je - sus

moved, all mo - tion's source, you, from the morn till
eve - ning that shall last; that, by a ho - ly
Christ, our Lord Most High, whom with the Spi - rit

eve - ning's ray, through all its chan - ges guide the day:
death at - tained, e - ter - nal glo - ry may be gained.
we a - dore for ev - er and for ev - er - more.

Words: Ambrose of Milan (340-397); tr. John Mason Neale (1818-1866), alt.
St. 3, James Waring McCrady (b. 1938)
Music: *Te lucis ante terminum,* plainsong, Mode 8, *Antiphonale Sarisburiense,* Vol. II

LM

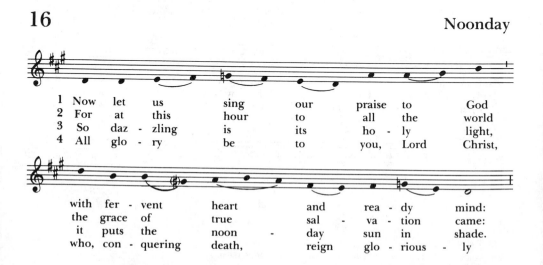

1 Now let us sing our praise to God
2 For at this hour to all the world
3 So daz - zling is its ho - ly light,
4 All glo - ry be to you, Lord Christ,

with fer - vent heart and rea - dy mind:
the grace of true sal - va - tion came:
it puts the noon - day sun in shade.
who, con - quering death, reign glo - rious - ly

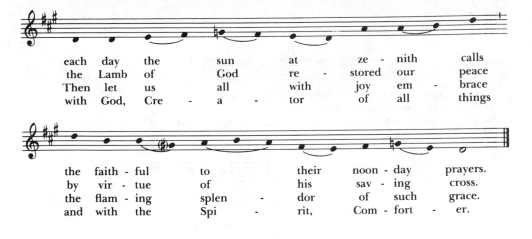

each day the sun at ze - nith calls
the Lamb of God re - stored our peace
Then let us all with joy em - brace
with God, Cre - a - tor of all things

the faith - ful to their noon - day prayers.
by vir - tue of his sav - ing cross.
the flam - ing splen - dor of such grace.
and with the Spi - rit, Com - fort - er.

Words: Latin; ver. *Hymnal 1982*. St. 4, Anne K. LeCroy (b. 1930)
Music: *Dicamus laudes Domino*, plainsong, Mode 5, Nevers MS., 13th cent.

LM

Noonday 17

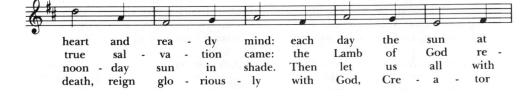

1 Now let us sing our praise to God with fer - vent
2 For at this hour to all the world the grace of
3 So daz - zling is its ho - ly light, it puts the
4 All glo - ry be to you, Lord Christ, who, con - quering

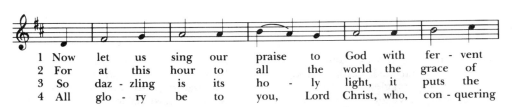

heart and rea - dy mind: each day the sun at
true sal - va - tion came: the Lamb of God re -
noon - day sun in shade. Then let us all with
death, reign glo - rious - ly with God, Cre - a - tor

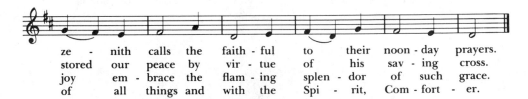

ze - nith calls the faith - ful to their noon - day prayers.
stored our peace by vir - tue of his sav - ing cross.
joy em - brace the flam - ing splen - dor of such grace.
of all things and with the Spi - rit, Com - fort - er.

Words: Latin; ver. *Hymnal 1982*. St. 4, Anne K. LeCroy (b. 1930)
Music: *Solemnis haec festivitas*, melody from *Graduale*, 1685

LM

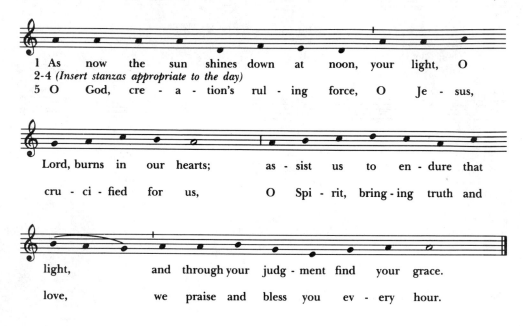

1 As now the sun shines down at noon, your light, O
2-4 *(Insert stanzas appropriate to the day)*
5 O God, cre - a - tion's rul - ing force, O Je - sus,

Lord, burns in our hearts; as - sist us to en - dure that

cru - ci - fied for us, O Spi - rit, bring - ing truth and

light,   and through your judg - ment find your grace.

love,   we praise and bless you ev - ery hour.

Monday and Thursday

2 The sun stood still for Joshua
while he contended, Lord, for you;
so may we struggle faithfully
and seek our victory in your peace.

3 At noon you hung upon the cross
betrayed, forsaken, all alone;
help us to share your pain and grief,
and, sharing, know life's victory won.

4 At noon you came to Jacob's well,
athirst and spent, you asked for aid;
to us, like her who saw your need,
your living water give to drink.

Tuesday and Saturday

2 Elijah taunted Baal at noon;
he knew you, Lord, would answer him;
may we, too, trust your sovereign power
when we must act in day's hard light.

3 On Golgotha the sky turned dark;
all shadows of the morn and eve
converged to shield frail human eyes
from all the woe you bore for us.

4 At noontime Paul beheld your light,
so bright it cancelled out the sun;
you blinded and converted him:
O turn us now to see your face.

2 By noon's bright light, destruction stalks;
  ten thousand perish at our side;
  held by your unrelenting grace,
  let us cling always to your love.

3 The dark midday could not conceal
  your cry of awful agony;
  teach us to hear its echoes still
  in every human misery.

4 In noonday vision Peter saw
  that all you made was pure and clean;
  grant us that same revealing light
  that we may see your world is good.

Words: Charles P. Price (b. 1920) and Carl P. Daw, Jr. (b. 1944)
Music: *Jesu dulcis memoria*, plainsong, Mode 2

LM

Noonday 19

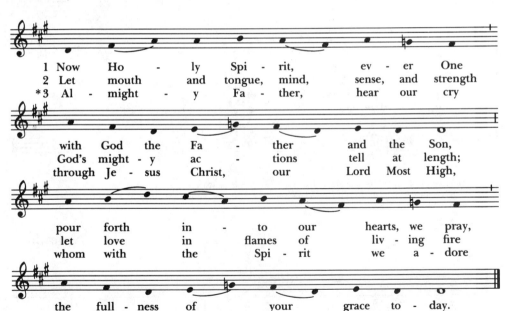

```
1 Now  Ho    -  ly   Spi - rit,        ev - er   One
2 Let  mouth    and  tongue,  mind,    sense,  and  strength
*3 Al  might  - y    Fa - ther,        hear  our  cry

   with  God   the   Fa   -  ther     and  the  Son,
   God's might - y   ac   -  tions     tell  at  length;
   through Je - sus  Christ,   our     Lord  Most High,

   pour  forth  in  - to   our   hearts,  we   pray,
   let   love   in   flames of    liv - ing  fire
   whom  with   the  Spi - rit    we   a - dore

   the   full - ness  of    your  grace  to - day.
   the   hearts of   all    the   world  in - spire.
   for   ev  - er   and    for   ev - er - more.
```

Words: Ambrose of Milan (340-397); *ver. Hymnal 1982*. St. 3, James Waring McCrady (b. 1938)
Music: *Nunc Sancte nobis Spiritus*, plainsong, Mode 5, Engelberg MS, 14th cent.

LM

1 Now Ho - ly Spi - rit, ev - er One with God the
2 Let mouth and tongue, mind, sense, and strength God's might - y
*3 Al - might - y Fa - ther, hear our cry through Je - sus

Fa - ther and the Son, pour forth in - to our
ac - tions tell at length; let love in flames of
Christ, our Lord Most High, whom with the Spi - rit

hearts, we pray, the full - ness of your grace to - day.
liv - ing fire the hearts of all the world in - spire.
we a - dore for ev - er and for ev - er - more.

Words: Ambrose of Milan (340-397); ver. *Hymnal 1982.* St. 3, James Waring McCrady (b. 1938)
Music: *Wareham,* melody William Knapp (1698-1768), alt.; harm *Hymns Ancient and Modern,* 1875,
after James Turle (1802-1882)

LM

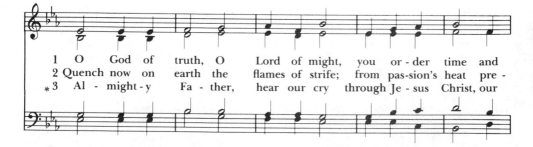

1 O God of truth, O Lord of might, you or - der time and
2 Quench now on earth the flames of strife; from pas - sion's heat pre -
*3 Al - might - y Fa - ther, hear our cry through Je - sus Christ, our

change a - right, you send the ear - ly morn - ing
serve our life; and while you keep our bo - dy
Lord Most High, whom with the Spi - rit we a -

ray, and light the glow of per - fect day:
whole, pour heal - ing peace up - on our soul.
dore for ev - er and for ev - er - more.

Words: Ambrose of Milan (340-397); tr. John Mason Neale (1818-1866), alt.
St. 3, James Waring McCrady (b. 1938)
Music: *Song 34*, melody and bass Orlando Gibbons (1583-1625); as adapted and harmonized in
The English Hymnal, 1906

LM

Noonday

22

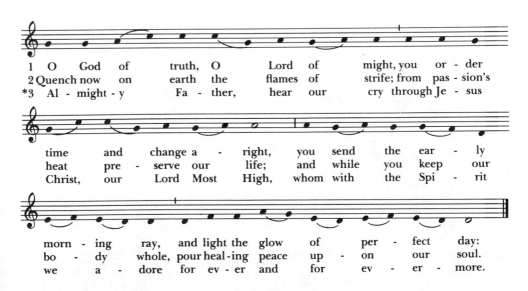

1 O God of truth, O Lord of might, you or - der
2 Quench now on earth the flames of strife; from pas - sion's
*3 Al - might - y Fa - ther, hear our cry through Je - sus

time and change a - right, you send the ear - ly
heat pre - serve our life; and while you keep our
Christ, our Lord Most High, whom with the Spi - rit

morn - ing ray, and light the glow of per - fect day:
bo - dy whole, pour heal - ing peace up - on our soul.
we a - dore for ev - er and for ev - er - more.

Words: Ambrose of Milan (340-397); tr. John Mason Neale (1818-1866), alt.
St. 3, James Waring McCrady (b. 1938)
Music: *Rector potens, verax Deus*, plainsong, Mode 1, *Klosterneuburger Hymnar*, 1336

LM

1 The fleet-ing day is near-ly gone;
2 At prayer time, near the Tem-ple gate,
3 With "It is fi-nished" on your lips,
4 O God, cre-a-tion's rul-ing force,

we har-vest what the morn-ing sowed.
A-pos-tles made a lame man walk.
at that ninth hour you died for us.
O Je-sus, cru-ci-fied for us,

Now grant us un-di-mi-nished strength
They gave him heal-ing in your Name;
In-spire us by your dy-ing breath
O Spi-rit, bring-ing power and health,

to stand and do what still re-mains.
now give us grace to walk your way.
to live for you and do your will.
we praise and bless you ev-ery hour.

Words: Charles P. Price (b. 1920)
Music: *Du meiner Seelen*, from *Cantica Spiritualia*, 1847

LM

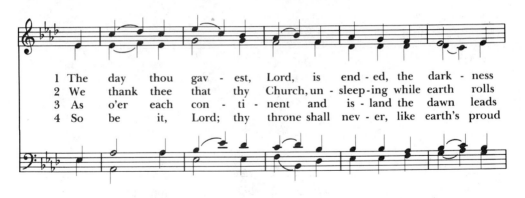

1 The day thou gav - est, Lord, is end - ed, the dark - ness
2 We thank thee that thy Church, un - sleep-ing while earth rolls
3 As o'er each con - ti - nent and is - land the dawn leads
4 So be it, Lord; thy throne shall nev - er, like earth's proud

falls at thy be - hest; to thee our morn - ing hymns a -
on - ward in - to light, through all the world her watch is
on an - oth - er day, the voice of prayer is nev - er
em - pires, pass a - way; thy king - dom stands, and grows for

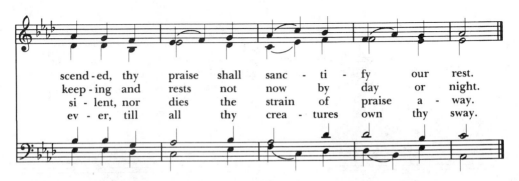

scend - ed, thy praise shall sanc - ti - fy our rest.
keep - ing and rests not now by day or night.
si - lent, nor dies the strain of praise a - way.
ev - er, till all thy crea - tures own thy sway.

This hymn may be used in the morning by omitting stanza 1.

Words: John Ellerton (1826-1893)
Music: *St. Clement,* Clement Cottevill Scholefield (1839-1904)

98. 98

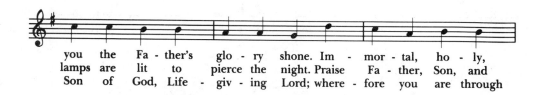

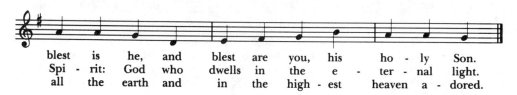

1 O gra - cious Light, Lord Je - sus Christ, in
2 Now sun - set comes, but light shines forth, the
3 Wor - thy are you of end - less praise, O

you the Fa - ther's glo - ry shone. Im - mor - tal, ho - ly,
lamps are lit to pierce the night. Praise Fa - ther, Son, and
Son of God, Life - giv - ing Lord; where - fore you are through

blest is he, and blest are you, his ho - ly Son.
Spi - rit: God who dwells in the e - ter - nal light.
all the earth and in the high - est heaven a - dored.

This hymn may be sung unaccompanied as a four-part canon at a distance of one measure.

Words: Greek, 3rd cent.; tr. F. Bland Tucker (1895-1984); para. of *O Gracious Light*
Music: *The Eighth Tune*, Thomas Tallis (1505?-1585)

LM

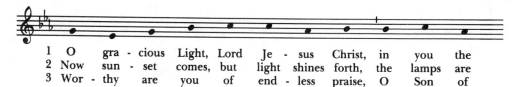

1 O gra - cious Light, Lord Je - sus Christ, in you the
2 Now sun - set comes, but light shines forth, the lamps are
3 Wor - thy are you of end - less praise, O Son of

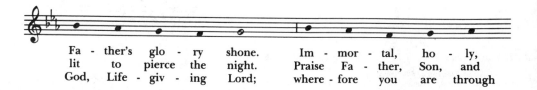

Fa - ther's glo - ry shone. Im - mor - tal, ho - ly,
lit to pierce the night. Praise Fa - ther, Son, and
God, Life - giv - ing Lord; where - fore you are through

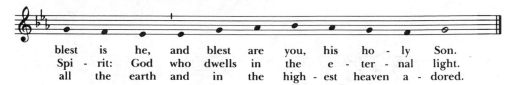

blest	is	he,	and	blest	are	you,	his	ho - ly	Son.
Spi - rit:	God	who	dwells	in	the	e - ter - nal	light.
all	the	earth	and	in	the	high - est	heaven a - dored.

This melody may be sung in rhythmic form: ♪ ♩ ♪ ♩

Words: Greek, 3rd cent.; tr. F. Bland Tucker (1895-1984); para. of *O Gracious Light*
Music: *Conditor alme siderum*, plainsong, Mode 4

LM

Evening

27

1 O		blest Cre	a - tor,	source	of	light,
2 You		joined the	morn and	eve -	ning	ray;
3 Lest		we, be -	set by	doubt	and	strife,
4 E -	ter - nal	Fa - ther,	help	us	rise
5 De -	fend us,	Fa - ther,	through	the	night,

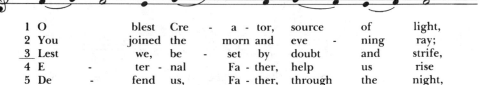

1 you	gave	the	day	with	splen -	dor	bright,
2 you	found	it	good	and	called	it	'day.'
3 for -	get	your	bless -	ed	gift	of	life,
4 and	strive	to	gain	the	heaven -	ly	prize;
5 and	with	your	Son,	and	Spi -	rit	bright

1 when	on	the	new	and	liv - ing	earth
2 But	now	the	threat - ening	dark - ness	nears—
3 and	an - guished	and	in	mind dis - tressed,
4 for	you	a - lone	can	make us	strong
5 the	Tri - ni - ty	whom	we	a - dore—

1 you	brought	all	things	to	glo -	rious	birth.
2 we	pray	you,	Fa -	ther,	calm	our	fears.
3 be	crushed	by	guilt,	by	sin	op -	pressed.
4 to	turn	from	sin	and	cease	from	wrong.
5 be	with	us	now	and	ev -	er -	more.

Words: Latin, 6th cent.; tr. Anne LeCroy (b. 1930), alt.
Music: *Lucis creator optime*, plainsong, Mode 8, Worcester MS., 13th cent.

LM

1 O blest Cre - a - tor, source of light, you gave the
2 You joined the morn and eve - ning ray; you found it
3 Lest we, be - set by doubt and strife, for - get your
4 E - ter - nal Fa - ther, help us rise and strive to
*5 De - fend us, Fa - ther, through the night, and with your

1 day with splen - dor bright, when on the new and
2 good and called it 'day.' But now the threat - ening
3 bless - ed gift of life, and an - guished and in
4 gain the heaven - ly prize; for you a - lone can
5 Son, and Spi - rit bright the Tri - ni - ty whom

1 liv - ing earth you brought all things to glo - rious birth.
2 dark - ness nears— we pray you, Fa - ther, calm our fears.
3 mind dis - tressed, be crushed by guilt, by sin op - pressed.
4 make us strong to turn from sin and cease from wrong.
5 we a - dore— be with us now and ev - er - more.

Words: Latin, 6th cent.; tr. Anne K. LeCroy (b. 1930), alt.
Music: *Bromley*, Franz Joseph Haydn (1732-1809), alt.

LM

1 O Trin - i - ty of bless - ed light, O U - ni -
2 To thee our morn - ing song of praise, to thee our
3 To God the Fa - ther, heaven - ly Light, to Christ re -

ty of prince - ly might, the fier - y sun now
eve - ning prayer we raise; O grant us with thy
vealed in earth - ly night, to God the Ho - ly

goes his way; shed thou with - in our hearts thy ray.
saints on high to praise thee through e - ter - ni - ty.
Ghost we raise our e - qual and un - ceas - ing praise.

Words: Latin, 6th cent.; tr. John Mason Neale (1818-1866). St. 3, Charles Coffin (1676-1749);
     tr. John Chandler (1806-1876)
Music: *Bromley*, Franz Joseph Haydn (1732-1809), alt.

LM

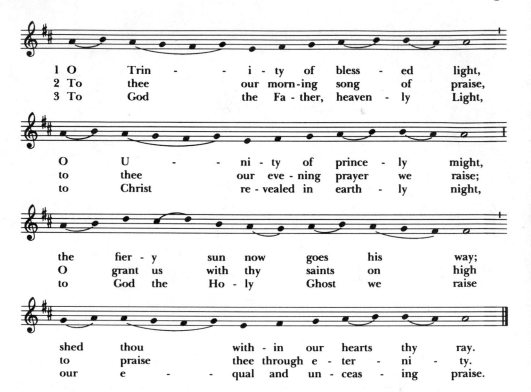

1 O Trin - - i - ty of bless - ed light,
2 To thee our morn-ing song of praise,
3 To God the Fa - ther, heaven - ly Light,

O U - - ni - ty of prince - ly might,
to thee our eve - ning prayer we raise;
to Christ re - vealed in earth - ly night,

the fier - y sun now goes his way;
O grant us with thy saints on high
to God the Ho - ly Ghost we raise

shed thou with - in our hearts thy ray.
to praise thee through e - ter - ni - ty.
our e - - qual and un - ceas - ing praise.

Words: Latin, 6th cent.; tr. John Mason Neale (1818-1866). St. 3, Charles Coffin (1676-1749);
      tr. John Chandler (1806-1876)
Music: *O lux beata Trinitas*, plainsong, Mode 8   LM

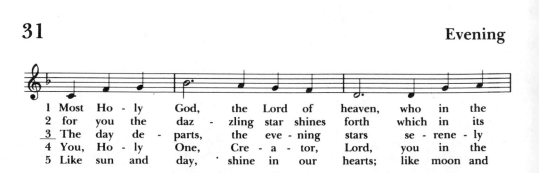

1 Most Ho - ly God, the Lord of heaven, who in the
2 for you the daz - zling star shines forth which in its
3 The day de - parts, the eve - ning stars se - rene - ly
4 You, Ho - ly One, Cre - a - tor, Lord, you in the
5 Like sun and day, shine in our hearts; like moon and

1 high arched sky has placed the sun that flames up from the
2 gleam - ing path de - clares the won - ders of your glo - rious
3 light the dark - ening sky; the moon with cool re - flect - ed
4 pri - mal world once set the bound-aries of the day and
5 night, give lov - ing peace. Free us from bonds of blind - ing

1 east and brings the splen - dors of the dawn:
2 power, and beck - ons us to wor - ship you.
3 glow will bring the si - lenc - es of night.
4 night and or - dered sea - sons in their round.
5 sin and guide us on our path to you.

Words: Latin; tr. Anne K. LeCroy (b. 1930)
Music: *Dunedin*, Vernon Griffiths (b. 1894)   LM

Evening   32

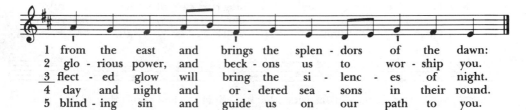

1 Most Ho - ly God, the Lord of heaven, who in the
2 for you the daz - zling star shines forth which in its
3 The day de - parts, the eve - ning stars se - rene - ly
4 You, Ho - ly One, Cre - a - tor, Lord, you in the
5 Like sun and day, shine in our hearts; like moon and

1 high - arched sky has placed the sun that flames up
2 gleam - ing path de - clares the won - ders of your
3 light the dark - ening sky; the moon with cool re -
4 pri - mal world once set the bound - aries of the
5 night, give lov - ing peace. Free us from bonds of

1 from the east and brings the splen - dors of the dawn:
2 glo - rious power, and beck - ons us to wor - ship you.
3 flect - ed glow will bring the si - lenc - es of night.
4 day and night and or - dered sea - sons in their round.
5 blind - ing sin and guide us on our path to you.

Words: Latin; tr. Anne K. LeCroy (b. 1930)
Music: *Immense caeli Conditor*, plainsong, Mode 1; Kempton MS., circa 11th cent., ver Schola
Antiqua, 1983   LM

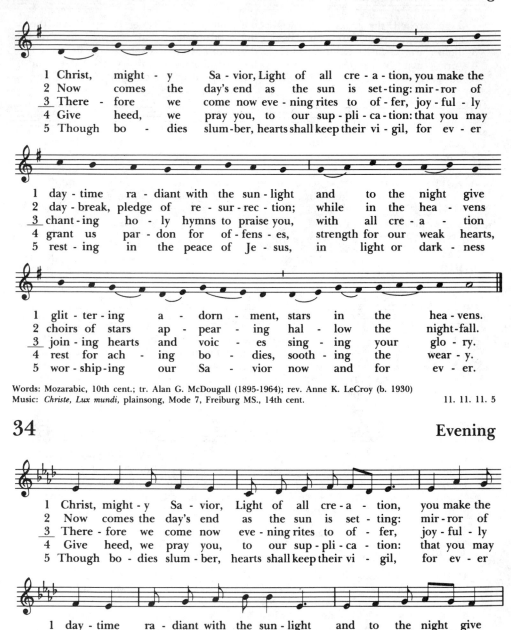

1 Christ, might - y Sa - vior, Light of all cre - a - tion, you make the
2 Now comes the day's end as the sun is set-ting: mir-ror of
3 There - fore we come now eve - ning rites to of - fer, joy - ful - ly
4 Give heed, we pray you, to our sup - pli - ca - tion: that you may
5 Though bo - dies slum-ber, hearts shall keep their vi - gil, for ev - er

1 day - time ra - diant with the sun - light and to the night give
2 day - break, pledge of re - sur - rec - tion; while in the hea - vens
3 chant - ing ho - ly hymns to praise you, with all cre - a - tion
4 grant us par - don for of - fens - es, strength for our weak hearts,
5 rest - ing in the peace of Je - sus, in light or dark - ness

1 glit - ter - ing a - dorn - ment, stars in the hea - vens.
2 choirs of stars ap - pear - ing hal - low the night-fall.
3 join - ing hearts and voic - es sing - ing your glo - ry.
4 rest for ach - ing bo - dies, sooth - ing the wear - y.
5 wor - ship - ing our Sa - vior now and for ev - er.

Words: Mozarabic, 10th cent.; tr. Alan G. McDougall (1895-1964); rev. Anne K. LeCroy (b. 1930)
Music: *Christe, Lux mundi*, plainsong, Mode 7, Freiburg MS., 14th cent.   11. 11. 11. 5

1 Christ, might - y Sa - vior, Light of all cre - a - tion, you make the
2 Now comes the day's end as the sun is set - ting: mir - ror of
3 There - fore we come now eve - ning rites to of - fer, joy - ful - ly
4 Give heed, we pray you, to our sup - pli - ca - tion: that you may
5 Though bo - dies slum - ber, hearts shall keep their vi - gil, for ev - er

1 day - time ra - diant with the sun - light and to the night give
2 day - break, pledge of re - sur - rec - tion; while in the hea - vens
3 chant - ing ho - ly hymns to praise you, with all cre - a - tion
4 grant us par - don for of - fens - es, strength for our weak hearts,
5 rest - ing in the peace of Je - sus, in light or dark - ness

1 glit-ter-ing a-dorn-ment,	stars	in	the hea-	vens.
2 choirs of stars ap-pear-ing	hal-low		the night-	fall.
3 join-ing hearts and voic-es	sing-ing		your glo-	ry.
4 rest for ach-ing bo-dies,	sooth-ing		the wear-	y.
5 wor-ship-ing our Sa-vior	now	and	for ev-er.	

Words: Mozarabic, 10th cent.; tr. Alan G. McDougall (1895-1964); rev. Anne K. LeCroy (b. 1930)
Music: *Innisfree Farm*, Richard Wayne Dirksen (b. 1921)

11. 11. 11. 5

Evening 35

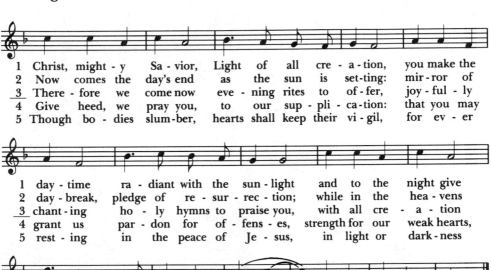

1 Christ, might-y Sa-vior,	Light of all cre-a-tion,	you make the
2 Now comes the day's end	as the sun is set-ting:	mir-ror of
3 There-fore we come now	eve-ning rites to of-fer,	joy-ful-ly
4 Give heed, we pray you,	to our sup-pli-ca-tion:	that you may
5 Though bo-dies slum-ber,	hearts shall keep their vi-gil,	for ev-er

1 day-time	ra-diant with the sun-light	and to the	night give
2 day-break,	pledge of re-sur-rec-tion;	while in the	hea-vens
3 chant-ing	ho-ly hymns to praise you,	with all cre-a-tion
4 grant us	par-don for of-fens-es,	strength for our	weak hearts,
5 rest-ing	in the peace of Je-sus,	in light or	dark-ness

1 glit-ter-ing a-dorn-ment,	stars	in the hea-	vens.
2 choirs of stars ap-pear-ing	hal-	low the night-	fall.
3 join-ing hearts and voi-ces	sing-	ing your glo-	ry.
4 rest for ach-ing bo-dies,	sooth-	ing the wear-	y.
5 wor-ship-ing our Sa-vior	now	and for ev-	er.

Words: Mozarabic, 10th cent.; tr. Alan G. McDougall; (1895-1964) rev. Anne K. LeCroy (b. 1930)
Music: *Mighty Savior*, David Hurd (b. 1950)

11. 11. 11. 5

1 O glad-some Light, O grace of God the Fa-ther's face,
2 Now, ere day fad - eth quite, we see the eve-ning light,
3 To thee of right be - longs all praise of ho-ly songs,

the e - ter - nal splen-dor wear - ing; ce - les - tial, ho - ly, blest,
our wont - ed hymn out - pour - ing; Fa - ther of might un - known,
O Son of God, Life - giv - er; thee, there-fore, O Most High,

our Sa - vior Je - sus Christ, joy - ful in thine ap - pear - ing.
thee, his in - car - nate Son, and Ho - ly Spirit a - dor - ing.
the world doth glo - ri - fy, and shall ex - alt for ev - er.

Words: Greek, 3rd cent.; tr. Robert Seymour Bridges (1844-1930); para. of *O Gracious Light*
Music: *Le Cantique de Siméon*, melody Louis Bourgeois (1510?-1561?);
  harm. Claude Goudimel (1514-1572)

667. 667

1 O bright-ness of the im-mor-tal Fa-ther's face, most ho - ly,
2 the sun is sink-ing now, and one by one the lamps of
3 Worth - y art thou at all times to re - ceive our hal - lowed

heaven - ly, blest, Lord Je - sus Christ, in whom his
eve - ning shine; we hymn the e - ter - nal Fa - ther,
prais - es, Lord. O Son of God, be thou, in

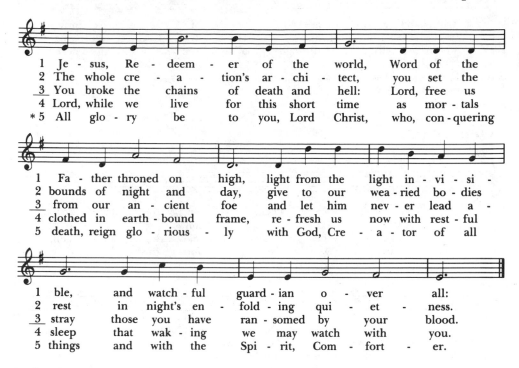

1 Je - sus, Re - deem - er of the world, Word of the
2 The whole cre - a - tion's ar - chi - tect, you set the
3 You broke the chains of death and hell: Lord, free us
4 Lord, while we live for this short time as mor - tals
*5 All glo - ry be to you, Lord Christ, who, con - quering

1 Fa - ther throned on high, light from the light in - vi - si -
2 bounds of night and day, give to our wea - ried bo - dies
3 from our an - cient foe and let him nev - er lead a -
4 clothed in earth - bound frame, re - fresh us now with rest - ful
5 death, reign glo - rious - ly with God, Cre - a - tor of all

1 ble, and watch - ful guard - ian o - ver all:
2 rest in night's en - fold - ing qui - et - ness.
3 stray those you have ran - somed by your blood.
4 sleep that wak - ing we may watch with you.
5 things and with the Spi - rit, Com - fort - er.

Words: Latin, 10th cent.; ver. *Hymnal 1982*. St. 5, Anne K. LeCroy (b. 1930)
Music: *Wilderness*, Reginald Sparshatt Thatcher (1888-1957)

LM

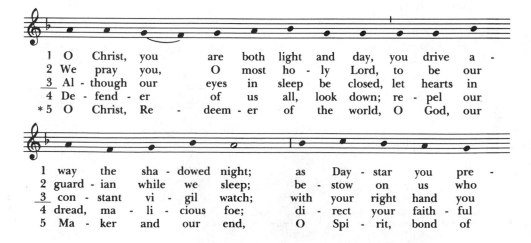

1 O Christ, you are both light and day, you drive a -
2 We pray you, O most ho - ly Lord, to be our
3 Al - though our eyes in sleep be closed, let hearts in
4 De - fend - er of us all, look down; re - pel our
*5 O Christ, Re - deem - er of the world, O God, our

1 way the sha - dowed night; as Day - star you pre -
2 guard - ian while we sleep; be - stow on us who
3 con - stant vi - gil watch; with your right hand you
4 dread, ma - li - cious foe; di - rect your faith - ful
5 Ma - ker and our end, O Spi - rit, bond of

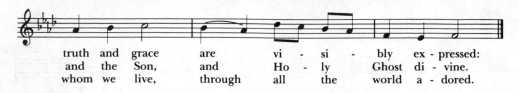

truth and grace   are   vi - si - bly ex - pressed:
and the Son,   and   Ho - ly Ghost di - vine.
whom we live,   through   all the world a - dored.

Words: Greek, 3rd cent.; tr. Edward W. Eddis (1825-1905); para. of *O Gracious Light*
Music: *Evening Hymn*, Gerald Near (b. 1942)

10 6. 10 6

Compline

38

1 Je - sus,   Re - deem - er of the world,
2 The whole cre - a - tion's ar - chi - tect,
3 You broke the chains of death and hell:
4 Lord, while we live for this short time
*5 All glo - ry be to you, Lord Christ,

1 Word of the Fa - ther throned on high,
2 you set the bounds of night and day;
3 Lord, free us from our an - cient foe
4 as mor - tals clothed in earth - bound frame,
5 who, con - quering death, reign glo - rious - ly

1 light from the light in - vi - si - ble,
2 give to our wea - ried bo - dies rest
3 and let him nev - er lead a - stray
4 re - fresh us now with rest - ful sleep
5 with God, Cre - a - tor of all things

1 and watch - ful guard - ian o - ver all:
2 in night's en - fold - ing qui - et - ness.
3 those you have ran - somed by your blood.
4 that wak - ing we may watch with you.
5 and with the Spi - rit, Com - fort - er.

Words: Latin, 10th cent.; ver *Hymnal 1982*. St. 5, Anne K. LeCroy (b. 1930)
Music: *Jesu, nostra redemptio*, plainsong, Mode 8, Worcester MS., 13th cent.

LM

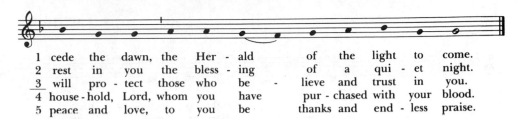

1	cede	the	dawn,	the	Her - ald	of	the	light	to	come.
2	rest	in	you	the	bless - ing	of	a	qui - et		night.
3	will	pro - tect	those	who	be - lieve	and	trust	in		you.
4	house - hold,	Lord,	whom	you	have	pur - chased	with	your		blood.
5	peace	and	love,	to	you	be	thanks	and	end - less	praise.

Words: Latin, 6th cent.; ver. *Hymnal 1982*. St. 5, Charles P. Price (b. 1920)
Music: *Christe, qui Lux es et dies*, plainsong, Mode 2, *Mailander Hymnen*, 15th cent.

LM

Compline

41

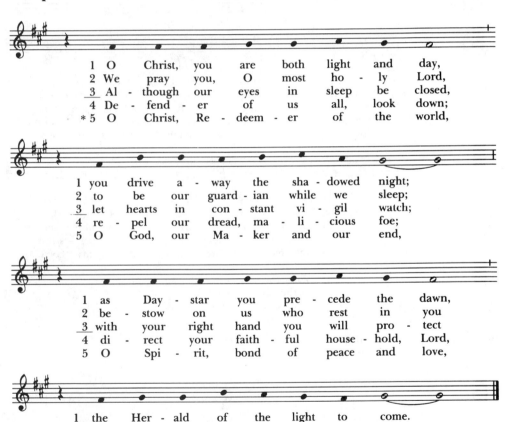

1	O	Christ,	you	are	both	light	and	day,
2	We	pray	you,	O	most	ho - ly		Lord,
3	Al - though	our	eyes	in	sleep	be		closed,
4	De - fend - er	of	us	all,	look			down;
*5	O	Christ,	Re - deem - er	of	the			world,

1	you	drive	a - way	the	sha - dowed			night;
2	to	be	our	guard - ian	while	we		sleep;
3	let	hearts	in	con - stant	vi - gil			watch;
4	re - pel	our	dread,	ma - li - cious				foe;
5	O	God,	our	Ma - ker	and	our		end,

1	as	Day - star	you	pre - cede	the			dawn,
2	be - stow	on	us	who	rest	in		you
3	with	your	right	hand	you	will	pro -	tect
4	di - rect	your	faith - ful	house - hold,				Lord,
5	O	Spi - rit,	bond	of	peace	and		love,

1	the	Her - ald	of	the	light	to		come.
2	the	bless - ing	of	a	qui - et			night.
3	those	who	be - lieve	and	trust	in		you.
4	whom	you	have	pur - chased	with	your		blood.
5	to	you	be	thanks	and	end - less		praise.

Words: Latin, 6th cent.; ver. *Hymnal 1982*. St. 5, Charles P. Price (b 1920)
Music: *Compline*, David Hurd (b. 1950)

LM

1 Now the day is o - ver, night is draw - ing nigh,
2 Je - sus, give the wear - y calm and sweet re - pose;
3 Grant to lit - tle child - ren vis - ions bright of thee;
4 Com - fort ev - ery suf - ferer watch - ing late in pain;
5 Through the long night watch - es may thine an - gels spread

1 sha - dows of the eve - ning steal a - cross the sky.
2 with thy tend - erest bless - ing may our eye - lids close.
3 guard the sail - ors toss - ing on the deep, blue sea.
4 those who plan some e - vil from their sin re - strain.
5 their white wings a - bove me, watch - ing round my bed.

1 eve - ning steal a - cross the sky.
2 bless - ing may our eye - lids close.
3 toss - ing on the deep, blue sea.
4 e - vil from their sin re - strain.
5 bove me, watch - ing round my bed.

6 When the morning wakens,
   then may I arise
Pure, and fresh, and sinless
   in thy holy eyes.

Words: Sabine Baring-Gould (1834-1924), alt.
Music: *Merrial*, Joseph Barnby (1838-1896)

65.65

43 Compline

1 All praise to thee, my God, this night, for
2 For - give me, Lord, for thy dear Son, the
3 O may my soul on thee re - pose, and
4 Praise God, from whom all bless - ings flow; praise

all the bless-ings of the light: keep me, O keep me,
ill that I this day have done; that with the world, my -
with sweet sleep mine eye-lids close; sleep that shall me more
him, all crea-tures here be-low; praise him a-bove, ye

King of kings, be-neath thine own al - might-y wings.
self, and thee, I, ere I sleep, at peace may be.
vi - gorous make to serve my God when I a-wake.
heaven-ly host: praise Fa - ther, Son, and Ho - ly Ghost.

This hymn may be sung unaccompanied as a four-part canon at the distance of one measure.

Words: Thomas Ken (1637-1711)
Music: *The Eighth Tune*, Thomas Tallis (1505?-1585)

LM

Compline 44

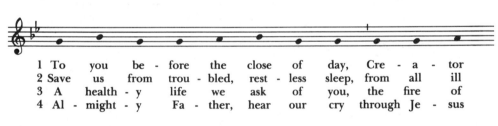

1 To you be - fore the close of day, Cre - a - tor
2 Save us from trou - bled, rest - less sleep, from all ill
3 A health - y life we ask of you, the fire of
4 Al - might - y Fa - ther, hear our cry through Je - sus

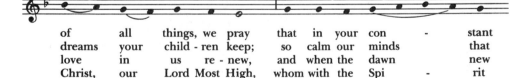

of all things, we pray that in your con - stant
dreams your child - ren keep; so calm our minds that
love in us re - new, and when the dawn new
Christ, our Lord Most High, whom with the Spi - rit

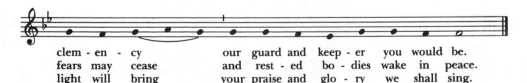

clem - en - cy our guard and keep - er you would be.
fears may cease and rest - ed bo - dies wake in peace.
light will bring your praise and glo - ry we shall sing.
we a - dore for ev - er and for ev - er - more.

Words: Latin, 6th cent.; ver. *Hymnal 1982*. St. 4, James Waring McCrady (b. 1938)
Music: *Te lucis ante terminum*, plainsong, Mode 8, *Antiphonale Sarisburiense*, Vol. II

LM

1 To you be - fore the close of day, Cre - a - tor
2 Save us from trou - bled, rest - less sleep, from all ill
3 A health - y life we ask of you, the fire of
4 Al - might - y Fa - ther, hear our cry through Je - sus

of all things, we pray that in your con - stant
dreams your child - ren keep; so calm our minds that
love in us re - new, and when the dawn new
Christ, our Lord Most High, whom with the Spi - rit

clem - en - cy our guard and keep - er you would be.
fears may cease and rest - ed bo - dies wake in peace.
light will bring your praise and glo - ry we shall sing.
we a - dore for ev - er and for ev - er - more.

Words: Latin, 6th cent.; ver. *Hymnal 1982*. St. 4, James Waring McCrady (b. 1938)
Music: *Te lucis ante terminum*, plainsong, Mode 8

                                                                          LM

1 The du - teous day now clos - eth, each flower and tree re -
2 Now all the heaven-ly splen - dor breaks forth in star - light
3 Though long our mor - tal blind - ness has missed God's lov - ing -

pos - eth, shade creeps o'er wild and wood: let
ten - der from myr - iad worlds un - known; and
kind - ness and plunged us in - to strife; yet

us, as night is fall - ing, on God our Ma - ker
we, this mar - vel see - ing, for - get our sel - fish
when life's day is o - ver, shall death's fair night dis -

call - - ing, give thanks to him, the Giv - er good.
be - - ing for joy of beau - ty not our own.
cov - - er the fields of ev - er - last - ing life.

Words: Paul Gerhardt (1607-1676); tr. Robert Seymour Bridges (1844-1930) and others
Music: *O Welt, ich muss dich lassen*, melody att. Heinrich Isaac (1450?-1517);
   harm. Johann Sebastian Bach (1685-1750)   776. 778

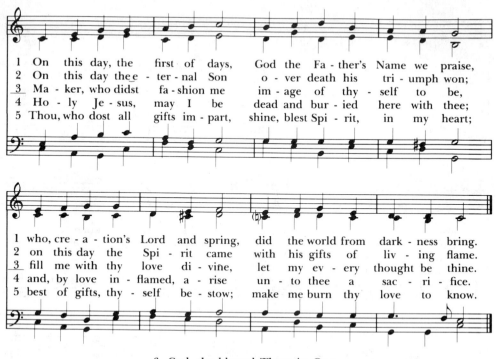

1 On this day, the first of days, God the Fa-ther's Name we praise,
2 On this day the e-ter-nal Son o-ver death his tri-umph won;
3 Ma-ker, who didst fa-shion me im-age of thy-self to be,
4 Ho-ly Je-sus, may I be dead and bur-ied here with thee;
5 Thou, who dost all gifts im-part, shine, blest Spi-rit, in my heart;

1 who, cre-a-tion's Lord and spring, did the world from dark-ness bring.
2 on this day the Spi-rit came with his gifts of liv-ing flame.
3 fill me with thy love di-vine, let my ev-ery thought be thine.
4 and, by love in-flamed, a-rise un-to thee a sac-ri-fice.
5 best of gifts, thy-self be-stow; make me burn thy love to know.

6 God, the blessed Three in One,
dwell within my heart alone;
thou dost give thyself to me:
help me give myself to thee.

Words: Latin; tr. Henry Williams Baker (1821-1877), alt.
Music: *Gott sei Dank*, melody from *Geistreiches Gesangbuch*, 1704;
    adapt. and harm. William Henry Havergal (1793-1870), alt.

                                                                                                          77. 77

1 O day of ra-diant glad - ness, O day of joy and
2 This day at the cre - a - - tion, the light first had its
3 This day, God's peo-ple meet - ing, his Ho-ly Scrip-ture
4 That light our hope sus - tain - ing, we walk the pil-grim

light, O balm of care and sad - - ness, most
birth; this day for our sal - va - - tion Christ
hear; his liv - ing pres - ence greet - - ing, through
way, at length our rest at - tain - - ing, our

beau - ti - ful, most bright; this day the high and
rose from depths of earth; this day our Lord vic -
Bread and Wine made near. We jour - ney on, be -
end - less Sab - bath day. We sing to thee our

low - ly, through a - ges joined in tune, sing,
to - rious the Spi - rit sent from heaven, and
liev - ing, re - newed with heaven - ly might, from
prais - es, O Fa - ther, Spi - rit, Son; the

"Ho - ly, ho - ly, ho - ly," to the great God Tri - une.
thus this day most glo - rious a tri - ple light was given.
grace more grace re - ceiv - ing on this blest day of light.
Church her voice up - rais - es to thee, blest Three in One.

Words: Sts. 1-2, Christopher Wordsworth (1807-1885), alt.; st. 3, Charles P. Price (b. 1920);
st. 4, *Hymnal 1982*
Music: *Es flog ein kleins Waldvögelein*, German folk song;
harm. George Ratcliffe Woodward (1848-1934)

76. 76. D

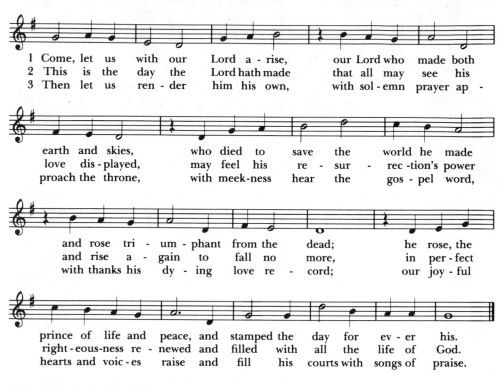

1 Come, let us with our Lord a - rise, our Lord who made both
2 This is the day the Lord hath made that all may see his
3 Then let us ren - der him his own, with sol - emn prayer ap -

earth and skies, who died to save the world he made
love dis - played, may feel his re - sur - rec - tion's power
proach the throne, with meek - ness hear the gos - pel word,

and rose tri - um - phant from the dead; he rose, the
and rise a - gain to fall no more, in per - fect
with thanks his dy - ing love re - cord; our joy - ful

prince of life and peace, and stamped the day for ev - er his.
right - eous - ness re - newed and filled with all the life of God.
hearts and voic - es raise and fill his courts with songs of praise.

Words: Charles Wesley (1707-1788)
Music: *Meadville*, Walter Pelz (b. 1926); adapt. W. Thomas Jones (b. 1956)

88. 88. 88

Unison or harmony

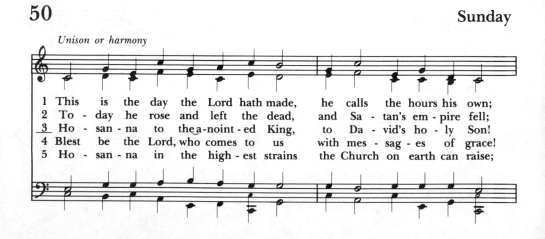

1 This is the day the Lord hath made, he calls the hours his own;
2 To - day he rose and left the dead, and Sa - tan's em - pire fell;
3 Ho - san - na to the a - noint - ed King, to Da - vid's ho - ly Son!
4 Blest be the Lord, who comes to us with mes - sag - es of grace!
5 Ho - san - na in the high - est strains the Church on earth can raise;

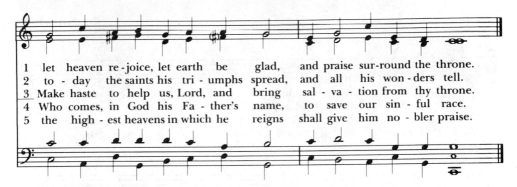

1 let heaven re-joice, let earth be glad, and praise sur-round the throne.
2 to - day the saints his tri - umphs spread, and all his won - ders tell.
3 Make haste to help us, Lord, and bring sal - va - tion from thy throne.
4 Who comes, in God his Fa - ther's name, to save our sin - ful race.
5 the high - est heavens in which he reigns shall give him no - bler praise.

Words: Isaac Watts (1674-1748), alt.
Music: *London New*, melody from *The Psalms of David in Prose and Meeter*, 1635, alt.;
   harm. John Playford (1623-1686)

CM

Sunday 51

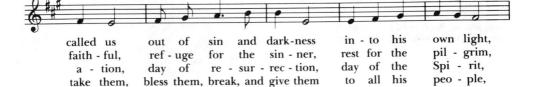

1 We the Lord's peo - ple, heart and voice u - nit - ing, praise him who
2 This is the Lord's house, home of all his peo - ple, school for the
3 This is the Lord's day, day of God's own mak - ing, day of cre -
4 In the Lord's ser - vice bread and wine are of - fered, that Christ may

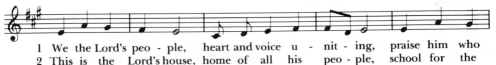

called us out of sin and dark-ness in - to his own light,
faith - ful, ref - uge for the sin - ner, rest for the pil - grim,
a - tion, day of re - sur - rec - tion, day of the Spi - rit,
take them, bless them, break, and give them to all his peo - ple,

that he might a - noint us a roy - al priest-hood.
ha - ven for the wea - ry; all find a wel - come.
sign of hea - ven's ban - quet, day for re - joic - ing.
his own life im - part - ing, food ev - er - last - ing.

Words: John E. Bowers (b. 1923), alt.
Music: *Decatur Place*, Richard Wayne Dirksen (b. 1921)

11. 11. 11. 5

52

1 This day at thy cre - at - ing word
2 This day the Lord for sin - ners slain
3 This day the Ho - ly Spi - rit came
4 All praise to God the Fa - ther be,

first o'er the earth the light was poured;
in might vic - to - rious rose a - gain;
with fier - y tongues of clo - ven flame;
all praise, e - ter - nal Son, to thee,

O Lord, this day up - on us shine
O Je - sus, may we lift - ed be
O Spi - rit, fill our hearts this day
whom, with the Spi - rit, we a - dore

and fill our souls with light di - vine.
from death of sin to life in thee!
with grace to hear and grace to pray.
for ev - er and for ev - er - more.

Words: William Walsham How (1823-1897), alt.
Music: *Rushford*, Henry G. Ley (1887-1962)

LM

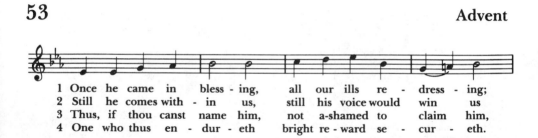

53

1 Once he came in bless - ing, all our ills re - dress - ing;
2 Still he comes with - in us, still his voice would win us
3 Thus, if thou canst name him, not a-shamed to claim him,
4 One who thus en - dur - eth bright re - ward se - cur - eth.

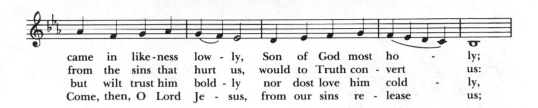

came   in   like-ness   low - ly,   Son   of   God   most   ho   -   ly;
from   the   sins that   hurt   us,   would to   Truth con - vert   us:
but   wilt   trust him   bold - ly   nor   dost love   him   cold   -   ly,
Come, then, O   Lord   Je - sus,   from   our   sins   re - lease   us;

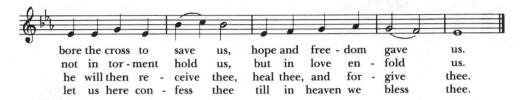

bore   the   cross   to   save   us,   hope   and   free - dom   gave   us.
not   in   tor - ment   hold   us,   but   in   love   en - fold   us.
he   will then   re - ceive   thee,   heal thee, and   for - give   thee.
let   us   here   con - fess   thee   till   in   heaven   we   bless   thee.

Words: Jan Roh (1485?-1547); tr. Catherine Winkworth (1827-1878), alt.
Music: *Gottes Sohn ist kommen*, melody Michael Weisse (d. 1534)

66. 66. 66

Advent

54

1 Sa   -   vior   of   the   na   -   tions,   come!   Vir   -   gin's
2 Won   -   drous   birth!   Oh,   won   -   drous   child   of   the
3 Thus   on   earth   the   Word   ap   -   pears,   grac   -   ing
4 Come,   O   Fa   -   ther's   sav   -   ing   Son,   who   o'er

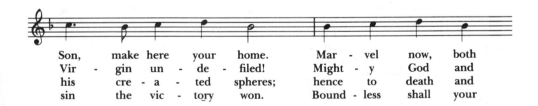

Son,   make here   your   home.   Mar   -   vel   now,   both
Vir   -   gin un   -   de   -   filed!   Might   -   y   God   and
his   cre   -   a   -   ted   spheres;   hence   to   death   and
sin   the   vic   -   tory   won.   Bound - less   shall   your

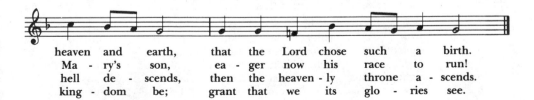

heaven   and   earth,   that   the   Lord   chose   such   a   birth.
Ma   -   ry's   son,   ea   -   ger   now   his   race   to   run!
hell   de   -   scends,   then   the   heaven - ly   throne   a - scends.
king - dom   be;   grant   that   we   its   glo   -   ries   see.

Words: Martin Luther (1483-1546) after Ambrose of Milan (340-397);
    tr. William M. Reynolds (1812-1876) and James Waring McCrady (b. 1938)
Music: *Nun komm, der Heiden Heiland*, melody from *Erfurt Enchiridia*, 1524

77. 77

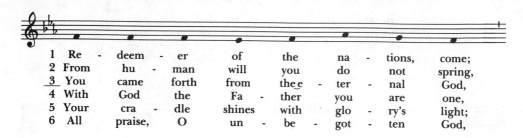

1 Re - deem - er of the na - tions, come;
2 From hu - man will you do not spring,
3 You came forth from the e - ter - nal God,
4 With God the Fa - ther you are one,
5 Your cra - dle shines with glo - ry's light;
6 All praise, O un - be - got - ten God,

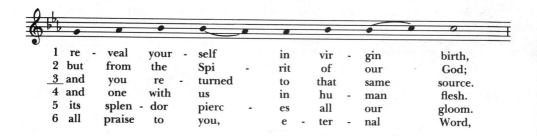

1 re - veal your - self in vir - gin birth,
2 but from the Spi - rit of our God;
3 and you re - turned to that same source.
4 and one with us in hu - man flesh.
5 its splen - dor pierc - es all our gloom.
6 all praise to you, e - ter - nal Word,

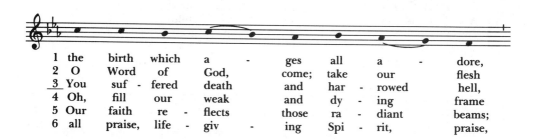

1 the birth which a - ges all a - dore,
2 O Word of God, come; take our flesh
3 You suf - fered death and har - rowed hell,
4 Oh, fill our weak and dy - ing frame
5 Our faith re - flects those ra - diant beams;
6 all praise, life - giv - ing Spi - rit, praise,

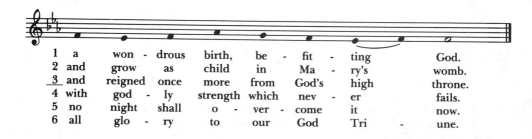

1 a won - drous birth, be - fit - ting God.
2 and grow as child in Ma - ry's womb.
3 and reigned once more from God's high throne.
4 with god - ly strength which nev - er fails.
5 no night shall o - ver - come it now.
6 all glo - ry to our God Tri - une.

Words: Att. Ambrose of Milan (340-397); tr. Charles P. Price (b. 1920)
Music: *Veni Redemptor gentium*, plainsong, Mode 1, Einsiedeln MS., 12th cent.

LM

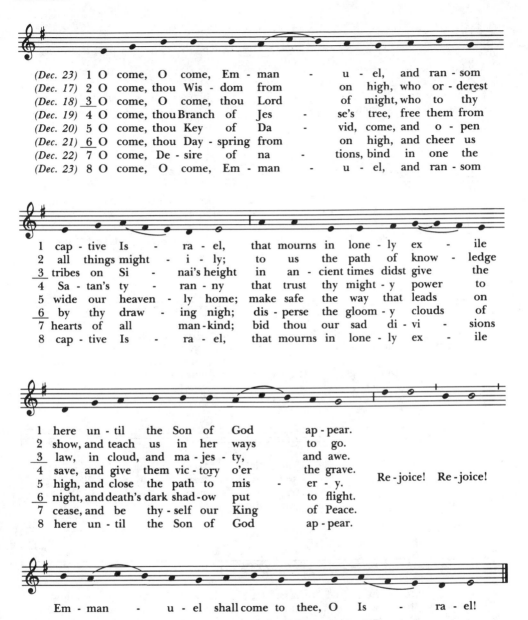

1 (Dec. 23) O come, O come, Emmanuel, and ransom captive Israel, that mourns in lonely exile here until the Son of God appear.
2 (Dec. 17) O come, thou Wisdom from on high, who orderest all things mightily; to us the path of knowledge show, and teach us in her ways to go.
3 (Dec. 18) O come, O come, thou Lord of might, who to thy tribes on Sinai's height in ancient times didst give the law, in cloud, and majesty, and awe.
4 (Dec. 19) O come, thou Branch of Jesse's tree, free them from Satan's tyranny that trust thy mighty power to save, and give them victory o'er the grave.
5 (Dec. 20) O come, thou Key of David, come, and open wide our heavenly home; make safe the way that leads on high, and close the path to misery.
6 (Dec. 21) O come, thou Day-spring from on high, and cheer us by thy drawing nigh; disperse the gloomy clouds of night, and death's dark shadow put to flight.
7 (Dec. 22) O come, Desire of nations, bind in one the hearts of all mankind; bid thou our sad divisions cease, and be thyself our King of Peace.
8 (Dec. 23) O come, O come, Emmanuel, and ransom captive Israel, that mourns in lonely exile here until the Son of God appear.

Re-joice! Re-joice! Emmanuel shall come to thee, O Israel!

The stanzas may be used as antiphons with "The Song of Mary" on the dates given.

Words: Latin, ca. 9th cent.; ver. *Hymnal 1940*, alt.
Music: *Veni, veni, Emmanuel*, plainsong, Mode 1, *Processionale*, 15th cent.;
adapt. Thomas Helmore (1811-1890)

LM with Refrain

1 Lo! he comes, with clouds de - scend - ing, once for
2 Ev - ery eye shall now be - hold him, robed in
3 Those dear to - kens of his pas - sion still his
4 Yea, a - men! let all a - dore thee, high on

our sal - va - tion slain; thou - sand thou - sand
dread - ful ma - jes - ty; those who set at
daz - zling bo - dy bears, cause of end - less
thine e - ter - nal throne; Sa - vior, take the

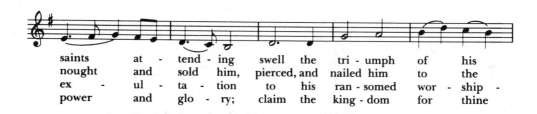

saints at - tend - ing swell the tri - umph of his
nought and sold him, pierced, and nailed him to the
ex - ul - ta - tion to his ran - somed wor - ship -
power and glo - ry; claim the king - dom for thine

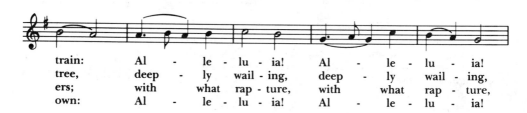

train: Al - le - lu - ia! Al - le - lu - ia!
tree, deep - ly wail - ing, deep - ly wail - ing,
ers; with what rap - ture, with what rap - ture,
own: Al - le - lu - ia! Al - le - lu - ia!

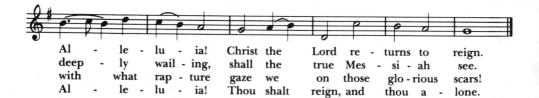

Al - le - lu - ia! Christ the Lord re - turns to reign.
deep - ly wail - ing, shall the true Mes - si - ah see.
with what rap - ture gaze we on those glo - rious scars!
Al - le - lu - ia! Thou shalt reign, and thou a - lone.

Words: Charles Wesley (1707-1788)
Music: *Helmsley*, melody Augustine Arne (1710-1778)

87. 87 12 7

1 Lo! he comes, with clouds de - scend - ing, once for our sal -
2 Ev - ery eye shall now be - hold him, robed in dread - ful
3 Those dear to - kens of his pas - sion still his daz - zling
4 Yea, a - men! let all a - dore thee, high on thine e -

va - tion slain; thou - sand thou - sand saints at - tend - ing
ma - jes - ty; those who set at nought and sold him,
bo - dy bears, cause of end - less ex - ul - ta - tion
ter - nal throne; Sa - vior, take the power and glo - ry;

swell the tri - umph of his train: Al - le - lu - ia!
pierced, and nailed him to the tree, deep - ly wail - ing,
to his ran - somed wor - ship - ers; with what rap - ture,
claim the king - dom for thine own: Al - le - lu - ia!

Al - le - lu - ia! Christ the Lord re - turns to reign.
deep - ly wail - ing, shall the true Mes - si - ah see.
with what rap - ture gaze we on those glo - rious scars!
Al - le - lu - ia! Thou shalt reign, and thou a - lone.

Words: Charles Wesley (1707-1788)
Music: *St. Thomas*, melody att. John Francis Wade (1711-1786);
   harm. att. Vincent Francis Novello (1781-1861)

87. 87. 87

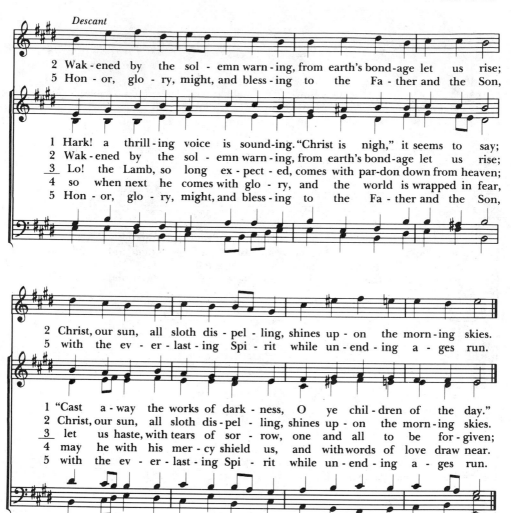

Descant

2 Wak-ened by the sol-emn warn-ing, from earth's bond-age let us rise;
5 Hon-or, glo-ry, might, and bless-ing to the Fa-ther and the Son,

1 Hark! a thrill-ing voice is sound-ing. "Christ is nigh," it seems to say;
2 Wak-ened by the sol-emn warn-ing, from earth's bond-age let us rise;
3 Lo! the Lamb, so long ex-pect-ed, comes with par-don down from heaven;
4 so when next he comes with glo-ry, and the world is wrapped in fear,
5 Hon-or, glo-ry, might, and bless-ing to the Fa-ther and the Son,

2 Christ, our sun, all sloth dis-pel-ling, shines up-on the morn-ing skies.
5 with the ev-er-last-ing Spi-rit while un-end-ing a-ges run.

1 "Cast a-way the works of dark-ness, O ye chil-dren of the day."
2 Christ, our sun, all sloth dis-pel-ling, shines up-on the morn-ing skies.
3 let us haste, with tears of sor-row, one and all to be for-given;
4 may he with his mer-cy shield us, and with words of love draw near.
5 with the ev-er-last-ing Spi-rit while un-end-ing a-ges run.

Words: Latin, ca. 6th cent.; tr. *Hymns Ancient and Modern,* 1861, alt.
Music: *Merton,* William Henry Monk (1823-1889); desc. Alan Gray (1855-1935)

87. 87

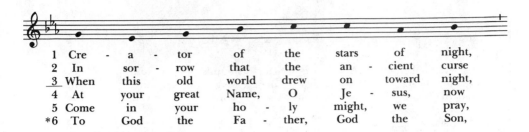

1 Cre - a - tor of the stars of night,
2 In sor - row that the an - cient curse
3 When this old world drew on toward night,
4 At your great Name, O Je - sus, now
5 Come in your ho - ly might, we pray,
*6 To God the Fa - ther, God the Son,

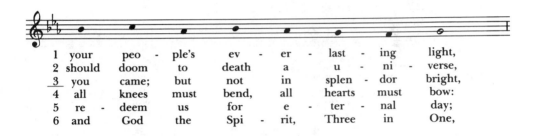

1 your peo - ple's ev - er - last - ing light,
2 should doom to death a u - ni - verse,
3 you came; but not in splen - dor bright,
4 all knees must bend, all hearts must bow:
5 re - deem us for e - ter - nal day;
6 and God the Spi - rit, Three in One,

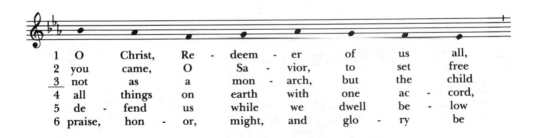

1 O Christ, Re - deem - er of us all,
2 you came, O Sa - vior, to set free
3 not as a mon - arch, but the child
4 all things on earth with one ac - cord,
5 de - fend us while we dwell be - low
6 praise, hon - or, might, and glo - ry be

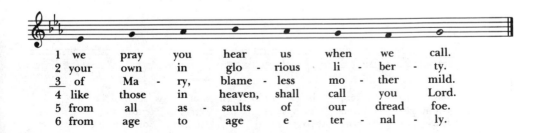

1 we pray you hear us when we call.
2 your own in glo - rious li - ber - ty.
3 of Ma - ry, blame - less mo - ther mild.
4 like those in heaven, shall call you Lord.
5 from all as - saults of our dread foe.
6 from age to age e - ter - nal - ly.

Words: Latin, 9th cent.; ver. *Hymnal 1940*, alt.
Music: *Conditor alme siderum*, plainsong, Mode 4

LM

1 "Sleep-ers, wake!" A voice a-stounds us, the
2 Zi - on hears the watch - men sing - ing; her
3 Lamb of God, the heavens a - dore you; let

shout of ram - part - guards sur - rounds us: "A -
heart with joy - ful hope is spring - ing, she
saints and an - gels sing be - fore you, as

wake, Je - ru - sa - lem, a - rise!" Mid - night's peace their
wakes and hur - ries through the night. Forth he comes, her
harps and cym - bals swell the sound. Twelve great pearls, the

cry has bro - ken, their ur - gent sum - mons clear - ly spo -
Bride - groom glo - rious in strength of grace, in truth vic - to -
ci - ty's por - tals: through them we stream to join the im - mor -

ken: "The   time   has   come,   O   maid - ens wise!
rious: her   star   is   risen,   her   light grows bright.
tals   as   we   with   joy   your   throne sur - round.

Rise   up,   and give us   light;   the   Bride - groom is   in
Now come,   most wor - thy Lord,   God's   Son,   In - car - nate
No   eye   has known the sight,   no   ear   heard such de -

sight. Al - le - lu - ia!   Your lamps pre - pare and
Word, Al - le - lu - ia!   We   fol - low all   and
light: Al - le - lu - ia!   There - fore we   sing   to

has - ten there, that   you   the   wed - ding feast may share."
heed your call   to   come   in - to   the ban - quet hall.
greet our King; for   ev - er   let   our   prais - es ring.

Words: Philipp Nicolai (1556-1608); tr. Carl P. Daw, Jr. (b. 1944)
Music: *Wachet auf,* melody Hans Sachs (1494-1576); adapt. Philipp Nicolai (1556-1608);
    arr. and harm. Johann Sebastian Bach (1685-1750)

Irr.

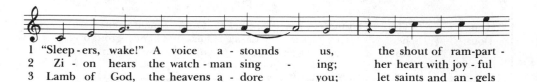

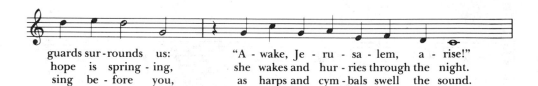

1 "Sleep - ers, wake!" A voice a - stounds us, the shout of ram-part -
2 Zi - on hears the watch - man sing - ing; her heart with joy - ful
3 Lamb of God, the heavens a - dore you; let saints and an - gels

guards sur - rounds us: "A - wake, Je - ru - sa - lem, a - rise!"
hope is spring - ing, she wakes and hur - ries through the night.
sing be - fore you, as harps and cym - bals swell the sound.

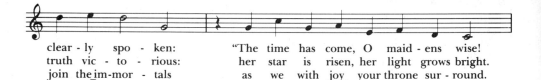

Mid - night's peace their cry has bro - ken, their ur - gent sum - mons
Forth he comes, her Bride-groom glo - rious in strength of grace, in
Twelve great pearls, the ci - ty's por - tals: through them we stream to

clear - ly spo - ken: "The time has come, O maid - ens wise!"
truth vic - to - rious: her star is risen, her light grows bright.
join the im-mor - tals as we with joy your throne sur - round.

Rise up, and give us light; the Bride - groom is in sight.
Now come, most wor - thy Lord, God's Son, In - car - nate Word,
No eye has known the sight, no ear heard such de - light:

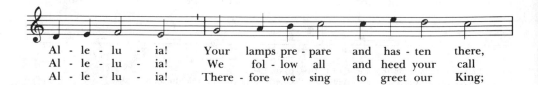

Al - le - lu - ia! Your lamps pre - pare and has - ten there,
Al - le - lu - ia! We fol - low all and heed your call
Al - le - lu - ia! There - fore we sing to greet our King;

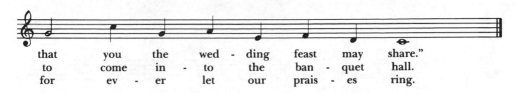

that	you	the	wed -	ding	feast	may	share."
to	come	in -	to	the	ban -	quet	hall.
for	ev -	er	let	our	prais -	es	ring.

Words: Philipp Nicolai (1556-1608); tr. Carl P. Daw, Jr. (b. 1944)
Music: *Wachet auf*, melody Hans Sachs (1494-1576); adapt. Philipp Nicolai (1556-1608)   Irr.

Advent   63

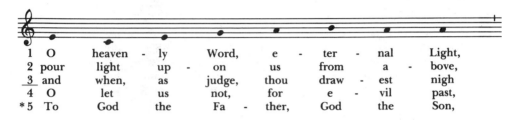

1 O	heaven -	ly	Word,	e -	ter -	nal	Light,
2 pour	light	up -	on	us	from	a -	bove,
3 and	when,	as	judge,	thou	draw -	est	nigh
4 O	let	us	not,	for	e -	vil	past,
*5 To	God	the	Fa -	ther,	God	the	Son,

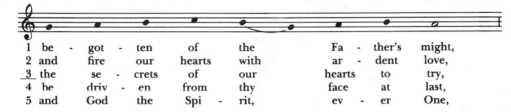

1 be -	got -	ten	of	the	Fa -	ther's	might,
2 and	fire	our	hearts	with	ar -	dent	love,
3 the	se -	crets	of	our	hearts	to	try,
4 be	driv -	en	from	thy	face	at	last,
5 and	God	the	Spi -	rit,	ev -	er	One,

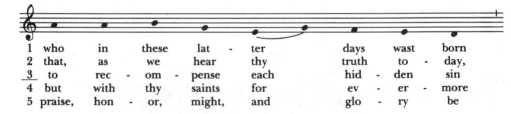

1 who	in	these	lat -	ter	days	wast	born
2 that,	as	we	hear	thy	truth	to -	day,
3 to	rec -	om -	pense	each	hid -	den	sin
4 but	with	thy	saints	for	ev -	er -	more
5 praise,	hon -	or,	might,	and	glo -	ry	be

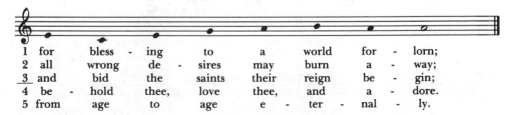

1 for	bless -	ing	to	a	world	for -	lorn;
2 all	wrong	de -	sires	may	burn	a -	way;
3 and	bid	the	saints	their	reign	be -	gin;
4 be -	hold	thee,	love	thee,	and	a -	dore.
5 from	age	to	age	e -	ter -	nal -	ly.

Words: Latin, ca. 7th cent.; tr. *Hymnal 1982*
Music: *Verbum supernum prodiens*, plainsong, Mode 2, Nevers MS., 13th cent.   LM

1 O heaven - ly Word, e - ter - nal Light, be - got - ten
2 pour light up - on us from a - bove, and fire our
3 and when, as judge, thou draw - est nigh the se - crets
4 O let us not, for e - vil past, be driv - en
*5 To God the Fa - ther, God the Son, and God the

1 of the Fa - ther's might, who in these lat - ter days wast
2 hearts with ar - dent love, that, as we hear thy truth to -
3 of our hearts to try, to rec - om - pense each hid - den
4 from thy face at last, but with thy saints for ev - er -
5 Spi - rit, ev - er One, praise, hon - or, might, and glo - ry

1 born for bless - ing to a world for - lorn;
2 day, all wrong de - sires may burn a - way;
3 sin and bid the saints their reign be - gin;
4 more be - hold thee, love thee, and a - dore.
5 be from age to age e - ter - nal - ly.

Words: Latin, ca. 7th cent.; tr. *Hymnal 1982*
Music: *O Heiland, reiss*, melody from *Rheinfelsisches Deutsches Catholisches Gesangbuch*, 1666   LM

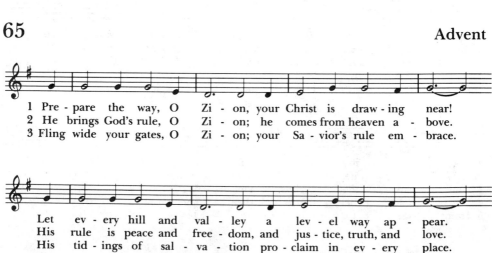

1 Pre - pare the way, O Zi - on, your Christ is draw - ing near!
2 He brings God's rule, O Zi - on; he comes from heaven a - bove.
3 Fling wide your gates, O Zi - on; your Sa - vior's rule em - brace.

Let ev - ery hill and val - ley a lev - el way ap - pear.
His rule is peace and free - dom, and jus - tice, truth, and love.
His tid - ings of sal - va - tion pro - claim in ev - ery place.

Greet One who comes in glo - ry, fore - told in sa - cred sto - ry.
Lift high your praise re - sound-ing, for grace and joy a - bound-ing.
All lands will bow be - fore him, their voic - es will a - dore him.

Refrain

Oh, blest is Christ that came in God's most ho - ly name.

Words: Frans Mikael Franzen (1772-1847); tr. composite; adapt. Charles P. Price (b. 1920)
Music: *Bereden väg för Herran,* melody from *Then Swenska Psalmboken,* 1697
76. 76. 77 with Refrain

Advent   66

1 Come, thou long - ex - pect-ed Je - sus, born to set thy peo - ple free;
2 Is - rael's strength and con - so - la - tion, hope of all the earth thou art:
3 Born thy peo - ple to de - liv - er, born a child, and yet a king,
4 By thine own e - ter - nal Spi - rit rule in all our hearts a - lone;

from our fears and sins re - lease us, let us find our rest in thee.
dear de - sire of ev - ery na - tion, joy of ev - ery long - ing heart.
born to reign in us for ev - er, now thy gra-cious king - dom bring.
by thine all - suf - fi - cient mer - it raise us to thy glo - rious throne.

Words: Charles Wesley (1707-1788)
Music: *Stuttgart,* melody from *Psalmodia Sacra, oder Andächtige und Schöne Gesange,* 1715;
adapt. and harm. William Henry Havergal (1793-1870), alt.
87. 87

1 Com - fort, com - fort ye my peo - ple, speak ye peace, thus
2 Hark, the voice of one that cri - eth in the des - ert
3 Make ye straight what long was crook - ed, make the rough - er

saith our God; com - fort those who sit in dark - ness
far and near, call - ing us to new re - pent - ance
pla - ces plain; let your hearts be true and hum - ble,

mourn - ing 'neath their sor - rows' load. Speak ye to Je -
since the king - dom now is here. Oh, that warn - ing
as be - fits his ho - ly reign. For the glo - ry

ru - sa - lem of the peace that waits for them;
cry o - bey! Now pre - pare for God a way;
of the Lord now o'er earth is shed a - broad;

tell her that her sins I cov - er,
let the val - leys rise to meet him
and all flesh shall see the to - ken

and her war - fare now is o - ver.
and the hills bow down to greet him.
that the word is nev - er bro - ken.

Words: Johann G. Olearius (1611-1684); tr. Catherine Winkworth (1827-1878), alt.
Music: *Psalm 42*, melody Claude Goudimel (1514-1572)

87. 87. 77. 88

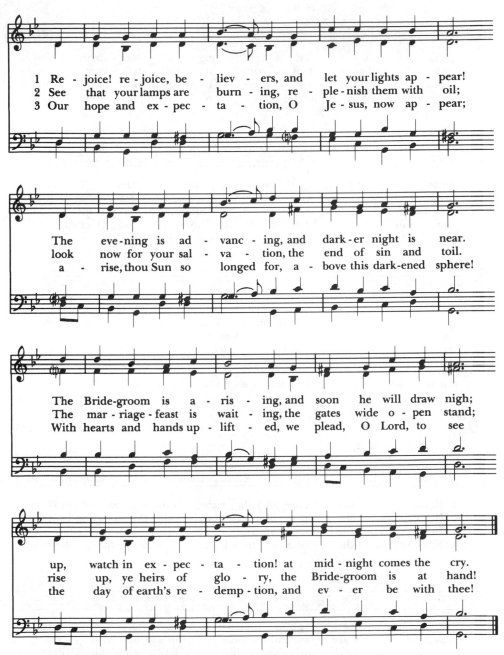

1 Re - joice! re - joice, be - liev - ers, and let your lights ap - pear!
2 See that your lamps are burn - ing, re - ple - nish them with oil;
3 Our hope and ex - pec - ta - tion, O Je - sus, now ap - pear;

The eve-ning is ad - vanc - ing, and dark - er night is near.
look now for your sal - va - tion, the end of sin and toil.
a - rise, thou Sun so longed for, a - bove this dark-ened sphere!

The Bride-groom is a - ris - ing, and soon he will draw nigh;
The mar - riage-feast is wait - ing, the gates wide o - pen stand;
With hearts and hands up - lift - ed, we plead, O Lord, to see

up, watch in ex - pec - ta - tion! at mid - night comes the cry.
rise up, ye heirs of glo - ry, the Bride-groom is at hand!
the day of earth's re - demp - tion, and ev - er be with thee!

Words: Laurentius Laurenti (1660-1722); tr. Sarah B. Findlater (1823-1907), alt.
Music: *Llangloffan*, melody from *Hymnau a Thonau er Gwasanaeth yr Eglwys yng Nghymru*, 1865

76. 76 D

69

Advent

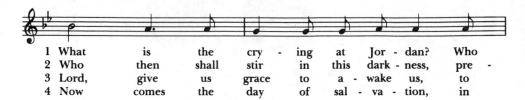

```
1 What      is    the   cry - ing   at   Jor - dan?   Who
2 Who       then  shall stir  in    this dark - ness, pre -
3 Lord,     give  us    grace to   a - wake us,       to
4 Now       comes the   day   of   sal - va - tion,   in
```

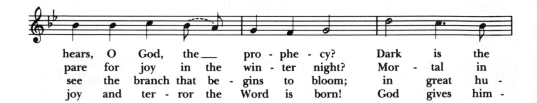

```
hears, O   God,  the __  pro - phe - cy?   Dark is  the
pare for   joy   in the  win - ter  night?  Mor - tal in
see   the  branch that be - gins to  bloom;  in  great hu -
joy   and  ter - ror the  Word is   born!   God gives him -
```

```
sea - son,  dark   our   hearts and shut __  to   mys - ter - y.
dark - ness  we    lie   down, blind - heart - ed  see - ing no  light.
mil - i - ty  is   hid   all heaven in a  lit - tle room.
self  in - to our   lives; O   let __ sal - va - tion dawn!
```

Words: Carol Christopher Drake (b. 1933), alt.
Music: *St. Mark's, Berkeley*, Irish melody from *Danta De: Hymns to God, Ancient and Modern*

88. 86

70

Advent

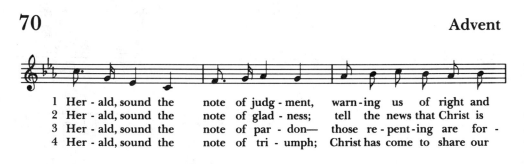

```
1 Her - ald, sound the   note of judg - ment,  warn - ing us  of right and
2 Her - ald, sound the   note of glad - ness;   tell  the news that Christ is
3 Her - ald, sound the   note of par - don—   those re - pent - ing are for -
4 Her - ald, sound the   note of tri - umph;   Christ has come to share our
```

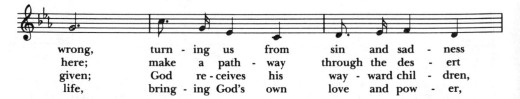

```
wrong,  turn - ing us    from   sin  and  sad - ness
here;   make  a  path - way   through the des - ert
given;  God  re - ceives his   way - ward chil - dren,
life,   bring - ing God's own   love  and  pow - er,
```

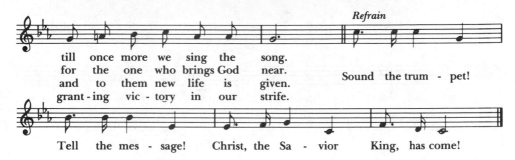

till once more we sing the song.
for the one who brings God near.
and to them new life is given.
grant-ing vic-to-ry in our strife.

Sound the trum - pet!

Tell the mes - sage! Christ, the Sa - vior King, has come!

Words: Moir A. J. Waters (1906-1980), alt.
Music: *Herald, Sound*, Robert Powell (b. 1932)

87. 87 with Refrain

Advent

71

1 Hark! the glad sound! the Sa - vior comes, the Sa - vior
2 He comes, the pris - oners to re - lease in Sa - tan's
3 He comes, the bro - ken heart to bind, the bleed-ing
4 Our glad ho - san - nas, Prince of Peace, thy wel - come

prom - ised long: let ev - ery heart pre -
bond - age held; the gates of brass be -
soul to cure; and with the trea - sures
shall pro - claim; and heaven's e - ter - nal

pare a throne, and ev - ery voice a song.
fore him burst, the i - ron fet - ters yield.
of his grace to en - rich the hum - ble poor.
arch - es ring with thy be - lov - ed Name.

Words: Philip Doddridge (1702-1751)
Music: *Bristol*, from *The Whole Booke of Psalmes*, 1621

CM

Descant

4 Our glad ho-san-nas, Prince of Peace, thy wel-come

1 Hark! the glad sound! the Sa - vior comes, the Sa - vior
2 He comes, the pris - oners to re - lease in Sa - tan's
3 He comes, the bro - ken heart to bind, the bleed - ing
4 Our glad ho-san-nas, Prince of Peace, thy wel-come

shall pro - claim; and heaven's e - ter - nal

prom - ised long; let ev - ery heart pre -
bond - age held; the gates of brass be -
soul to cure; and with the trea - sures
shall pro - claim; and heaven's e - ter - nal

arch - es ring with thy be - lov ed Name.

pare a throne, and ev - ery voice a song.
fore him burst, the i - ron fet - ters yield.
of his grace to en - rich the hum - ble poor.
arch - es ring with thy be - lov - ed Name.

Words: Philip Doddridge (1702-1751)
Music: *Richmond*, melody Thomas Haweis (1734-1820); adapt. Samuel Webbe, Jr. (1770-1843);
harm. *The English Hymnal*, 1906; desc. Craig Sellar Lang (1891-1971)

CM

1 The King shall come when morn-ing dawns and
2 Not, as of old, a lit-tle child, to
3 The King shall come when morn-ing dawns and
4 and let the end-less bliss be-gin, by
5 The King shall come when morn-ing dawns and

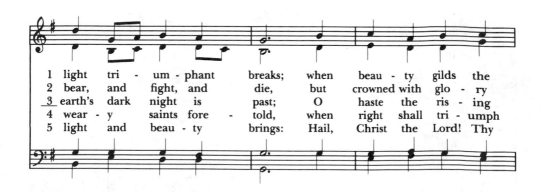

1 light tri-um-phant breaks; when beau-ty gilds the
2 bear, and fight, and die, but crowned with glo-ry
3 earth's dark night is past; O haste the ris-ing
4 wear-y saints fore-told, when right shall tri-umph
5 light and beau-ty brings: Hail, Christ the Lord! Thy

1 east-ern hills and life to joy a-wakes.
2 like the sun that lights the morn-ing sky.
3 of that morn, the day that e'er shall last;
4 o-ver wrong, and truth shall be ex-tolled.
5 peo-ple pray, come quick-ly, King of kings.

Words: Greek; tr. John Brownlie (1859-1925), alt.
Music: *St. Stephen*, William Jones (1726-1800), alt.

CM

Descant

3 Blest be the King whose com-ing is in the name of

1 Blest be the King whose com-ing is in the name of
2 Blest be the King whose com-ing is in the name of
3 Blest be the King whose com-ing is in the name of
4 Blest be the King whose com-ing is in the name of

God! He on-ly to the hum-ble re-veals the face of

God! For him let doors be o-pened, no hearts a-gainst him
God! By those who tru-ly lis-ten his voice is tru-ly
God! He on-ly to the hum-ble re-veals the face of
God! He of-fers to the bur-dened the rest and grace they

God. All power is his, all glo-ry! All

barred! Not robed in roy-al splen-dor, in
heard; pi-ty the proud and haugh-ty, who
God. All power is his, all glo-ry! All
need. Gen-tle is he and hum-ble! And

1 There's a voice in the wil - der - ness cry - ing, a ___
2 O ___ Zi - on, that bring - est good tid - ings, get thee
3 but the word of our God ___ en - dur - eth, the ___

call from the ways un - trod: Pre - pare in the des - ert a
up to the heights and sing! Pro - claim to a des - o - late
arm of the Lord is strong; he stands in the midst ___ of

high - way, a high - way for our God! The ___
peo - ple the com - ing of their King. Like the
na - tions, and he will right the wrong. He shall

val - leys shall be ex - alt - ed, the
flowers of the field they ___ per - ish, like
feed his ___ flock like a shep - herd, the

lof - ty hills brought low; make straight all the crook - ed
grass our works de - cay, the power and ___ pomp of
lambs he'll gent - ly hold; to pas - tures of peace he'll

pla - ces where the Lord our ___ God ___ may go!
na - tions shall ___ pass like a dream ___ a - way;
lead them, and ___ bring them ___ safe to his fold.

Words: James Lewis Milligan (1876-1961), alt.
Music: *Ascension*, Henry Hugh Bancroft (b. 1904)

Irr.

things are in his hand, all a-ges and all

power and pomp, comes he; but clad as are the
have not learned to heed the Christ who is the
things are in his hand, all a-ges and all
light his yoke shall be, for he would have us

peo-ples, till time it-self shall end!

poor-est, such his hu-mil-i-ty!
Prom-ise, who has a-tone-ment made.
peo-ples, till time it-self shall end!
bear it so he can make us free!

Words: Federico J. Pagura (b. 1923); tr. F. Pratt Green (b. 1903), alt.
Music: *Valet will ich dir geben*, melody Melchior Teschner (1584-1635) alt.;
    harm. and desc. Ronald Arnatt (b. 1930)

76. 76 D

1 On Jor - dan's bank the Bap - tist's cry an -
2 Then cleansed be ev - ery breast from sin; make
3 For thou art our sal - va - tion, Lord, our
4 To heal the sick stretch out thine hand, and
5 All praise, e - ter - nal Son, to thee, whose

1 noun - ces that the Lord is nigh; a - wake and heark - en,
2 straight the way for God with - in, and let each heart pre -
3 ref - uge, and our great re - ward; with - out thy grace we
4 bid the fall - en sin - ner stand; shine forth, and let thy
5 ad - vent doth thy peo - ple free; whom with the Fa - ther

1 for he brings glad tid - ings of the King of kings.
2 pare a home where such a might - y guest may come.
3 waste a - way like flowers that with - er and de - cay.
4 light re - store earth's own true love - li - ness once more.
5 we a - dore and Ho - ly Spi - rit ev - er - more.

Words: Charles Coffin (1676-1749); tr. Charles Winfred Douglas (1867-1944),
    after John Chandler (1806-1876); alt.
Music: *Winchester New,* melody from *Musicalishes Hand-Buch,* 1690;
    harm. William Henry Monk (1823-1889), alt.

LM

1 From east to west, from shore to shore, let
2 Be - hold, the world's cre - a - tor wears the
3 For this how won - drous - ly he wrought! A
4 And while the an - gels in the sky sang
5 All glo - ry for this bless - ed morn to

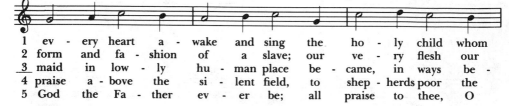

1 ev - ery heart a - wake and sing the ho - ly child whom
2 form and fa - shion of a slave; our ve - ry flesh our
3 maid in low - ly hu - man place be - came, in ways be -
4 praise a - bove the si - lent field, to shep - herds poor the
5 God the Fa - ther ev - er be; all praise to thee, O

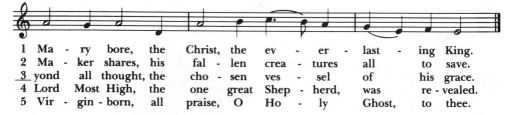

1 Ma - ry bore, the Christ, the ev - er - last - ing King.
2 Ma - ker shares, his fal - len crea - tures all to save.
3 yond all thought, the cho - sen ves - sel of his grace.
4 Lord Most High, the one great Shep - herd, was re - vealed.
5 Vir - gin - born, all praise, O Ho - ly Ghost, to thee.

Words: Caelius Sedulius (5th cent.); tr. John Ellerton (1826-1893), alt.
Music: *Vom Himmel kam der Engel Schar*, melody source unknown

LM

Unison or harmony

1 O lit - tle town of Beth - le - hem, how still we see thee lie!
2 For Christ is born of Ma - ry; and gath - ered all a - bove,
3 How si - lent - ly, how si - lent - ly, the won - drous gift is given!
*4 Where child-ren pure and hap - py pray to the bless - ed Child,
5 O ho - ly Child of Beth - le - hem, de - scend to us, we pray;

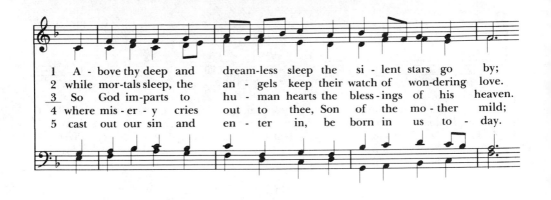

1 A - bove thy deep and dream-less sleep the si - lent stars go by;
2 while mor-tals sleep, the an - gels keep their watch of won-dering love.
3 So God im-parts to hu - man hearts the bless - ings of his heaven.
4 where mis - er - y cries out to thee, Son of the mo - ther mild;
5 cast out our sin and en - ter in, be born in us to - day.

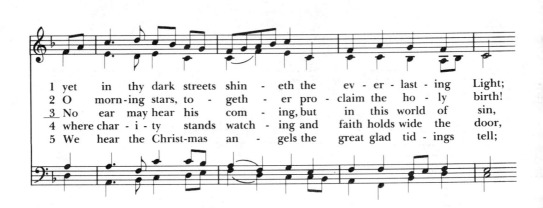

1 yet in thy dark streets shin - eth the ev - er - last - ing Light;
2 O morn-ing stars, to - geth - er pro - claim the ho - ly birth!
3 No ear may hear his com - ing, but in this world of sin,
4 where char - i - ty stands watch - ing and faith holds wide the door,
5 We hear the Christ-mas an - gels the great glad tid - ings tell;

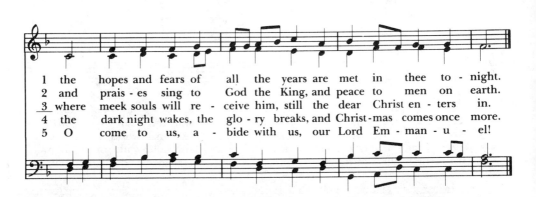

1 the hopes and fears of all the years are met in thee to - night.
2 and prais - es sing to God the King, and peace to men on earth.
3 where meek souls will re - ceive him, still the dear Christ en - ters in.
4 the dark night wakes, the glo - ry breaks, and Christ-mas comes once more.
5 O come to us, a - bide with us, our Lord Em - man - u - el!

Words: Phillips Brooks (1835-1893)
Music: *Forest Green*, English melody; adapt. and harm. Ralph Vaughan Williams (1872-1958)   CMD

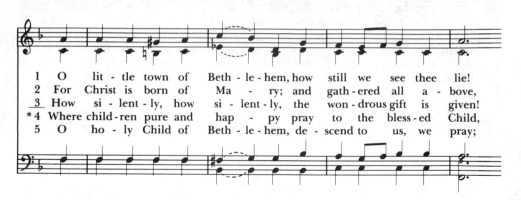

1 O lit - tle town of Beth - le - hem, how still we see thee lie!
2 For Christ is born of Ma - ry; and gath - ered all a - bove,
3 How si - lent - ly, how si - lent - ly, the won - drous gift is given!
*4 Where child - ren pure and hap - py pray to the bless - ed Child,
5 O ho - ly Child of Beth - le - hem, de - scend to us, we pray;

1 A - bove thy deep and dream - less sleep the si - lent stars go by;
2 while mor - tals sleep, the an - gels keep their watch of won - dering love.
3 So God im - parts to hu - man hearts the bless - ings of his heaven.
4 where mis - er - y cries out to thee, Son of the mo - ther mild;
5 cast out our sin and en - ter in, be born in us to - day.

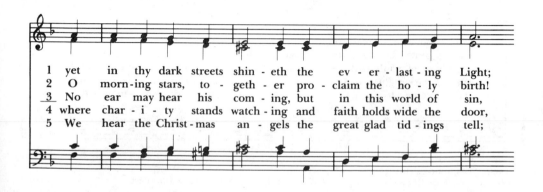

1 yet in thy dark streets shin - eth the ev - er - last - ing Light;
2 O morn - ing stars, to - geth - er pro - claim the ho - ly birth!
3 No ear may hear his com - ing, but in this world of sin,
4 where char - i - ty stands watch - ing and faith holds wide the door,
5 We hear the Christ - mas an - gels the great glad tid - ings tell;

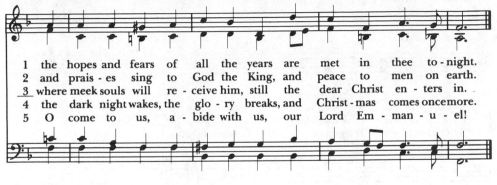

1 the hopes and fears of all the years are met in thee to-night.
2 and prais-es sing to God the King, and peace to men on earth.
3 where meek souls will re-ceive him, still the dear Christ en-ters in.
4 the dark night wakes, the glo-ry breaks, and Christ-mas comes once more.
5 O come to us, a-bide with us, our Lord Em-man-u-el!

Words: Phillips Brooks (1835-1893)
Music: *St. Louis*, Lewis H. Redner (1831-1908)

CMD

Christmas

80

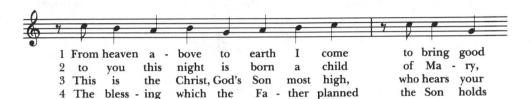

1 From heaven a - bove to earth I come to bring good
2 to you this night is born a child of Ma - ry,
3 This is the Christ, God's Son most high, who hears your
4 The bless - ing which the Fa - ther planned the Son holds

news to ev - ery - one! Glad tid - ings of great
cho - sen vir - gin mild; this new - born child of
sad and bit - ter cry; he will him - self your
in his in - fant hand, that in his king - dom,

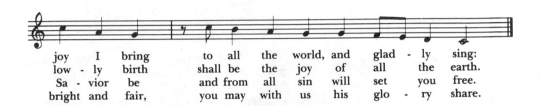

joy I bring to all the world, and glad - ly sing:
low - ly birth shall be the joy of all the earth.
Sa - vior be and from all sin will set you free.
bright and fair, you may with us his glo - ry share.

Words: Martin Luther (1483-1546); tr. *Lutheran Book of Worship*, 1978
Music: *Vom Himmel hoch*, melody from *Geistliche lieder auffs new gebessert und gemehrt*, 1539

LM

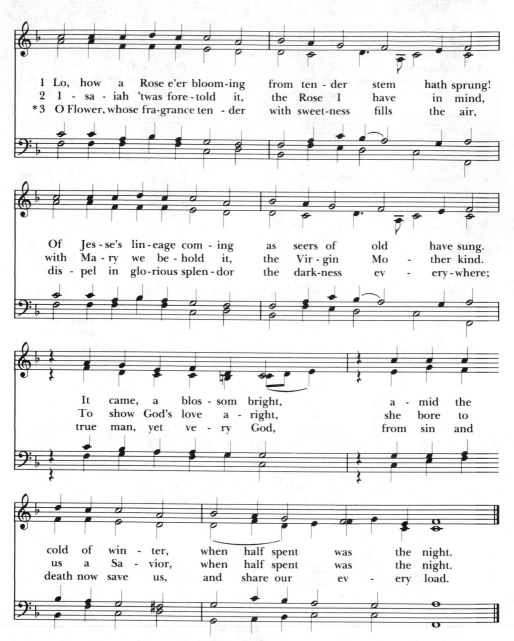

1 Lo, how a Rose e'er bloom-ing from ten - der stem hath sprung!
2 I - sa - iah 'twas fore-told it, the Rose I have in mind,
*3 O Flower, whose fra-grance ten - der with sweet-ness fills the air,

Of Jes - se's lin-eage com - ing as seers of old have sung.
with Ma - ry we be-hold it, the Vir - gin Mo - ther kind.
dis - pel in glo-rious splen-dor the dark-ness ev - ery-where;

It came, a blos-som bright, a - mid the
To show God's love a - right, she bore to
true man, yet ve - ry God, from sin and

cold of win - ter, when half spent was the night.
us a Sa - vior, when half spent was the night.
death now save us, and share our ev - ery load.

Words: St. 1-2, German, 15th cent.; tr. Theodore Baker (1851-1934). st. 3, Friedrich Layritz (1808-1859);
    tr. Harriet Reynolds Krauth Spaeth (1845-1925); ver. *Hymnal 1940*
Music: *Es ist ein Ros*, melody from *Alte Catholische Geistliche Kirchengesäng*, 1599;
    harm. Michael Praetorius (1571-1621)

76. 76. 676

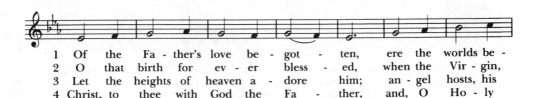

1 Of the Fa - ther's love be - got - ten, ere the worlds be -
2 O that birth for ev - er bless - ed, when the Vir - gin,
3 Let the heights of heaven a - dore him; an - gel hosts, his
4 Christ, to thee with God the Fa - ther, and, O Ho - ly

gan to be, he is Al - pha and O - me - ga,
full of grace, by the Ho - ly Ghost con - ceiv - ing,
prais - es sing; powers, do - min - ions, bow be - fore him,
Ghost, to thee, hymn and chant and high thanks - giv - ing,

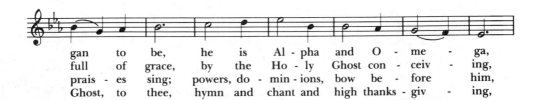

he the source, the end - ing he, of the things that
bore the Sa - vior of our race; and the Babe, the
and ex - tol our God and King; let no tongue on
and un - wea - ried prais - es be; hon - or, glo - ry

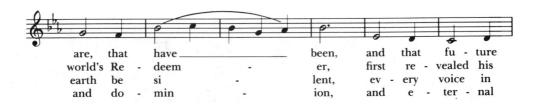

are, that have _____ been, and that fu - ture
world's Re - deem - er, first re - vealed his
earth be si - lent, ev - ery voice in
and do - min - ion, and e - ter - nal

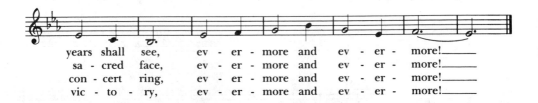

years shall see, ev - er - more and ev - er - more! _____
sa - cred face, ev - er - more and ev - er - more! _____
con - cert ring, ev - er - more and ev - er - more! _____
vic - to - ry, ev - er - more and ev - er - more! _____

This hymn may be performed in equal note values: ♩ ♩ ♩

Words: Marcus Aurelius Clemens Prudentius (348-410?); tr. John Mason Neale (1818-1866)
and Henry Williams Baker (1821-1877), alt.
Music: *Divinum mysterium*, Sanctus trope, 11th cent.; adapt. *Piae Cantiones*, 1582

87. 87. 87 with Refrain

1 O come, all ye faith - ful, joy - ful and tri - um - phant, O
2 God from God, Light from Light e - ter - nal,
3 Sing, choirs of an - gels, sing in ex - ul - ta - tion,
*4 See how the shep - herds, sum-moned to his cra - dle,
*5 Child, for us sin - ners poor and in the man - ger,

1 come ye, O come ye to Beth - le - hem;
2 lo! he ab - hors not the Vir - gin's womb;
3 sing, all ye ci - ti - zens of heaven a - bove;
4 leav - ing their flocks, draw nigh to gaze;
5 we would em - brace thee, with love and awe;

1 come, and be - hold him, born the King of an - gels;
2 on - ly - be - got - ten Son of the Fa - ther;
3 glo - ry to God, glo - ry in the high - est;
4 we too will thith - er bend our joy - ful foot - steps;
5 who would not love thee, lov - ing us so dear - ly?

Refrain

O come, let us a - dore him, O come, let us a -

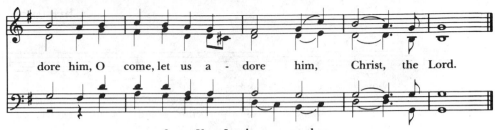

dore him, O come, let us a - dore him, Christ, the Lord.

6   Yea, Lord, we greet thee,
born this happy morning;
Jesus, to thee be glory given;
Word of the Father,
now in flesh appearing;

Refrain

Words: John Francis Wade (1711-1786); tr. Frederick Oakeley (1802-1880) and others
Music: *Adeste fideles,* present form of melody att. John Francis Wade (1711-1786);
    harm. *The English Hymnal,* 1906

Irr.

Christmas   84

1 Love came down at Christ - mas, love all love - ly, love di - vine;
2 Wor-ship we the God - head, love in-car - nate, love di - vine;
3 Love shall be our to - ken; love be yours and love be mine,

love was born at Christ - mas: star and an - gels gave the sign.
wor - ship we our Je - sus, but where-with for sa - cred sign?
love to God and neigh - bor, love for plea and gift and sign.

Words: Christina Rossetti (1830-1894), alt.
Music: *Gartan,* melody from *Petrie Collection of Irish Melodies, Part II,* 1902;
    harm. David Evans (1874-1948)

67. 67

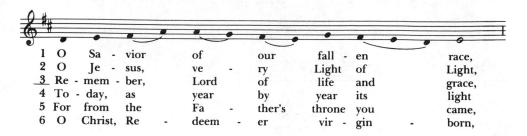

1	O	Sa - vior	of	our	fall - en	race,
2	O	Je - sus,	ve - ry	Light of	Light,
3	Re - mem - ber,	Lord	of	life and	grace,
4	To - day,	as	year	by	year its	light
5	For	from	the	Fa - ther's	throne you	came,
6	O	Christ, Re - deem - er	vir - gin - born,

1	O	Bright - ness	of	the	Fa - ther's	face,
2	our	con - stant	star	in	sin's	deep	night;
3	how	once, to	save	our	fall - en	race,
4	bathes	all	the	world	in	ra - diance	bright,
5	his	ban - ished	chil - dren	to	re - claim;
6	let	songs	of	praise	your	Name	a - dorn,

1	O	Son	who	shared	the	Fa - ther's	might
2	now	hear	the	prayers	your	peo - ple	pray
3	you	put	our	hu - man	ves - ture	on
4	one	pre - cious	truth	out - shines	the	sun:
5	and	earth	and	sea	and	sky	re - vere
6	whom	with	the	Fa - ther	we	a - dore

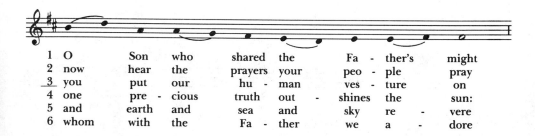

1	be - fore	the	world	knew	day	or	night,
2	through-out	the	world	this	ho - ly	day.
3	and	came	to	us	as	Ma - ry's	son.
4	sal - va - tion	comes	from	you	a - lone.
5	the	love	of	him	who	sent	you	here.
6	and	Ho - ly	Spi - rit	ev - er - more.

Words: Latin, ca. 6th cent.; tr. Gilbert E. Doan (b. 1930)
Music: *Christe, Redemptor omnium*, plainsong, Mode 1

LM

1. O Sa - vior of our fall - en race,
2. O Je - sus, ve - ry Light of Light,
3. Re - mem - ber, Lord of life and grace,
4. To - day, as year by year its light
5. For from the Fa - ther's throne you came,
6. O Christ, Re - deem - er vir - gin - born,

1. O Bright - ness of the Fa - ther's face,
2. our con - stant star in sin's deep night;
3. how once, to save our fall - en race,
4. bathes all the world in ra - diance bright,
5. his ban - ished chil - dren to re - claim;
6. let songs of praise your Name a - dorn,

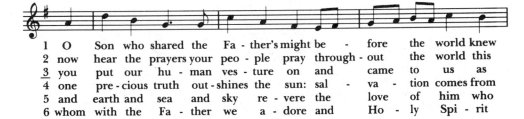

1. O Son who shared the Fa - ther's might be - fore the world knew
2. now hear the prayers your peo - ple pray through - out the world this
3. you put our hu - man ves - ture on and came to us as
4. one pre - cious truth out - shines the sun: sal - va - tion comes from
5. and earth and sea and sky re - vere the love of him who
6. whom with the Fa - ther we a - dore and Ho - ly Spi - rit

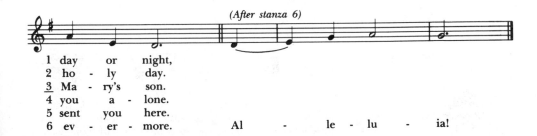

(After stanza 6)

1. day or night,
2. ho - ly day.
3. Ma - ry's son.
4. you a - lone.
5. sent you here.
6. ev - er - more.   Al - le - lu - ia!

Words: Latin, ca. 6th cent.; tr. Gilbert E. Doan (b. 1930)
Music: *Gonfalon Royal*, Percy Carter Buck (1871-1947)

LM

1 Hark! the her - ald an - gels sing glo - ry to the new - born King!
2 Christ, by high - est heaven a - dored; Christ, the ev - er - last - ing Lord;
3 Mild he lays his glo - ry by, born that we no more may die,

Peace on earth and mer - cy mild, God and sin - ners rec - on - ciled!
late in time be - hold him come, off - spring of the Vir - gin's womb.
born to raise us from the earth, born to give us sec - ond birth.

Joy - ful, all ye na - tions, rise, join the tri - umph of the skies;
Veiled in flesh the God - head see; hail the in - car - nate De - i - ty.
Risen with heal - ing in his wings, light and life to all he brings,

with the an - gel - ic host pro - claim Christ is born in Beth - le - hem!
Pleased as man with us to dwell; Je - sus, our Em - man - u - el!
hail, the Sun of Right - eous - ness! hail, the heaven - born Prince of Peace!

Hark! the her-ald an-gels sing glo-ry to the new-born King!

Words: Charles Wesley (1707-1788), alt.
Music: *Mendelssohn,* Felix Mendelssohn (1809-1847); adapt. William
H. Cummings (1831-1915)

77. 77. D with Refrain

Christmas

88

1 Sing, O sing, this bless-ed morn, un - to us a child is born,
2 God from God, and Light from Light, comes with mer - cies in-fi - nite,
3 God with us, Em-man - u - el, deigns for ev - er now to dwell;
4 God comes down that we may rise, lift - ed by him to the skies;
5 O re - new us, Lord, we pray, with thy Spi - rit day by day,

1 un - to us a son is given, God him - self comes down from heaven.
2 from high heaven he comes to earth, one with us in hu - man birth.
3 he on Ad - am's fall - en race sheds the full - ness of his grace.
4 Christ is born for us that we born a - gain in him may be.
5 that we ev - er one may be with the Fa - ther and with thee.

Refrain

Sing, O sing, this bless-ed morn, Je - sus Christ to - day is born.

Words: Christopher Wordsworth (1807-1885), alt.
Music: *England's Lane,* English melody; adapt. and harm. Geoffrey Turton Shaw (1879-1943)

77. 77. 77

1 It came up- on the mid - night clear, that
2 Still through the clov - en skies they come with
3 Yet with the woes of sin and strife the
4 For lo! the days are haste - ning on, by

glo - rious song of old, from an - gels bend - ing
peace - ful wings un - furled, and still their heaven - ly
world has suf - fered long; be - neath the heaven - ly
pro - phets seen of old, when with the ev - er -

near the earth to touch their harps of gold:
mu - sic floats o'er all the wea - ry world;
hymn have rolled two thou - sand years of wrong;
cir - cling years shall come the time fore - told,

"Peace on the earth, good will to men, from
a - bove its sad and low - ly plains they
and war - ring hu - man - kind hears not the
when peace shall o - ver all the earth its

heaven's all - gra - cious King." The world in sol - emn
bend on hov - ering wing, and ev - er o'er its
tid - ings which they bring; O hush the noise and
an - cient splen - dors fling, and all the world give

still - ness lay to hear the an - gels sing.
Ba - bel - sounds the bless - ed an - gels sing.
cease your strife and hear the an - gels sing!
back the song which now the an - gels sing.

Words: Edmund H. Sears (1810-1876), alt.
Music: *Carol*, Richard Storrs Willis (1819-1900)

CMD

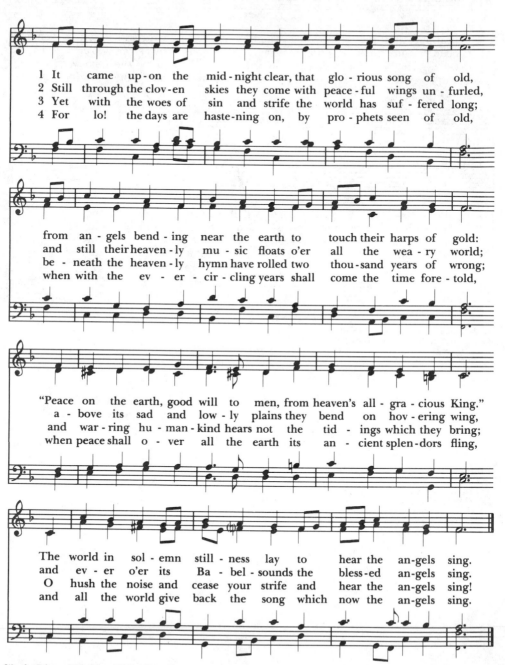

1 It came up-on the mid-night clear, that glo-rious song of old,
2 Still through the clov-en skies they come with peace-ful wings un-furled,
3 Yet with the woes of sin and strife the world has suf-fered long;
4 For lo! the days are haste-ning on, by pro-phets seen of old,

from an-gels bend-ing near the earth to touch their harps of gold:
and still their heaven-ly mu-sic floats o'er all the wea-ry world;
be-neath the heaven-ly hymn have rolled two thou-sand years of wrong;
when with the ev-er-cir-cling years shall come the time fore-told,

"Peace on the earth, good will to men, from heaven's all-gra-cious King."
a-bove its sad and low-ly plains they bend on hov-ering wing,
and war-ring hu-man-kind hears not the tid-ings which they bring;
when peace shall o-ver all the earth its an-cient splen-dors fling,

The world in sol-emn still-ness lay to hear the an-gels sing.
and ev-er o'er its Ba-bel-sounds the bless-ed an-gels sing.
O hush the noise and cease your strife and hear the an-gels sing!
and all the world give back the song which now the an-gels sing.

Words: Edmund H. Sears (1810-1876), alt.
Music: *Noel*, English melody; adapt. Arthur Seymour Sullivan (1842-1900)

CMD

Break forth, O beau-teous heaven-ly light, and ush-er in the morn - ing; O shep - herds, greet that glo - rious sight, our Lord a crib a - dorn - ing. This child, this lit - tle help - less boy, shall be our con - fi - dence and joy, the power of Sa - tan break - ing, our peace e - ter - nal mak - ing.

Words: Johann Rist (1607-1667); ver. *Hymnal 1982*
Music: *Ermuntre dich*, melody Johann Schop (d. 1665?), alt.;
     harm. Johann Sebastian Bach (1685-1750)

87. 87. 88. 77

1 On this day earth shall ring
2 His the doom, ours the mirth;
3 God's bright star, o'er his head,
4 On this day an - gels sing;

with the song chil - dren sing to the Lord, Christ our King,
when he came down to earth Beth - le - hem saw his birth;
Wise Men three to him led; kneel they low by his bed,
with their song earth shall ring, prais - ing Christ, hea - ven's King,

born on earth to save us; him the Fa - ther gave us.
ox and ass be - side him from the cold would hide him.
lay their gifts be - fore him, praise him and a - dore him.
born on earth to save us; peace and love he gave us.

Refrain

Id - e - o - o - o, Id - e - o - o - o,

Id - e - o glo - ri - a in ex - cel - sis De - o!

"Ideo gloria in excelsis Deo!" is Latin for "Therefore, glory to God in the highest!"

Words: *Piae Cantiones*, 1582; tr. Jane M. Joseph (1894-1929)
Music: *Personent hodie*, melody from *Piae Cantiones*, 1582

666. 66 with Refrain

1 An - gels, from the realms of glo - ry, wing your flight o'er all the earth; ye, who sang cre - a - tion's sto - ry, now pro - claim Mes - si - ah's birth:

2 Shep - herds in the field a - bid - ing, watch - ing o'er your flocks by night, God with you is now re - sid - ing; yon - der shines the in - fant Light:

3 Sa - ges, leave your con - tem - pla - tions; bright - er vi - sions beam a - far: seek the great De - sire of na - tions; ye have seen his na - tal star:

4 Saints be - fore the al - tar bend - ing, watch - ing long in hope and fear, sud - den - ly the Lord, de - scend - ing, in his tem - ple shall ap - pear:

Refrain

come and wor - ship, come and wor - ship, wor - ship Christ, the new - born King.

Words: James Montgomery (1771-1854), alt.
Music: *Regent Square*, Henry Thomas Smart (1813-1879)

87. 87. 87

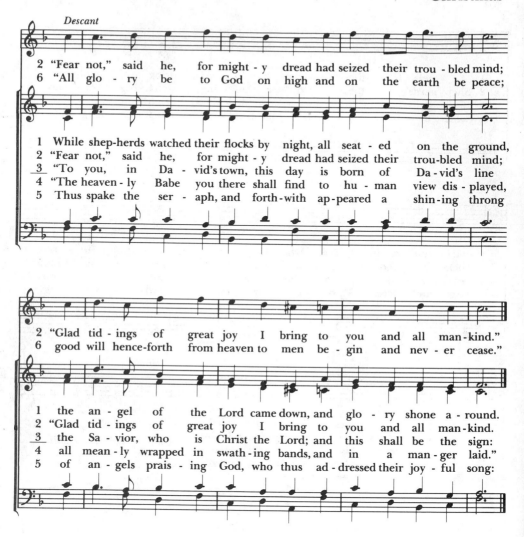

Descant

2 "Fear not," said he, for might-y dread had seized their trou-bled mind;
6 "All glo-ry be to God on high and on the earth be peace;

1 While shep-herds watched their flocks by night, all seat-ed on the ground,
2 "Fear not," said he, for might-y dread had seized their trou-bled mind;
3 "To you, in Da-vid's town, this day is born of Da-vid's line
4 "The heaven-ly Babe you there shall find to hu-man view dis-played,
5 Thus spake the ser-aph, and forth-with ap-peared a shin-ing throng

2 "Glad tid-ings of great joy I bring to you and all man-kind."
6 good will hence-forth from heaven to men be-gin and nev-er cease."

1 the an-gel of the Lord came down, and glo-ry shone a-round.
2 "Glad tid-ings of great joy I bring to you and all man-kind.
3 the Sa-vior, who is Christ the Lord; and this shall be the sign:
4 all mean-ly wrapped in swath-ing bands, and in a man-ger laid."
5 of an-gels prais-ing God, who thus ad-dressed their joy-ful song:

6 "All glory be to God on high
   and on the earth be peace;
good will henceforth from heaven to men
   begin and never cease."

Words: Nahum Tate (1625-1715)
Music: *Winchester Old,* melody from *The Whole Booke of Psalmes,* 1592; harm. *Hymns Ancient and Modern,* 1922; desc. Craig Sellar Lang (1891-1971)

CM

Stanzas 1, 3, and 5 in unison

1 While shep - herds watched their flocks by night, all
2 "Fear not," said he, for might - y dread had
3 "To you, in Da - vid's town, this day is
4 "The heaven - ly Babe you there shall find to
5 Thus spake the ser - aph, and forth - with ap -

1 seat - ed on the ground, the an - gel of the
2 seized their trou - bled mind; "Glad tid - ings of great
3 born of Da - vid's line the Sa - vior, who is
4 hu - man view dis - played, all mean - ly wrapped in
5 peared a shin - ing throng of an - gels prais - ing

1 Lord came down, and glo - ry shone a - round.
2 joy I bring to you and all man - kind.
3 Christ the Lord; and this shall be the sign:
4 swath - ing bands, and in a man - ger laid."
5 God, who thus ad - dressed their joy - ful song:

6 "All glory be to God on high
   and on the earth be peace;
   good will henceforth from heaven to men
   begin and never cease."

Words: Nahum Tate (1625-1715)
Music: *Hampton*, McNeil Robinson II (b. 1943)

CM

1 An - gels we have heard on high, sing - ing sweet - ly through the night,
2 Shep - herds, why this ju - bi - lee? Why these songs of hap - py cheer?
3 Come to Beth - le - hem and see him whose birth the an - gels sing;
4 See him in a man - ger laid whom the an - gels praise a - bove;

and the moun - tains in re - ply ech - o - ing their brave de - light.
What great bright - ness did you see? What glad tid - ings did you hear?
come, a - dore on bend - ed knee Christ, the Lord, the new - born King.
Ma - ry, Jo - seph, lend your aid, while we raise our hearts in love.

Refrain

Glo - - - - - - - - ri - a

in ex - cel - sis De - o. Glo - - - - -

Words: French carol; tr. James Chadwick (1813-1882), alt.
Music: *Gloria*, French carol; arr. Edward Shippen Barnes (1887-1958)

77. 77 with Refrain

Christmas

97

1 Dost thou in a man-ger lie, who hast all cre - a - ted,
2 "For the world a love su - preme brought me to this sta - ble;
3 Christ we praise with voic - es bold, laud and hon - or rais - ing;

stretch-ing in - fant hands on high, Sa - vior, long a - wait - ed?
all cre - a - tion to re - deem I a - lone am a - ble.
for these mer - cies man - i - fold join the hosts in prais - ing:

If a mon-arch, where thy state? Where thy court on thee to wait?
By this low - ly birth of mine, sin - ner, rich - es shall be thine,
Fa - ther, glo - ry be to thee for the won - drous char - i - ty

Scep - ter, crown, and sphere? Here no re - gal pomp we see,
match-less gifts and free; will - ing - ly this yoke I take,
of thy Son, our Lord. Bet - ter wit - ness to thy worth,

nought but need and pen - u - ry: why thus cra - dled here?
and this sac - ri - fice I make, heap - ing joys for thee."
pur - er praise than ours on earth, an - gels' songs af - ford.

Words: Jean Mauburn (1460-1503); tr. Elizabeth Rundle Charles (1828-1896) and others
Music: *Dies est laetitiae*, melody from *Piae Cantiones*, 1582

76. 76. 775. 775

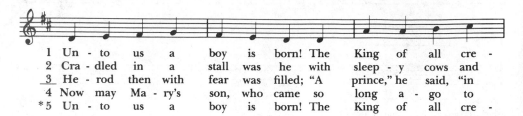

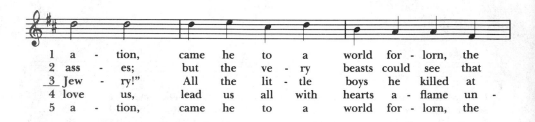

1 Un - to   us   a   boy   is   born! The   King   of   all   cre -
2 Cra - dled in   a   stall   was   he   with   sleep - y   cows   and
3 He - rod   then with fear   was filled; "A   prince," he   said, "in
4 Now may Ma - ry's   son, who came so   long   a - go   to
*5 Un - to us   a   boy   is   born! The   King   of   all   cre -

1 a - tion,   came he   to   a   world   for - lorn, the
2 ass - es;   but   the   ve - ry   beasts could see   that
3 Jew - ry!"   All   the   lit - tle   boys   he   killed at
4 love   us,   lead us   all   with   hearts a - flame un -
5 a - tion,   came he   to   a   world   for - lorn, the

1 Lord of   ev - ery   na -   tion.
2 he   all men sur - pass -   es.
3 Beth-lehem in his   fu -   ry.
4 to   the joys a - bove   us.
5 Lord of   ev - ery   na -   tion.

Words: Latin carol, 15th cent.; tr. Percy Dearmer (1867-1936), alt.
Music: *Puer nobis nascitur*, melody from *Piae Cantiones*, 1582

77. 77

Refrain

Go   tell   it on   the moun - tain,   o - ver the hills and

ev - ery - where; go tell it on the moun - tain, that

Je - sus Christ is born!

1 While shep - herds kept their
2 The shep - herds feared and
3 Down in a low - ly

watch - ing o'er si - lent flocks by night, be -
trem - bled when lo! a - bove the earth rang
man - ger the hum - ble Christ was born, and

Repeat Refrain

hold, through-out the hea - vens there shone a ho - ly light.
out the an - gel cho - rus that hailed our Sa - vior's birth.
God sent us sal - va - tion that bless - ed Christ - mas morn.

Words: Afro-American spiritual, 19th cent.; adapt. John W. Work (b. 1901)
Music: *Go Tell It on the Mountain,* Afro-American spiritual, 19th cent.;
    arr. Horace Clarence Boyer (b. 1935)

76. 76 with Refrain

1 Joy to the world! the Lord is come: let earth re -
2 Joy to the world! the Sa - vior reigns; let us our
*3 No more let sins and sor - rows grow, nor thorns in -
4 He rules the world with truth and grace, and makes the

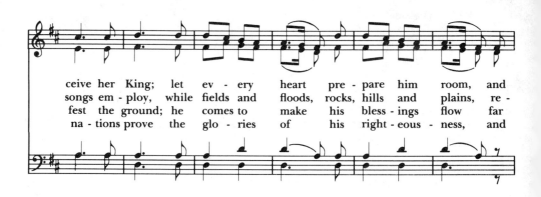

ceive her King; let ev - ery heart pre - pare him room, and
songs em - ploy, while fields and floods, rocks, hills and plains, re -
fest the ground; he comes to make his bless - ings flow far
na - tions prove the glo - ries of his right - eous - ness, and

heaven and na - ture sing, and heaven and na - ture
peat the sound - ing joy, re - peat the sound - ing
as the curse is found, far as the curse is
won - ders of his love, and won - ders of his

1 and heaven and na - ture sing, and
2 re - peat the sound - ing joy, re -
3 far as the curse is found, far
4 and won - ders of his love, and

sing,   and   heaven,   and   heaven   and   na - ture   sing.
joy,   re - peat,   re - peat   the   sound-ing   joy.
found,   far   as,   far   as   the   curse   is   found.
love,   and   won - ders,   won - ders   of   his   love.

heaven and na - ture   sing,
peat   the sound-ing   joy,
as   the curse   is   found,
won - ders of   his   love,

Words: Isaac Watts (1674-1748), alt.
Music: *Antioch*, George Frideric Handel (1685-1759); adapt. and arr. Lowell Mason (1792-1872)   CM with Repeat

Christmas   101

1 A - way   in   a   man - ger,   no   crib   for   his   bed,
2 The   cat - tle   are   low - ing,   the   ba - by   a - wakes,
*3 Be   near me,   Lord   Je - sus;   I   ask   thee   to   stay

the   lit - tle   Lord   Je - sus   laid   down   his   sweet   head.
but   lit - tle   Lord   Je - sus   no   cry - ing   he   makes.
close   by   me   for   ev - er,   and   love   me   I   pray.

The   stars   in   the   bright sky   looked   down where   he   lay,
I   love   thee,   Lord   Je - sus!   Look   down from   the   sky,
Bless   all   the   dear   chil - dren   in   thy   ten - der   care,

the   lit - tle   Lord   Je - sus   a - sleep   on   the   hay.
and   stay   by   my   side   un - til   morn - ing   is   nigh.
and   fit   us   for   hea - ven   to   live   with   thee   there.

Words: Traditional carol
Music: *Cradle Song*, melody William James Kirkpatrick (1838-1921)   11 11. 11 11

1 Once in roy - al Da - vid's ci - ty stood a
2 He came down to earth from hea - ven, who is
*3 We, like Ma - ry, rest con - found - ed that a
4 For he is our life - long pat - tern; dai - ly,
*5 And our eyes at last shall see him, through his
6 Not in that poor low - ly sta - ble, with the

1 low - ly cat - tle shed, where a mo - ther laid her
2 God and Lord of all, and his shel - ter was a
3 sta - ble should dis - play hea - ven's Word, the world's cre -
4 when on earth he grew, he was tempt - ed, scorned, re -
5 own re - deem - ing love; for that child who seemed so
6 ox - en stand - ing round, we shall see him; but in

1 ba - by in a man - ger for his bed: Ma - ry
2 sta - ble, and his cra - dle was a stall; with the
3 a - tor, cra - dled there on Christ - mas Day, yet this
4 ject - ed, tears and smiles like us he knew. Thus he
5 help - less is our Lord in heaven a - bove; and he
6 hea - ven, where his saints his throne sur - round: Christ, re -

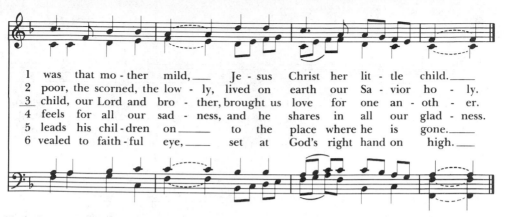

1 was that mo-ther mild,___ Je-sus Christ her lit-tle child.___
2 poor, the scorned, the low-ly, lived on earth our Sa-vior ho-ly.
3 child, our Lord and bro-ther, brought us love for one an-oth-er.
4 feels for all our sad-ness, and he shares in all our glad-ness.
5 leads his chil-dren on___ to the place where he is gone.___
6 vealed to faith-ful eye,___ set at God's right hand on high.___

Words: Sts. 1-2 and 4-6, Cecil Frances Alexander (1818-1895), alt.;
      st. 3, James Waring McCrady (b. 1938)
Music: *Irby*, melody Henry John Gauntlett (1805-1876); harm. Arthur Henry Mann (1850-1929)   87. 87. 77

Christmas   103

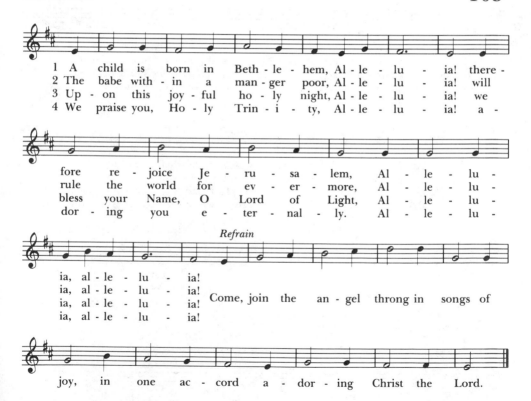

1 A child is born in Beth-le-hem, Al-le-lu-ia! there-
2 The babe with-in a man-ger poor, Al-le-lu-ia! will
3 Up-on this joy-ful ho-ly night, Al-le-lu-ia! we
4 We praise you, Ho-ly Trin-i-ty, Al-le-lu-ia! a-

fore re-joice Je-ru-sa-lem, Al-le-lu-
rule the world for ev-er-more, Al-le-lu-
bless your Name, O Lord of Light, Al-le-lu-
dor-ing you e-ter-nal-ly. Al-le-lu-

Refrain

ia, al-le-lu-ia!
ia, al-le-lu-ia!
ia, al-le-lu-ia!   Come, join the an-gel throng in songs of
ia, al-le-lu-ia!

joy, in one ac-cord a-dor-ing Christ the Lord.

Words: Latin, 14th cent.; tr. Ruth Fox Hume (1922-1980), alt.
Music: *Puer natus in Bethlehem*, plainsong, Mode 1.
    Benedictine Processional, 14th cent.   88 with Alleluias and Refrain

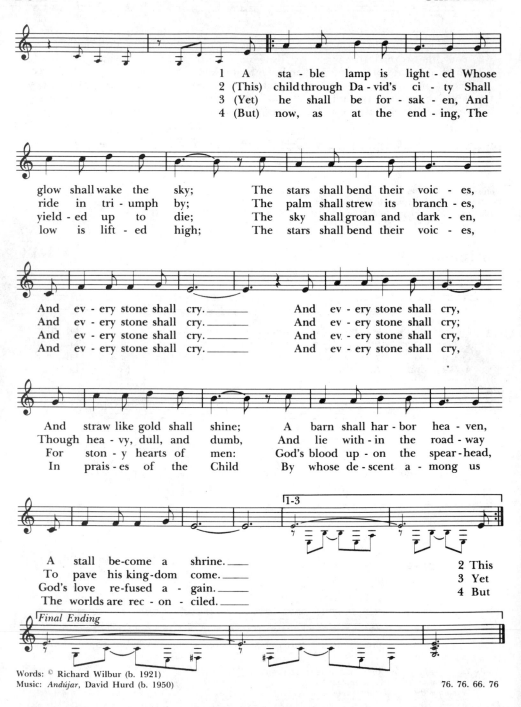

1 A sta - ble lamp is light - ed Whose
2 (This) child through Da - vid's ci - ty Shall
3 (Yet) he shall be for - sak - en, And
4 (But) now, as at the end - ing, The

glow shall wake the sky; The stars shall bend their voic - es,
ride in tri - umph by; The palm shall strew its branch - es,
yield - ed up to die; The sky shall groan and dark - en,
low is lift - ed high; The stars shall bend their voic - es,

And ev - ery stone shall cry.____ And ev - ery stone shall cry,
And ev - ery stone shall cry.____ And ev - ery stone shall cry;
And ev - ery stone shall cry.____ And ev - ery stone shall cry,
And ev - ery stone shall cry.____ And ev - ery stone shall cry,

And straw like gold shall shine; A barn shall har - bor hea - ven,
Though hea - vy, dull, and dumb, And lie with - in the road - way
For ston - y hearts of men: God's blood up - on the spear - head,
In prais - es of the Child By whose de - scent a - mong us

1-3

A stall be - come a shrine.___
To pave his king - dom come.___
God's love re - fused a - gain.___
The worlds are rec - on - ciled.___

2 This
3 Yet
4 But

Final Ending

Words: © Richard Wilbur (b. 1921)
Music: *Andújar*, David Hurd (b. 1950)

76. 76. 66. 76

1 God rest you mer - ry, gen - tle-men, let noth-ing you dis - may;
2 From God our heaven - ly Fa - ther a bless-ed an-gel came
3 "Fear not, then," said the an - gel, "Let noth-ing you af - fright;
4 Now to the Lord sing prais - es, all you with - in this place,

re - mem-ber Christ our Sa - vior was born on Christ-mas Day,
and un - to cer - tain shep - herds brought tid - ings of the same:
this day is born a Sa - vior of a pure vir - gin bright,
and with true love and char - i - ty each o - ther now em - brace;

to save us all from Sa - tan's power when we were gone a - stray.
how that in Beth - le - hem was born the Son of God by name.
to free all those who trust in him from Sa - tan's power and might."
this ho - ly tide of Christ - mas doth bring re - deem-ing grace.

Refrain

O tid - ings of com - fort and joy, com-fort and

joy; O tid - ings of com - fort and joy!

Words: London carol, 18th cent.
Music: *God Rest You Merry*, melody from *Little Book of Christmas Carols*, ca. 1850   76. 76. 86 with Refrain

1 Chris - tians, a - wake, sa - lute the hap - py morn
2 Then to the watch - ful shep - herds it was told,
*3 He spoke, and straight - way the ce - les - tial choir
*4 In Beth - le - hem the hap - py shep - herds sought
5 Let us, like these good shep - herds, then em - ploy

1 where - on the Sa - vior of the world was born;
2 who heard the an - gel - ic her - ald's voice: "Be - hold,
3 in hymns of joy, un - known be - fore, con - spire;
4 to see the won - der God for us had wrought,
5 our grate - ful voic - es to pro - claim the joy;

1 rise to a - dore the mys - ter - y of love,
2 I bring good tid - ings of a Sa - vior's birth
3 the prais - es of re - deem - ing love they sang,
4 and found, with Jo - seph and the bless - ed maid,
5 trace we the Babe, who hath re - trieved our loss,

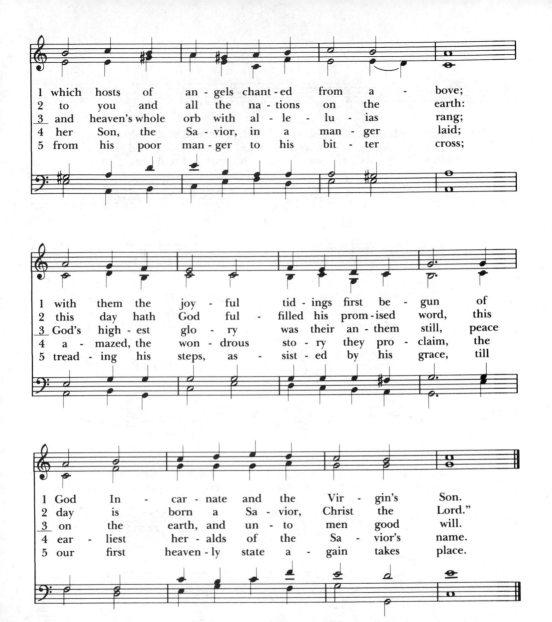

1 which hosts of an - gels chant - ed from a - bove;
2 to you and all the na - tions on the earth:
3 and heaven's whole orb with al - le - lu - ias rang;
4 her Son, the Sa - vior, in a man - ger laid;
5 from his poor man - ger to his bit - ter cross;

1 with them the joy - ful tid - ings first be - gun of
2 this day hath God ful - filled his prom - ised word, this
3 God's high - est glo - ry was their an - them still, peace
4 a - mazed, the won - drous sto - ry they pro - claim, the
5 tread - ing his steps, as - sist - ed by his grace, till

1 God In - car - nate and the Vir - gin's Son.
2 day is born a Sa - vior, Christ the Lord."
3 on the earth, and un - to men good will.
4 ear - liest her - alds of the Sa - vior's name.
5 our first heaven - ly state a - gain takes place.

6 Then may we hope, the angelic thrones among,
   to sing, redeemed, a glad triumphal song;
   he that was born upon this joyful day
   around us all his glory shall display;
   saved by his love, incessant we shall sing
   eternal praise to heaven's almighty King.

Words: John Byrom (1692-1763), alt.
Music: *Yorkshire*, John Wainwright (1723-1768)

10 10. 10 10. 10 10

1 Good Christian friends, rejoice with heart and soul and voice;
2 Good Christian friends, rejoice with heart and soul and voice;
3 Good Christian friends, rejoice with heart and soul and voice;

give ye heed to what we say: Jesus Christ is born today;
now ye hear of endless bliss; Jesus Christ was born for this!
now ye need not fear the grave: Jesus Christ was born to save!

ox and ass before him bow, and he is in the manger now.
He hath opened heaven's door, and we are blest for evermore.
Calls you one and calls you all to gain his everlasting hall.

Christ is born today! Christ is born today!
Christ was born for this! Christ was born for this!
Christ was born to save! Christ was born to save!

Words: John Mason Neale (1818-1866), alt.
Music: *In dulci jubilo*, German carol, 14th cent.; harm. Charles Winfred Douglas (1867-1944)

66. 77. 78. 55

1 Now yield we thanks and praise to Christ en-throned in glo - ry,
2 What tri - bute shall we pay to him who came in weak - ness,

and on this day of days tell out re - demp-tion's sto - ry,
and in a man - ger lay to teach his peo - ple meek - ness?

who tru - ly have be - lieved that on this bless - ed morn,
Let ev - ery house be bright; let prais - es nev - er cease;

in ho - li - ness con - ceived, the Son of God was born.
with mer - cies in - fi - nite our Christ hath brought us peace.

Words: Howard Chandler Robbins (1876-1952)
Music: *Was frag' ich nach der Welt*, melody Ahasuerus Fritsch (1629-1701);
harm. Johann Sebastian Bach (1685-1750)

67. 67. 66. 66

1 The first No - well the an - gel did say
2 They look - ed up and saw a star
3 And by the light of that same star
4 This star drew nigh to the north - west,
5 Then en - tered in those wise men three

1 was to cer - tain poor shep - herds in fields as they lay;
2 shin - ing in the east be - yond them far,
3 three wise men came from coun - try far;
4 o'er Beth - le - hem it took its rest,
5 full rev - erent - ly up - on their knee,

1 in fields as they lay, keep - ing their sheep,
2 and to the earth it gave great light,
3 to seek for a king was their in - tent,
4 and there it did both stop and stay
5 and of - fered there in his pres - ence

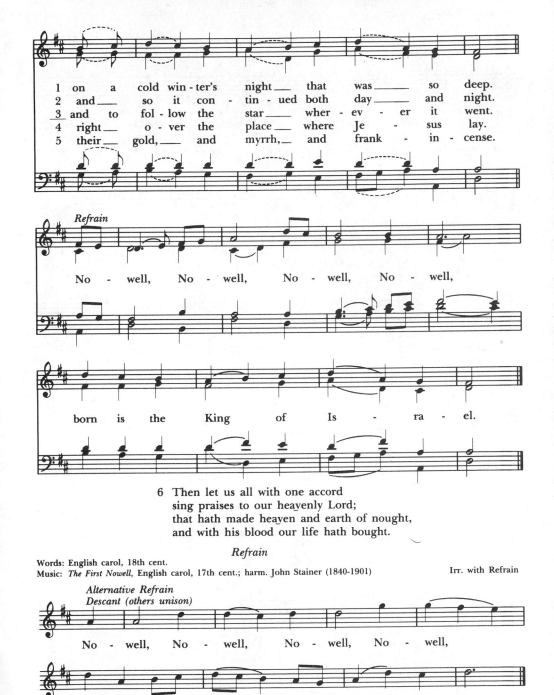

1 on a cold win-ter's night___ that was___ so deep.
2 and___ so it con-tin-ued both day___ and night.
3 and to fol-low the star___ wher-ev-er it went.
4 right___ o-ver the place___ where Je-sus lay.
5 their___ gold,___ and myrrh,___ and frank-in-cense.

Refrain

No - well, No - well, No - well, No - well,

born is the King of Is - ra - el.

6 Then let us all with one accord
  sing praises to our heavenly Lord;
  that hath made heaven and earth of nought,
  and with his blood our life hath bought.

Refrain

Words: English carol, 18th cent.
Music: *The First Nowell,* English carol, 17th cent.; harm. John Stainer (1840-1901)

Irr. with Refrain

Alternative Refrain
Descant (others unison)

No - well, No - well, No - well, No - well,

born is the King of Is - ra - el.

Music: *The First Nowell,* English carol, 17th cent.; desc. Healey Willan (1880-1968)

1 The snow lay on the ground, the stars shone bright,
2 'Twas Ma - ry, daugh - ter pure of ho - ly Anne,
3 Saint Jo - seph, too, was by to tend the child;
4 And thus that man - ger poor be - came a throne;

when Christ our Lord was born on Christ - mas night. Ve -
that brought in - to this world the God made man. She
to guard him, and pro - tect his mo - ther mild; the
for he whom Ma - ry bore was God the Son. O

ni - te a - do - re - mus Do - mi - num. Ve -
laid him in a stall at Beth - le - hem; the
an - gels hov - ered round, and sang this song, Ve -
come, then, let us join the heaven - ly host; to

Refrain

ni - te a - do - re - mus Do - mi - num.
ass and ox - en shared the roof with them.
ni - te a - do - re - mus Do - mi - num. Ve -
praise the Fa - ther, Son, and Ho - ly Ghost.

ni - te a - do - re - mus Do - mi - num. Ve -

ni - te a - do - re - mus Do - mi - num.

Words: Source unknown, 19th cent.
Music: *Venite adoremus*, melody adapt. Charles Winfred Douglas (1867-1944)

Irr. with Refrain

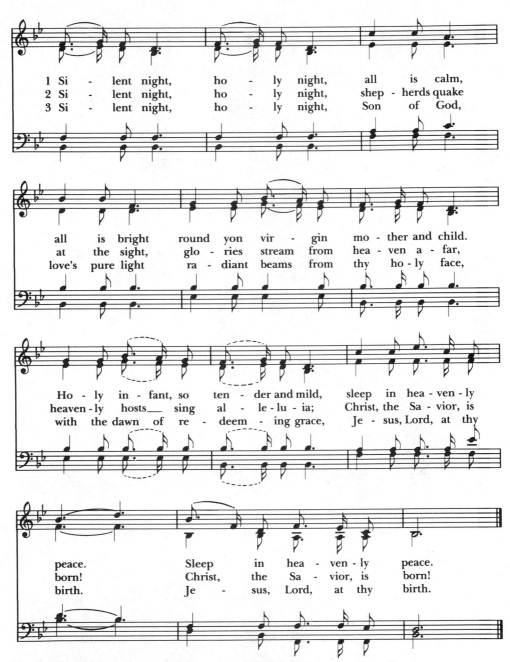

1 Si - lent night, ho - ly night, all is calm,
2 Si - lent night, ho - ly night, shep - herds quake
3 Si - lent night, ho - ly night, Son of God,

all is bright round yon vir - gin mo - ther and child.
at the sight, glo - ries stream from hea - ven a - far,
love's pure light ra - diant beams from thy ho - ly face,

Ho - ly in - fant, so ten - der and mild, sleep in hea - ven - ly
heaven - ly hosts____ sing al - le - lu - ia; Christ, the Sa - vior, is
with the dawn of re - deem - ing grace, Je - sus, Lord, at thy

peace. Sleep in hea - ven - ly peace.
born! Christ, the Sa - vior, is born!
birth. Je - sus, Lord, at thy birth.

Words: Joseph Mohr (1792-1848); tr. John Freeman Young (1820-1885)
Music: *Stille Nacht*, melody Franz Xaver Gruber (1787-1863); harm. Carl H. Reinecke (1824-1910)

Irr.

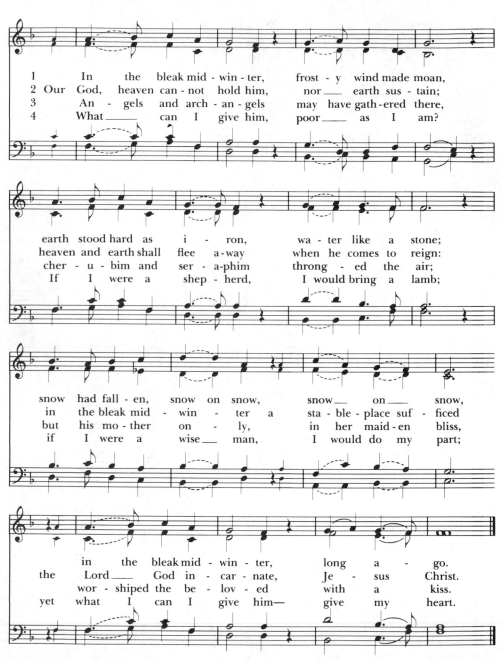

1 In the bleak mid - win - ter, frost - y wind made moan,
2 Our God, heaven can - not hold him, nor ___ earth sus - tain;
3 An - gels and arch - an - gels may have gath - ered there,
4 What ___ can I give him, poor ___ as I am?

earth stood hard as i - ron, wa - ter like a stone;
heaven and earth shall flee a - way when he comes to reign:
cher - u - bim and ser - a - phim throng - ed the air;
If I were a shep - herd, I would bring a lamb;

snow had fall - en, snow on snow, snow ___ on ___ snow,
in the bleak mid - win - ter a sta - ble - place suf - ficed
but his mo - ther on - ly, in her maid - en bliss,
if I were a wise ___ man, I would do my part;

in the bleak mid - win - ter, long a - go.
the Lord ___ God in - car - nate, Je - sus Christ.
wor - shiped the be - lov - ed with a kiss.
yet what I can I give him— give my heart.

Words: Christina Rossetti (1830-1894)
Music: *Cranham*, Gustav Theodore Holst (1874-1934)

Irr.

Introduction/Interlude

1 Duér-
2 No

1 Oh,
2 You

1 me - te, Ni - ño lin - do, en los bra - zos del a -
2 te - mas al rey He - ro - des que na - da te ha de ha -

1 sleep now, ho - ly ba - by, with your head a - gainst my
2 need not fear King He - rod, he will bring no harm to

1 mor mien - tras que duer-me y des - can - sa la
2 cer; en los bra - zos de tu ma - dre y ahí

1 breast; mean - while the pangs of my sor - row are
2 you; so rest in the arms of your mo - ther who

Refrain

1 pe - na de mi do - lor.
2 na - die te ha de o - fen - der. A la ru, a la

1 soothed and put to rest.
2 sings you a la ru.

mè, a la ru, a la mè, a la ru, a la

mè, a la ru, a la ru, a la mè.

Words: Hispanic folk song; tr. John Donald Robb (b. 1892), alt.
Music: *A la ru*, Hispanic folk melody; arr. John Donald Robb (b. 1892)

Irr. with Refrain

Optional Introduction

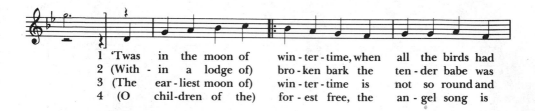

1 'Twas in the moon of win - ter - time, when all the birds had
2 (With - in a lodge of) bro - ken bark the ten - der babe was
3 (The ear - liest moon of) win - ter - time is not so round and
4 (O chil-dren of the) for - est free, the an - gel song is

fled, that God the Lord of all the earth sent
found, a rag - ged robe of rab - bit skin en -
fair as was the ring of glo - ry on the
true; the ho - ly child of earth and heaven is

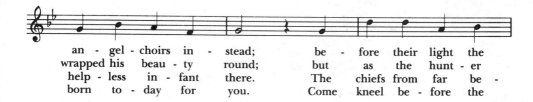

an - gel - choirs in - stead; be - fore their light the
wrapped his beau - ty round; but as the hunt - er
help - less in - fant there. The chiefs from far be -
born to - day for you. Come kneel be - fore the

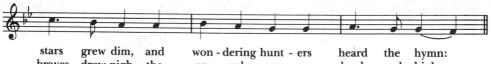

stars grew dim, and won - dering hunt - ers heard the hymn:
braves drew nigh, the an - gel - song rang loud and high:
fore him knelt with gifts of fox and bea - ver - pelt.
ra - diant boy, who brings you beau - ty, peace, and joy.

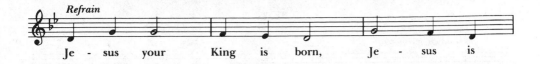

Refrain

Je - sus your King is born, Je - sus is

(Fine) Optional Interlude [1-3]

born, in ex - cel-sis glo-ri - a.

2 With - in a lodge of
3 The ear - liest moon of
4 O chil - dren of the

Final Ending   8va

Words: Jesse Edgar Middleton (1872-1960), alt.
Music: *Une jeune pucelle*, French folk melody, 16th cent.

86. 86. 88 with Refrain

Unison or harmony

1 What child is this, who, laid to rest, on
2 Why lies he in such mean es - tate where
3 So bring him in - cense, gold, and myrrh, come,

Ma - ry's lap is sleep - ing? Whom an - gels greet with
ox and ass are feed - ing? Good Chris - tian, fear: for
peas - ant, king, to own him; the King of kings sal -

an - thems sweet, while shep - herds watch are keep - ing?
sin - ners here the si - lent Word is plead - ing.
va - tion brings, let lov - ing hearts en - throne him.

Refrain

This, this is Christ the King, whom shep - herds

guard and an - gels sing; haste, haste to

bring him laud, the babe, the son of Ma - ry.

Words: William Chatterton Dix (1837-1898)

Music: *Greensleeves*, **English melody; harm.** *Christmas Carols New and Old*, **1871, alt.**

87. 87 with Refrain

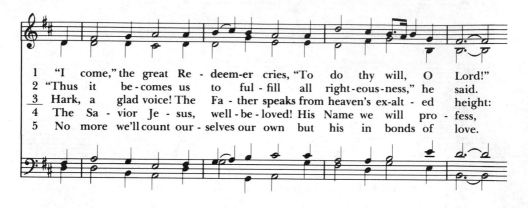

1 "I come," the great Re - deem-er cries, "To do thy will, O Lord!"
2 "Thus it be - comes us to ful - fill all right-eous-ness," he said.
3 Hark, a glad voice! The Fa - ther speaks from heaven's ex-alt - ed height:
4 The Sa - vior Je - sus, well - be - loved! His Name we will pro - fess,
5 No more we'll count our - selves our own but his in bonds of love.

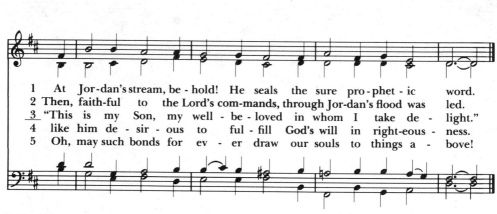

1 At Jor-dan's stream, be - hold! He seals the sure pro-phet - ic word.
2 Then, faith-ful to the Lord's com-mands, through Jor-dan's flood was led.
3 "This is my Son, my well - be - loved in whom I take de - light."
4 like him de - sir - ous to ful - fill God's will in right-eous - ness.
5 Oh, may such bonds for ev - er draw our souls to things a - bove!

Words: *Christian Hymnbook*, 1865, alt.
Music: *This Endris Nyght*, English melody; harm. Ralph Vaughan Williams (1872-1958)
CM

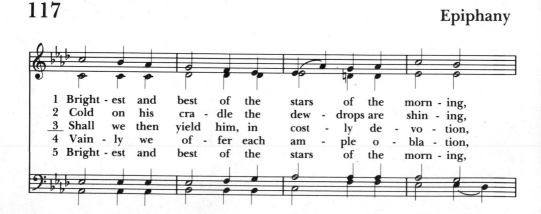

1 Bright - est and best of the stars of the morn - ing,
2 Cold on his cra - dle the dew - drops are shin - ing,
3 Shall we then yield him, in cost - ly de - vo - tion,
4 Vain - ly we of - fer each am - ple o - bla - tion,
5 Bright - est and best of the stars of the morn - ing,

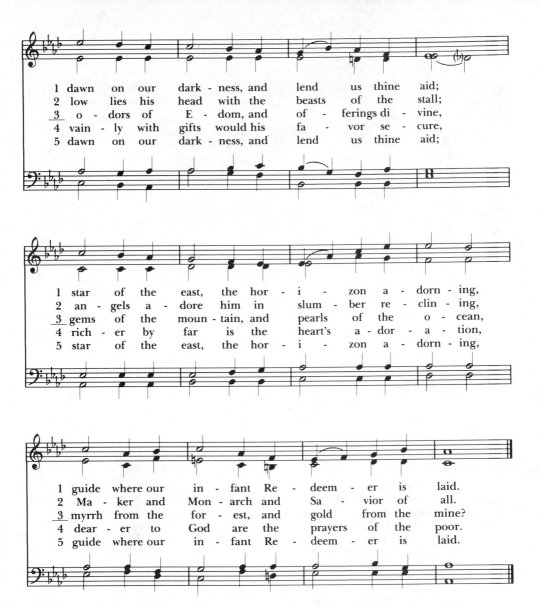

1 dawn on our dark - ness, and lend us thine aid;
2 low lies his head with the beasts of the stall;
3 o - dors of E - dom, and of - ferings di - vine,
4 vain - ly with gifts would his fa - vor se - cure,
5 dawn on our dark - ness, and lend us thine aid;

1 star of the east, the hor - i - zon a - dorn - ing,
2 an - gels a - dore him in slum - ber re - clin - ing,
3 gems of the moun - tain, and pearls of the o - cean,
4 rich - er by far is the heart's a - dor - a - tion,
5 star of the east, the hor - i - zon a - dorn - ing,

1 guide where our in - fant Re - deem - er is laid.
2 Ma - ker and Mon - arch and Sa - vior of all.
3 myrrh from the for - est, and gold from the mine?
4 dear - er to God are the prayers of the poor.
5 guide where our in - fant Re - deem - er is laid.

Words: Reginald Heber (1783-1826), alt.
Music: *Morning Star*, James Proctor Harding (1850-1911)

11 10. 11 10

Unison (Harmony on following pages)

1 Bright - est and best of the stars of the morn - ing,
2 Cold on his cra - dle the dew - drops are shin - ing,
3 Shall we then yield him, in cost - ly de - vo - tion,
4 Vain - ly we of - fer each am - ple o - bla - tion,
*5 Bright - est and best of the stars of the morn - ing,

1 dawn on our dark - ness, and lend us thine aid;
2 low lies his head with the beasts of the stall;
3 o - dors of E - dom, and of - ferings di - vine,
4 vain - ly with gifts would his fa - vor se - cure,
5 dawn on our dark - ness, and lend us thine aid;

1 star of the east, the hor - i - zon a - dorn - ing,
2 an - gels a - dore him in slum - ber re - clin - ing,
3 gems of the moun - tain, and pearls of the o - cean,
4 rich - er by far is the heart's a - dor - a - tion,
5 star of the east, the hor - i - zon a - dorn - ing,

1 guide where our in - fant Re - deem - er is laid.
2 Ma - ker and Mon - arch and Sa - vior of all.
3 myrrh from the for - est, and gold from the mine?
4 dear - er to God are the prayers of the poor.
5 guide where our in - fant Re - deem - er is laid.

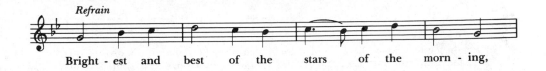

Bright - est and best of the stars of the morn - ing,

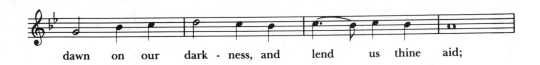

dawn on our dark - ness, and lend us thine aid;

star of the east, the hor - i - zon a - dorn - ing,

guide where our in - fant Re - deem - er is laid.

Words: Reginald Heber (1783-1826), alt.
Music: *Star in the East,* from *The Southern Harmony,* 1835

11 10. 11 10 with Refrain

Harmony (the melody is in the tenor)

1 Bright - est and best of the stars of the morn - ing,
2 Cold on his cra - dle the dew - drops are shin - ing,
3 Shall we then yield him, in cost - ly de - vo - tion,
4 Vain - ly we of - fer each am - ple o - bla - tion,
*5 Bright - est and best of the stars of the morn - ing,

1 dawn on our dark - ness, and lend us thine aid;
2 low lies his head with the beasts of the stall;
3 o - dors of E - dom, and of - ferings di - vine,
4 vain - ly with gifts would his fa - vor se - cure,
5 dawn on our dark - ness, and lend us thine aid;

1 star of the east, the hor - i - zon a - dorn - ing,
2 an - gels a - dore him in slum - ber re - clin - ing,
3 gems of the moun - tain, and pearls of the o - cean,
4 rich - er by far is the heart's a - dor - a - tion,
5 star of the east, the hor - i - zon a - dorn - ing,

1 guide where our in - fant Re - deem - er is laid.
2 Ma - ker and Mon - arch and Sa - vior of all.
3 myrrh from the for - est, and gold from the mine?
4 dear - er to God are the prayers of the poor.
5 guide where our in - fant Re - deem - er is laid.

Refrain

Bright-est and best of the stars of the morn-ing,

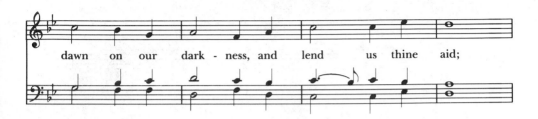

dawn on our dark-ness, and lend us thine aid;

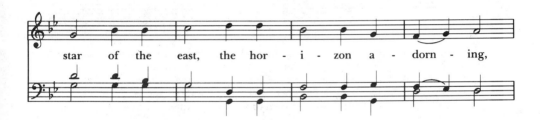

star of the east, the hor-i-zon a-dorn-ing,

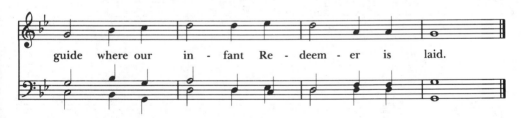

guide where our in-fant Re-deem-er is laid.

Words: Reginald Heber (1783-1826), alt.
Music: *Star in the East*, from *The Southern Harmony*, 1835

11 10. 11 10 with Refrain

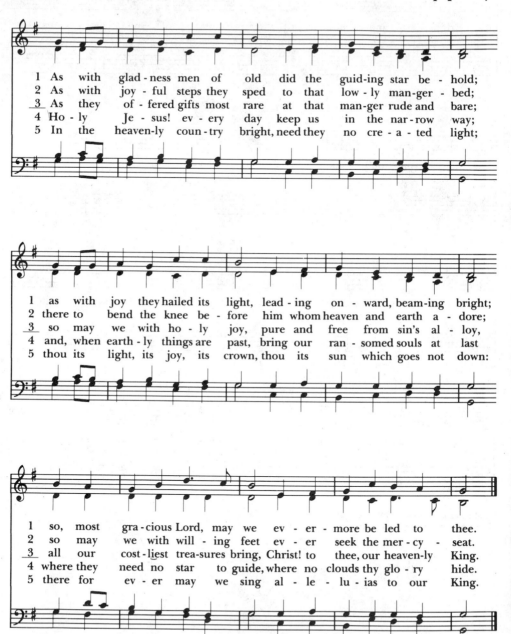

1 As with glad-ness men of old did the guid-ing star be-hold;
2 As with joy-ful steps they sped to that low-ly man-ger-bed;
3 As they of-fered gifts most rare at that man-ger rude and bare;
4 Ho-ly Je-sus! ev-ery day keep us in the nar-row way;
5 In the heaven-ly coun-try bright, need they no cre-a-ted light;

1 as with joy they hailed its light, lead-ing on-ward, beam-ing bright;
2 there to bend the knee be-fore him whom heaven and earth a-dore;
3 so may we with ho-ly joy, pure and free from sin's al-loy,
4 and, when earth-ly things are past, bring our ran-somed souls at last
5 thou its light, its joy, its crown, thou its sun which goes not down:

1 so, most gra-cious Lord, may we ev-er-more be led to thee.
2 so may we with will-ing feet ev-er seek the mer-cy-seat.
3 all our cost-liest trea-sures bring, Christ! to thee, our heaven-ly King.
4 where they need no star to guide, where no clouds thy glo-ry hide.
5 there for ev-er may we sing al-le-lu-ias to our King.

Music: William Chatterton Dix (1837-1898)
Music: *Dix*, melody Conrad Kocher (1786-1872); arr. William Henry Monk (1823-1889);
  harm. *The English Hymnal*, 1906

77. 77. 77

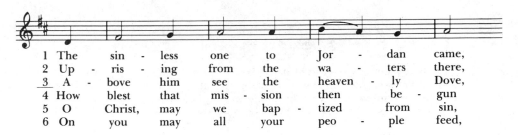

1 The sin - less one to Jor - dan came,
2 Up - ris - ing from the wa - ters there,
3 A - bove him see the heaven - ly Dove,
4 How blest that mis - sion then be - gun
5 O Christ, may we bap - tized from sin,
6 On you may all your peo - ple feed,

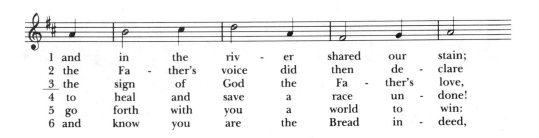

1 and in the riv - er shared our stain;
2 the Fa - ther's voice did then de - clare
3 the sign of God the Fa - ther's love,
4 to heal and save a race un - done!
5 go forth with you a world to win:
6 and know you are the Bread in - deed,

1 God's right - eous - ness he thus ful - filled,
2 that Christ, the Son of God, had come
3 now by the Ho - ly Spi - rit shed
4 Straight to the wil - der - ness he goes
5 grant us the Ho - ly Spi - rit's power
6 who gives e - ter - nal life to those

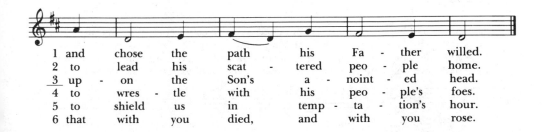

1 and chose the path his Fa - ther willed.
2 to lead his scat - tered peo - ple home.
3 up - on the Son's a - noint - ed head.
4 to wres - tle with his peo - ple's foes.
5 to shield us in temp - ta - tion's hour.
6 that with you died, and with you rose.

Words: George B. Timms (b. 1910), alt.
Music: *Solemnis haec festivitas*, melody from *Graduale*, 1685

LM

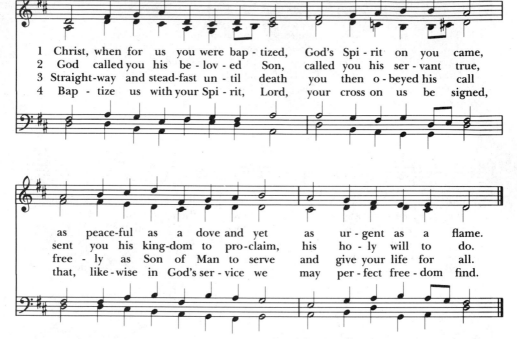

1 Christ, when for us you were bap - tized, God's Spi - rit on you came,
2 God called you his be - lov - ed Son, called you his ser - vant true,
3 Straight-way and stead-fast un - til death you then o - beyed his call
4 Bap - tize us with your Spi - rit, Lord, your cross on us be signed,

as peace-ful as a dove and yet as ur - gent as a flame.
sent you his king-dom to pro-claim, his ho - ly will to do.
free - ly as Son of Man to serve and give your life for all.
that, like-wise in God's ser - vice we may per - fect free - dom find.

Words: F. Bland Tucker (1895-1984), rev.
Music: *Caithness*, melody from *The Psalmes of David in Prose and Meeter*, 1635;
      harm. *The English Hymnal*, 1906

CM

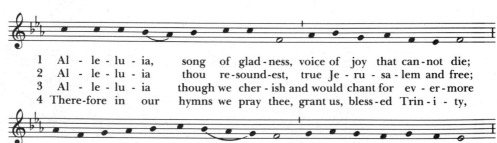

1 Al - le - lu - ia,   song of glad - ness, voice of joy that can - not die;
2 Al - le - lu - ia   thou re - sound - est, true Je - ru - sa - lem and free;
3 Al - le - lu - ia   though we cher - ish and would chant for ev - er - more
4 There-fore in our   hymns we pray thee, grant us, bless - ed Trin - i - ty,

al - le - lu - ia is the an - them ev - er raised by choirs on high;
al - le - lu - ia, joy - ful mo - ther, all thy chil - dren sing with thee;
al - le - lu - ia in our sing - ing, let us for a while give o'er,
at the last to keep thine Eas - ter with thy faith - ful saints on high;

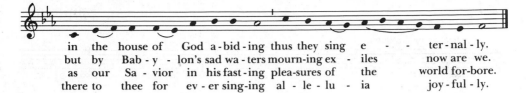

in the house of God a-bid-ing thus they sing e - - ter-nal-ly.
but by Bab - y - lon's sad wa - ters mourn-ing ex - iles now are we.
as our Sa - vior in his fast-ing plea-sures of the world for-bore.
there to thee for ev - er sing-ing al - le - lu - ia joy-ful-ly.

Words: Latin, 11th cent; tr. John Mason Neale (1818-1866), alt.
Music: *Urbs beata Jerusalem*, plainsong, Mode 2

87. 87. 87

Epiphany

123

1 Al - le - lu - ia, song of glad-ness, voice of joy that
2 Al - le - lu - ia thou re - sound-est, true Je - ru - sa -
3 Al - le - lu - ia though we cher - ish and would chant for
4 There - fore in our hymns we pray thee, grant us, bless - ed

can - not die; al - le - lu - ia is the an - them
lem and free; al - le - lu - ia, joy - ful mo - ther,
ev - er - more al - le - lu - ia in our sing - ing,
Trin - i - ty, at the last to keep thine Eas - ter,

ev - er raised by choirs on high; in the house of
all thy chil - dren sing with thee; but by Bab - y -
let us for a while give o'er, as our Sa - vior
with thy faith - ful saints on high; there to thee for

God a - bid - ing thus they sing e - ter - nal - ly.
lon's sad wa - ters mourn-ing ex - iles now are we.
in his fast - ing plea - sures of the world for - bore.
ev - er sing - ing al - le - lu - ia joy - ful - ly.

Words: Latin, 11th cent.; tr. John Mason Neale (1818-1866), alt.
Music: *Tibi Christe, splendor Patris*, plainsong, Mode 2,
Nevers MS, 13th cent.; ver. Schola Antiqua 1983

Music: Melody rhythmic version © 1984, Schola Antiqua Inc. Used by permission.

87. 87. 87

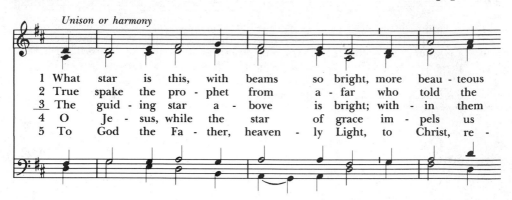

Unison or harmony

1 What star is this, with beams so bright, more beau - teous
2 True spake the pro - phet from a - far who told the
3 The guid - ing star a - bove is bright; with - in them
4 O Je - sus, while the star of grace im - pels us
5 To God the Fa - ther, heaven - ly Light, to Christ, re -

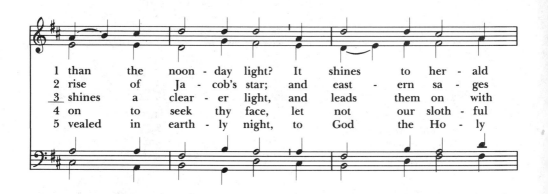

1 than the noon - day light? It shines to her - ald
2 rise of Ja - cob's star; and east - ern sa - ges
3 shines a clear - er light, and leads them on with
4 on to seek thy face, let not our sloth - ful
5 vealed in earth - ly night, to God the Ho - ly

1 forth the King, and Gen - tiles to his crib to bring.
2 with a - maze up - on the won - drous to - ken gaze.
3 power be - nign to seek the Giv - er of the sign.
4 hearts re - fuse the guid - ance of thy light to use.
5 Ghost we raise our e - qual and un - ceas - ing praise.

Words: Charles Coffin (1676-1749); tr. *Hymns Ancient and Modern*, 1861, after John Chandler (1807-1876), alt.
Music: *Puer nobis*, melody from Trier MS., 15th cent.; adapt. Michael Praetorius (1571-1621);
      harm. *Hymns Ancient and Modern*, Revised

LM

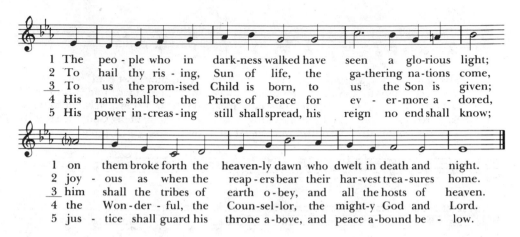

1 The peo-ple who in dark-ness walked have seen a glo-rious light;
2 To hail thy ris-ing, Sun of life, the ga-thering na-tions come,
3 To us the prom-ised Child is born, to us the Son is given;
4 His name shall be the Prince of Peace for ev-er-more a-dored,
5 His power in-creas-ing still shall spread, his reign no end shall know;

1 on them broke forth the heaven-ly dawn who dwelt in death and night.
2 joy-ous as when the reap-ers bear their har-vest trea-sures home.
3 him shall the tribes of earth o-bey, and all the hosts of heaven.
4 the Won-der-ful, the Coun-sel-lor, the might-y God and Lord.
5 jus-tice shall guard his throne a-bove, and peace a-bound be-low.

Words: John Morison (1749-1798), alt.; para. of Isaiah 9:2-7
Music: *Perry*, Leo Sowerby (1895-1968)

CM

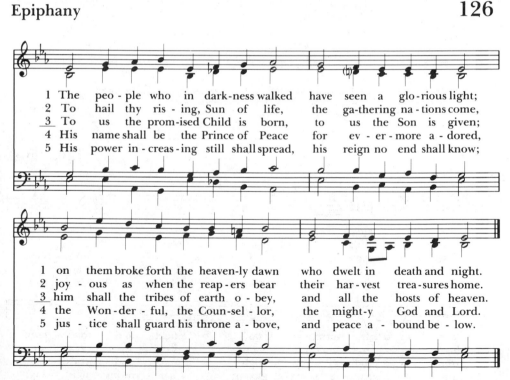

1 The peo-ple who in dark-ness walked have seen a glo-rious light;
2 To hail thy ris-ing, Sun of life, the ga-thering na-tions come,
3 To us the prom-ised Child is born, to us the Son is given;
4 His name shall be the Prince of Peace for ev-er-more a-dored,
5 His power in-creas-ing still shall spread, his reign no end shall know;

1 on them broke forth the heaven-ly dawn who dwelt in death and night.
2 joy-ous as when the reap-ers bear their har-vest trea-sures home.
3 him shall the tribes of earth o-bey, and all the hosts of heaven.
4 the Won-der-ful, the Coun-sel-lor, the might-y God and Lord.
5 jus-tice shall guard his throne a-bove, and peace a-bound be-low.

Words: John Morison (1749-1798), alt.; para. of Isaiah 9:2-7
Music: *Dundee*, melody *The CL Psalmes of David*, 1615; harm. Thomas Ravenscroft (1592?-1635?), alt.

CM

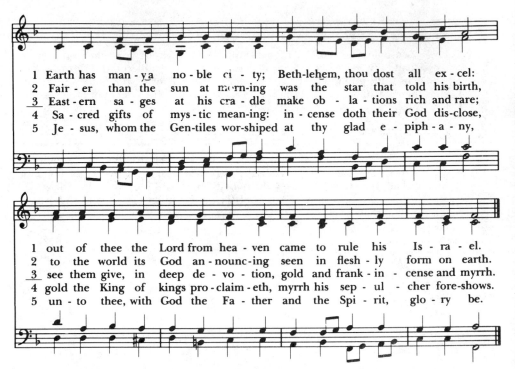

1 Earth has man - y a no - ble ci - ty; Beth-lehem, thou dost all ex - cel:
2 Fair - er than the sun at morn-ing was the star that told his birth,
3 East - ern sa - ges at his cra - dle make ob - la - tions rich and rare;
4 Sa - cred gifts of mys - tic mean-ing: in - cense doth their God dis-close,
5 Je - sus, whom the Gen-tiles wor-shiped at thy glad e - piph - a - ny,

1 out of thee the Lord from hea - ven came to rule his Is - ra - el.
2 to the world its God an - nounc-ing seen in flesh - ly form on earth.
3 see them give, in deep de - vo - tion, gold and frank - in - cense and myrrh.
4 gold the King of kings pro - claim - eth, myrrh his sep - ul - cher fore-shows.
5 un - to thee, with God the Fa - ther and the Spi - rit, glo - ry be.

Words: Marcus Aurelius Clemens Prudentius (348-410?); tr. *Hymns Ancient and Modern*, 1861, alt.
Music: *Stuttgart*, melody from *Psalmodia Sacra, oder Andächtige und Schöne Gesange*, 1715;
adapt. William Henry Havergal (1793-1870); harm. K. D. Smith (b. 1928)

87. 87

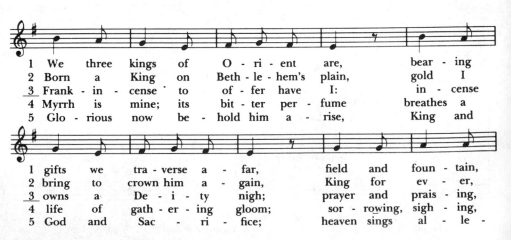

1 We three kings of O - ri - ent are, bear - ing
2 Born a King on Beth - le - hem's plain, gold I
3 Frank - in - cense to of - fer have I: in - cense
4 Myrrh is mine; its bit - ter per - fume breathes a
5 Glo - rious now be - hold him a - rise, King and

1 gifts we tra - verse a - far, field and foun - tain,
2 bring to crown him a - gain, King for ev - er,
3 owns a De - i - ty nigh; prayer and prais - ing,
4 life of gath - er - ing gloom; sor - rowing, sigh - ing,
5 God and Sac - ri - fice; heaven sings al - le -

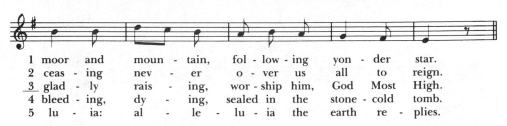

1 moor and moun - tain, fol - low - ing yon - der star.
2 ceas - ing nev - er o - ver us all to reign.
3 glad - ly rais - ing, wor - ship him, God Most High.
4 bleed - ing, dy - ing, sealed in the stone - cold tomb.
5 lu - ia: al - le - lu - ia the earth re - plies.

Refrain

O_____ star of won - der, star of night,

star with roy - al beau - ty bright; west - ward lead - ing,

still pro - ceed - ing, guide us to thy per - fect light!

Interlude

The stanzas may be sung by three soloists: 1 and 5 by the ensemble; 2-4 by individuals; and the refrain by all.

Words: John Henry Hopkins, Jr. (1820-1891), alt.
Music: *Three Kings of Orient*, John Henry Hopkins, Jr. (1820-1891)

88. 446 with Refrain

1 Christ up-on the moun-tain peak   stands a-lone in
2 Trem-bling at his feet we saw   Mo - ses and E -
3 Swift the cloud of glo - ry came.   God pro-claim-ing
4 This is God's be - lov - ed Son!   Law and pro-phets

glo - ry blaz-ing; let us, if we dare to speak,
li - jah speak-ing. All the pro-phets and the Law
in its thun-der Je - sus as his Son by name!
fade be - fore him; first and last and on - ly One,

with the saints and an - gels praise him. Al - le - lu - ia!
shout through them their joy - ful greet-ing. Al - le - lu - ia!
Na - tions cry a - loud in won - der! Al - le - lu - ia!
let cre - a - tion now a - dore him! Al - le - lu - ia!

Words: Brian A. Wren (b. 1936)
Music: *Mowsley*, Cyril Vincent Taylor (b. 1907)   78. 78 with Alleluia

1 Christ up - on the moun-tain peak   stands a - lone in glo - ry
2 Trem-bling at his feet we saw   Mo - ses and E - li - jah
3 Swift the cloud of glo - ry came.   God pro-claim-ing in its
4 This is God's be - lov - ed Son!   Law and pro-phets fade be -

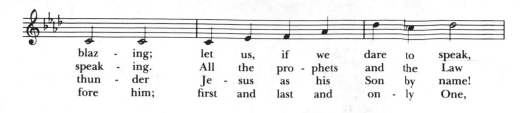

blaz - ing; let us, if we dare to speak,
speak - ing. All the pro - phets and the Law
thun - der Je - sus as his Son by name!
fore him; first and last and on - ly One,

with the saints and an - gels praise him. Al - le - lu - ia!
shout through them their joy - ful greet - ing. Al - le - lu - ia!
Na - tions cry a - loud in won - der! Al - le - lu - ia!
let cre - a - tion now a - dore him! Al - le - lu - ia!

Words: Brian A. Wren (b. 1936)
Music: *Shillingford*, Peter Cutts (b. 1937)

78. 78 with Alleluia

Epiphany

131

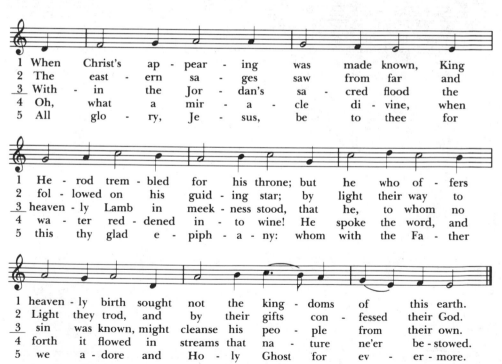

1 When Christ's ap - pear - ing was made known, King
2 The east - ern sa - ges saw from far and
3 With - in the Jor - dan's sa - cred flood the
4 Oh, what a mir - a - cle di - vine, when
5 All glo - ry, Je - sus, be to thee for

1 He - rod trem - bled for his throne; but he who of - fers
2 fol - lowed on his guid - ing star; by light their way to
3 heaven - ly Lamb in meek - ness stood, that he, to whom no
4 wa - ter red - dened in - to wine! He spoke the word, and
5 this thy glad e - piph - a - ny: whom with the Fa - ther

1 heaven - ly birth sought not the king - doms of this earth.
2 Light they trod, and by their gifts con - fessed their God.
3 sin was known, might cleanse his peo - ple from their own.
4 forth it flowed in streams that na - ture ne'er be - stowed.
5 we a - dore and Ho - ly Ghost for ev - er - more.

Words: Caelius Sedulius (5th cent.); st. 1, tr. *The Hymn Book of the Anglican Church of Canada
     and the United Church of Canada*, 1971; sts. 2-5, tr. John Mason Neale (1818-1866), alt.
Music: *Vom Himmel kam der Engel Schar*, melody source unknown

LM

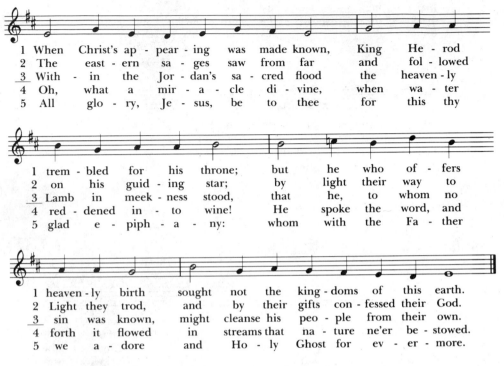

1 When Christ's ap - pear - ing was made known, King He - rod
2 The east - ern sa - ges saw from far and fol - lowed
3 With - in the Jor - dan's sa - cred flood the heaven - ly
4 Oh, what a mir - a - cle di - vine, when wa - ter
5 All glo - ry, Je - sus, be to thee for this thy

1 trem - bled for his throne; but he who of - fers
2 on his guid - ing star; by light their way to
3 Lamb in meek - ness stood, that he, to whom no
4 red - dened in - to wine! He spoke the word, and
5 glad e - piph - a - ny: whom with the Fa - ther

1 heaven - ly birth sought not the king - doms of this earth.
2 Light they trod, and by their gifts con - fessed their God.
3 sin was known, might cleanse his peo - ple from their own.
4 forth it flowed in streams that na - ture ne'er be - stowed.
5 we a - dore and Ho - ly Ghost for ev - er - more.

Words: Caelius Sedulius (5th cent.); st. 1, tr. *The Hymn Book of the Anglican Church of Canada
and the United Church of Canada*, 1971; sts. 2-5, tr. John Mason Neale (1818-1866), alt.
Music: *Erhalt uns, Herr*, melody from *Geistliche Lieder*, 1543

LM

1 O Light of Light, Love giv - en birth; Je - sus, Re -
2 Two pro - phets, who had faith to see, with your e -
3 May all who seek to praise a - right through pur - er

deem - er of the earth: more bright than day your face did
lect found com - pa - ny; the heavens a - bove your glo - ry
lives show forth your light. To you, the King of glo - ry,

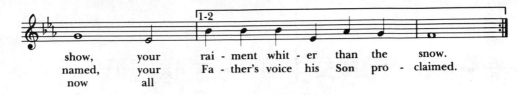

show,	your	rai	- ment	whit	- er	than	the	snow.
named,	your	Fa	- ther's	voice	his	Son	pro	- claimed.
now	all							

Final Ending

faith - ful hearts a - dor - ing bow.

Words: Latin, 10th cent.; tr. Laurence Housman (1865-1959), alt.
Music: *Elmhurst*, Cary Ratcliff (b. 1953)

LM

Epiphany

134

1 O	Light	of	Light,	Love	giv	- en	birth;
2 Two	pro	- phets,	who	had	faith	to	see,
3 May	all	who	seek	to	praise	a	- right

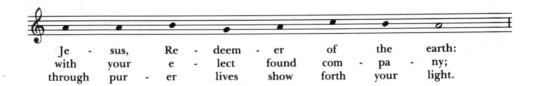

Je	- sus,	Re	- deem	- er	of	the	earth:
with	your	e	- lect	found	com	- pa	- ny;
through	pur	- er	lives	show	forth	your	light.

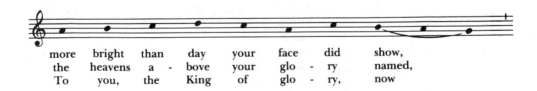

more	bright	than	day	your	face	did	show,
the	heavens	a	- bove	your	glo	- ry	named,
To	you,	the	King	of	glo	- ry,	now

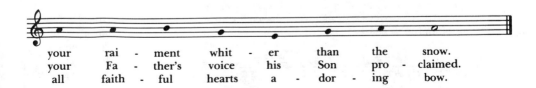

your	rai	- ment	whit	- er	than	the	snow.
your	Fa	- ther's	voice	his	Son	pro	- claimed.
all	faith	- ful	hearts	a	dor	- ing	bow.

Words: Latin, 10th cent.; tr. Laurence Housman (1865-1959), alt.
Music: *Jesu dulcis memoria*, plainsong, Mode 2

LM

1 Songs of thank-ful - ness and praise, Je - sus, Lord, to thee we raise,
2 Man - i - fest at Jor - dan's stream, Pro - phet, Priest, and King su - preme;
3 Man - i - fest in mak - ing whole pal - sied limbs and faint - ing soul;
4 Man - i - fest on moun - tain height, shin - ing in re - splen-dent light,

man - i - fest - ed by the star to the sa - ges from a - far;
and at Ca - na, wed - ding-guest, in thy God - head man - i - fest;
man - i - fest in val - iant fight, quell - ing all the dev - il's might;
where dis - ci - ples filled with awe thy trans - fi - gured glo - ry saw.

branch of roy - al Da - vid's stem in thy birth at Beth - le - hem;
man - i - fest in power di - vine, chang - ing wa - ter in - to wine;
man - i - fest in gra - cious will, ev - er bring - ing good from ill;
When from there thou led - dest them stead - fast to Je - ru - sa - lem,

an - thems be to thee ad - dressed, God in man made man - i - fest.
an - thems be to thee ad - dressed, God in man made man - i - fest.
an - thems be to thee ad - dressed, God in man made man - i - fest.
cross and Eas - ter Day at - test God in man made man - i - fest.

Words: Sts. 1-3, Christopher Wordsworth (1807-1885); st. 4, F. Bland Tucker (1895-1984)
Music: *Salzburg*, melody Jakob Hintze (1622-1702); harm. Johann Sebastian Bach (1685-1750)

77. 77. D

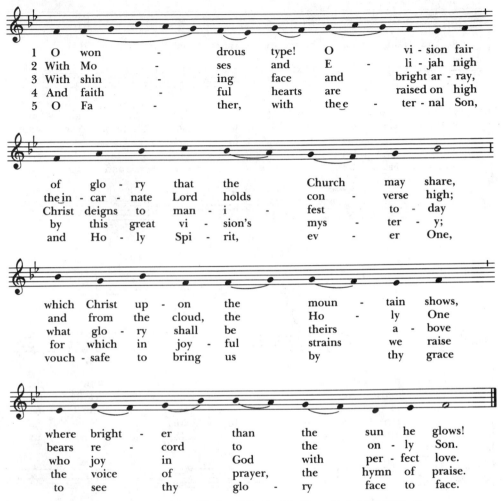

1 O won - drous type! O vi - sion fair
2 With Mo - ses and E - li - jah nigh
3 With shin - ing face and bright ar - ray,
4 And faith - ful hearts are raised on high
5 O Fa - ther, with the e - ter - nal Son,

of glo - ry that the Church may share,
the in - car - nate Lord holds con - verse high;
Christ deigns to man - i - fest to - day
by this great vi - sion's mys - ter - y;
and Ho - ly Spi - rit, ev - er One,

which Christ up - on the moun - tain shows,
and from the cloud, the Ho - ly One
what glo - ry shall be theirs a - bove
for which in joy - ful strains we raise
vouch - safe to bring us by thy grace

where bright - er than the sun he glows!
bears re - cord to the on - ly Son.
who joy in God with per - fect love.
the voice of prayer, the hymn of praise.
to see thy glo - ry face to face.

Words: Latin, 15th cent.; tr. *Hymns Ancient and Modern*, 1861, after John Mason Neale (1818-1866), alt.
Music: *Aeterne Rex altissime*, plainsong, Mode 1

LM

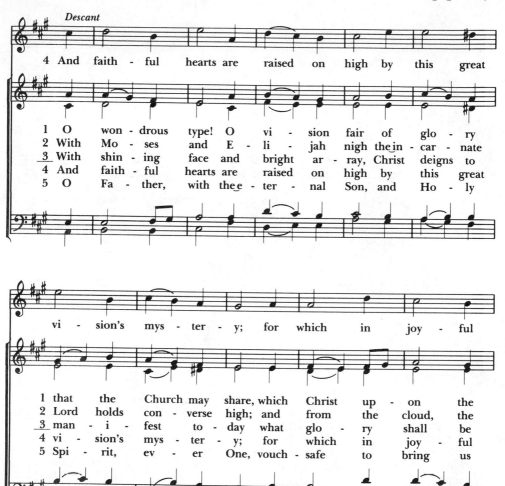

Descant

4 And faith - ful hearts are raised on high by this great

1 O won - drous type! O vi - sion fair of glo - ry
2 With Mo - ses and E - li - jah nigh the in - car - nate
3 With shin - ing face and bright ar - ray, Christ deigns to
4 And faith - ful hearts are raised on high by this great
5 O Fa - ther, with the e - ter - nal Son, and Ho - ly

1 that the Church may share, which Christ up - on the
2 Lord holds con - verse high; and from the cloud, the
3 man - i - fest to - day what glo - ry shall be
4 vi - sion's mys - ter - y; for which in joy - ful
5 Spi - rit, ev - er One, vouch - safe to bring us

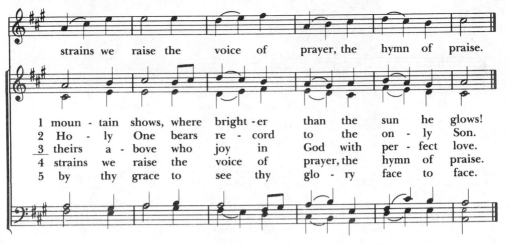

strains we raise the voice of prayer, the hymn of praise.

1 moun - tain shows, where bright - er than the sun he glows!
2 Ho - ly One bears re - cord to the on - ly Son.
3 theirs a - bove who joy in God with per - fect love.
4 strains we raise the voice of prayer, the hymn of praise.
5 by thy grace to see thy glo - ry face to face.

Words: Latin, 15th cent.; tr. *Hymns Ancient and Modern*, 1861, after John Mason Neale (1818-1866), alt.
Music: *Wareham*, melody William Knapp (1698-1768), alt.; harm. *Hymns Ancient and Modern*, 1875,
    after James Turle (1802-1882); desc. Sydney Hugo Nicholson (1875-1947)

LM

Epiphany

138

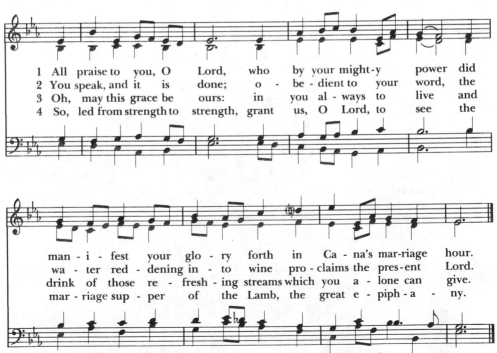

1 All praise to you, O Lord, who by your might-y power did
2 You speak, and it is done; o - be - dient to your word, the
3 Oh, may this grace be ours: in you al - ways to live and
4 So, led from strength to strength, grant us, O Lord, to see the

man - i - fest your glo - ry forth in Ca - na's mar-riage hour.
wa - ter red - dening in - to wine pro - claims the pres - ent Lord.
drink of those re - fresh - ing streams which you a - lone can give.
mar - riage sup - per of the Lamb, the great e - piph - a - ny.

Words: Hyde W. Beadon (1812-1891), alt.
Music: *Carlisle*, Charles Lockhart (1745-1815)

SM

1 When Jesus went to Jordan's stream his Father's will obeying, and was baptized by John, there came a voice from heaven saying, "This is my dear beloved Son upon whom rests my favor." And till God's will is fully done he will not bend or waver, for he is Christ the Savior.

2 The Holy Spirit then was shown, a dove on him descending; the Triune God is thus made known in Christ as love unending. He taught, he healed, he raised the dead, yet, in his great endeavor but death could hold him never. He rose, and lives for ever.

3 He came by water and by blood to heal our lost condition; he cleanses, reconciles to God, and gives the Great Commission. Then let us not heed worldly lies nor rest upon our merit, but trust in Christ who will baptize with water and the Spirit that we may life inherit.

Words: Martin Luther (1483-1546); para. F. Bland Tucker (1895-1984), rev.
Music: *Christ unser Herr zum Jordan kam*, melody from *Geystliche gesangk Buchleyn*, 1524

87. 87. 87. 877

1 Wilt thou for-give that sin, where I be - gun,
2 Wilt thou for-give that sin, by which I won
3 I have a sin of fear that when I've spun

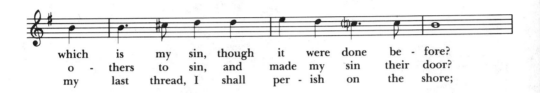

which is my sin, though it were done be - fore?
o - thers to sin, and made my sin their door?
my last thread, I shall per - ish on the shore;

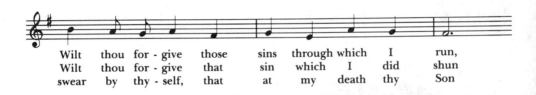

Wilt thou for-give those sins through which I run,
Wilt thou for-give that sin which I did shun
swear by thy - self, that at my death thy Son

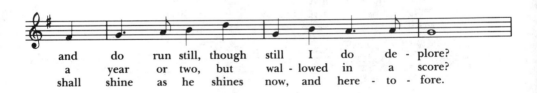

and do run still, though still I do de - plore?
a year or two, but wal - lowed in a score?
shall shine as he shines now, and here - to - fore.

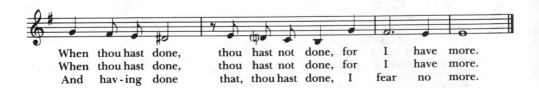

When thou hast done, thou hast not done, for I have more.
When thou hast done, thou hast not done, for I have more.
And hav - ing done that, thou hast done, I fear no more.

Words: John Donne (1573-1631)
Music: *Donne*, melody John Hilton (1599-1657), alt.

10 10. 10 10. 84

harmony

1 Wilt thou for-give that sin, where I be - gun,
2 Wilt thou for-give that sin, by which I won
3 I have a sin of fear that when I've spun

which is my sin, though it were done be - fore?
o - thers to sin, and made my sin their door?
my last thread, I shall per - ish on the shore;

Wilt thou for-give those sins through which I run,
Wilt thou for-give that sin which I did shun
swear by thy-self, that at my death thy Son

and do run still, though still I do de-plore?
a year or two, but wal - lowed in a score?
shall shine as he shines now, and here - to-fore.

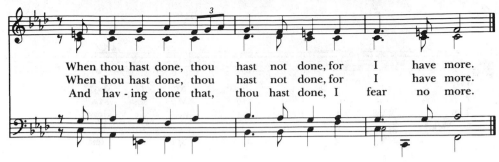

When thou hast done, thou hast not done, for I have more.
When thou hast done, thou hast not done, for I have more.
And hav - ing done that, thou hast done, I fear no more.

Words: John Donne (1573-1631)
Music: *So giebst du nun*, melody from *Geist und Lehr-reiches Kirchen und Haus Buch*, 1694;
harm. Johann Sebastian Bach (1685-1750)

10 10. 10 10. 84

Lent

142

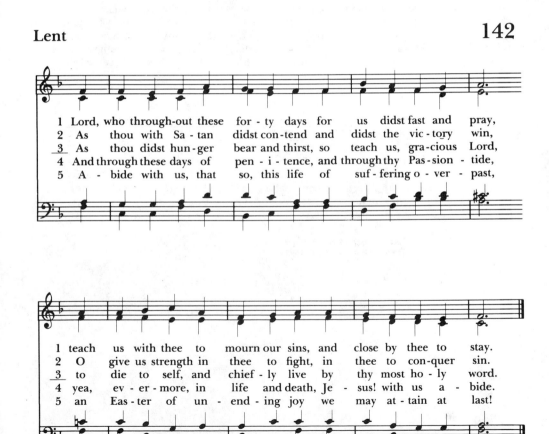

1 Lord, who through-out these for - ty days for us didst fast and pray,
2 As thou with Sa - tan didst con-tend and didst the vic - to - ry win,
3 As thou didst hun - ger bear and thirst, so teach us, gra - cious Lord,
4 And through these days of pen - i - tence, and through thy Pas - sion - tide,
5 A - bide with us, that so, this life of suf - fering o - ver - past,

1 teach us with thee to mourn our sins, and close by thee to stay.
2 O give us strength in thee to fight, in thee to con-quer sin.
3 to die to self, and chief - ly live by thy most ho - ly word.
4 yea, ev - er - more, in life and death, Je - sus! with us a - bide.
5 an Eas - ter of un - end - ing joy we may at - tain at last!

Words: Claudia Frances Hernaman (1838-1898)
Music: *St. Flavian*, melody from *Day's Psalter*, 1562; adapt. and harm. Richard Redhead (1820-1901)

CM

143

1 The glo - ry of these for - ty days we
2 A - lone and fast - ing Mo - ses saw the
3 So Dan - iel trained his mys - tic sight, de -
4 Then grant us, Lord, like them to be full
*5 O Fa - ther, Son, and Spi - rit blest, to

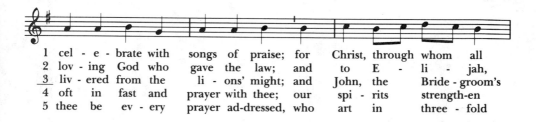

1 cel - e - brate with songs of praise; for Christ, through whom all
2 lov - ing God who gave the law; and to E - li - jah,
3 liv - ered from the li - ons' might; and John, the Bride - groom's
4 oft in fast and prayer with thee; our spi - rits strength-en
5 thee be ev - ery prayer ad-dressed, who art in three - fold

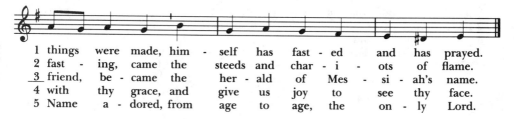

1 things were made, him - self has fast - ed and has prayed.
2 fast - ing, came the steeds and char - i - ots of flame.
3 friend, be - came the her - ald of Mes - si - ah's name.
4 with thy grace, and give us joy to see thy face.
5 Name a - dored, from age to age, the on - ly Lord.

Words: Latin, 6th cent.; tr. Maurice F. Bell (1862-1947), alt.
Music: *Erhalt uns, Herr,* melody from *Geistliche Lieder,* 1543

LM

1 Lord Je - sus, Sun of Right - eous - ness, shine
2 Give guid - ance to our wan - dering ways, for -
3 Lord, grant that we in pen - i - tence may
4 Now near - er draws the day of days when
5 The u - ni - verse your glo - ry shows, blest

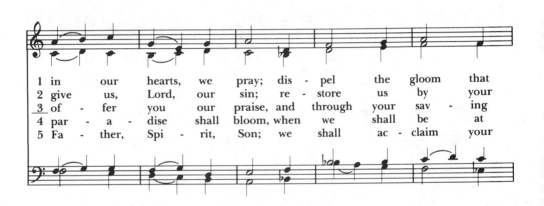

1 in our hearts, we pray; dis - pel the gloom that
2 give us, Lord, our sin; re - store us by your
3 of - fer you our praise, and through your sav - ing
4 par - a - dise shall bloom, when we shall be at
5 Fa - ther, Spi - rit, Son; we shall ac - claim your

1 shades our minds and be to us as day.
2 lov - ing care to peace and joy with - in.
3 sac - ri - fice re - ceive your gift of grace.
4 one with you, Lord, ris - en from the tomb.
5 ma - jes - ty, e - ter - nal Three in One.

Words: Latin; tr. Anne K. LeCroy (b. 1930)
Music: *Cornhill*, Harold Darke (1888-1976), alt.

CM

145

Lent

1 Now quit your care and anx - ious fear and wor - ry; for
2 To bow the head in sack-cloth and in ash - es, or
3 For is not this the fast that I have cho - sen? (The
4 For right - eous - ness and peace will show their fa - ces to
5 Then shall your light break forth as doth the morn - ing; your

1 schemes are vain and fret - ting brings no gain. Lent calls to
2 rend the soul, such grief is not Lent's goal; but to be
3 pro - phet spoke) To shat - ter ev - ery yoke, of wick - ed -
4 those who feed the hun - gry in their need, and wrongs re -
5 health shall spring, the friends you make shall bring God's glo - ry

1 prayer, to trust and ded - i - ca - tion; God brings new beau - ty
2 led to where God's glo - ry flash - es, his beau - ty to come
3 ness the griev - ous bands to loos - en, op - pres - sion put to
4 dress, who build the old waste pla - ces, and in the dark-ness
5 bright, your way through life a - dorn - ing; and love shall be the

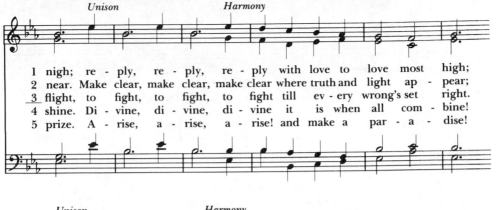

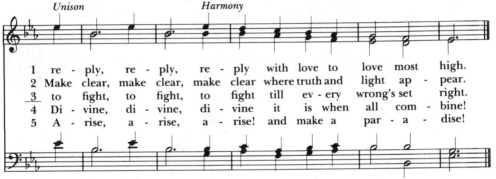

Words: Percy Dearmer (1867-1936), alt.
Music: *Quittez, Pasteurs,* French carol; harm. Martin Fallas Shaw (1875-1958)

Irr.

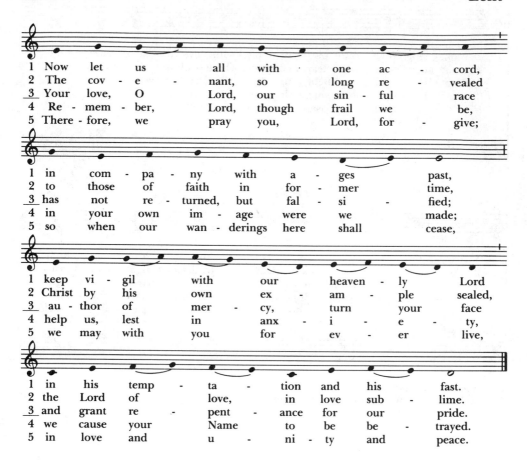

1 Now let us all with one ac - cord,
2 The cov - e - nant, so long re - vealed
3 Your love, O Lord, our sin - ful race
4 Re - mem - ber, Lord, though frail we be,
5 There - fore, we pray you, Lord, for - give;

1 in com - pa - ny with a - ges past,
2 to those of faith in for - mer time,
3 has not re - turned, but fal - si - fied;
4 in your own im - age were we made;
5 so when our wan - derings here shall cease,

1 keep vi - gil with our heaven - ly Lord
2 Christ by his own ex - am - ple sealed,
3 au - thor of mer - cy, turn your face
4 help us, lest in anx - i - e - ty,
5 we may with you for ev - er live,

1 in his temp - ta - tion and his fast.
2 the Lord of love, in love sub - lime.
3 and grant re - pent - ance for our pride.
4 we cause your Name to be be - trayed.
5 in love and u - ni - ty and peace.

Words: Att. Gregory the Great (540-604); tr. *Praise the Lord*, 1972, alt.
Music: *Ex more docti mystico*, plainsong, Mode 2, Verona MS., 12th cent.

LM

1 Now let us all with one ac - cord, in
2 The cov - e - nant, so long re - vealed to
3 Your love, O Lord, our sin - ful race has
4 Re - mem - ber, Lord, though frail we be, in
5 There - fore, we pray you, Lord, for - give; so

1 com-pa-ny with a-ges past, keep vi-gil with our
2 those of faith in for-mer time, Christ by his own ex -
3 not re-turned, but fal-si-fied; au-thor of mer-cy,
4 your own im-age were we made; help us, lest in anx -
5 when our wan-derings here shall cease, we may with you for

1 heaven-ly Lord in his temp-ta-tion and his fast.
2 am-ple sealed, the Lord of love, in love sub-lime.
3 turn your face and grant re-pent-ance for our pride.
4 i-e-ty, we cause your Name to be be-trayed.
5 ev-er live, in love and u-ni-ty and peace.

Words: Att. Gregory the Great (540-604); tr. *Praise the Lord*, 1972, alt.
Music: *Bourbon*, melody att. Freeman Lewis (1780-1859)

LM

Lent

148

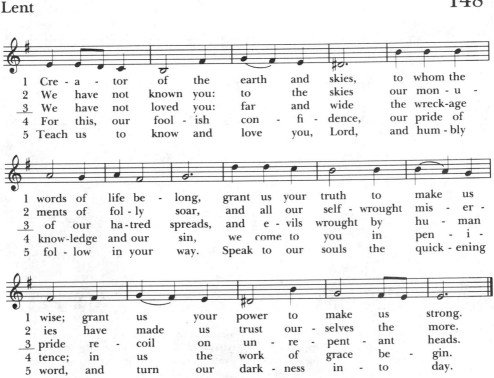

1 Cre-a-tor of the earth and skies, to whom the
2 We have not known you: to the skies our mon-u -
3 We have not loved you: far and wide the wreck-age
4 For this, our fool-ish con-fi-dence, our pride of
5 Teach us to know and love you, Lord, and hum-bly

1 words of life be-long, grant us your truth to make us
2 ments of fol-ly soar, and all our self-wrought mis-er -
3 of our ha-tred spreads, and e-vils wrought by hu-man
4 know-ledge and our sin, we come to you in pen-i -
5 fol-low in your way. Speak to our souls the quick-ening

1 wise; grant us your power to make us strong.
2 ies have made us trust our-selves the more.
3 pride re-coil on un-re-pent-ant heads.
4 tence; in us the work of grace be-gin.
5 word, and turn our dark-ness in-to day.

Words: Donald W. Hughes (1911-1967), alt.
Music: *Uffingham*, melody Jeremiah Clarke (1670-1707), alt.

LM

Unison or harmony

1 E - ter - nal Lord of love, be - hold your Church
2 So dai - ly dy - ing to the way of self,
3 If dead in you, so in you we a - rise,

walk - ing once more the pil - grim way of Lent,
so dai - ly liv - ing to your way of Lent love,
you the first - born of all the faith - ful dead;

led by your cloud by day, by night your fire,
we walk the road, Lord Je - sus, that you trod,
and as through ston - y ground the green shoots break,

moved by your love and toward your pres - ence bent:
know - ing our - selves bap - tized in - to your death:
glo - rious in spring - time dress of leaf and flower,

far off yet here— the goal of all de - sire.
so we are dead and live with you in God.
so in the Fa - ther's glo - ry shall we wake.

Words: Thomas H. Cain (b. 1931)
Music: *Old 124th*, melody *Pseaumes octante trois de David*, 1551;
  harm. Charles Winfred Douglas (1867-1944)

10 10. 10 10 10

Lent

150

1 For - ty days and for - ty nights thou wast fast - ing in the wild;
2 Should not we thy sor - row share and from world-ly joys ab - stain,
3 Then if Sa - tan on us press, Je - sus, Sa - vior, hear our call!
4 So shall we have peace di - vine: ho - lier glad-ness ours shall be;
5 Keep, O keep us, Sa - vior dear, ev - er con-stant by thy side;

1 for - ty days and for - ty nights tempt - ed, and yet un - de - filed.
2 fast - ing with un - ceas - ing prayer, strong with thee to suf - fer pain?
3 Vic - tor in the wil - der - ness, grant we may not faint nor fall!
4 round us, too, shall an - gels shine, such as min - is - tered to thee.
5 that with thee we may ap - pear at the e - ter - nal Eas - ter - tide.

Words: George Hunt Smyttan (1822-1870), alt.
Music: *Aus der Tiefe rufe ich*, melody att. Martin Herbst (1654-1681), alt.;
  harm. William Henry Monk (1823-1889)

77. 77

1 From deep-est woe I cry to thee; Lord, hear me, I im-
2 Thou grant-est par-don through thy love; thy grace a - lone a-
3 And thus my hope is in the Lord, and not in my own

plore thee! Bend down thy gra - cious ear to me;
vail - eth. Our works could ne'er our guilt re - move;
mer - it; I rest up - on his faith - ful word

I lay my sins be - fore thee.
yea, e'en the sins best life fail - eth.
to them of con - trite spi - rit.

If thou re - mem - ber-est ev - ery sin,
For none may boast them - selves of aught,
That he is mer - ci - ful and just,

if nought but just re - ward we win,
but must con - fess thy grace hath wrought
here is my com - fort and my trust;

could we a - bide thy pres - ence?
what - e'er in them is wor - thy.
his help I wait with pa - tience.

Words: Martin Luther (1483-1546); tr. Catherine Winkworth (1827-1878), alt.; based on Psalm 130
Music: *Aus tiefer Not,* melody att. Martin Luther (1483-1546)

87. 87. 887

1 Kind Ma-ker of the world, O hear the fer-vent
2 Each heart is man-i-fest to thee; thou know-est
3 Spare us, O Lord, who now con-fess our sins and
4 Give us the dis-ci-pline that springs from ab-sti-
5 Grant, O thou bless-ed Trin-i-ty; grant, O un-

1 prayer, with man-y a tear poured forth by all the
2 our in-fir-mi-ty; now we re-pent, and
3 all our wick-ed-ness, and, for the glo-ry
4 nence in out-ward things with in-ward fast-ing,
5 chang-ing U-ni-ty; that this our fast of

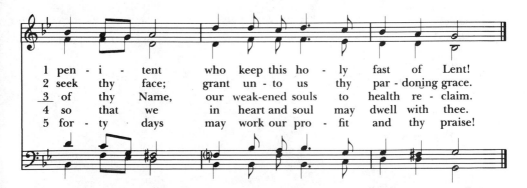

1 pen-i-tent who keep this ho-ly fast of Lent!
2 seek thy face; grant un-to us thy par-don-ing grace.
3 of thy Name, our weak-ened souls to health re-claim.
4 so that we in heart and soul may dwell with thee.
5 for-ty days may work our pro-fit and thy praise!

Words: Att. Gregory the Great (540-604); ver. *Hymnal 1940*, alt.
Music: *A la venue de Noël*, melody from *Fleurs des noëls*, 1535

LM

Opening Anthem

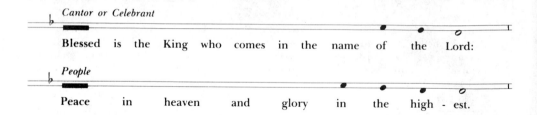

Cantor or Celebrant

Blessed is the King who comes in the name of the Lord:

People

Peace in heaven and glory in the high - est.

Blessing over the Branches

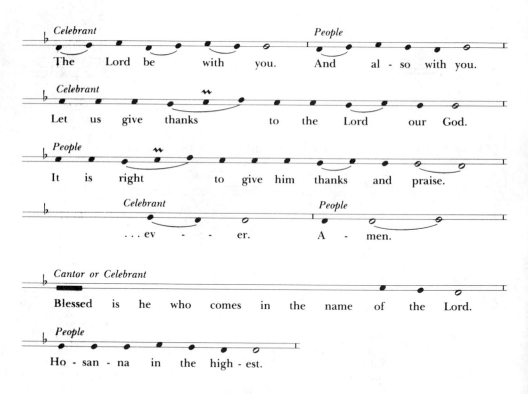

Celebrant   *People*

The Lord be with you. And al - so with you.

Celebrant

Let us give thanks to the Lord our God.

People

It is right to give him thanks and praise.

Celebrant   *People*

... ev - - er. A - men.

Cantor or Celebrant

Blessed is he who comes in the name of the Lord.

People

Ho - san - na in the high - est.

At the Procession

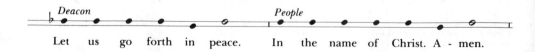

Deacon   *People*

Let us go forth in peace. In the name of Christ. A - men.

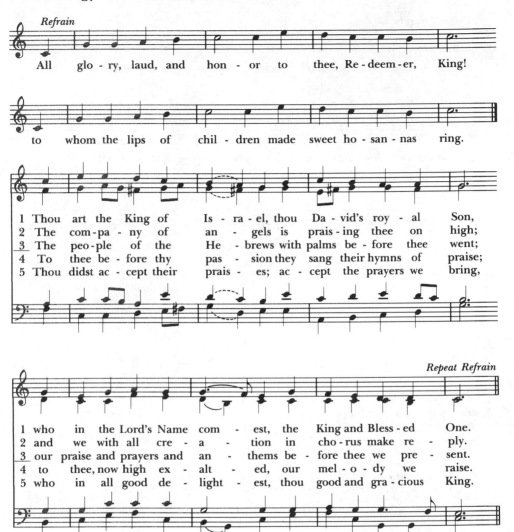

All glo-ry, laud, and hon-or to thee, Re-deem-er, King!
to whom the lips of chil-dren made sweet ho-san-nas ring.

1 Thou art the King of Is-ra-el, thou Da-vid's roy-al Son,
2 The com-pa-ny of an-gels is prais-ing thee on high;
3 The peo-ple of the He-brews with palms be-fore thee went;
4 To thee be-fore thy pas-sion they sang their hymns of praise;
5 Thou didst ac-cept their prais-es; ac-cept the prayers we bring,

Repeat Refrain

1 who in the Lord's Name com-est, the King and Bless-ed One.
2 and we with all cre-a-tion in cho-rus make re-ply.
3 our praise and prayers and an-thems be-fore thee we pre-sent.
4 to thee, now high ex-alt-ed, our mel-o-dy we raise.
5 who in all good de-light-est, thou good and gra-cious King.

The stanzas may be sung by choir alone or alternately by contrasted groups; all sing the refrain.

Words: Theodulph of Orleans (d. 821); tr. John Mason Neale (1818-1866), alt.
Music: *Valet will ich dir geben*, melody Melchior Teschner (1584-1635), alt.;
    harm. Wiliam Henry Monk (1823-1889)

76. 76. D

Refrain (sung by all)

All glo-ry, laud, and hon-or to thee, Re-deem-er, King!

to whom the lips of chil-dren made sweet ho-san-nas ring.

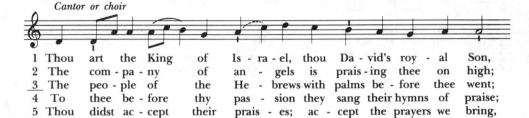

Cantor or choir

1 Thou art the King of Is-ra-el, thou Da-vid's roy-al Son,
2 The com-pa-ny of an-gels is prais-ing thee on high;
3 The peo-ple of the He-brews with palms be-fore thee went;
4 To thee be-fore thy pas-sion they sang their hymns of praise;
5 Thou didst ac-cept their prais-es; ac-cept the prayers we bring,

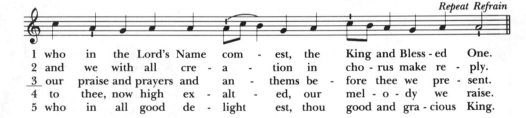

Repeat Refrain

1 who in the Lord's Name com-est, the King and Bless-ed One.
2 and we with all cre-a-tion in cho-rus make re-ply.
3 our praise and prayers and an-thems be-fore thee we pre-sent.
4 to thee, now high ex-alt-ed, our mel-o-dy we raise.
5 who in all good de-light-est, thou good and gra-cious King.

Words: Theodulph of Orleans (d. 821); tr. John Mason Neale (1818-1866), alt.
Music: *Gloria, laus, et honor*, plainsong, Mode 1, Einsiedeln MS. and St. Gall MS., 10th cent.;
　　　ver. Schola Antiqua, 1983　　　　　　　　　　　　　76. 76 with Refrain
Music: Melody rhythmic version © 1984, Schola Antiqua Inc. Used by permission.

1 Ride on! ride on in ma-jes-ty! Hark! all the
2 Ride on! ride on in ma-jes-ty! In low-ly
3 Ride on! ride on in ma-jes-ty! The an-gel
4 Ride on! ride on in ma-jes-ty! Thy last and
5 Ride on! ride on in ma-jes-ty! In low-ly

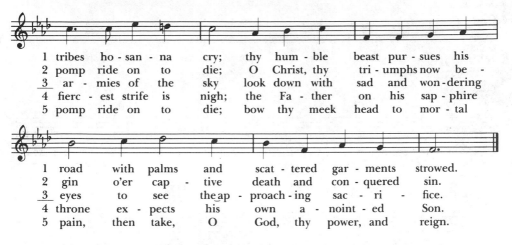

1	tribes	ho - san - na	cry;	thy	hum - ble	beast	pur - sues	his
2	pomp	ride on to	die;	O	Christ, thy	tri - umphs	now	be -
3	ar -	mies of the	sky	look	down with	sad	and	won-dering
4	fierc -	est strife is	nigh;	the	Fa - ther	on	his	sap - phire
5	pomp	ride on to	die;	bow	thy meek	head	to	mor - tal

1	road	with	palms	and	scat - tered	gar - ments	strowed.
2	gin	o'er	cap -	tive	death and	con - quered	sin.
3	eyes	to	see	the ap -	proach - ing	sac - ri -	fice.
4	throne	ex -	pects	his	own a -	noint - ed	Son.
5	pain,	then	take,	O	God, thy	power, and	reign.

Words: Henry Hart Milman (1791-1868), alt.
Music: *The King's Majesty*, Graham George (b. 1912)

LM

The Liturgy of the Palms: Processional 157

Antiphon (at the beginning)

Ho - san - na in the high - est. Bless - ed is he who comes

in the name of the Lord. Ho - san - na in the high-est.

(The phrase "Hosanna in the highest" may be repeated as a Refrain after each verse.)

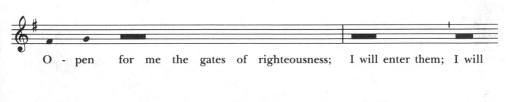

O - pen for me the gates of righteousness; I will enter them; I will

offer thanks to the Lord. [R] "This is the gate of the Lord; he who is righteous

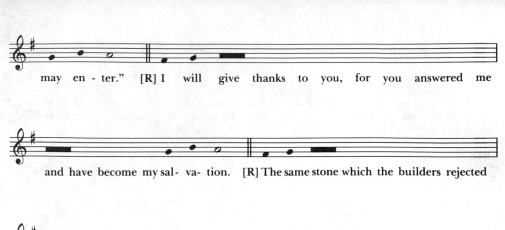

may en - ter." [R] I will give thanks to you, for you answered me

and have become my sal- va- tion. [R] The same stone which the builders rejected

has become the chief cor-ner-stone. [R] This is the Lord's doing, and it is

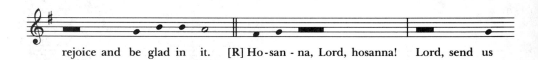

marve - lous in our eyes. [R] On this day the Lord has acted; we will

rejoice and be glad in it. [R] Ho-san - na, Lord, hosanna! Lord, send us

now suc-cess. [R] Bless-ed is he who comes in the name of the Lord; we bless you

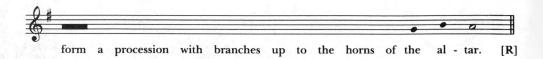

from the house of the Lord. [R] God is the Lord; he has shined upon us;

form a procession with branches up to the horns of the al - tar. [R]

"You are my God, and I will thank you; you are my God, and I will ex-alt you." [R]

Give thanks to the Lord, for he is good; his mercy endures for ev - er. [R]

Antiphon (at the end)

Ho - san - na in the high - est. Bless - ed is he who comes

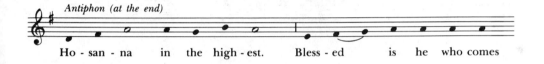

in the name of the Lord. Ho - san - na in the high - est.

Words: Psalm 118:19-29
Music: Ancient Gallican chant; adapt. Howard E. Galley (b. 1929)

1 Ah, ho-ly Je-sus, how hast thou of-fend-ed, that man to judge thee hath in hate pre-tend-ed? By foes de-rid-ed, by thine own re-ject-ed, O most af-flict-ed.

2 Who was the guilt-y? Who brought this up-on thee? A-las, my trea-son, Je-sus, hath un-done thee. 'Twas I, Lord Je-sus, I it was de-nied thee: I cru-ci-fied thee.

3 Lo, the Good Shep-herd for the sheep is of-fered; the slave hath sin-ned, and the Son hath suf-fered; for our a-tone-ment, while we noth-ing heed-ed, God in-ter-ced-ed.

4 For me, kind Je-sus, was thy in-car-na-tion, thy mor-tal sor-row, and thy life's ob-la-tion; thy death of an-guish and thy bit-ter pas-sion, for my sal-va-tion.

5 There-fore, kind Je-sus, since I can-not pay thee, I do a-dore thee, and will ev-er pray thee, think on thy pi-ty and thy love un-swerv-ing, not my de-serv-ing.

Words: Johann Heermann (1585-1647); tr. Robert Seymour Bridges (1844-1930)
Music: *Herzliebster Jesu*, Johann Cruger (1598-1662), alt.

11 11. 11 5

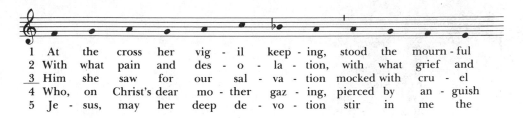

1 At the cross her vig - il keep - ing, stood the mourn - ful
2 With what pain and des - o - la - tion, with what grief and
3 Him she saw for our sal - va - tion mocked with cru - el
4 Who, on Christ's dear mo - ther gaz - ing, pierced by an - guish
5 Je - sus, may her deep de - vo - tion stir in me the

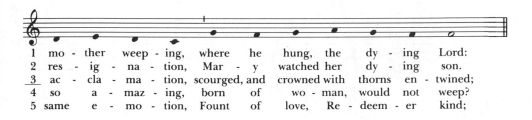

1 mo - ther weep - ing, where he hung, the dy - ing Lord:
2 res - ig - na - tion, Mar - y watched her dy - ing son.
3 ac - cla - ma - tion, scourged, and crowned with thorns en - twined;
4 so a - maz - ing, born of wo - man, would not weep?
5 same e - mo - tion, Fount of love, Re - deem - er kind;

1 there she wait - ed in her an - guish, see - ing Christ in
2 Deep the woe of her af - flic - tion, when she saw the
3 saw him then from judg - ment tak - en, and in death by
4 Who, on Christ's dear mo - ther think - ing, such a cup of
5 that my heart fresh ar - dor gain - ing, and a pur - er

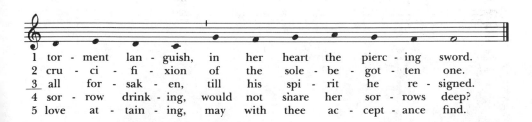

1 tor - ment lan - guish, in her heart the pierc - ing sword.
2 cru - ci - fi - xion of the sole - be - got - ten one.
3 all for - sak - en, till his spi - rit he re - signed.
4 sor - row drink - ing, would not share her sor - rows deep?
5 love at - tain - ing, may with thee ac - cept - ance find.

Words: Latin, 13th cent.; ver. *Hymnal 1982*
Music: *Stabat Mater dolorosa*, melody from *Maintzisch Gesangbuch*, 1661

1 Cross of Je - sus, cross of sor - row, where the
2 Here the King of all the a - ges, throned in
3 O mys - ter - ious con - de - scend - ing! O a -
4 Cross of Je - sus, cross of sor - row, where the

blood of Christ was shed, per - fect Man on
light ere worlds could be, robed in mor - tal
ban - don - ment sub - lime! Ve - ry God him -
blood of Christ was shed, per - fect Man on

thee did suf - fer, per - fect God on thee has bled!
flesh is dy - ing, cru - ci - fied by sin for me.
self is bear - ing all the suf - fer - ings of time!
thee did suf - fer, per - fect God on thee has bled!

Words: William J. Sparrow-Simpson (1860-1952)
Music: *Cross of Jesus*, John Stainer (1840-1901)

87. 87

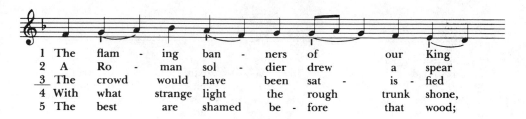

1 The flam - ing ban - ners of our King
2 A Ro - man sol - dier drew a spear
3 The crowd would have been sat - is - fied
4 With what strange light the rough trunk shone,
5 The best are shamed be - fore that wood;

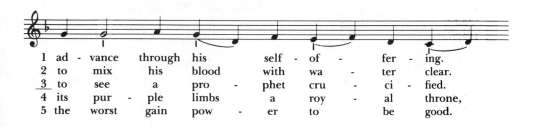

1 ad - vance through his self - of - fer - ing.
2 to mix his blood with wa - ter clear.
3 to see a pro - phet cru - ci - fied.
4 its pur - ple limbs a roy - al throne,
5 the worst gain pow - er to be good.

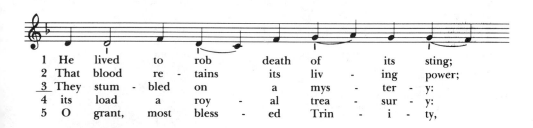

1 He lived to rob death of its sting;
2 That blood re - tains its liv - ing power;
3 They stum - bled on a mys - ter - y:
4 its load a roy - al trea - sur - y:
5 O grant, most bless - ed Trin - i - ty,

1 he died e - ter - nal life to bring.
2 the wa - ter cleans - es to this hour.
3 Mes - si - ah reign - ing from a tree.
4 the ran - som of a world set free.
5 that all may share the vic - to - ry.

Words: Venantius Honorius Fortunatus (540?-600?); para. John Webster Grant (b. 1919)
Music: *Vexilla Regis prodeunt,* plainsong, Mode 1, Rome MS., 12th cent.;
    ver. Schola Antiqua, 1983
Music: Melody rhythmic version © 1984, Schola Antiqua Inc. Used by permission.

LM

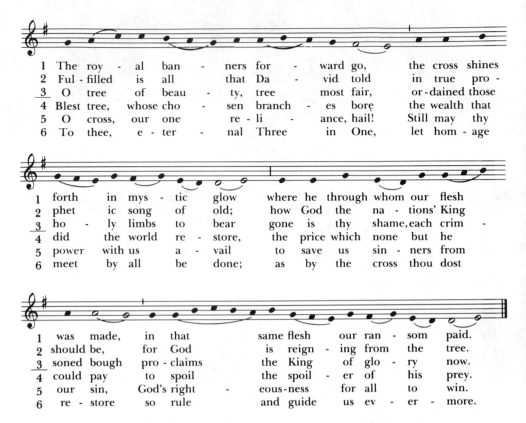

1 The roy-al ban-ners for-ward go, the cross shines
2 Ful-filled is all that Da-vid told in true pro-
3 O tree of beau-ty, tree most fair, or-dained those
4 Blest tree, whose cho-sen branch-es bore the wealth that
5 O cross, our one re-li-ance, hail! Still may thy
6 To thee, e-ter-nal Three in One, let hom-age

1 forth in mys-tic glow where he through whom our flesh
2 phet-ic song of old; how God the na-tions' King
3 ho-ly limbs to bear gone is thy shame, each crim-
4 did the world re-store, the price which none but he
5 power with us a-vail to save us sin-ners from
6 meet by all be done; as by the cross thou dost

1 was made, in that same flesh our ran-som paid.
2 should be, for God is reign-ing from the tree.
3 soned bough pro-claims the King of glo-ry now.
4 could pay to spoil the spoil-er of his prey.
5 our sin, God's right-eous-ness for all to win.
6 re-store so rule and guide us ev-er-more.

Words: Venantius Honorius Fortunatus (540?-600?); ver. *Hymnal 1982*
Music: *Vexilla Regis prodeunt*, plainsong, Mode 1, Rome MS., 12th cent.   LM

1 Sun-set to sun-rise chang-es now, for
2 E'en though the sun with-holds its light, lo!
3 Here in o'er-whelm-ing fi-nal strife the

1 God doth make his world a-new; on the Re-deem-er's
2 a more heaven-ly lamp shines here, and from the cross on
3 Lord of life hath vic-to-ry, and sin is slain, and

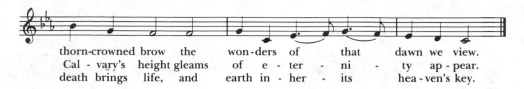

thorn-crowned brow the won-ders of that dawn we view.
Cal - vary's height gleams of e - ter - ni - ty ap - pear.
death brings life, and earth in - her - its hea - ven's key.

Words: Clement of Alexandria (170?-220?); para. Howard Chandler Robbins (1876-1952), alt.
Music: *Kedron*, melody att. Elkanah Kelsay Dare (1782-1826)   LM

Holy Week   164

1 A - lone thou go - est forth, O Lord, in
2 Our sins, not thine, thou bear - est, Lord; make
3 This is earth's dark - est hour, but thou dost
4 Grant us with thee to suf - fer pain that,

sac - ri - fice to die; is this thy sor - row
us thy sor - row feel, till through our pit - y
light and life re - store; then let all praise be
as we share this hour, thy cross may bring us

nought to us who pass un - heed - ing by?
and our shame love an - swers love's ap - peal.
giv - en thee who liv - est ev - er - more.
to thy joy and re - sur - rec - tion power.

Words: Peter Abelard (1079-1142); tr. F. Bland Tucker (1895-1984)
Music: *Bangor*, from *A Compleat Melody or Harmony of Zion*, 1734   CM

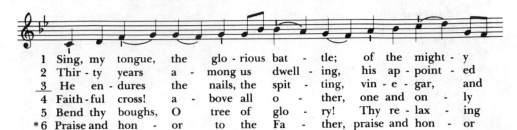

1 Sing, my tongue, the glo-rious bat - tle; of the might-y
2 Thir-ty years a - mong us dwell - ing, his ap-point-ed
3 He en-dures the nails, the spit - ting, vin-e-gar, and
4 Faith-ful cross! a - bove all o - ther, one and on - ly
5 Bend thy boughs, O tree of glo-ry! Thy re-lax - ing
*6 Praise and hon - or to the Fa - ther, praise and hon - or

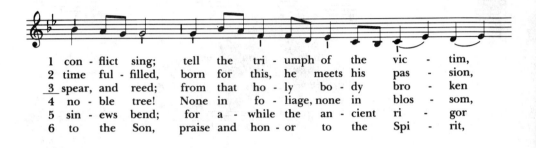

1 con - flict sing; tell the tri - umph of the vic - tim,
2 time ful - filled, born for this, he meets his pas - sion,
3 spear, and reed; from that ho - ly bo - dy bro - ken
4 no - ble tree! None in fo - liage, none in blos - som,
5 sin - ews bend; for a - while the an - cient ri - gor
6 to the Son, praise and hon - or to the Spi - rit,

1 to his cross thy tri - bute bring. Je - sus Christ, the
2 this the Sa - vior free - ly willed: on the cross the
3 blood and wa - ter forth pro - ceed: earth, and stars, and
4 none in fruit thy peer may be: sweet - est wood and
5 that thy birth be - stowed, sus - pend; and the King of
6 ev - er Three and ev - er One: one in might and

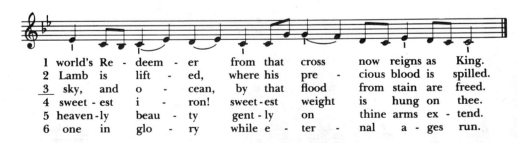

1 world's Re - deem - er from that cross now reigns as King.
2 Lamb is lift - ed, where his pre - cious blood is spilled.
3 sky, and o - cean, by that flood from stain are freed.
4 sweet - est i - ron! sweet-est weight is hung on thee.
5 heaven-ly beau - ty gent - ly on thine arms ex - tend.
6 one in glo - ry while e - ter - nal a - ges run.

Words: Venantius Honorius Fortunatus (540?-600?); ver. *Hymnal 1982*, after John Mason Neale (1818-1866)
Music: *Pange lingua*, plainsong, Mode 1, St. Gall MS., 10th cent.; ver. Schola Antiqua, 1983
87. 87. 87

Music: Melody rhythmic version © 1984, Schola Antiqua Inc. Used by permission.

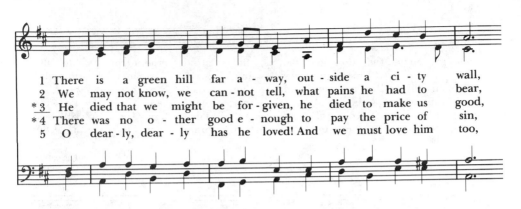

167

1 There is a green hill far a - way, out - side a ci - ty wall,
2 We may not know, we can - not tell, what pains he had to bear,
*3 He died that we might be for - given, he died to make us good,
*4 There was no o - ther good e - nough to pay the price of sin,
5 O dear - ly, dear - ly has he loved! And we must love him too,

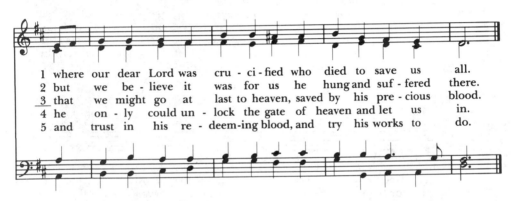

1 where our dear Lord was cru - ci - fied who died to save us all.
2 but we be - lieve it was for us he hung and suf - fered there.
3 that we might go at last to heaven, saved by his pre - cious blood.
4 he on - ly could un - lock the gate of heaven and let us in.
5 and trust in his re - deem - ing blood, and try his works to do.

Words: Cecil Frances Alexander (1818-1895), alt.
Music: *Horsley*, William Horsley (1774-1858)

CM

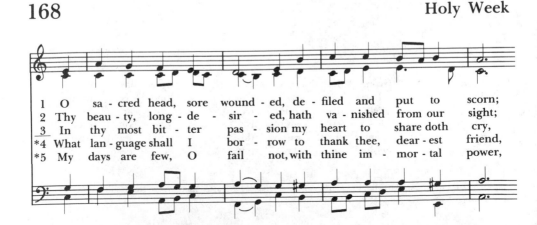

168

1 O sa - cred head, sore wound - ed, de - filed and put to scorn;
2 Thy beau - ty, long - de - sir - ed, hath va - nished from our sight;
3 In thy most bit - ter pas - sion my heart to share doth cry,
*4 What lan - guage shall I bor - row to thank thee, dear - est friend,
*5 My days are few, O fail not, with thine im - mor - tal power,

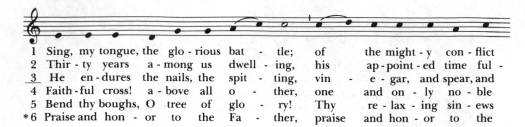

```
1 Sing, my tongue, the glo - rious bat - tle;  of   the might - y con - flict
2 Thir - ty years a - mong us dwell - ing,  his  ap - point - ed time ful -
3 He en - dures the nails, the spit - ting,  vin - e - gar, and spear, and
4 Faith - ful cross! a - bove all o - ther,  one  and on - ly no - ble
5 Bend thy boughs, O tree of glo - ry!  Thy  re - lax - ing sin - ews
*6 Praise and hon - or to the Fa - ther,  praise and hon - or to the
```

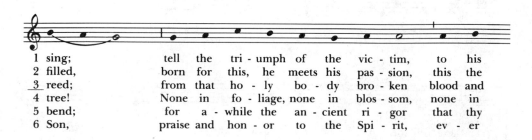

```
1 sing;         tell the tri - umph of the vic - tim,  to his
2 filled,        born for this, he meets his pas - sion, this the
3 reed;         from that ho - ly bo - dy bro - ken blood and
4 tree!         None in fo - liage, none in blos - som, none in
5 bend;         for a - while the an - cient ri - gor  that thy
6 Son,         praise and hon - or to the Spi - rit,  ev - er
```

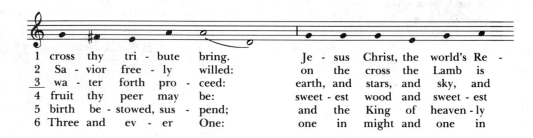

```
1 cross thy tri - bute bring.   Je - sus Christ, the world's Re -
2 Sa - vior free - ly willed:   on  the cross the Lamb is
3 wa - ter forth pro - ceed:   earth, and stars, and sky, and
4 fruit thy peer may be:   sweet - est wood and sweet - est
5 birth be - stowed, sus - pend;   and the King of heaven - ly
6 Three and ev - er One:   one  in might and one in
```

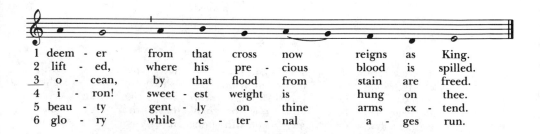

```
1 deem - er   from that cross now   reigns as King.
2 lift - ed,   where his pre - cious   blood is spilled.
3 o - cean,   by that flood from   stain are freed.
4 i - ron!   sweet - est weight is   hung on thee.
5 beau - ty   gent - ly on thine   arms ex - tend.
6 glo - ry   while e - ter - nal   a - ges run.
```

Words: Venantius Honorius Fortunatus (540?-600?); ver. *Hymnal 1982*, after John Mason Neale (1818-1866)
Music: *Pange lingua*, plainsong, Mode 3, Sarum Melody

87. 87

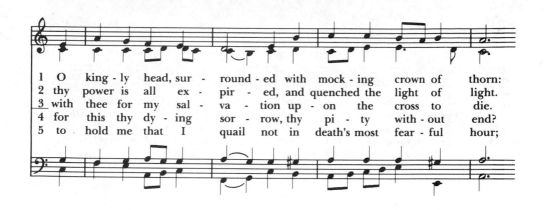

1 O king-ly head, sur - round-ed with mock-ing crown of thorn:
2 thy power is all ex - pir - ed, and quenched the light of light.
3 with thee for my sal - va - tion up - on the cross to die.
4 for this thy dy - ing sor - row, thy pi - ty with - out end?
5 to hold me that I quail not in death's most fear - ful hour;

1 what sor - row mars thy gran - deur? Can death thy bloom de - flower?
2 Ah me! for whom thou di - est, hide not so far thy grace:
3 Ah, keep my heart thus mov - ed to stand thy cross be - neath,
4 Oh, make me thine for ev - er! and should I faint - ing be,
5 that I may fight be - friend - ed, and see in my last strife

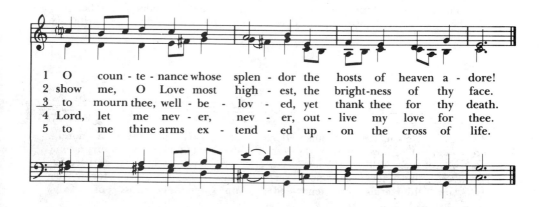

1 O coun - te-nance whose splen - dor the hosts of heaven a - dore!
2 show me, O Love most high - est, the bright-ness of thy face.
3 to mourn thee, well - be - lov - ed, yet thank thee for thy death.
4 Lord, let me nev - er, nev - er, out - live my love for thee.
5 to me thine arms ex - tend - ed up - on the cross of life.

Words: Paul Gerhardt (1607-1676); sts. 1-3 and 5, tr. Robert Seymour Bridges (1844-1930);
st. 4, tr. James Waddell Alexander (1804-1859), alt.
Music: *Herzlich tut mich verlangen* [Passion Chorale], Hans Leo Hassler (1564-1612);
adapt. and harm. Johann Sebastian Bach (1685-1750)

76. 76. D

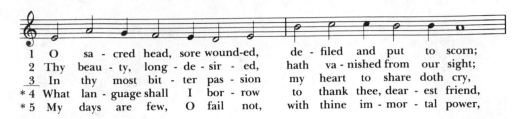

1 O sa - cred head, sore wound-ed,   de - filed and put to scorn;
2 Thy beau - ty, long - de - sir - ed,   hath va - nished from our sight;
3 In thy most bit - ter pas - sion   my heart to share doth cry,
* 4 What lan - guage shall I bor - row   to thank thee, dear - est friend,
* 5 My days are few, O fail not,   with thine im - mor - tal power,

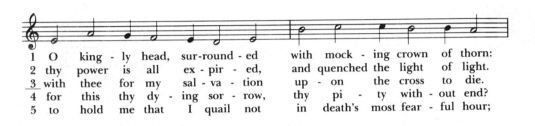

1 O king - ly head, sur-round - ed   with mock - ing crown of thorn:
2 thy power is all ex - pir - ed,   and quenched the light of light.
3 with thee for my sal - va - tion   up - on the cross to die.
4 for this thy dy - ing sor - row,   thy pi - ty with - out end?
5 to hold me that I quail not   in death's most fear - ful hour;

1 what sor - row mars thy gran - deur? Can death thy bloom de - flower?
2 Ah me! for whom thou di - est, hide not so far thy grace:
3 Ah, keep my heart thus mov - ed to stand thy cross be - neath,
4 Oh, make me thine for - ev - er! and should I faint-ing be,
5 that I may fight be - friend - ed, and see in my last strife

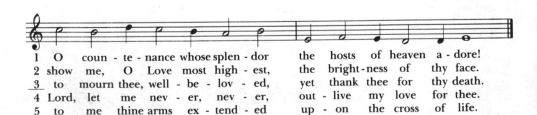

1 O coun - te - nance whose splen - dor   the hosts of heaven a - dore!
2 show me, O Love most high - est,   the bright-ness of thy face.
3 to mourn thee, well - be - lov - ed,   yet thank thee for thy death.
4 Lord, let me nev - er, nev - er,   out - live my love for thee.
5 to me thine arms ex - tend - ed   up - on the cross of life.

Words: Paul Gerhardt (1607-1676); sts. 1-3 and 5, tr. Robert Seymour Bridges (1844-1930);
     st. 4, tr. James Waddell Alexander (1804-1859), alt.
Music: *Herzlich tut mich verlangen,* Hans Leo Hassler (1564-1612)   76. 76. D

1 To mock your reign, O dear-est Lord, they made a crown of thorns;
2 In mock ac-claim, O gra-cious Lord, they snatched a pur-ple cloak,
3 A scep-tered reed, O pa-tient Lord, they thrust in-to your hand,

set you with taunts a-long that road from which no one re-turns.
your pas-sion turned, for all they cared, in-to a sol-dier's joke.
and act-ed out their grim cha-rade to its ap-point-ed end.

They did not know, as we do now, that glo-rious is your crown;
They did not know, as we do now, that though we mer-it blame
They did not know, as we do now, though em-pires rise and fall,

that thorns would flower up-on your brow, your sor-rows heal our own.
you will your robe of mer-cy throw a-round our na-ked shame.
your King-dom shall not cease to grow till love em-bra-ces all.

*The bracketed notes are to be treated as triplet groups.

Words: F. Pratt Green (b. 1903), alt.
Music: *The Third Tune*, Thomas Tallis (1505?-1585); ed. John Wilson (b. 1905)   CMD
Words: Copyright © 1973 by Hope Publishing Company. All Rights Reserved. Used by Permission.

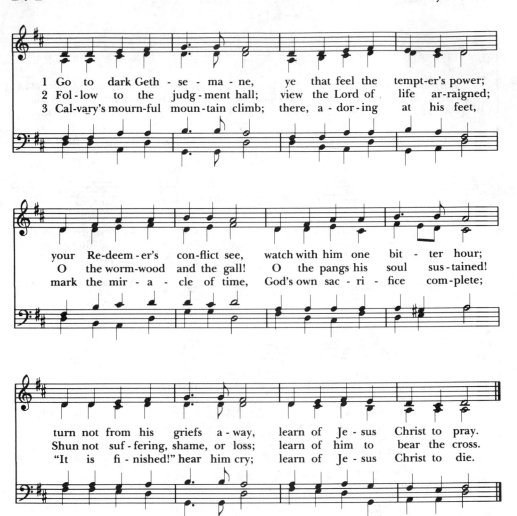

1 Go to dark Geth - se - ma - ne, ye that feel the tempt-er's power;
2 Fol - low to the judg - ment hall; view the Lord of life ar-raigned;
3 Cal-vary's mourn-ful moun-tain climb; there, a - dor - ing at his feet,

your Re-deem - er's con-flict see, watch with him one bit - ter hour;
O the worm-wood and the gall! O the pangs his soul sus-tained!
mark the mir - a - cle of time, God's own sac - ri - fice com-plete;

turn not from his griefs a - way, learn of Je - sus Christ to pray.
Shun not suf - fering, shame, or loss; learn of him to bear the cross.
"It is fi - nished!" hear him cry; learn of Je - sus Christ to die.

Words: James Montgomery (1771-1854)
Music: *Petra*, Richard Redhead (1820-1901)

77. 77. 77

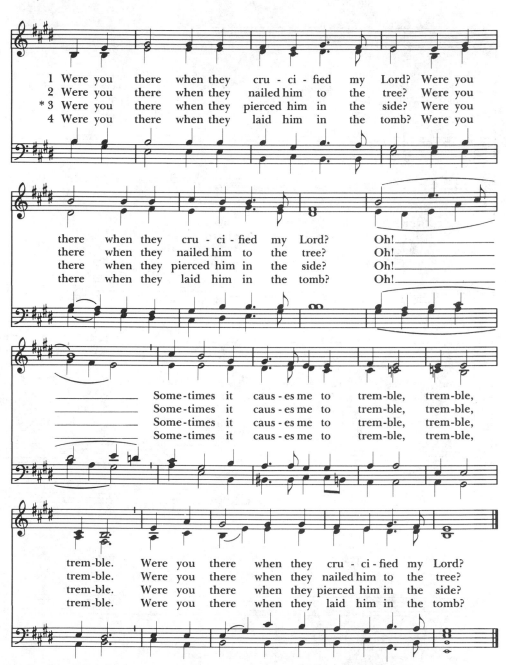

1 Were you there when they cru - ci - fied my Lord? Were you
2 Were you there when they nailed him to the tree? Were you
*3 Were you there when they pierced him in the side? Were you
4 Were you there when they laid him in the tomb? Were you

there when they cru - ci - fied my Lord? Oh!
there when they nailed him to the tree? Oh!
there when they pierced him in the side? Oh!
there when they laid him in the tomb? Oh!

Some - times it caus - es me to trem - ble, trem - ble,
Some - times it caus - es me to trem - ble, trem - ble,
Some - times it caus - es me to trem - ble, trem - ble,
Some - times it caus - es me to trem - ble, trem - ble,

trem - ble. Were you there when they cru - ci - fied my Lord?
trem - ble. Were you there when they nailed him to the tree?
trem - ble. Were you there when they pierced him in the side?
trem - ble. Were you there when they laid him in the tomb?

Words: Afro-American spiritual
Music: *Were You There*, Afro-American spiritual; harm. Charles Winfred Douglas (1867-1944)

Irr.

1 O sorrow deep! Who would not weep
2 The Paschal Lamb, like I-saac's ram,
3 Blest shall they be e-ter-nal-ly
4 O Je-sus blest, my help and rest,

with heart-felt pain and sigh-ing!
in blood was of-fered for us,
who pon-der in their weep-ing
with tears I pray thee, hear me:

slightly slower

God the Fa-ther's on-ly Son
pour-ing out his life that he
that the glo-rious Prince of Life
now, and e-ven un-to death,

in the tomb is ly-ing.
might to life re-store us.
should in death be sleep-ing.
dear-est Lord, be near me.

Words: St. 1, Friedrich von Spee (1591-1635); tr. Charles Winfred Douglas (1867-1944).
St. 2-3, James Waring McCrady (b. 1938). St. 4, Johann Rist (1607-1667);
tr. Charles Winfred Douglas (1867-1944)
Music: *O Traurigkeit*, melody and bass *Himlischer Lieder*, 1641, alt.; harm. *Hymnal 1982*

447. 76

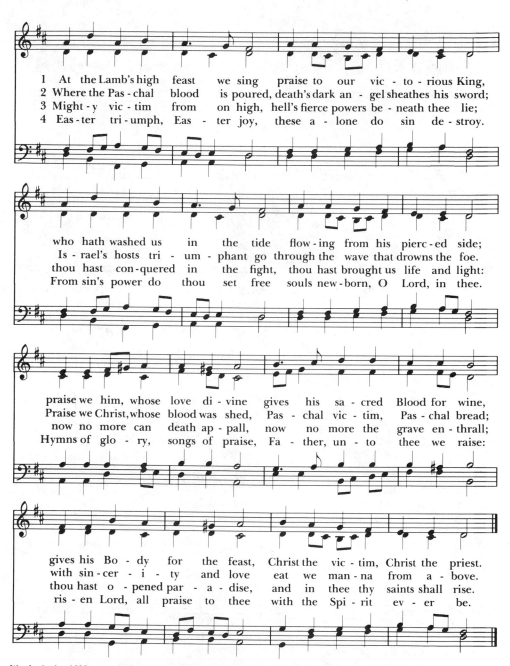

1 At the Lamb's high feast we sing praise to our vic - to - rious King,
2 Where the Pas - chal blood is poured, death's dark an - gel sheathes his sword;
3 Might - y vic - tim from on high, hell's fierce powers be - neath thee lie;
4 Eas - ter tri - umph, Eas - ter joy, these a - lone do sin de - stroy.

who hath washed us in the tide flow - ing from his pierc - ed side;
Is - rael's hosts tri - um - phant go through the wave that drowns the foe.
thou hast con - quered in the fight, thou hast brought us life and light:
From sin's power do thou set free souls new - born, O Lord, in thee.

praise we him, whose love di - vine gives his sa - cred Blood for wine,
Praise we Christ, whose blood was shed, Pas - chal vic - tim, Pas - chal bread;
now no more can death ap - pall, now no more the grave en - thrall;
Hymns of glo - ry, songs of praise, Fa - ther, un - to thee we raise:

gives his Bo - dy for the feast, Christ the vic - tim, Christ the priest.
with sin - cer - i - ty and love eat we man - na from a - bove.
thou hast o - pened par - a - dise, and in thee thy saints shall rise.
ris - en Lord, all praise to thee with the Spi - rit ev - er be.

Words: Latin, 1632; tr. Robert Campbell (1814-1868), alt.
Music: *Salzburg*, melody Jakob Hintze (1622-1702); harm. Johann Sebastian Bach (1685-1750)

77. 77. D

Refrain

Hail thee, fes - ti - val day! blest day that art hal-lowed for -
ev - er, day where-on Christ a - rose, break - ing the
king - dom of death.

First time only

death.

1 Lo, the fair beau - ty of earth, from the death of the
3 Dai - ly the love - li - ness grows, a - dorned with the
5 God the Cre - a - tor, the Lord, who rul - est the
7 Spi - rit of life and of power, now flow in us,

win - ter a - ris - ing! Ev - ery good
glo - ry of blos - som; hea - ven her
earth and the hea - vens, guard us from
fount of our be - ing, light that dost

Repeat Refrain

gift of the year now with its Mas - ter re - turns:
gates un - bars, fling - ing her in - crease of light:
harm with - out, cleanse us from e - vil with - in:
light - en all, life that in all dost a - bide:

2 He who was nailed to the cross is Lord and the
4 Rise from the grave now, O Lord, who art au - thor of
6 Je - sus the health of the world, en - light - en our
8 Praise to the Giv - er of good! Thou Love who art

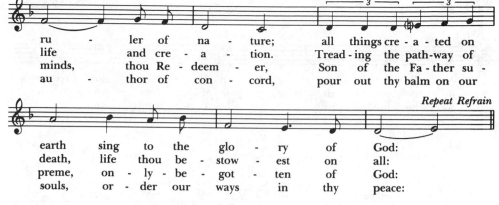

ru -	ler of na -	ture;	all things cre - a - ted on
life	and cre - a -	tion.	Tread - ing the path-way of
minds,	thou Re - deem - er,	Son	of the Fa - ther su -
au -	thor of con -	cord,	pour out thy balm on our

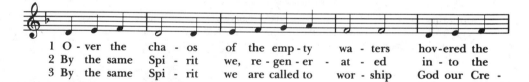

Repeat Refrain

earth	sing to the glo - ry of	God:
death,	life thou be - stow - est on	all:
preme,	on - ly - be - got - ten of	God:
souls,	or - der our ways in thy	peace:

The refrain may be sung once by choir alone and repeated by all. The stanzas may be sung by choir alone, alternately by contrasted groups, or by all.

Words: Venantius Honorius Fortunatus (540?-600?); tr. *The English Hymnal*, 1906, alt.
Music: *Salve festa dies*, Ralph Vaughan Williams (1872-1958)

79. 77 with Refrain

Easter 176

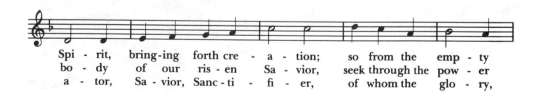

1 O - ver the cha - os of the emp - ty wa - ters hov-ered the
2 By the same Spi - rit we, re - gen - er - at - ed in - to the
3 By the same Spi - rit we are called to wor - ship God our Cre -

Spi - rit, bring-ing forth cre - a - tion; so from the emp - ty
bo - dy of our ris - en Sa - vior, seek through the pow - er
a - tor, Sa - vior, Sanc - ti - fi - er, of whom the glo - ry,

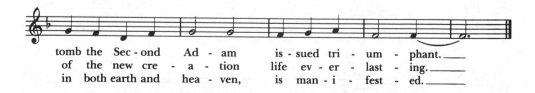

tomb the Sec - ond Ad - am is - sued tri - um - phant.____
of the new cre - a - tion life ev - er - last - ing.____
in both earth and hea - ven, is man - i - fest - ed.____

Words: Sts. 1-2, *A Monastic Breviary*, 1976; st. 3, *Hymnal 1982*
Music: *West Park*, Robert Roth (b. 1928)

11 11. 11 5

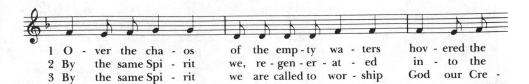

177

1 O - ver the cha - os of the emp - ty wa - ters hov - ered the
2 By the same Spi - rit we, re - gen - er - at - ed in - to the
3 By the same Spi - rit we are called to wor - ship God our Cre -

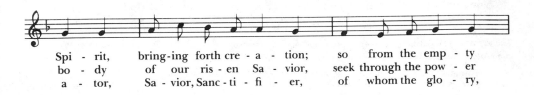

Spi - rit, bring-ing forth cre - a - tion; so from the emp - ty
bo - dy of our ris - en Sa - vior, seek through the pow - er
a - tor, Sa - vior, Sanc - ti - fi - er, of whom the glo - ry,

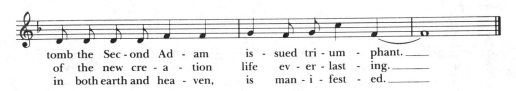

tomb the Sec - ond Ad - am is - sued tri - um - phant._____
of the new cre - a - tion life ev - er - last - ing._____
in both earth and hea - ven, is man - i - fest - ed._____

Words: Sts. 1-2, *A Monastic Breviary*, 1976; st. 3, Hymnal 1982
Music: *Bickford*, Hank Beebe (b. 1926)

11 11. 11 5

178

Descant

Al - le - lu - ia, al - le -

Refrain

Al - le - lu - ia, al - le - lu - ia! Give thanks to the

lu - ia, al - le - lu - ia!

ris - en Lord. Al - le - lu - ia, al - le - lu - ia! Give

1-4   **Final Ending**

Praise   to   his   Name.   Name.

praise   to   his   Name.   Name.

1 Je - sus   is   Lord   of   all   the   earth.
2 Spread the   good   news   o'er   all   the   earth:
3 We   have   been   cru - ci - fied   with   Christ.
4 Come, let   us   praise   the   liv - ing   God,

Repeat Refrain

He   is   the   King   of   cre - a - tion.
Je - sus   has   died   and   has   ris - en.
Now   we   shall   live___   for   ev - er.   Al - le -
joy - ful - ly   sing   to   our   Sa - vior.

The descant may be sung after stanzas 3 and 4.

Words: Donald Fishel (b. 1950)
Music: *Alleluia No. 1*, Donald Fishel (b. 1950); arr. Betty Pulkingham (b. 1928),
    Charles Mallory (b. 1950) and George Mims (b. 1938)

887. 85

1 "Wel - come, hap - py morn-ing!" age to age shall say:
*2 Earth her joy con - fess - es, cloth-ing her for spring,
*3 Months in due suc - ces - sion, days of length-en-ing light,
4 Ma - ker and Re - deem - er, life and health of all,
5 Thou, of life the au - thor, death didst un - der - go,

1 hell to - day is van - quished, heaven is won to - day!
2 all fresh gifts re - turned with her re - turn - ing King:
3 hours and pass - ing mo - ments praise thee in their flight.
4 thou from heaven be - hold - ing hu - man na - ture's fall,
5 tread the path of dark - ness, sav - ing strength to show;

1 Lo! the dead is liv - ing, God for ev - er - more!
2 bloom in ev - ery mea - dow, leaves on ev - ery bough,
3 Bright-ness of the morn - ing, sky and fields and sea,
4 of the Fa - ther's God - head true and on - ly Son,
5 come then, true and faith - ful, now ful - fill thy word,

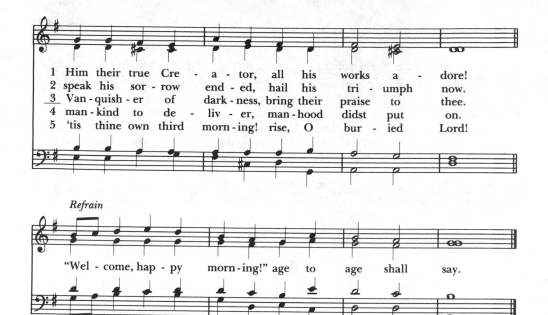

1 Him their true Cre - a - tor, all his works a - dore!
2 speak his sor - row end - ed, hail his tri - umph now.
3 Van - quish - er of dark - ness, bring their praise to thee.
4 man - kind to de - liv - er, man - hood didst put on.
5 'tis thine own third morn - ing! rise, O bur - ied Lord!

Refrain

"Wel - come, hap - py morn - ing!" age to age shall say.

6 Loose the souls long prisoned, bound with Satan's chain;
   all that now is fallen raise to life again;
   show thy face in brightness, bid the nations see;
   bring again our daylight: day returns with thee!

   Refrain

Words: Venantius Honorius Fortunatus (540?-600?); tr. John Ellerton (1826-1893), alt.
Music: *Fortunatus*, Arthur Seymour Sullivan (1842-1900)

11 11. 11 11. 11

1 He is ris - en, he is ris - en! Tell it out with
2 Come, ye sad and fear - ful - heart - ed, with glad smile and
*3 Come, with high and ho - ly hymn - ing, hail our Lord's tri -
4 He is ris - en, he is ris - en! He hath o - pened

joy - ful voice: he has burst his three days' pris - on;
ra - diant brow! Death's long sha - dows have de - part - ed;
um - phant day; not one dark - some cloud is dim - ming
hea - ven's gate: we are free from sin's dark pris - on,

let the whole wide earth re - joice: death is con - quered,
Je - sus' woes are o - ver now, and the pas - sion
yon - der glo - rious morn - ing ray, break - ing o'er the
ris - en to a ho - lier state; and a bright - er

we are free, Christ has won the vic - to - ry.
that he bore— sin and pain can vex no more.
pur - ple east, sym - bol of our Eas - ter feast.
Eas - ter beam on our long - ing eyes shall stream.

Words: Cecil Frances Alexander (1818-1895), alt.
Music: *Unser Herrscher*, Joachim Neander (1650-1680)

87. 87. 77

Descant

4 Soon shall each rap - tured tongue his

1 A - wake and sing the song of his
2 Sing of his dy - ing love, his
3 You pil - grims on the road to
4 Soon shall each rap - tured tongue his

end - less praise pro - claim, and sing in sweet - er

Mo - ses and the Lamb; wake ev - ery heart and
re - sur - rec - tion power; sing how he in - ter -
Zi - on's ci - ty, sing, re - joic - ing in the
end - less praise pro - claim, and sing in sweet - er

notes the song of Mo - ses and the Lamb.

ev - ery tongue to praise the Sa - vior's name.
cedes a - bove for those whose sins he bore.
Lamb of God, to Christ the e - ter - nal King.
notes the song of Mo - ses and the Lamb.

Words: William Hammond (1719-1783), alt.
Music: *St. Ethelwald*, William Henry Monk (1823-1889); desc. Cyril Winn (1884-1973)

SM

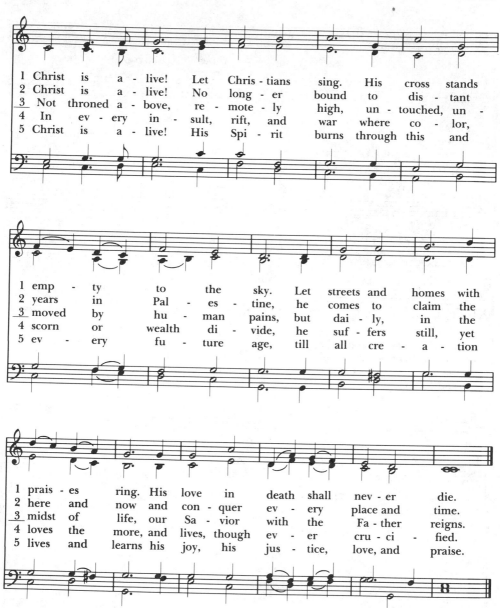

1 Christ is a - live! Let Chris - tians sing. His cross stands
2 Christ is a - live! No long - er bound to dis - tant
3 Not throned a - bove, re - mote - ly high, un - touched, un -
4 In ev - ery in - sult, rift, and war where co - lor,
5 Christ is a - live! His Spi - rit burns through this and

1 emp - ty to the sky. Let streets and homes with
2 years in Pal - es - tine, he comes to claim the
3 moved by hu - man pains, but dai - ly, in the
4 scorn or wealth di - vide, he suf - fers still, yet
5 ev - ery fu - ture age, till all cre - a - tion

1 prais - es ring. His love in death shall nev - er die.
2 here and now and con - quer ev - ery place and time.
3 midst of life, our Sa - vior with the Fa - ther reigns.
4 loves the more, and lives, though ev - er cru - ci - fied.
5 lives and learns his joy, his jus - tice, love, and praise.

Words: Brian A. Wren (b. 1936), rev.
Music: *Truro*, melody from *Psalmodia Evangelica, Part II*, 1789; harm. Lowell Mason (1792-1872), alt.

LM

1. Chris-tians, to the Pas-chal vic-tim of-fer your thank-ful prais-es!

2. A lamb the sheep re-deem-eth: Christ, who on-ly is sin-less, rec-on-cil-eth sin-ners to the Fa-ther.

3. Death and life have con-tend-ed in that com-bat stu-pen-dous: the Prince of life, who died, reigns im-mor-tal.

4. Speak, Ma-ry, de-clar-ing what thou saw-est, way-far-ing:

5. "The tomb of Christ, who is liv-ing, the glo-ry of Je-sus' re-sur-rec-tion;

6. bright an-gels at-test-ing, the shroud and nap-kin rest-ing.

7. Yea, Christ my hope is a-

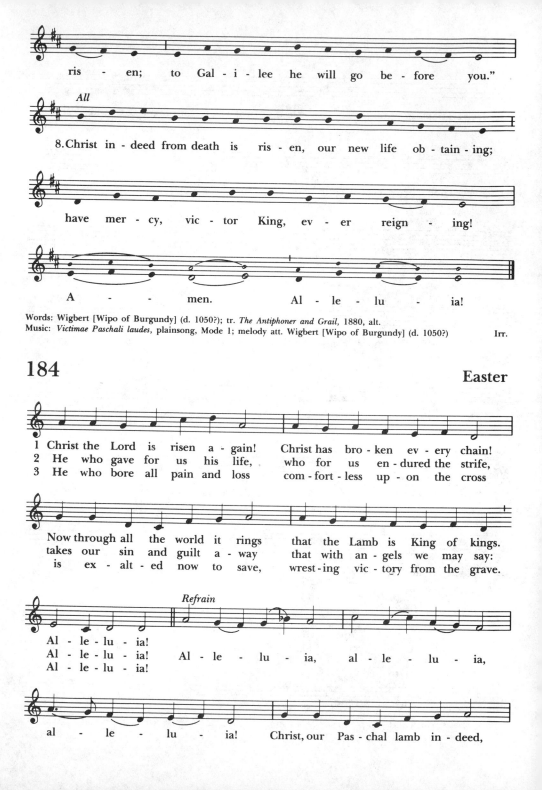

ris - en; to Gal - i - lee he will go be - fore you."

All

8. Christ in - deed from death is ris - en, our new life ob - tain - ing;

have mer - cy, vic - tor King, ev - er reign - ing!

A - men. Al - le - lu - ia!

Words: Wigbert [Wipo of Burgundy] (d. 1050?); tr. *The Antiphoner and Grail*, 1880, alt.
Music: *Victimae Paschali laudes*, plainsong, Mode 1; melody att. Wigbert [Wipo of Burgundy] (d. 1050?)   Irr.

184

Easter

1 Christ the Lord is risen a - gain! Christ has bro - ken ev - ery chain!
2 He who gave for us his life, who for us en - dured the strife,
3 He who bore all pain and loss com - fort - less up - on the cross

Now through all the world it rings that the Lamb is King of kings.
takes our sin and guilt a - way that with an - gels we may say:
is ex - alt - ed now to save, wrest - ing vic - to - ry from the grave.

Refrain

Al - le - lu - ia!
Al - le - lu - ia! Al - le - lu - ia, al - le - lu - ia,
Al - le - lu - ia!

al - le - lu - ia! Christ, our Pas - chal lamb in - deed,

Christ, to - day your peo - ple feed. Al - le - lu - ia!

Words: Michael Weisse (1480-1534); tr. Catherine Winkworth (1827-1878), alt.
Music: *Christ ist erstanden*, melody from *Geistliche Lieder*, 1533

77. 77. 4 with Refrain

Easter

185

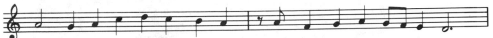

1 Christ Je - sus lay in death's strong bands   for our of - fens - es giv - en;
2 It was a strange and dread-ful strife   when life and death con - tend - ed;
3 So let us keep the fes - ti - val   to which the Lord in - vites us;
4 Then let us feast this ho - ly day   on the true bread of hea - ven;

but now at God's right hand he stands   and brings us life from hea - ven;
the vic - to - ry re - mained with life,   the reign of death was end - ed;
Christ is him - self the joy of all,   the sun that warms and lights us;
the word of grace hath purged a - way   the old and wick - ed lea - ven;

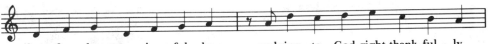

there-fore let us joy - ful be,   and sing to God right thank-ful - ly
stripped of power, no more he reigns,   an emp - ty form a - lone re - mains;
by his grace he doth im - part   e - ter - nal sun-shine to the heart;
Christ a - lone our souls will feed,   he is our meat and drink in - deed;

loud songs of al - le - lu - ia!   Al - le - lu - ia!
his sting is lost for ev - er!   Al - le - lu - ia!
the night of sin is end - ed!   Al - le - lu - ia!
faith lives up - on no o - ther!   Al - le - lu - ia!

Words: Martin Luther (1483-1546); tr. Richard Massie (1800-1887), alt.
Music: *Christ lag in Todesbanden*, melody from *Geystliche gesangk Buchleyn*, 1524

87. 87. 78. 74

1 Christ Je - sus lay in death's strong bands for
2 It was a strange and dread - ful strife when
3 So let us keep the fes - ti - val to
4 Then let us feast this ho - ly day on

our of - fens - es giv - en; but now at God's right
life and death con - tend - ed; the vic - to - ry re -
which the Lord in - vites us; Christ is him - self the
the true bread of hea - ven; the word of grace hath

hand he stands and brings us life from hea - ven;
mained with life, the reign of death was end - ed;
joy of all, the sun that warms and lights us;
purged a - way the old and wick - ed lea - ven;

there - fore let us joy - ful be, and sing to
stripped of power, no more he reigns, an emp - ty
by his grace he doth im - part e - ter - nal
Christ a - lone our souls will feed, he is our

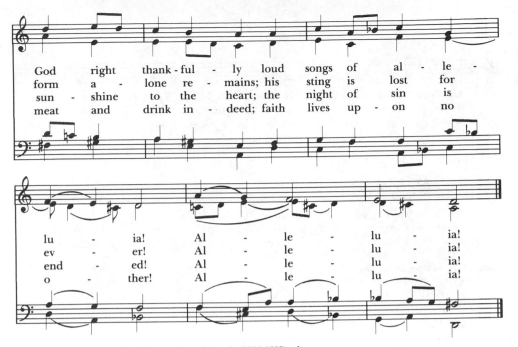

God right thank-ful-ly loud songs of al le -
form a - lone re - mains; his sting is lost for
sun - shine to the heart; the night of sin is
meat and drink in - deed; faith lives up - on no

lu - ia! Al - le - lu - ia!
ev - er! Al - le - lu - ia!
end - ed! Al - le - lu - ia!
o - ther! Al - le - lu - ia!

Words: Martin Luther (1483-1546); tr. Richard Massie (1800-1887), alt.
Music: *Christ lag in Todesbanden*, melody from *Geystliche gesangk Buchleyn*, 1524;
adapt. and harm. Johann Sebastian Bach (1685-1750)

87. 87. 78. 74

Easter

187

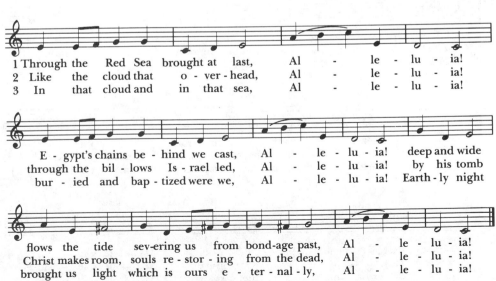

1 Through the Red Sea brought at last, Al - le - lu - ia!
2 Like the cloud that o - ver - head, Al - le - lu - ia!
3 In that cloud and in that sea, Al - le - lu - ia!

E - gypt's chains be - hind we cast, Al - le - lu - ia! deep and wide
through the bil - lows Is - rael led, Al - le - lu - ia! by his tomb
bur - ied and bap - tized were we, Al - le - lu - ia! Earth-ly night

flows the tide sev-ering us from bond-age past, Al - le - lu - ia!
Christ makes room, souls re - stor - ing from the dead, Al - le - lu - ia!
brought us light which is ours e - ter - nal-ly, Al - le - lu - ia!

Words: Ronald A. Knox (1888-1957)
Music: *Straf mich nicht*, melody from *Hundert Arien*, 1694

76. 76. 676

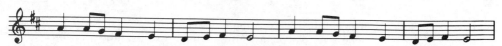

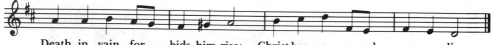

1 Love's re-deem-ing work is done, fought the fight, the bat-tle won.
2 Lives a-gain our glo-rious King; where, O death, is now thy sting?
3 Soar we now where Christ has led, fol-lowing our ex-alt-ed Head;

Death in vain for-bids him rise; Christ has o-pened par-a-dise.
Once he died our souls to save, where thy vic-to - ry, O grave?
made like him, like him we rise, ours the cross, the grave, the skies.

Words: Charles Wesley (1707-1788), alt.
Music: *Savannah*, from *Harmonia Sacra*, ca. 1760

77. 77

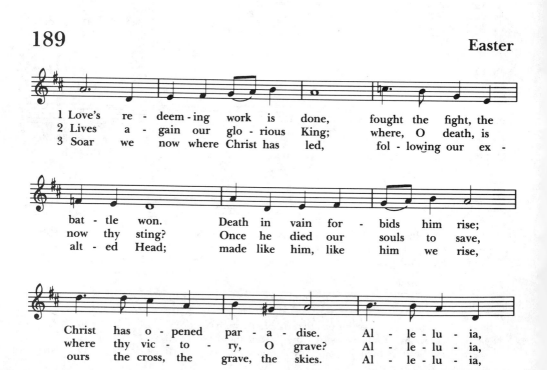

1 Love's re-deem-ing work is done, fought the fight, the
2 Lives a-gain our glo-rious King; where, O death, is
3 Soar we now where Christ has led, fol-low-ing our ex-

bat-tle won. Death in vain for-bids him rise;
now thy sting? Once he died our souls to save,
alt-ed Head; made like him, like him we rise,

Christ has o-pened par-a-dise. Al-le-lu-ia,
where thy vic-to-ry, O grave? Al-le-lu-ia,
ours the cross, the grave, the skies. Al-le-lu-ia,

al - le - lu - ia! _____
al - le - lu - ia! _____
al - le - lu - (ia!)   ia! _____

Words: Charles Wesley (1707-1788), alt.
Music: *Resurrexit*, Robert Sherlaw Johnson (b. 1932)

77. 77 with Alleluias

Easter

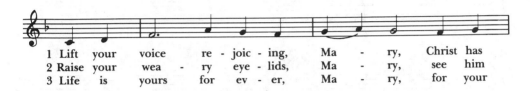

1 Lift your voice re - joic - ing, Ma - ry, Christ has
2 Raise your wea - ry eye - lids, Ma - ry, see him
3 Life is yours for ev - er, Ma - ry, for your

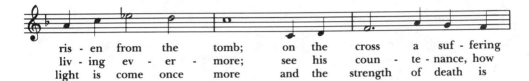

ris - en from the tomb; on the cross a suf - fering
liv - ing ev - er - more; see his coun - te - nance, how
light is come once more and the strength of death is

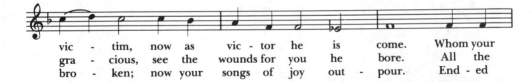

vic - tim, now as vic - tor he is come. Whom your
gra - cious, see the wounds for you he bore. All the
bro - ken; now your songs of joy out - pour. End - ed

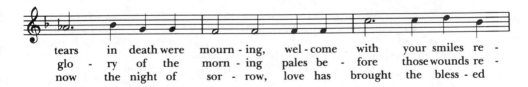

tears in death were mourn - ing, wel - come with your smiles re -
glo - ry of the morn - ing pales be - fore those wounds re -
now the night of sor - row, love has brought the bless - ed

turn - ing. Let your al - le - lu - ias rise!
deem - ing. Let your al - le - lu - ias rise!
mor - row. Let your al - le - lu - ias rise!

Words: Latin; tr. Elizabeth Rundle Charles (1828-1896), alt.
Music: *Fisk of Gloucester*, Thomas Foster (b. 1938)

87. 87. 887

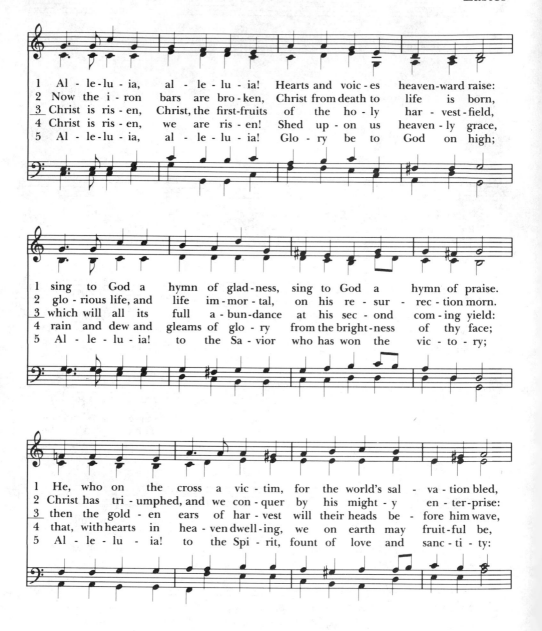

1 Al - le - lu - ia,   al - le - lu - ia!   Hearts and voic - es   heaven-ward raise:
2 Now the i - ron   bars are bro - ken,   Christ from death to   life   is   born,
3 Christ is ris - en,   Christ, the first-fruits   of   the   ho - ly   har - vest - field,
4 Christ is ris - en,   we   are ris - en!   Shed up - on us   heaven - ly grace,
5 Al - le - lu - ia,   al - le - lu - ia!   Glo - ry be to   God   on high;

1 sing   to God a   hymn of glad - ness,   sing to God a   hymn of praise.
2 glo - rious life, and   life im - mor - tal,   on his re - sur - rec - tion morn.
3 which will all its   full   a - bun-dance   at his sec - ond   com - ing yield:
4 rain and dew and   gleams of glo - ry   from the bright - ness   of   thy face;
5 Al - le - lu - ia!   to   the Sa - vior   who has won   the   vic - to - ry;

1 He, who on   the   cross a vic - tim,   for   the world's sal - va - tion bled,
2 Christ has tri - umphed, and we con - quer   by   his might - y   en - ter-prise:
3 then the gold - en   ears of har - vest   will their heads be - fore him wave,
4 that, with hearts in   hea - ven dwell - ing,   we on earth may   fruit-ful be,
5 Al - le - lu - ia!   to   the Spi - rit,   fount of love and   sanc - ti - ty:

1 Je - sus Christ, the King of glo - ry, now is ris - en from the dead.
2 we with him to life e - ter - nal by his re - sur - rec - tion rise.
3 ri -pened by his glo - rious sun -shine from the fur-rows of the grave.
4 and by an - gel hands be gath-ered, and be ev - er, Lord, with thee.
5 Al - le - lu - ia, al - le - lu - ia! to the Tri -une Ma - jes - ty.

Words: Christopher Wordsworth (1807-1885), alt.
Music: *Lux eoi,* Arthur Seymour Sullivan (1842-1900)

87. 87. D

Unison or harmony

1 This joy-ful Eas - ter - tide, a - way with sin and
2 Death's flood hath lost its chill, since Je - sus crossed the
3 My flesh in hope shall rest, and for a sea - son

sor - row! My Love, the Cru - ci - fied, hath
riv - er: Lord of all life, from ill my
slum - ber, till trump from east to west shall

sprung to life this mor - row.
pass - ing life de - liv - er. Had Christ, that once was
wake the dead in num - ber.

Refrain

slain, ne'er burst his three-day pris - on, our faith had been in

vain; but now is Christ a - ris - en, a - ris - en, a -

ris - en, a - ris - - - en.

Words: George R. Woodward (1848-1934), alt.
Music: *Vruechten*, melody from *Psalmen*, 1685; harm. Charles Wood (1866-1926)

67. 67 with Refrain

Easter

1 That Eas - ter day with joy was bright, the
2 His ris - en flesh with ra - diance glowed; his
3 O Je - sus, King of gen - tle - ness, do
4 O Lord of all, with us a - bide in
5 All praise, O ris - en Lord, we give to

1 sun shone out with fair - er light, when, to their long - ing
2 wound - ed hands and feet he showed; those scars their sol - emn
3 thou thy - self our hearts pos - sess that we may give thee
4 this our joy - ful Eas - ter - tide; from ev - ery wea - pon
5 thee, who, dead, a - gain dost live; to God the Fa - ther

1 eyes re - stored, the a - pos - tles saw their ris - en Lord.
2 wit - ness gave that Christ was ris - en from the grave.
3 all our days the will - ing tri - bute of our praise.
4 death can wield thine own re - deemed for ev - er shield.
5 e - qual praise, and God the Ho - ly Ghost, we raise.

Words: Latin, 5th cent.; ver. *Hymnal 1940*
Music: *Puer nobis*, melody from Trier MS., 15th cent.; adapt. Michael Praetorius (1571-1621)

LM

1 Je - sus lives! thy ter - rors now can no long - er, death, ap -
2 Je - sus lives! for us he died; then, a - lone to Je - sus
3 Je - sus lives! our hearts know well nought from us his love shall
4 Je - sus lives! to him the throne o - ver all the world is

pall us; Je - sus lives! by this we know thou, O
liv - ing, pure in heart may we a - bide, glo - ry
sev - er; life, nor death, nor powers of hell tear us
giv - en: may we go where he has gone, rest and

grave, canst not en - thrall us. Al - le - lu - ia!
to our Sa - vior giv - ing. Al - le - lu - ia!
from his keep - ing ev - er. Al - le - lu - ia!
reign with him in hea - ven. Al - le - lu - ia!

Words: Christian Furchtegott Gellert (1715-1769); tr. Frances Elizabeth Cox (1812-1897), alt.
Music: *St. Albinus*, Henry John Gauntlett (1805-1876)

78. 78 with Alleluia

1 Je - sus lives! thy ter - rors now can no long - er,
2 Je - sus lives! for us he died; then, a - lone to
3 Je - sus lives! our hearts know well nought from us his
4 Je - sus lives! to him the throne o - ver all the

death, ap - pall us; Je - sus lives! by this we know
Je - sus liv - ing, pure in heart may we a - bide,
love shall sev - er; life, nor death, nor powers of hell
world is giv - en: may we go where he has gone,

thou, O grave, canst not en - thrall us. Al - le - lu - ia!
glo - ry to our Sa - vior giv - ing. Al - le - lu - ia!
tear us from his keep - ing ev - er. Al - le - lu - ia!
rest and reign with him in hea - ven. Al - le - lu - ia!

Words: Christian Furchtegott Gellert (1715-1769); tr. Frances Elizabeth Cox (1812-1897), alt.
Music: *Mowsley*, Cyril Vincent Taylor (b. 1907)

78. 78 with Alleluia

1 Look there! the Christ, our Bro-ther, comes re-
2 Good Je-sus Christ in-side his pain looked
3 Good Je-sus Christ, our Bro-ther, died in
4 Look there! the Christ, our Bro-ther, comes re-

splen-dent from the gal-lows tree ____ and what he brings in
down Gol-go-tha's ston-y slope ____ and let the blood flow
dark-est hurt up-on the tree ____ to of-fer us the
splen-dent from the gal-lows tree ____ and what he brings in

his hurt hands is life on life for you and me. ____
from his flesh to fill the springs of liv-ing hope. ____
worlds of light that live in-side the Trin-i-ty. ____
his hurt hands is life on life for you and me. ____

Refrain

Joy! (joy) joy! (joy) joy to the heart and all in this good day's dawn-

- ing! Joy! (joy) joy! (joy) joy to the heart and

all in this good day's dawn - ing!

Words: John Bennett (b. 1920), alt.
Music: *Petrus*, William Albright (b. 1944)

LM with Refrain

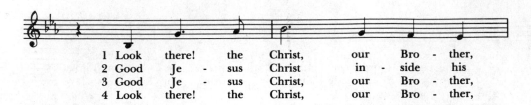

1 Look there! the Christ, our Bro - ther,
2 Good Je - sus Christ in - side his
3 Good Je - sus Christ, our Bro - ther,
4 Look there! the Christ, our Bro - ther,

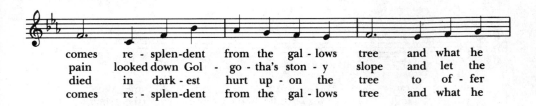

comes re - splen-dent from the gal - lows tree and what he
pain looked down Gol - go - tha's ston - y slope and let the
died in dark - est hurt up - on the tree to of - fer
comes re - splen-dent from the gal - lows tree and what he

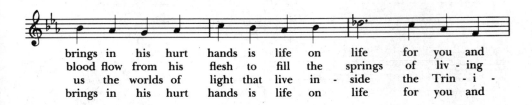

brings in his hurt hands is life on life for you and
blood flow from his flesh to fill the springs of liv - ing
us the worlds of light that live in - side the Trin - i -
brings in his hurt hands is life on life for you and

Refrain

me. Joy! joy!_____ joy to the
hope.
ty.
me.

heart and all in this good day's dawn - ing!

Words: John Bennett (b. 1920), alt.
Music: *Grand Prairie*, Peter Cutts (b. 1937)

LM with Refrain

Music: Copyright © 1984 by Hope Publishing Company. All Rights Reserved. Used by Permission.

1 Thou hal - lowed cho - sen morn of praise, that best and great - est
2 Come, let us taste the vine's new fruit, for heaven - ly joy pre -

shin - est: fair Eas - ter, queen of all the days, of
par - ing; to - day the branch - es with the root in

sea - sons, best, di - vin - est! Christ rose from death; and
re - sur - rec - tion shar - ing: whom as true God our

we a - dore for ev - er and for ev - er - more.
hymns a - dore for ev - er and for ev - er - more.

Words: John of Damascus (8th cent.); tr. John Mason Neale (1818-1866), alt.
Music: *Mach's mit mir, Gott,* melody from *Das ander Theil des andern newen Operis Geistlicher
Deutscher Lieder,* 1605; adapt., att., and harm. Johann Hermann Schein (1586-1630)

87. 87. 88

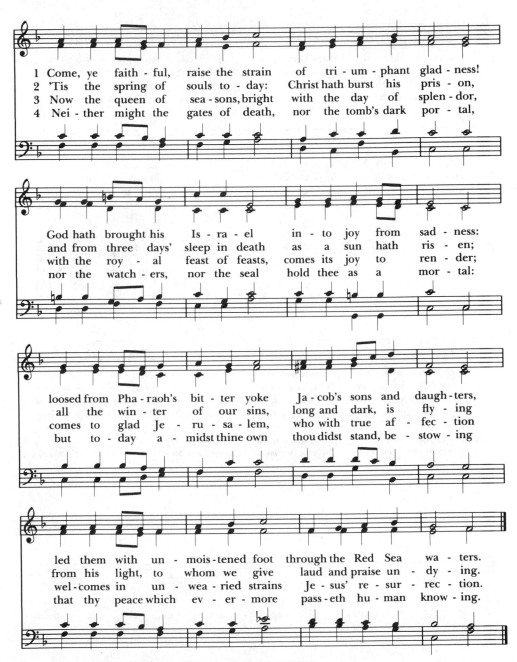

1 Come, ye faith-ful, raise the strain of tri-um-phant glad-ness!
2 'Tis the spring of souls to-day: Christ hath burst his pris-on,
3 Now the queen of sea-sons, bright with the day of splen-dor,
4 Nei-ther might the gates of death, nor the tomb's dark por-tal,

God hath brought his Is-ra-el in-to joy from sad-ness:
and from three days' sleep in death as a sun hath ris-en;
with the roy-al feast of feasts, comes its joy to ren-der;
nor the watch-ers, nor the seal hold thee as a mor-tal:

loosed from Pha-raoh's bit-ter yoke Ja-cob's sons and daugh-ters,
all the win-ter of our sins, long and dark, is fly-ing
comes to glad Je-ru-sa-lem, who with true af-fec-tion
but to-day a-midst thine own thou didst stand, be-stow-ing

led them with un-mois-tened foot through the Red Sea wa-ters.
from his light, to whom we give laud and praise un-dy-ing.
wel-comes in un-wea-ried strains Je-sus' re-sur-rec-tion.
that thy peace which ev-er-more pass-eth hu-man know-ing.

Words: John of Damascus (8th cent.); tr. John Mason Neale (1818-1866), alt.
Music: *St. Kevin*, Arthur Seymour Sullivan (1842-1900)

76. 76. D

200

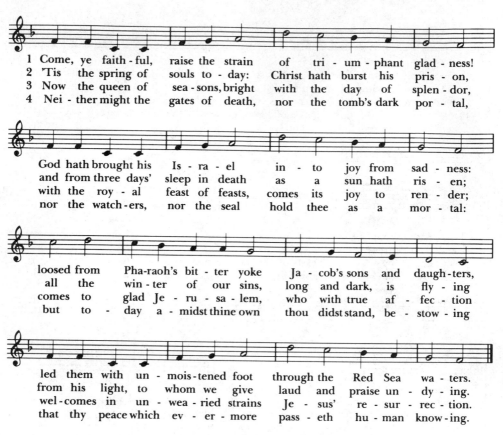

1 Come, ye faith-ful, raise the strain of tri-um-phant glad-ness!
2 'Tis the spring of souls to-day: Christ hath burst his pris-on,
3 Now the queen of sea-sons, bright with the day of splen-dor,
4 Nei-ther might the gates of death, nor the tomb's dark por-tal,

God hath brought his Is-ra-el in-to joy from sad-ness:
and from three days' sleep in death as a sun hath ris-en;
with the roy-al feast of feasts, comes its joy to ren-der;
nor the watch-ers, nor the seal hold thee as a mor-tal:

loosed from Pha-raoh's bit-ter yoke Ja-cob's sons and daugh-ters,
all the win-ter of our sins, long and dark, is fly-ing
comes to glad Je-ru-sa-lem, who with true af-fec-tion
but to-day a-midst thine own thou didst stand, be-stow-ing

led them with un-mois-tened foot through the Red Sea wa-ters.
from his light, to whom we give laud and praise un-dy-ing.
wel-comes in un-wea-ried strains Je-sus' re-sur-rec-tion.
that thy peace which ev-er-more pass-eth hu-man know-ing.

Words: John of Damascus (8th cent.); tr. John Mason Neale (1818-1866), alt.
Music: *Gaudeamus pariter*, melody from *Medieval [German or] Bohemian Carol Melody*, 1544

76. 76. D

201

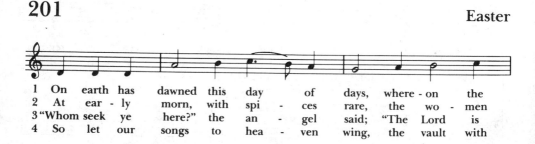

1 On earth has dawned this day of days, where-on the
2 At ear-ly morn, with spi-ces rare, the wo-men
3 "Whom seek ye here?" the an-gel said; "The Lord is
4 So let our songs to hea-ven wing, the vault with

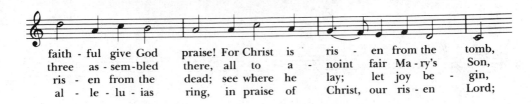

faith - ful give God praise! For Christ is ris - en from the tomb,
three as - sem - bled there, all to a - noint fair Ma - ry's Son,
ris - en from the dead; see where he lay; let joy be - gin,
al - le - lu - ias ring, in praise of Christ, our ris - en Lord;

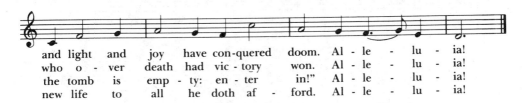

and light and joy have con - quered doom. Al - le - lu - ia!
who o - ver death had vic - tory won. Al - le - lu - ia!
the tomb is emp - ty: en - ter in!" Al - le - lu - ia!
new life to all he doth af - ford. Al - le - lu - ia!

Words: Nikolaus Hermann (1480?-1561); tr. Charles Sanford Terry (1864-1936), alt.
Music: *Erschienen ist der herrlich Tag*, melody Nikolaus Hermann (1480?-1561)

LM with Alleluia

Easter

202

1 The Lamb's high ban - quet called to share, ar - rayed in
2 Pro - tect - ed in the Pas - chal night from the de -
3 Now Christ our Pass - o - ver is slain, the Lamb of
4 O all - suf - fi - cient Sac - ri - fice, be - neath thee
5 All praise be thine, O ris - en Lord, from death to

1 gar - ments white and fair, the Red Sea past, we
2 stroy - ing an - gel's might, in tri - umph went the
3 God with - out a stain; his flesh, the true un -
4 hell de - feat - ed lies; thy cap - tive peo - ple
5 end - less life re - stored; all praise to God the

1 now would sing to Je - sus our tri - um - phant King.
2 ran - somed free from Pha - raoh's cru - el ty - ran - ny.
3 lea - vened bread, is free - ly of - fered in our stead.
4 are set free, and end - less life re - stored in thee.
5 Fa - ther be and Ho - ly Ghost e - ter - nal - ly.

Words: Latin, 7th-8th cent.; tr. John Mason Neale (1818-1866) and others
Music: *Ad cenam Agni providi*, plainsong, Mode 8, Paris MS., 12th cent.; ver. A. Gregory Murray (b. 1905)

LM

Antiphon (at the beginning)

Al - le - lu - ia, al - le - lu - ia!

Al - le - lu - ia, al - le - lu - ia!

1 O sons and daugh-ters, let us sing! The King of heaven, the
2 That Eas - ter morn, at break of day, the faith - ful wo - men
3 An an - gel clad in white they see, who sat and spake un -
4 That night the a - pos - tles met in fear; a - midst them came their
5 On this most ho - ly day of days, to God your hearts and

1 glo - rious King, o'er death and hell rose tri - umph - ing.
2 went their way to seek the tomb where Je - sus lay.
3 to the three, "Your Lord doth go to Gal - i - lee."
4 Lord most dear, and said, "My peace be on all here."
5 voic - es raise, in laud and ju - bi - lee and praise.

1 Al - le - lu - ia, al - le - lu - ia!
2 Al - le - lu - ia, al - le - lu - ia!
3 Al - le - lu - ia, al - le - lu - ia!
4 Al - le - lu - ia, al - le - lu - ia!
5 Al - le - lu - ia, al - le - lu - ia! [Ant.]

Al - le - lu - ia, al - le - lu - ia!

Al - le - lu - ia, al - le - lu - ia!

Words: Att. Jean Tisserand (15th cent.); tr. John Mason Neale (1818-1866)
Music: *O filii et filiae*, melody from *Airs sur les hymnes sacrez, odes et noëls*, 1623; harm.
Hymnal 1982

888 with Alleluias

Easter

204

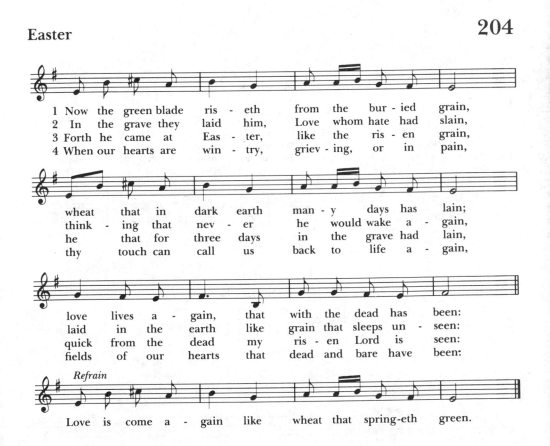

1 Now the green blade ris - eth from the bur - ied grain,
2 In the grave they laid him, Love whom hate had slain,
3 Forth he came at Eas - ter, like the ris - en grain,
4 When our hearts are win - try, griev - ing, or in pain,

wheat that in dark earth man - y days has lain;
think - ing that nev - er he would wake a - gain,
he that for three days in the grave had lain,
thy touch can call us back to life a - gain,

love lives a - gain, that with the dead has been:
laid in the earth like grain that sleeps un - seen:
quick from the dead my ris - en Lord is seen:
fields of our hearts that dead and bare have been:

Refrain

Love is come a - gain like wheat that spring-eth green.

Words: John Macleod Campbell Crum (1872-1958), alt.
Music: *Noël nouvelet*, medieval French carol

11 10. 10 11

1 Good Chris-tians all, re - joice and sing! Now is the
*2 The Lord of life is risen to - day! Sing songs of
3 Praise we in songs of vic - to - ry that love, that
4 Your Name we bless, O ris - en Lord, and sing to -
5 To God the Fa - ther, God the Son, to God the

1 tri - umph of our King! To all the world glad news we bring:
2 praise a - long his way; let all the earth re - joice and say:
3 life which can - not die, and sing with hearts up - lift - ed high:
4 day with one ac - cord the life laid down, the life re - stored:
5 Spi - rit, al - ways One, we sing for life in us be - gun:

Al - le - lu - ia, al - le - lu - ia, al - le - lu - ia!

Al - le - lu - ia, al - le - lu - ia, al - le - lu - ia!

Al - le - lu - ia, al - le - lu - ia, al - le - lu - ia!

Words: Cyril A. Alington (1872-1955), alt. St. 5, Norman Mealy (b. 1923)
Music: *Gelobt sei Gott*, Melchior Vulpius (1560?-1616)

888 with Alleluias

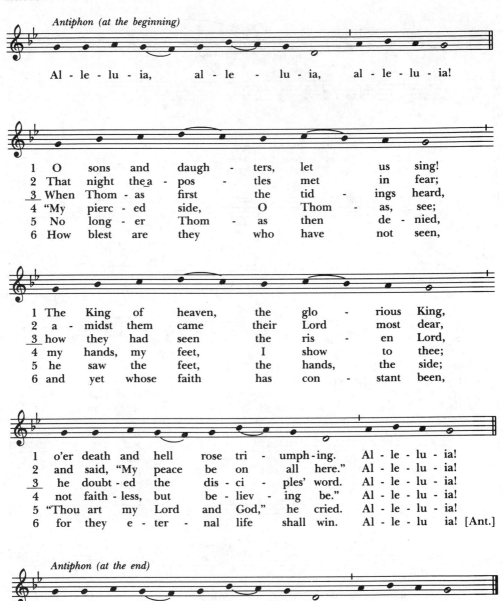

Antiphon (at the beginning)

Al - le - lu - ia, al - le - lu - ia, al - le - lu - ia!

1 O sons and daugh - ters, let us sing!
2 That night the a - pos - tles met in fear;
3 When Thom - as first the tid - ings heard,
4 "My pierc - ed side, O Thom - as, see;
5 No long - er Thom - as then de - nied,
6 How blest are they who have not seen,

1 The King of heaven, the glo - rious King,
2 a - midst them came their Lord most dear,
3 how they had seen the ris - en Lord,
4 my hands, my feet, I show to thee;
5 he saw the feet, the hands, the side;
6 and yet whose faith has con - stant been,

1 o'er death and hell rose tri - umph - ing. Al - le - lu - ia!
2 and said, "My peace be on all here." Al - le - lu - ia!
3 he doubt - ed the dis - ci - ples' word. Al - le - lu - ia!
4 not faith - less, but be - liev - ing be." Al - le - lu - ia!
5 "Thou art my Lord and God," he cried. Al - le - lu - ia!
6 for they e - ter - nal life shall win. Al - le - lu - ia! [Ant.]

Antiphon (at the end)

Al - le - lu - ia, al - le - lu - ia, al - le - lu - ia!

This hymn is for the Second Sunday of Easter and St. Thomas' Day.

Words: Att. Jean Tisserand (15th cent.); tr. John Mason Neale (1818-1866)
Music: *O filii et filiae,* melody from *Airs sur les hymnes sacrez, odes et noëls,* 1623

888 with Alleluias

Descant

1 Je - sus Christ is risen to - day, Al - le - lu - ia!
2 Hymns of praise then let us sing, Al - le - lu - ia!
3 But the pains which he en - dured, Al - le - lu - ia!
4 Sing we to our God a - bove, Al - le - lu - ia!

our tri - um - phant ho - ly day, Al - le - lu - ia!
un - to Christ, our heaven - ly King, Al - le - lu - ia!
our sal - va - tion have pro - cured, Al - le - lu - ia!
praise e - ter - nal as his love, Al - le - lu - ia!

who did once up - on the cross, Al - le - lu - ia!
who en - dured the cross and grave, Al - le - lu - ia!
now a - bove the sky he's King, Al - le - lu - ia!
praise him, all ye heaven - ly host, Al - le - lu - ia!

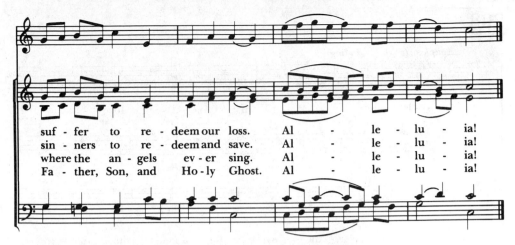

suf - fer to re - deem our loss. Al - le - lu - ia!
sin - ners to re - deem and save. Al - le - lu - ia!
where the an - gels ev - er sing. Al - le - lu - ia!
Fa - ther, Son, and Ho - ly Ghost. Al - le - lu - ia!

Words: Latin, 14th cent.; tr. *Lyra Davidica*, 1708, alt. St. 4, Charles Wesley (1707-1788)
Music: *Easter Hymn*, from *Lyra Davidica*, 1708; adapt. *The Compleat Psalmodist*, 1749, alt.;
desc. *Hymns Ancient and Modern, Revised*, 1950

77. 77 with Alleluias

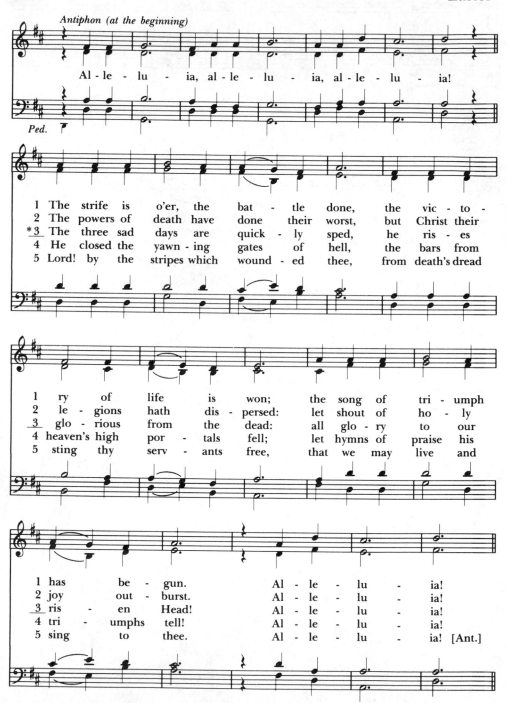

Antiphon (at the beginning)

Al - le - lu - ia, al - le - lu - ia, al - le - lu - ia!

Ped.

1 The strife is o'er, the bat - tle done, the vic - to -
2 The powers of death have done their worst, but Christ their
*3 The three sad days are quick - ly sped, he ris - es
4 He closed the yawn - ing gates of hell, the bars from
5 Lord! by the stripes which wound - ed thee, from death's dread

1 ry of life is won; the song of tri - umph
2 le - gions hath dis - persed: let shout of ho - ly
3 glo - rious from the dead: all glo - ry to our
4 heaven's high por - tals fell; let hymns of praise his
5 sting thy serv - ants free, that we may live and

1 has be - gun. Al - le - lu - ia!
2 joy out - burst. Al - le - lu - ia!
3 ris - en Head! Al - le - lu - ia!
4 tri - umphs tell! Al - le - lu - ia!
5 sing to thee. Al - le - lu - ia! [Ant.]

Al - le - lu - ia, al - le - lu - ia, al - le - lu - ia!

Ped.

Words: Latin, 1695; tr. Francis Pott (1832-1909), alt.
Music: *Victory*, Giovanni Pierluigi da Palestrina (1525-1594); adapt. and arr.
William Henry Monk (1823-1889)

888 with Alleluias

Easter

209

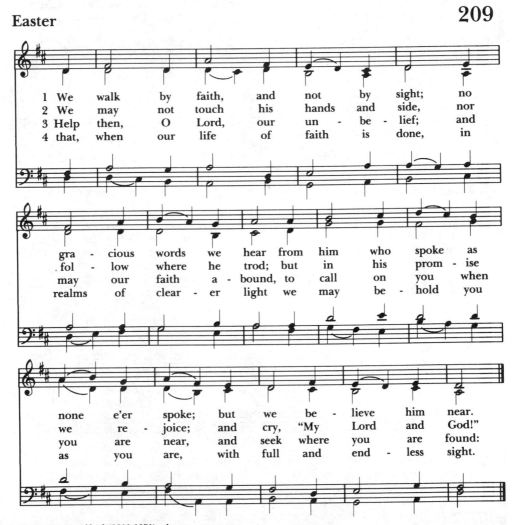

1 We walk by faith, and not by sight; no
2 We may not touch his hands and side, nor
3 Help then, O Lord, our un - be - lief; and
4 that, when our life of faith is done, in

gra - cious words we hear from him who spoke as
fol - low where he trod; but in his prom - ise
may our faith a - bound, to call on you when
realms of clear - er light we may be - hold you

none e'er spoke; but we be - lieve him near.
we re - joice; and cry, "My Lord and God!"
you are near, and seek where you are found:
as you are, with full and end - less sight.

Words: Henry Alford (1810-1871), alt.
Music: *St. Botolph*, Gordon Slater (1896-1979)

CM

Descant

3 Now let the heavens be joy - ful, let earth her song be - gin,

1 The day of re - sur - rec - tion! Earth, tell it out a - broad;
2 Our hearts be pure from e - vil, that we may see a - right
3 Now let the heavens be joy - ful, let earth her song be - gin,

the round world keep high tri - umph, and all that is there - in;

the Pass - o - ver of glad - ness, the Pass - o - ver of God.
the Lord in rays e - ter - nal of re - sur - rec - tion light;
the round world keep high tri - umph, and all that is there - in;

let all things seen and un - seen their notes to - geth - er blend,

From death to life e - ter - nal, from earth un - to the sky,
and, lis - tening to his ac - cents, may hear so calm and plain
let all things seen and un - seen their notes to - geth - er blend,

for Christ the Lord is ris - en, our joy that hath no end.

our Christ hath brought us o - ver with hymns of vic - to - ry.
his own "All hail!" and, hear - ing, may raise the vic - tor strain.
for Christ the Lord is ris - en, our joy that hath no end.

Words: John of Damascus (8th cent.); tr. John Mason Neale (1818-1866), alt.
Music: *Ellacombe*, from *Gesangbuch . . . der Herzogl. Wirtembergischen katholischen Hofkapelle*, 1784, alt.;
adapt. *Katholisches Gesangbuch*, 1863; harm. William Henry Monk (1823-1889);
desc. Cyril Winn (1884-1973)

76. 76. D

Easter

211

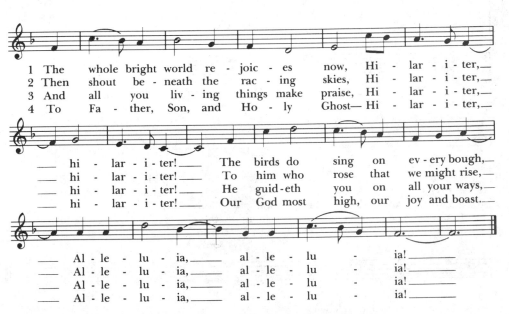

1 The whole bright world re - joic - es now, Hi - lar - i - ter,—
2 Then shout be - neath the rac - ing skies, Hi - lar - i - ter,—
3 And all you liv - ing things make praise, Hi - lar - i - ter,—
4 To Fa - ther, Son, and Ho - ly Ghost— Hi - lar - i - ter,—

— hi - lar - i - ter! The birds do sing on ev - ery bough,—
— hi - lar - i - ter! To him who rose that we might rise,—
— hi - lar - i - ter! He guid - eth you on all your ways,—
— hi - lar - i - ter! Our God most high, our joy and boast.—

— Al - le - lu - ia,— al - le - lu - ia!—
— Al - le - lu - ia,— al - le - lu - ia!—
— Al - le - lu - ia,— al - le - lu - ia!—
— Al - le - lu - ia,— al - le - lu - ia!—

"Hilariter" is Latin for "joyfully" and is pronounced "hi-lair-i-tair" in this hymn.

Words: Friedrich von Spee (1591-1635); tr. Percy Dearmer (1867-1936)
Music: *Hilariter*, Richard Wayne Dirksen (b. 1921)

LM

1 A - wake, a - rise, lift up your voice, let
2 Oh, with what glad - ness and sur - prise the
3 those hands of lib - eral love in - deed in
4 His en - e - mies had sealed the stone as
5 O Dead a - rise! O Friend - less stand by

1 Eas - ter mu - sic swell; re - joice in Christ, a -
2 saints their Sa - vior greet; nor will they trust their
3 in - fi - nite de - gree, those feet still free to
4 Pi - late gave them leave, lest dead and friend - less
5 ser - a - phim a - dored! O Sol - i - tude a -

1 gain re - joice and on his prais - es dwell.
2 ears and eyes but by his hands and feet,
3 move and bleed for mil - lions and for me.
4 and a - lone he should their skill de - ceive.
5 gain com - mand your host from heaven re - stored!

Words: Christopher Smart (1722-1771), alt.
Music: *Richmond*, melody Thomas Haweis (1734-1820); adapt. Samuel Webbe, Jr. (1770-1843);
harm. *The English Hymnal*, 1906

CM

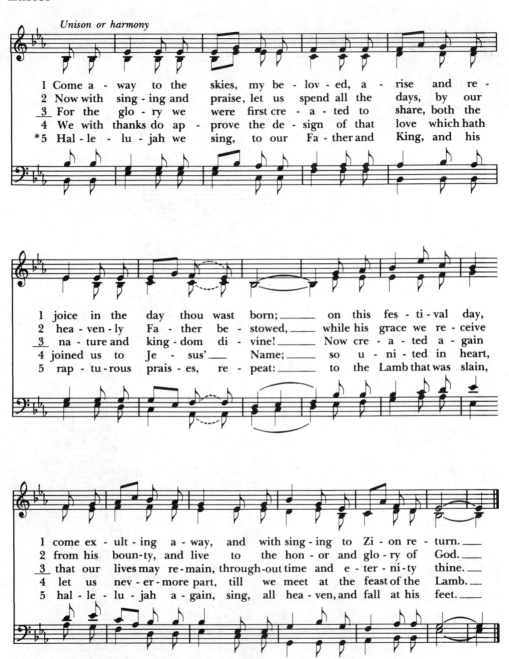

Unison or harmony

1 Come a - way to the skies, my be - lov - ed, a - rise and re-
2 Now with sing - ing and praise, let us spend all the days, by our
3 For the glo - ry we were first cre - a - ted to share, both the
4 We with thanks do ap - prove the de - sign of that love which hath
*5 Hal - le - lu - jah we sing, to our Fa - ther and King, and his

1 joice in the day thou wast born;____ on this fes - ti - val day,
2 hea - ven - ly Fa - ther be - stowed,____ while his grace we re - ceive
3 na - ture and king - dom di - vine!____ Now cre - a - ted a - gain
4 joined us to Je - sus'____ Name;____ so u - ni - ted in heart,
5 rap - tu - rous prais - es, re - peat:____ to the Lamb that was slain,

1 come ex - ult - ing a - way, and with sing - ing to Zi - on re - turn.____
2 from his boun - ty, and live to the hon - or and glo - ry of God.____
3 that our lives may re - main, through-out time and e - ter - ni - ty thine.____
4 let us nev - er - more part, till we meet at the feast of the Lamb.____
5 hal - le - lu - jah a - gain, sing, all hea - ven, and fall at his feet.____

Words: Charles Wesley (1707-1788)
Music: *Middlebury*, melody from *The Southern Harmony*; harm. Jack W. Burnam (b. 1946)

669. 669

1 Hail the day that sees him rise, Al - le - lu - ia!
2 There the glo-rious tri-umph waits; Al - le - lu - ia!
*3 See! he lifts his hands a - bove; Al - le - lu - ia!
4 Lord be-yond our mor-tal sight, Al - le - lu - ia!

glo-rious to his na-tive skies; Al - le - lu - ia!
lift your heads, e-ter-nal gates! Al - le - lu - ia!
See! he shows the prints of love: Al - le - lu - ia!
raise our hearts to reach thy height, Al - le - lu - ia!

Christ, a-while to mor-tals given, Al - le - lu - ia!
Wide un-fold the ra-diant scene; Al - le - lu - ia!
Hark! his gra-cious lips be-stow, Al - le - lu - ia!
there thy face un-cloud-ed see, Al - le - lu - ia!

en-ters now the high-est heaven! Al - le - lu - ia!
take the King of glo-ry in! Al - le - lu - ia!
bless-ings on his Church be-low. Al - le - lu - ia!
find our heaven of heavens in thee. Al - le - lu - ia!

Words: Charles Wesley (1707-1788), alt.
Music: *Llanfair*, Robert Williams (1781-1821)

77. 77 with Alleluias

1 See the Con-queror mounts in tri-umph; see the King in
2 He who on the cross did suf-fer, he who from the
3 Thou hast raised our hu-man na-ture on the clouds to

roy - al state, rid - ing on the clouds, his
grave a - rose, he has van - quished sin and
God's right hand: there we sit in heaven - ly

char - iot, to his heaven - ly pal - ace gate!
Sa - tan; he by death has spoiled his foes.
pla - ces, there with thee in glo - ry stand.

Hark! the choirs of an - gel voic - es joy - ful
While he lifts his hands in bless - ing, he is
Je - sus reigns, a - dored by an - gels; Man with

al - le - lu - ias sing, and the por - tals
part - ed from his friends; while their ea - ger
God is on the throne; might - y Lord, in

high are lift - ed to re - ceive their heaven - ly King.
eyes be - hold him, he up - on the clouds a - scends.
thine as - cen - sion, we by faith be - hold our own.

Words: Christopher Wordsworth (1807-1885), alt.
Music: *In Babilone*, melody from *Oude en Nieuwe Hollantse Boerenlities en Contradanseu*, 1710

87. 87. D

Refrain

Hail thee, fes-ti-val day! blest day that art hal-lowed for
ev - er, day when the Christ a - scends, high in the
hea - vens to reign. *First time only* reign.

1 He who was nailed to the cross is Lord and the
3 God the Cre-a - tor, the Lord who rul - est the
5 Spi - rit of life and of power, now flow in us,

ru - ler of na - ture; all things cre -
earth and the hea - vens, guard us from
fount of our be - ing, light that dost

a - ted on earth sing to the glo - ry of God:
harm with - out, cleanse us from e - vil with - in:
light - en all, life that in all dost a - bide:

Repeat Refrain

2 Dai - ly the love - li - ness grows, a - dorned with the
4 Je - sus the health of the world, en - light - en our
6 Praise to the Giv - er of good! Thou Love who art

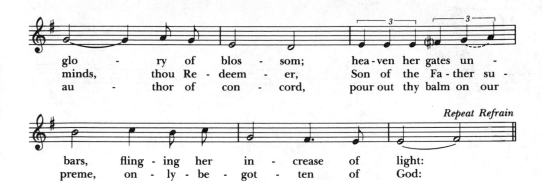

glo	- ry of	blos - som;	hea-ven her gates un -	
minds,	thou Re - deem - er,	Son of the Fa - ther su -		
au	- thor of con - cord,	pour out thy balm on our		

Repeat Refrain

bars,	fling - ing her	in - crease of	light:
preme,	on - ly - be - got - ten of	God:
souls,	or - der our ways in thy	peace:

*The refrain may be sung once by choir alone and repeated by all. The stanzas may be sung alternately
by contrasted groups, or by all.*

Words: Venantius Honorius Fortunatus (540?-600?); tr. *The English Hymnal*, 1906, alt.
Music: *Salve festa dies*, Ralph Vaughan Williams (1872-1958)

79. 77 with Refrain

Ascension   217

1 A	hymn	of	glo - ry	let	us	sing,	new	hymns through -
2 You	are	a	pre - sent	joy,	O	Lord;	you	will be
3 O	ris - en	Christ, a -	scend - ed	Lord,	all		praise to

out	the	world shall ring;	by	a	new	way	none
ev - er	our	re - ward;	and	great	the	light	in
you	let	earth ac - cord,	who	are,	while	end - less

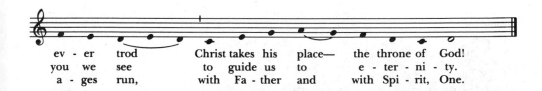

ev - er	trod	Christ takes his	place—	the throne of	God!
you we	see	to guide us	to	e - ter - ni - ty.
a - ges	run,	with Fa - ther and	with Spi - rit, One.

Words: The Venerable Bede (673-735); sts. 1-2, tr. Elizabeth Rundle Charles (1828-1896), alt.; st. 3,
     tr. Benjamin Webb (1819-1885), alt.
Music: *Jam lucis orto sidere*, plainsong, Mode 1, *Mailander Hymnen*, 15th cent.

LM

Fanfare

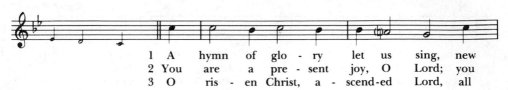

1 A   hymn   of   glo - ry   let   us   sing,   new
2 You   are   a   pre - sent   joy,   O   Lord;   you
3 O   ris - en Christ,   a - scend-ed   Lord,   all

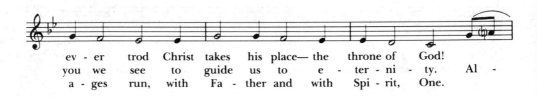

hymns through-out   the   world shall ring;   by   a   new way   none
will   be   ev - er   our   re - ward; and   great the light   in
praise   to   you   let   earth ac - cord, who   are, while end - less

ev - er   trod Christ takes   his place— the   throne of   God!
you we   see   to   guide   us   to   e - ter - ni - ty.   Al -
a - ges   run, with   Fa - ther and with   Spi - rit,   One.

- le - lu - ia,   al - le - lu - ia,   al - le -

lu - ia,   al - le - lu - ia,   al - le - lu - ia!

The fanfare may be used as introduction, interlude or conclusion.

Words: The Venerable Bede (673-735); sts. 1-2, tr. Elizabeth Rundle Charles (1828-1896), alt.; st. 3,
      tr. Benjamin Webb (1819-1885), alt.

Music: *Deo gracias*, English ballad melody, Trinity College MS., 15th cent.   LM with Alleluias

Ascension

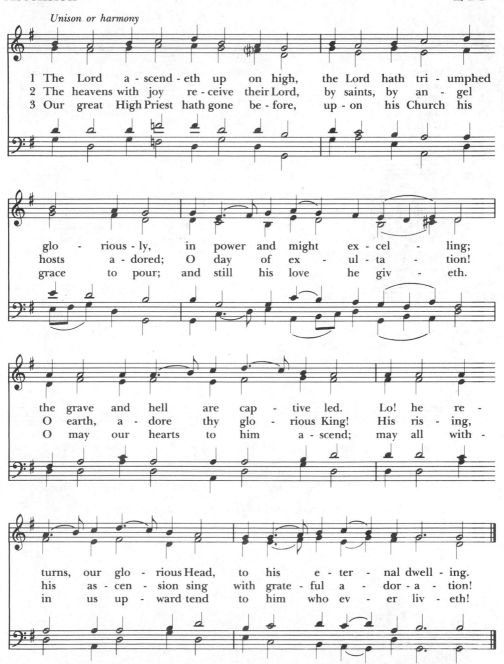

Unison or harmony

1 The Lord a-scend-eth up on high, the Lord hath tri-umphed
2 The heavens with joy re-ceive their Lord, by saints, by an-gel
3 Our great High Priest hath gone be-fore, up-on his Church his

glo-rious-ly, in power and might ex-cel - ling;
hosts a-dored; O day of ex-ul-ta - tion!
grace to pour; and still his love he giv - eth.

the grave and hell are cap-tive led. Lo! he re -
O earth, a-dore thy glo-rious King! His ris-ing,
O may our hearts to him a-scend; may all with -

turns, our glo-rious Head, to his e-ter-nal dwell-ing.
his as-cen-sion sing with grate-ful a-dor-a-tion!
in us up-ward tend to him who ev-er liv-eth!

Words: Arthur T. Russell (1806-1874), alt.
Music: *Ach Herr, du allerhöchster Gott*, Michael Praetorius (1571-1621)

887. 887

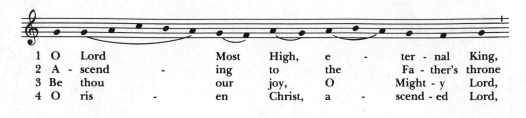

1 O Lord Most High, e - ter - nal King,
2 A - scend - ing to the Fa - ther's throne
3 Be thou our joy, O Might - y Lord,
4 O ris - en Christ, a - scend - ed Lord,

by thee re - deemed thy praise we sing.
thou claim'st the king - dom as thine own;
as thou wilt be our great re - ward;
all praise to thee let earth ac - cord,

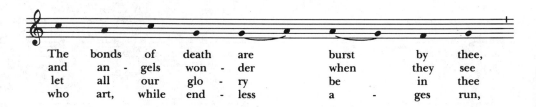

The bonds of death are burst by thee,
and an - gels won - der when they see
let all our glo - ry be in thee
who art, while end - less a - ges run,

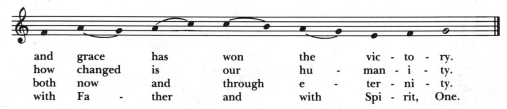

and grace has won the vic - to - ry.
how changed is our hu - man - i - ty.
both now and through e - ter - ni - ty.
with Fa - ther and with Spi - rit, One.

Words: Medieval Latin; sts. 1-3, tr. F. Bland Tucker (1895-1984); st. 4, tr. Benjamin Webb (1819-1885)
Music: *Aeterne Rex altissime*, plainsong, Mode 1

LM

Ascension

1 O Lord Most High, e - ter - nal King, _____ by
2 A - scend - ing to the Fa - ther's throne _____ thou
3 Be thou our joy, O might - y Lord, _____ as
4 O ris - en Christ, a - scend - ed Lord, _____ all

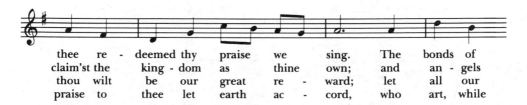

thee re - deemed thy praise we sing. The bonds of
claim'st the king - dom as thine own; and an - gels
thou wilt be our great re - ward; let all our
praise to thee let earth ac - cord, who art, while

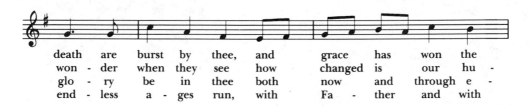

death are burst by thee, and grace has won the
won - der when they see how changed is our hu -
glo - ry be in thee both now and through e -
end - less a - ges run, with Fa - ther and with

After stanza 4

vic - to - ry.
man - i - ty.
ter - ni - ty.
Spi - rit, One. Al - le - lu - ia!

Words: Medieval Latin; sts. 1-3, tr. F. Bland Tucker (1895-1984); st. 4, tr. Benjamin Webb (1819-1885)
Music: *Gonfalon Royal*, Percy Carter Buck (1871-1947)   LM

1 Re - joice, the Lord of life a - scends
2 No more his mor - tal form we see;
3 He reigns, but with a love that shares
4 He reigns in heaven un - til the hour

in tri - umph from earth's bat - tle - field:
he reigns in - vis - i - ble but near:
the trou - bles of our earth - ly life;
when he, who once was cru - ci - fied,

his strife with hu - man ha - tred ends,
for in the midst of two or three
he takes up - on his heart the cares,
shall come in all love's glo - rious power

as sin and death their con - quests yield.
he makes his glo - rious pres - ence clear.
the pain, and shame of hu - man strife.
to rule the world for which he died.

Words: Albert F. Bayly (1901-1984)
Music: *Parker*, Horatio Parker (1864-1919)

LM

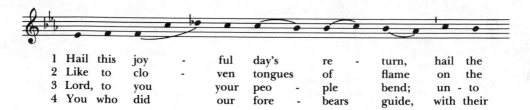

1 Hail this joy - ful day's re - turn, hail the
2 Like to clo - ven tongues of flame on the
3 Lord, to you your peo - ple bend; un - to
4 You who did our fore - bears guide, with their

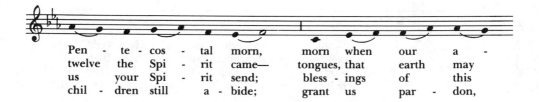

Pen - te - cos - tal morn, morn when our a -
twelve the Spi - rit came— tongues, that earth may
us your Spi - rit send; bless - ings of this
chil - dren still a - bide; grant us par - don,

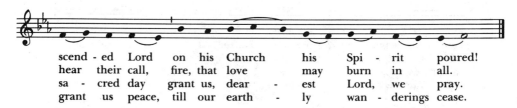

scend - ed Lord on his Church his Spi - rit poured!
hear their call, fire, that love may burn in all.
sa - cred day grant us, dear - est Lord, we pray.
grant us peace, till our earth - ly wan - derings cease.

Words: Att. Hilary of Poitiers (4th cent.); tr. Robert Campbell (1814-1868), alt.
Music: *Beata nobis gaudia*, plainsong, Mode 1, *Zisterzienser Hymnar*, 14th cent.

77. 77

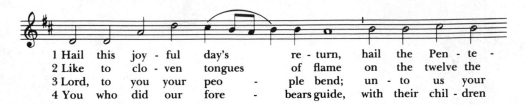

1 Hail this joy - ful day's   re - turn, hail the Pen - te -
2 Like to clo - ven tongues   of flame on the twelve the
3 Lord, to you your peo - ple bend; un - to us your
4 You who did our fore - bears guide, with their chil - dren

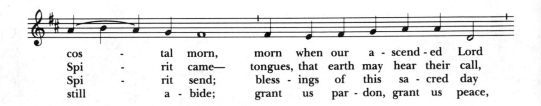

cos - tal morn,   morn when our a - scend - ed Lord
Spi - rit came—   tongues, that earth may hear their call,
Spi - rit send;   bless - ings of this sa - cred day
still a - bide;   grant us par - don, grant us peace,

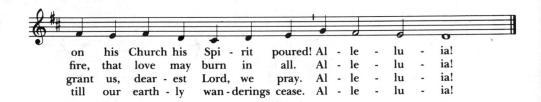

on his Church his Spi - rit poured! Al - le - lu - ia!
fire, that love may burn in all. Al - le - lu - ia!
grant us, dear - est Lord, we pray. Al - le - lu - ia!
till our earth - ly wan - derings cease. Al - le - lu - ia!

Words: Att. Hilary of Poitiers (4th cent.); tr. Robert Campbell (1824-1868), alt.
Music: *Sonne der Gerechtigkeit*, melody from *Bohemian Brethren, Kirchengeseng,* 1566   77. 77 with Alleluia

Refrain

Hail thee, fes - ti - val day! blest day that art hal-lowed for

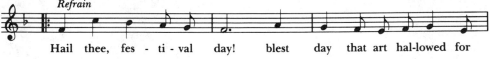

ev - er, day when the Ho - ly Ghost shone in the

First time only | 2

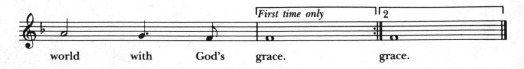

world with God's grace.   grace.

1 Lo, in the like - ness of fire, on those who a -
3 Hark! for in myr - i - ad tongues Christ's own, his___

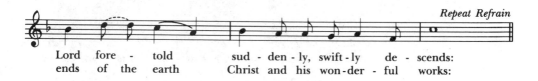

wait his ap - pear - ing, he whom the
cho - sen a - pos - tles, preach to the

Repeat Refrain

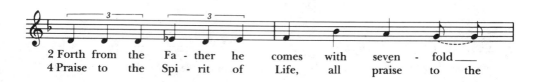

Lord fore - told sud - den - ly, swift - ly de - scends:
ends of the earth Christ and his won - der - ful works:

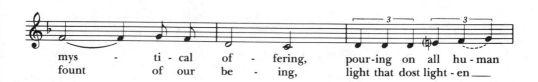

2 Forth from the Fa - ther he comes with sev - en - fold___
4 Praise to the Spi - rit of Life, all praise to the

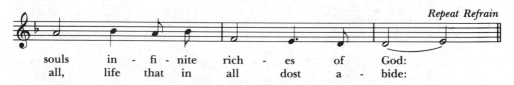

mys - ti - cal of - fering, pour - ing on all hu - man
fount of our be - ing, light that dost light - en___

Repeat Refrain

souls in - fi - nite rich - es of God:
all, life that in all dost a - bide:

The refrain may be sung once by choir alone and repeated by all. The stanzas may be sung by choir alone, alternately by contrasted groups, or by all.

Words: Venantius Honorius Fortunatus (540?-600?); tr. *English Hymnal*, 1906, alt.
Music: *Salve festa dies*, Ralph Vaughan Williams (1872-1958)

Irr.

1. Come, thou Ho - ly Spi - rit bright; come with thy ce - les - tial light;

pour on us thy love di - vine. Come, pro - tec - tor of the poor;

come, thou source of bless - ings sure; come with - in our hearts to shine.

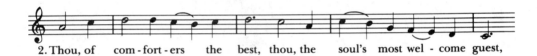

2. Thou, of com - fort - ers the best, thou, the soul's most wel - come guest,

of our peace thou art the sign. In our la - bor, be our aid;

in our sum - mer, cool - ing shade. Ev - ery bit - ter tear re - fine.

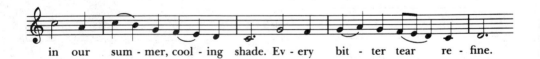

3. Bright-er than the noon - day sun, fill our lives which Christ has won;

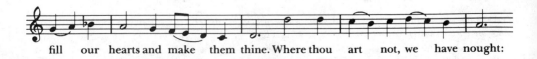

fill our hearts and make them thine. Where thou art not, we have nought:

all our word and deed and thought twist-ed from thy true de-sign.

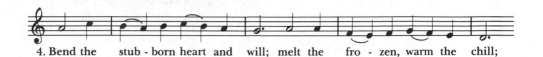

4. Bend the stub-born heart and will; melt the fro-zen, warm the chill;

rule us by thy judg-ment's line. Cleanse us with thy heal-ing power;

what is bar-ren bring to flower; to thy love our sins con-sign.

5. To thy peo-ple who a-dore and con-fess thee ev-er-more,

thy blest sev-en-fold gift as-sign. Grant us thy sal-va-tion, Lord,

bound-less mer-cy our re-ward, joys which earth and heaven en-twine.

Words: Latin, 12th cent.; tr. Charles P. Price (b. 1920)
Music: *Veni Sancte Spiritus*, plainsong, Mode 1, *Dublin Troper*, ca. 1360

777. 777

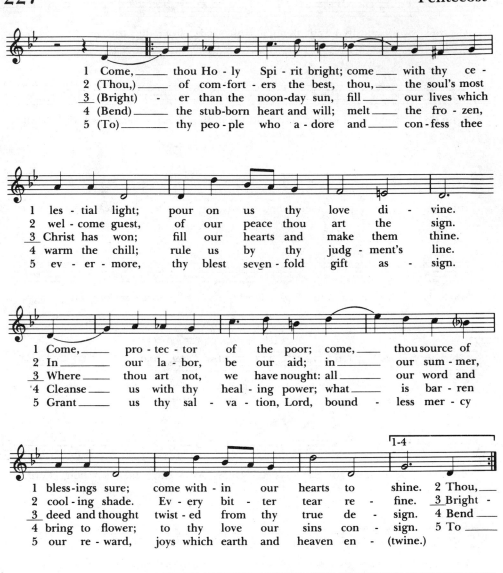

1 Come, _____ thou Ho - ly Spi - rit bright; come _____ with thy ce -
2 (Thou,) _____ of com-fort - ers the best, thou, _____ the soul's most
3 (Bright) - er than the noon-day sun, fill _____ our lives which
4 (Bend) _____ the stub-born heart and will; melt _____ the fro - zen,
5 (To) _____ thy peo - ple who a - dore and _____ con - fess thee

1 les - tial light; pour on us thy love di - vine.
2 wel - come guest, of our peace thou art the sign.
3 Christ has won; fill our hearts and make them thine.
4 warm the chill; rule us by thy judg - ment's line.
5 ev - er - more, thy blest seven - fold gift as - sign.

1 Come, _____ pro - tec - tor of the poor; come, _____ thou source of
2 In _____ our la - bor, be our aid; in _____ our sum - mer,
3 Where _____ thou art not, we have nought: all _____ our word and
4 Cleanse _____ us with thy heal - ing power; what _____ is bar - ren
5 Grant _____ us thy sal - va - tion, Lord, bound - less mer - cy

[1-4]

1 bless-ings sure; come with - in our hearts to shine. 2 Thou, ____
2 cool - ing shade. Ev - ery bit - ter tear re - fine. 3 Bright -
3 deed and thought twist - ed from thy true de - sign. 4 Bend ____
4 bring to flower; to thy love our sins con - sign. 5 To _____
5 our re - ward, joys which earth and heaven en - (twine.)

Final Ending

5 twine.

Words: Latin, 12th cent.; tr. Charles P. Price (b. 1920)
Music: *Arbor Street*, William Albright (b. 1944)

777. 777

1 Ho - ly Spi - rit, font of light, fo - cus of God's glo - ry bright,
2 Source of strength and sure re - lief, com - fort - er in time of grief,
3 En - ter each as - pir - ing heart, oc - cu - py its in - most part
4 With your soft, re - fresh - ing rains break our drought, re - move our stains;
5 As your prom - ise we be - lieve, make us rea - dy to re - ceive

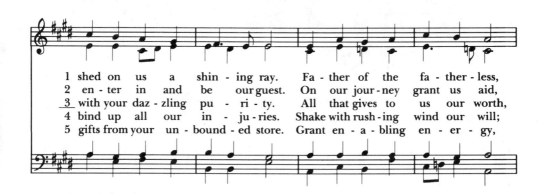

1 shed on us a shin - ing ray. Fa - ther of the fa - ther - less,
2 en - ter in and be our guest. On our jour - ney grant us aid,
3 with your daz - zling pu - ri - ty. All that gives to us our worth,
4 bind up all our in - ju - ries. Shake with rush - ing wind our will;
5 gifts from your un - bound - ed store. Grant en - a - bling en - er - gy,

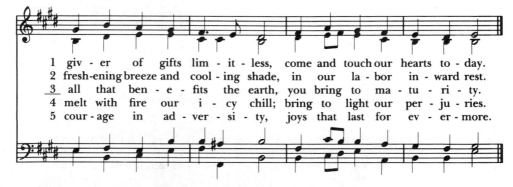

1 giv - er of gifts lim - it - less, come and touch our hearts to - day.
2 fresh - ening breeze and cool - ing shade, in our la - bor in - ward rest.
3 all that ben - e - fits the earth, you bring to ma - tu - ri - ty.
4 melt with fire our i - cy chill; bring to light our per - ju - ries.
5 cour - age in ad - ver - si - ty, joys that last for ev - er - more.

Words: Latin, 12th cent.; tr. John Webster Grant (b. 1919), alt.
Music: *Webbe*, melody from *An Essay on the Church Plain Chant*, 1782; adapt. att. Samuel Webbe
(1740-1816), alt.; harm. *Hymns Ancient and Modern*, 1916

77. 77. 77

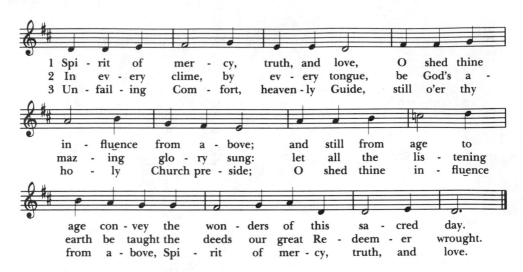

1 Spi - rit of mer - cy, truth, and love, O shed thine
2 In ev - ery clime, by ev - ery tongue, be God's a -
3 Un - fail - ing Com - fort, heaven - ly Guide, still o'er thy

in - fluence from a - bove; and still from age to
maz - ing glo - ry sung: let all the lis - tening
ho - ly Church pre - side; O shed thine in - fluence

age con - vey the won - ders of this sa - cred day.
earth be taught the deeds our great Re - deem - er wrought.
from a - bove, Spi - rit of mer - cy, truth, and love.

Words: Anon., *Psalms, Hymns, and Anthems*, 1774, alt.
Music: *Cornish*, M. Lee Suitor (b. 1942)   LM

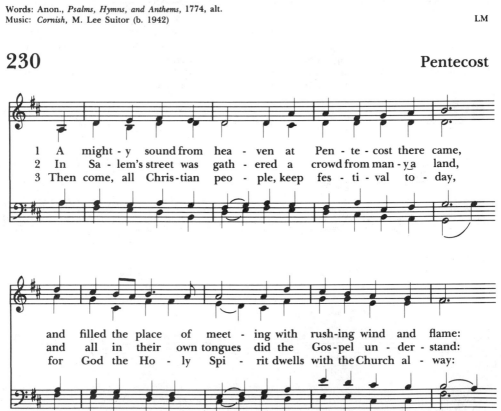

1 A might - y sound from hea - ven at Pen - te - cost there came,
2 In Sa - lem's street was gath - ered a crowd from man - y a land,
3 Then come, all Chris - tian peo - ple, keep fes - ti - val to - day,

and filled the place of meet - ing with rush-ing wind and flame:
and all in their own tongues did the Gos - pel un - der - stand:
for God the Ho - ly Spi - rit dwells with the Church al - way:

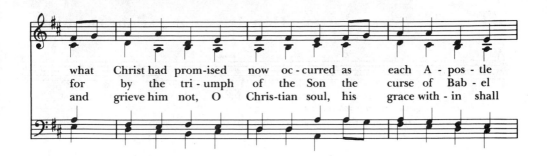

what Christ had prom-ised now oc-curred as each A-pos-tle
for by the tri-umph of the Son the curse of Bab-el
and grieve him not, O Chris-tian soul, his grace with-in shall

spoke the word be-neath the Spi-rit's thun - der, and to the
was un-done when God did send the Spi - rit; so to the
make you whole in bo-dy, mind, and spi - rit, un-til you

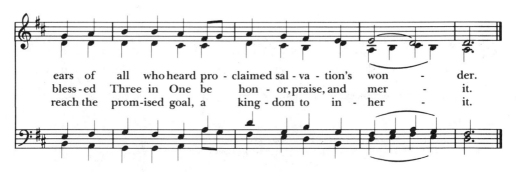

ears of all who heard pro-claimed sal-va-tion's won - der.
bless-ed Three in One be hon-or, praise, and mer - it.
reach the prom-ised goal, a king-dom to in-her - it.

Words: George B. Timms (b. 1910), alt.
Music: *Song of the Holy Spirit*, Dutch melody; harm. Alec Wyton (b. 1921)   76. 76. 887. 87

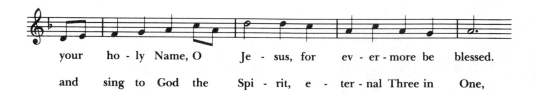

1 By all your saints still striv - ing, for all your saints at rest,
2 *(Insert the stanza appropriate to the day)*
3 Then let us praise the Fa - ther and wor - ship God the Son

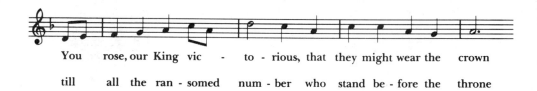

your ho - ly Name, O Je - sus, for ev - er - more be blessed.

and sing to God the Spi - rit, e - ter - nal Three in One,

You rose, our King vic - to - rious, that they might wear the crown

till all the ran - somed num - ber who stand be - fore the throne

and ev - er shine in splen - dor re - flect - ed from your throne.

a - scribe all power and glo - ry and praise to God a - lone.

Saints' Days.

Words: Horatio Bolton Nelson (1823-1913); ver. *Hymnal 1982*
Music: *King's Lynn*, English melody; adapt. Ralph Vaughan Williams (1872-1958)   76. 76. D

Saint Andrew *November 30*

All praise, O Lord, for Andrew,
    the first to follow you;
he witnessed to his brother,
    "This is Messiah true."
You called him from his fishing
    upon Lake Galilee;
he rose to meet your challenge,
    "Leave all and follow me."

Saint Thomas *December 21*

All praise, O Lord, for Thomas
    whose short-lived doubtings prove
your perfect two-fold nature,
    the depth of your true love.
To all who live with questions
    a steadfast faith afford;
and grant us grace to know you,
    made flesh, yet God and Lord.

Saint Stephen *December 26*

All praise, O Lord, for Stephen
　　who, martyred, saw you stand
to help in time of torment,
　　to plead at God's right hand.
Like you, our suffering Savior,
　　his enemies he blessed,
with "Lord, receive my spirit,"
　　his faith, in death, confessed.

Saint John *December 27*

For John, your loved disciple,
　　exiled to Patmos' shore,
and for his faithful record,
　　we praise you evermore;
praise for the mystic vision
　　his words to us unfold.
Instill in us his longing,
　　your glory to behold.

The Holy Innocents *December 28*

Praise for your infant martyrs,
　　whom your mysterious love
called early from life's conflicts
　　to share your peace above.
O Rachel, cease your weeping;
　　they're free from pain and cares.
Lord, grant us crowns as brilliant
　　and lives as pure as theirs.

Confession of Saint Peter *January 18*

We praise you, Lord, for Peter,
　　so eager and so bold:
thrice falling, yet repentent,
　　thrice charged to feed your fold.
Lord, make your pastors faithful
　　to guard your flock from harm
and hold them when they waver
　　with your almighty arm.

Conversion of Saint Paul *January 25*

Praise for the light from heaven
　　and for the voice of awe,
praise for the glorious vision
　　the persecutor saw.
O Lord, for Paul's conversion,
　　we bless your Name today.
Come shine within our darkness
　　and guide us in the Way.

Saint Matthias *February 24*

For one in place of Judas,
　　the apostles sought God's choice:
the lot fell to Matthias
　　for whom we now rejoice.
May we like true apostles
　　your holy Church defend,
and not betray our calling
　　but serve you to the end.

Saint Joseph *March 19*

All praise, O God, for Joseph,
　　the guardian of your Son,
who saved him from King Herod
　　when safety there was none.
He taught the trade of builder,
　　when they to Nazareth came,
and Joseph's love made "Father"
　　to be, for Christ, God's Name.

Saint Mark *April 25*

For Mark, O Lord, we praise you,
　　the weak by grace made strong:
his witness in his Gospel
　　becomes victorious song.
May we, in all our weakness,
　　receive your power divine,
and all, as faithful branches
　　grow strong in you, the Vine.

Saint Philip and Saint James *May 1*

We praise you, Lord, for Philip,
　　blest guide to Greek and Jew,
and for young James the faithful,
　　who heard and followed you.
O grant us grace to know you,
　　the victor in the strife,
that we with all your servants
　　may wear the crown of life.

Saint Barnabas *June 11*

For Barnabas we praise you,
　　who kept your law of love
and, leaving earthly treasures,
　　sought riches from above.
O Christ, our Lord and Savior,
　　let gifts of grace descend,
that your true consolation
　　may through the world extend.

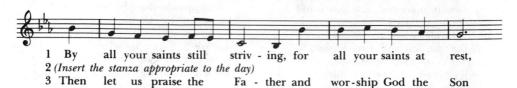

1 By   all your saints still   striv - ing, for   all your saints at   rest,
2 *(Insert the stanza appropriate to the day)*
3 Then   let us praise the   Fa - ther and   wor-ship God the   Son

your   ho - ly Name, O   Je - sus for   ev - er - more be   blessed.

and   sing to God the   Spi - rit, e - ter - nal   Three in   One,

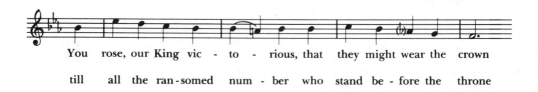

You   rose, our King vic - to - rious, that   they might wear the   crown

till   all the ran-somed   num - ber who   stand be - fore the   throne

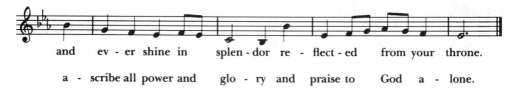

and   ev - er shine in   splen - dor re - flect - ed   from your   throne.

a - scribe all power and   glo - ry and   praise to   God a - lone.

Saints' Days.

Words: Horatio Bolton Nelson (1823-1913); ver. *Hymnal 1982*
Music: *Nyland,* Finnish folk melody; adapt. David Evans (1874-1948)   76. 76. D

The Nativity of Saint John the Baptist *June 24*

All praise for John the Baptist,
    forerunner of the Word,
our true Elijah, making
    a highway for the Lord.
The last and greatest prophet,
    he saw the dawning ray
of light that grows in splendor
    until the perfect day.

Saint Peter and Saint Paul *June 29*

We praise you for Saint Peter;
  we praise you for Saint Paul.
They taught both Jew and Gentile
  that Christ is all in all.
To cross and sword they yielded
  and saw the kingdom come:
O God, your two apostles,
  won life through martyrdom.

Saint Mary Magdalene *July 22*

All praise for Mary Magdalene,
  whose wholeness was restored
by you, her faithful Master,
  her Savior and her Lord.
On Easter morning early,
  a word from you sufficed:
her faith was first to see you,
  her Lord, the risen Christ.

Saint James *July 25*

O Lord, for James, we praise you,
  who fell to Herod's sword.
He drank the cup of suffering
  and thus fulfilled your word.
Lord, curb our vain impatience
  for glory and for fame,
equip us for such sufferings
  as glorify your Name.

Saint Mary the Virgin *August 15*

We sing with joy of Mary
  whose heart with awe was stirred
when, youthful and unready,
  she heard the angel's word;
yet she her voice upraises,
  God's glory to proclaim,
as once for our salvation
  your mother she became.

Saint Bartholomew *August 24*

Praise for your blest apostle
  surnamed Bartholomew;
we know not his achievements
  but know that he was true,
for he at the ascension
  was an apostle still.
May we discern your presence
  and seek, like him, your will.

Saint Matthew *September 21*

We praise you, Lord, for Matthew,
  whose gospel words declare
that, worldly gain forsaking,
  your path of life we share.
From all unrighteous mammon,
  O raise our eyes anew,
that we, whate'er our station
  may rise and follow you.

Saint Luke *October 18*

For Luke, beloved physician,
  all praise, whose Gospel shows
the healer of the nations,
  the one who shares our woes.
Your wine and oil, O Savior,
  upon our spirits pour,
and with true balm of Gilead
  anoint us evermore.

Saint James of Jerusalem *October 23*

Praise for the Lord's own brother,
  James of Jerusalem;
he saw the risen Savior
  and placed his faith in him.
Presiding at the council
  that set the Gentiles free,
he welcomed them as kindred
  on equal terms to be.

Saint Simon and Saint Jude *October 28*

Praise, Lord, for your apostles,
  Saint Simon and Saint Jude.
One love, one hope, impelled them
  to tread the way, renewed.
May we with zeal as earnest
  the faith of Christ maintain,
be bound in love together,
  and life eternal gain.

All Saints' Day *November 1*

Apostles, prophets, martyrs,
  and all the noble throng
who wear the spotless raiment
  and raise the ceaseless song:
for them and those whose witness
  is only known to you—
by walking in their footsteps
  we give you praise anew.

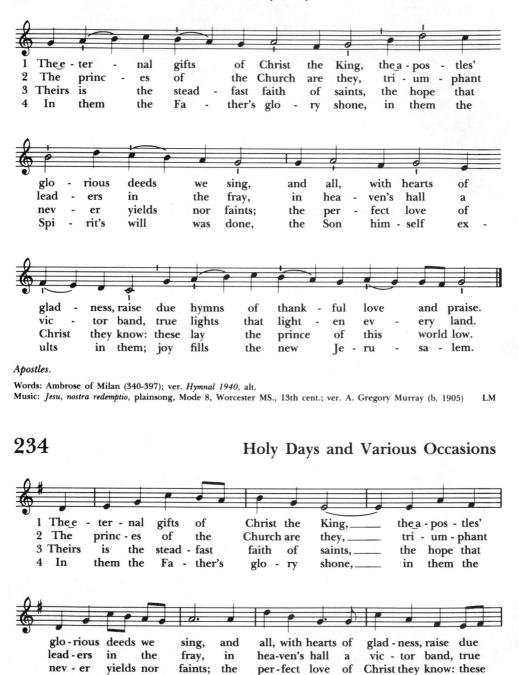

1 The e - ter - nal gifts of Christ the King, the a - pos - tles'
2 The princ - es of the Church are they, tri - um - phant
3 Theirs is the stead - fast faith of saints, the hope that
4 In them the Fa - ther's glo - ry shone, in them the

glo - rious deeds we sing, and all, with hearts of
lead - ers in the fray, in hea - ven's hall a
nev - er yields nor faints; the per - fect love of
Spi - rit's will was done, the Son him - self ex -

glad - ness, raise due hymns of thank - ful love and praise.
vic - tor band, true lights that light - en ev - ery land.
Christ they know: these lay the prince of this world low.
ults in them; joy fills the new Je - ru - sa - lem.

Apostles.

Words: Ambrose of Milan (340-397); ver. *Hymnal 1940*, alt.
Music: *Jesu, nostra redemptio*, plainsong, Mode 8, Worcester MS., 13th cent.; ver. A. Gregory Murray (b. 1905)　　　LM

1 The e - ter - nal gifts of Christ the King, the a - pos - tles'
2 The princ - es of the Church are they, tri - um - phant
3 Theirs is the stead - fast faith of saints, the hope that
4 In them the Fa - ther's glo - ry shone, in them the

glo - rious deeds we sing, and all, with hearts of glad - ness, raise due
lead - ers in the fray, in hea - ven's hall a vic - tor band, true
nev - er yields nor faints; the per - fect love of Christ they know: these
Spi - rit's will was done, the Son him - self ex - ults in them; joy

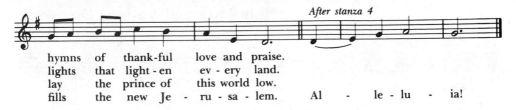

After stanza 4

hymns	of	thank-ful	love and praise.	
lights	that	light-en	ev-ery land.	
lay	the	prince of	this world low.	
fills	the	new Je-ru-sa-lem.	Al - le - lu - ia!	

Apostles.

Words: Ambrose of Milan (340-397); ver. *Hymnal 1940*, alt.
Music: *Gonfalon Royal*, Percy Carter Buck (1871-1947)

LM

Holy Days and Various Occasions

235

1 Come sing, ye choirs ex-ult - ant, those mes-sen-gers of God,
2 In one har-mo-nious wit - ness the cho-sen four com-bine,
3 Four-square on this foun-da - tion the Church of Christ re-mains,

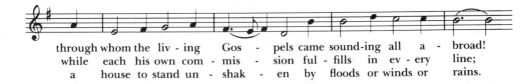

through whom the liv-ing Gos - pels came sound-ing all a - broad!
while each his own com-mis - sion ful-fills in ev-ery line;
a house to stand un-shak - en by floods or winds or rains.

Whose voice pro-claimed sal-va - tion that poured up-on the night,
as, in the pro-phet's vi - sion from out the am-ber flame
How blest this ha-bi-ta - tion of gos-pel li-ber-ty,

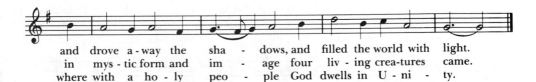

and drove a-way the sha - dows, and filled the world with light.
in mys-tic form and im - age four liv-ing crea-tures came.
where with a ho-ly peo - ple God dwells in U-ni-ty.

Evangelists.

Words: Latin, 12th cent.; tr. Jackson Mason (1833-1889), alt.
Music: *Ach Gott, vom Himmelreiche*, melody Michael Praetorius (1571-1621)

76. 76. D

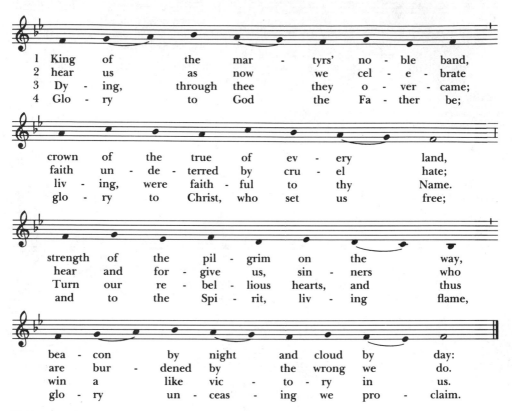

1 King of the mar - tyrs' no - ble band,
2 hear us as now we cel - e - brate
3 Dy - ing, through thee they o - ver - came;
4 Glo - ry to God the Fa - ther be;

crown of the true of ev - ery land,
faith un - de - terred by cru - el hate;
liv - ing, were faith - ful to thy Name.
glo - ry to Christ, who set us free;

strength of the pil - grim on the way,
hear and for - give us, sin - ners who
Turn our re - bel - lious hearts, and thus
and to the Spi - rit, liv - ing flame,

bea - con by night and cloud by day:
are bur - dened by the wrong we do.
win a like vic - to - ry in us.
glo - ry un - ceas - ing we pro - claim.

Martyrs.

Words: Latin; tr. John Webster Grant (b. 1919), alt.
Music: *Jesu, nostra redemptio,* plainsong, Mode 8, Worcester MS., 13th cent.   LM

237   Holy Days and Various Occasions

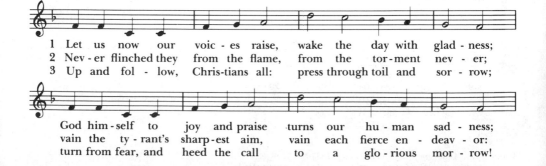

1 Let us now our voic - es raise, wake the day with glad - ness;
2 Nev - er flinched they from the flame, from the tor - ment nev - er;
3 Up and fol - low, Chris-tians all: press through toil and sor - row;

God him - self to joy and praise turns our hu - man sad - ness;
vain the ty - rant's sharp-est aim, vain each fierce en - deav - or:
turn from fear, and heed the call to a glo - rious mor - row!

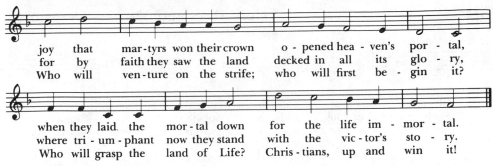

joy that mar-tyrs won their crown o - pened hea - ven's por - tal,
for by faith they saw the land decked in all its glo - ry,
Who will ven-ture on the strife; who will first be - gin it?

when they laid. the mor-tal down for the life im - mor - tal.
where tri - um - phant now they stand with the vic - tor's sto - ry.
Who will grasp the land of Life? Chris - tians, up and win it!

Martyrs.

Words: Joseph the Hymnographer (9th cent.); tr. John Mason Neale (1818-1866), alt.
Music: *Gaudeamus pariter,* melody from *Medieval [German or] Bohemian Carol Melody,* 1544

76. 76. D

Holy Days and Various Occasions

238

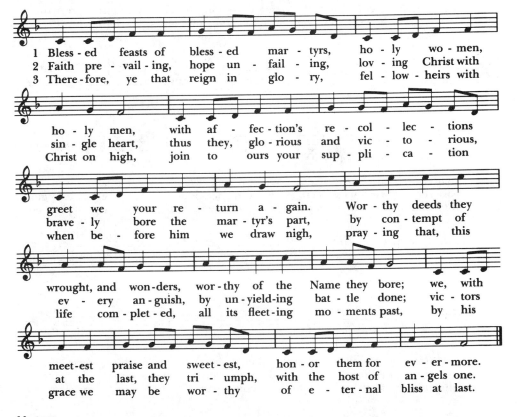

1 Bless - ed feasts of bless - ed mar - tyrs, ho - ly wo - men,
2 Faith pre - vail - ing, hope un - fail - ing, lov - ing Christ with
3 There-fore, ye that reign in glo - ry, fel - low - heirs with

ho - ly men, with af - fec - tion's re - col - lec - tions
sin - gle heart, thus they, glo - rious and vic - to - rious,
Christ on high, join to ours your sup - pli - ca - tion

greet we your re - turn a - gain. Wor - thy deeds they
brave - ly bore the mar - tyr's part, by con - tempt of
when be - fore him we draw nigh, pray - ing that, this

wrought, and won-ders, wor - thy of the Name they bore; we, with
ev - ery an - guish, by un - yield-ing bat - tle done; vic - tors
life com - plet - ed, all its fleet-ing mo - ments past, by his

meet-est praise and sweet - est, hon - or them for ev - er - more.
at the last, they tri - umph, with the host of an - gels one.
grace we may be wor - thy of e - ter - nal bliss at last.

Martyrs.

Words: Latin, 12th cent.; tr. John Mason Neale (1818-1866), alt.
Music: *Holy Manna,* melody from *The Southern Harmony,* 1835

87. 87. D

Unison or harmony

1 Bless - ed feasts of bless - ed mar-tyrs, ho - ly wo - men,
2 Faith pre - vail - ing, hope un - fail - ing, lov - ing Christ with
3 There-fore, ye that reign in glo - ry, fel - low - heirs with

ho - ly men, with af - fec-tion's re - col - lec-tions greet we
sin - gle heart, thus they, glo - rious and vic - to-rious, brave-ly
Christ on high, join to ours your sup - pli - ca-tion when be -

your re - turn a - gain. Wor-thy deeds they wrought, and won-ders,
bore the mar - tyr's part, by con - tempt of ev - ery an - guish,
fore him we draw nigh, pray-ing that, this life com - plet - ed,

wor - thy of the Name they bore; we, with meet - est
by un - yield-ing bat - tle done; vic - tors at the
all its fleet - ing mo - ments past, by his grace we

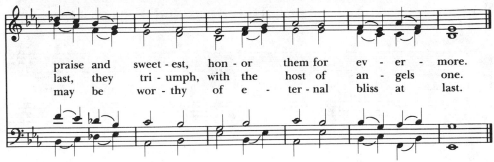

praise and sweet-est, hon-or them for ev - er - more.
last, they tri - umph, with the host of an - gels one.
may be wor-thy of e - ter-nal bliss at last.

Martyrs.

Words: Latin, 12th cent.; tr. John Mason Neale (1818-1866), alt.
Music: *Alta Trinità beata*, melody from *Laudi Spirituali*, 14th cent.; adapt. and
harm. Charles Burney (1726-1814)

87. 87. D

Holy Days and Various Occasions

240

1 Heark-en to the an-them glo - rious of the mar - tyrs
2 Liv - ing, they pro - claimed sal - va - tion, heaven - en - dowed with
3 Christ, for cru - el trai - tors plead - ing, tri - umphed in his
4 Take from him what ye will give him, of his full - ness

robed in white; they, like Christ, in death vic - to - rious
grace and power; and they died in im - i - ta - tion
part - ing breath o'er all mir - a - cles pre - ced - ing
grace for grace; strive to think him, speak him, live him,

dwell for ev - er in the light.
of their Sa - vior's fi - nal hour.
his in - es - ti - ma - ble death.
till you find him face to face.

Martyrs. The C♯ applies to the final stanza only.

Words: Christopher Smart (1722-1771), alt.
Music: *Faciem ejus videtis*, David Thompson Childs (b. 1938)

87. 87

Descant

4 Take from him what ye will give him, of his

1 Heark - en to the an - them glo - rious of the
2 Liv - ing, they pro - claimed sal - va - tion, heaven - en -
3 Christ, for cru - el trai - tors plead - ing, tri - umphed
4 Take from him what ye will give him, of his

full - ness grace for grace; strive to think him,

mar - tyrs robed in white; they, like Christ, in
dowed with grace and power; and they died in
in his part - ing breath o'er all mir - a -
full - ness grace for grace; strive to think him,

speak him, live him, till you find him face to face.

death vic - to - rious dwell for ev - er in the light.
im - i - ta - tion of their Sa - vior's fi - nal hour.
cles pre - ced - ing his in - es - ti - ma - ble death.
speak him, live him, till you find him face to face.

Martyrs.

Words: Christopher Smart (1722-1771), alt.
Music: *Laus Deo*, Richard Redhead (1820-1901); desc. Percy William Whitlock (1903-1946)   87. 87

1 How oft, O Lord, thy face hath shone on doubt-ing souls whose
2 He loved thee well, and firm-ly said, "Come, let us go, and
3 His breth-ren's word he would not take, but craved to touch those
4 He saw thee risen; at once he rose to full be-lief's un-
5 O Sa-vior, make thy pres-ence known to all who doubt thy

1 wills were true! Thou Christ of Pe-ter and of John,
2 die with him"; yet when thine Eas-ter-news was spread,
3 hands of thine; when thou didst thine ap-pear-ance make,
4 cloud-ed height; and still through his con-fes-sion flows
5 Word and thee; and teach us in that Word a-lone

1 thou art the Christ of Thom-as too.
2 mid all its light his faith was dim.
3 he saw, and hailed his Lord Di-vine.
4 to Chris-tian souls thy life and light.
5 to find the truth that sets us free.

Saint Thomas (December 21).

Words: William Bright (1824-1901), alt.
Music: *Jacob,* Jane Manton Marshall (b. 1924)

LM

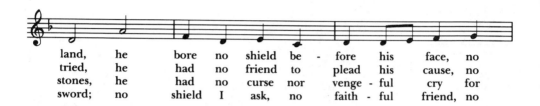

1 When Ste-phen, full of power and grace, went forth through-out the
2 When Ste-phen preached a - gainst the laws and by those laws was
3 When Ste-phen, young and doomed to die, fell crushed be - neath the
4 Let me, O Lord, thy cause de - fend, a knight with - out a

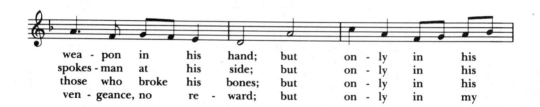

land, he bore no shield be - fore his face, no
tried, he had no friend to plead his cause, no
stones, he had no curse nor venge - ful cry for
sword; no shield I ask, no faith - ful friend, no

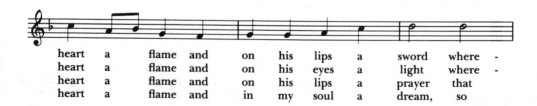

wea - pon in his hand; but on - ly in his
spokes - man at his side; but on - ly in his
those who broke his bones; but on - ly in his
ven - geance, no re - ward; but on - ly in my

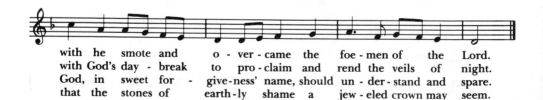

heart a flame and on his lips a sword where -
heart a flame and on his eyes a light where -
heart a flame and on his lips a prayer that
heart a flame and in my soul a dream, so

with he smote and o - ver - came the foe - men of the Lord.
with God's day - break to pro - claim and rend the veils of night.
God, in sweet for - give-ness' name, should un - der - stand and spare.
that the stones of earth-ly shame a jew - eled crown may seem.

Saint Stephen (December 26).

Words: Jan Struther (1901-1953), alt.
Music: *Salvation,* melody from *Kentucky Harmony,* 1816   CMD

1 Come, pure hearts, in joy-ful mea-sure sing of those who
2 See the riv-ers four that glad-den, with their streams, the
3 O that we, thy truth con-fess-ing, and thy ho-ly

spread the trea-sure in the ho-ly Gos-pels shrined;
bet-ter E-den plant-ed by our Lord most dear;
word pos-sess-ing, Je-sus may thy love a-dore;

bless-ed tid-ings of sal-va-tion, peace on earth their
Christ the foun-tain, these the wa-ters; drink, O Zi-on's
un-to thee our voic-es rais-ing, thee with all thy

proc-la-ma-tion, love from God to lost man-kind.
sons and daugh-ters, drink, and find sal-va-tion here.
ran-somed prais-ing, ev-er and for ev-er-more.

Evangelists.

Words: Latin, 12th cent.; tr. *Hymns Ancient and Modern*, 1861, after Robert Campbell (1814-1868), alt.
Music: *Alles ist an Gottes Segen*, melody att. Johann Balthasar König (1691-1758), alt.;
    harm. Johan Löhner (1645-1705), after chorale version by Johann Sebastian Bach (1685-1750)   887. 887

1 Praise God for John, e - van - ge - list, who bore the Spi - rit's
2 Your great I AM's Saint John re - cords, signs of your grace di -
3 O Word made flesh, your deeds and words re - fresh our hearts like

sword, whose words re - flect, like ea - gles' wings, the
vine: "I am the way, the truth, the life; the
dew. Our thanks we raise that all John wrote bears

glo - ry of our Lord. Your bright - ness, O e -
light; the liv - ing vine; your soul's true bread; thirst -
wit - ness, Lord, to you. We praise you that John's

ter - nal Word, A - pos - tle John un - furled, the
quench - ing stream. All these I am, and more: the
voice still lives your glo - ry to pro - claim where -

full - ness of your grace and truth for us and all the world.
faith - ful shep - herd of the flock, the sheep-fold's on - ly door."
by your Spi - rit gives us life, the faith to bear your Name.

Saint John (December 27).

Words: F. Samuel Janzow (b. 1913)
Music: *Noel*, English melody; adapt. Arthur Seymour Sullivan (1842-1900)

CMD

Holy Days and Various Occasions

246

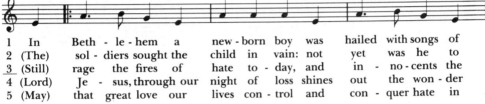

1 In Beth - le - hem a new - born boy was hailed with songs of
2 (The) sol - diers sought the child in vain: not yet was he to
3 (Still) rage the fires of hate to - day, and in - no - cents the
4 (Lord) Je - sus, through our night of loss shines out the won - der
5 (May) that great love our lives con - trol and con - quer hate in

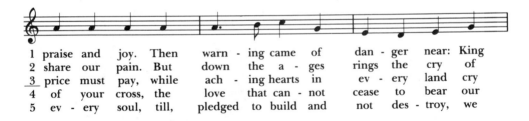

1 praise and joy. Then warn - ing came of dan - ger near: King
2 share our pain. But down the a - ges rings the cry of
3 price must pay, while ach - ing hearts in ev - ery land cry
4 of your cross, the love that can - not cease to bear our
5 ev - ery soul, till, pledged to build and not des - troy, we

|1-4   ‖Final Ending

1 He - rod's troops would soon ap - pear. ———— | 2 The
2 those who saw their chil - dren die. ———— | 3 Still
3 out "We can - not un - der - stand!" ———— | 4 Lord
4 hu - man an - guish ev - ery - where. ———— | 5 May
5 share your pain and find your joy. ————

Holy Innocents (December 28).

Words: Rosamond E. Herklots (b. 1905)
Music: *In Bethlehem*, Wilbur Held (b. 1914)

LM

Burden

Lul - ly, lul - lay, thou lit - tle tin - y child, bye - bye, lul -
ly lul - lay.

1 O sis - ters, too, how may we do
2 He - rod the King, in his ra - ging
3 That woe is me, poor child for thee!

for to pre - serve this day this poor young - ling for
charg - ed he hath this day his men of might, in
And ev - ery morn and day, for thy part - ing nor

Repeat Burden after verse 3

whom we sing bye - bye, lul - ly lul - lay?
his own sight, all young chil - dren to slay.
say nor sing bye - bye, lul - ly lul - lay.

Holy Innocents (December 28).

Words: Coventry carol, 15th cent.
Music: *Coventry Carol*, melody from *Pageant of the Shearmen and Tailors*, 15th cent.;
      harm. Martin Fallas Shaw (1875-1958)

44. 6 D with Refrain

1 To the Name of our sal - va - tion laud and hon - or
2 Je - sus is the Name we trea - sure; Name be - yond what
3 'Tis the Name that who - so preach - eth speaks like mu - sic
4 There-fore we, in love a - dor - ing, this most bless - ed

let us pay, which for man - y a gen - er - a - tion
words can tell; Name of glad - ness, Name of plea - sure,
to the ear; who in prayer this Name be - seech - eth
Name re - vere, ho - ly Je - sus, thee im - plor - ing

hid in God's fore - know-ledge lay; but with ho - ly
ear and heart de - light - ing well; Name of sweet-ness,
sweet - est com - fort find - eth near; who its per - fect
so to write it in us here that here - af - ter,

ex - ul - ta - tion we may sing a - loud to - day.
pass - ing mea - sure, sav - ing us from sin and hell.
wis - dom reach - eth, heaven - ly joy pos - ess - eth here.
heaven-ward soar - ing, we may sing with an - gels there.

Holy Name; New Year (January 1).

Words: Latin, 15th cent.; tr. *Hymns Ancient and Modern,* 1861
Music: *Oriel,* Caspar Ett (1788-1847)

87. 87. 87

1 To the Name of our sal - va - tion laud and hon - or
2 Je - sus is the Name we trea - sure; Name be - yond what
3 'Tis the Name that who - so preach - eth speaks like mu - sic
4 There - fore we, in love a - dor - ing, this most bless - ed

let us pay, which for man - y a gen - er - a - tion
words can tell; Name of glad - ness, Name of plea - sure,
to the ear; who in prayer this Name be - seech - eth
Name re - vere, ho - ly Je - sus, thee im - plor - ing

hid in God's fore - know - ledge lay; but with ho - ly
ear and heart de - light - ing well; Name of sweet - ness,
sweet - est com - fort find - eth near; who its per - fect
so to write it in us here that here - af - ter,

ex - ul - ta - tion we may sing a - loud to - day.
pass - ing mea - sure, sav - ing us from sin and hell.
wis - dom reach - eth, heaven - ly joy pos - sess - eth here.
heaven - ward soar - ing, we may sing with an - gels there.

Holy Name; New Year (January 1).

Words: Latin, 15th cent.; tr. *Hymns Ancient and Modern,* 1861
Music: *Grafton,* melody from *Chants ordinaires de l'Office Divin,* 1881;
　　　　harm. *Songs of Praise,* 1925

87. 87. 87

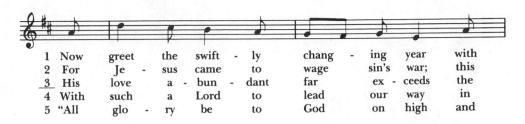

1 Now greet the swift - ly chang - ing year with
2 For Je - sus came to wage sin's war; this
3 His love a - bun - dant far ex - ceeds the
4 With such a Lord to lead our way in
5 "All glo - ry be to God on high and

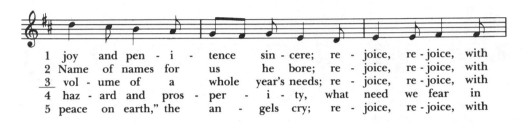

1 joy and pen - i - tence sin - cere; re - joice, re - joice, with
2 Name of names for us he bore; re - joice, re - joice, with
3 vol - ume of a whole year's needs; re - joice, re - joice, with
4 haz - ard and pros - per - i - ty, what need we fear in
5 peace on earth," the an - gels cry; re - joice, re - joice, with

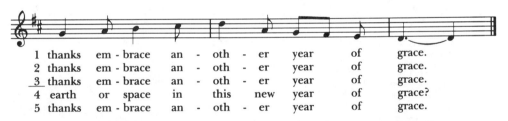

1 thanks em - brace an - oth - er year of grace.
2 thanks em - brace an - oth - er year of grace.
3 thanks em - brace an - oth - er year of grace.
4 earth or space in this new year of grace?
5 thanks em - brace an - oth - er year of grace.

Holy Name; New Year (January 1). The melody may be sung in canon at a distance of one measure.

Words: Slovak, 17th cent.; tr. Jaroslav J. Vajda (b. 1919), alt.
Music: *Sixth Night*, Alfred V. Fedak (b. 1953)

88. 86

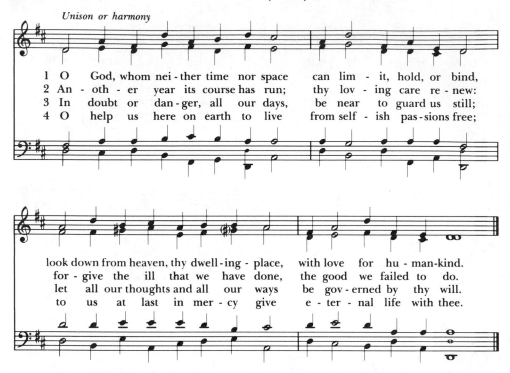

Unison or harmony

1 O God, whom nei-ther time nor space   can lim - it, hold, or bind,
2 An-oth-er year its course has run;   thy lov - ing care re-new:
3 In doubt or dan-ger, all our days,   be near to guard us still;
4 O help us here on earth to live   from self - ish pas-sions free;

look down from heaven, thy dwell-ing-place,   with love for hu-man-kind.
for-give the ill that we have done,   the good we failed to do.
let all our thoughts and all our ways   be gov-erned by thy will.
to us at last in mer-cy give   e - ter - nal life with thee.

Holy Name; New Year (January 1). This hymn may be used at other times by omitting stanza 2.

Words: Horace Smith (1836-1922) and others
Music: *London New*, melody from *The Psalmes of David in Prose and Meeter*, 1635, alt.;
    harm. John Playford (1623-1686)

CM

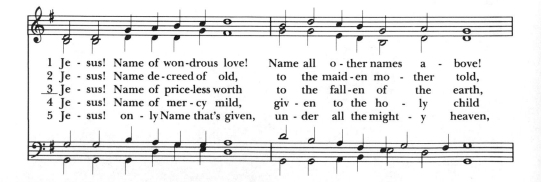

1 Je - sus! Name of won-drous love!   Name all o - ther names a - bove!
2 Je - sus! Name de-creed of old,   to the maid-en mo - ther told,
3 Je - sus! Name of price-less worth   to the fall-en of the earth,
4 Je - sus! Name of mer-cy mild,   giv - en to the ho - ly child
5 Je - sus! on - ly Name that's given,   un - der all the might - y heaven,

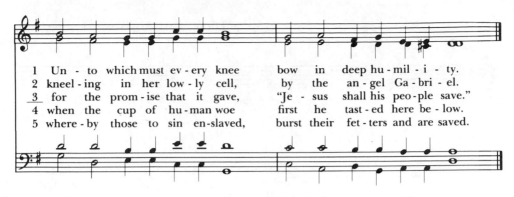

1. Un-to which must ev-ery knee   bow in   deep hu-mil-i-ty.
2. kneel-ing in her low-ly cell,   by the   an-gel Ga-bri-el.
3. for the prom-ise that it gave, "Je-sus   shall his peo-ple save."
4. when the cup of hu-man woe   first he   tast-ed here be-low.
5. where-by those to sin en-slaved, burst their fet-ters and are saved.

6 Jesus! Name of wondrous love!
Human Name of God above;
pleading only this we flee,
helpless, O our God, to thee.

Holy Name; New Year (January 1).

Words: William Walsham How (1823-1897), alt.
Music: *Louez Dieu,* from *Les cent cinquante Pseaumes de David,* 1564

77. 77

Holy Days and Various Occasions   253

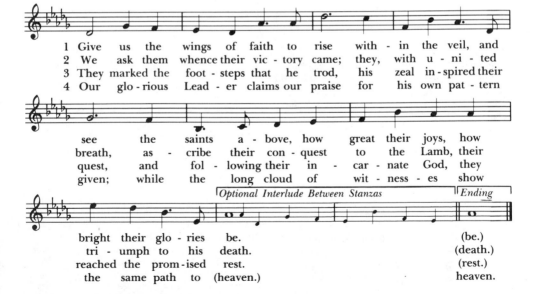

1. Give   us   the   wings of faith to   rise   with-in the veil, and
2. We   ask them whence their vic-tory came;   they, with u-ni-ted
3. They marked the   foot-steps that he trod,   his   zeal in-spired their
4. Our   glo-rious Lead-er claims our praise for   his own pat-tern

see   the   saints a-bove, how great their joys, how
breath, as-cribe their con-quest to the Lamb, their
quest, and fol-lowing their in-car-nate God, they
given; while the long cloud of wit-ness-es show

Optional Interlude Between Stanzas   *Ending*

bright their glo-ries be.   (be.)
tri-umph to his death.   (death.)
reached the prom-ised rest.   (rest.)
the same path to (heaven.)   heaven.

Saints' Days; All Saints' Day (November 1).

Words: Isaac Watts (1674-1748), alt.
Music: *San Rocco,* Derek Williams (b. 1945)

CM

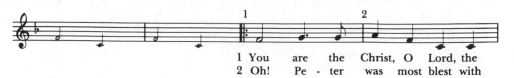

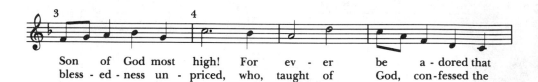

1 You   are   the   Christ, O   Lord, the
2 Oh!   Pe - ter   was   most blest with

Son   of God most   high!   For   ev - er   be   a - dored that
bless - ed - ness un - priced,   who,   taught of   God,   con-fessed the

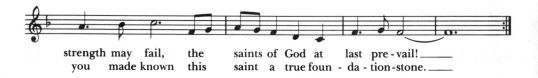

Name   in   earth   and   sky,   in   which, though mor - tal
God - head   in   the   Christ!   For   of   your   Church, Lord,

strength may   fail,   the   saints of God at   last pre - vail!
you   made known   this   saint a true foun - da - tion-stone.

Confession of Saint Peter (January 18). This hymn may be sung as a two- or four-part canon with entrances alternating between treble and male voices.

Words: William Walsham How (1823-1897), alt.
Music: *Wyngate Canon,* Richard Wayne Dirksen (b. 1921)

66. 66. 88

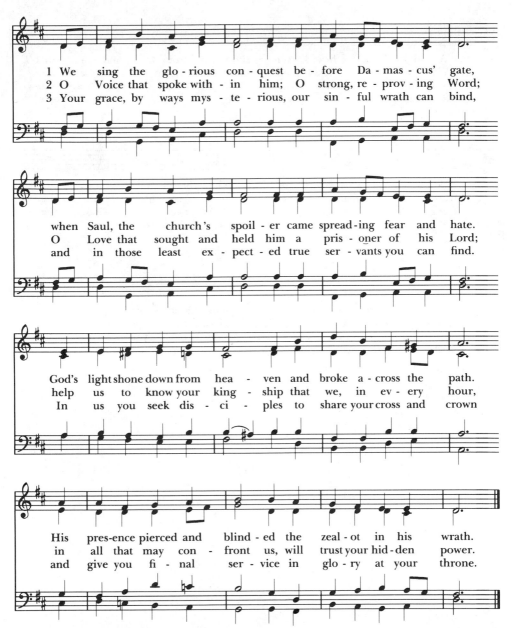

1 We sing the glorious conquest before Damascus' gate,
when Saul, the church's spoiler came spreading fear and hate.
God's light shone down from heaven and broke across the path.
His presence pierced and blinded the zealot in his wrath.

2 O Voice that spoke within him; O strong, reproving Word;
O Love that sought and held him a prisoner of his Lord;
help us to know your kingship that we, in every hour,
in all that may confront us, will trust your hidden power.

3 Your grace, by ways mysterious, our sinful wrath can bind,
and in those least expected true servants you can find.
In us you seek disciples to share your cross and crown
and give you final service in glory at your throne.

Conversion of Saint Paul (January 25).

Words: John Ellerton (1826-1893), alt.
Music: *Munich*, melody from *Neu-vermehrtes und zu Ubung Christl. Gottseligkeit eingerichtetes Meiningisches Gesangbuch*, 1693; adapt. and harm. Felix Mendelssohn (1809-1847)

76. 76. D

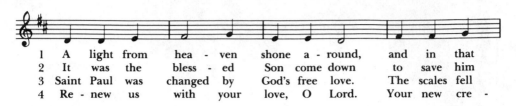

1 A light from hea - ven shone a - round, and in that
2 It was the bless - ed Son come down to save him
3 Saint Paul was changed by God's free love. The scales fell
4 Re - new us with your love, O Lord. Your new cre -

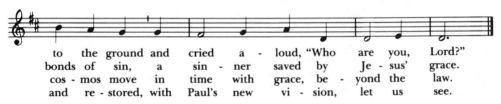

light a voice was heard. Then Saul fell blind - ed
from his fear - ful ways and free him from the
from his eyes, he saw the love of God, the
a - tion let us be; re - deemed for ev - er

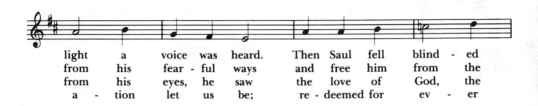

to the ground and cried a - loud, "Who are you, Lord?"
bonds of sin, a sin - ner saved by Je - sus' grace.
cos - mos move in time with grace, be - yond the law.
and re - stored, with Paul's new vi - sion, let us see.

Conversion of Saint Paul (January 25).

Words: Gracia Grindal (b. 1943), alt.
Music: *Cornish,* M. Lee Suitor (b. 1942)   LM

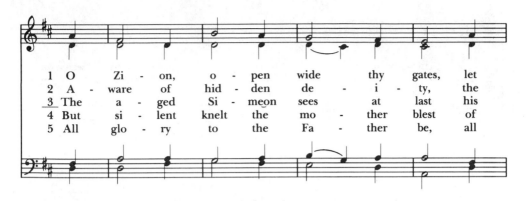

1. O Zi - on, o - pen wide thy gates, let
2. A - ware of hid - den de - i - ty, the
3. The a - ged Si - meon sees at last his
4. But si - lent knelt the mo - ther blest of
5. All glo - ry to the Fa - ther be, all

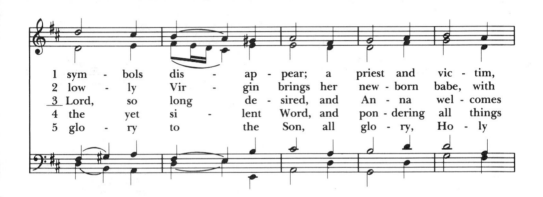

1. sym - bols dis - ap - pear; a priest and vic - tim,
2. low - ly Vir - gin brings her new - born babe, with
3. Lord, so long de - sired, and An - na wel - comes
4. the yet si - lent Word, and pon - dering all things
5. glo - ry to the Son, all glo - ry, Ho - ly

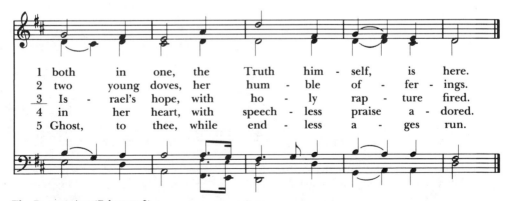

1. both in one, the Truth him - self, is here.
2. two young doves, her hum - ble of - fer - ings.
3. Is - rael's hope, with ho - ly rap - ture fired.
4. in her heart, with speech - less praise a - dored.
5. Ghost, to thee, while end - less a - ges run.

The Presentation (February 2).

Words: Jean Baptiste de Santeüil (1630-1697); tr. Edward Caswall (1814-1878), alt.
Music: *Edmonton*, from *Harmonia Sacra*, ca. 1760

CM

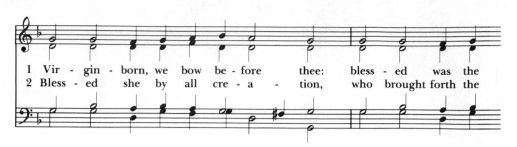

1 Vir - gin - born, we bow be - fore   thee: bless - ed   was   the
2 Bless - ed   she   by   all   cre - a -   tion,   who   brought forth the

womb that bore   thee; __ Ma - ry,   Mo - ther meek and   mild, __
world's sal - va -   tion, and   bless - ed   they, for   ev - er blest,   who

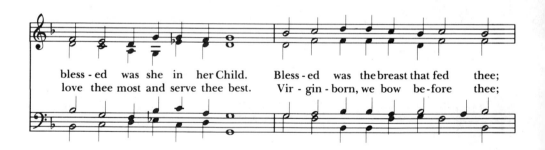

bless - ed   was she in her Child.   Bless - ed   was the breast that fed   thee;
love thee most and serve thee best.   Vir - gin - born, we bow be - fore   thee;

bless - ed   was   the hand that led   thee;   bless - ed   was   the
bless - ed   was   the womb that bore   thee;   Ma - ry,   Mo - ther

par - ent's eye that watched thy slum-bering in - fan - cy.
meek and mild,_____ bless - ed was she in her Child.

The Presentation (February 2); The Annunciation (March 25).

Words: Reginald Heber (1783-1826)
Music: *Psalm 86,* Claude Goudimel (1514-1572), alt.

88. 77. D

Holy Days and Various Occasions

259

1 Hail to the Lord who comes, comes to his tem - ple gate;
2 but, borne up - on the throne of Ma - ry's gen - tle breast,
3 There Jo - seph at her side in rev - erent won - der stands;
4 O Light of all the earth, thy chil - dren wait for thee!

not with his an - gel host, not in his king - ly state;
watched by her du - teous love, in her fond arms at rest,
and, filled with ho - ly joy, old Si - meon in his hands
Come to thy tem - ples here, that we, from sin set free,

no shouts pro-claim him nigh, no crowds his com - ing wait;
thus to his Fa - ther's house he comes, the heaven - ly guest.
takes up the prom-ised child, the glo - ry of all lands.
be - fore thy Fa - ther's face may all pre - sent - ed be!

The Presentation (February 2).

Words: John Ellerton (1826-1893), alt.
Music: *Old 120th,* melody from *The Whole Booke of Psalmes,* 1570; harm. Thomas Ravenscroft (1592?-1635?),
after Richard Allison (16th cent.); adapt. Ralph Vaughan Williams (1872-1958)

66. 66. 66

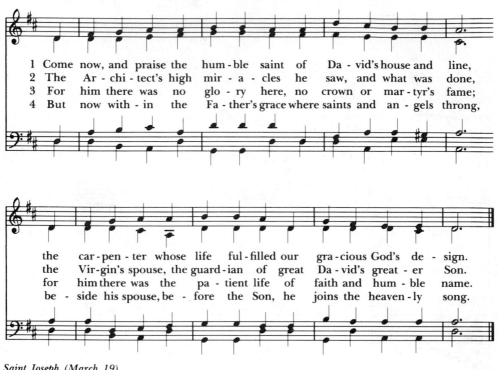

1 Come now, and praise the hum-ble saint of Da-vid's house and line,
2 The Ar-chi-tect's high mir-a-cles he saw, and what was done,
3 For him there was no glo-ry here, no crown or mar-tyr's fame;
4 But now with-in the Fa-ther's grace where saints and an-gels throng,

the car-pen-ter whose life ful-filled our gra-cious God's de-sign.
the Vir-gin's spouse, the guard-ian of great Da-vid's great-er Son.
for him there was the pa-tient life of faith and hum-ble name.
be-side his spouse, be-fore the Son, he joins the heaven-ly song.

Saint Joseph (March 19).

Words: George W. Williams (b. 1922)
Music: *Tallis' Ordinal*, Thomas Tallis (1505?-1585)   CM

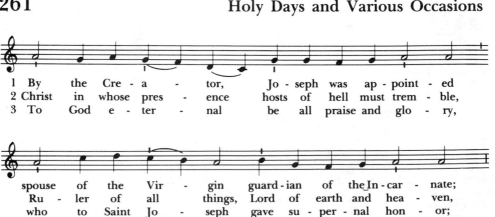

1 By the Cre-a-tor, Jo-seph was ap-point-ed
2 Christ in whose pres-ence hosts of hell must trem-ble,
3 To God e-ter-nal be all praise and glo-ry,

spouse of the Vir-gin guard-ian of the In-car-nate;
Ru-ler of all things, Lord of earth and hea-ven,
who to Saint Jo-seph gave su-per-nal hon-or;

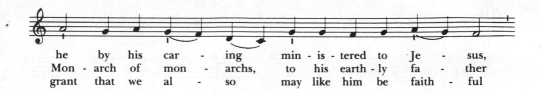

he	by	his	car -	ing	min - is - tered	to	Je -		sus,
Mon -	arch	of	mon -	archs,	to his earth - ly	fa -			ther
grant	that	we	al -	so	may like him be	faith -			ful

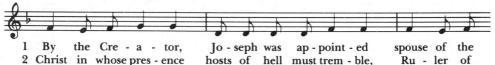

source	of	sal -	va -	tion.
free -	ly	was	sub -	ject.
in	our	o -	be -	dience.

Saint Joseph (March 19).

Words: Hieronimo Casanate (d. 1700); tr. *Hymnal 1982*
Music: *Caelitum Joseph*, plainsong, Mode 1; ver. Schola Antiqua, 1983   11 11. 11 5

Holy Days and Various Occasions   262

1 By   the Cre - a - tor,   Jo - seph was ap - point - ed   spouse of the
2 Christ in whose pres - ence hosts of hell must trem - ble,   Ru - ler of
3 To   God e - ter - nal   be all praise and glo - ry,   who to Saint

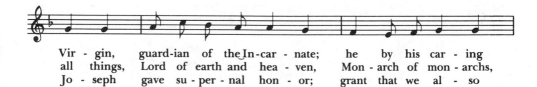

Vir - gin,   guard-ian of the In - car - nate;   he   by his car - ing
all things, Lord of earth and hea - ven,   Mon - arch of mon - archs,
Jo - seph   gave su - per - nal hon - or;   grant that we al - so

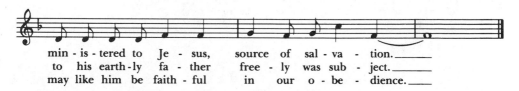

min - is - tered to Je - sus,   source of sal - va - tion.____
to   his earth - ly fa - ther   free - ly was sub - ject.____
may like him be faith - ful   in   our o - be - dience.____

Saint Joseph (March 19).

Words: Hieronimo Casanate (d. 1700); tr. *Hymnal 1982*
Music: *Bickford*, Hank Beebe (b. 1926)   11 11. 11 5

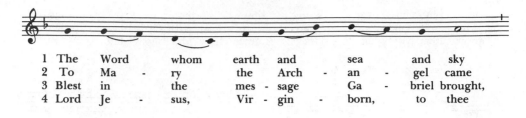

1 The Word whom earth and sea and sky
2 To Ma - ry the Arch - an - gel came
3 Blest in the mes - sage Ga - briel brought,
4 Lord Je - sus, Vir - gin - born, to thee

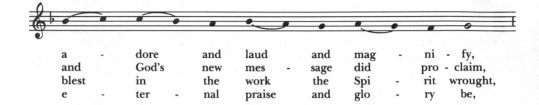

a - dore and laud and mag - ni - fy,
and God's new mes - sage did pro - claim,
blest in the work the Spi - rit wrought,
e - ter - nal praise and glo - ry be,

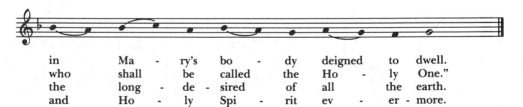

whose might they show, whose praise they tell,
"Hail, Ma - ry, you shall bear a son
most blest to bring to hu - man birth
whom with the Fa - ther we a - dore

in Ma - ry's bo - dy deigned to dwell.
who shall be called the Ho - ly One."
the long - de - sired of all the earth.
and Ho - ly Spi - rit ev - er - more.

The Annunciation (March 25).

Words: Latin, 7th-8th cent.; sts. 1 and 3-4, tr. *Hymns Ancient and Modern*, 1861,
     after John Mason Neale (1818-1866); st. 2 tr. Anne K. LeCroy (b. 1930)
Music: *Quem terra, pontus, aethera*, plainsong, Mode 2, Nevers MS, 13th cent.   LM

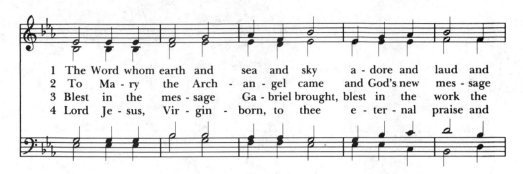

1 The Word whom earth and sea and sky a - dore and laud and
2 To Ma - ry the Arch - an - gel came and God's new mes - sage
3 Blest in the mes - sage Ga - briel brought, blest in the work the
4 Lord Je - sus, Vir - gin - born, to thee e - ter - nal praise and

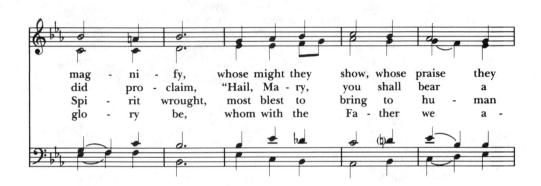

mag - ni - fy, whose might they show, whose praise they
did pro - claim, "Hail, Ma - ry, you shall bear a
Spi - rit wrought, most blest to bring to hu - man
glo - ry be, whom with the Fa - ther we a -

tell, in Ma - ry's bo - dy deigned to dwell.
son who shall be called the Ho - ly One."
birth the long - de - sired of all the earth.
dore and Ho - ly Spi - rit ev - er - more.

The Annunciation (March 25).

Words: Latin, 7th-8th cent.; sts. 1 and 3-4, tr. *Hymns Ancient and Modern*, 1861,
after John Mason Neale (1818-1866); st. 2, tr. Anne K. LeCroy (b. 1930)
Music: *Song 34*, melody and bass Orlando Gibbons (1583-1625); harm. as adapted and
harmonized in *The English Hymnal*, 1906

LM

1 The an - gel Ga - bri - el from hea - ven came,
2 "For know a bless - ed Mo - ther thou shalt be,
3 Then gen - tle Ma - ry meek - ly bowed her head,
4 Of her, Em - man - u - el, the Christ, was born

his wings as drift - ed snow, his eyes as flame;
all gen - er - a - tions laud and hon - or thee,
"To me be as it pleas - eth God," she said,
in Beth - le - hem, all on a Christ - mas morn,

"All hail," said he, "thou low - ly maid - en Ma - ry,
thy Son shall be Em - man - u - el, by seers fore - told,
"my soul shall laud and mag - ni - fy his ho - ly Name."
and Chris - tian folk through - out the world will ev - er say—

most high - ly fa - vored la - dy," Glo - ri - a!
most high - ly fa - vored la - dy," Glo - ri - a!
Most high - ly fa - vored la - dy, Glo - ri - a!
"Most high - ly fa - vored la - dy," Glo - ri - a!

The Annunciation (March 25).

Words: Basque carol; para. Sabine Baring-Gould (1834-1924)
Music: *Gabriel's Message*, Basque carol; harm. Edgar Pettman (1865-1943)

♩. = 66
10 10. 12 10

Burden

No - va, no - va. A - ve fit ex E - va.

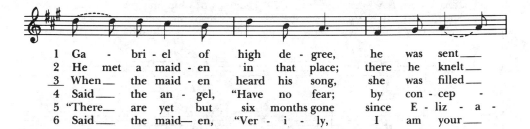

1 Ga - bri - el of high de - gree, he was sent___
2 He met a maid - en in that place; there he knelt___
3 When___ the maid - en heard his song, she was filled___
4 Said___ the an - gel, "Have no fear; by con - cep -
5 "There___ are yet but six months gone since E - liz - a -
6 Said___ the maid—en, "Ver - i - ly, I am your___

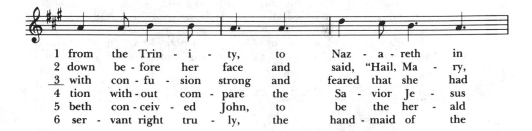

1 from the Trin - i - ty, to Naz - a - reth in
2 down be - fore her face and said, "Hail, Ma - ry,
3 with con - fu - sion strong and feared that she had
4 tion with - out com - pare the Sa - vior Je - sus
5 beth con - ceiv - ed John, to be the her - ald
6 ser - vant right tru - ly, the hand - maid of the

Repeat Burden

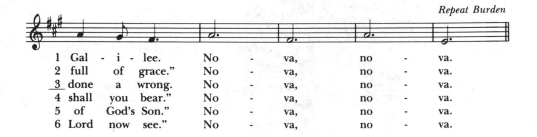

1 Gal - i - lee. No - va, no - va.
2 full of grace." No - va, no - va.
3 done a wrong. No - va, no - va.
4 shall you bear." No - va, no - va.
5 of God's Son." No - va, no - va.
6 Lord now see." No - va, no - va.

The Annunciation (March 25). The following burden and final line may be used with each stanza:
"Tidings! Tidings! Promise of salvation!" and "Tidings! Tidings!".

Words: Hunterian MS. 83, 15th cent.; adapt. Carl P. Daw, Jr. (b. 1944)
Music: *Nova, nova,* melody Hunterian MS., 15th cent.   Irr. with Refrain

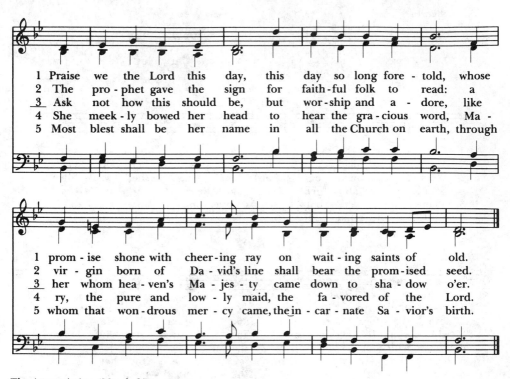

1 Praise we the Lord this day, this day so long fore-told, whose
2 The pro-phet gave the sign for faith-ful folk to read: a
3 Ask not how this should be, but wor-ship and a-dore, like
4 She meek-ly bowed her head to hear the gra-cious word, Ma-
5 Most blest shall be her name in all the Church on earth, through

1 prom-ise shone with cheer-ing ray on wait-ing saints of old.
2 vir-gin born of Da-vid's line shall bear the prom-ised seed.
3 her whom hea-ven's Ma-jes-ty came down to sha-dow o'er.
4 ry, the pure and low-ly maid, the fa-vored of the Lord.
5 whom that won-drous mer-cy came, the in-car-nate Sa-vior's birth.

The Annunciation (March 25).

Words: Anon., *Hymns for the Festivals and Saints' Days of the Church of England*, 1846, alt.
Music: *St. George*, Henry John Gauntlett (1805-1876)   SM

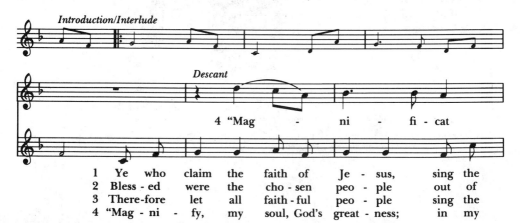

Introduction/Interlude

Descant

4 "Mag - ni - fi - cat

1 Ye who claim the faith of Je - sus, sing the
2 Bless - ed were the cho - sen peo - ple out of
3 There-fore let all faith-ful peo - ple sing the
4 "Mag - ni - fy, my soul, God's great - ness; in my

an - i - ma me - a

won - ders that were done   when the love of God the
whom the Lord did come;   bless - ed was the land of
hon - or of her name;   let the Church, in her fore -
Sa - vior I re - joice;   all the a - ges call me

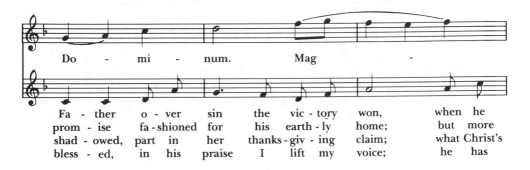

Do - mi - num.   Mag -

Fa - ther o - ver sin the vic - to - ry won,   when he
prom - ise fa - shioned for his earth - ly home;   but more
shad - owed, part in her thanks - giv - ing claim;   what Christ's
bless - ed, in his praise I lift my voice;   he has

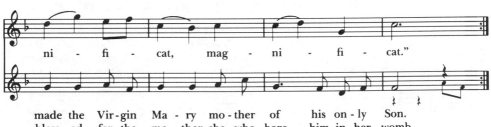

ni - fi - cat, mag - ni - fi - cat."

made the Vir - gin Ma - ry mo - ther of his on - ly Son.
bless - ed far the mo - ther, she who bore him in her womb.
mo - ther sang in glad - ness let Christ's peo - ple sing the same:
cast down all the might - y, and the low - ly are his choice."

Conclusion

The Annunciation (March 25); The Visitation (May 31).

Words: Sts. 1-3, Vincent Stuckey Stratton Coles (1845-1929), alt; st. 4, F. Bland
    Tucker (1895-1984), metrical *Magnificat*
Music: *Julion*, David Hurd (b. 1950)

87. 87. 87

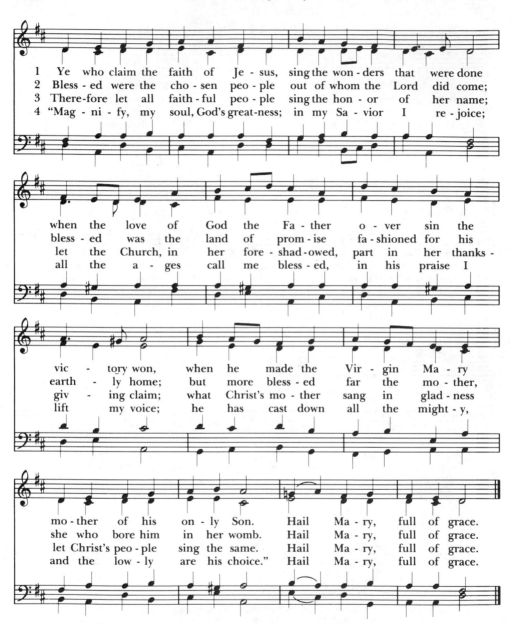

1 Ye who claim the faith of Je - sus, sing the won - ders that were done
2 Bless - ed were the cho - sen peo - ple out of whom the Lord did come;
3 There-fore let all faith - ful peo - ple sing the hon - or of her name;
4 "Mag - ni - fy, my soul, God's great-ness; in my Sa - vior I re - joice;

when the love of God the Fa - ther o - ver sin the
bless - ed was the land of prom - ise fa - shioned for his
let the Church, in her fore - shad - owed, part in her thanks -
all the a - ges call me bless - ed, in his praise I

vic - tory won, when he made the Vir - gin Ma - ry
earth - ly home; but more bless - ed far the mo - ther,
giv - ing claim; what Christ's mo - ther sang in glad - ness
lift my voice; he has cast down all the might - y,

mo - ther of his on - ly Son. Hail Ma - ry, full of grace.
she who bore him in her womb. Hail Ma - ry, full of grace.
let Christ's peo - ple sing the same. Hail Ma - ry, full of grace.
and the low - ly are his choice." Hail Ma - ry, full of grace.

The Annunciation (March 25); The Visitation (May 31).

Words: Sts. 1-3, Vincent Stuckey Stratton Coles (1845-1929), alt; st. 4, F. Bland
        Tucker (1895-1984), metrical *Magnificat*
Music: *Den des Vaters Sinn geboren*, melody from *Hundert Arien*, 1694;
        harm. Conrad Kocher (1786-1872)

87. 87. 87 with Refrain

1 Ga - briel's mes - sage does a - way Sa - tan's curse and
2 He that comes de - spised shall reign; he that can - not
3 Weak - ness shall the strong con - found; by the hands, in
4 Art by art shall be as - sailed; to the cross shall

Sa - tan's sway, out of dark - ness brings our Day:
die, be slain; death by death its death shall gain:
grave clothes wound, Ad - am's chains shall be un - bound:
Life be nailed; from the grave shall hope be hailed:

Refrain

so, be - hold, all the gates of heaven un - fold.

The Annunciation (March 25).

Words: *Piae Cantiones*, 1582; tr. John Mason Neale (1818-1866)
Music: *Angelus emittitur*, melody from *Piae Cantiones*, 1582;
    harm. Richard Runciman Terry (1865-1938)

777 with Refrain

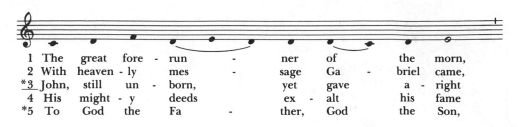

1 The great fore - run - ner of the morn,
2 With heaven - ly mes - sage Ga - briel came,
*3 John, still un - born, yet gave a - right
4 His might - y deeds ex - alt his fame
*5 To God the Fa - ther, God the Son,

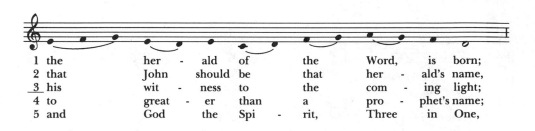

1 the her - ald of the Word, is born;
2 that John should be that her - ald's name,
3 his wit - ness to the com - ing light;
4 to great - er than a pro - phet's name;
5 and God the Spi - rit, Three in One,

1 and faith - ful hearts shall nev - er fail
2 and with pro - phet - ic ut - terance told
3 and Christ, the Sun of all the earth,
4 of wo - man born shall nev - er be
5 praise, hon - or, might, and glo - ry be

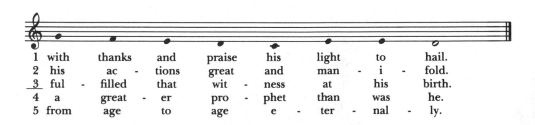

1 with thanks and praise his light to hail.
2 his ac - tions great and man - i - fold.
3 ful - filled that wit - ness at his birth.
4 a great - er pro - phet than was he.
5 from age to age e - ter - nal - ly.

The Nativity of Saint John the Baptist (June 24).

Words: The Venerable Bede (673-735); tr. John Mason Neale (1818-1866), alt.
Music: *Ut queant laxis*, plainsong, Mode 2, Solesmes Version

LM

Unison or harmony

1 The great fore-run - ner of the morn, the
2 With heaven-ly mes - sage Ga - briel came, that
*3 John, still un - born, yet gave a - right his
4 His might - y deeds ex - alt his fame to
*5 To God the Fa - ther, God the Son, and

1 her - ald of the Word, is born; and faith-ful hearts shall
2 John should be that her - ald's name, and with pro - phet - ic
3 wit - ness to the com - ing light; and Christ, the Sun of
4 great - er than a pro - phet's name; of wo - man born shall
5 God the Spi - rit, Three in One, praise, hon - or, might, and

1 nev - er fail with thanks and praise his light to hail.
2 ut - terance told his ac - tions great and man - i - fold.
3 all the earth, ful - filled that wit - ness at his birth.
4 nev - er be a great - er pro - phet than was he.
5 glo - ry be from age to age e - ter - nal - ly.

The Nativity of Saint John the Baptist (June 24).

Words: The Venerable Bede (673-735); tr. John Mason Neale (1818-1866), alt.
Music: *The Truth From Above*, English melody; harm. Ralph Vaughan Williams (1872-1958)

LM

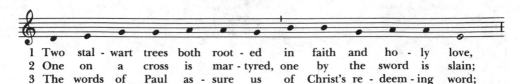

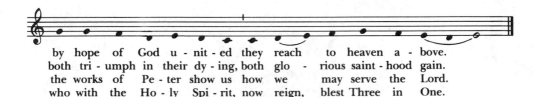

1 Two stal-wart trees both root-ed in faith and ho-ly love,
2 One on a cross is mar-tyred, one by the sword is slain;
3 The words of Paul as-sure us of Christ's re-deem-ing word;
*4 All glo-ry to the Fa-ther, all glo-ry to the Son,

by hope of God u-nit-ed they reach to heaven a-bove.
both tri-umph in their dy-ing, both glo-rious saint-hood gain.
the works of Pe-ter show us how we may serve the Lord.
who with the Ho-ly Spi-rit, now reign, blest Three in One.

Saint Peter and Saint Paul (June 29).

Words: Latin; tr. Anne K. LeCroy (b. 1930)
Music: *Ave caeli janua*, plainsong, Mode 4, Moissac MS., 12th cent.   76. 76

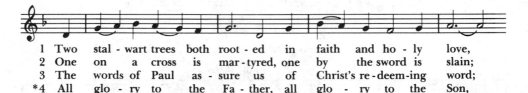

1 Two stal-wart trees both root-ed in faith and ho-ly love,
2 One on a cross is mar-tyred, one by the sword is slain;
3 The words of Paul as-sure us of Christ's re-deem-ing word;
*4 All glo-ry to the Fa-ther, all glo-ry to the Son,

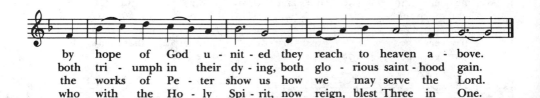

by hope of God u-nit-ed they reach to heaven a-bove.
both tri-umph in their dy-ing, both glo-rious saint-hood gain.
the works of Pe-ter show us how we may serve the Lord.
who with the Ho-ly Spi-rit, now reign, blest Three in One.

Saint Peter and Saint Paul (June 29).

Words: Latin; tr. Anne K. LeCroy (b. 1930)
Music: *De eersten zijn de laatsten*, Frederik August Mehrtens (b. 1922)   76. 76

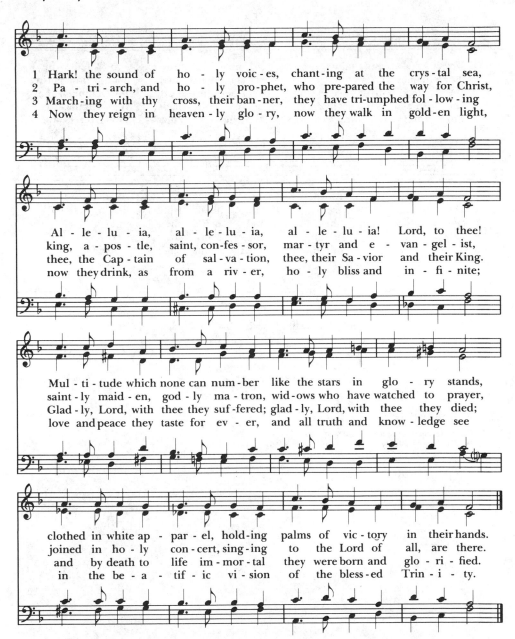

1 Hark! the sound of ho - ly voic - es, chant-ing at the crys-tal sea,
2 Pa - tri - arch, and ho - ly pro-phet, who pre-pared the way for Christ,
3 March-ing with thy cross, their ban-ner, they have tri-umphed fol - low - ing
4 Now they reign in heaven-ly glo - ry, now they walk in gold-en light,

Al - le - lu - ia, al - le - lu - ia, al - le - lu - ia! Lord, to thee!
king, a - pos - tle, saint, con-fes - sor, mar - tyr and e - van - gel - ist,
thee, the Cap - tain of sal - va - tion, thee, their Sa - vior and their King.
now they drink, as from a riv - er, ho - ly bliss and in - fi - nite;

Mul - ti - tude which none can num - ber like the stars in glo - ry stands,
saint - ly maid - en, god - ly ma - tron, wid - ows who have watched to prayer,
Glad - ly, Lord, with thee they suf-fered; glad - ly, Lord, with thee they died;
love and peace they taste for ev - er, and all truth and know - ledge see

clothed in white ap - par - el, hold-ing palms of vic - to - ry in their hands.
joined in ho - ly con - cert, sing-ing to the Lord of all, are there.
and by death to life im - mor - tal they were born and glo - ri - fied.
in the be - a - tif - ic vi - sion of the bless-ed Trin - i - ty.

Saints' Days; All Saints' Day (November 1).

Words: Christopher Wordsworth (1807-1885)
Music: *Moultrie*, Gerard Francis Cobb (1838-1904)

87. 87. D

1 For thy blest saints, a no-ble throng, who fell by
2 For James who left his fa-ther's side, not lin-gering
3 he stood with thee be - side the dead; he climbed the
4 he knelt be - neath the ol - ive shade; he drank thy
5 Lord, may we learn to drink thy cup, and meek and

1 fire and sword, or ear - ly died or
2 by the sea: he heard what could not
3 mount with thee, and saw the glo - ry
4 cup of pain; and slain by He - rod's
5 firm be found, when thou shalt come to

1 flour - ished long, we praise thy Name, O Lord.
2 be de - nied, thy sum - mons, "Fol - low me";
3 round thy head, one of thy cho - sen three;
4 flash - ing blade, he saw thy face a - gain.
5 take us up where thine e - lect are crowned.

Saint James (July 25).

Words: Cecil Frances Alexander (1818-1895), alt.
Music: *Dunlap's Creek,* melody Freeman Lewis (1780-1859)

CM

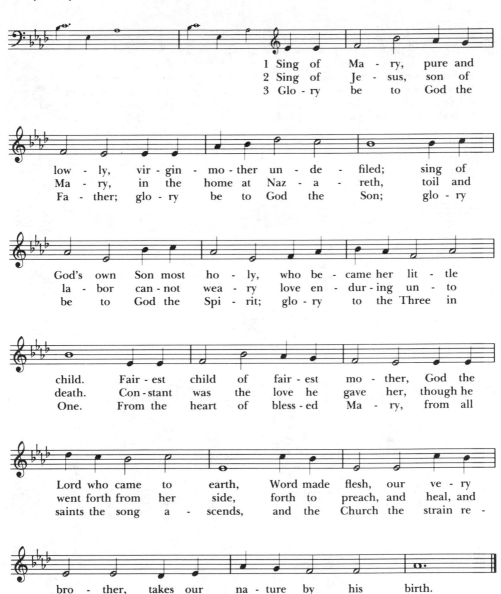

1 Sing of Ma-ry, pure and low-ly, vir-gin-mo-ther un-de-filed; sing of God's own Son most ho-ly, who be-came her lit-tle child. Fair-est child of fair-est mo-ther, God the Lord who came to earth, Word made flesh, our ve-ry bro-ther, takes our na-ture by his birth.

2 Sing of Je-sus, son of Ma-ry, in the home at Naz-a-reth, toil and la-bor can-not wea-ry love en-dur-ing un-to death. Con-stant was the love he gave her, though he went forth from her side, forth to preach, and heal, and suf-fer, till on Cal-va-ry he died.

3 Glo-ry be to God the Fa-ther; glo-ry be to God the Son; glo-ry be to God the Spi-rit; glo-ry to the Three in One. From the heart of bless-ed Ma-ry, from all saints the song a-scends, and the Church the strain re-ech-oes un-to earth's re-mot-est ends.

Saint Mary the Virgin (August 15).

Words: Roland Ford Palmer (b. 1891)
Music: *Raquel*, Skinner Chávez-Melo (b. 1944)

87. 87. D

1 Sing we of the bless-ed Mo-ther who re-ceived the an-gel's
2 Sing we, too, of Ma-ry's sor-rows, of the sword that pierced her
3 Sing a-gain the joys of Ma-ry when she saw the ris-en
4 Sing the chief-est joy of Ma-ry when on earth her work was

word, and o-be-dient to the sum-mons bore in
through, when be-neath the cross of Je-sus she his
Lord, and in prayer with Christ's a-pos-tles, wait-ed
done, and the Lord of all cre-a-tion brought her

love the in-fant Lord; sing we of the joys of
weight of suf-fering knew, looked up-on her Son and
on his prom-ised word; from on high the blaz-ing
to his heaven-ly home; where, raised high with saints and

Ma-ry at whose breast the child was fed who is
Sa-vior reign-ing from the aw-ful tree, saw the
glo-ry of the Spi-rit's pres-ence came, heaven-ly
an-gels, in Je-ru-sa-lem a-bove, she be-

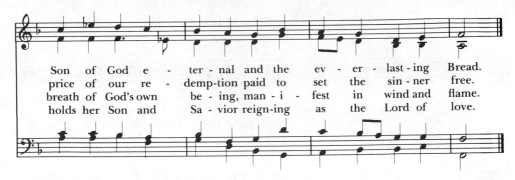

Son of God e - ter - nal and the ev - er - last - ing Bread.
price of our re - demp-tion paid to set the sin - ner free.
breath of God's own be - ing, man - i - fest in wind and flame.
holds her Son and Sa - vior reign-ing as the Lord of love.

Saint Mary the Virgin (August 15).

Words: George B. Timms (b. 1910), alt.
Music: *Rustington*, Charles Hubert Hastings Parry (1848-1918)

87. 87. D

Holy Days and Various Occasions

279

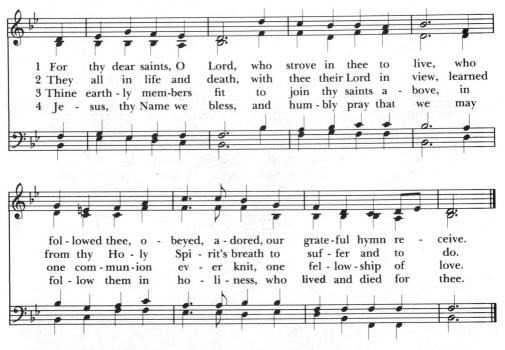

1 For thy dear saints, O Lord, who strove in thee to live, who
2 They all in life and death, with thee their Lord in view, learned
3 Thine earth-ly mem-bers fit to join thy saints a - bove, in
4 Je - sus, thy Name we bless, and hum - bly pray that we may

fol - lowed thee, o - beyed, a - dored, our grate-ful hymn re - ceive.
from thy Ho - ly Spi - rit's breath to suf - fer and to do.
one com - mun-ion ev - er knit, one fel - low-ship of love.
fol - low them in ho - li-ness, who lived and died for thee.

Saints' Days; All Saints' Day (November 1).

Words: Richard Mant (1776-1848), alt.
Music: *St. George*, Henry John Gauntlett (1805-1876)

SM

1 God of saints, to whom the num-ber of the star - ry
2 In the roll of your a - pos - tles stands the name Bar -
3 All his faith and prayer and pa - tience, all his toil - ing
4 There are named the bless - ed faith-ful of the new Je -

host is known: man - y saints by earth for -
thol - o - mew, for this faith - ful saint we
and his strife, all are veiled from us, but
ru - sa - lem. When Christ comes a - gain in

got - ten live for ev - er round your throne.
of - fer, year by year, our thanks to you.
writ - ten in the Lamb's great book of life.
glo - ry, num - ber us, we pray, with them.

Saint Bartholomew (August 24).

Words: John Ellerton (1826-1893), alt.
Music: *Halton Holgate*, William Boyce (1711-1779)

87. 87

Saint Matthew (September 21).

Words: William Bright (1824-1901), alt.
Music: *Breslau*, melody from *Lochamer Gesangbuch*, 1450?, alt. harm. after Felix Mendelssohn (1809-1847)   LM

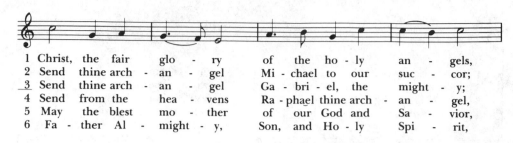

1 Christ, the fair glo - ry of the ho - ly an - gels,
2 Send thine arch - an - gel Mi - chael to our suc - cor;
3 Send thine arch - an - gel Ga - bri - el, the might - y;
4 Send from the hea - vens Ra - phael thine arch - an - gel,
5 May the blest mo - ther of our God and Sa - vior,
6 Fa - ther Al - might - y, Son, and Ho - ly Spi - rit,

1 ma - ker of all things, ru - ler of all
2 peace - ma - ker bless - ed, may he ban - ish
3 her - ald of hea - ven, may he, from us
4 health - bring - er bless - ed, aid - ing ev - ery
5 may the ce - les - tial com - pa - ny of
6 God ev - er bless - ed, hear our thank - ful

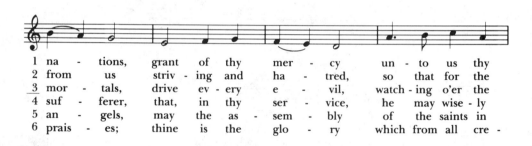

1 na - tions, grant of thy mer - cy un - to us thy
2 from us striv - ing and ha - tred, so that for the
3 mor - tals, drive ev - ery e - vil, watch - ing o'er the
4 suf - ferer, that, in thy ser - vice, he may wise - ly
5 an - gels, may the as - sem - bly of the saints in
6 prais - es; thine is the glo - ry which from all cre -

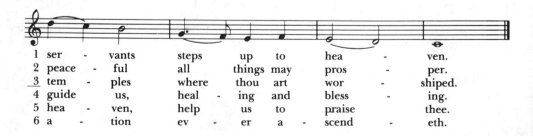

1 ser - vants steps up to hea - ven.
2 peace - ful all things may pros - per.
3 tem - ples where thou art wor - shiped.
4 guide us, heal - ing and bless - ing.
5 hea - ven, help us to praise thee.
6 a - tion ev - er a - scend - eth.

Saint Michael and All Angels (September 29).

Words: Rabanus Maurus (776-856); ver. *Hymnal 1940*, alt.
Music: *Caelites plaudant*, melody from *Antiphoner*, 1728

11 11. 11 5

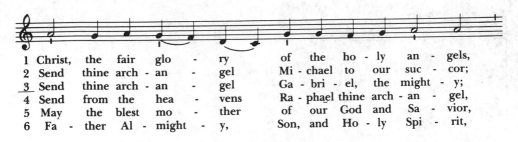

1 Christ, the fair glo - ry of the ho - ly an - gels,
2 Send thine arch - an - gel Mi - chael to our suc - cor;
3 Send thine arch - an - gel Ga - bri - el, the might - y;
4 Send from the hea - vens Ra - pha_el thine arch - an - gel,
5 May the blest mo - ther of our God and Sa - vior,
6 Fa - ther Al - might - y, Son, and Ho - ly Spi - rit,

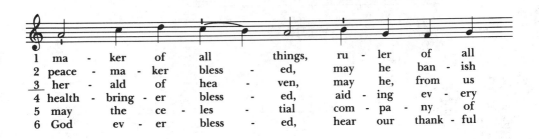

1 ma - ker of all things, ru - ler of all
2 peace - ma - ker bless - ed, may he ban - ish
3 her - ald of hea - ven, may he, from us
4 health - bring - er bless - ed, aid - ing ev - ery
5 may the ce - les - tial com - pa - ny of
6 God ev - er bless - ed, hear our thank - ful

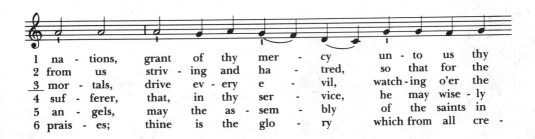

1 na - tions, grant of thy mer - cy un - to us thy
2 from us striv - ing and ha - tred, so that for the
3 mor - tals, drive ev - ery e - vil, watch - ing o'er the
4 suf - ferer, that, in thy ser - vice, he may wise - ly
5 an - gels, may the as - sem - bly of the saints in
6 prais - es; thine is the glo - ry which from all cre -

1 ser - vants steps up to hea - ven.
2 peace - ful all things may pros - per.
3 tem - ples where thou art wor - shipped.
4 guide us, heal - ing and bless - ing.
5 hea - ven help us to praise thee.
6 a - tion ev - er a - scend - eth.

Saint Michael and All Angels (September 29).

Words: Rabanus Maurus (776-856); ver. *Hymnal 1940*, alt.
Music: *Caelitum Joseph*, plainsong, Mode 1; ver. Schola Antiqua, 1983

11 11. 11 5

1 O ye im - mor - tal throng of an - gels round the
2 Ye saw the heaven-born child in hu - man flesh ar -
3 Ye in the wil - der - ness be - held the Tempt - er
4 In dark Geth - sem - a - ne the night be - fore he
5 Ye thronged to Cal - va - ry and pressed with sad de -

1 throne, join with our earth - bound song to
2 rayed, so in - no - cent and mild while
3 spoiled, un - masked in ev - ery dress, in
4 died, ye saw his ag - o - ny, ye
5 sire that awe - ful sight to see— the

1 make the Sa - vior known. On earth ye knew his
2 in the man - ger laid. "Glo - ry to God and
3 ev - ery com - bat foiled. With great de - light ye
4 heard the plaint he cried. When hope was dim, and
5 Lord of life ex - pire. E'en an - gel eyes slow

1	won - drous	grace,	his	beau - teous face	in	heaven	ye	view.
2	peace	on	earth," for	such a birth	ye	sang	a -	loud.
3	crowned his	head	when	Sa - tan fled	the	Sa -	vior's	might.
4	pain and	grief	be -	yond be - lief,	ye	tend - ed		him.
5	tears did	shed:	ye	mourned the dead	in	sad	sur -	prise.

6 Around his sacred tomb
   a willing watch ye kept;
till out from death's vast room,
   up from the grave, he leapt.
     Ye rolled the stone,
      and all adored
       your rising Lord
     with joy unknown.

7 When all arrayed in light
   the shining conqueror rode,
ye hailed his wondrous flight
   up to the throne of God.
     And waved around
      your golden wings,
      and struck your strings
     of sweetest sound.

8 The joyous notes pursue
   and louder anthems raise;
while mortals sing with you
   their own Redeemer's praise.
     With equal flame
      and equal art,
      do thou my heart
     extol his Name.

Saint Michael and All Angels (September 29).

Words: Sts. 1-3 and 5-8, Philip Doddridge (1702-1751), alt.; st. 4, Charles P. Price (b. 1920)
Music: *Croft's 136th,* melody and bass William Croft (1678-1727);
    harm. *More Hymns for Today*

66. 66. 44. 44

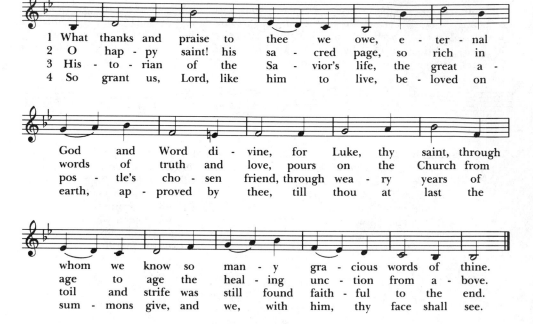

1 What thanks and praise to thee we owe, e-ter-nal
2 O hap-py saint! his sa-cred page, so rich in
3 His-to-rian of the Sa-vior's life, the great a-
4 So grant us, Lord, like him to live, be-loved on

God and Word di-vine, for Luke, thy saint, through
words of truth and love, pours on the Church from
pos-tle's cho-sen friend, through wea-ry years of
earth, ap-proved by thee, till thou at last the

whom we know so man-y gra-cious words of thine.
age to age the heal-ing unc-tion from a-bove.
toil and strife was still found faith-ful to the end.
sum-mons give, and we, with him, thy face shall see.

Saint Luke (October 18).

Words: William Dalrymple Maclagan (1826-1910), alt.
Music: *Deus tuorum militum*, melody from *Antiphoner*, 1753; adapt. *The English Hymnal*, 1906, alt.   LM

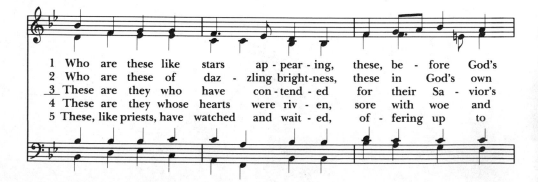

1 Who are these like stars ap-pear-ing, these, be-fore God's
2 Who are these of daz-zling bright-ness, these in God's own
3 These are they who have con-tend-ed for their Sa-vior's
4 These are they whose hearts were riv-en, sore with woe and
5 These, like priests, have watched and wait-ed, of-fering up to

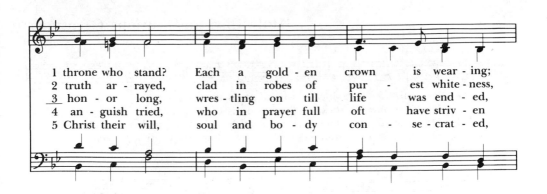

1 throne who stand? Each a gold - en crown is wear - ing;
2 truth ar - rayed, clad in robes of pur - est white - ness,
3 hon - or long, wres - tling on till life was end - ed,
4 an - guish tried, who in prayer full oft have striv - en
5 Christ their will, soul and bo - dy con - se - crat - ed,

1 who are all this glo - rious band? Al - le - lu - ia!
2 robes whose lus - ter ne'er shall fade, ne'er be touched by
3 fol - lowing not the sin - ful throng; these, who well the
4 with the God they glo - ri - fied; now, their pain - ful
5 day and night they serve him still. Now in God's most

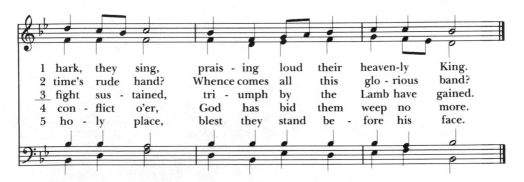

1 hark, they sing, prais - ing loud their heaven - ly King.
2 time's rude hand? Whence comes all this glo - rious band?
3 fight sus - tained, tri - umph by the Lamb have gained.
4 con - flict o'er, God has bid them weep no more.
5 ho - ly place, blest they stand be - fore his face.

All Saints' Day (November 1).

Words: Theobald Heinrich Schenck (1656-1727); tr. Frances Elizabeth Cox (1812-1897), alt.
Music: *Zeuch mich, zeuch mich,* melody from *Geistreiches Gesang-buch,* 1698;
     harm. William Henry Monk (1823-1889), alt.

87. 87. 77

1 For all the saints, who from their la - bors rest, who
2 Thou wast their rock, their for - tress, and their might: ____
3 O may thy sol - diers, faith - ful, true, and bold, ____
4 O blest com - mun - ion, fel - low - ship di - vine! ____

thee ____ by faith be - fore the world con - fessed, thy
thou, Lord, their Cap - tain in the well - fought fight; ____
fight as the saints who no - bly fought of old, and
We feeb - ly strug - gle, they in glo - ry shine; yet

Name, O ____ Je - sus, be for ev - er blessed.
thou, in the dark - ness drear, the one true Light.
win, with ____ them, the vic - tor's crown of gold.
all are ____ one in thee, for all are thine.

Al - le - lu - ia, al - le - lu - ia!

*5 And when the strife is fierce, the war-fare long, steals on the ear the
*6 The gold - en eve - ning bright-ens in the west; soon, soon to faith-ful

dis-tant tri-umph song, and hearts are____ brave a-gain, and arms are
war-riors com-eth rest;____ sweet is the calm of par-a-dise the

strong.
blest. Al - le-lu - ia. al - le-lu - ia!

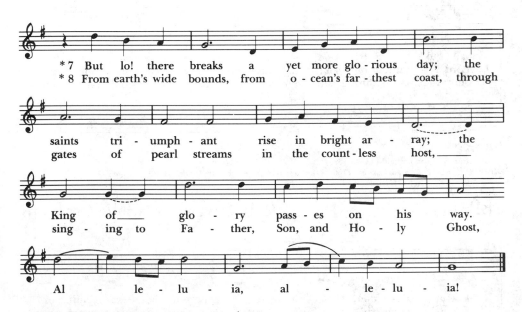

*7 But lo! there breaks a yet more glo-rious day; the
*8 From earth's wide bounds, from o-cean's far-thest coast, through

saints tri-umph-ant rise in bright ar - ray; the
gates of pearl streams in the count-less host,____

King of____ glo - ry pass-es on his way.
sing-ing to Fa - ther, Son, and Ho-ly Ghost,

Al - le-lu - ia, al - le-lu - ia!

All Saints' Day (November 1).

Words: William Walsham How (1823-1897)
Music: *Sine Nomine*, Ralph Vaughan Williams (1872-1958)

10 10 10 with Alleluias

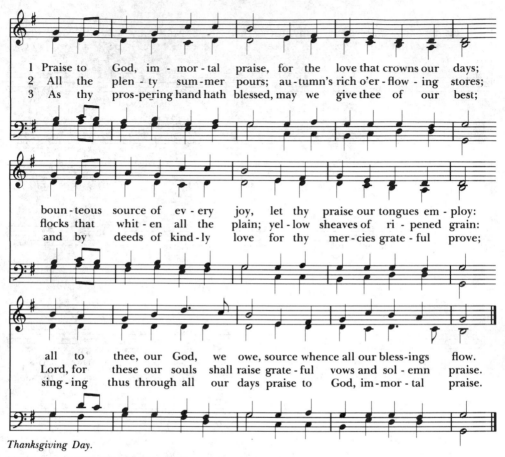

1 Praise to God, im-mor-tal praise, for the love that crowns our days;
2 All the plen-ty sum-mer pours; au-tumn's rich o'er-flow-ing stores;
3 As thy pros-pering hand hath blessed, may we give thee of our best;

boun-teous source of ev-ery joy, let thy praise our tongues em-ploy:
flocks that whit-en all the plain; yel-low sheaves of ri-pened grain:
and by deeds of kind-ly love for thy mer-cies grate-ful prove;

all to thee, our God, we owe, source whence all our bless-ings flow.
Lord, for these our souls shall raise grate-ful vows and sol-emn praise.
sing-ing thus through all our days praise to God, im-mor-tal praise.

Thanksgiving Day.

Words: Anna Laetitia Barbauld (1743-1825)
Music: *Dix*, melody Conrad Kocher (1786-1872); arr. William Henry Monk (1823-1889);
    harm. *The English Hymnal*, 1906   77. 77. 77

289   Holy Days and Various Occasions

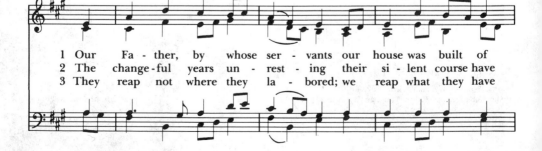

1 Our Fa-ther, by whose ser-vants our house was built of
2 The change-ful years un-rest-ing their si-lent course have
3 They reap not where they la-bored; we reap what they have

old,   whose   hand hath crowned her   chil - dren with
sped,   new   com-rades ev - er   bring - ing in
sown: our   har - vest may be   gar - nered by

bless-ings man - i - fold,   for   thine un - fail - ing
com-rades' steps to tread: and   some are long for -
a - ges yet un - known.   The   days of old have

mer - cies far - strewn a - long our way,   with
got - ten, long spent their hopes and fears;   safe
dowered us with gifts be - yond all praise: our

all who passed be - fore us, we praise thy Name to - day.
rest they in thy keep - ing, who chan-gest not with years.
Fa-ther, make us faith - ful to serve the com - ing days.

On the Anniversary of the Dedication of a Church.

Words: George Wallace Briggs (1875-1959)
Music: *Wolvercote*, William Harold Ferguson (1874-1950)

76. 76. D

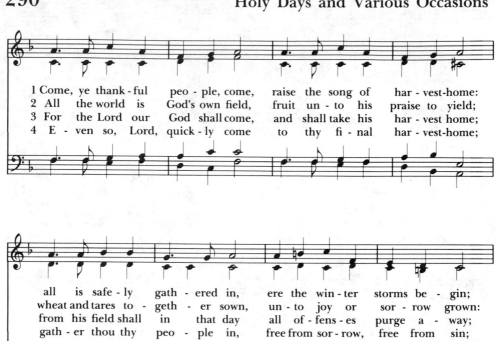

1 Come, ye thank-ful people, come, raise the song of har-vest-home:
2 All the world is God's own field, fruit un-to his praise to yield;
3 For the Lord our God shall come, and shall take his har-vest home;
4 E-ven so, Lord, quick-ly come to thy fi-nal har-vest-home;

all is safe-ly gath-ered in, ere the win-ter storms be-gin;
wheat and tares to-geth-er sown, un-to joy or sor-row grown:
from his field shall in that day all of-fens-es purge a-way;
gath-er thou thy peo-ple in, free from sor-row, free from sin;

Descant

4 there, for ev-er pur-i-fied, in thy pres-ence

1 God, our Ma-ker, doth pro-vide for our wants to
2 first the blade, and then the ear, then the full corn
3 give his an-gels charge at last in the fire the
4 there, for ev-er pur-i-fied, in thy pres-ence

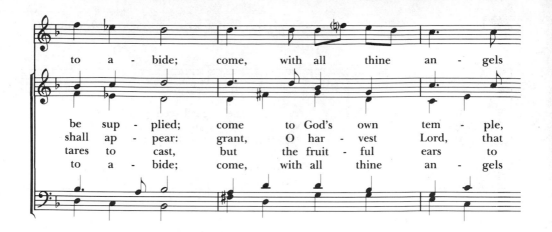

to a - bide; come, with all thine an - gels

be sup - plied; come to God's own tem - ple,
shall ap - pear: grant, O har - vest Lord, that
tares to cast, but the fruit - ful ears to
to a - bide; come, with all thine an - gels

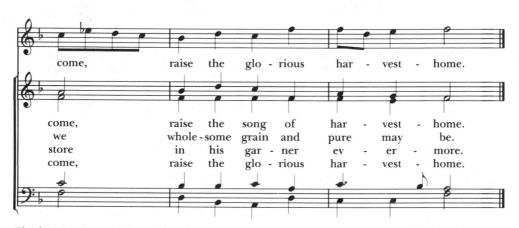

come, raise the glo - rious har - vest - home.

come, raise the song of har - vest - home.
we whole - some grain and pure may be.
store in his gar - ner ev - er - more.
come, raise the glo - rious har - vest - home.

Thanksgiving Day.

Words: Henry Alford (1810-1871), alt.
Music: *St. George's, Windsor,* George Job Elvey (1816-1893); desc. Craig Sellar Lang (1891-1971)   77. 77. D

1 We plow the fields, and scat - ter the good seed on the land,
2 He on - ly is the Ma - ker of all things near and far;
3 We thank thee, then, O Fa - ther, for all things bright and good,

but it is fed and wa - tered by God's al - might - y hand;
he paints the way-side flow - er, he lights the eve - ning star;
the seed - time and the har - vest, our life, our health, our food:

he sends the snow in win - ter, the warmth to swell the grain,
the winds and waves o - bey him, by him the birds are fed;
the gifts we have to of - fer are what thy love im - parts,

the breez-es and the sun - shine, and soft re - fresh - ing rain.
much more to us, his chil - dren, he gives our dai - ly bread.
but chief-ly thou de - sir - est our hum - ble thank-ful hearts.

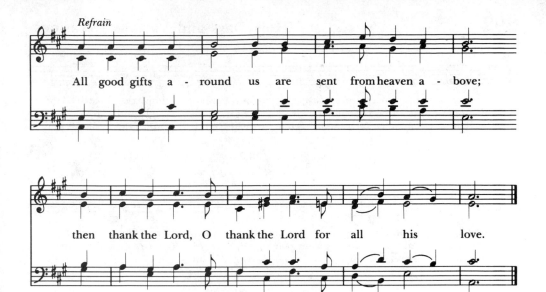

Thanksgiving Day.

Words: Matthias Claudius (1740-1815); tr. Jane Montgomery Campbell (1817-1878), alt.
Music: *Wir pflugen*, Johann Abraham Peter Schulz (1747-1800)

76. 76. D with Refrain

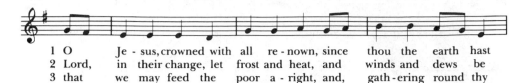

1 O Je - sus, crowned with all re - nown, since thou the earth hast
2 Lord, in their change, let frost and heat, and winds and dews be
3 that we may feed the poor a - right, and, gath - ering round thy

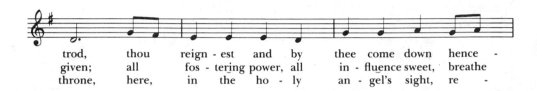

trod, thou reign - est and by thee come down hence -
given; all fos - tering power, all in - fluence sweet, breathe
throne, here, in the ho - ly an - gel's sight, re -

forth the gifts of God. Thine is the health and
from the boun - teous heaven. At - tem - per fair with
pay thee of thine own: That we may praise thee

thine the wealth that in our halls a - bound, and
gen - tle air the sun - shine and the rain, that
all our days, and with the Fa - ther's Name, and

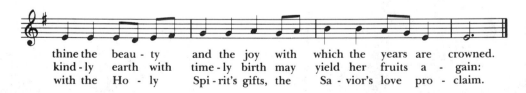

thine the beau - ty and the joy with which the years are crowned.
kind - ly earth with time - ly birth may yield her fruits a - gain:
with the Ho - ly Spi - rit's gifts, the Sa - vior's love pro - claim.

Rogation Days.

Words: Edward White Benson (1829-1896), alt.
Music: *Kingsfold*, English melody; adapt. Ralph Vaughan Williams (1872-1958)

CMD

1 I sing a song of the saints of God, _____ pa-tient and brave and true, who___ toiled and___ fought and___ lived and died for the Lord they___ loved and knew. And___ one was a doc-tor, and one was a queen, and one was a shep-herd-ess on the___ green: they were all of them saints of ___ God— and I mean, God help-ing, to be one too.

2 They loved their Lord so___ dear, so dear, and___ his love___ made them strong; and they fol-lowed the right, for___ Je-sus' sake, the___ whole of their good lives long. And___ one was a sold-ier, and one was a priest, and one was___ slain by a fierce wild___ beast: and there's not an-y rea-son— no, not the least, why I should-n't be one too.

3 They lived not on-ly in a-ges past, there are hund-reds of thou-sands still, the___ world is___ bright with the joy-ous saints who___ love to do Je-sus' will. You can meet them in school, or in lanes, or at sea, in church, or in trains, or in shops, or at tea, for the saints of___ God are just folk like___ me, and I mean to be one too.

Saints' Days; All Saints' Day (November 1).

Words: Lesbia Scott (b. 1898), alt.
Music: *Grand Isle,* John Henry Hopkins (1861-1945)

Irr.

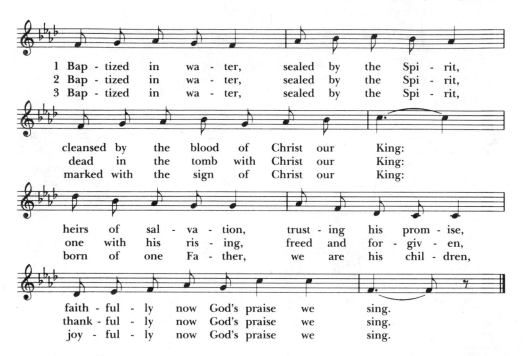

1 Bap - tized in wa - ter, sealed by the Spi - rit,
2 Bap - tized in wa - ter, sealed by the Spi - rit,
3 Bap - tized in wa - ter, sealed by the Spi - rit,

cleansed by the blood of Christ our King:
dead in the tomb with Christ our King:
marked with the sign of Christ our King:

heirs of sal - va - tion, trust - ing his prom - ise,
one with his ris - ing, freed and for - giv - en,
born of one Fa - ther, we are his chil - dren,

faith - ful - ly now God's praise we sing.
thank - ful - ly now God's praise we sing.
joy - ful - ly now God's praise we sing.

Words: Michael Saward (b. 1932)
Music: *Point Loma*, David Charles Walker (b. 1938)

558. 558

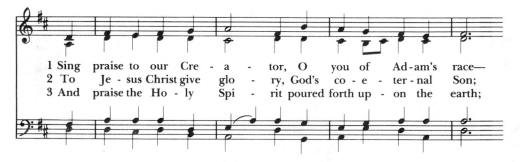

1 Sing praise to our Cre - a - tor, O you of Ad - am's race—
2 To Je - sus Christ give glo - ry, God's co - e - ter - nal Son;
3 And praise the Ho - ly Spi - rit poured forth up - on the earth;

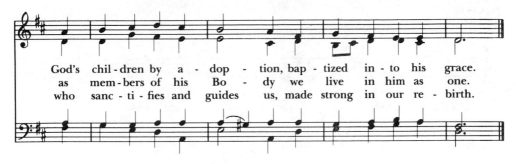

God's chil-dren by a - dop - tion, bap - tized in - to his grace.
as mem-bers of his Bo - dy we live in him as one.
who sanc - ti - fies and guides us, made strong in our re - birth.

Words: Mark Evans (b. 1916), alt.
Music: *Christus, der ist mein Leben*, melody Melchior Vulpius (1560?-1616);
harm. after Melchior Vulpius (1560?-1616)

76. 76

Holy Baptism

296

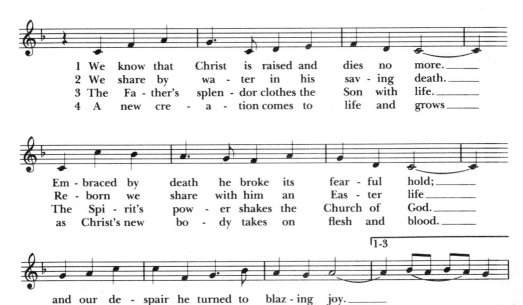

1 We know that Christ is raised and dies no more.____
2 We share by wa - ter in his sav - ing death.____
3 The Fa - ther's splen - dor clothes the Son with life.____
4 A new cre - a - tion comes to life and grows____

Em - braced by death he broke its fear - ful hold;____
Re - born we share with him an Eas - ter life.____
The Spi - rit's pow - er shakes the Church of God.____
as Christ's new bo - dy takes on flesh and blood.____

[1-3

and our de - spair he turned to blaz - ing joy.____
as liv - ing mem - bers of a liv - ing Christ.____
Bap-tized we live with God the Three in One.____ Al - le -
The u - ni - verse re - stored and whole will sing:____

||Final Ending

lu - ia! ___ Al - le - lu - ia! A - men.

Words: John Brownlow Geyer (b. 1932), alt.
Music: *Engelberg*, Charles Villiers Stanford (1852-1924)

10 10 10 with Alleluia

1 De - scend, O Spi - rit, purg - ing flame, brand
2 For - bid us not this sec - ond birth; grant

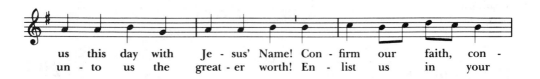

us this day with Je - sus' Name! Con - firm our faith, con -
un - to us the great - er worth! En - list us in your

sume our doubt; sign us as Christ's, with - in, with - out.
ser - vice, Lord; bap - tize all na - tions with your Word.

Words: Scott Francis Brenner (b. 1903), alt.
Music: *Erhalt uns, Herr*, melody from *Geistliche Lieder*, 1543   LM

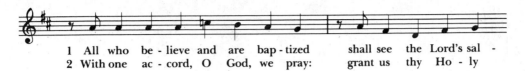

1 All who be - lieve and are bap - tized   shall see the Lord's sal -
2 With one ac - cord, O God, we pray: grant us thy Ho - ly

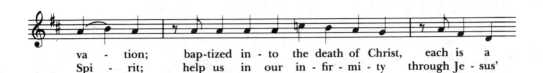

va - tion;   bap-tized in - to the death of Christ,   each is   a
Spi - rit;   help us in our in - fir - mi - ty   through Je - sus'

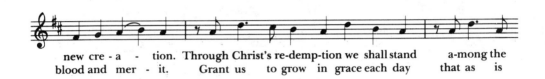

new cre - a - tion. Through Christ's re-demp-tion we shall stand   a-mong the
blood and mer - it.   Grant us   to grow in grace each day   that as   is

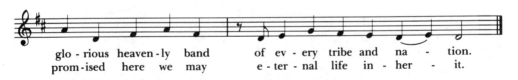

glo - rious heaven - ly band   of ev - ery tribe and na - tion.
prom-ised here we may   e - ter - nal life in - her - it.

Words: Thomas Hansen Kingo (1634-1703); tr. George Alfred Taylor Rygh (1860-1942), alt.
Music: *Es ist das Heil*, Hans Leo Hassler (1564-1612), alt.

87. 87. 887

1 Spi - rit of God, un - leashed on earth
2 You came in power; the Church was born;
3 With burn - ing words of vic - to - ry won

with rush of wind and roar of flame!
O Ho - ly Spi - rit, come a - gain!
in - spire our hearts grown cold with fear,

With tongues of fire saints spread good news;
From liv - ing wa - ters raise new saints;
re - vive in us bap - tis - mal grace,

earth, kin - dling, blazed her loud ac - claim.
let new tongues hail the ris - en Lord.
and fan our smol - dering lives to flame.

Words: John W. Arthur (1922-1980), alt.
Music: *Lledrod*, melody from *Llyfr Tonau Cynnulleidfaol*, 1859

LM

1 Glo - ry, love, and praise, and hon - or for our food
2 Thank-ful for our ev - ery bless - ing, let us sing
3 He dis-pels our sin and sad - ness, life im - parts,

now be - stowed ren - der we the Do - nor.
Christ the Spring, nev - er, nev - er ceas - ing.
cheers our hearts, fills with food and glad - ness.

Boun-teous God, we now con - fess thee: God, who thus
Source of all our gifts and gra - ces, Christ we own;
Who him - self for all hath giv - en, us he feeds,

bless - est us, right it is to bless thee.
Christ a - lone calls for all our prais - es.
us he leads to a feast in hea - ven.

Words: Charles Wesley (1707-1788), alt.
Music: *Benifold*, Francis B. Westbrook (1903-1975)

8. 33. 6. D

Bread of the world, in mer-cy bro-ken, Wine of the
soul, in mer-cy shed, by whom the words of life were
spo-ken, and in whose death our sins are dead:
look on the heart by sor-row bro-ken, look on the
tears by sin-ners shed; and be thy feast to us the
to-ken that by thy grace our souls are fed.

Words: Reginald Heber (1783-1826)
Music: *Rendez à Dieu*, melody att. Louis Bourgeois (1510?-1561?)

98. 98. D

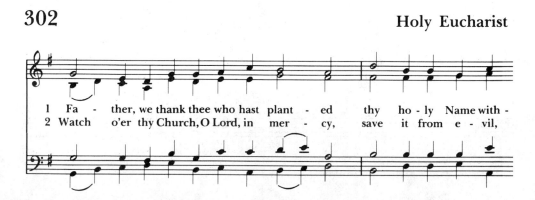

1 Fa - ther, we thank thee who hast plant - ed thy ho - ly Name with -
2 Watch o'er thy Church, O Lord, in mer - cy, save it from e - vil,

in our hearts. Know-ledge and faith and life im-mor-tal Je-sus thy
guard it still, per-fect it in thy love, u-nite it, cleansed and con-

Son to us im-parts. Thou, Lord, didst make all for thy plea-sure,
formed un-to thy will. As grain, once scat-tered on the hill-sides,

didst give us food for all our days, giv-ing in Christ the
was in this bro-ken bread made one, so from all lands thy

Bread e-ter-nal; thine is the power, be thine the praise.
Church be gath-ered in-to thy king-dom by thy Son.

Words: Greek, ca. 110; tr. F. Bland Tucker (1895-1984), rev.
Music: *Rendez a Dieu*, melody and harm. att. Louis Bourgeois (1510?-1561?)

98. 98. D

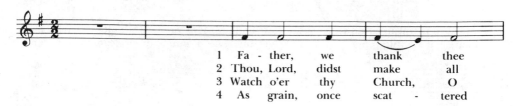

1 Fa - ther, we thank thee
2 Thou, Lord, didst make all
3 Watch o'er thy Church, O
4 As grain, once scat - tered

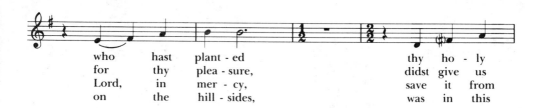

who hast plant - ed   thy ho - ly
for thy plea - sure,   didst give us
Lord, in mer - cy,   save it from
on the hill - sides,   was in this

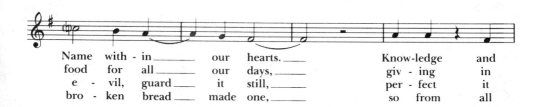

Name with - in___ our hearts.___ Know-ledge and
food for all___ our days,___ giv - ing in
e - vil, guard___ it still,___ per - fect it
bro - ken bread___ made one,___ so from all

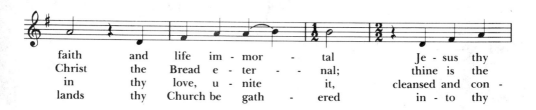

faith and life im - mor - tal   Je - sus thy
Christ the Bread e - ter - - nal;   thine is the
in thy love, u - nite it,   cleansed and con -
lands thy Church be gath - ered   in - to thy

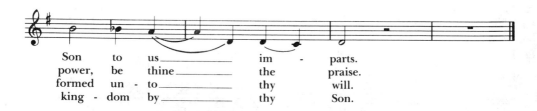

Son to us___ im - parts.
power, be thine___ the praise.
formed un - to___ thy will.
king - dom by___ thy Son.

Words: Greek, ca. 110; tr. F. Bland Tucker (1895-1984), rev.
Music: *Albright*, William Albright (b. 1944)

                                                              98. 98

Unison or harmony

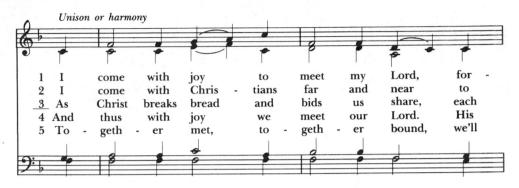

1 I come with joy to meet my Lord, for -
2 I come with Chris - tians far and near to
3 As Christ breaks bread and bids us share, each
4 And thus with joy we meet our Lord. His
5 To - geth - er met, to - geth - er bound, we'll

1 giv - en, loved, and free, in awe and won - der
2 find, as all are fed, the new com - mu - ni -
3 proud di - vi - sion ends. That love that made us
4 pres - ence, al - ways near, is in such friend - ship
5 go our dif - ferent ways, and as his peo - ple

1 to re - call his life laid down for me.
2 ty of love in Christ's com - mun - ion bread.
3 makes us one, and stran - gers now are friends.
4 bet - ter known: we see and praise him here.
5 in the world we'll live and speak his praise.

Words: Brian A. Wren (b. 1936), alt.
Music: *Land of Rest*, American folk melody; adapt. and harm. Annabel Morris Buchanan (1889-1983)   CM

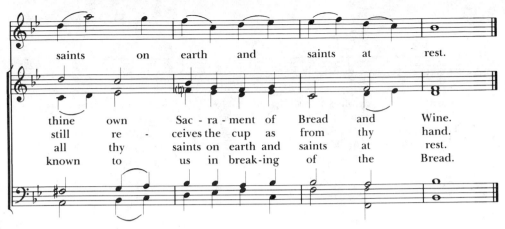

saints on earth and saints at rest.

thine	own	Sac - ra - ment of	Bread	and		Wine.
still	re -	ceives the cup as	from	thy		hand.
all	thy	saints on earth and	saints	at		rest.
known	to	us in break-ing	of	the		Bread.

Words: George Wallace Briggs (1875-1959), alt.
Music: *Rosedale*, Leo Sowerby (1895-1968)

10 10. 10 10

Holy Eucharist

306

1 Come,	ris - en	Lord,	and	deign	to	be	our	guest;
2 We	meet, as	in	that	up - per	room	they	met;
3 One	bo - dy	we,	one	Bo - dy	who	par -	take,
4 One	with each	o - ther,	Lord,	for	one	in	thee,

nay,	let us	be	thy	guests; the	feast	is	thine;
thou	at the	ta -	ble,	bless - ing,	yet	dost	stand;
one	Church u -	nit -	ed	in	com - mun -	ion	blest;
who	art one	Sa -	vior	and	one	liv - ing	Head;

thy -	self	at	thine own	board make	man - i -	fest
"This	is	my	Bo - dy";	so	thou	giv - est	yet:
one	Name	we	bear, one	Bread	of	life we	break,
then	o -	pen	thou our	eyes,	that	we may	see;

in	thine own	Sac - ra -	ment	of	Bread	and	Wine.
faith	still	re - ceives	the	cup	as	from thy	hand.
with	all thy	saints	on	earth	and	saints at	rest.
be	known to	us	in	break - ing	of	the	Bread.

Words: George Wallace Briggs (1875-1959), alt.
Music: *Sursum Corda*, Alfred Morton Smith (1879-1971)

10 10. 10 10

1 Lord, en-throned in heaven-ly splen-dor, first-be-
*2 Here our hum-blest hom-age pay we, here in
*3 Though the low-liest form doth veil thee as of
4 Pas-chal Lamb, thine of-fering, fi-nished once for
5 Life-im-part-ing heaven-ly Man-na, smit-ten

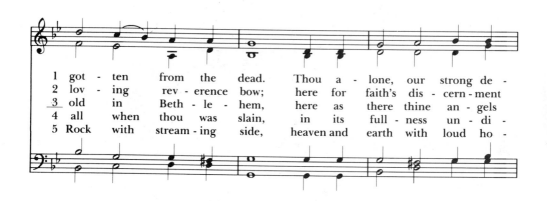

1 got-ten from the dead. Thou a-lone, our strong de-
2 lov-ing rev-erence bow; here for faith's dis-cern-ment
3 old in Beth-le-hem, here as there thine an-gels
4 all when thou was slain, in its full-ness un-di-
5 Rock with stream-ing side, heaven and earth with loud ho-

Al - le -

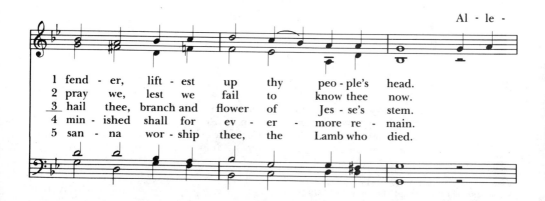

1 fend-er, lift-est up thy peo-ple's head.
2 pray we, lest we fail to know thee now.
3 hail thee, branch and flower of Jes-se's stem.
4 min-ished shall for ev-er-more re-main.
5 san-na wor-ship thee, the Lamb who died.

lu - ia! Al - le - lu - ia! Al - le -

Al - le - lu - ia! Al - le - lu - ia!

lu - ia!

Al - le - lu - ia!

1 Je - sus, true and liv - ing
2 Thou art here, we ask not
3 We in wor - ship join with
4 Cleans - ing us from ev - ery
5 Ris - en, a - scend - ed, glo - ri -

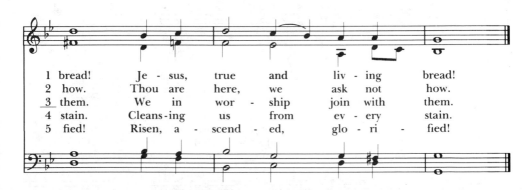

1 bread! Je - sus, true and liv - ing bread!
2 how. Thou are here, we ask not how.
3 them. We in wor - ship join with them.
4 stain. Cleans - ing us from ev - ery stain.
5 fied! Ris - en, a - scend - ed, glo - ri - fied!

Words: George Hugh Bourne (1840-1925), alt.
Music: *Bryn Calfaria*, melody William Owen (1813-1893); harm. *Christian Hymns*, 1977

87. 87. 12 77

Unison or harmony

1 O Food to pil - grims giv - en, O Bread of
2 O stream of love past tell - ing, O pur - est
3 O Je - sus, by thee bid - den, we here a -

life from hea - ven, O Man - na from on high!
foun - tain, well - ing from out the Sa - vior's side!
dore thee, hid - den in forms of bread and wine.

We hun - ger; Lord, sup - ply us, nor thy de -
We faint with thirst; re - vive us, of thine a -
Grant when the veil is riv - en, we may be -

lights de - ny us, whose hearts to thee draw nigh.
bun - dance give us, and all we need pro - vide.
hold, in hea - ven, thy coun - te - nance di - vine.

Words: Latin, 1661; tr. John Athelstan Laurie Riley (1858-1945), alt.
Music: *Psalm 6*, from *Les cent cinquante Pseaumes de David*, 1564, alt.

776. D

1 O Food to pil-grims giv - en, O Bread of life from
2 O stream of love past tell - ing, O pur - est foun - tain,
3 O Je - sus, by thee bid - den, we here a - dore thee,

hea - ven, O Man - na from on high! We
well - ing from out the Sa - vior's side! We
hid - den in forms of bread and wine. Grant

hun - ger; Lord, sup - ply us, nor thy de - lights de -
faint with thirst; re - vive us, of thine a - bun - dance
when the veil is riv - en, we may be - hold, in

ny us, whose hearts to thee draw nigh.
give us, and all we need pro - vide.
hea - ven, thy coun - te - nance di - vine.

Words: Latin, 1661; tr. John Athelstan Laurie Riley (1858-1945), alt.
Music: *O Welt, ich muss dich lassen*, present form of melody att. Heinrich Isaac (1450?-1517), alt.;
harm. Johann Sebastian Bach (1685-1750)

776 D

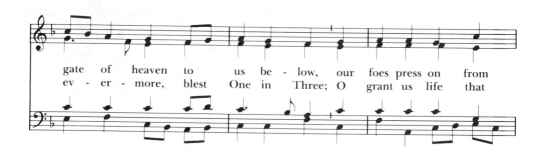

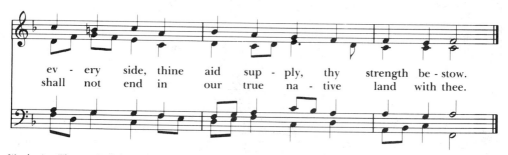

Words: Att. Thomas Aquinas (1225?-1274); tr. Edward Caswall (1814-1878), alt.
Music: *Herr Jesu Christ*, melody from *Cantionale Germanicum*, 1628; adapt. and harm.
    Johann Sebastian Bach (1685-1750)

LM

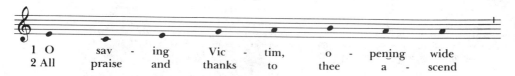

the gate of heaven to us be - low,
for ev - er - more, blest One in Three;

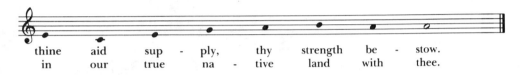

our foes press on from ev - ery side,
O grant us life that shall not end

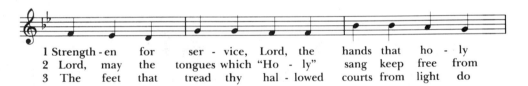

thine aid sup - ply, thy strength be - stow.
in our true na - tive land with thee.

Words: Att. Thomas Aquinas (1225?-1274); tr. Edward Caswall (1814-1878), alt.
Music: *Verbum supernum prodiens*, plainsong, Mode 2, Nevers MS., 13th cent.

LM

Holy Eucharist

312

1 Strength - en for ser - vice, Lord, the hands that ho - ly
2 Lord, may the tongues which "Ho - ly" sang keep free from
3 The feet that tread thy hal - lowed courts from light do

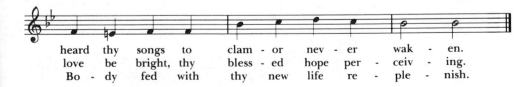

things have tak - en; let ears that now have
all de - ceiv - ing; the eyes which saw thy
thou not ban - ish; the bo - dies by thy

heard thy songs to clam - or nev - er wak - en.
love be bright, thy bless - ed hope per - ceiv - ing.
Bo - dy fed with thy new life re - ple - nish.

Words: Syriac Liturgy of Malabar; tr. Charles William Humphreys (1840-1921);
alt. Percy Dearmer (1867-1936)
Music: *Malabar*, David McKinley Williams (1887-1978)

87. 87

1 Let thy Blood in mer - cy poured, let thy gra - cious
2 Thou didst die that I might live; bless - ed Lord, thou
3 By the thorns that crowned thy brow, by the spear-wound
4 Wilt thou own the gift I bring? All my pen - i -

Bo - dy bro - ken, be to me, O gra - cious Lord,
cam'st to save me; all that love of God could give
and the nail - ing, by the pain and death, I now
tence I give thee; thou art my ex - alt - ed King,

Refrain

of thy bound-less love the to - ken.
Je - sus by his sor - rows gave me.
claim, O Christ, thy love un - fail - ing.   Thou didst give thy -
of thy match-less love for - give me.

self for me, now I give my - self to thee.

Words: John Brownlie (1859-1925)
Music: *Jesus, meine Zuversicht*, melody Johann Cruger (1598-1662);
    harm. after *The Chorale Book for England*, 1863

78. 78. 77

1 Hum - bly I a - dore thee, Ver - i - ty un - seen,
2 Taste and touch and vi - sion to dis - cern thee fail;
3 O me - mo - rial won - drous of the Lord's own death;
4 Je - sus, whom now hid - den, I by faith be - hold,

who thy glo - ry hid - est 'neath these sha - dows mean;
faith, that comes by hear - ing, pierc - es through the veil.
liv - ing Bread that giv - est all thy crea - tures breath,
what my soul doth long for, that thy word fore - told:

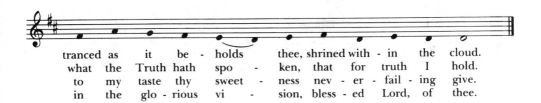

lo, to thee sur - ren - dered, my whole heart is bowed,
I be - lieve what - e'er the Son of God hath told;
grant my spi - rit ev - er by thy life may live,
face to face thy splen - dor, I at last shall see,

tranced as it be - holds thee, shrined with - in the cloud.
what the Truth hath spo - ken, that for truth I hold.
to my taste thy sweet - ness nev - er - fail - ing give.
in the glo - rious vi - sion, bless - ed Lord, of thee.

Words: Att. Thomas Aquinas (1225?-1274); sts. 1-3, tr. *Hymnal 1940*; st. 4, tr. *Hymnal 1982*
Music: *Adoro devote*, French church melody, Mode 5, *Processionale*, 1697   11 11. 11 11

Unison or harmony

1 Thou, who at thy first Eu-cha-rist didst pray
2 For all thy Church, O Lord, we in-ter-cede;
3 So, Lord, at length when sac-ra-ments shall cease,

that all thy Church might be for ev-er one,
make thou our sad di-vi-sions soon to cease;
may we be one with all thy Church a-bove,

grant us at ev-ery Eu-cha-rist to say
draw us the near-er each to each, we plead,
one with thy saints in one un-bro-ken peace,

with long-ing heart and soul, "Thy will be done."
by draw-ing all to thee, O Prince of Peace;
one with thy saints in one un-bound-ed love;

O	may	we	all	one	bread,	one	bo	-	dy	be,
thus	may	we	all	one	bread,	one	bo	-	dy	be,
more	bless	- ed	still,	in	peace	and	love	to	be

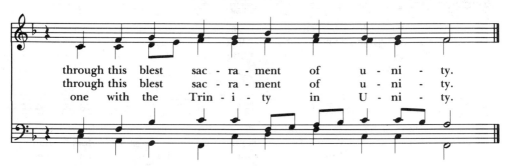

through this	blest	sac	- ra	- ment	of	u	- ni	-	ty.
through this	blest	sac	- ra	- ment	of	u	- ni	-	ty.
one	with the	Trin	- i	- ty	in	U	- ni	-	ty.

Words: William Harry Turton (1856-1938)
Music: *Song 1*, melody and bass Orlando Gibbons (1583-1625);
harm. *Hymns for Church and School*, 1964

10 10. 10 10. 10 10

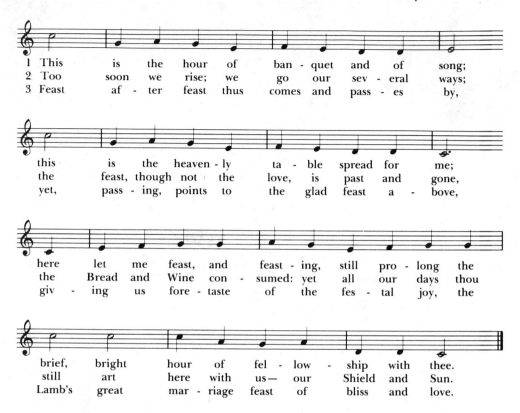

1 This is the hour of ban - quet and of song;
2 Too soon we rise; we go our sev - eral ways;
3 Feast af - ter feast thus comes and pass - es by,

this is the heaven - ly ta - ble spread for me;
the feast, though not the love, is past and gone,
yet, pass - ing, points to the glad feast a - bove,

here let me feast, and feast - ing, still pro - long the
the Bread and Wine con - sumed: yet all our days thou
giv - ing us fore - taste of the fes - tal joy, the

brief, bright hour of fel - low - ship with thee.
still art here with us— our Shield and Sun.
Lamb's great mar - riage feast of bliss and love.

Words: Horatius Bonar (1808-1889), alt.
Music: *Canticum refectionis*, David McKinley Williams (1887-1978)

10 10. 10 10

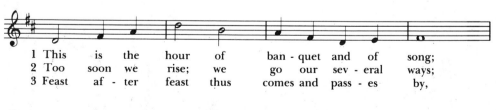

1 This is the hour of ban - quet and of song;
2 Too soon we rise; we go our sev - eral ways;
3 Feast af - ter feast thus comes and pass - es by,

this is the heaven - ly ta - ble spread for me;
the feast, though not the love, is past and gone,
yet, pass - ing, points to the glad feast a - bove,

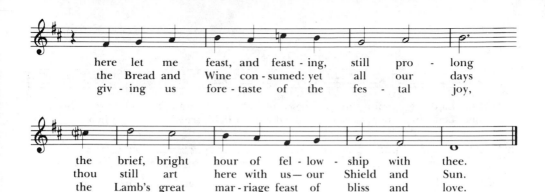

here let me feast, and feast-ing, still pro - long
the Bread and Wine con - sumed: yet all our days
giv - ing us fore - taste of the fes - tal joy,

the brief, bright hour of fel - low - ship with thee.
thou still art here with us— our Shield and Sun.
the Lamb's great mar - riage feast of bliss and love.

Words: Horatius Bonar (1808-1889), alt.
Music: *Morestead*, Sidney Watson (b. 1903)

10 10. 10 10

Holy Eucharist

318

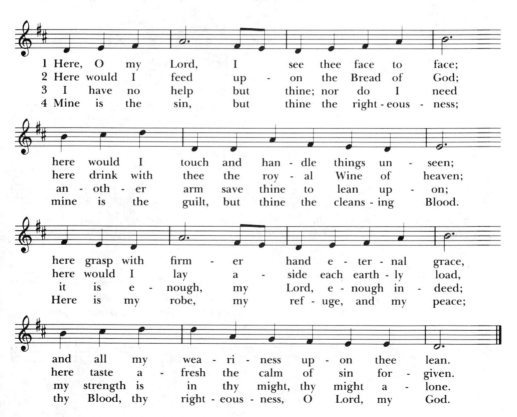

1 Here, O my Lord, I see thee face to face;
2 Here would I feed up - on the Bread of God;
3 I have no help but thine; nor do I need
4 Mine is the sin, but thine the right - eous - ness;

here would I touch and han - dle things un - seen;
here drink with thee the roy - al Wine of heaven;
an - oth - er arm save thine to lean up - on;
mine is the guilt, but thine the cleans - ing Blood.

here grasp with firm - er hand e - ter - nal grace,
here would I lay a - side each earth - ly load,
it is e - nough, my Lord, e - nough in - deed;
Here is my robe, my ref - uge, and my peace;

and all my wea - ri - ness up - on thee lean.
here taste a - fresh the calm of sin for - given.
my strength is in thy might, thy might a - lone.
thy Blood, thy right - eous - ness, O Lord, my God.

Words: Horatius Bonar (1808-1889)
Music: *Nyack*, Warren Swenson (b. 1937)

10 10. 10 10

1 You, Lord, we praise in songs of cel - e - bra - tion for this
2 You, Lord, in our stead to the grave de - scend - ed when by

feast of our sal - va - tion. Here at your
sin our life was end - ed. No great - er

ta - ble ev - ery life you nour - ish; by your grace we
love than this to you could bind us; dai - ly still your

all may flour - ish. Ky - ri - e e - le - i - son.
mer - cies find us. Ky - ri - e e - le - i - son.

In the light of your In - car - na - tion, all cre -
Bind our hearts as one we im - plore you, who a -

a - tion knows the love of God, and in
dore you and con - fess your Name. Thus may

you finds re - lease that we all might
we ev - er be yours in peace and

live in peace. Ky - ri - e e - le - i - son.____
u - ni - ty. Ky - ri - e e - le - i - son.____

Words: Russell Schulz-Widmar (b. 1944), based on German folk hymn and Martin Luther (1483-1546)
Music: *Gott sei gelobet*, melody from *Miltenberger Processionale*, 15th cent. adapt. *Geistliche Gesangbüchlein*, 1524   Irr.

1 Zi - on, praise thy Sa - vior, sing - ing hymns with ex - ul -
Hon - or Christ, thy voice up - rais - ing, who sur - pass - eth

ta - tion ring - ing, praise thy King and Shep - herd true.
all thy prais - ing; nev - er canst thou reach his due.

2 Let the Bread, life - giv - ing, liv - ing, be our
as of old the Lord pro - vid - ed when the

theme of glad thanks - giv - ing, now in truth be - fore thee set;
twelve, di - vine - ly guid - ed, at the ho - ly ta - ble met.

3 What he did, at sup - per seat - ed, Christ or - dained to
4 Full and clear sing out thy prais - ing, gra - cious hymns of

be re - peat - ed, his me - mo - rial ne'er to cease;
joy up - rais - ing in thy heart and soul to - day;

his com - mand for guid - ance tak - ing, bread and wine we
for to - day the new ob - la - tion of the new King's

hal - low, mak - ing thus our sac - ri - fice of peace.
rev - e - la - tion bids us feast in glad ar - ray.

*5 Ve - ry Bread, good Shep-herd, tend us, Je - sus, of thy love
*6 thou, who all things canst and know - est, who on earth such food

be - friend us, Lord, re - fresh us and de - fend us, thine e -
be - stow - est, grant us, with thy saints, though low - est, where the

ter - nal good-ness send us in the land of life to see:
heaven-ly feast thou show - est, fel - low - heirs and guests to be.

*When stanzas 5 and 6 are omitted, stanzas 1 through 4 may be sung to the tune of stanza 1,
or the tunes of stanzas 1 and 2 may be repeated for stanzes 3 and 4.*

Words: Att. Thomas Aquinas (1225?-1274); tr. *Hymnal 1940*; rev. *Hymnal 1982*
Music: *Lauda Sion Salvatorem*, plainsong, Mode 7, 12th cent.

887. 887

321

Holy Eucharist

1 My God, thy ta - ble now is spread, thy cup with
2 O let thy ta - ble hon - ored be, and fur - nished
3 Drawn by thy quick-ening grace, O Lord, in count - less
4 Nor let thy spread-ing Gos - pel rest till through the

love doth o - ver - flow; be all thy chil - dren
well with joy - ful guests; and may each soul sal -
num - bers let them come and gath - er from their
world thy truth has run, till with this Bread shall

thith - er led, and let them thy sweet mer - cies know.
va - tion see, that here its sa - cred pledg - es tastes.
Fa - ther's board the Bread that lives be - yond the tomb.
all be blessed who see the light or feel the sun.

Words: Sts. 1-3, Philip Doddridge (1702-1751), alt.; st. 4, Issac Watts (1674-1748), alt.
Music: *Rockingham*, melody from *Second Supplement to Psalmody in Miniature*, ca. 1780;
harm. Edward Miller (1731-1807); adapt. Samuel Webbe, Jr. (1770-1843)

LM

Holy Eucharist

322

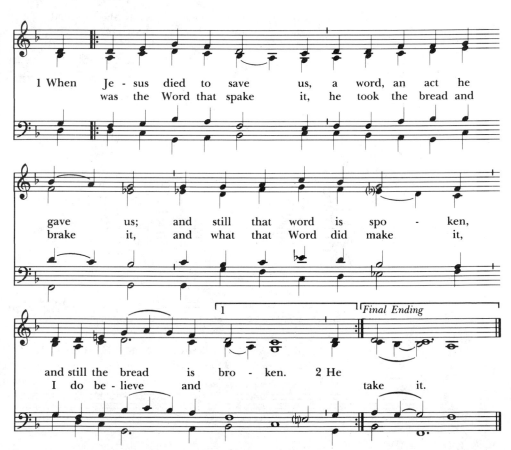

1 When Je - sus died to save us, a word, an act he
was the Word that spake it, he took the bread and

gave us; and still that word is spo - ken,
brake it, and what that Word did make it,

Final Ending

and still the bread is bro - ken. 2 He
I do be - lieve and take it.

Words: St. 1, F. Bland Tucker (1895-1984); st. 2, att. John Donne (1573-1631)
Music: *Tucker*, David Hurd (b. 1950)

77. 77

1 Bread of heaven, on thee we feed, for thy Flesh is
2 Vine of heaven, thy Blood sup-plies this blest cup of

meat in-deed; ev-er may our souls be fed
sac-ri-fice; Lord, thy wounds our heal-ing give,

with this true and liv-ing Bread; day by day with
to thy cross we look and live: Je-sus, may we

strength sup-plied, through the life of him who died.
ev-er be graft-ed, root-ed, built in thee.

Words: Josiah Conder (1789-1855), alt.
Music: *Jesu, Jesu, du mein Hirt*, melody Paul Heinlein (1626-1686); harm. *The English Hymnal*, 1906

77. 77. 77

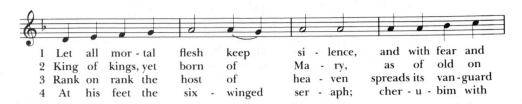

1 Let all mor - tal flesh keep si - lence, and with fear and
2 King of kings, yet born of Ma - ry, as of old on
3 Rank on rank the host of hea - ven spreads its van - guard
4 At his feet the six - winged ser - aph; cher - u - bim with

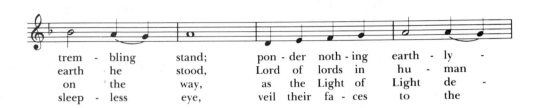

trem - bling stand; pon - der noth - ing earth - ly -
earth he stood, Lord of lords in hu - man
on 'the way, as the Light of Light de -
sleep - less eye, veil their fa - ces to the

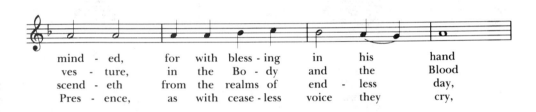

mind - ed, for with bless - ing in his hand
ves - ture, in the Bo - dy and the Blood
scend - eth from the realms of end - less day,
Pres - ence, as with cease - less voice they cry,

Christ our God to earth de - scend - eth,
he will give to all the faith - ful
that the powers of hell may va - nish
"Al - le - lu - ia, al - le - lu - ia!

our full hom - age to de - mand.
his own self for heaven - ly food.
as the dark - ness clears a - way.
Al - le - lu - ia, Lord Most High!"

Words: Liturgy of St. James; para. Gerard Moultrie (1829-1885)
Music: *Picardy*, French carol, 17th cent.; melody from *Chansons populaires des Provinces de France*, 1860   87. 87. 87

1 Let us break bread to-geth-er on our knees;
2 Let us drink wine to-geth-er on our knees;

let us break bread to-geth-er on our knees;
let us drink wine to-geth-er on our knees;

Refrain

when I fall on my knees, with my face to the ris-ing sun,

O Lord, have mer-cy on me.

3 Let us praise God to-geth-er on our knees;

let us praise God to-geth-er on our knees;

Refrain

when I fall on my knees, with my face to the ris-ing sun,

O Lord, have mer-cy on me.

Words: Afro-American spiritual
Music: *Let Us Break Bread*, Afro-American spiritual; **arr.** David Hurd (b. 1950)

10 10 with Refrain

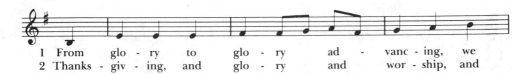

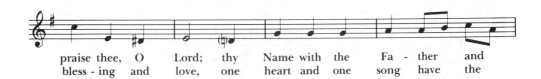

1 From glo - ry to glo - ry ad - vanc - ing, we
2 Thanks - giv - ing, and glo - ry and wor - ship, and

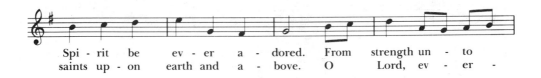

praise thee, O Lord; thy Name with the Fa - ther and
bless - ing and love, one heart and one song have the

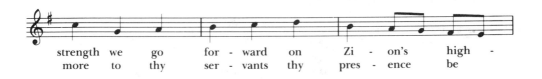

Spi - rit be ev - er a - dored. From strength un - to
saints up - on earth and a - bove. O Lord, ev - er -

strength we go for - ward on Zi - on's high -
more to thy ser - vants thy pres - ence be

way, to ap - pear be - fore God in the
nigh; ev - er fit us by ser - vice on

ci - ty of in - fi - nite day.
earth for thy ser - vice on high.

The small notes in the vocal part are recommended for stanza 2.

Words: Liturgy of St. James; tr. Charles William Humphreys (1840-1921)
Music: *St. Keverne*, Craig Sellar Lang (1891-1971)

14 14. 14 15

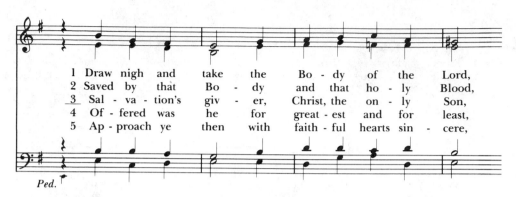

1 Draw nigh and take the Bo-dy of the Lord,
2 Saved by that Bo - dy and that ho - ly Blood,
3 Sal - va - tion's giv - er, Christ, the on - ly Son,
4 Of - fered was he for great - est and for least,
5 Ap - proach ye then with faith - ful hearts sin - cere,

Ped.

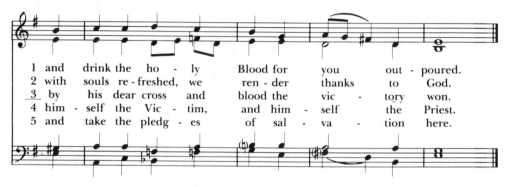

1 and drink the ho - ly Blood for you out - poured.
2 with souls re - freshed, we ren - der thanks to God.
3 by his dear cross and blood the vic - tory won.
4 him - self the Vic - tim, and him - self the Priest.
5 and take the pledg - es of sal - va - tion here.

6 He that his saints in this world rules and shields
   to all believers life eternal yields;

7 with heavenly bread he makes the hungry whole,
   gives living waters to the thirsting soul.

8 Alpha-Omega, unto whom shall bow
   all nations at the doom, is with us now.

Words: *Bangor Antiphoner*, ca. 690; tr. John Mason Neale (1818-1866), alt.
Music: *Palmer Church*, David Ashley White (b. 1944)

10. 10

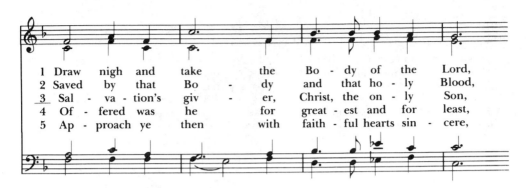

1 Draw nigh and take the Bo - dy of the Lord,
2 Saved by that Bo - dy and that ho - ly Blood,
3 Sal - va - tion's giv - er, Christ, the on - ly Son,
4 Of - fered was he for great - est and for least,
5 Ap - proach ye then with faith - ful hearts sin - cere,

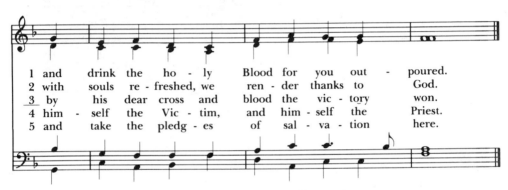

1 and drink the ho - ly Blood for you out - poured.
2 with souls re - freshed, we ren - der thanks to God.
3 by his dear cross and blood the vic - tory won.
4 him - self the Vic - tim, and him - self the Priest.
5 and take the pledg - es of sal - va - tion here.

6 He that his saints in this world rules and shields
to all believers life eternal yields;

7 with heavenly bread he makes the hungry whole,
gives living waters to the thirsting soul.

8 Alpha-Omega, unto whom shall bow
all nations at the doom, is with us now.

Words: *Bangor Antiphoner*, ca. 690; tr. John Mason Neale (1818-1866), alt.
Music: *Song 46*, melody and most of the bass from a longer tune by Orlando Gibbons (1583-1625); harm. *The English Hymnal*, 1906

10. 10

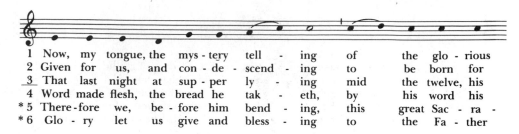

1 Now, my tongue, the mys-tery tell - ing of the glo-rious
2 Given for us, and con-de-scend - ing to be born for
3 That last night at sup-per ly - ing mid the twelve, his
4 Word made flesh, the bread he tak - eth, by his word his
*5 There-fore we, be-fore him bend - ing, this great Sac-ra-
*6 Glo-ry let us give and bless - ing to the Fa-ther

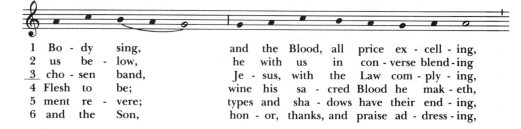

1 Bo - dy sing, and the Blood, all price ex - cell-ing,
2 us be - low, he with us in con-verse blend-ing,
3 cho-sen band, Je - sus, with the Law com-ply-ing,
4 Flesh to be; wine his sa - cred Blood he mak-eth,
5 ment re - vere; types and sha - dows have their end-ing,
6 and the Son, hon - or, thanks, and praise ad-dress-ing,

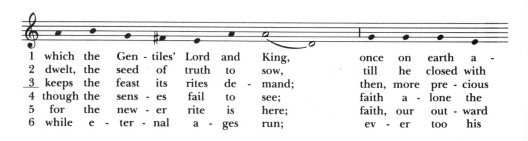

1 which the Gen-tiles' Lord and King, once on earth a-
2 dwelt, the seed of truth to sow, till he closed with
3 keeps the feast its rites de - mand; then, more pre-cious
4 though the sens - es fail to see; faith a - lone the
5 for the new - er rite is here; faith, our out-ward
6 while e - ter-nal a - ges run; ev - er too his

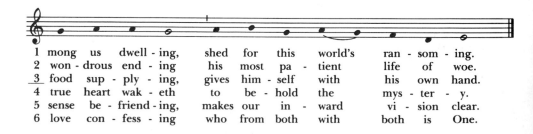

1 mong us dwell-ing, shed for this world's ran-som-ing.
2 won-drous end-ing, his most pa - tient life of woe.
3 food sup-ply-ing, gives him-self with his own hand.
4 true heart wak-eth, to be-hold the mys-ter - y.
5 sense be-friend-ing, makes our in - ward vi - sion clear.
6 love con-fess-ing, who from both with both is One.

Words: Att. Thomas Aquinas (1225?-1274); ver. *Hymnal 1940*, rev.
Music: *Pange lingua*, plainsong, Mode 3, Worcester MS, 13th cent.

87. 87. 87

5 There-fore we, be-fore him bend - ing,
6 Glo - ry let us give and bless - ing

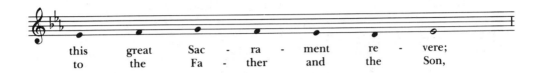

this great Sac - ra - ment re - vere;
to the Fa - ther and the Son,

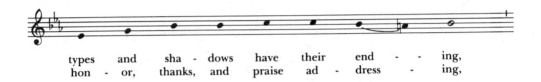

types and sha - dows have their end - - ing,
hon - or, thanks, and praise ad - dress - ing,

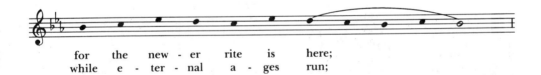

for the new - er rite is here;
while e - ter - nal a - ges run;

faith, our out - ward sense be - friend - ing,
ev - er too his love con - fess - - ing

makes our in - ward vi - sion clear.
who from both with both is One.

These are stanzas from the hymns found at 329 and 331.

Words: Att. Thomas Aquinas (1225?-1274); ver. *Hymnal 1940*
Music: *Tantum ergo Sacramentum*, plainsong, Mode 5, *Zisterzienser Hymnar*, 14th cent.

87. 87. 87

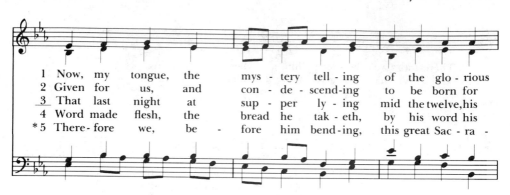

1 Now, my tongue, the mys - tery tell - ing of the glo - rious
2 Given for us, and con - de - scend-ing to be born for
3 That last night at sup - per ly - ing mid the twelve, his
4 Word made flesh, the bread he tak - eth, by his word his
*5 There - fore we, be - fore him bend-ing, this great Sac - ra -

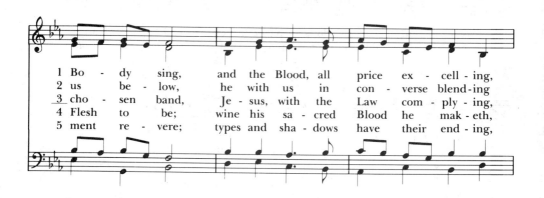

1 Bo - dy sing, and the Blood, all price ex - cell - ing,
2 us be - low, he with us in con - verse blend-ing
3 cho - sen band, Je - sus, with the Law com - ply - ing,
4 Flesh to be; wine his sa - cred Blood he mak - eth,
5 ment re - vere; types and sha - dows have their end - ing,

1 which the Gen-tiles' Lord and King; once on earth a -
2 dwelt, the seed of truth to sow, till he closed with
3 keeps the feast its rites de - mand; then, more pre - cious
4 though the sens - es fail to see; faith a - lone the
5 for the new - er rite is here; faith, our out - ward

1 mong us dwell-ing, shed for this world's ran - som - ing.
2 won - drous end - ing his most pa - tient life of woe.
3 food sup - ply - ing, gives him - self with his own hand.
4 true heart wak - eth to be - hold the mys - te - ry.
5 sense be - friend-ing, makes our in - ward vi - sion clear.

*6 Glory let us give and blessing
to the Father and the Son,
honor, thanks, and praise addressing,
while eternal ages run;
ever too his love confessing
who from both with both is One.

Words: Att. Thomas Aquinas (1225?-1274); ver. *Hymnal 1940*, rev.
Music: *Grafton*, melody from *Chants ordinaires de l'Office Divin*, 1881; harm. *Songs of Praise*, 1925   87. 87. 87

Holy Eucharist   332

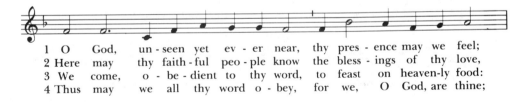

1 O God, un - seen yet ev - er near, thy pres - ence may we feel;
2 Here may thy faith - ful peo - ple know the bless - ings of thy love,
3 We come, o - be - dient to thy word, to feast on heaven-ly food:
4 Thus may we all thy word o - bey, for we, O God, are thine;

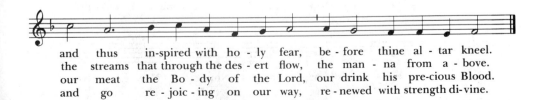

and thus in-spired with ho - ly fear, be - fore thine al - tar kneel.
the streams that through the des - ert flow, the man - na from a - bove.
our meat the Bo - dy of the Lord, our drink his pre-cious Blood.
and go re - joic - ing on our way, re - newed with strength di-vine.

Words: Edward Osler (1798-1863)
Music: *St. Flavian*, from *Day's Psalter*, 1562   CM

Now the si - lence Now the peace Now the emp - ty

hands up - lift - ed Now the kneel - ing Now the plea

Now the Fa - ther's arms in wel - come Now the hear - ing

Now the power Now the ves - sel brimmed for pour - ing

Now the Bo - dy Now the Blood Now the joy - ful

cel - e - bra - tion Now the wed - ding Now the songs

Now the heart for - giv - en leap - ing Now the Spi - rit's

vis - i - ta - tion Now the Son's e - piph - a - ny

Now the Fa - ther's bless - ing Now Now Now

Words: Jaroslav J. Vajda (b. 1919)
Music: *Now*, Carl Flentge Schalk (b. 1929)
Irr.

1 Praise the Lord, rise up re - joic - ing, wor - ship, thanks, de -
2 Scat - tered flock, one shep - herd shar - ing, lost and lone - ly,
3 Sins for - giv - en, wrongs for - giv - ing, we go forth a -

vo - tion voic - ing; glo - ry be to God on high!
one voice hear - ing, ears at - ten - tive to your word;
lert and liv - ing in your Spi - rit, strong and free.

Christ, your cross and pas - sion shar - ing, by this Eu - cha -
by your Blood new life re - ceiv - ing, in your Bo - dy,
Part - ners in your new cre - a - tion, seek - ing peace in

rist de - clar - ing yours the fi - nal vic - to - ry.
firm be - liev - ing, we are yours, and you the Lord.
ev - ery na - tion, may we faith - ful fol - lowers be.

Words: Howard Charles Adie Gaunt (b. 1902), alt.
Music: *Alles ist an Gottes Segen*, melody att. Johann Balthasar König (1691-1758), alt.;
harm. Johann Löhner (1645-1705), after chorale ver. Johann Sebastian Bach (1685-1750)

887. 887

1   I   am the bread   of   life; ____   they who
2 (The)   Bread that__   I   will   give__   is   my
3 (Un-)   less_____   you   eat__   of   the
4   I   am the re - sur - rec - tion,____
5 (Yes,)   Lord____   we   be - lieve__   that__

1 come   to   me shall   not__   hun - ger;   they who be -
2 Flesh   for   the   life   of   the   world, __   and   they who
3 Flesh   of   the   Son   of __   Man____   and __
4 I____   am   the __   life. __   They who be -
5 you____   are   the __   Christ, ____   the __

1 lieve   in me shall   not   thirst.   No   one can come   to
2 eat____   of   this   bread,   they   shall__ live   for
3 drink____   of   his   Blood,   you   shall   not have life   with -
4 lieve____   in   me,   e - ven__   if   they
5 Son____   of   God   who____   has

1 me____   un - less   the__   Fa - ther   draw   them.
2 ev - er,____   they   shall__ live   for   ev - er.
3 in   you,   you   shall   not have life   with - in   you.
4 die,____   they   shall__ live   for   ev - er.
5 come__   in - to____   the__   world. __

Descant

And I will   raise   them   up,   and I will   raise   them

Refrain

And I will   raise   them   up,   and I will   raise   them

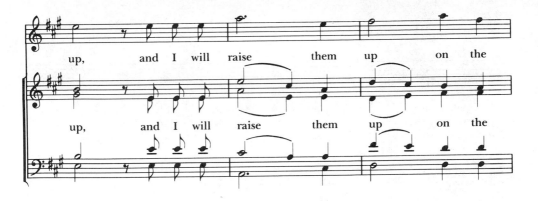

up, and I will raise them up on the

up, and I will raise them up on the

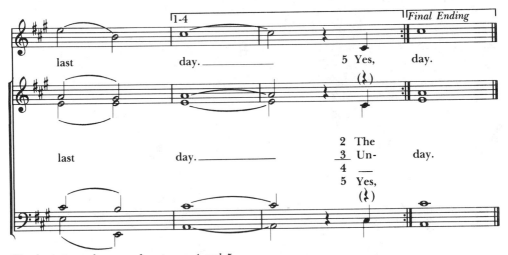

last day. 5 Yes, day.

last day.
2 The
3 Un- day.
4
5 Yes,

The descant may be sung after stanzas 4 and 5.

Words: Suzanne Toolan (b. 1927); adapt. of John 6
Music: *I Am the Bread of Life*, Suzanne Toolan (b. 1927); arr. Betty Pulkingham (b. 1928)

Irr. with Refrain

1 Come with us, O bless - ed Je - sus, with us ev - er -
*2 Come with us, O might - y Sa - vior, God from God, and
*3 Come with us, O King of glo - ry, by an - gel - ic

more to be; and though leav - ing now thine
Light from Light; thou art God, thy glo - ry
voic - es praised; in our hearts as in thy

al - tar, let us nev - er - more leave thee.
veil - ing, so that we may bear the sight.
hea - ven, be en - rap - tured an - thems raised.

Be thou one with us for ev - er, in our life thy
Now we go to seek and serve thee, through our work as
Let the might - y cho - rus ev - er sing its glad ex -

love di - vine   our own flesh and blood has
through our prayer; grant us light to see and
ul - tant songs; let its hymn be heard for

tak - en,   and   to us thou giv - est thine.
know thee, in thy peo - ple ev - ery - where.
ev - er— peace for which cre - a - tion longs.

Words: John Henry Hopkins, Jr. (1820-1891) and Charles P. Price (b. 1920)
Music: *Werde munter*, Johann Schop (d. 1665?); arr. and harm.
    Johann Sebastian Bach (1685-1750)

87. 87. D

1 And now, O Fa - ther, mind - ful of the love that
2 Look Fa - ther, look on his a - noint - ed face, and
*3 And then for those, our dear - est and our best, by
*4 And so we come; O draw us to thy feet, most

bought us, once for all, on Cal - vary's tree, and hav - ing with us
on - ly look on us as found in him; look not on our mis -
this pre - vail - ing pres-ence we ap - peal; O fold them clos - er
pa - tient Sa - vior, who canst love us still! And by this food, so

him that pleads a - bove, we here pre - sent, we here spread
us - ings of thy grace, our prayer so lan - guid, and our
to thy mer - cy's breast! O do thine ut - most for their
awe - some and so sweet, de - liv - er us from ev - ery

forth to thee, that on - ly of - fering per - fect in thine
faith so dim: for lo! be - tween our sins and their re -
soul's true weal! From taint - ing mis - chief keep them pure and
touch of ill: in thine own ser - vice make us glad and

eyes, the one true, pure, im - mor - tal sac - ri - fice.
ward, we set the pas - sion of thy Son our Lord.
clear, and crown thy gifts with strength to per - se - vere.
free, and grant us nev - er - more to part from thee.

Words: William Bright (1824-1901), alt.
Music: *Unde et memores*, William Henry Monk (1823-1889)

10 10. 10 10. 10 10

Holy Eucharist

338

Unison or harmony

1 Where - fore, O Fa - ther, we thy hum - ble ser - vants here bring be -
2 See now thy chil - dren, ma - king in - ter - ces - sion through him our

fore thee Christ thy well - be - lov - ed, All - per - fect Of - fering,
Sa - vior, Son of God in - car - nate, for all thy peo - ple,

sac - ri - fice im - mor - tal, spot - less ob - la - tion.
liv - ing and de - part - ed, plead - ing be - fore thee.

Words: William Henry Hammond Jervois (1852-1905)
Music: *Lobet den Herren*, melody Johann Cruger (1598-1662); harm. Friedrich Layriz (1808-1859)

11 11. 11 5

1 Deck thy-self, my soul, with glad - ness, leave the
2 Sun, who all my life dost bright - en; Light, who
3 Je - sus, Bread of life, I pray thee, let me

gloom-y haunts of sad - ness, come in - to the day-light's
dost my soul en - light - en; Joy, the best that an - y
glad - ly here o - bey thee; nev - er to my hurt in -

splen - dor, there with joy thy prais - es ren - der
know - eth; Fount, whence all my be - ing flow - eth:
vit - ed, be thy love with love re - quit - ed;

un - to him whose grace un - bound - ed hath this
at thy feet I cry, my Ma - ker, let me
from this ban - quet let me mea - sure, Lord, how

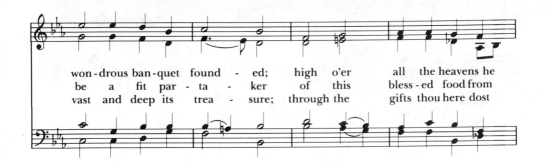

won-drous ban-quet found - ed; high o'er all the heavens he
be a fit par - ta - ker of this bless - ed food from
vast and deep its trea - sure; through the gifts thou here dost

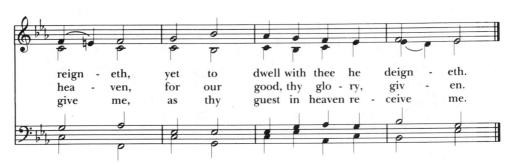

reign - eth, yet to dwell with thee he deign - eth.
hea - ven, for our good, thy glo - ry, giv - en.
give me, as thy guest in heaven re - ceive me.

Words: Johann Franck (1618-1677); tr. Catherine Winkworth (1827-1878), alt.
Music: *Schmücke dich*, melody Johann Cruger (1598-1662); harm. *The English Hymnal*, 1906   LMD

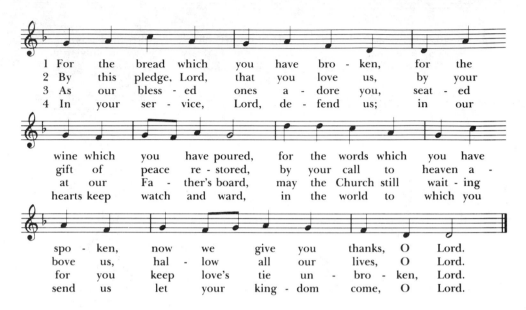

1 For the bread which you have bro - ken, for the
2 By this pledge, Lord, that you love us, by your
3 As our bless - ed ones a - dore you, seat - ed
4 In your ser - vice, Lord, de - fend us; in our

wine which you have poured, for the words which you have
gift of peace re - stored, by your call to heaven a -
at our Fa - ther's board, may the Church still wait - ing
hearts keep watch and ward, in the world to which you

spo - ken, now we give you thanks, O Lord.
bove us, hal - low all our lives, O Lord.
for you keep love's tie un - bro - ken, Lord.
send us let your king - dom come, O Lord.

Words: Louis F. Benson (1855-1930), alt.
Music: *Beng-Li*, I-to Loh (b. 1936)

87. 87

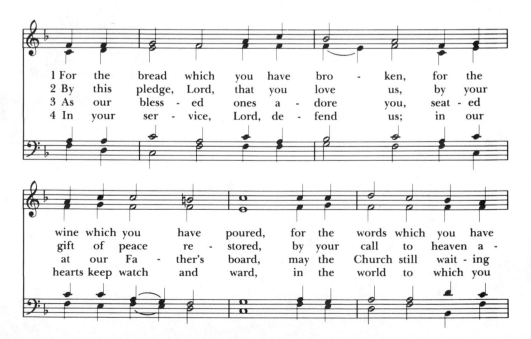

1 For the bread which you have bro - ken, for the
2 By this pledge, Lord, that you love us, by your
3 As our bless - ed ones a - dore you, seat - ed
4 In your ser - vice, Lord, de - fend us; in our

wine which you have poured, for the words which you have
gift of peace re - stored, by your call to heaven a -
at our Fa - ther's board, may the Church still wait - ing
hearts keep watch and ward, in the world to which you

spo	- ken,	now	we	give	you	thanks,	O	Lord.
bove	us,	hal	- low	all	our	lives,	O	Lord.
for	you	keep	love's	tie	un - bro	-	ken,	Lord.
send	us	let	your	king - dom	come,		O	Lord.

Words: Louis F. Benson (1855-1930), alt.
Music: *Omni die*, melody from *Gross Catolisch Gesangbuch*, 1631;
    harm. William Smith Rockstro (1823-1895)

87. 87

Holy Eucharist

342

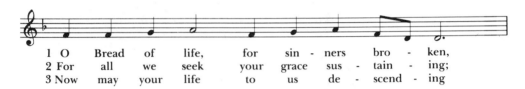

1 O	Bread	of	life,	for	sin	- ners	bro	- ken,
2 For	all	we	seek	your	grace	sus	- tain	- ing;
3 Now	may	your	life	to	us	de	- scend	- ing

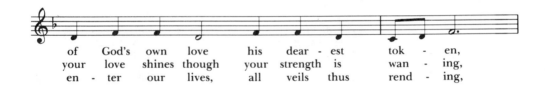

of	God's	own	love	his	dear	- est	tok	- en,
your	love	shines	though	your	strength	is	wan	- ing,
en	- ter	our	lives,	all	veils	thus	rend	- ing,

we	hear	the	words	so	gen	- tly	spo	- ken,
thus	by	your	death	our	life	ob	- tain	- ing.
Em	- man - u	- el,	our	joy	un	- end	- ing.

"Do	this	for	me	in	my	re	- mem	- brance."
"Come	un	- to	me,	you	hea	- vy	la	- den."
"I	am	with	you,	this	day	and	ev	- er."

Words: Timothy T'ing Fang Lew (1892-1947); tr. Frank W. Price (1895-1974), alt.
Music: *Sheng En*, melody Su Yin-Lan (20th cent.)

99. 99

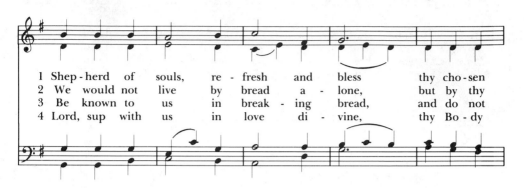

1 Shep-herd of souls, re-fresh and bless thy cho-sen
2 We would not live by bread a-lone, but by thy
3 Be known to us in break-ing bread, and do not
4 Lord, sup with us in love di-vine, thy Bo-dy

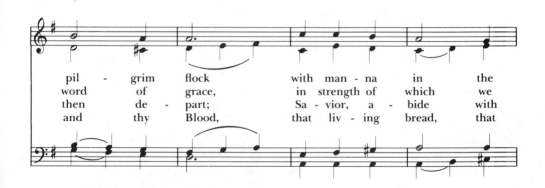

pil-grim flock with man-na in the
word of grace, in strength of which we
then de-part; Sa-vior, a-bide with
and thy Blood, that liv-ing bread, that

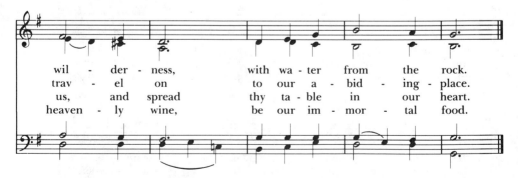

wil-der-ness, with wa-ter from the rock.
trav-el on to our a-bid-ing-place.
us, and spread thy ta-ble in our heart.
heaven-ly wine, be our im-mor-tal food.

Words: James Montgomery (1771-1854), alt.
Music: *St. Agnes*, melody John Bacchus Dykes (1823-1876); harm. Richard Proulx (b. 1937),
     after John Bacchus Dykes (1823-1876)   CM

Holy Eucharist

344

1 Lord, dis - miss us with thy bless - ing; fill our hearts with
2 Thanks we give and a - dor - a - tion for thy Gos - pel's
3 so that when thy love shall call us, Sa - vior, from the

joy and peace; let us each, thy love pos - sess - ing,
joy - ful sound: may the fruits of thy sal - va - tion
world a - way, fear of death shall not ap - pall us,

tri - umph in re - deem - ing grace: O re - fresh us,
in our hearts and lives a - bound: ev - er faith - ful,
glad thy sum - mons to o - bey. May we ev - er,

O re - fresh us, trav - eling through this wil - der - ness.
ev - er faith - ful to thy truth may we be found;
may we ev - er reign with thee in end - less day.

Words: Att. John Fawcett (1739/40-1817)
Music: *Sicilian Mariners*, Sicilian melody; first published
The European Magazine and London Review, 1792, alt.

87. 87. 87

345

1 Sa - vior, a - gain to thy dear Name we raise
*2 Grant us thy peace up - on our home-ward way;
3 Grant us thy peace through - out our earth - ly life;
4 thy peace in life, the balm of ev - ery pain;

with one ac - cord our part - ing hymn of praise;
with thee be - gan, with thee shall end the day:
peace to thy Church from er - ror and from strife;
thy peace in death, the hope to rise a - gain;

guard thou the lips from sin, the hearts from shame,
from harm and dan - ger keep thy chil - dren free,
peace to our land, the fruit of truth and love;
then, when thy voice shall bid our con - flict cease,

that in this house have called up - on thy Name.
for dark and light are both a - like to thee.
peace in each heart, thy Spi - rit from a - bove:
call us, O Lord, to thine e - ter - nal peace.

Words: John Ellerton (1826-1893), alt.
Music: *Ellers*, Edward John Hopkins (1818-1901)

10 10. 10 10

Unison or harmony

1 Com - plet - ed, Lord, the Ho - ly Mys - ter - ies,
2 Here we have tast - ed in - fi - nite de - lights,
3 Through God's good grace these Mys - ter - ies are ours,

as far as lies with - in our mor - tal power!
be - held a - far that life which soon shall be;
or - dained by thee, the ev - er - last - ing Son;

Thy death re - mem - bered, feed - ing thus on thee,
oh, count us wor - thy, Christ, thy joys to share
blest by the Spi - rit, breath and flame of life,

we here have known the re - sur - rec - tion hour.
for ev - er in e - ter - ni - ty with thee.
to whom be praise while end - less a - ges run.

Words: Liturgy of St. Basil; tr. Cyril E. Pocknee (1906-1980)
Music: *Song 4*, Orlando Gibbons (1583-1625), harm. *The English Hymnal*, 1906, alt.

10 10. 10 10

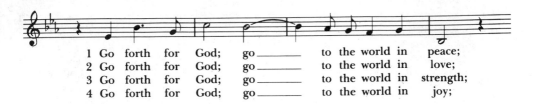

1 Go forth for God; go _____ to the world in peace;
2 Go forth for God; go _____ to the world in love;
3 Go forth for God; go _____ to the world in strength;
4 Go forth for God; go _____ to the world in joy;

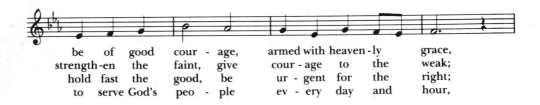

be of good cour - age, armed with heaven - ly grace,
strength-en the faint, give cour - age to the weak;
hold fast the good, be ur - gent for the right;
to serve God's peo - ple ev - ery day and hour,

in God's good Spi - rit dai - - ly to in - crease,
help the af - flict - ed; rich - ly from a - bove
ren - der to no one e - - vil; Christ at length
and serv - ing Christ, our ev - - ery gift em - ploy,

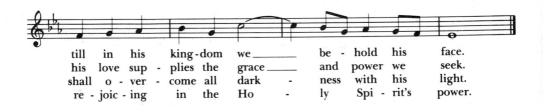

till in his king-dom we _____ be - hold his face.
his love sup - plies the grace _____ and power we seek.
shall o - ver - come all dark - ness with his light.
re - joic - ing in the Ho - ly Spi - rit's power.

Words: John Raphael Peacey (1896-1971) and *English Praise*, 1975, alt.
Music: *Litton*, Erik Routley (1917-1982)

10 10. 10 10

1 Lord, we have come at your own in-vi-ta-tion,
2 Here, at your ta-ble, con-firm our in-ten-tion
3 When, at your ta-ble, each time of re-turn-ing,
4 So, in the world where each du-ty as-signed us

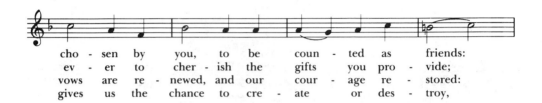

cho-sen by you, to be coun-ted as friends:
ev-er to cher-ish the gifts you pro-vide;
vows are re-newed, and our cour-age re-stored:
gives us the chance to cre-ate or des-troy,

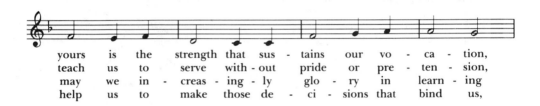

yours is the strength that sus-tains our vo-ca-tion,
teach us to serve with-out pride or pre-ten-sion,
may we in-creas-ing-ly glo-ry in learn-ing
help us to make those de-ci-sions that bind us,

ours a com-mit-ment we know nev-er ends.
led by your Spi-rit, de-fend-er and guide.
all that it means to ac-cept you as Lord.
Lord, to your-self, in o-be-dience and joy.

Words: F. Pratt Green (b. 1903), rev.
Music: *O quanta qualia*, melody from *Antiphoner*, 1681, harm. Percy C. Buck, *A Plainsong Hymnal*, 1932   10 10. 10 10
Words: Copyright © 1979 by Hope Publishing Company. All Rights Reserved. Used by Permission.

1 Ho - ly Spi - rit, Lord of love, who de - scend - ed
2 When the sa - cred vow is made, when the hands are

from a - bove, gifts of bless - ing to be - stow
on them laid, come in this most sol - emn hour

on your wait - ing Church be - low, once a - gain in
with your strength-en-ing gift of power. Give them light, your

love draw near to your ser - vants gath - ered here; from their
truth to see; give them life, your own to be; dai - ly

bright bap - tis - mal day you have led them on their way.
power to con-quer sin; pa - tient faith, the crown to win.

Words: William Dalrymple Maclagen (1826-1910), alt.
Music: *Aberystwyth*, Joseph Parry (1841-1903)

77. 77. D

Marriage

350

1 O God of love, _____ to thee we bow,
2 What-ev - er comes _____ to be their share _____
3 E - ter - nal love, _____ with them a - bide; _____

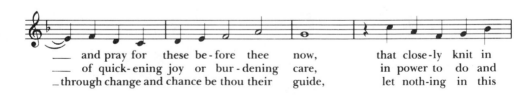

_____ and pray for these be-fore thee now, that close-ly knit in
_____ of quick-ening joy or bur-dening care, in power to do and
_ through change and chance be thou their guide, let noth-ing in this

ho - ly vow, they may in thee be one.
grace to bear, may they in thee be one.
life di - vide those whom thou mak - est one.

Words: William Vaughan Jenkins (1868-1920), alt.
Music: *St. Mary Magdalene*, Gerre Hancock (b. 1934)

888. 6

1 May the grace of Christ our Sa - vior, and the
2 Thus may they a - bide in un - ion with each

Fa - ther's bound - less love, with the Ho - ly
o - ther and the Lord, and pos - sess, in

Spi - rit's fa - vor, rest up - on them from a - bove.
sweet com - mun - ion, joys which earth can - not af - ford.

Words: John Newton (1725-1807), alt.
Music: *Halton Holgate*, William Boyce (1711-1779)

87. 87

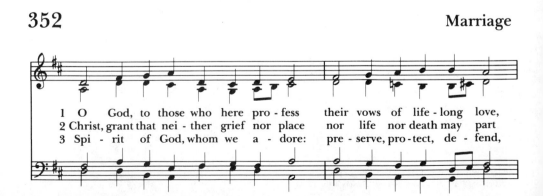

1 O God, to those who here pro - fess their vows of life - long love,
2 Christ, grant that nei - ther grief nor place nor life nor death may part
3 Spi - rit of God, whom we a - dore: pre - serve, pro - tect, de - fend,

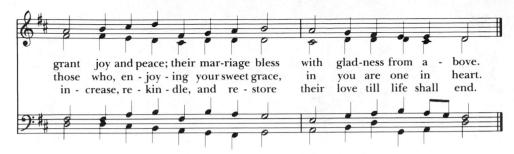

grant joy and peace; their mar-riage bless with glad-ness from a - bove.
those who, en - joy - ing your sweet grace, in you are one in heart.
in - crease, re - kin - dle, and re - store their love till life shall end.

Words: Sts. 1 and 3, Charles P. Price (b. 1920); st. 2, Charles Wesley (1707-1788), alt.
Music: *Caithness*, melody from *The Psalmes of David in Prose and Meeter*, 1635;
    harm. *The English Hymnal*, 1906

CM

Marriage

353

1 Your love, O God, has called us here, for all love
2 O gra - cious God, you con - se - crate all that is
3 O God of love, in - spire our life, re - veal your

finds its source in you, the per - fect love that
love - ly, good, and true. Bless those who in your
will in all we do; join ev - ery hus - band,

casts out fear, the love that Christ makes ev - er new.
pres - ence wait and ev - ery day their love re - new.
ev - ery wife in mu - tual love and love for you.

Words: Russell Schulz-Widmar (b. 1944)
Music: *Wareham*, melody William Knapp (1698-1768); harm. *Hymns Ancient and Modern*, 1875,
    after James Turle (1802-1882)

LM

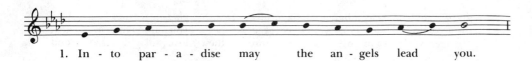

1. In - to par - a - dise may the an - gels lead you.

At your com - ing may the mar-tyrs re - ceive you,

and bring you in - to the ho - ly ci - ty Je - ru - sa - lem.

2. May the choirs of an - gels wel - come you,

and with Laz - a - rus who once was poor

may you have peace ev - er - last - ing.

Words: Latin; tr. *The Book of Common Prayer*, 1979, and Theodore Marier (b. 1912)
Music: *In paradisum*, plainsong, Mode 7 and Mode 8; *Graduale Romanum*, 1974

Irr.

Give rest, O Christ, to your ser-vant(s) with your saints, where sor-row and pain are no more, nei-ther

Fine

sigh-ing, but life ev-er-last-ing.

You on-ly are im-mor-tal, the cre-a-tor and ma-ker of man-kind; and we are mor-tal,

Words: Eastern Orthodox Memorial Service; tr. *The Book of Common Prayer*, 1979
Music: *Kontakion [Kievan chant]*, from Eastern Orthodox Memorial Service; ed. Walter Parratt (1841-1924), alt.　　Irr.

Burial　　356

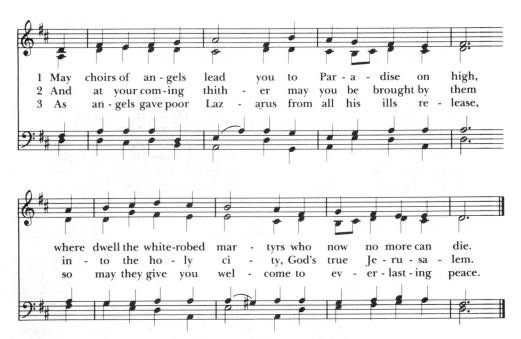

1 May choirs of an-gels lead you to Par-a-dise on high,
2 And at your com-ing thith-er may you be brought by them
3 As an-gels gave poor Laz-arus from all his ills re-lease,

where dwell the white-robed mar-tyrs who now no more can die.
in-to the ho-ly ci-ty, God's true Je-ru-sa-lem.
so may they give you wel-come to ev-er-last-ing peace.

Words: Latin; tr. F. Bland Tucker (1895-1984)
Music: *Christus, der ist mein Leben*, melody Melchior Vulpius (1560?-1616);
　　harm. after Melchior Vulpius (1560?-1616)　　　　76. 76

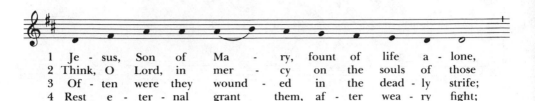

1 Je - sus, Son of Ma - ry, fount of life a - lone,
2 Think, O Lord, in mer - cy on the souls of those
3 Of - ten were they wound - ed in the dead - ly strife;
4 Rest e - ter - nal grant them, af - ter wea - ry fight;

now we hail thee pres - ent on thine al - tar throne.
who, in faith gone from us, now in death re - pose.
heal them, Good Phy - si - cian, with the balm of life.
shed on them the ra - diance of thy heaven - ly light.

Hum - bly we a - dore thee, Lord of end - less might,
Here mid stress and con - flict toils can nev - er cease;
Ev - ery taint of e - vil, frail - ty and de - cay,
Lead them on - ward, up - ward, to the ho - ly place,

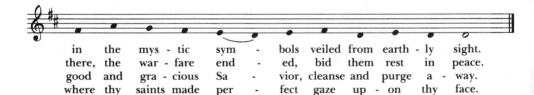

in the mys - tic sym - bols veiled from earth - ly sight.
there, the war - fare end - ed, bid them rest in peace.
good and gra - cious Sa - vior, cleanse and purge a - way.
where thy saints made per - fect gaze up - on thy face.

Words: Edmund Stuart Palmer (1856-1931)
Music: *Adoro devote*, French church melody, Mode 5, *Processionale*, 1697

11 11. 11 11

1 Christ the Vic - to - ri - ous, give to your ser - vants
2 On - ly Im - mor - tal One, Might - y Cre - a - tor!
3 God - spo - ken pro - phe - cy, word at cre - a - tion:
4 Christ the Vic - to - ri - ous, give to your ser - vants

rest with your saints in the re - gions of light.
We are your crea - tures and chil - dren of earth.
"You came from dust and to dust shall re - turn."
rest with your saints in the re - gions of light.

Grief and pain end - ed, and sigh - ing no long - er,
From earth you formed us, both glo - rious and mor - tal,
Yet at the grave shall we raise up our glad song,
Grief and pain end - ed, and sigh - ing no long - er,

there may they find ev - er - last - ing life.
and to the earth shall we all re - turn.
"Al - le - lu - ia, al - le - lu - ia!"
there may they find ev - er - last - ing life.

Words: Carl P. Daw, Jr. (b. 1944)
Music: *Russia*, Alexis Lvov (1799-1870)

11 10. 11 9

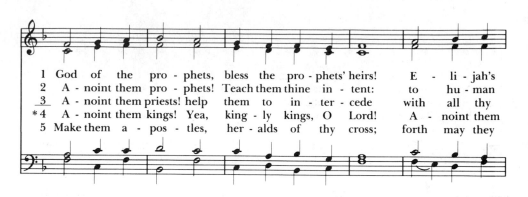

1 God of the pro - phets, bless the pro - phets' heirs!　E - li - jah's
2 A - noint them pro - phets! Teach them thine in - tent:　to　hu - man
3 A - noint them priests! help them to in - ter - cede　with　all　thy
*4 A - noint them kings! Yea, king - ly kings, O Lord!　A - noint them
5 Make them a - pos - tles, her - alds of thy cross;　forth　may they

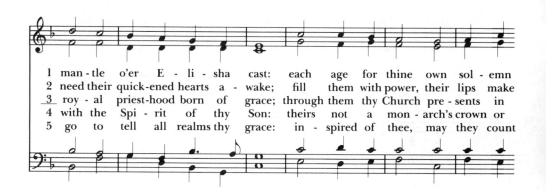

1 man - tle o'er E - li - sha cast: each age for thine own sol - emn
2 need their quick-ened hearts a - wake; fill them with power, their lips make
3 roy - al priest-hood born of grace; through them thy Church pre - sents in
4 with the Spi - rit of thy Son: theirs not a mon - arch's crown or
5 go to tell all realms thy grace: in - spired of thee, may they count

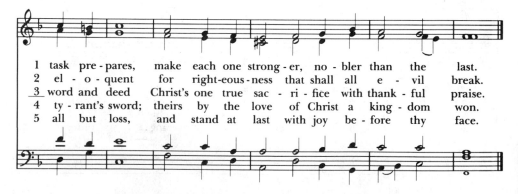

1 task pre - pares, make each one strong - er, no - bler than the last.
2 el - o - quent for right-eous - ness that shall all e - vil break.
3 word and deed Christ's one true sac - ri - fice with thank - ful praise.
4 ty - rant's sword; theirs by the love of Christ a king - dom won.
5 all but loss, and stand at last with joy be - fore thy face.

Words: St. 1-2 and 4-5, Denis Wortman (1835-1922), alt.; st. 3, Carl P. Daw, Jr. (b. 1944)
Music: *Toulon*, melody from *Pseaumes octante trois de David*, 1551, abridged;
　　　harm. Charles Winfred Douglas (1867-1944)

10 10. 10 10

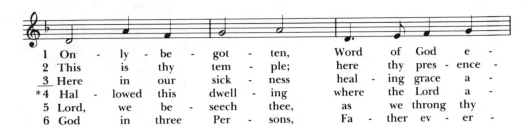

1 On - ly - be - got - ten, Word of God e -
2 This is thy tem - ple; here thy pres - ence -
3 Here in our sick - ness heal - ing grace a -
*4 Hal - lowed this dwell - ing where the Lord a -
5 Lord, we be - seech thee, as we throng thy
6 God in three Per - sons, Fa - ther ev - er -

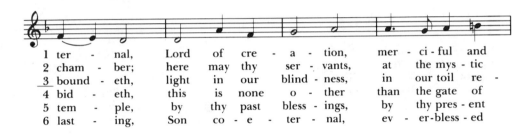

1 ter - nal, Lord of cre - a - tion, mer - ci - ful and
2 cham - ber; here may thy ser - vants, at the mys - tic
3 bound - eth, light in our blind - ness, in our toil re -
4 bid - eth, this is none o - ther than the gate of
5 tem - ple, by thy past bless - ings, by thy pres - ent
6 last - ing, Son co - e - ter - nal, ev - er-bless - ed

1 might - y, hear now thy ser - vants, when their joy - ful
2 ban - quet, hum - bly a - dor - ing, take thy Bo - dy
3 fresh - ment: sin is for - giv - en, hope o'er fear pre -
4 hea - ven; strang - ers and pil - grims, seek - ing homes e -
5 boun - ty, fa - vor thy chil - dren, and with ten - der
6 Spi - rit, thine be the glo - ry, praise, and a - dor -

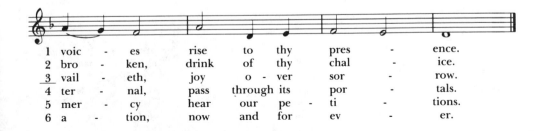

1 voic - es rise to thy pres - ence.
2 bro - ken, drink of thy chal - ice.
3 vail - eth, joy o - ver sor - row.
4 ter - nal, pass through its por - tals.
5 mer - cy hear our pe - ti - tions.
6 a - tion, now and for ev - er.

Words: Latin, ca. 9th cent.; tr. Maxwell Julius Blacker (1822-1888)
Music: *Rouen*, melody from *Vesperale*, 1746

11 11. 11 5

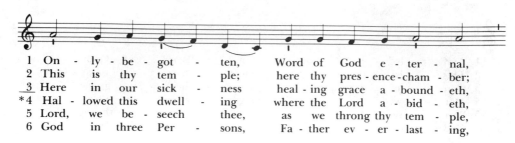

1 On - ly - be - got - ten, Word of God e - ter - nal,
2 This is thy tem - ple; here thy pres - ence - cham - ber;
3 Here in our sick - ness heal - ing grace a - bound - eth,
*4 Hal - lowed this dwell - ing where the Lord a - bid - eth,
5 Lord, we be - seech thee, as we throng thy tem - ple,
6 God in three Per - sons, Fa - ther ev - er - last - ing,

1 Lord of cre - a - tion, mer - ci - ful and might - y,
2 here may thy ser - vants, at the mys - tic ban - quet,
3 light in our blind - ness, in our toil re - fresh - ment:
4 this is none o - ther than the gate of hea - ven;
5 by thy past bless - ings, by thy pres - ent boun - ty,
6 Son co - e - ter - nal, ev - er - bless - ed Spi - rit,

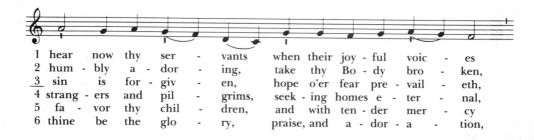

1 hear now thy ser - vants when their joy - ful voic - es
2 hum - bly a - dor - ing, take thy Bo - dy bro - ken,
3 sin is for - giv - en, hope o'er fear pre - vail - eth,
4 strang - ers and pil - grims, seek - ing homes e - ter - nal,
5 fa - vor thy chil - dren, and with ten - der mer - cy
6 thine be the glo - ry, praise, and a - dor - a - tion,

1 rise to thy pres - ence.
2 drink of thy chal - ice.
3 joy o - ver sor - row.
4 pass through its por - tals.
5 hear our pe - ti - tions.
6 now and for ev - er.

Words: Latin, ca. 9th cent.; tr. Maxwell Julius Blacker (1822-1888)
Music: *Caelitum Joseph*, plainsong, Mode 1; ver. Schola Antiqua, 1983
Music: Melody rhythmic version © 1984, Schola Antiqua Inc. Used by Permission.

11 11. 11 5

1 Ho-ly, ho-ly ho-ly! Lord___ God Al-might-y!
*2 Ho-ly, ho-ly, ho-ly! All the saints a-dore thee,
3 Ho-ly, ho-ly ho-ly! Though the dark-ness hide thee,
4 Ho-ly, ho-ly, ho-ly! Lord___ God Al-might-y!

Ear-ly in the morn-ing our song shall rise to thee:
cast-ing down their gold-en crowns a-round the glass-y sea;
though the sin-ful hu-man eye thy glo-ry may not see,
All thy works shall praise thy Name, in earth, and sky, and sea;

Ho-ly, ho-ly, ho-ly! Mer-ci-ful and might-y,
cher-u-bim and ser-a-phim fall-ing down be-fore thee,
on-ly thou art ho-ly; there is none be-side thee,
Ho-ly, ho-ly, ho-ly! Mer-ci-ful and might-y,

God in three Per-sons, bless-ed Trin-i-ty.
which wert, and art, and ev-er-more shalt be.
per-fect in power, in love, and pu-ri-ty.
God in three Per-sons, bless-ed Trin-i-ty.

Words: Reginald Heber (1783-1826), alt.
Music: *Nicaea*, John Bacchus Dykes (1823-1876)

11 12. 12 10

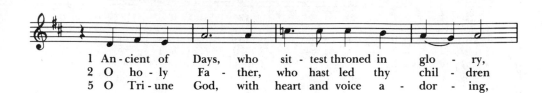

1 An-cient of Days, who sit-test throned in glo - ry,
2 O ho-ly Fa - ther, who hast led thy chil - dren
5 O Tri-une God, with heart and voice a - dor - ing,

to thee all knees are bent, all voic - es pray;
in all the a - ges with the fire and cloud,
praise we the good - ness that doth crown our days;

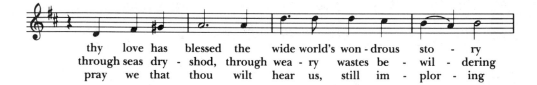

thy love has blessed the wide world's won - drous sto - ry
through seas dry - shod, through wea - ry wastes be - wil - dering
pray we that thou wilt hear us, still im - plor - ing

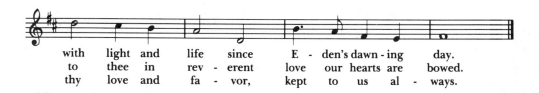

with light and life since E - den's dawn - ing day.
to thee in rev - erent love our hearts are bowed.
thy love and fa - vor, kept to us al - ways.

3 O ho-ly Je - sus, Lord of our sal - va - tion,
4 O Ho-ly Ghost, the Lord and the Life - giv - er,

ped.

call - ing the least, the last, the lost to thee,
thine is the quick - ening power that gives in - crease:

sum-mon-ing all to share thy new cre - a - tion,
from thee have flowed, as from a might - y riv - er,

ped.

thou, Lord, by death hast won life's vic - to - ry.
our faith and hope, our fel - low-ship and peace.

Words: William Croswell Doane (1832-1913), alt.
Music: *Coburn*, Alec Wyton (b. 1921)

11 10. 11 10

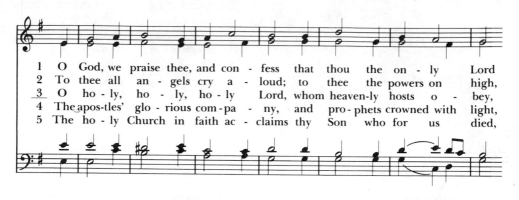

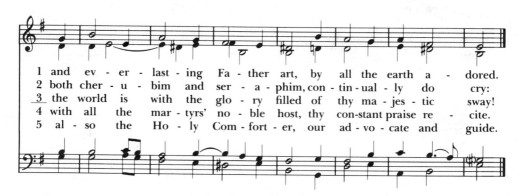

1 O God, we praise thee, and con - fess that thou the on - ly Lord
2 To thee all an - gels cry a - loud; to thee the powers on high,
3 O ho - ly, ho - ly, ho - ly Lord, whom heaven-ly hosts o - bey,
4 The apos-tles' glo - rious com-pa - ny, and pro - phets crowned with light,
5 The ho - ly Church in faith ac - claims thy Son who for us died,

1 and ev - er - last - ing Fa - ther art, by all the earth a - dored.
2 both cher - u - bim and ser - a - phim, con - tin - ual - ly do cry:
3 the world is with the glo - ry filled of thy ma - jes - tic sway!
4 with all the mar - tyrs' no - ble host, thy con-stant praise re - cite.
5 al - so the Ho - ly Com - fort - er, our ad - vo - cate and guide.

*6 Thou art the King of glory, Christ,
    the everlasting Son;
humbly thou cam'st to set us free,
    nor Virgin womb didst shun.

*7 When thou hadst overcome death's sting
    and opened heaven's door,
thou didst ascend to God's right hand
    in glory evermore.

*8 When thou shalt come to be our judge,
    bring us whom thou hast bought
to dwell on high with all thy saints
    in joy surpassing thought.

The G♯ may be reserved for the final stanza.

Words: Para. of *Te Deum;* sts. 1-5, *A Supplement to the New Version of the Psalms of David,* 1698, alt.;
    sts. 6-8, ver. *Hymnal 1982*
Music: *Manchester,* melody and bass Thomas Ravenscroft (1592?-1635?); harm. *Hymnal 1982*

CM

1 Come, thou al - might - y King, help us thy Name to sing,
2 Come, thou in - car - nate Word, by heaven and earth a - dored;
3 Come, ho - ly Com - fort - er, thy sa - cred wit - ness bear
4 To Thee, great One in Three, the high - est prais - es be,

help us to praise. Fa - ther whose love un - known all things cre -
our prayer at - tend: come, and thy peo - ple bless; come, give thy
in this glad hour: thou, who al - might - y art, now rule in
hence ev - er - more; thy sov - ereign ma - jes - ty may we in

at - ed own, build in our hearts thy throne, An - cient of Days.
word suc - cess; stab - lish thy right - eous - ness, Sa - vior and friend.
ev - ery heart, and ne'er from us de - part, Spi - rit of power.
glo - ry see, and to e - ter - ni - ty love and a - dore.

Words: Anon., ca. 1757, alt.
Music: *Moscow* Felice de Giardini (1716-1796); harm. *The New Hymnal,* 1916,
based on *Hymns Ancient and Modern,* 1875, and Lowell Mason (1792-1872)

664. 6664

1 Ho - ly God, we praise thy Name, Lord of all, we bow be - fore thee;
2 Hark, the loud ce - les - tial hymn an - gel choirs a - bove are rais - ing;
3 Lo, the a - po - sto - lic train join, thy sa - cred Name to hal - low;
4 Ho - ly Fa - ther, ho - ly Son, Ho - ly Spi - rit, Three we name thee,
*5 Christ, thou art our glor - ious King, Son of God en - throned in splen - dor;

all on earth thy scep - ter claim, all in heaven a - bove a - dore thee;
cher - u - bim and ser - a - phim, in un - ceas - ing cho - rus prais - ing,
pro - phets swell the loud re - frain, and the white robed mar - tyrs fol - low;
while in es - sence on - ly One, un - di - vid - ed God we claim thee;
but de - liv - er - ance to bring thou all hon - ors didst sur - ren - der,

in - fi - nite thy vast do - main, ev - er - last - ing is thy reign.
fill the heavens with sweet ac - cord: ho - ly, ho - ly, ho - ly Lord!
and, from morn till set of sun, through the Church the song goes on.
then, a - dor - ing, bend the knee and con - fess the mys - ter - y.
and wast of a vir - gin born hum - bly on that bless - ed morn.

6 Thou didst take the sting from death,
    Son of God, as Savior given;
on the cross thy dying breath
    opened wide the realm of heaven.
In the glory of that land
thou art set at God's right hand.

7 As our judge thou wilt appear.
    Savior, who hast died to win us.
help thy servants, drawing near.
    Lord, renew our hearts within us.
Grant that with thy saints we may
dwell in everlasting day.

Words: Para. of *Te Deum*, Sts. 1-4, Ignaz Franz (1719-1790); tr. Clarence Walworth (1820-1900).
    Sts. 5-7, F. Bland Tucker (1895-1984)
Music: *Grosser Gott* melody from *Katholisches Gesangbuch*, 1686; alt. *Cantate*, 1851;
    harm. Charles Winfred Douglas (1867-1944), after Conrad Kocher (1786-1872)   78. 78. 77

The Holy Trinity

1 Round the Lord in glo - ry seat - ed cher - u - bim and ser - a - phim
2 Heaven is still with glo - ry ring - ing, earth takes up the an - gels' cry,
3 "Lord, thy glo - ry fills the hea - ven, earth is with thy full - ness stored;

filled his tem - ple, and re - peat - ed each to each the al - ter - nate hymn:
"Ho - ly, ho - ly, ho - ly," sing - ing, "Lord of hosts, the Lord Most High."
un - to thee be glo - ry giv - en, ho - ly, ho - ly, ho - ly, Lord."

"Lord, thy glo - ry fills the hea - ven, earth is with thy full - ness stored;
With his ser - aph train be - fore him, with his ho - ly Church be - low,
Thus thy glo - rious Name con - fess - ing, with thine an - gel hosts we cry

un - to thee be glo - ry giv - en, ho - ly, ho - ly, ho - ly Lord."
thus u - nite we to a - dore him, bid we thus our an - them flow:
"Ho - ly, ho - ly, ho - ly," bless - ing thee, the Lord of hosts Most High.

Words: Richard Mant (1776-1848)
Music: *Rustington*, Charles Hubert Hastings Parry (1848-1918)

87. 87. D

Descant

4 God the Lord, through ev — ery na-tion let thy won-drous

1 Ho - ly Fa - ther, great Cre - a - tor, source of mer - cy,
2 Ho - ly Je - sus, Lord of glo - ry, whom an - gel - ic
3 Ho - ly Spi - rit, Sanc - ti - fi - er, come with unc - tion
4 God the Lord, through ev - ery na - tion let thy won-drous

mer - cies shine. In the song of thy sal - va - tion

love, and peace, look up - on the Me - di - a - tor,
hosts pro - claim, while we hear thy won - drous sto - ry,
from a - bove, touch our hearts with sa - cred fire,
mer - cies shine. In the song of thy sal - va - tion

ev - ery tongue and race com - bine. Great Je - ho - vah,

clothe us with his right-eous - ness; heaven - ly Fa - ther,
meet and wor - ship in thy Name, dear Re-deem - er,
fill them with the Sa - vior's love. Source of com - fort,
ev - ery tongue and race com - bine. Great Je - ho - vah,

great Je-ho-vah, form our hearts _____ and make them thine.

heaven - ly Fa - ther, through the Sa - vior hear and bless.
dear Re-deem - er, in our hearts thy peace pro - claim.
Source of com - fort, cheer us with the Sa - vior's love.
great Je - ho - vah, form our hearts and make them thine.

Words: Alexander Viets Griswold (1766-1843), alt.
Music: *Regent Square*, Henry Thomas Smart (1813-1879); desc. Craig Sellar Lang (1891-1971)

87. 87. 87

The Holy Trinity   369

1 How won-drous great, how glo - rious bright must our Cre - a - tor be,
2 Our soar-ing spi - rits up - ward rise to reach the burn-ing throne
3 Our rea - son stretch-es all its wings, and climbs a - bove the skies;
4 While all the heaven-ly powers con - spire e - ter - nal praise to sing,

who dwells a - midst the daz - zling light of vast e - ter - ni - ty.
and long to see the bless - ed Three in the Al - might - y One.
but still how far be-neath thy feet our ground-ling know-ledge lies!
let faith in hum-ble notes a - dore the great mys - te - rious King.

Words: Isaac Watts (1674-1748), alt; st. 3, alt. Caryl Micklem (b. 1925)
Music: *Shorney*, Alec Wyton (b. 1921)

CM

1. I bind un-to my-self to-day the strong Name of the Trin-i-ty, by in-vo-ca-tion of the same, the Three in One, and One in Three.

2. I bind this day to me for ev-er, by power of
*3. I bind un-to my-self the power_ of the great
*4. I bind un-to my-self to-day__ the vir-tues
*5. I bind un-to my-self to-day__ the power of

faith, Christ's In-car-na-tion; his bap-tism in the
love of cher-u-bim;__ the sweet "Well done" in
of the star-lit heaven_ the glo-rious sun's life-
God to hold and lead,__ his eye to watch, his

Jor-dan riv-er; his death on cross for my sal-va-tion;
judg-ment hour;__ the ser-vice of the ser-a-phim;__
giv-ing ray,__ the white-ness of the moon at even,__
might to stay,__ his ear to heark-en, to my need;__

his burst-ing from the spic-èd tomb; his rid-ing
con-fess-ors' faith, a-pos-tles' word, the pa-tri-archs'
the flash-ing of the light-ning free, the whirl-ing
the wis-dom of my God to teach, his hand to

up   the   heaven - ly   way;   his   com - ing   at   the
prayers,   the   pro - phets' scrolls; all   good   deeds   done   un -
wind's   tem - pes - tuous shocks, the   sta - ble   earth,   the
guide,   his   shield to   ward;   the   word   of   God   to

day   of   doom: I   bind un - to   my - self to - day.
to   the   Lord,   and   pu - ri - ty   of   vir - gin   souls.
deep salt   sea,   a - round the   old   e - ter - nal   rocks.
give me   speech,   his   heaven - ly   host   to   be   my   guard.

*6. Christ be   with   me, Christ with - in   me, Christ be - hind me,
Christ be - neath   me, Christ a - bove me, Christ in   qui - et,

Christ be - fore   me, Christ be - side   me, Christ to
Christ in   dan - ger, Christ in   hearts of   all   that

win   me, Christ to com - fort   and re - store   me,
love   me, Christ in mouth of   friend and stran - ger.

7. I bind unto myself the Name, the strong Name of the Trinity, by invocation of the same, the Three in One, and One in Three. Of whom all nature hath creation, eternal Father, Spirit, Word: praise to the Lord of my salvation, salvation is of Christ the Lord.

Words: Att. Patrick (372-466); tr. Cecil Frances Alexander (1818-1895)
Music: *St. Patrick's Breastplate*, Irish melody; adapt. Charles Villiers Stanford (1852-1924).
St. 6, *Deirdre*, Irish melody; harm. Ralph Vaughan Williams (1872-1958)

LMD

1 Thou, whose al-might-y word cha-os and dark-ness heard,
2 Thou who didst come to bring on thy re-deem-ing wing
3 Spi-rit of truth and love, life-giv-ing, ho-ly Dove,
4 Ho-ly and bless-ed Three, glo-ri-ous Trin-i-ty,

and took their flight; hear us, we hum-bly pray, and, where the
heal-ing and sight, health to the sick in mind, sight to the
speed forth thy flight! Move on the wa-ters' face bear-ing the
wis-dom, love, might; bound-less as o-cean's tide, roll-ing in

Gos-pel day sheds not its glo-rious ray, let there be light!
in-ly blind, now to all hu-man-kind, let there be light!
gifts of grace, and, in earth's dark-est place, let there be light!
full-est pride, through the world far and wide, let there be light!

Words: John Marriott (1780-1825), alt.
Music: *Moscow*, Felice de Giardini (1716-1796); harm. *The New Hymnal*, 1916,
based on *Hymns Ancient and Modern*, 1875, and Lowell Mason (1792-1872)

664. 6664

1 Praise to the living God! All praised be his Name
2 Formless, all lovely forms declare his loveliness;
3 His Spirit floweth free, high surging where it will:
4 Eternal life hath he implanted in the soul;

who was, and is, and is to be, for ay the same.
holy, no holiness of earth can his express.
in prophet's word he spoke of old; he speaketh still.
his love shall be our strength and stay while ages roll.

The one eternal God ere aught that now appears:
Lo, he is Lord of all. Creation speaks his praise,
Established is his law, and changeless it shall stand,
Praise to the living God! All praised be his Name

the first, the last, beyond all thought his timeless years!
and everywhere above, below, his will obeys.
deep writ upon the human heart, on sea, on land.
who was, and is, and is to be, for ay the same.

Words: Medieval Jewish liturgy; tr. Max Landsberg (1845-1928) and Newton M. Mann (1836-1926)
Music: *Leoni*, Hebrew melody; harm. *Hymns Ancient and Modern*, 1875, alt.

66. 84. D

1 Praise the Lord! ye heavens a - dore him; praise him an - gels in the height;
2 Praise the Lord! for he is glo - rious; nev - er shall his prom-ise fail;

sun and moon, re - joice be - fore him; praise him, all ye stars of light.
God hath made his saints vic - to - rious; sin and death shall not pre - vail.

Praise the Lord! for he hath spo-ken; worlds his might - y voice o - beyed;
Praise the God of our sal - va-tion! Hosts on high, his power pro - claim;

laws which nev - er shall be bro-ken for their guid-ance he hath made.
heaven and earth, and all cre - a - tion, laud and mag - ni - fy his Name.

Words: Anon. *Foundling Hospital Psalms and Hymns*, 1797; para. of Psalm 148
Music: *Daniel's Tune*, David N. Johnson (b. 1922)

87. 87. D

Praise to God 374

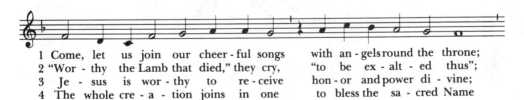

1 Come, let us join our cheer - ful songs with an - gels round the throne;
2 "Wor - thy the Lamb that died," they cry, "to be ex - alt - ed thus";
3 Je - sus is wor - thy to re - ceive hon - or and power di - vine;
4 The whole cre - a - tion joins in one to bless the sa - cred Name

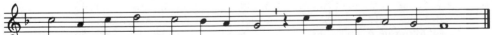

ten thou-sand thou - sand are their tongues, but all their joys are one.
"Wor - thy the Lamb," our lips re - ply, "for he was slain for us."
may bless-ings, more than we can give, be, Lord, for ev - er thine.
of him that sits up - on the throne, and to a - dore the Lamb.

Words: Isaac Watts (1674-1748); para. of *A Song of the Lamb*
Music: *Nun danket all und bringet Ehr*, melody att. Johann Cruger (1598-1662), alt.

CM

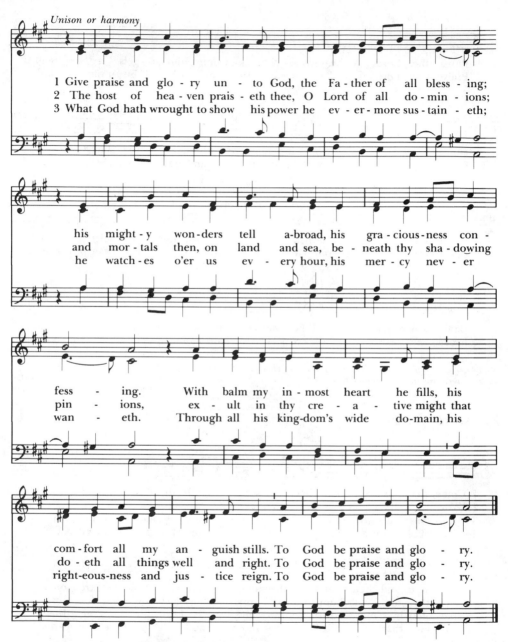

Unison or harmony

1 Give praise and glo - ry un - to God, the Fa - ther of all bless - ing;
2 The host of hea - ven prais - eth thee, O Lord of all do - min - ions;
3 What God hath wrought to show his power he ev - er - more sus - tain - eth;

his might - y won - ders tell a - broad, his gra - cious - ness con -
and mor - tals then, on land and sea, be - neath thy sha - dowing
he watch - es o'er us ev - ery hour, his mer - cy nev - er

fess - ing. With balm my in - most heart he fills, his
pin - ions, ex - ult in thy cre - a - tive might that
wan - eth. Through all his king - dom's wide do - main, his

com - fort all my an - guish stills. To God be praise and glo - ry.
do - eth all things well and right. To God be praise and glo - ry.
right - eous - ness and jus - tice reign. To God be praise and glo - ry.

Words: Johann Jacob Schütz (1640-1690); tr. Arthur William Farlander (1898-1952)
and Charles Winfred Douglas (1867-1944), alt.
Music: *Du Lebensbrot, Herr Jesu Christ,* Peter Sohren (1630?-1692?);
adapt. Johann Anastasius Freylinghausen (1670-1739), alt.

87. 87. 887

Praise to God

376

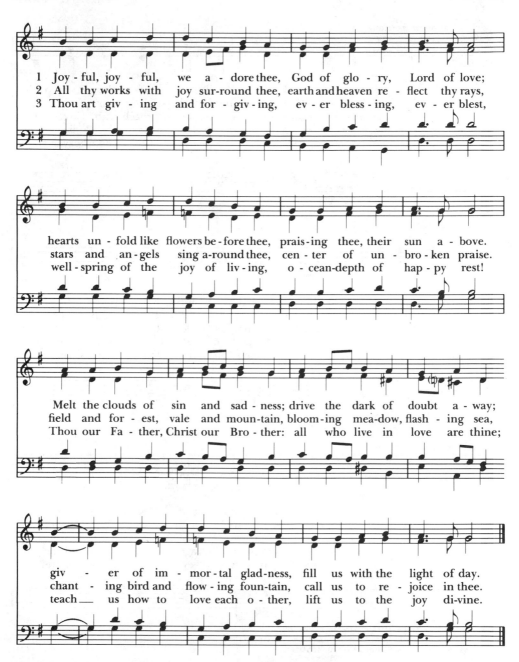

1 Joy - ful, joy - ful, we a - dore thee, God of glo - ry, Lord of love;
2 All thy works with joy sur-round thee, earth and heaven re - flect thy rays,
3 Thou art giv - ing and for - giv-ing, ev - er bless - ing, ev - er blest,

hearts un - fold like flowers be - fore thee, prais-ing thee, their sun a - bove.
stars and an - gels sing a-round thee, cen - ter of un - bro - ken praise.
well - spring of the joy of liv - ing, o - cean-depth of hap - py rest!

Melt the clouds of sin and sad - ness; drive the dark of doubt a - way;
field and for - est, vale and moun-tain, bloom-ing mea-dow, flash - ing sea,
Thou our Fa - ther, Christ our Bro - ther: all who live in love are thine;

giv - er of im - mor-tal glad-ness, fill us with the light of day.
chant - ing bird and flow - ing foun-tain, call us to re - joice in thee.
teach us how to love each o - ther, lift us to the joy di-vine.

Words: Henry Van Dyke (1852-1933)
Music: *Hymn to Joy*, Ludwig van Beethoven (1770-1827); adapt. Edward Hodges (1796-1867), alt.

87. 87. D

Unison or harmony

1 All peo - ple that on earth do dwell, sing to the Lord with
2 Know that the Lord is God in - deed; with - out our aid he
3 O en - ter then his gates with praise, ap - proach with joy his
4 For why? the Lord our God is good, his mer - cy is for
*5 To Fa - ther, Son, and Ho - ly Ghost, the God whom heaven and

1 cheer - ful voice: him serve with mirth, his praise forth
2 did us make: we are his folk, he doth us
3 courts un - to; praise, laud, and bless his Name al -
4 ev - er sure; his truth at all times firm - ly
5 earth a - dore, from men and from the an - gel

1 tell, come ye be - fore him and re - - joice.
2 feed, and for his sheep he doth us take.
3 ways, for it is seem - ly so to do.
4 stood, and shall from age to age en - - dure.
5 host be praise and glo - ry ev - er - - more.

Words: William Kethe (d. 1608?); para. of Psalm 100
Music: *Old 100th*, melody from *Pseaumes octante trois de David*, 1551, alt.;
harm. after Louis Bourgeois (1510?-1561?)

LM

Praise to God

Fauxbourdon (the melody is in the tenor)

1 All peo-ple that on earth do dwell, sing to the Lord with
2 Know that the Lord is God in-deed; with-out our aid he
3 O en-ter then his gates with praise, ap-proach with joy his
4 For why? the Lord our God is good, his mer-cy is for
*5 To Fa-ther, Son, and Ho-ly Ghost, the God whom heaven and

1 cheer - ful voice: him serve with mirth, his praise forth
2 did us make: we are his folk, he doth us
3 courts un - to; praise, laud, and bless his Name al -
4 ev - - er sure; his truth at all times firm - ly
5 earth a - dore, from men and from the an - gel

1 tell, come ye be - fore him and re - joice.
2 feed, and for his sheep he doth us take.
3 ways, for it is seem - ly so to do.
4 stood, and shall from age to age en - dure.
5 host be praise and glo - ry ev - er - more.

Words: William Kethe (d. 1608?); para. of Psalm 100
Music: *Old 100th*, melody from *Pseaumes octante trois de David*, 1551, alt.;
fauxbourdon and harm. by John Dowland (1563-1626), alt.

LM

379

1 God is Love, let heaven a - dore him; God is Love, let
2 God is Love; and love en - folds us, all the world in
3 God is Love; and though with blind-ness sin af - flicts all

earth re - joice; let cre - a - tion sing be - fore him
one em - brace: with un - fail - ing grasp God holds us,
hu - man life, God's e - ter - nal lov - ing - kind-ness

and ex - alt him with one voice. God who laid the earth's foun-
ev - ery child of ev - ery race. And when hu - man hearts are
guides us through our earth - ly strife. Sin and death and hell shall

da - tion, God who spread the heavens a - bove, God who breathes through
break-ing un - der sor - row's i - ron rod, then we find that
nev - er o'er us fi - nal tri - umph gain; God is Love, so

all cre - a - tion: God is Love, e - ter - nal Love.
self - same ach - ing deep with - in the heart of God.
Love for ev - er o'er the u - ni - verse must reign.

Words: Timothy Rees (1874-1939), alt.
Music: *Abbot's Leigh*, Cyril Vincent Taylor (b. 1907)

87. 87. D

Praise to God

380

1 From all that dwell be - low the skies let
2 E - ter - nal are thy mer - cies, Lord, and
*3 Praise God, from whom all bless - ings flow; praise

the Cre - a - tor's praise a - rise! Let the Re - deem - er's
truth e - ter - nal is thy word: thy praise shall sound from
him, all crea - tures here be - low; praise him a - bove, ye

Name be sung through ev - ery land, by ev - ery tongue!
shore to shore till suns shall rise and set no more.
heaven - ly host: praise Fa - ther, Son, and Ho - ly Ghost.

Words: Isaac Watts (1674-1748), para. of Psalm 117. St. 3, Thomas Ken (1637-1711)
Music: *Old 100th*, melody from *Pseaumes octante trois de David*, 1551, alt.;
    harm. after Louis Bourgeois (1510?-1561?)

LM

381

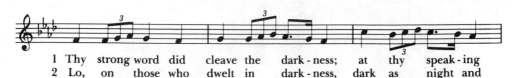

1 Thy strong word did cleave the dark - ness; at thy speak - ing
2 Lo, on those who dwelt in dark - ness, dark as night and
3 Thy strong word be - speaks us right - eous; bright with thine own
4 God the Fa - ther, Light - Cre - a - tor, to thee laud and

it was done; for cre - a - ted light we thank thee,
deep as death, broke the light of thy sal - va - tion,
ho - li - ness, glo - rious now, we press toward glo - ry,
hon - or be; to thee, Light of Light be - got - ten,

while thine or - dered sea - sons run: Al - le - lu - ia, al - le -
breathed thine own life - giv - ing breath: Al - le - lu - ia, al - le -
and our lives our hopes con - fess: Al - le - lu - ia, al - le -
praise be sung e - ter - nal - ly; Ho - ly Spi - rit, Light - Re -

lu - ia! Praise to thee who light dost send! Al - le - lu - ia,
lu - ia! Praise to thee who light dost send! Al - le - lu - ia,
lu - ia! Praise to thee who light dost send! Al - le - lu - ia,
veal - er, glo - ry, glo - ry be to thee; mor - tals, an - gels,

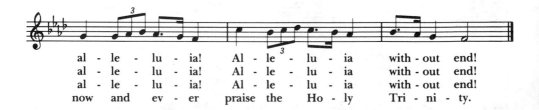

al - le - lu - ia! Al - le - lu - ia with - out end!
al - le - lu - ia! Al - le - lu - ia with - out end!
al - le - lu - ia! Al - le - lu - ia with - out end!
now and ev - er praise the Ho - ly Tri - ni - ty.

The Alleluias in stanzas 1-3 may be sung antiphonally.

Words: Martin H. Franzman (1907-1976)
Music: *Ton-y-Botel*, Thomas John Williams (1869-1944)

87. 87. D

Praise to God

382

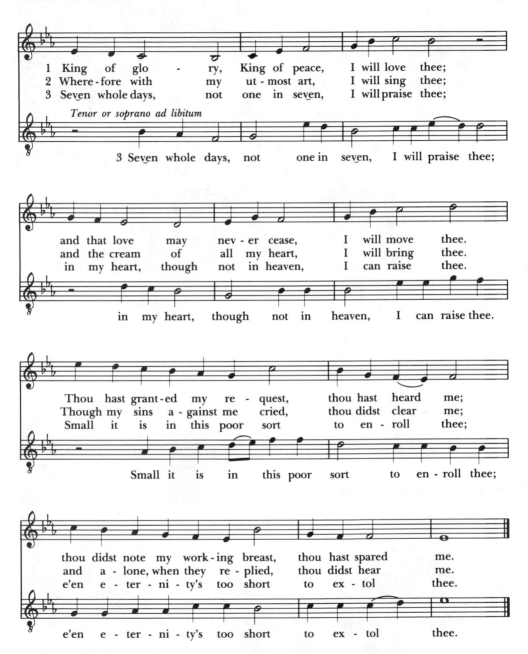

1 King of glo - ry, King of peace, I will love thee;
2 Where - fore with my ut - most art, I will sing thee;
3 Seven whole days, not one in seven, I will praise thee;

Tenor or soprano ad libitum

3 Seven whole days, not one in seven, I will praise thee;

and that love may nev - er cease, I will move thee.
and the cream of all my heart, I will bring thee.
in my heart, though not in heaven, I can raise thee.

in my heart, though not in heaven, I can raise thee.

Thou hast grant - ed my re - quest, thou hast heard me;
Though my sins a - gainst me cried, thou didst clear me;
Small it is in this poor sort to en - roll thee;

Small it is in this poor sort to en - roll thee;

thou didst note my work - ing breast, thou hast spared me.
and a - lone, when they re - plied, thou didst hear me.
e'en e - ter - ni - ty's too short to ex - tol thee.

e'en e - ter - ni - ty's too short to ex - tol thee.

Words: George Herbert (1593-1633)
Music: *General Seminary*, David Charles Walker (b. 1938)

74. 74. D

1 Fair-est Lord Je-sus, Ru-ler of all na-ture, O thou of
2 Fair are the mea-dows, fair-er still the wood-lands, robed in the
3 Fair is the sun-shine, fair-er still the moon-light, and all the

God and man the Son; thee will I cher-ish,
bloom-ing garb of spring: Je-sus is fair-er,
twink-ling, star-ry host: Je-sus shines bright-er,

thee will I hon-or, thou, my soul's glo-ry, joy, and crown.
Je-sus is pur-er, who makes the woe-ful heart to sing.
Je-sus shines pur-er, than all the an-gels heaven can boast.

Words: German composite; tr. pub. New York, 1850, alt.
Music: *St. Elizabeth*, melody from *Schlesische Volkslieder*, 1842; harm. Thomas Tertius Noble (1867-1953)   568. 558

1 Fair-est Lord Je-sus, Ru-ler of all na-ture, ___
2 Fair are the mea-dows, fair-er still the wood-lands, ___
3 Fair is the sun-shine, fair-er still the moon-light, and

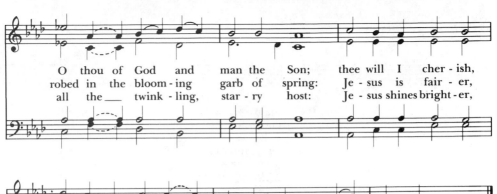

O thou of God and man the Son; thee will I cher - ish,
robed in the bloom - ing garb of spring: Je - sus is fair - er,
all the____ twink - ling, star - ry host: Je - sus shines bright - er,

thee will I hon - or,____ thou, my soul's glo - ry, joy, and crown.
Je - sus is pur - er, who makes the____ woe - ful heart to sing.
Je - sus shines pur - er, than all the____ an - gels heaven can boast.

Words: German composite; tr. pub. New York, 1850, alt.
Music: *Schönster Herr Jesu*, melody from *Münster Gesangbuch*, 1677; harm. *The English Hymnal*, 1906   568. 558

Praise to God   385

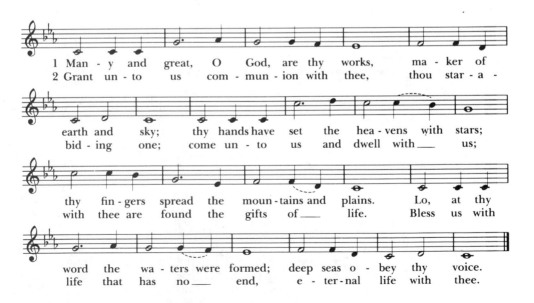

1 Man - y and great, O God, are thy works, ma - ker of
2 Grant un - to us com - mun - ion with thee, thou star - a -

earth and sky; thy hands have set the hea - vens with stars;
bid - ing one; come un - to us and dwell with____ us;

thy fin - gers spread the moun - tains and plains. Lo, at thy
with thee are found the gifts of____ life. Bless us with

word the wa - ters were formed; deep seas o - bey thy voice.
life that has no____ end, e - ter - nal life with thee.

Words: Joseph R. Renville ca. 1835; tr. Philip Frazier (1892-1964), alt.
Music: *Dakota Indian Chant Dakota Indian Chant [Lacquiparle]*, Native American melody   96. 99. 96

1 We sing of God, the might-y source of all things; the stu-
*2 Tell them I AM, the Lord God said, to Mo-ses while on
3 Glo-rious the sun in mid ca-reer; glo-rious the as-sem-bled
4 Glo-rious, most glo-rious, is the crown of him that brought sal-

pen-dous force on which all strength de - pends; from
earth in dread and smit-ten to the heart, at
fires ap-pear; glo - rious the com-et's train: glo-
va-tion down by meek-ness, Ma-ry's son; seers

whose right arm, be - neath whose eyes, all pe - ri-od, power, and
once, a - bove, be - neath, a - round, all na - ture with-out
rious the trum-pet and a - larm; glo - rious the al-might-y
that stu-pen-dous truth be-lieved, and now the match-less

en - ter - prise com - men - ces, reigns, and ends.
voice or sound re - plied, O Lord, thou art.
stretched-out arm; glo - rious the en-rap-tured main:
deed's a - chieved, de - ter - mined, dared, and done.

Words: Christopher Smart (1722-1771), alt.
Music: *Cornwall*, Samuel Sebastian Wesley (1810-1876)

886. 886

Praise to God

387

1 We sing of God, the might - y source of all things;
the stu - pen - dous force on which all strength de - pends;
from whose right arm, be - neath whose eyes, all pe - ri-od,
power, and en - ter - prise com - men - ces, reigns, and ends.

*2 Tell them I AM, the Lord God said, to Mo - ses
while on earth in dread and smit - ten to the heart,
at once, a - bove, be - neath, a - round, all na - ture
with - out voice or sound re - plied, O Lord, thou art.

3 Glo - rious the sun in mid ca - reer; glo - rious the as -
sem - bled fires ap - pear; glo - rious the com - et's train:
glo - rious the trum - pet and a - larm; glo - rious the al -
might - y stretched-out arm; glo - rious the en-rap - tured main:

4 Glo - rious, most glo - rious, is the crown of him that
brought sal - va - tion down by meek - ness, Ma - ry's son;
seers that stu - pen - dous truth be - lieved, and now the
match - less deed's a - chieved, de - ter - mined, dared, and done.

Words: Christopher Smart (1722-1771), alt.
Music: *Magdalen College*, William Hayes (1706-1777)

886. 886

388

Praise to God

1 O worship the King, all glo - rious a - bove!
2 O tell of his might! O sing of his grace!
3 The earth, with its store of won - ders un - told,
4 Thy boun - ti - ful care, what tongue can re - cite?
5 Frail chil - dren of dust, and fee - ble as frail,

1 O grate - ful - ly sing his power and his love!
2 Whose robe is the light, whose can - o - py space.
3 Al - might - y, thy power hath found - ed of old,
4 It breathes in the air; it shines in the light;
5 in thee do we trust, nor find thee to fail;

1 Our shield and de - fend - er, the An - cient of Days,
2 His char - iots of wrath the deep thun - der - clouds form,
3 hath stab - lished it fast by a change - less de - cree,
4 it streams from the hills, it de - scends to the plain,
5 thy mer - cies, how ten - der! how firm to the end!

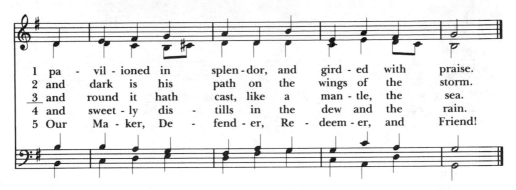

1 pa - vil - ioned in splen - dor, and gird - ed with praise.
2 and dark is his path on the wings of the storm.
3 and round it hath cast, like a man - tle, the sea.
4 and sweet - ly dis - tills in the dew and the rain.
5 Our Ma - ker, De - fend - er, Re - deem - er, and Friend!

Words: Robert Grant (1779-1838)
Music: *Hanover*, att. William Croft (1678-1727)

10 10. 11 11

Praise to God 389

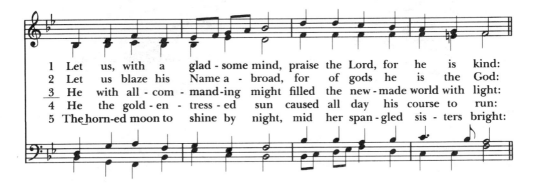

1 Let us, with a glad - some mind, praise the Lord, for he is kind:
2 Let us blaze his Name a - broad, for of gods he is the God:
3 He with all - com - mand - ing might filled the new - made world with light:
4 He the gold - en - tress - ed sun caused all day his course to run:
5 The horn - ed moon to shine by night, mid her span - gled sis - ters bright:

Refrain

for his mer - cies ay en - dure, ev - er faith - ful, ev - er sure.

6 All things living he doth feed,
his full hand supplies their need:

Refrain

7 Let us, with a gladsome mind,
praise the Lord, for he is kind:

Refrain

Words: John Milton (1608-1674); para. Psalm 136
Music: *Monkland*, John Antes (1740-1811), as edited by J. Wilkes in *Hymns Ancient and Modern*, 1861

77. 77

Descant

4 Praise to the Lord! O let all that is in me a-
dore him! All that hath life and breath come now with
prais-es be-fore him! Let the a-men sound from his

1 Praise to the Lord, the Al-might-y, the King of cre-
2 Praise to the Lord; o-ver all things he glo-rious-ly
3 Praise to the Lord, who doth pros-per thy way and de-
4 Praise to the Lord! O let all that is in me a-

a - tion; O my soul, praise him, for he is thy
reign - eth: borne as on ea-gle-wings, safe-ly his
fend thee; sure-ly his good-ness and mer-cy shall
dore him! All that hath life and breath come now with

health and sal - va - tion: join the great throng, psal-ter-y,
saints he sus-tain - eth. Hast thou not seen how all thou
ev - er at-tend thee; pon-der a-new what the Al-
prais-es be-fore him! Let the a-men sound from his

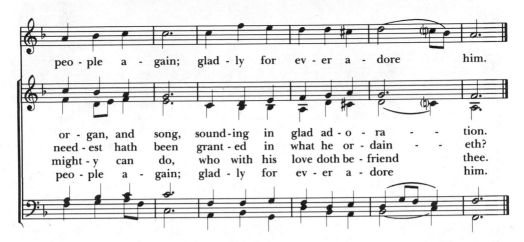

peo - ple a - gain; glad - ly for ev - er a - dore him.

or - gan, and song, sound-ing in glad ad - o - ra - - tion.
need - est hath been grant - ed in what he or - dain - - eth?
might - y can do, who with his love doth be - friend thee.
peo - ple a - gain; glad - ly for ev - er a - dore him.

Words: Joachim Neander (1650-1680); tr. *Hymnal 1940*, alt.
Music: *Lobe den Herren*, melody from *Erneuerten Gesangbuch*, 1665;
    harm. *The Chorale Book for England*, 1863; desc. Craig Sellar Lang (1891-1971)   14 14. 478

391

1 Be - fore the Lord's e - ter - nal throne, ye
2 His sov - ereign power with - out our aid formed
3 We are his peo - ple, we his care, our
4 We'll crowd thy gates with thank - ful songs, high
5 Wide as the world is thy com - mand, vast

1 na - tions, bow with sa - cred joy; know that the Lord is
2 us of clay and gave us breath; and when like wan - dering
3 souls, and all our mor - tal frame: what last - ing hon - ors
4 as the heaven our voic - es raise; and earth, with her ten
5 as e - ter - ni - ty thy love; firm as a rock thy

1 God a - lone; he can cre - ate, and he des - troy.
2 sheep we strayed, he saved us from the power of death.
3 shall we rear, al - might - y Ma - ker, to thy Name?
4 thou - sand tongues, shall fill thy courts with sound - ing praise.
5 truth must stand, when roll - ing years shall cease to move.

Words: Isaac Watts (1674-1748), alt.; para. of Psalm 100
Music: *Winchester New,* melody from *Musicalishes Hand-Buch,* 1690;
   harm. William Henry Monk (1823-1889)

LM

392

Praise to God

1 Come, we that love the Lord, and let our joys be known; join
2 Let those re - fuse to sing that nev - er knew our God; but
3 The heirs of grace have found glo - ry be - gun be - low; ce -
4 Then let our song a - bound and let our tears be dry; we're

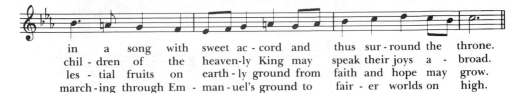

in a song with sweet ac-cord and thus sur-round the throne.
chil-dren of the heaven-ly King may speak their joys a-broad.
les-tial fruits on earth-ly ground from faith and hope may grow.
march-ing through Em-man-uel's ground to fair-er worlds on high.

Refrain

Ho-san-na, ho-san-na! Re-joice, give thanks and sing.

Words: Isaac Watts (1674-1748), alt.
Music: *Vineyard Haven*, Richard Wayne Dirksen (b. 1921)

SM with Refrain

Praise to God 393

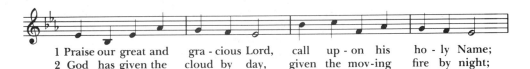

1 Praise our great and gra-cious Lord, call up-on his ho-ly Name;
2 God has given the cloud by day, given the mov-ing fire by night;

rais-ing hymns in glad ac-cord, all his might-y acts pro-claim:
guides his Is-rael on their way from the dark-ness in-to light.

how he leads his cho-sen un-to Ca-naan's prom-ised land,
God it is who grants us sure re-treat and ref-uge nigh;

how the word we have heard firm and change-less still shall stand.
light of dawn leads us on: 'tis the Day-spring from on high.

Words: Harriet Auber (1773-1862), alt.
Music: *Maoz Zur*, Hebrew melody; adapt. Eric Werner (b. 1901)

77. 77. 67. 67

394

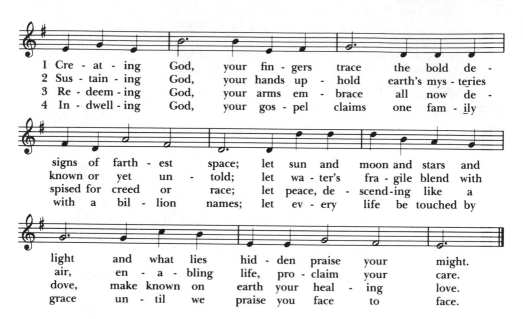

1 Cre - at - ing God, your fin - gers trace the bold de -
2 Sus - tain - ing God, your hands up - hold earth's mys - teries
3 Re - deem - ing God, your arms em - brace all now de -
4 In - dwell - ing God, your gos - pel claims one fam - i - ly

signs of farth - est space; let sun and moon and stars and
known or yet un - told; let wa - ter's fra - gile blend with
spised for creed or race; let peace, de - scend-ing like a
with a bil - lion names; let ev - ery life be touched by

light and what lies hid - den praise your might.
air, en - a - bling life, pro - claim your care.
dove, make known on earth your heal - ing love.
grace un - til we praise you face to face.

Words: Jeffery Rowthorn (b. 1934), alt.
Music: *Wilderness*, Reginald Sparshatt Thatcher (1888-1957)

LM

395

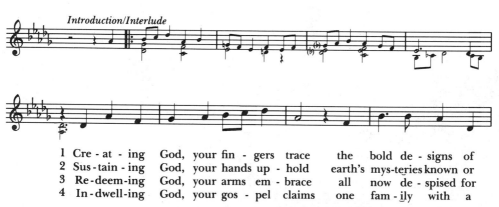

Introduction/Interlude

1 Cre - at - ing God, your fin - gers trace the bold de - signs of
2 Sus - tain - ing God, your hands up - hold earth's mys-teries known or
3 Re - deem-ing God, your arms em - brace all now de - spised for
4 In - dwell-ing God, your gos - pel claims one fam - i - ly with a

farth-est space; let sun and moon and stars and light and
yet un-told; let wa-ter's fra-gile blend with air, en-
creed or race; let peace, de-scend-ing like a dove, make
bil-lion names; let ev-ery life be touched by grace un-

what lies hid - den praise_____ your might.
a-bling life, pro - claim_____ your care.
known on earth your heal - ing love.
til we praise you face_____ to face.

Words: Jeffery Rowthorn (b. 1934), alt.
Music: *King*, David Hurd (b. 1950)

LM

Praise to God

396

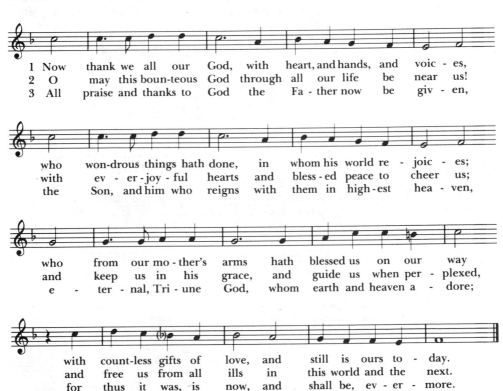

1 Now thank we all our God, with heart, and hands, and voic - es,
2 O may this boun-teous God through all our life be near us!
3 All praise and thanks to God the Fa - ther now be giv - en,

who won-drous things hath done, in whom his world re - joic - es;
with ev - er-joy-ful hearts and bless-ed peace to cheer us;
the Son, and him who reigns with them in high-est hea - ven,

who from our mo-ther's arms hath blessed us on our way
and keep us in his grace, and guide us when per - plexed,
e - ter - nal, Tri - une God, whom earth and heaven a - dore;

with count-less gifts of love, and still is ours to - day.
and free us from all ills in this world and the next.
for thus it was, is now, and shall be, ev - er - more.

Words: Martin Rinckart (1586-1649); tr. Catherine Winkworth (1827-1878), alt.
Music: *Nun danket alle Gott*, melody Johann Cruger (1598-1662)

67. 67. 66. 66

1 Now thank we all our God, with heart, and hands, and voic - es,
2 O may this boun - teous God through all our life be near us!
3 All praise and thanks to God the Fa - ther now be giv - en,

who won-drous things hath done, in whom his world re - joic - es;
with ev - er - joy - ful hearts and bless - ed peace to cheer us;
the Son, and him who reigns with them in high-est hea - ven,

who from our mo - ther's arms hath blessed us on our way
and keep us in his grace, and guide us when per - plexed,
e - ter - nal, Tri - une God, whom earth and heaven a - dore;

with count-less gifts of love, and still is ours to - day.
and free us from all ills in this world and the next.
for thus it was, is now, and shall be, ev - er - more.

Words: Martin Rinckart (1586-1649); tr. Catherine Winkworth (1827-1878), alt.
Music: *Nun danket alle Gott*, melody Johann Crüger (1598-1662);
    harm. William Henry Monk (1823-1889), after Felix Mendelssohn (1809-1847)   67. 67. 66. 66

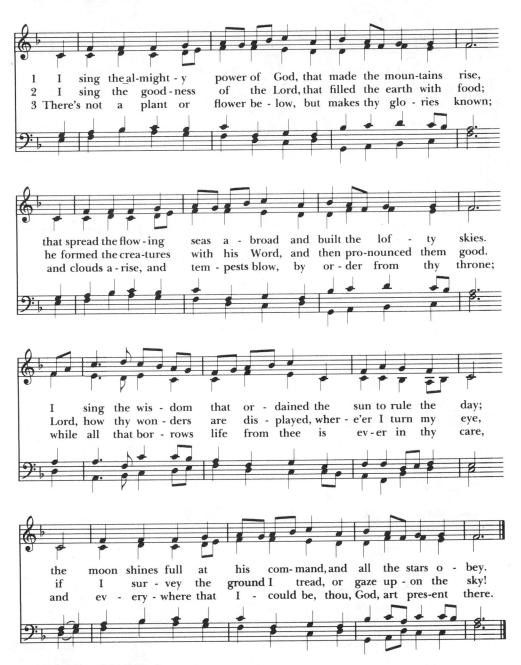

1 I sing the al-might-y power of God, that made the moun-tains rise,
2 I sing the good-ness of the Lord, that filled the earth with food;
3 There's not a plant or flower be-low, but makes thy glo-ries known;

that spread the flow-ing seas a-broad and built the lof-ty skies.
he formed the crea-tures with his Word, and then pro-nounced them good.
and clouds a-rise, and tem-pests blow, by or-der from thy throne;

I sing the wis-dom that or-dained the sun to rule the day;
Lord, how thy won-ders are dis-played, wher-e'er I turn my eye,
while all that bor-rows life from thee is ev-er in thy care,

the moon shines full at his com-mand, and all the stars o-bey.
if I sur-vey the ground I tread, or gaze up-on the sky!
and ev-ery-where that I - could be, thou, God, art pres-ent there.

Words: Isaac Watts (1674-1748), alt.
Music: *Forest Green*, English melody; adapt. and harm. Ralph Vaughan Williams (1872-1958)　　　CMD

Descant

3 Your heaven-ly Fa - ther praise, ac - claim his

1 To God with glad - ness sing, your Rock and Sa - vior
2 He cra - dles in his hand the heights and depths of
3 Your heaven - ly Fa - ther praise, ac - claim his on - ly

on - ly Son, your voic - es raise to him who

bless; in - to his tem - ple bring your songs of
earth; he made the sea and land, he brought the
Son, your voice in hom - age raise to him who

makes all one, O Dove on

thank - - ful - - ness! O God of might, to
world to birth! O God Most High, we
makes all one! O Dove of peace, on

us de - scend, joy_____ in - crease!

you we sing, en - throned as King on hea - ven's height!
are your sheep; on us you keep your shep - herd's eye!
us de - scend that strife may end and joy in - crease!

Words: James Quinn (b. 1919), alt.; para. of Psalm 95 (Venite)
Music: *Camano*, Richard Proulx (b. 1937)

66. 66. 44. 44

Praise to God

1 All crea-tures of our God and King, lift up your voic-es, let us
*2 Great rush-ing winds and breez-es soft, you clouds that ride the heavens a-
*3 Swift flow-ing wa-ter, pure and clear, make mu-sic for your Lord to
4 Dear mo-ther earth, you day by day un-fold your bless-ings on our
5 All you with mer-cy in your heart, for-giv-ing o-thers, take your
*6 And e-ven you, most gen-tle death, wait-ing to hush our fi-nal
7 Let all things their cre-a-tor bless, and wor-ship him in hum-ble-

1 sing: Al-le-lu-ia, al-le-lu-ia! Bright burn-ing
2 loft, O___ praise him, Al-le-lu-ia! Fair ris-ing
3 hear, Al-le-lu-ia, al-le-lu-ia! Fire, so in-
4 way, O___ praise him, Al-le-lu-ia! All flowers and
5 part, O___ sing now: Al-le-lu-ia! All you that
6 breath, O___ praise him, Al-le-lu-ia! You lead back
7 ness, O___ praise him, Al-le-lu-ia! Praise God the

1 sun with gold-en beams, pale sil-ver moon that gen-tly gleams,
2 morn, with praise re-joice, stars night-ly shin-ing, find a voice,
3 tense and fierce-ly bright, you give to us both warmth and light,
4 fruits that in you grow, let them his glo-ry al-so show:
5 pain and sor-row bear, praise God, and cast on him your care,
6 home the child of God, for Christ our Lord that way has trod:
7 Fa-ther, praise the Son, and praise the Spi-rit, Three in One:

Refrain

O praise him, O praise him, Al-le-lu-ia,

al-le-lu-ia, al-le-lu-ia!

The refrain may be sung antiphonally, by phrase; all join in the final Alleluia.

Words: Francis of Assisi (1182-1226); tr. William H. Draper (1855-1933), alt.
Music: *Lasst uns erfreuen,* melody from *Auserlesene Catholische Geistliche Kirchengeseng,* 1623;
adapt. Ralph Vaughan Williams (1872-1958)

88. 44. 88 with Refrain

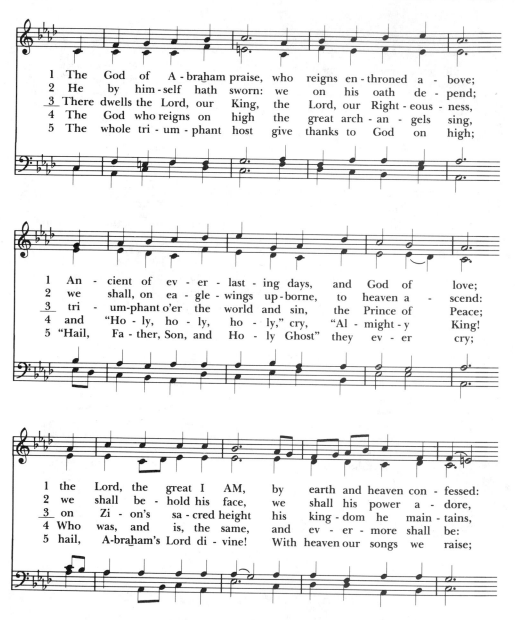

1 The God of A-braham praise, who reigns en-throned a - bove;
2 He by him-self hath sworn: we on his oath de-pend;
3 There dwells the Lord, our King, the Lord, our Right-eous-ness,
4 The God who reigns on high the great arch-an-gels sing,
5 The whole tri-um-phant host give thanks to God on high;

1 An - cient of ev - er - last-ing days, and God of love;
2 we shall, on ea - gle-wings up-borne, to heaven a - scend:
3 tri - um-phant o'er the world and sin, the Prince of Peace;
4 and "Ho - ly, ho - ly, ho - ly," cry, "Al - might-y King!
5 "Hail, Fa - ther, Son, and Ho - ly Ghost" they ev - er cry;

1 the Lord, the great I AM, by earth and heaven con - fessed:
2 we shall be - hold his face, we shall his power a - dore,
3 on Zi - on's sa - cred height his king - dom he main - tains,
4 Who was, and is, the same, and ev - er - more shall be:
5 hail, A-braham's Lord di - vine! With heaven our songs we raise;

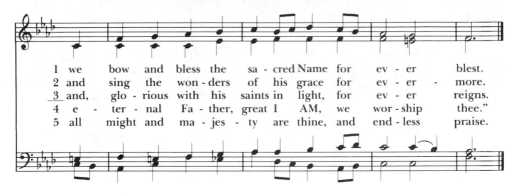

1 we bow and bless the sa-cred Name for ev-er blest.
2 and sing the won-ders of his grace for ev-er - more.
3 and, glo-rious with his saints in light, for ev-er reigns.
4 e-ter-nal Fa-ther, great I AM, we wor-ship thee."
5 all might and ma-jes-ty are thine, and end-less praise.

Words: Thomas Olivers (1725-1799), alt.
Music: *Leoni*, Hebrew melody; harm. *Hymns Ancient and Modern*, 1875, alt.

66. 84. D

Praise to God

402

Let all the world in ev-ery cor-ner sing, my God and King! King!

1 The heavens are not too high, his praise may thith-er fly; the
2 The Church with psalms must shout, no door can keep them out; but,

earth is not too low, his prais-es there may grow.
a-bove all, the heart must bear the lon-gest part.

Words: George Herbert (1593-1633)
Music: *Augustine*, Erik Routley (1917-1982)

66. 66 with Refrain

403

Praise to God

Introduction

I

Let all the world in ev - ery cor - ner sing, my God and

II

King! Let all the world in ev - ery cor - ner sing, my God and

All

King!
1 The heavens are not too high, his praise may thith - er
2 The Church with psalms must shout, no door can keep them

fly; the earth is not too low, his prais - es there may grow.
out; but, a - bove all, the heart must bear the long - est part.

Let all the world in ev - ery cor - ner sing, my God and

1 *Final Ending*

King! King! A - - men.

Words: George Herbert (1593-1633)
Music: *MacDougall*, Calvin Hampton (1938-1984)

66. 66 with Refrain

Praise to God

1 We will extol you, ever-blessed Lord; your holy
2 Age shall to age pass on the endless song, tell-ing the
3 You, Lord, are gra-cious, mer-ci-ful to all, close to your

Name for ev-er be a-dored; each day we live our
won-ders which to you be-long, your might-y acts with
chil-dren when on you they call; and slow to an-ger,

psalm to you we raise; you, God and King, are wor-thy of all
joy and fear re-late; praise we your glo-ry while on you we
mer-ci-ful and kind, in your com-pas-sion we your bless-ings

praise, great and un-search-a-ble in all your ways.
wait, glad in the know-ledge of your love so great.
find. We love you with our heart and strength and mind.

The first stanza may be repeated at the end.

Words: J. Nichol Grieve, alt.; para. of Psalm 145
Music: *Old 124th*, melody from *Pseaumes octante trois de David*, 1551;
harm. Charles Winfred Douglas (1867-1944)

10 10. 10 10 10

Praise to God

Descant

All things bright and beau - ti - ful, crea-tures great and small,

Refrain

All things bright and beau - ti - ful, all crea-tures great and small,

all things wise and won - der - ful, God made them all.

all things wise and won - der - ful, the Lord God made them all.

1 Each lit - tle flower that o - pens, each lit - tle bird that sings,
2 The pur - ple - head - ed moun-tain, the riv - er run - ning by,
3 The cold wind in the win - ter, the pleas-ant sum - mer sun,
4 He gave us eyes to see them, and lips that we might tell

Repeat Refrain

he made their glow-ing col - ors, he made their ti - ny wings.
the sun - set, and the morn - ing that bright-ens up the sky.
the ripe fruits in the gar - den, he made them ev - ery one.
how great is God Al - might - y, who has made all things well.

Words: Cecil Frances Alexander (1818-1895)
Music: *Royal Oak*, melody from *The Dancing Master*, 1686;
    adapt. Martin Fallas Shaw (1875-1958); desc. Richard Proulx (b. 1937)

76. 76 with Refrain

Praise to God

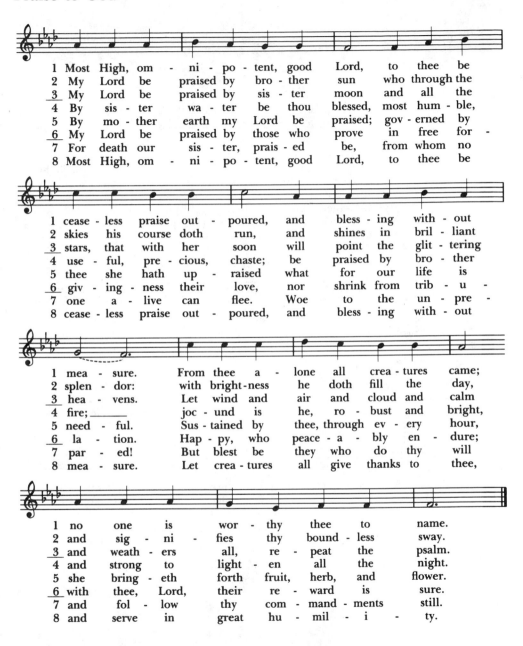

1 Most High, om - ni - po - tent, good Lord, to thee be
2 My Lord be praised by bro - ther sun who through the
3 My Lord be praised by sis - ter moon and all the
4 By sis - ter wa - ter be thou blessed, most hum - ble,
5 By mo - ther earth my Lord be praised; gov - erned by
6 My Lord be praised by those who prove in free for -
7 For death our sis - ter, prais - ed be, from whom no
8 Most High, om - ni - po - tent, good Lord, to thee be

1 cease - less praise out - poured, and bless - ing with - out
2 skies his course doth run, and shines in bril - liant
3 stars, that with her soon will point the glit - tering
4 use - ful, pre - cious, chaste; be praised by bro - ther
5 thee she hath up - raised what for our life is
6 giv - ing - ness their love, nor shrink from trib - u -
7 one a - live can flee. Woe to the un - pre -
8 cease - less praise out - poured, and bless - ing with - out

1 mea - sure. From thee a - lone all crea - tures came;
2 splen - dor: with bright - ness he doth fill the day,
3 hea - vens. Let wind and air and cloud and calm
4 fire; joc - und is he, ro - bust and bright,
5 need - ful. Sus - tained by thee, through ev - ery hour,
6 la - tion. Hap - py, who peace - a - bly en - dure;
7 par - ed! But blest be they who do thy will
8 mea - sure. Let crea - tures all give thanks to thee,

1 no one is wor - thy thee to name.
2 and sig - ni - fies thy bound - less sway.
3 and weath - ers all, re - peat the psalm.
4 and strong to light - en all the night.
5 she bring - eth forth fruit, herb, and flower.
6 with thee, Lord, their re - ward is sure.
7 and fol - low thy com - mand - ments still.
8 and serve in great hu - mil - i - ty.

This hymn may be sung by alternating groups, with all singing the first and final stanzas.

Words: Francis of Assisi (1182-1226); tr. Howard Chandler Robbins (1876-1952), alt.
Music: *Assisi*, Alfred Morton Smith (1879-1971)

887. 88

407

1 Most High, om - ni - po - tent, good Lord, to thee be
2 (My Lord be) praised by bro - ther sun who through the
3 (My Lord be) praised by sis - ter moon and all the
4 (By sis - ter) wa - ter be thou blessed, most hum - ble,
5 (By mo - ther) earth my Lord be praised; gov - erned by
6 (My Lord be) praised by those who prove in free for -
7 (For death our) sis - ter, prais - ed be, from whom no
8 (Most High, om) - ni - po - tent, good Lord, to thee be

1 cease-less praise out - poured, and bless - ing with - out mea - sure.
2 skies his course doth run, and shines in bril - liant splen - dor:
3 stars, that with her soon will point the glit - tering hea - vens.
4 use - ful, pre - cious, chaste; be praised by bro - ther fire;
5 thee she hath up - raised what for our life is need - ful.
6 giv - ing-ness their love, nor shrink from trib - u - la - tion.
7 one a - live can flee. Woe to the un - pre - par - ed!
8 cease-less praise out - poured, and bless - ing with - out mea - sure.

1 From thee a - lone all crea - tures came; no one is
2 with bright-ness he doth fill the day, and sig - ni -
3 Let wind and air and cloud and calm and weath - ers
4 joc - und is he, ro - bust and bright, and strong to
5 Sus - tained by thee, through ev - ery hour, she bring - eth
6 Hap - py, who peace - a - bly en - dure; with thee, Lord,
7 But blest be they who do thy will and fol - low
8 Let crea - tures all give thanks to thee, and serve in

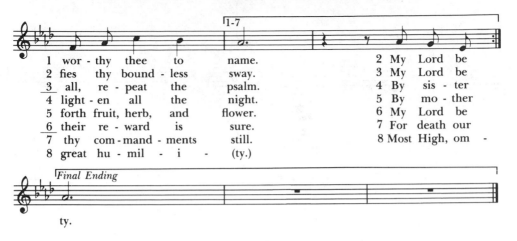

2	My	Lord be
3	My	Lord be
4	By	sis - ter
5	By	mo - ther
6	My	Lord be
7	For	death our
8	Most	High, om -

Final Ending

ty.

This hymn may be sung by alternating groups, with all singing the first and final stanzas.

Words: Francis of Assisi (1182-1226); tr. Howard Chandler Robbins (1876-1952), alt.
Music: *Lukkason*, Calvin Hampton (1938-1984)

887. 88

Praise to God

408

1 Sing praise to God who reigns a - bove, the God of all cre -
2 What God's al - might - y power hath made, his gra-cious mer - cy
3 Let all who name Christ's ho - ly Name give God all praise and

a - tion, the God of power, the God of love, the God of
keep - eth; by morn-ing glow or eve-ning shade his watch-ful
glo - ry; let all who know his power pro-claim a - loud the

our sal - va - tion; with heal-ing balm my soul he fills, and
eye ne'er sleep - eth. With - in the king-dom of his might, lo!
won - drous sto - ry! Cast each false i - dol from its throne, the

ev - ery faith-less mur-mur stills: to God all praise and glo - ry.
all is just and all is right: to God all praise and glo - ry.
Lord is God, and he a - lone: to God all praise and glo - ry.

Words: Johann Jacob Schütz (1640-1690); tr. Frances Elizabeth Cox (1812-1897), alt.
Music: *Mit Freuden zart*, melody from "Une pastourelle gentille," 1529;
 adapt. *Pseaumes cinquante de David*, 1547, and *Kirchengesang darinnen die Heubtartickel
 des Christlichen Glaubens gefasset*, 1566

87. 87. 887

Unison or harmony

1 The spa - cious fir - - ma - ment on high,
2 Soon as the eve - ning shades pre - vail,
3 What though in sol - emn si - lence all

with all the blue e - ther - eal sky,
the moon takes up the won - drous tale,
move round the dark ter - res - trial ball?

and span - gled heavens, a shin - ing frame,
and night - ly to the lis - tening earth
What though no re - - al voice nor sound

their great O - rig - i - nal pro - claim.
re - peats the sto - ry of her birth:
a - mid their ra - diant orbs be found?

The un-wea - ried sun from day to day
whilst all the stars that round her burn,
In rea - son's ear they all re - joice,

does his Cre - a - tor's power dis - play;
and all the plan - ets in their turn,
and ut - ter forth a glo - rious voice;

and pub - lish - es to ev - ery land
con - firm the ti - dings, as they roll
for ev - er sing - ing as they shine,

the work of an al - might - y hand.
and spread the truth from pole to pole.
"The hand that made us is di - vine."

Words: Joseph Addison (1672-1719); para. of Psalm 19:1-6
Music: *Creation*, Franz Joseph Haydn (1732-1809);
    adapt. *Dulcimer, or New York Collection of Sacred Music*, 1850, alt.

LMD

Unison or harmony

1 Praise, my soul, the King of hea - ven; to his feet thy tri - bute bring;
2 Praise him for his grace and fa - vor to his peo - ple in dis - tress;
3 Fa - ther - like he tends and spares us; well our fee - ble frame he knows;
4 An - gels, help us to a - dore him; ye be - hold him face to face;

ran - somed, healed, re - stored, for - giv - en, ev - er - more his prais - es sing:
praise him still the same as ev - er, slow to chide, and swift to bless:
in his hand he gen - tly bears us, res - cues us from all our foes.
sun and moon, bow down be - fore him, dwell - ers all in time and space.

Al - le - lu - ia, al - le - lu - ia! Praise the ev - er - last - ing King.
Al - le - lu - ia, al - le - lu - ia! Glo - rious in his faith - ful - ness.
Al - le - lu - ia, al - le - lu - ia! Wide - ly yet his mer - cy flows.
Al - le - lu - ia, al - le - lu - ia! Praise with us the God of grace.

Words: Henry Francis Lyte (1793-1847), alt.
Music: *Lauda anima*, John Goss (1800-1880)

87. 87. 87

Descant for use with unison singing

4 An - gels, help us to a - dore him; ye be - hold him face to face;

sun and moon, bow down be - fore him, dwell - ers all in time and space.

Al - le - lu - ia, al - le - lu - ia! Praise——with us the God of grace.

Music: *Lauda anima*, desc. Craig Sellar Lang (1891-1971)

Praise to God

411

1 O bless the Lord, my soul! His grace to thee pro - claim!
2 O bless the Lord, my soul! His mer - cies bear in mind!
3 He will not al - ways chide; he will with pa - tience wait;
4 He par - dons all thy sins, pro - longs thy fee - ble breath;
5 He clothes thee with his love, up - holds thee with his truth;

1 And all that is with - in me join to bless his ho - ly Name!
2 For - get not all his ben - e - fits! The Lord to thee is kind.
3 his wrath is ev - er slow to rise and rea - dy to a - bate.
4 he heal - eth thine in - fir - mi - ties and ran - soms thee from death.
5 and like the ea - gle he re - news the vi - gor of thy youth.

6 Then bless his holy Name,
   whose grace hath made thee whole,
   whose loving-kindness crowns thy days:
   O bless the Lord, my soul!

Words: James Montgomery (1771-1854); para. of Psalm 103:1-5
Music: *St. Thomas (Williams)*, melody Aaron Williams (1731-1776); harm. Lowell Mason (1792-1872)   SM

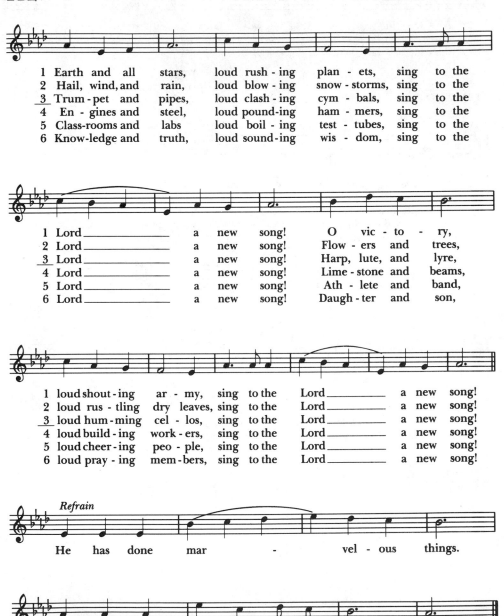

1 Earth and all stars, loud rush-ing plan-ets, sing to the
2 Hail, wind, and rain, loud blow-ing snow-storms, sing to the
3 Trum-pet and pipes, loud clash-ing cym-bals, sing to the
4 En-gines and steel, loud pound-ing ham-mers, sing to the
5 Class-rooms and labs loud boil-ing test-tubes, sing to the
6 Know-ledge and truth, loud sound-ing wis-dom, sing to the

1 Lord_____ a new song! O vic-to-ry,
2 Lord_____ a new song! Flow-ers and trees,
3 Lord_____ a new song! Harp, lute, and lyre,
4 Lord_____ a new song! Lime-stone and beams,
5 Lord_____ a new song! Ath-lete and band,
6 Lord_____ a new song! Daugh-ter and son,

1 loud shout-ing ar-my, sing to the Lord_____ a new song!
2 loud rus-tling dry leaves, sing to the Lord_____ a new song!
3 loud hum-ming cel-los, sing to the Lord_____ a new song!
4 loud build-ing work-ers, sing to the Lord_____ a new song!
5 loud cheer-ing peo-ple, sing to the Lord_____ a new song!
6 loud pray-ing mem-bers, sing to the Lord_____ a new song!

Refrain

He has done mar - vel-ous things.

I, too, will praise him with a new song!

Words: Herbert F. Brokering (b. 1926)
Music: *Earth and All Stars*, David N. Johnson (b. 1922)

45. 7. D with Refrain

1 New songs of cel - e - bra - tion ren - der to him who
2 Joy - ful - ly, heart - i - ly re - sound - ing, let ev - ery
3 Riv - ers and seas and tor - rents roar - ing, hon - or the

has great won - ders done; awed by his love his
in - stru - ment and voice peal out the praise of
Lord with wild ac - claim; moun - tains and stones look

foes sur - ren - der and fall be - fore the Might - y One.
grace a - bound - ing, call - ing the whole world to re - joice.
up a - dor - ing and find a voice to praise his Name.

He has made known his great sal - va - tion which
Trum - pets and or - gans set in mo - tion such
Right - eous, com - mand - ing, ev - er glo - rious, prais -

all his friends with joy con - fess; he has re - vealed to
sounds as make the hea - vens ring: all things that live in
es be his that nev - er cease; just is our God, whose

ev - ery na - tion his ev - er - last - ing right - eous - ness.
earth and o - cean, make mu - sic for your might - y King.
truth vic - to - rious es - tab - lish - es the world in peace.

Words: Erik Routley (1917-1982); para. of Psalm 98
Music: *Rendez à Dieu*, melody att. Louis Bourgeois (1510?-1561?)

98. 98. D

Descant

6 All thy works, O Lord, shall bless thee; thee shall all thy

1 God, my King, thy might con - fess - ing, ev - er will I
2 Hon - or great our God be - fit - teth; who his ma - jes -
3 They shall talk of all thy glo - ry, on thy might and
4 Nor shall fail from mem-ory's trea - sure works by love and
5 Full of kind - ness and com - pas - sion, slow to an - ger,

saints a - dore: King su - preme shall they con - fess thee,

1 bless thy Name; day by day thy throne ad - dress-ing,
2 ty can reach? Age to age his works trans - mit - teth,
3 great - ness dwell, speak of thy dread acts the sto - ry,
4 mer - cy wrought, works of love sur - pass - ing mea - sure,
5 vast in love, God is good to all cre - a - tion;

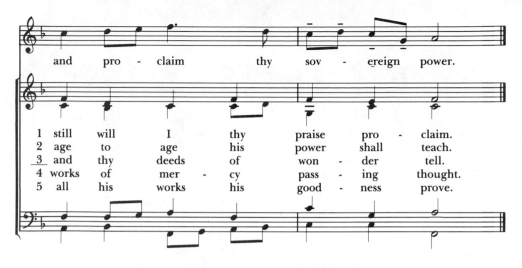

and pro - claim thy sov - ereign power.

1 still will I thy praise pro - claim.
2 age to age his power shall teach.
3 and thy deeds of won - der tell.
4 works of mer - cy pass - ing thought.
5 all his works his good - ness prove.

6 All thy works, O Lord, shall bless thee;
thee shall all thy saints adore:
King supreme shall they confess thee,
and proclaim thy sovereign power.

Words: Richard Mant (1776-1848); para. of Psalm 145:1-12
Music: *Stuttgart*, melody from *Psalmodia Sacra, oder Andächtige und Schöne Gesänge*, 1715;
adapt. and harm. William Henry Havergal (1793-1870); desc. John Wilson (b. 1905)

87. 87

Praise to God

415

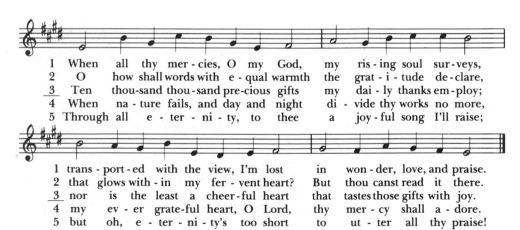

1 When all thy mer - cies, O my God, my ris - ing soul sur - veys,
2 O how shall words with e - qual warmth the grat - i - tude de - clare,
3 Ten thou-sand thou-sand pre-cious gifts my dai - ly thanks em - ploy;
4 When na - ture fails, and day and night di - vide thy works no more,
5 Through all e - ter - ni - ty, to thee a joy - ful song I'll raise;

1 trans - port - ed with the view, I'm lost in won - der, love, and praise.
2 that glows with - in my fer - vent heart? But thou canst read it there.
3 nor is the least a cheer - ful heart that tastes those gifts with joy.
4 my ev - er grate-ful heart, O Lord, thy mer - cy shall a - dore.
5 but oh, e - ter - ni - ty's too short to ut - ter all thy praise!

Words: Joseph Addison (1672-1719), alt.
Music: *Durham*, melody and bass Thomas Ravenscroft (1592?-1635?)

CM

1 For the beau - ty of the earth, for the beau - ty of the skies,
2 For the beau - ty of each hour of the day and of the night,
3 For the joy of ear and eye, for the heart and mind's de - light,
4 For the joy of hu-man love, bro-ther, sis - ter, par - ent, child,
5 For the Church which ev - er - more lift-eth ho - ly hands a - bove,

1 for the love which from our birth o - ver and a - round us lies,
2 hill and vale, and tree and flower, sun and moon, and stars of light,
3 for the mys - tic har - mo - ny link-ing sense to sound and sight,
4 friends on earth, and friends a - bove, for all gen - tle thoughts and mild,
5 of - fering up on ev - ery shore thy pure sac - ri - fice of love,

Refrain

Christ our God, to thee we raise this our hymn of grate-ful praise.

6   For each perfect gift of thine
     to the world so freely given,
     faith and hope and love divine,
       peace on earth and joy in heaven

Refrain

Words: Folliot Sandford Pierpoint (1835-1917), alt.
Music: *Lucerna Laudoniae*, David Evans (1874-1948)

77. 77 with Refrain

Praise to God

417

Antiphon

This is the feast of vic-to-ry for our God.

Al - le - lu - ia, al - le - lu - ia, al - le - lu - ia!

1 Wor - thy is Christ, the Lamb who was slain,_____ whose
2 Pow - er, rich - es, wis - dom, and strength,___ and
3 Sing___ with all the peo - ple of God,_____ and
4 Bless - ing, hon - or, glo - ry, and might be to
5 For___ the Lamb_____ who was slain has be -

1 blood set us free___ to be peo - ple of God. [Ant.]
2 hon - or,___ bless - ing, and glo - ry are his. [Ant.]
3 join in the hymn of all cre - a - - - tion. [Ant.]
4 God and the Lamb for ev - er. A - - - men. [Ant.]
5 gun his___ reign.___ Al - le - lu - - - ia! [Ant.]

Final Antiphon

This is the feast of vic-to-ry for our God.

Al - le - lu - ia, al - le - lu - ia, al - le - lu - ia!

Words: Revelation 5:12-13; adapt. John W. Arthur (1922-1980)
Music: *Festival Canticle*, Richard Hillert (b. 1923)

Irr. with Refrain

418

Antiphon

This is the feast of vic-to-ry for our God. Al-le-lu-ia, al - - - le-lu-ia!

1. Wor-thy is Christ, the Lamb who was slain, whose blood set us free to be peo-ple of God. [Ant.]

2. Pow-er, rich-es, wis-dom and strength, and hon-or, bless-ing, and glo-ry are his. [Ant.]

3. Sing with all the peo-ple of God, and join in the hymn of all cre-a-tion. [Ant.]

4. Bless - ing, hon - or, glo - ry, and might be to God and the Lamb for ev - er. A - men. [Ant.]

5. For the Lamb who was slain has be - gun his reign. Al - le - lu - ia! [Ant.]

Final Antiphon

This is the feast of vic - to - ry for our God. Al - le - lu - ia, al - le - lu - ia!

Words: Revelation 5:12-13; adapt. John W. Arthur (1922-1980)
Music: *Raymond*, Peter R. Hallock (b. 1923)

Irr. with Refrain

1 Lord of all be - ing, throned a - far, thy glo - ry
2 Sun of our life, thy quick - ening ray sheds on our
3 Lord of all life, be - low, a - bove, whose light is
4 Grant us thy truth to make us free, and kin - dling

flames from sun and star; cen - ter and soul of
path the glow of day; star of our hope, thy
truth, whose warmth is love, be - fore thy ev - er -
hearts that burn for thee, till all thy liv - ing

ev - ery sphere, yet to each lov - ing heart how near!
soft - ened light cheers the long watch - es of the night.
blaz - ing throne we ask no lus - ter of our own.
al - tars claim one ho - ly light, one heaven - ly flame.

Words: Oliver Wendell Holmes (1809-1894)
Music: *Mendon*, melody from *Methodist Harmonist*, 1821; adapt. Lowell Mason (1792-1872)   LM

420   Praise to God

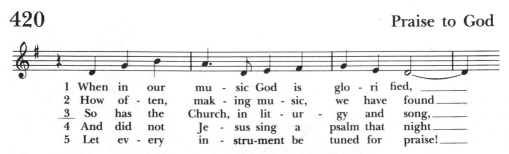

1 When in our mu - sic God is glo - ri fied, _____
2 How of - ten, mak - ing mu - sic, we have found _____
3 So has the Church, in lit - ur - gy and song, _____
4 And did not Je - sus sing a psalm that night _____
5 Let ev - ery in - stru - ment be tuned for praise! _____

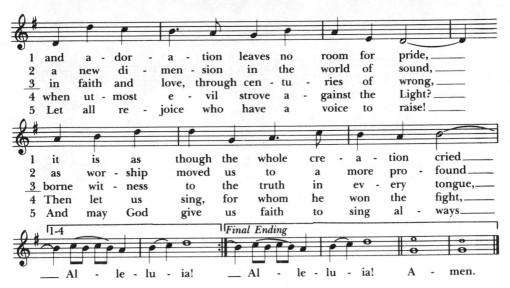

1 and a - dor - a - tion leaves no room for pride,____
2 a new di - men - sion in the world of sound,____
3 in faith and love, through cen - tu - ries of wrong,____
4 when ut - most e - vil strove a - gainst the Light?____
5 Let all re - joice who have a voice to raise!____

1 it is as though the whole cre - a - tion cried____
2 as wor - ship moved us to a more pro - found____
3 borne wit - ness to the truth in ev - ery tongue,____
4 Then let us sing, for whom he won the fight,____
5 And may God give us faith to sing al - ways____

1-4 / *Final Ending*

___ Al - le - lu - ia! ___ Al - le - lu - ia! A - men.

Words: F. Pratt Green (b. 1903)
Music: *Engelberg*, Charles Villiers Stanford (1852-1924)

10 10 10 with Alleluia

Praise to God

421

1 All glo - ry be to God on high, and peace on earth from
2 O Lamb of God, Lord Je - sus Christ, whom God the Fa - ther
3 You on - ly are the Ho - ly One, who came for our sal -

hea - ven, and God's good will un - fail - ing - ly be
gave us, who for the world was sac - ri - ficed up -
va - tion, and on - ly you are God's true Son, who

to all peo - ple giv - en. We bless, we wor - ship you, we raise for
on the cross to save us; and, as you sit at God's right hand and
was be - fore cre - a - tion. You, on - ly, Christ, as Lord we own and,

your great glo - ry thanks and praise, O God, Al - might - y Fa - ther.
we for judg-ment there must stand, have mer - cy, Lord, up - on us.
with the Spi - rit, you a - lone share in the Fa - ther's glo - ry.

Words: Nikolaus Decius (1490?-1541); tr. F. Bland Tucker (1895-1984), rev.;
para. of *Gloria in excelsis*
Music: *Allein Gott in der Höh*, melody att. Nikolaus Decius (1490?-1541);

87. 87. 887

422

Praise to God

1 Not far be-yond the sea, nor high a-bove the heavens, but
2 Root-ed and ground-ed in thy love, with saints on earth and
3 Help us to press on toward that mark, and, though our vi-sion

ve-ry high thy voice, O God, is heard. For
saints a-bove we join in full ac-cord: to
now is dark, to live by what we see. So,

each new step of faith we take thou hast more truth and
know the breadth, length, depth, and height, the cru-ci-fied and
when we see thee face to face, thy truth and light our

light to break forth from thy Ho-ly Word.
ris-en might of Christ, the in-car-nate Word.
dwell-ing-place for ev-er-more shall be.

Words: George B. Caird (b. 1917), alt.
Music: *Cornwall*, Samuel Sebastian Wesley (1810-1876)

886. 886

1 Im - mor - tal, in - vis - i - ble, God on - ly wise,
2 Un - rest - ing, un - hast - ing, and si - lent as light,
3 To all life thou giv - est, to both great and small;
4 Thou reign - est in glo - ry, thou rul - est in light,

in light in - ac - ces - si - ble hid from our eyes,
nor want - ing, nor wast - ing, thou rul - est in might;
in all life thou liv - est, the true life of all;
thine an - gels a - dore thee, all veil - ing their sight;

most bless - ed, most glo - rious, the An - cient of Days,
thy jus - tice like moun - tains high soar - ing a - bove
we blos - som and flour - ish, like leaves on the tree,
all laud we would ren - der: O help us to see

al - might - y, vic - tor - ious, thy great Name we praise.
thy clouds, which are foun - tains of good - ness and love.
then with - er and per - ish; but nought chan - geth thee.
'tis on - ly the splen - dor of light hid - eth thee.

Words: Walter Chalmers Smith (1824-1908), alt.
Music: *St. Denio*, Welsh hymn, from *Caniadau y Cyssegr*, 1839; adapt. John Roberts (1822-1877);
    harm. *The English Hymnal*, 1906, alt.

11 11. 11 11

1 For the fruit of all cre - a - tion, thanks be to
2 In the just re - ward of la - bor, God's will be
3 For the har - vests of the Spi - rit, thanks be to

God. For his gifts to ev - ery na - tion,
done. In the help we give our neigh - bor,
God. For the good we all in - her - it,

thanks be to God. For the plow - ing, sow - ing, reap - ing,
God's will be done. In our world-wide task of car - ing
thanks be to God. For the won - ders that as - tound us,

si - lent growth while we are sleep - ing, fu - ture needs in
for the hun - gry and de - spair - ing, in the har - vests
for the truths that still con-found us, most of all that

earth's safe - keep - ing, thanks be to God.
we are shar - ing, God's will be done.
love has found us, thanks be to God.

Words: F. Pratt Green (b. 1903), alt.
Music: *East Acklam*, Francis Jackson (b. 1917)

84. 84. 888. 4

425   Praise to God

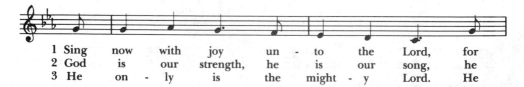

1 Sing now with joy un - to the Lord, for
2 God is our strength, he is our song, he
3 He on - ly is the might - y Lord. He

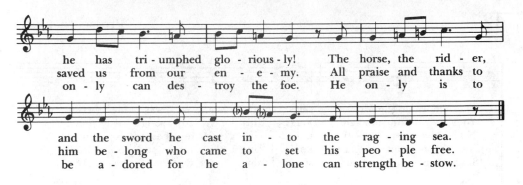

he has tri-umphed glo-rious-ly! The horse, the rid-er,
saved us from our en-e-my. All praise and thanks to
on-ly can des-troy the foe. He on-ly is to

and the sword he cast in-to the rag-ing sea.
him be-long who came to set his peo-ple free.
be a-dored for he a-lone can strength be-stow.

Words: Anon., ca. 1976, alt.; based on Exodus 15:1-2
Music: *Adon Olam*, Eliezer Gerovitch (1844-1914)

LM

Praise to God

426

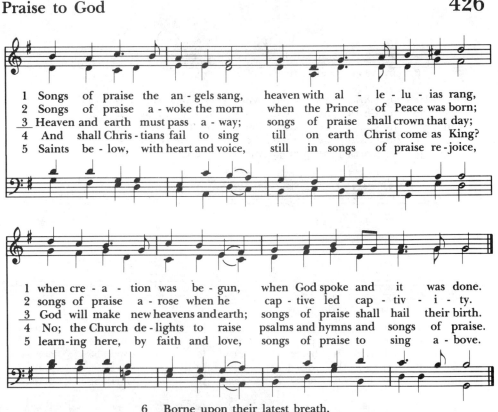

1 Songs of praise the an-gels sang, heaven with al - le - lu - ias rang,
2 Songs of praise a - woke the morn when the Prince of Peace was born;
3 Heaven and earth must pass a - way; songs of praise shall crown that day;
4 And shall Chris-tians fail to sing till on earth Christ come as King?
5 Saints be - low, with heart and voice, still in songs of praise re - joice,

1 when cre - a - tion was be - gun, when God spoke and it was done.
2 songs of praise a - rose when he cap - tive led cap - tiv - i - ty.
3 God will make new heavens and earth; songs of praise shall hail their birth.
4 No; the Church de - lights to raise psalms and hymns and songs of praise.
5 learn-ing here, by faith and love, songs of praise to sing a - bove.

6 Borne upon their latest breath,
   songs of praise shall conquer death;
   then, amidst eternal joy,
   songs of praise their powers employ.

Words: James Montgomery (1771-1854), alt.
Music: *Northampton*, Charles John King (1859-1934)

77. 77

1 When morn-ing gilds the skies, my heart, a-wak-ing, cries,
2 When mirth for mu-sic longs, this is my song of songs:
3 No love-lier an-ti-phon in all high heaven is known
4 Ye na-tions of man-kind, in this your con-cord find:
5 Sing, suns and stars of space, sing, ye that see his face,

1 may Je-sus Christ be praised! When eve-ning sha-dows fall,
2 may Je-sus Christ be praised! God's ho-ly house of prayer
3 than, Je-sus Christ be praised! There to the e-ter-nal Word
4 may Je-sus Christ be praised! Let all the earth a-round
5 sing, Je-sus Christ be praised! God's whole cre-a-tion o'er,

1 this rings my cur-few call, may Je-sus Christ be praised!
2 hath none that can com-pare with: Je-sus Christ be praised!
3 the e-ter-nal psalm is heard: may Je-sus Christ be praised!
4 ring joy-ous with the sound: may Je-sus Christ be praised!
5 both now and ev-er-more shall Je-sus Christ be praised!

Words: German, ca. 1800; tr. Robert Seymour Bridges (1844-1930), alt.
Music: *Laudes Domini*, Joseph Barnby (1838-1896)

666. 666

1 O all ye works of God, now come to thank him
2 O sun and moon and stars of heaven, your end - less
3 O heat and cold, O night and day, O storms and
4 O earth and sea, O all that live in wa - ter
5 O let his peo - ple bless the Lord like right - eous

1 and a - dore; O an - gels, sing and
2 praise out - pour; O chang - ing sea - sons,
3 thun - der's roar, O fields and for - ests,
4 or on shore, O men and wo - men,
5 souls of yore; let those of ho - ly,

1 bless the Lord and praise him ev - er - more.
2 bless the Lord and praise him ev - er - more.
3 bless the Lord and praise him ev - er - more.
4 bless the Lord and praise him ev - er - more.
5 hum - ble heart come praise him ev - er - more.

6   So let us glorify and bless
the God we bow before,
the Father, Holy Spirit, Son,
and praise him evermore.

Words: F. Bland Tucker (1895-1984), rev.; para. of *A Song of Creation*
Music: *Irish*, melody from *Hymns and Sacred Poems*, 1749; harm. *The English Hymnal*, 1906   CM

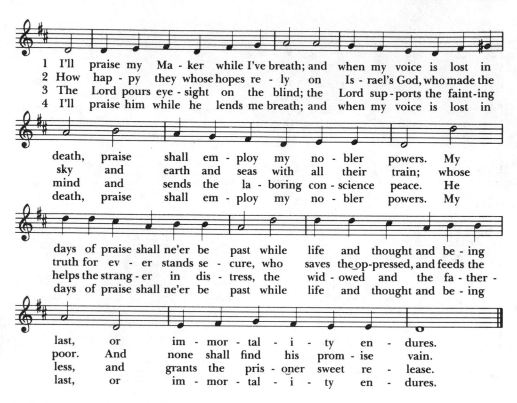

1 I'll praise my Ma - ker while I've breath; and when my voice is lost in
2 How hap - py they whose hopes re - ly on Is - rael's God, who made the
3 The Lord pours eye - sight on the blind; the Lord sup - ports the faint - ing
4 I'll praise him while he lends me breath; and when my voice is lost in

death, praise shall em - ploy my no - bler powers. My
sky and earth and seas with all their train; whose
mind and sends the la - boring con - science peace. He
death, praise shall em - ploy my no - bler powers. My

days of praise shall ne'er be past while life and thought and be - ing
truth for ev - er stands se - cure, who saves the op-pressed, and feeds the
helps the strang - er in dis - tress, the wid - owed and the fa - ther -
days of praise shall ne'er be past while life and thought and be - ing

last, or im - mor - tal - i - ty en - dures.
poor. And none shall find his prom - ise vain.
less, and grants the pris - oner sweet re - lease.
last, or im - mor - tal - i - ty en - dures.

Words: Isaac Watts (1674-1748); alt. by John Wesley (1703-1791), alt.; para. of Psalm 146
Music: *Old 113th*, melody from *Strassburger Kirchenamt*, 1525

88. 88. 88

1 Come, O come, our voic - es raise, sound - ing
2 Sound the trum - pet, touch the lute, let no
3 Come ye all be - fore his face, in this
4 Let, in praise of God, the sound run a
5 So this huge wide orb we see shall one
6 Thus our song shall o - ver - climb all the

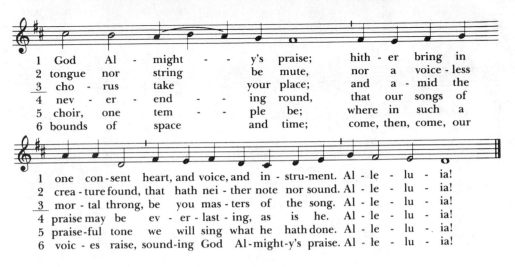

1 God	Al	might - -	y's praise;	hith - er	bring in
2 tongue	nor	string	be mute,	nor	a voice - less
3 cho - rus	take	your place;	and	a - mid the
4 nev - er -	end - -	ing round,	that	our songs of
5 choir,	one	tem - -	ple be;	where in	such a
6 bounds	of	space	and time;	come, then, come, our

1 one con - sent	heart, and voice, and	in - stru - ment. Al - le - lu - ia!
2 crea - ture found,	that hath nei - ther note	nor sound. Al - le - lu - ia!
3 mor - tal throng,	be you mas - ters of	the song. Al - le - lu - ia!
4 praise may be	ev - er - last - ing, as	is he. Al - le - lu - ia!
5 praise - ful tone	we will sing what he	hath done. Al - le - lu - ia!
6 voic - es raise,	sound - ing God Al - might - y's praise. Al - le - lu - ia!

Words: George Wither (1588-1667), alt.
Music: *Sonne der Gerechtigkeit*, melody from *Bohemian Brethren, Kirchengeseng*, 1566

77. 77 with Alleluia

Praise to God

431

1 The	stars	de - clare his	glo - ry; the	vault of hea - ven	springs
2 The	dawn	re - turns in	splen - dor, the	hea - vens burn and	blaze,
3 So	shine	the Lord's com -	mand - ments to	make the sim - ple	wise;
4 So	or -	der too this	life of mine, di -	rect it all my	days;

mute	wit - ness of the	Mas - ter's hand in	all cre - at - ed	things, and
the	ris - ing sun re -	news the race that	mea - sures all our	**days**, and
more sweet	than hon - ey	to the taste, more	rich than an - y	prize, a
the	med - i - ta - tions	of my heart be	in - no - cence and	praise, my

through the	si - lenc - es	of	space their	sound - less mu - sic	sings. _____
writes in	fire a - cross the	skies God's	ma - jes - ty and	praise. _____
law of	love with - in	our hearts, a	light be - fore our	eyes. _____
rock, and	my re - deem - ing	Lord, in	all my words and	ways. _____

Words: Timothy Dudley-Smith (b. 1926); para. of Psalm 19
Music: *Aldine*, Richard Proulx (b. 1937)

76. 86. 86

1 O praise ye the Lord! Praise him in the height;
2 O praise ye the Lord! Praise him up-on earth,
*3 O praise ye the Lord! All things that give sound;
4 O praise ye the Lord! Thanks-giv-ing and song

re - joice in his word, ye an - gels of light;
in tune - ful ac - cord, all ye of new birth;
each ju - bi - lant chord re - ech - o a - round;
to him be out - poured all a - ges a - long!

ye hea - vens, a - dore him by whom ye were made,
praise him who hath brought you his grace from a - bove,
loud or - gans, his glo - ry forth tell in deep tone,
For love in cre - a - tion, for hea - ven re - stored,

and wor - ship be - fore him, in bright - ness ar - rayed.
praise him who hath taught you to sing of his love.
and sweet harp, the sto - ry of what he hath done.
for grace of sal - va - tion, O praise ye the Lord!

Words: Henry Williams Baker (1821-1877), alt.; based on Psalms 148 and 150
Music: *Laudate Dominum*, Charles Hubert Hastings Parry (1848-1918)

10 10. 11 11

Praise to God

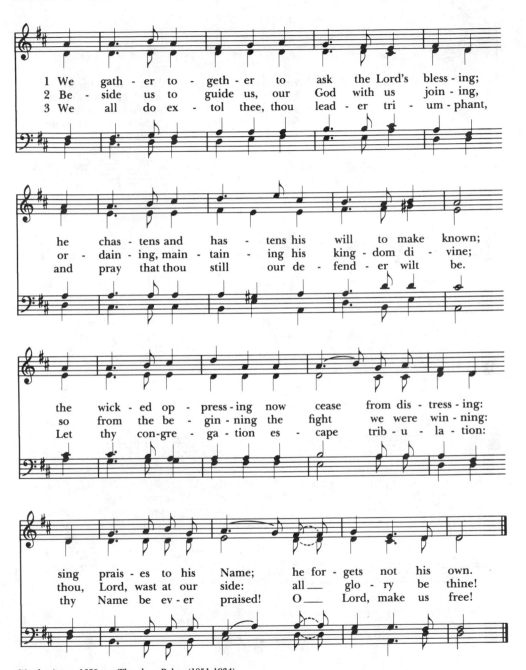

1 We gath-er to-geth-er to ask the Lord's bless-ing;
2 Be-side us to guide us, our God with us join-ing,
3 We all do ex-tol thee, thou lead-er tri-um-phant,

he chas-tens and has-tens his will to make known;
or-dain-ing, main-tain-ing his king-dom di-vine;
and pray that thou still our de-fend-er wilt be.

the wick-ed op-press-ing now cease from dis-tress-ing:
so from the be-gin-ning the fight we were win-ning:
Let thy con-gre-ga-tion es-cape trib-u-la-tion:

sing prais-es to his Name; he for-gets not his own.
thou, Lord, wast at our side: all glo-ry be thine!
thy Name be ev-er praised! O Lord, make us free!

Words: Anon. 1625; tr. Theodore Baker (1851-1934)
Music: *Kremser*, from *Nederlandtsch Gedenckclank*, 1626; arr. Eduard Kremser (1838-1914)

12 11. 12 11

434

Jesus Christ our Lord

1 Nature with open volume stands to spread her
2 But in the grace that rescued man his brightest
3 Here his whole Name appears complete; nor wit can
4 Oh, the sweet wonders of that cross where Christ my
5 I would for ever speak his Name in sounds to

1 Maker's praise abroad and every labor of his
2 form of glory shines; here, on the cross, 'tis fairest
3 guess, nor reason prove which of the letters best is
4 Savior loved and died! Her noblest life my spirit
5 mortal ears unknown, with angels join to praise the

1 hands shows something worthy of a God.
2 drawn in precious blood and crimson lines.
3 writ, the power, the wisdom, or the love.
4 draws from his dear wounds and bleeding side.
5 Lamb and worship at his Father's throne!

The G♯ in the final chord should be reserved for stanza 5.

Words: Isaac Watts (1674-1748)
Music: *Eltham*, melody Nathaniel Gawthorn (18th cent.); harm. Samuel Sebastian Wesley (1810-1876)

LM

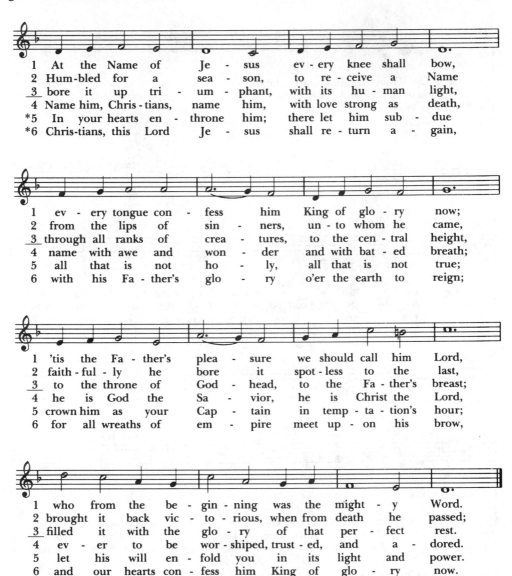

1 At the Name of Je - sus ev - ery knee shall bow,
2 Hum-bled for a sea - son, to re - ceive a Name
3 bore it up tri - um - phant, with its hu - man light,
4 Name him, Chris - tians, name him, with love strong as death,
*5 In your hearts en - throne him; there let him sub - due
*6 Chris-tians, this Lord Je - sus shall re - turn a - gain,

1 ev - ery tongue con - fess him King of glo - ry now;
2 from the lips of sin - ners, un - to whom he came,
3 through all ranks of crea - tures, to the cen - tral height,
4 name with awe and won - der and with bat - ed breath;
5 all that is not ho - ly, all that is not true;
6 with his Fa - ther's glo - ry o'er the earth to reign;

1 'tis the Fa - ther's plea - sure we should call him Lord,
2 faith - ful - ly he bore it spot - less to the last,
3 to the throne of God - head, to the Fa - ther's breast;
4 he is God the Sa - vior, he is Christ the Lord,
5 crown him as your Cap - tain in temp - ta - tion's hour;
6 for all wreaths of em - pire meet up - on his brow,

1 who from the be - gin - ning was the might - y Word.
2 brought it back vic - to - rious, when from death he passed;
3 filled it with the glo - ry of that per - fect rest.
4 ev - er to be wor - shiped, trust - ed, and a - dored.
5 let his will en - fold you in its light and power.
6 and our hearts con - fess him King of glo - ry now.

Words: Caroline Maria Noel (1817-1877), alt.
Music: *King's Weston*, Ralph Vaughan Williams (1872-1958)

65. 65. D

1 Lift up your heads, ye might - y gates; be - hold the
2 O blest the land, the ci - ty blest, where Christ the
3 Fling wide the por - tals of your heart; make it a
*4 Re - deem - er come! I o - pen wide my heart to
5 So come, my Sov - ereign; en - ter in! Let new and

1 King of glo - ry waits! The King of kings is
2 ru - ler is con - fessed! O hap - py hearts and
3 tem - ple, set a - part from earth - ly use for
4 thee: here, Lord, a - bide! Let me thy in - ner
5 no - bler life be - gin; thy Ho - ly Spi - rit

1 draw - ing near; the Sa - vior of the world is here.
2 hap - py homes to whom this King of tri - umph comes!
3 heaven's em - ploy, a - dorned with prayer and love and joy.
4 pres - ence feel: thy grace and love in me re - veal.
5 guide us on, un - til the glo - rious crown be won.

Words: Georg Weissel (1590-1635); tr. Catherine Winkworth (1827-1878)
Music: *Truro*, melody from *Psalmodia Evangelica, Part II*, 1789; harm. Lowell Mason (1792-1872), alt.   LM

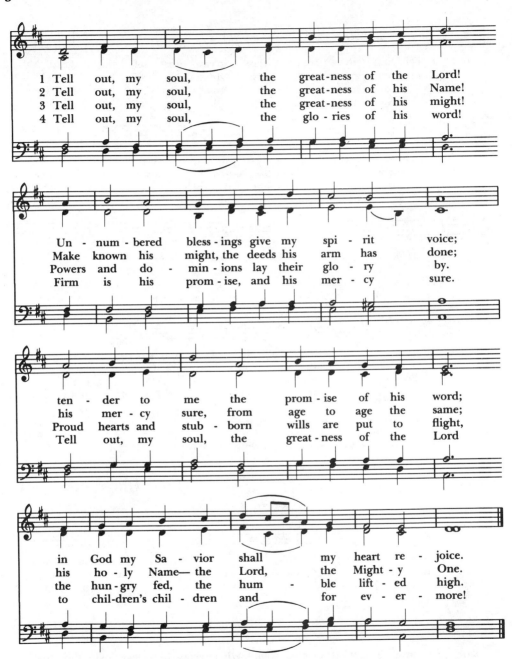

1 Tell out, my soul, the great-ness of the Lord!
2 Tell out, my soul, the great-ness of his Name!
3 Tell out, my soul, the great-ness of his might!
4 Tell out, my soul, the glo-ries of his word!

Un - num - bered bless-ings give my spi - rit voice;
Make known his might, the deeds his arm has done;
Powers and do - min-ions lay their glo - ry by.
Firm is his prom - ise, and his mer - cy sure.

ten - der to me the prom - ise of his word;
his mer - cy sure, from age to age the same;
Proud hearts and stub - born wills are put to flight,
Tell out, my soul, the great - ness of the Lord

in God my Sa - vior shall my heart re - joice.
his ho - ly Name— the Lord, the Might - y One.
the hun - gry fed, the hum - ble lift - ed high.
to chil-dren's chil - dren and for ev - er - more!

Words: Timothy Dudley-Smith (b. 1926); based on *The Song of Mary*
Music: *Birmingham*, from *Repository of Sacred Music, Part II*, 1813; harm. *Songs of Praise*, 1925

10 10. 10 10

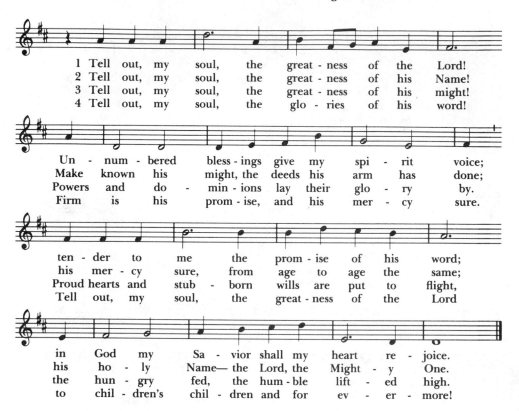

1 Tell out, my soul, the great-ness of the Lord!
2 Tell out, my soul, the great-ness of his Name!
3 Tell out, my soul, the great-ness of his might!
4 Tell out, my soul, the glo-ries of his word!

Un-num-bered bless-ings give my spi-rit voice;
Make known his might, the deeds his arm has done;
Powers and do-min-ions lay their glo-ry by.
Firm is his prom-ise, and his mer-cy sure.

ten-der to me the prom-ise of his word;
his mer-cy sure, from age to age the same;
Proud hearts and stub-born wills are put to flight,
Tell out, my soul, the great-ness of the Lord

in God my Sa-vior shall my heart re-joice.
his ho-ly Name— the Lord, the Might-y One.
the hun-gry fed, the hum-ble lift-ed high.
to chil-dren's chil-dren and for ev-er-more!

Words: Timothy Dudley-Smith (b. 1926); based on *The Song of Mary*
Music: *Woodlands*, Walter Greatorex (1877-1949)

10 10. 10 10

Words: Copyright © 1962 by Hope Publishing Company. All Rights Reserved. Used by Permission.

439
Jesus Christ our Lord

Unison

1 What won-drous love is this, O my soul, O my soul! What
2 To God and to the Lamb, I will sing, I will sing, to
3 And when from death I'm free, I'll sing on, I'll sing on, and

won-drous love is this, O my soul! What won-drous love is this that
God and to the Lamb, I will sing. To God and to the Lamb who
when from death I'm free, I'll sing on. And when from death I'm free I'll

caused the Lord of bliss to lay a - side his crown for my
is the great I AM, while mil - lions join the theme, I will
sing and joy - ful be, and through e - ter - ni - ty I'll sing

soul, for my soul, to lay a - side his crown for my soul.
sing, I will sing, while mil - lions join the theme I will sing.
on, I'll sing on, and through e - ter - ni - ty I'll sing on.

Harmony (the melody is in the tenor)

1 What won-drous love is this, O my soul, O my soul! What
2 To God and to the Lamb, I will sing, I will sing, to
3 And when from death I'm free, I'll sing on, I'll sing on, and

won-drous love is this, O my soul! What won-drous love is this that
God and to the Lamb, I will sing. To God and to the Lamb who
when from death I'm free, I'll sing on. And when from death I'm free I'll

caused the Lord of bliss to lay a - side his crown for my
is the great I AM, while mil - lions join the theme, I will
sing and joy - ful be, and through e - ter - ni - ty I'll sing

soul, for my soul, to lay a - side his crown for my soul.
sing, I will sing, while mil - lions join the theme I will sing.
on, I'll sing on, and through e - ter - ni - ty I'll sing on.

Words: American folk hymn, ca. 1835
Music: *Wondrous Love,* from *The Southern Harmony,* 1835

12 9. 12. 12 9

1 Bless-ed Je-sus, at thy word we are gath-ered all to
2 All our know-ledge, sense, and sight lie in deep-est dark-ness
3 Gra-cious Lord, thy-self im-part! Light of Light, from God pro-

hear thee; let our hearts and souls be stirred
shroud - ed, till thy Spi - rit breaks our night
ceed - ing, o - pen thou our ears and heart,

now to seek and love and fear thee; by thy teach - ings
with the beams of truth un - cloud - ed; thou a - lone to
help us by thy Spi - rit's plead - ing. Hear the cry thy

pure and ho - ly, drawn from earth to love thee sole - ly.
God canst win us; thou must work all good with - in us.
Church up - rais - es; hear, and bless our prayers and prais - es.

Words: Tobias Clausnitzer (1619-1684); tr. Catherine Winkworth (1827-1878), alt.
Music: *Liebster Jesu*, melody Johann Rudolph Ahle (1625-1673); alt. *Das grosse Cantional
oder Kirchen-Gesangbuch*, 1687; harm. George Herbert Palmer (1846-1926)

78. 78. 88

1 In the cross of Christ I glory, tower - ing
2 When the woes of life o'er - take me, hopes de -
3 When the sun of bliss is beam - ing light and
4 Bane and bless - ing, pain and plea - sure, by the
*5 In the cross of Christ I glory, tower - ing

1 o'er the wrecks of time; all the light of
2 ceive, and fears an - noy, nev - er shall the
3 love up - on my way, from the cross the
4 cross are sanc - ti - fied; peace is there that
5 o'er the wrecks of time; all the light of

1 sa - cred sto - ry gath - ers round its head sub - lime.
2 cross for - sake me: lo, it glows with peace and joy.
3 ra - diance stream - ing adds new lus - ter to the day.
4 knows no mea - sure, joys that through all time a - bide.
5 sa - cred sto - ry gath - ers round its head sub - lime.

Words: John Bowring (1792-1872)
Music: *Rathbun*, Ithamar Conkey (1815-1867)

87. 87

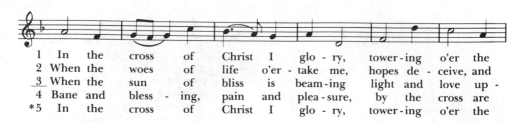

1 In the cross of Christ I glo-ry, tower-ing o'er the
2 When the woes of life o'er-take me, hopes de-ceive, and
3 When the sun of bliss is beam-ing light and love up-
4 Bane and bless-ing, pain and plea-sure, by the cross are
*5 In the cross of Christ I glo-ry, tower-ing o'er the

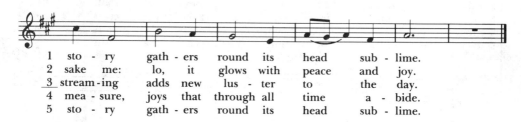

1 wrecks of time; all the light of sa - cred
2 fears an - noy, nev - er shall the cross for -
3 on my way, from the cross the ra - diance
4 sanc - ti - fied; peace is there that knows no
5 wrecks of time; all the light of sa - cred

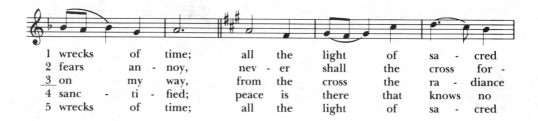

1 sto - ry gath - ers round its head sub - lime.
2 sake me: lo, it glows with peace and joy.
3 stream-ing adds new lus - ter to the day.
4 mea - sure, joys that through all time a - bide.
5 sto - ry gath - ers round its head sub - lime.

Words: John Bowring (1792-1872)
Music: *Tomter*, Bruce Neswick (b. 1956)

87. 87

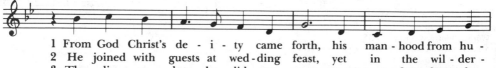

1 From God Christ's de - i - ty came forth, his man - hood from hu -
2 He joined with guests at wed - ding feast, yet in the wil - der -
3 The dis - so - lute he did not scorn, nor turn from those who
4 He did not dis - re - gard the sick; to sim - ple ones his
5 Who then, my Lord, com-pares to you? The Watch - er slept, the

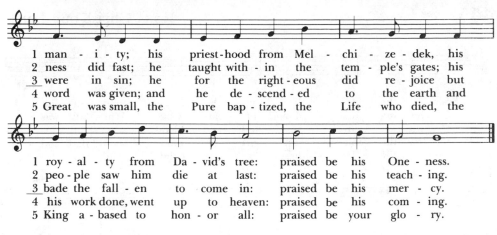

1 man - i - ty; his priest-hood from Mel - chi - ze - dek, his
2 ness did fast; he taught with - in the tem - ple's gates; his
3 were in sin; he for the right - eous did re - joice but
4 word was given; and he de - scend - ed to the earth and
5 Great was small, the Pure bap - tized, the Life who died, the

1 roy - al - ty from Da - vid's tree: praised be his One - ness.
2 peo - ple saw him die at last: praised be his teach - ing.
3 bade the fall - en to come in: praised be his mer - cy.
4 his work done, went up to heaven: praised be his com - ing.
5 King a - based to hon - or all: praised be your glo - ry.

Words: Ephrem of Edessa (4th cent.); tr. J. Howard Rhys (b. 1917);
adapt. and alt. F. Bland Tucker (1895-1984)
Music: *Salem Harbor*, Ronald Arnatt (b. 1930)

88. 88. 5

Jesus Christ our Lord

444

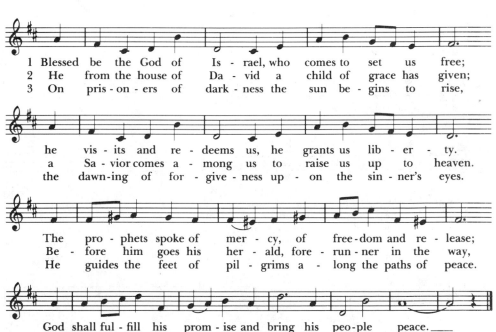

1 Blessed be the God of Is - rael, who comes to set us free;
2 He from the house of Da - vid a child of grace has given;
3 On pris - on - ers of dark - ness the sun be - gins to rise,

he vis - its and re - deems us, he grants us lib - er - ty.
a Sa - vior comes a - mong us to raise us up to heaven.
the dawn - ing of for - give - ness up - on the sin - ner's eyes.

The pro - phets spoke of mer - cy, of free - dom and re - lease;
Be - fore him goes his her - ald, fore - run - ner in the way,
He guides the feet of pil - grims a - long the paths of peace.

God shall ful - fill his prom - ise and bring his peo - ple peace. ___
the pro - phet of sal - va - tion, the har - bin - ger of Day. ___
O bless our God and Sa - vior with songs that nev - er cease. ___

Words: Michael A. Perry (b. 1942), alt.; para. of *The Song of Zechariah*
Music: *Thornbury*, Basil Harwood (1859-1949)

76. 76. D

1 Praise to the Ho - liest in the height, and in the
2 O lov - ing wis - dom of our God! When all was
3 O wis - est love! that flesh and blood, which did in
4 and that the high - est gift of grace should flesh and
5 Praise to the Ho - liest in the height, and in the

1 depth be praise; in all his words most
2 sin and shame, a sec - ond Ad - am
3 Ad - am fail, should strive a - fresh a -
4 blood re - fine: God's pres - ence and his
5 depth be praise; in all his words most

1 won - der - ful, most sure in all his ways!
2 to the fight and to the res - cue came.
3 gainst the foe, should strive, and should pre - vail!
4 ve - ry self, and es - sence all - di - vine.
5 won - der - ful, most sure in all his ways!

Words: John Henry Newman (1801-1890), alt.
Music: *Gerontius*, John Bacchus Dykes (1823-1876)

CM

1 Praise to the Ho - liest in the height, and in the depth be praise; in all his words most won - der - ful, most sure in all his ways!

2 O lov - ing wis - dom of our God! When all was sin and shame, a sec - ond Ad - am to the fight and to the res - cue came.

3 O wis - est love! that flesh and blood, which did in Ad - am fail, should strive a - fresh a - gainst the foe, should strive, and should pre - vail;

4 and that the high - est gift of grace should flesh and blood re - fine: God's pres - ence and his ve - ry self, and es - sence all - di - vine.

5 Praise to the Ho - liest in the height, and in the depth be praise; in all his words most won - der - ful most sure in all his ways!

Words: John Henry Newman (1801-1890), alt.
Music: *Newman*, Richard Runciman Terry (1865-1938)

CM

1 The Christ who died but rose a-gain tri-um-phant from the grave,
2 What now can sep-a-rate us from the love of Christ our Lord?
3 The trou-bles that are ours to bear are trials we can-not flee;
4 Thus noth-ing in the heights or depths, no power earth can af-ford,

now pleads our cause at God's right hand all - pow-er - ful to save.
Can per - se - cu - tion, na - ked - ness, or per - il, or the sword?
yet he who loved us from the first en - sures our vic - to - ry.
will sep - a - rate us from the love of Je - sus Christ our Lord.

Words: Granton Douglas Hay (b. 1943), alt.; based on *Paraphrases*, 1781; para. of Romans 8:34-39
Music: *St. Magnus*, melody from *Divine Companion*, 1707; harm. William Henry Monk (1823-1889),
after John Pyke Hullah (19th cent.)

CM

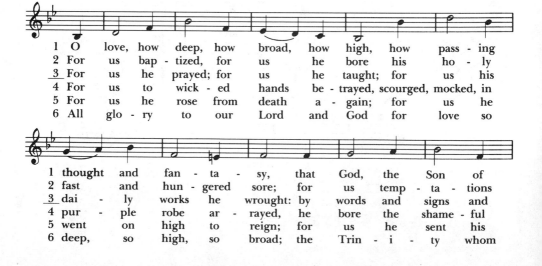

1 O love, how deep, how broad, how high, how pass - ing
2 For us bap - tized, for us he bore his ho - ly
3 For us he prayed; for us he taught; for us his
4 For us to wick - ed hands be - trayed, scourged, mocked, in
5 For us he rose from death a - gain; for us he
6 All glo - ry to our Lord and God for love so

1 thought and fan - ta - sy, that God, the Son of
2 fast and hun - gered sore; for us temp - ta - tions
3 dai - ly works he wrought: by words and signs and
4 pur - ple robe ar - rayed, he bore the shame - ful
5 went on high to reign; for us he sent his
6 deep, so high, so broad; the Trin - i - ty whom

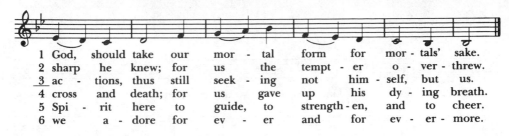

1 God, should take our mor - tal form for mor - tals' sake.
2 sharp he knew; for us the tempt - er o - ver - threw.
3 ac - tions, thus still seek - ing not him - self, but us.
4 cross and death; for us gave up his dy - ing breath.
5 Spi - rit here to guide, to strength - en, and to cheer.
6 we a - dore for ev - er and for ev - er - more.

Words: Latin, 15th cent.; tr. Benjamin Webb (1819-1885), alt.
Music: *Deus tuorum militum*, from *Antiphoner*, 1753; adapt. *The English Hymnal*, 1906, alt.   LM

Jesus Christ our Lord   449

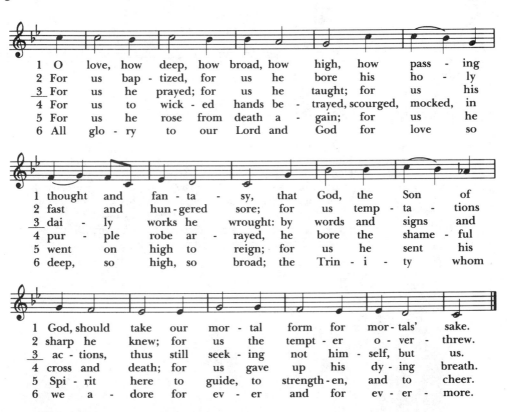

1 O love, how deep, how broad, how high, how pass - ing
2 For us bap - tized, for us he bore his ho - ly
3 For us he prayed; for us he taught; for us his
4 For us to wick - ed hands be - trayed, scourged, mocked, in
5 For us he rose from death a - gain; for us he
6 All glo - ry to our Lord and God for love so

1 thought and fan - ta - sy, that God, the Son of
2 fast and hun - gered sore; for us temp - ta - tions
3 dai - ly works he wrought: by words and signs and
4 pur - ple robe ar - rayed, he bore the shame - ful
5 went on high to reign; for us he sent his
6 deep, so high, so broad; the Trin - i - ty whom

1 God, should take our mor - tal form for mor - tals' sake.
2 sharp he knew; for us the tempt - er o - ver - threw.
3 ac - tions, thus still seek - ing not him - self, but us.
4 cross and death; for us gave up his dy - ing breath.
5 Spi - rit here to guide, to strength - en, and to cheer.
6 we a - dore for ev - er and for ev - er - more.

Words: Latin, 15th cent.; tr. Benjamin Webb (1819-1885), alt.
Music: *Deo gracias*, English ballad melody, Trinity College MS., 15th cent.   LM

6 Let ev - ery kin - dred, ev - ery tribe, on this ter - res - trial

1 All hail the power of Je - sus' Name! Let an - gels pros-trate
2 Crown him ye mar - tyrs of our God, who from his al - tar
3 Hail him, the Heir of Da - vid's line, whom Da - vid Lord did
*4 Ye heirs of Is - rael's cho - sen race, ye ran - somed of the
*5 Sin - ners, whose love can ne'er for - get the worm-wood and the

ball, to him a - scribe, and

1 fall; bring forth the roy - al di - a - dem, and
2 call: praise him whose way of pain ye trod, and
3 call, the God in - car - nate, Man di - vine, and
4 fall, hail him who saves you by his grace, and
5 gall, go, spread your tro - phies at his feet, and

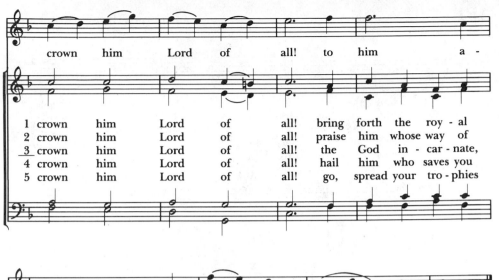

crown	him	Lord	of	all!	to	him	a -

1 crown him Lord of all! bring forth the roy - al
2 crown him Lord of all! praise him whose way of
3 crown him Lord of all! the God in - car - nate,
4 crown him Lord of all! hail him who saves you
5 crown him Lord of all! go, spread your tro - phies

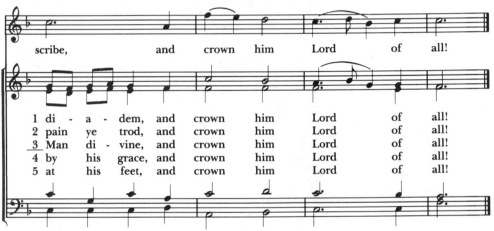

scribe, and crown him Lord of all!

1 di - a - dem, and crown him Lord of all!
2 pain ye trod, and crown him Lord of all!
3 Man di - vine, and crown him Lord of all!
4 by his grace, and crown him Lord of all!
5 at his feet, and crown him Lord of all!

6 Let every kindred, every tribe,
on this terrestrial ball,
to him all majesty ascribe,
and crown him Lord of all!

Words: Edward Perronet (1726-1792), alt.
Music: *Coronation*, Oliver Holden (1765-1844), alt.; desc. Michael E. Young (b. 1939)

86. 86. 86

1 All hail the power of Je - sus' Name! Let an - gels
2 Crown him, ye mar - tyrs of our God, who from his
3 Hail him, the Heir of Da - vid's line, whom Da - vid
*4 Ye heirs of Is - rael's cho - sen race, ye ran - somed
*5 Sin - ners, whose love can ne'er for - get the worm - wood

1 pros - trate fall; bring forth the roy - al di - a - dem,
2 al - tar call: praise him whose way of pain ye trod,
3 Lord did call, the God in - car - nate, Man di - vine,
4 of the fall, hail him who saves you by his grace,
5 and the gall, go, spread your tro - phies at his feet,

Refrain

and crown him, crown him, crown him, crown him Lord of all!

6 Let every kindred, every tribe,
on this terrestrial ball,
to him all majesty ascribe,

Refrain

Words: Edward Perronet (1726-1792), alt.
Music: *Miles Lane*, William Shrubsole (1760-1806)

868 with Refrain

1 Glo-rious the day when Christ was born to wear the
2 Glo-rious the day when Christ a-rose, the sur-est
3 Glo-rious the days of gos-pel grace when Christ re-
4 Glo-rious the day when Christ ful-fills what self re-

crown that Cae-sars scorn, whose life and death that
friend of all his foes; who for the sake of
stores the fal-len race, when doubt-ers kneel and
jects yet fee-bly wills; when that strong Light puts

love re-veal which mor-tals need and need to feel.
those he grieves tran-scends the world he nev-er leaves.
wa-verers stand, and faith a-chieves what rea-son planned.
out the sun and all is end-ed, all be-gun.

Refrain

Al-le-lu-ia! Al-le-lu-ia! Al-le-lu-ia!

Words: F. Pratt Green (b. 1903), rev.
Music: *Frohlockt mit Freud'*, Heinrich Schütz (1585-1672), alt.

LM with Refrain

1 As Jacob with travel was weary one day,
2 The ladder is long, it is strong and well-made,
3 Come, let us ascend! All may climb it who will,
4 And when we arrive at the haven of rest,

at night on a stone for a pillow he lay;
has stood hundreds of years and is not yet decayed;
for the angels of Jacob are guarding it still;
we shall hear the glad words, "Come to me all the blest,

he saw in a vision a ladder so high,
many millions have climbed it and reached Zion's hill,
and remember, each step that by faith we pass o'er,
here are regions of light, here are mansions of bliss."

that its foot was on earth and its top in the sky:
many millions by faith now are climbing it still:
many prophets and martyrs have trod it before:
Who would not want to climb such a ladder as this:

Refrain

Alleluia to Jesus, who died on the tree

and has raised up a ladder of mercy for me,

and has raised up a ladder of mercy for me.

Words: English carol, ca. 18th cent.
Music: *Jacob's Ladder*, English folk melody

Irr. with Refrain

Jesus Christ our Lord

454

Unison or harmony

1 Je - sus came, a - dored by an - gels, came with peace from realms on high; Je - sus came for our re - demp - tion, low - ly came on earth to die: Al - le - lu - ia, al - le - lu - ia! came in deep hu - mil - i - ty.

2 Je - sus comes a - gain in mer - cy, when our hearts are bowed with care; Je - sus comes a - gain in an - swer to our ear - nest heart - felt prayer: Al - le - lu - ia, al - le - lu - ia! comes to save us from de - spair.

3 Je - sus comes to hearts re - joic - ing, bring - ing news of sins for - given; Je - sus comes in sounds of glad - ness, lead - ing souls re - deemed to heaven; Al - le - lu - ia, al - le - lu - ia! now the gate of death is riven.

4 Je - sus comes on clouds tri - um - phant, when the heavens shall pass a - way; Je - sus comes a - gain in glo - ry; let us then our hom - age pay: Al - le - lu - ia, al - le - lu - ia! till the dawn of end - less day.

Words: Godfrey Thring (1823-1903), alt.
Music: *Lowry*, Gerald Near (b. 1942)

87. 87. 87

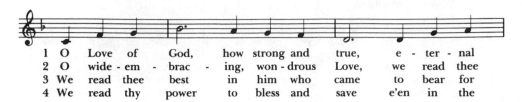

1 O Love of God, how strong and true, e - ter - nal
2 O wide - em - brac - ing, won - drous Love, we read thee
3 We read thee best in him who came to bear for
4 We read thy power to bless and save e'en in the

and yet ev - er new; un - com - pre - hend - ed and un -
in the sky a - bove; we read thee in the earth be -
us the cross of shame, sent by the Fa - ther from on
dark - ness of the grave; still more in re - sur - rec - tion

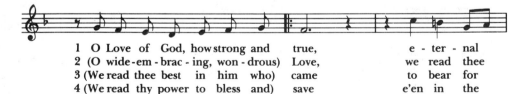

bought, be - yond all know - ledge and all thought.
low, in seas that swell and streams that flow.
high, our life to live, our death to die.
light we read the full - ness of thy might.

Words: Horatius Bonar (1808-1889)
Music: *Dunedin*, Vernon Griffiths (b. 1894)

LM

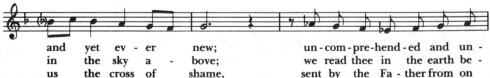

1 O Love of God, how strong and true, e - ter - nal
2 (O wide - em - brac - ing, won - drous) Love, we read thee
3 (We read thee best in him who) came to bear for
4 (We read thy power to bless and) save e'en in the

and yet ev - er new; un - com - pre - hend - ed and un -
in the sky a - bove; we read thee in the earth be -
us the cross of shame, sent by the Fa - ther from on
dark - ness of the grave; still more in re - sur - rec - tion

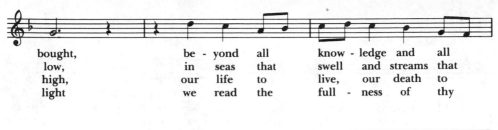

bought,	be - yond	all	know - ledge and	all
low,	in seas	that	swell and streams	that
high,	our life	to	live, our death	to
light	we read	the	full - ness	of thy

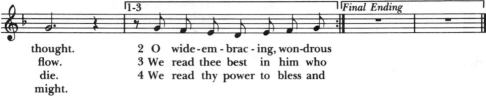

1-3   *Final Ending*

thought.	2 O wide-em-brac-ing, won-drous
flow.	3 We read thee best in him who
die.	4 We read thy power to bless and
might.	

Words: Horatius Bonar (1808-1899)
Music: *de Tar*, Calvin Hampton (1938-1984)

LM

Jesus Christ our Lord   457

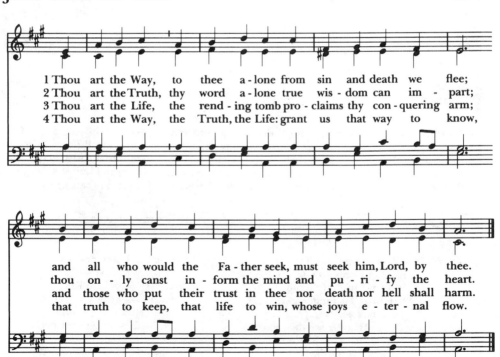

1 Thou art the Way, to thee a - lone from sin and death we flee;
2 Thou art the Truth, thy word a - lone true wis - dom can im - part;
3 Thou art the Life, the rend - ing tomb pro - claims thy con - quering arm;
4 Thou art the Way, the Truth, the Life: grant us that way to know,

and all who would the Fa - ther seek, must seek him, Lord, by thee.
thou on - ly canst in - form the mind and pu - ri - fy the heart.
and those who put their trust in thee nor death nor hell shall harm.
that truth to keep, that life to win, whose joys e - ter - nal flow.

Words: George Washington Doane (1799-1859), alt.
Music: *St. James*, Raphael Courteville (d. 1735)

CM

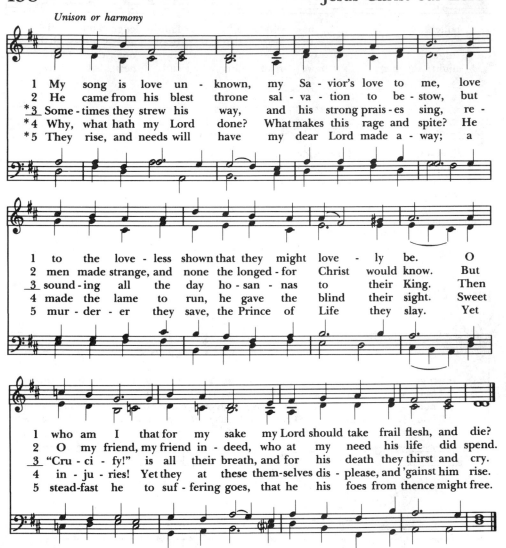

Unison or harmony

1 My song is love un - known, my Sa - vior's love to me, love
2 He came from his blest throne sal - va - tion to be - stow, but
*3 Some - times they strew his way, and his strong prais - es sing, re -
*4 Why, what hath my Lord done? What makes this rage and spite? He
*5 They rise, and needs will have my dear Lord made a - way; a

1 to the love - less shown that they might love - ly be. O
2 men made strange, and none the longed - for Christ would know. But
3 sound - ing all the day ho - san - nas to their King. Then
4 made the lame to run, he gave the blind their sight. Sweet
5 mur - der - er they save, the Prince of Life they slay. Yet

1 who am I that for my sake my Lord should take frail flesh, and die?
2 O my friend, my friend in - deed, who at my need his life did spend.
3 "Cru - ci - fy!" is all their breath, and for his death they thirst and cry.
4 in - ju - ries! Yet they at these them-selves dis - please, and 'gainst him rise.
5 stead-fast he to suf - fering goes, that he his foes from thence might free.

*6 In life no house, no home
　　my Lord on earth might have;
in death no friendly tomb
　　but what a stranger gave.
　　What may I say?
　　Heaven was his home;
　　but mine the tomb
wherein he lay.

7 Here might I stay and sing,
　　no story so divine:
never was love, dear King,
　　never was grief like thine.
　　This is my friend,
　　in whose sweet praise
　　I all my days
could gladly spend.

Words: Samuel Crossman (1624-1683), alt.
Music: *Love Unknown*, John Ireland (1879-1962)

66. 66. 44. 44

Jesus Christ our Lord

459

1 And have the bright im -
2 The heaven that hides him

men - si - ties re - ceived our ris - en Lord, where
from our sight knows nei - ther near nor far; an

light-years frame the Plei - a - des and point O - ri - on's
al - tar can - dle sheds its light as sure - ly as a

sword? Do flam - ing suns his foot - steps trace through
star: and where his lov - ing peo - ple meet to

cor - ri - dors sub - lime, the Lord of in - ter -
share the gift di - vine, there stands he with un -

Interlude/Conclusion

stel - lar space and Con - quer - or of time?
hur - ry - ing feet; there heaven - ly splen - dors shine.

Words: Howard Chandler Robbins (1876-1952)
Music: *Halifax*, George Frideric Handel (1685-1759); adapt. David Hurd (b. 1950)

CMD

1 Al - le - lu - ia! sing to Je - sus! his the
*2 Al - le - lu - ia! not as or - phans are we
3 Al - le - lu - ia! Bread of Hea - ven, thou on
4 Al - le - lu - ia! King e - ter - nal, thee the
*5 Al - le - lu - ia! sing to Je - sus! his the

1 scep - ter, his the throne; Al - le - lu - ia! his the
2 left in sor - row now; Al - le - lu - ia! he is
3 earth our food, our stay! Al - le - lu - ia! here the
4 Lord of lords we own: Al - le - lu - ia! born of
5 scep - ter his the throne; Al - le - lu - ia! his the

1 tri - umph, his the vic - to - ry a - lone; Hark! the
2 near us, faith be - lieves, nor ques - tions how: though the
3 sin - ful flee to thee from day to day: In - ter -
4 Ma - ry, earth thy foot - stool, heaven thy throne: thou with -
5 tri - umph, his the vic - to - ry a - lone; Hark! the

1 songs of peace - ful Zi - on thun - der like a
2 cloud from sight re - ceived him, when the for - ty
3 ces - sor, friend of sin - ners, earth's Re - deem - er,
4 in the veil hast en - tered, robed in flesh, our
5 songs of ho - ly Zi - on thun - der like a

1 might - y flood; Je - sus out of ev - ery
2 days were o'er, shall our hearts for - get his
3 plead for me, where the songs of all the
4 great High Priest: thou on earth both Priest and
5 might - y flood; Je - sus out of ev - ery

1 na - tion hath re - deemed us by his blood.
2 prom - ise, "I am with you ev - er - more"?
3 sin - less sweep a - cross the crys - tal sea.
4 Vic - tim in the eu - cha - ris - tic feast.
5 na - tion hath re - deemed us by his blood.

Words: William Chatterton Dix (1837-1898)
Music: *Hyfrydol*, Rowland Hugh Prichard (1811-1887)

87. 87. D

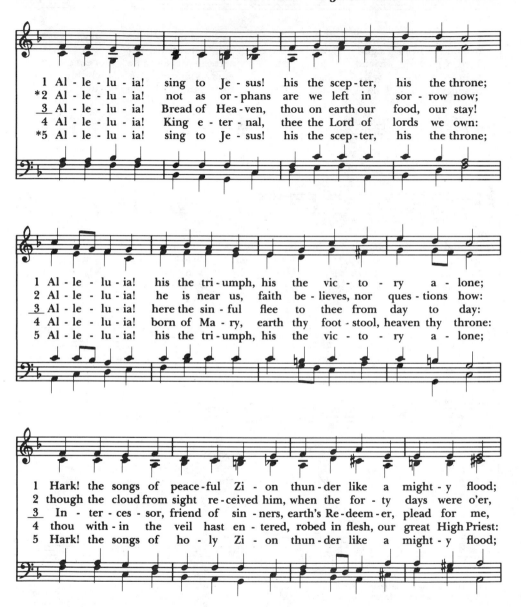

1 Al - le - lu - ia! sing to Je - sus! his the scep - ter, his the throne;
*2 Al - le - lu - ia! not as or - phans are we left in sor - row now;
3 Al - le - lu - ia! Bread of Hea - ven, thou on earth our food, our stay!
4 Al - le - lu - ia! King e - ter - nal, thee the Lord of lords we own:
*5 Al - le - lu - ia! sing to Je - sus! his the scep - ter, his the throne;

1 Al - le - lu - ia! his the tri - umph, his the vic - to - ry a - lone;
2 Al - le - lu - ia! he is near us, faith be - lieves, nor ques - tions how:
3 Al - le - lu - ia! here the sin - ful flee to thee from day to day:
4 Al - le - lu - ia! born of Ma - ry, earth thy foot - stool, heaven thy throne:
5 Al - le - lu - ia! his the tri - umph, his the vic - to - ry a - lone;

1 Hark! the songs of peace - ful Zi - on thun - der like a might - y flood;
2 though the cloud from sight re - ceived him, when the for - ty days were o'er,
3 In - ter - ces - sor, friend of sin - ners, earth's Re - deem - er, plead for me,
4 thou with - in the veil hast en - tered, robed in flesh, our great High Priest:
5 Hark! the songs of ho - ly Zi - on thun - der like a might - y flood;

1 Je - sus out of ev - ery na - tion hath re-deemed us by his blood.
2 shall our hearts for - get his prom - ise, "I am with you ev - er - more"?
3 where the songs of all the sin - less sweep a - cross the crys-tal sea.
4 thou on earth both Priest and Vic - tim in the eu - cha - ris - tic feast.
5 Je - sus out of ev - ery na - tion hath re-deemed us by his blood.

Words: William Chatterton Dix (1837-1898)
Music: *Alleluia*, Samuel Sebastian Wesley (1810-1876)

87. 87. D

Jesus Christ our Lord

462

1 The Lord will come and not be slow, his foot - steps can - not err;
2 Truth from the earth, like to a flower, shall bud and blos-som show;
3 Rise, God, judge thou the earth in might, this wick - ed earth re - dress;
4 The na - tions all whom thou hast made shall come, and all shall frame
5 For great thou art, and won-ders great by thy strong hand are done:

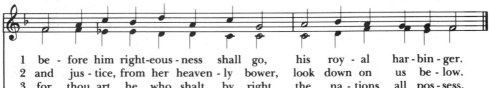

1 be - fore him right-eous - ness shall go, his roy - al har - bin - ger.
2 and jus - tice, from her heaven - ly bower, look down on us be - low.
3 for thou art he who shalt by right the na - tions all pos - sess.
4 to bow them low be - fore thee, Lord, and glo - ri - fy thy Name.
5 thou in thy ev - er - last - ing seat re - main - est God a - lone.

Words: John Milton (1608-1674), alt.
Music: *York*, melody from *The CL Psalmes of David*, 1615; adapt. *The Whole Booke of Psalmes*, 1621;
    harm. John Milton, Sr. (1563?-1647)

CM

1. He is the Way.   Fol-low him through the Land of Un-like -

ness;   you will see rare beasts ___ and have u - nique _____ ad -

ven - tures.   2. He is the Truth.   Seek him in the

King - dom of An - xi - e - ty: you will come to a great

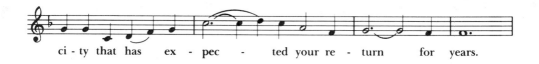

ci - ty that has ex - pec - ted your re - turn for years.

3. He is the Life.   Love him in the World of the Flesh: and

at your mar - riage all its oc - ca - sions shall dance for joy.

Words: W. H. Auden (1907-1973)
Music: *Hall*, David Hurd (b. 1950)

Irr.

1. He is the Way. Fol-low him through the Land of Un-like-ness;

you will see rare beasts and have u-nique ad - ven - tures.

2. He is the Truth. Seek him in the King-dom of Anx-i - e - ty:

you will come to a great ci - ty that has ex -

pect - ed your re - turn for years. 3. He is the

Life. Love him in the World of the Flesh: and at your

mar - riage all its oc - ca - sions shall dance for joy.

Words: W. H. Auden (1907-1973)
Music: *New Dance*, Richard Wetzel (b. 1935)

Irr.

Unison or harmony

1 E - ter - nal light, shine in my heart; e - ter - nal
2 E - ter - nal life, raise me from death; e - ter - nal
3 un - til by your most cost - ly grace, in - vit - ed

hope, lift up my eyes; e - ter - nal power, be
bright-ness, help me see; e - ter - nal Spi - rit,
by your ho - ly word, at last I come be -

my sup - port; e - ter - nal wis - dom, make me wise.
give me breath; e - ter - nal Sa - vior, come to me:
fore your face to know you, my e - ter - nal God.

Words: Christopher Idle (b. 1938); from a prayer of Alcuin (735?-804)
Music: *Ach bleib bei uns*, melody Samuel Scheidt (1587-1654); harm. Seth Calvisius (1556-1615)   LM

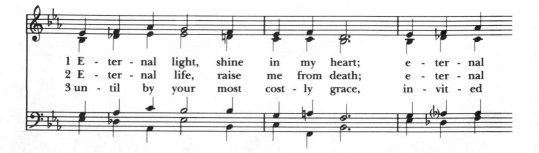

1 E - ter - nal light, shine in my heart; e - ter - nal
2 E - ter - nal life, raise me from death; e - ter - nal
3 un - til by your most cost - ly grace, in - vit - ed

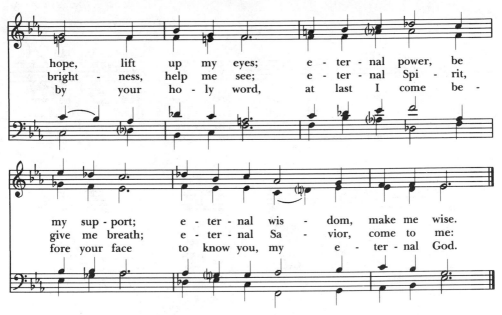

hope, lift up my eyes; e - ter - nal power, be
bright - ness, help me see; e - ter - nal Spi - rit,
by your ho - ly word, at last I come be -

my sup - port; e - ter - nal wis - dom, make me wise.
give me breath; e - ter - nal Sa - vior, come to me:
fore your face to know you, my e - ter - nal God.

Words: Christopher Idle (b. 1938); from a prayer by Alcuin (735?-804)
Music: *Jacob*, Jane Manton Marshall (b. 1924)

LM

Jesus Christ our Lord

467

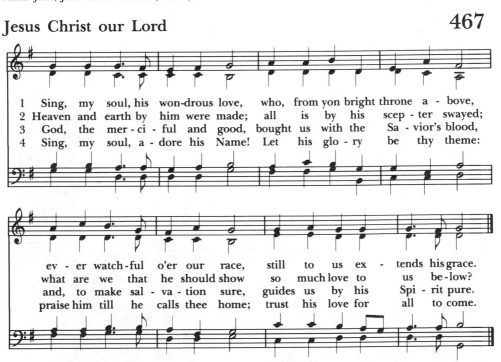

1 Sing, my soul, his won-drous love, who, from yon bright throne a - bove,
2 Heaven and earth by him were made; all is by his scep - ter swayed;
3 God, the mer - ci - ful and good, bought us with the Sa - vior's blood,
4 Sing, my soul, a - dore his Name! Let his glo - ry be thy theme:

ev - er watch-ful o'er our race, still to us ex - tends his grace.
what are we that he should show so much love to us be - low?
and, to make sal - va - tion sure, guides us by his Spi - rit pure.
praise him till he calls thee home; trust his love for all to come.

Words: Anon., 1800, alt.
Music: *St. Bees*, John Bacchus Dykes (1823-1876)

77. 77

468

1 It was poor lit-tle Je-sus, yes, yes;____ he was
2 It was poor lit-tle Je-sus, yes, yes;____ ____
3 It Little poor lit-tle Je-sus, yes, yes;____ they____
4 It was poor lit-tle Je-sus, yes, yes;____ he's____

born on____ Christ-mas, yes, yes;____ and __
child of____ Ma-ry, yes, yes;____ ____
nailed him to the cross, Lord, yes, yes;____ they____
ris-en from __ dark-ness, yes, yes;____ he's __

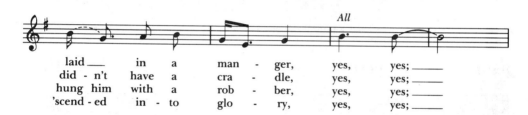

laid____ in a man-ger, yes, yes;____
did-n't have a cra-dle, yes, yes;____
hung him with a rob-ber, yes, yes;____
'scend-ed in-to glo-ry, yes, yes;____

was-n't that a pi-ty and a shame, Lord, Lord,
was-n't that a pi-ty and a shame, Lord, Lord,
was-n't that a pi-ty and a shame, Lord, Lord,
no__ more a pi-ty and a shame, Lord, Lord,

was-n't that a pi-ty and a shame?_____
was-n't that a pi-ty and a shame?_____
was-n't that a pi-ty and a shame?_____
no__ more a pi-ty and a shame._____

Words: Afro-American spiritual
Music: *Poor Little Jesus*, Afro-American spiritual; melody from *Songs and Games of American Children*, 1884-1911

Irr. with Refrain

1 There's a wide-ness in God's mer - cy like the wide-ness
2 There is no place where earth's sor - rows are more felt than
3 For the love of God is broad - er than the mea - sure

of the sea; there's a kind - ness in his jus -
up in heaven; there is no place where earth's fail -
of the mind; and the heart of the E - ter -

tice, which is more than lib - er - ty. There is wel - come
ings have such kind - ly judg - ment given. There is plen - ti -
nal is most won - der - ful - ly kind. If our love were

for the sin - ner, and more gra - ces for the good; there is mer - cy
ful re - demp - tion in the blood that has been shed; there is joy for
but more faith - ful, we should take him at his word; and our life would

Interlude/Conclusion

with the Sa - vior; there is heal - ing in his blood.
all the mem - bers in the sor - rows of the Head.
be thanks - giv - ing for the good-ness of the Lord.

Words: Frederick William Faber (1814-1863), alt.
Music: *St. Helena*, Calvin Hampton (1938-1984)

87. 87. D

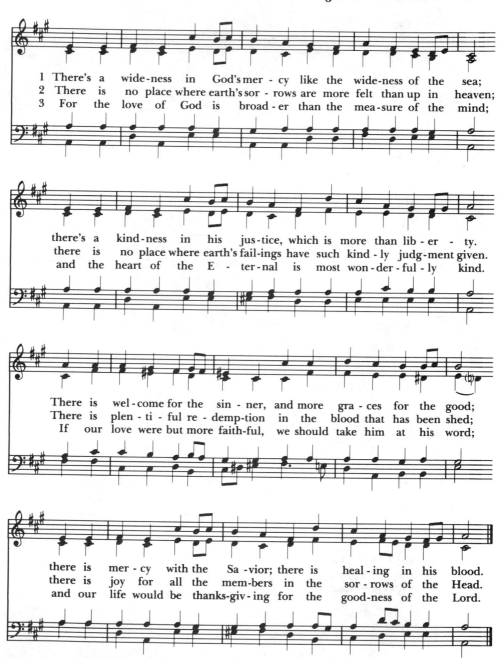

1 There's a wide-ness in God's mer-cy like the wide-ness of the sea;
2 There is no place where earth's sor-rows are more felt than up in heaven;
3 For the love of God is broad-er than the mea-sure of the mind;

there's a kind-ness in his jus-tice, which is more than lib-er-ty.
there is no place where earth's fail-ings have such kind-ly judg-ment given.
and the heart of the E-ter-nal is most won-der-ful-ly kind.

There is wel-come for the sin-ner, and more gra-ces for the good;
There is plen-ti-ful re-demp-tion in the blood that has been shed;
If our love were but more faith-ful, we should take him at his word;

there is mer-cy with the Sa-vior; there is heal-ing in his blood.
there is joy for all the mem-bers in the sor-rows of the Head.
and our life would be thanks-giv-ing for the good-ness of the Lord.

Words: Frederick William Faber (1814-1863), alt.
Music: *Beecher*, John Zundel (1815-1882), alt.

87. 87. D

1 We sing the praise of him who died, of
2 In-scribed up-on the cross we see in
3 The cross: it takes our guilt a-way, and
4 It makes the cow-ard spi-rit brave, and
5 The balm of life, the cure of woe, the

1 him who died up-on the cross; the sin-ner's hope let
2 shin-ing let-ters, God is love: he bears our sins up-
3 holds the faint-ing spi-rit up; it cheers with hope the
4 nerves the fee-ble arm for fight; it takes its ter-ror
5 mea-sure and the pledge of love, the sin-ner's ref-uge

1 sin de-ride; for this we count the world but loss.
2 on the tree: he brings us mer-cy from a-bove.
3 gloom-y day, and sweet-ens ev-ery bit-ter cup.
4 from the grave, and gilds the bed of death with light.
5 here be-low, the an-gel's theme in heaven a-bove.

Words: Thomas Kelly (1769-1855), alt.
Music: *Breslau*, melody from *Lochamer Gesangbuch*, ca. 1450; harm. Felix Mendelssohn (1809-1847)

LM

1 Hope of the world, thou Christ of great com - pas - sion,
2 Hope of the world, God's gift from high - est hea - ven,
3 Hope of the world, a - foot on dust - y high - ways,
4 Hope of the world, who by thy cross didst save us
5 Hope of the world, O Christ, o'er death vic - to - rious,

1 speak to our fear - ful hearts by con - flict rent.
2 bring - ing to hun - gry souls the bread of life,
3 show - ing to wan - dering souls the path of light,
4 from death and dark de - spair, from sin and guilt,
5 who by this sign didst con - quer grief and pain,

1 Save us, thy peo - ple, from con - sum - ing pas - sion,
2 still let thy Spi - rit un - to us be giv - en
3 walk thou be - side us lest the tempt - ing by - ways
4 we rend - er back the love thy mer - cy gave us;
5 we would be faith - ful to thy gos - pel glo - rious;

1 who by our own false hopes and aims are spent.
2 to heal earth's wounds and end her bit - ter strife.
3 lure us a - way from thee to end - less night.
4 take thou our lives, and use them as thou wilt.
5 thou art our Lord! Thou dost for ev - er reign!

Words: Georgia Harkness (1891-1974)
Music: *Donne secours*, melody from *Trente quatre pseaumes de David*, 1551

11 10. 11 10

Jesus Christ our Lord

Descant

Lift high the cross, the love of Christ pro - claim

Refrain

Lift high the cross, the love of Christ pro - claim

till all the world a - dore his sa - cred Name.

till all the world a - dore his sa - cred Name.

1 Led on their way by this tri - um - phant sign,
2 Each new - born ser - vant of the Cru - ci - fied
3 O Lord, once lift - ed on the glo - rious tree,
4 So shall our song of tri - umph ev - er be:

Repeat Refrain

the hosts of God in con - quering ranks com - bine.
bears on the brow the seal of him who died.
as thou hast prom - ised, draw the world to thee.
praise to the Cru - ci - fied for vic - to - ry.

Words: George William Kitchin (1827-1912); alt. Michael Robert Newbolt (1874-1956)
Music: *Crucifer*, Sydney Hugo Nicholson (1875-1947); desc. Richard Proulx (b. 1937)

10 10 with Refrain

1 When I sur - vey the won - drous cross where the young
2 For - bid it, Lord, that I should boast, save in the
3 See, from his head, his hands, his feet, sor - row and
4 Were the whole realm of na - ture mine, that were an

Prince of Glo - ry died, my rich - est gain I
cross of Christ, my God: all the vain things that
love flow min - gled down! Did e'er such love and
of - fering far too small; love so a - maz - ing,

count but loss, and pour con - tempt on all my pride.
charm me most, I sac - ri - fice them to his blood.
sor - row meet, or thorns com - pose so rich a crown?
so di - vine, de - mands my soul, my life, my all.

Words: Isaac Watts (1674-1748)
Music: *Rockingham*, from *Second Supplement to Psalmody in Miniature*, ca. 1780; harm. Edward Miller (1731-1807)   LM

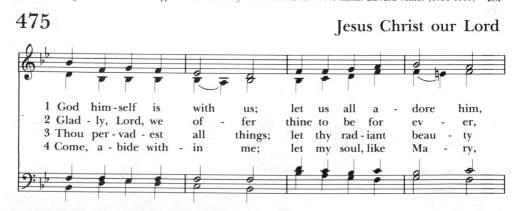

1 God him-self is with us; let us all a - dore him,
2 Glad - ly, Lord, we of - fer thine to be for ev - er,
3 Thou per - vad - est all things; let thy rad - iant beau - ty
4 Come, a - bide with - in me; let my soul, like Ma - ry,

and with awe ap-pear be - fore him. God is here with-
soul and life and each en - deav - or. Help us to sur-
light mine eyes to see my du - ty. As the ten - der
be thine earth - ly sanc - tu - ar - y. Come, in - dwell-ing

in us; souls in si - lence fear him, hum-bly, fer - vent-
rend - er earth's de - ceit - ful trea - sures, pride of life, and
flow - ers ea - ger - ly un - fold them, to the sun - light
Spi - rit, with trans - fi - guring splen - dor; love and hon - or

ly draw near him. Now his own who have known
sin - ful plea - sures: thou a - lone shalt be known
calm - ly hold them, so let me qui - et - ly
will I ren - der. Where I go here be - low,

God, in wor-ship low - ly, yield their spi - rits whol - ly.
Lord of all our be - ing, life's true way de - cree - ing.
in thy rays im - bue me; let thy light shine through me.
let me bow be - fore thee, know thee, and a - dore thee.

Words: Gerhardt Tersteegen (1697-1769); tr. *Hymnal 1940*, alt.;
st. 3, tr. Henry Sloane Coffin (1877-1954)
Music: *Tysk*, from *Psalm und Choralbuch*, 1719

668. 668. 666

1 Can we by search-ing find out God or for - mu - late his ways?
2 Al - though his be - ing is too bright for hu - man eyes to scan,
3 Our boast-ful - ness is turned to shame, our prof - it counts as loss,
4 There God breaks in up - on our search, makes birth and death his own;

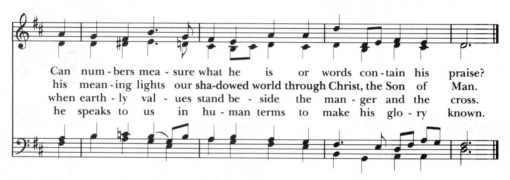

Can num - bers mea - sure what he is or words con - tain his praise?
his mean-ing lights our sha-dowed world through Christ, the Son of Man.
when earth - ly val - ues stand be - side the man - ger and the cross.
he speaks to us in hu - man terms to make his glo - ry known.

Words: Elizabeth Cosnett (b. 1936), alt.
Music: *Epworth*, melody att. Charles Wesley (1757-1834), alt.;
      harm. Martin Fallas Shaw (1875-1958), alt.

CM

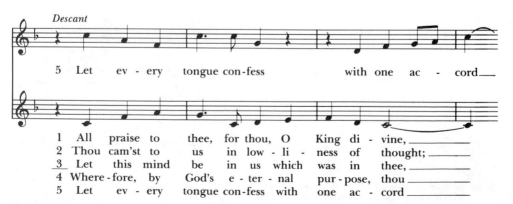

Descant

5 Let ev - ery tongue con-fess with one ac - cord___

1 All praise to thee, for thou, O King di - vine, ___
2 Thou cam'st to us in low - li - ness of thought; ___
3 Let this mind be in us which was in thee, ___
4 Where-fore, by God's e - ter - nal pur-pose, thou ___
5 Let ev - ery tongue con-fess with one ac - cord ___

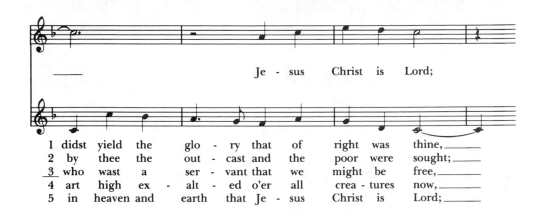

Je - sus   Christ   is   Lord;

1	didst	yield	the	glo	-	ry	that	of	right	was	thine,
2	by	thee	the	out	-	cast	and	the	poor	were	sought;
3	who	wast	a	ser	-	vant	that	we	might	be	free,
4	art	high	ex	-	alt	-	ed	o'er	all	crea - tures	now,
5	in	heaven	and	earth	that	Je	-	sus	Christ	is	Lord;

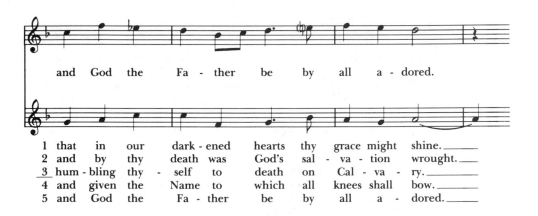

and   God   the   Fa - ther   be   by   all   a - dored.

1	that	in	our	dark - ened	hearts	thy	grace might	shine.
2	and	by	thy	death was	God's	sal - va - tion	wrought.
3	hum - bling	thy - self	to	death	on	Cal - va - ry.
4	and	given	the	Name to	which	all	knees shall	bow.
5	and	God	the	Fa - ther	be	by	all	a - dored.

Al - le - lu - ia!   A - men.

Al - le - lu - ia!   A - men.

Words: F. Bland Tucker (1895-1984)
Music: *Engelberg*, Charles Villiers Stanford (1852-1924); desc. Richard Proulx (b. 1937)   10 10 10 with Alleluia

1 Je - sus, our might - y Lord, our strength in sad - ness,___
2 Good shep-herd of your sheep, your own de - fend - ing,___
3 Glo - rious their life who sing, with glad thanks - giv - ing,___

the Fa - ther's con - quering Word, true source of glad - ness;___
in love your chil - dren keep to life un - end - ing.___
true hymns to Christ the King in all their liv - ing:___

your Name we glo - ri - fy, O Je - sus, throned on high;
You are your-self the Way: lead us then day by day
all who con - fess his Name, come then with hearts a - flame;

you gave your - self to die for our sal - va - tion.
in your own steps, we pray, O Lord most ho - ly.
the God of peace ac - claim as Lord and Sa - vior.

Words: Clement of Alexandria (170?-220?); para. F. Bland Tucker (1895-1984), rev.
Music: *Monk's Gate*, Sussex folk melody; adapt. Ralph Vaughan Williams (1872-1958)

11 11. 12 11

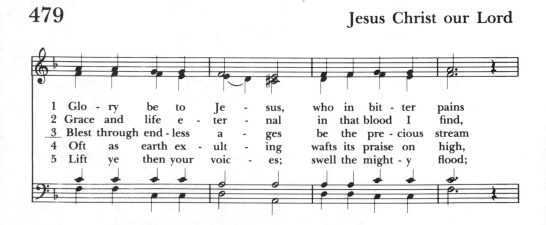

1 Glo - ry be to Je - sus, who in bit - ter pains
2 Grace and life e - ter - nal in that blood I find,
3 Blest through end - less a - ges be the pre - cious stream
4 Oft as earth ex - ult - ing wafts its praise on high,
5 Lift ye then your voic - es; swell the might - y flood;

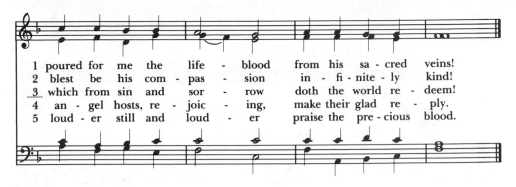

1 poured for me the life - blood from his sa - cred veins!
2 blest be his com - pas - sion in - fi - nite - ly kind!
3 which from sin and sor - row doth the world re - deem!
4 an - gel hosts, re - joic - ing, make their glad re - ply.
5 loud - er still and loud - er praise the pre - cious blood.

Words: Italian, 18th cent.; tr. Edward Caswall (1814-1878), alt.
Music: *Wem in Leidenstagen*, Friedrich Filitz (1804-1860)

65. 65

Jesus Christ our Lord

480

1 When Je - sus left his Fa-ther's throne, he chose an hum - ble birth;
2 Sweet were his words and kind his look, when mo-thers round him pressed;
3 When Je - sus in - to Zi - on rode, the chil - dren sang a - round;

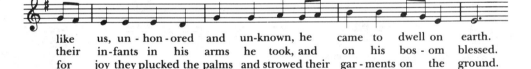

like us, un - hon - ored and un-known, he came to dwell on earth.
their in-fants in his arms he took, and on his bos - om blessed.
for joy they plucked the palms and strowed their gar - ments on the ground.

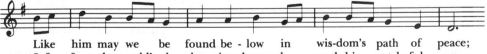

Like him may we be found be - low in wis-dom's path of peace;
Safe from the world's al - lur - ing harms, be - neath his watch-ful eye,
Ho - san - na our glad voic - es raise, ho - san - na to our King!

like him in grace and know-ledge grow as years and strength in - crease.
thus in the cir - cle of his arms may we for ev - er lie.
Should we for-get our Sa - vior's praise, the stones them-selves would sing.

Words: James Montgomery (1771-1854)
Music: *Kingsfold*, English folk melody; adapt. Ralph Vaughan Williams (1872-1958)

CMD

481

Jesus Christ our Lord

1 Re - joice, the Lord is King! Your Lord and King a - dore! Mor -
2 The Lord the Sa - vior reigns, the God of truth and love: when
3 His king-dom can - not fail; he rules o'er earth and heaven; the
4 Re - joice in glo - rious hope! Our Lord the Judge shall come, and

Refrain

tals, give thanks and sing, and tri - umph ev - er - more.
he had purged our stains, he took his seat a - bove. Lift
keys of death and hell to Christ the Lord are given.
take his ser - vants up to their e - ter - nal home.

1-3

up your heart! lift up your voice! Re - joice! a - gain I say, re -

Final Ending

joice! up your heart! lift up your voice! Re - joice! a -

gain I say, re - joice!

Words: Charles Wesley (1707-1788), alt.
Music: *Gopsal*, George Frideric Handel (1685-1759); arr. John Wilson (b. 1905)   66. 66 with Refrain

482

Jesus Christ our Lord

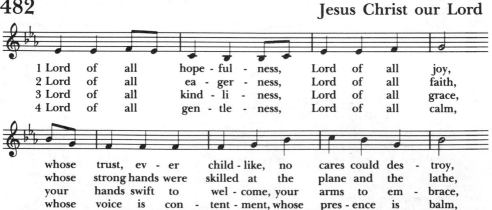

1 Lord of all hope - ful - ness, Lord of all joy,
2 Lord of all ea - ger - ness, Lord of all faith,
3 Lord of all kind - li - ness, Lord of all grace,
4 Lord of all gen - tle - ness, Lord of all calm,

whose trust, ev - er child - like, no cares could des - troy,
whose strong hands were skilled at the plane and the lathe,
your hands swift to wel - come, your arms to em - brace,
whose voice is con - tent - ment, whose pres - ence is balm,

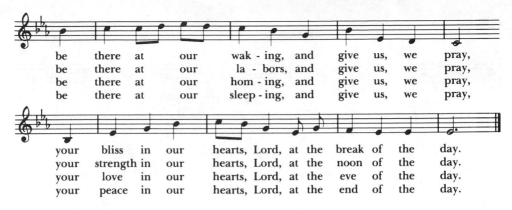

be there at our wak-ing, and give us, we pray,
be there at our la-bors, and give us, we pray,
be there at our hom-ing, and give us, we pray,
be there at our sleep-ing, and give us, we pray,

your bliss in our hearts, Lord, at the break of the day.
your strength in our hearts, Lord, at the noon of the day.
your love in our hearts, Lord, at the eve of the day.
your peace in our hearts, Lord, at the end of the day.

Words: Jan Struther (1901-1953)
Music: *Slane*, Irish ballad melody; adapt. *The Church Hymnary*, 1927

10 11. 11 12

Jesus Christ our Lord

483

1 The head that once was crowned with thorns is crowned with glo-ry now;
2 The high-est place that heaven af-fords is his, is his by right,
3 the joy of all who dwell a-bove, the joy of all be-low,
4 To them the cross with all its shame, with all its grace is given;
5 They suf-fer with their Lord be-low, they reign with him a-bove,

1 a roy-al di-a-dem a-dorns the might-y vic-tor's brow.
2 the King of kings, and Lord of lords, and heaven's e-ter-nal Light;
3 to whom he man-i-fests his love and grants his Name to know.
4 their name, an ev-er-last-ing name; their joy, the joy of heaven.
5 their prof-it and their joy to know the mys-ter-y of his love.

6 The cross he bore is life and health,
    though shame and death to him:
  his people's hope, his people's wealth,
    their everlasting theme.

Words: Thomas Kelly (1769-1855)
Music: *St. Magnus*, melody *Divine Companion*, 1707; harm. William Henry Monk (1823-1889),
    after John Pyke Hullah (19th cent.)

CM

1 Praise the Lord through ev - ery na - tion; his ho - ly
2 Je - sus, Lord, our Cap - tain glo - rious, o'er sin, and

arm hath wrought sal - va - tion; ex - alt him on his
death, and hell vic - to - rious, wis - dom and might to

Fa - ther's throne. Praise your King, ye Chris - tian le -
thee be - long: we con - fess, pro - claim, a - dore

gions, who now pre - pares in heaven - ly re -
thee; we bow the knee, we fall be - fore

gions un - fail - ing man - sions for his own: with
thee; thy love hence - forth shall be our song. The

voice and min - strel - sy ex - tol his ma - jes -
cross mean-while we bear, the crown ere-long to

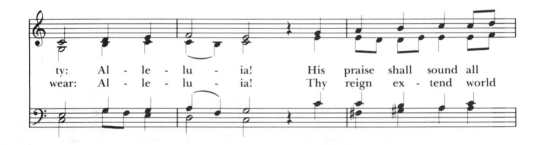

ty: Al - le - lu - ia! His praise shall sound all
wear: Al - le - lu - ia! Thy reign ex - tend world

na - ture round, and hymns on ev - ery tongue a - bound.
with - out end; let praise from all to thee a - scend.

Words: Rhijnvis Feith (1753-1824); para. James Montgomery (1771-1854), alt.
Music: *Wachet auf*, melody Hans Sachs (1494-1576); adapt. Philipp Nicolai (1556-1608);
    arr. and harm. Johann Sebastian Bach (1685-1750)

Irr.

1 Praise the Lord through ev - ery na - tion;
2 Je - sus, Lord, our Cap - tain glo - rious,

his ho - ly arm hath wrought sal - va - tion; ex - alt him
o'er sin, and death, and hell vic - to - rious, wis - dom and

on his Fa - ther's throne. Praise your King, ye Chris - tian
might to thee be - long: we con - fess, pro - claim, a -

le - gions, who now pre - pares in heaven - ly re - gions
dore thee; we bow the knee, we fall be - fore thee;

un - fail - ing man - sions for his own:
thy love hence - forth shall be our song.

with voice and min - strel - sy ex - tol his ma - jes - ty:
The cross mean - while we bear, the crown ere - long to wear:

Al - le - lu - ia! His praise shall sound all na - ture round,
Al - le - lu - ia! Thy reign ex - tend world with - out end;

and hymns on ev - ery tongue a - bound.
let praise from all to thee a - scend.

Words: Rhijnvis Feith (1753-1824); para. James Montgomery (1771-1854), alt.
Music: *Wachet auf,* melody Hans Sachs (1494-1576); adapt. Philipp Nicolai (1556-1608)   Irr.

1 Ho - sanna to the living Lord! Hosanna to the incarnate Word! To Christ, Creator Savior, King, let earth, let heaven, hosanna sing!

2 Hosanna Lord! thine angels cry; Hosanna Lord! thy saints reply; above, beneath us, and around, both dead and living swell the sound:

3 O Savior, with protecting care abide in this thy house of prayer, where we assembled in thy Name, in faith, thy parting promise claim.

4 But, chiefest, in our cleansed breast, Eternal! bid thy Spirit rest; and make our secret soul to be a temple pure and worthy thee.

5 So in the last and dreadful day, when earth and heaven shall melt away, thy flock, redeemed from sinful stain, shall swell the sound of praise again.

Refrain

Hosanna Lord! Hosanna in the highest!

Words: Reginald Heber (1783-1826), alt.
Music: *Hosanna*, John Bacchus Dykes (1823-1876)

LM with Refrain

487

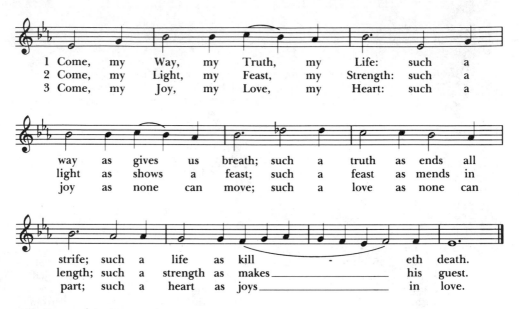

1 Come, my Way, my Truth, my Life: such a
2 Come, my Light, my Feast, my Strength: such a
3 Come, my Joy, my Love, my Heart: such a

way as gives us breath; such a truth as ends all
light as shows a feast; such a feast as mends in
joy as none can move; such a love as none can

strife; such a life as kill - eth death.
length; such a strength as makes his guest.
part; such a heart as joys in love.

Words: George Herbert (1593-1633)
Music: *The Call*, Ralph Vaughan Williams (1872-1958)

77. 77

488

1 Be thou my vi - sion, O Lord of my heart;
2 Be thou my wis - dom, and thou my true word;
3 High King of hea - ven, when vic - to - ry is won,

all else be nought to me, save that thou art—
I ev - er with thee and thou with me, Lord;
may I reach hea - ven's joys, bright hea - ven's Sun!

thou my best thought, by day or by night,
thou my great Fa - ther; thine own may I be;
Heart of my heart, what - ev - er be - fall,

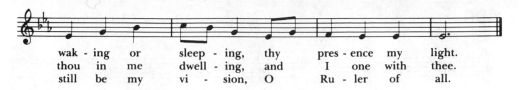

wak - ing or sleep - ing, thy pres - ence my light.
thou in me dwell - ing, and I one with thee.
still be my vi - sion, O Ru - ler of all.

Words: Irish, ca. 700; versified Mary Elizabeth Byrne (1880-1931);
tr. Eleanor H. Hull (1860-1935), alt.
Music: *Slane*, Irish ballad melody; adapt. *The Church Hymnary*, 1927

10 10. 9 10

Jesus Christ our Lord

489

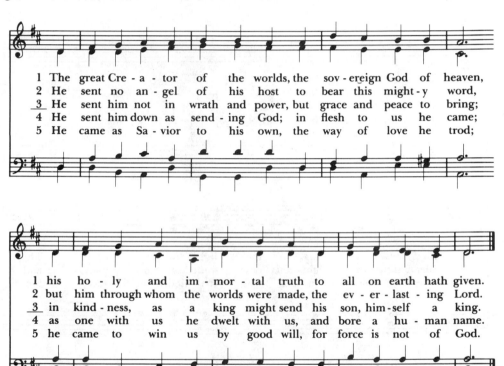

1 The great Cre - a - tor of the worlds, the sov - ereign God of heaven,
2 He sent no an - gel of his host to bear this might - y word,
3 He sent him not in wrath and power, but grace and peace to bring;
4 He sent him down as send - ing God; in flesh to us he came;
5 He came as Sa - vior to his own, the way of love he trod;

1 his ho - ly and im - mor - tal truth to all on earth hath given.
2 but him through whom the worlds were made, the ev - er - last - ing Lord.
3 in kind - ness, as a king might send his son, him - self a king.
4 as one with us he dwelt with us, and bore a hu - man name.
5 he came to win us by good will, for force is not of God.

6 Not to oppress, but summon all
their truest life to find,
in love God sent his Son to save,
not to condemn mankind.

Words: *Epistle to Diognetus*, ca. 150; tr. F. Bland Tucker (1895-1984), rev.
Music: *Tallis' Ordinal*, Thomas Tallis (1505?-1585)

CM

1 I want to walk as a child of the light.
2 I want to see___ the bright-ness of God.
3 I'm look-ing for___ the com-ing of Christ.

I want to fol-low Je - sus.
I want to look at Je - sus.
I want to be with Je - sus.

God set the stars to give light to the world. The
Clear sun of right-eous-ness, shine on my path, and
When we have run___ with pa-tience the race, we

star of my life___ is Je - sus.
show me the way to the Fa - ther.
shall know the joy___ of Je - sus.

In him there is no dark-ness at all. The night and the day are both a-like. The Lamb is the light of the ci-ty of God. Shine in my heart, Lord Je - sus.

Words: Kathleen Thomerson (b. 1934)
Music: *Houston*, Kathleen Thomerson (b. 1934)

Irr. with Refrain

1 Where is this stu - pen-dous stran-ger? Pro - phets, shep-herds, kings, ad - vise.
2 O Most Might - y! O Most Ho - ly! Far be - yond the ser-aph's thought:
3 O the mag - ni - tude of meek-ness! Worth from worth im - mor - tal sprung;
4 God all - boun-teous, all - cre - a - tive, whom no ills from good dis - suade,

Lead me to my Mas - ter's man - ger, show me where my Sa - vior lies.
art thou then so weak and low - ly as un-heed - ed pro - phets taught?
O the strength of in - fant weak-ness, if e - ter - nal is so young!
is in - car - nate, and a na - tive of the ve - ry world he made.

Words: Christopher Smart (1722-1771), alt.
Music: *Kit Smart*, Alec Wyton (b. 1921)

87. 87

Music: Copyright © 1969 by Hope Publishing Company. International Copyright Secured. All Rights Reserved. Used by Permission.

1 Sing, ye faith - ful, sing with glad - ness, wake your no - blest,
2 Sing how he came forth from hea - ven, bowed him-self to
3 So, he tast - ed death for mor - tals, he, of hu - man -
4 Now on high, yet ev - er with us, from his Fa - ther's

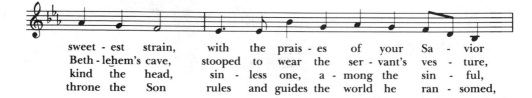

sweet - est strain, with the prais - es of your Sa - vior
Beth - le-hem's cave, stooped to wear the ser - vant's ves - ture,
kind the head, sin - less one, a - mong the sin - ful,
throne the Son rules and guides the world he ran - somed,

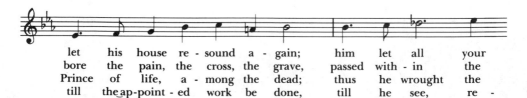

let his house re - sound a - gain; him let all your
bore the pain, the cross, the grave, passed with - in the
Prince of life, a - mong the dead; thus he wrought the
till the ap-point - ed work be done, till he see, re -

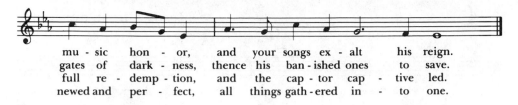

mu - sic hon - or, and your songs ex - alt his reign.
gates of dark - ness, thence his ban - ished ones to save.
full re - demp - tion, and the cap - tor cap - tive led.
newed and per - fect, all things gath - ered in - to one.

Words: John Ellerton (1826-1893), alt.
Music: *Finnian*, Christopher Dearnley (b. 1930)

87. 87. 87

Jesus Christ our Lord

493

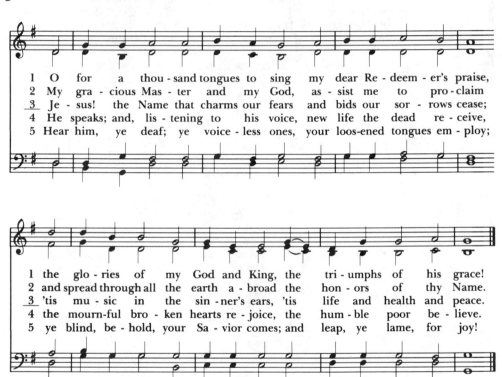

1 O for a thou-sand tongues to sing my dear Re-deem-er's praise,
2 My gra-cious Mas-ter and my God, as-sist me to pro-claim
3 Je-sus! the Name that charms our fears and bids our sor-rows cease;
4 He speaks; and, lis-tening to his voice, new life the dead re-ceive,
5 Hear him, ye deaf; ye voice-less ones, your loos-ened tongues em-ploy;

1 the glo-ries of my God and King, the tri-umphs of his grace!
2 and spread through all the earth a-broad the hon-ors of thy Name.
3 'tis mu-sic in the sin-ner's ears, 'tis life and health and peace.
4 the mourn-ful bro-ken hearts re-joice, the hum-ble poor be-lieve.
5 ye blind, be-hold, your Sa-vior comes; and leap, ye lame, for joy!

6 Glory to God and praise and love
be now and ever given
by saints below and saints above,
the Church in earth and heaven.

Words: Charles Wesley (1707-1788), alt.
Music: *Azmon*, Carl Gotthilf Gläser (1784-1829); adapt. and arr. Lowell Mason (1792-1872)

CM

Descant

5 Crown him the Lord of heaven, en-throned a-bove;

1 Crown him with man - y crowns, the Lamb up - on his throne; Hark!
2 Crown him the Son of God be - fore the worlds be - gan, and
3 Crown him the Lord of life, who tri - umphed o'er the grave, and
4 Crown him of lords the Lord, who o - ver all doth reign, who
5 Crown him the Lord of heaven, en-throned in worlds a - bove; crown

crown him to whom is given, the won - drous name of Love.

1 how the heaven - ly an - them drowns all mu - sic but its own; a-
2 ye, who tread where he hath trod, crown him the Son of man; who
3 rose vic - to - rious in the strife for those he came to save; his
4 once on earth, the in - car - nate Word, for ran - somed sin - ners slain, now
5 him the King, to whom is given, the won - drous name of Love. Crown

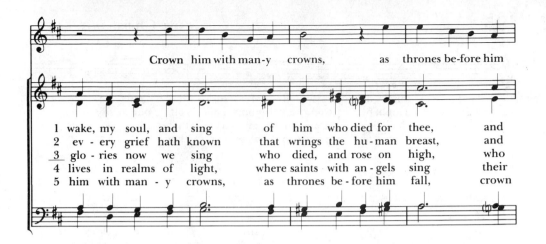

Crown him with man-y crowns, as thrones be-fore him

1 wake, my soul, and sing of him who died for thee, and
2 ev-ery grief hath known that wrings the hu-man breast, and
3 glo-ries now we sing who died, and rose on high, who
4 lives in realms of light, where saints with an-gels sing their
5 him with man-y crowns, as thrones be-fore him fall, crown

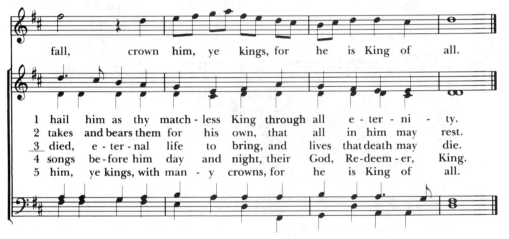

fall, crown him, ye kings, for he is King of all.

1 hail him as thy match-less King through all e-ter-ni-ty.
2 takes and bears them for his own, that all in him may rest.
3 died, e-ter-nal life to bring, and lives that death may die.
4 songs be-fore him day and night, their God, Re-deem-er, King.
5 him, ye kings, with man-y crowns, for he is King of all.

Words: Matthew Bridges (1800-1894)
Music: *Diademata*, George Job Elvey (1816-1893); desc. Richard Proulx (b. 1937)

SMD

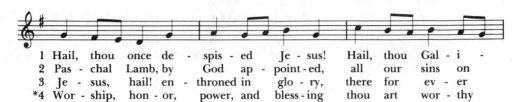

1 Hail, thou once de - spis - ed Je - sus! Hail, thou Gal - i -
2 Pas - chal Lamb, by God ap - point - ed, all our sins on
3 Je - sus, hail! en - throned in glo - ry, there for ev - er
*4 Wor - ship, hon - or, power, and bless - ing thou art wor - thy

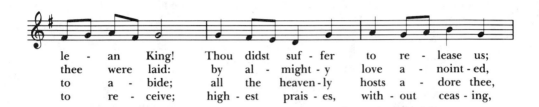

le - an King! Thou didst suf - fer to re - lease us;
thee were laid: by al - might - y love a - noint - ed,
to a - bide; all the heaven - ly hosts a - dore thee,
to re - ceive; high - est prais - es, with - out ceas - ing,

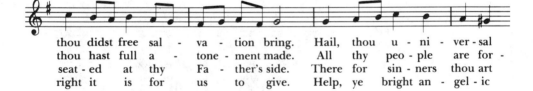

thou didst free sal - va - tion bring. Hail, thou u - ni - ver - sal
thou hast full a - tone - ment made. All thy peo - ple are for -
seat - ed at thy Fa - ther's side. There for sin - ners thou art
right it is for us to give. Help, ye bright an - gel - ic

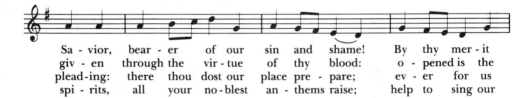

Sa - vior, bear - er of our sin and shame! By thy mer - it
giv - en through the vir - tue of thy blood: o - pened is the
plead - ing: there thou dost our place pre - pare; ev - er for us
spi - rits, all your no - blest an - thems raise; help to sing our

we find fa - vor: life is giv - en through thy Name.
gate of hea - ven, re - con - ciled are we with God.
in - ter - ced - ing, till in glo - ry we ap - pear.
Sa - vior's mer - its, help to chant Em - man - uel's praise!

Words: John Bakewell (1721-1819) and Martin Madan (1726-1790), alt.
Music: *In Babilone*, melody from *Oude en Nieuwe Hollantse Boerenlities en Contradanseu*, 1710

87. 87. D

1 How bright ap - pears the Morn-ing Star, with mer - cy beam -
2 Though cir - cled by the hosts on high, he deigned to cast
3 Re - joice, ye heavens; thou earth, re - ply; with praise, ye sin -

ing from a - far; the host of heaven re - joic - es;
a pit - y̆ing eye up - on his help - less crea - ture;
ners, fill the sky, for this his In - car - na - tion.

O right - eous Branch, O Jes - se's Rod! Thou Son of Man
the whole cre - a - tion's Head and Lord, by high-est ser -
In - car - nate God, put forth thy power, ride on, ride on,

and Son of God! We, too, will lift our voic - es:
a - phim a - dored, as - sumed our ve - ry na - ture;
great Con-quer - or, till all know thy sal - va - tion.

Je - sus, Je - sus! Ho - ly, ho - ly, yet most low - ly,
Je - sus, grant us, through thy mer - it, to in - her - it
A - men, a - men! Al - le - lu - ia, al - le - lu - ia!

draw thou near us; great Em - man - uel, come and hear us.
thy sal - va - tion; hear, O hear our sup - pli - ca - tion.
Praise be giv - en ev - er - more, by earth and hea - ven.

Words: William Mercer (1811-1873), after Philipp Nicolai (1556-1608)
Music: *Wie schön leuchtet,* melody att. Philipp Nicolai (1556-1608)

Irr.

1 How bright ap - pears the Morn-ing Star, with mer - cy beam-ing
2 Though cir - cled by the hosts on high, he deigned to cast a
3 Re - joice, ye heavens; thou earth, re - ply; with praise, ye sin - ners,

from a - far; the host of heaven re - joic - es;
pit - ying eye up - on his help - less crea - ture;
fill the sky, for this his In - car - na - tion.

O right-eous Branch, O Jes - se's Rod! Thou Son of Man and
the whole cre - a - tion's Head and Lord, by high-est ser - a -
In - car - nate God, put forth thy power, ride on, ride on, great

Son of God! We, too, will lift our voic - es:
phim a - dored, as - sumed our ve - ry na - ture;
Con - quer - or, till all know thy sal - va - tion.

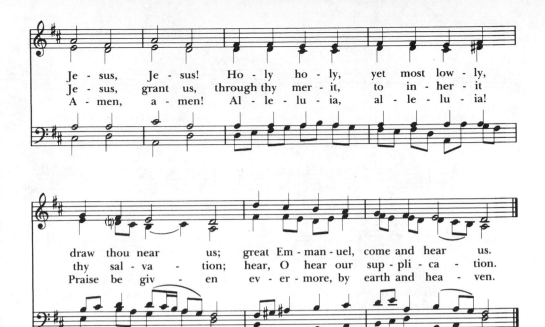

Je - sus, Je - sus! Ho - ly ho - ly, yet most low - ly,
draw thou near us; great Em - man - uel, come and hear us.

Je - sus, grant us, through thy mer - it, to in - her - it
thy sal - va - tion; hear, O hear our sup - pli - ca - tion.

A - men, a - men! Al - le - lu - ia, al - le - lu - ia!
Praise be giv - en ev - er - more, by earth and hea - ven.

Words: William Mercer (1811-1873), after Philipp Nicolai (1556-1608)
Music: *Wie schön leuchtet*, melody att. Philipp Nicolai, (1556-1608);
    arr. and harm. Johann Sebastian Bach (1685-1750)

Irr.

1 Be - neath the cross of Je - sus I fain would take my stand,
2 Up - on the cross of Je - sus mine eyes at times can see
3 I take, O cross, thy sha - dow for my a - bid - ing place;

the sha - dow of a might - y rock with - in a wea - ry land,
the ve - ry dy - ing form of one who suf - fered there for me;
I ask no o - ther sun - shine than the sun - shine of his face;

a home with - in the wil - der - ness, a rest up - on the way,
and from my smit - ten heart with tears two won - ders I con - fess:
con - tent to let my pride go by, to know no gain nor loss,

from the burn - ing of the noon - tide heat and the bur - den of the day.
the __ won - ders of re - deem - ing love and __ my un - wor - thi - ness.
my __ sin - ful self my on - ly shame, my __ glo - ry all the cross.

Words: Elizabeth Cecilia Clephane (1830-1869), alt.
Music: *St. Christopher*, Frederick Charles Maker (1844-1927)

76. 86. 86. 86

Jesus Christ our Lord

Unison or harmony

Lord God, you now have set your ser-vant free to go in
peace as prom-ised in your word; my eyes have seen the
Sa - vior, Christ the Lord, pre-pared by you for all the
world to see, to shine on na - tions trapped in dark - est night,
the glo - ry of your peo - ple, and their light.

Words: Rae E. Whitney (b. 1927); para. of The Song of Simeon
Music: *Song 1*, melody and bass Orlando Gibbons (1583-1625);
harm. *Hymns for Church and School*, 1964

10 10. 10 10. 10 10

1 Cre-a-tor Spi-rit, by whose aid the world's foun-
da-tions first were laid, come, vis-it ev-ery hum-ble
mind; come, pour thy joys on hu-man-kind; from sin and
sor-row set us free, and make thy tem-ples wor-thy thee.

2 O Source of un-cre-at-ed light, the Fa-ther's
prom-ised Par-a-clete, thrice ho-ly Fount, thrice ho-ly
Fire, our hearts with heaven-ly love in-spire; come, and thy
sa-cred unc-tion bring to sanc-ti-fy us while we sing.

3 Plen-teous of grace, come from on high, rich in thy
seven-fold en-er-gy; make us e-ter-nal truth re-
ceive, and prac-tice all that we be-lieve; give us thy-
self, that we may see the Fa-ther and the Son by thee.

Words: John Dryden (1631-1700); tr. of *Veni Creator Spiritus*
Music: *Surrey*, melody Henry Carey (1690?-1743)

88. 88. 88

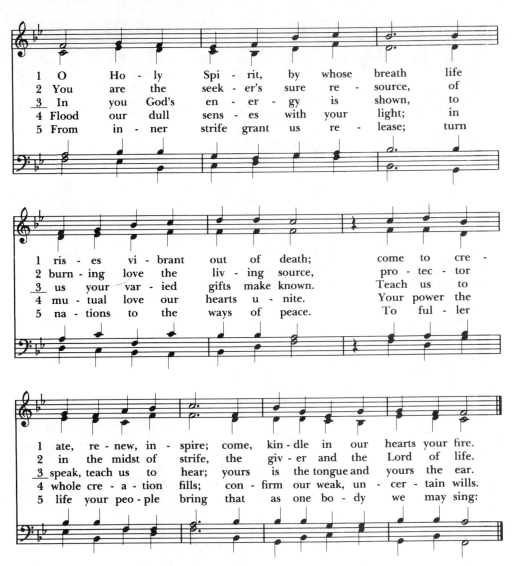

1 O Ho - ly Spi - rit, by whose breath life
2 You are the seek - er's sure re - source, of
3 In you God's en - er - gy is shown, to
4 Flood our dull sens - es with your light; in
5 From in - ner strife grant us re - lease; turn

1 ris - es vi - brant out of death; come to cre -
2 burn - ing love the liv - ing source, pro - tec - tor
3 us your var - ied gifts make known. Teach us to
4 mu - tual love our hearts u - nite. Your power the
5 na - tions to the ways of peace. To ful - ler

1 ate, re - new, in - spire; come, kin - dle in our hearts your fire.
2 in the midst of strife, the giv - er and the Lord of life.
3 speak, teach us to hear; yours is the tongue and yours the ear.
4 whole cre - a - tion fills; con - firm our weak, un - cer - tain wills.
5 life your peo - ple bring that as one bo - dy we may sing:

6 Praise to the Father, Christ, his Word,
and to the Spirit: God the Lord,
to whom all honor, glory be
both now and for eternity.

Words: Att. Rabanus Maurus (776-856); tr. John Webster Grant (b. 1919), alt.; para. of *Veni Creator Spiritus*
Music: *Komm, Gott Schöpfer*, melody from *Eyn Enchiridion*, 1524; harm. *The Lutheran Hymnal*, 1941   LM

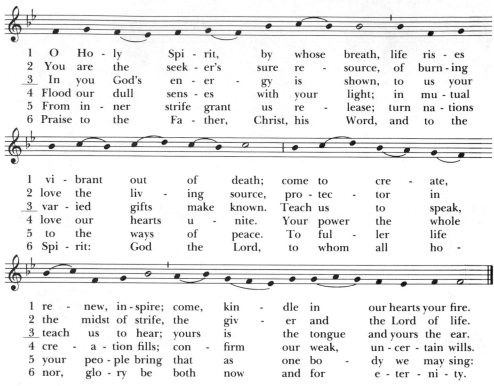

1 O Ho - ly Spi - rit, by whose breath, life ris - es
2 You are the seek - er's sure re - source, of burn - ing
3 In you God's en - er - gy is shown, to us your
4 Flood our dull sens - es with your light; in mu - tual
5 From in - ner strife grant us re - lease; turn na - tions
6 Praise to the Fa - ther, Christ, his Word, and to the

1 vi - brant out of death; come to cre - ate,
2 love the liv - ing source, pro - tec - tor in
3 var - ied gifts make known. Teach us to speak,
4 love our hearts u - nite. Your power the whole
5 to the ways of peace. To ful - ler life
6 Spi - rit: God the Lord, to whom all ho -

1 re - new, in - spire; come, kin - dle in our hearts your fire.
2 the midst of strife, the giv - er and the Lord of life.
3 teach us to hear; yours is the tongue and yours the ear.
4 cre - a - tion fills; con - firm our weak, un - cer - tain wills.
5 your peo - ple bring that as one bo - dy we may sing:
6 nor, glo - ry be both now and for e - ter - ni - ty.

Words: Att. Rabanus Maurus (776-856); tr. John Webster Grant (b. 1919), alt.;
　　　para. of *Veni Creator Spiritus*
Music: *Veni Creator Spiritus*, plainsong, Mode 8　　　　　　　　　　　　LM

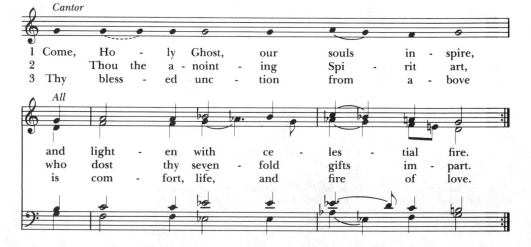

Cantor

1 Come, Ho - ly Ghost, our souls in - spire,
2 Thou the a - noint - ing Spi - rit art,
3 Thy bless - ed unc - tion from a - bove

All

and light - en with ce - les - tial fire.
who dost thy seven - fold gifts im - part.
is com - fort, life, and fire of love.

Cantor

4 En - a - ble with per - pet - ual light
5 A - noint and cheer our soil - ed face
6 Keep far our foes, give peace at home:
7 Teach us to know the Fa - ther, Son,

All

the dull - ness of our blind - ed sight.
with the a - bun - dance of thy grace.
where thou art guide, no ill can come.
and thee, of both, to be but One,

Cantor

8 that through the a - ges all a - long,

All

this may be our end - less song:

Cantor

9 praise to thy e - ter - nal mer - it,

All

Fa - ther, Son, and Ho - ly Spi - rit.

Words: Latin, 9th cent.; tr. John Cosin (1594-1672); para. of *Veni Creator Spiritus*.
Music: *Come Holy Ghost*, John Henry Hopkins Jr. (1820-1891); adapt. and harm. David Hurd (b. 1950)

88

504

1. Come, Ho - ly Ghost, our souls in - spire, and light - en
3. Thy bless - ed unc - tion from a - bove is com - fort,
5. A - noint and cheer our soil - ed face with the a -

with ce - les - tial fire. 2. Thou the a - noint - ing
life, and fire of love. 4. En - a - ble with per -
bun - dance of thy grace. 6. Keep far our foes, give

Spi - rit art, who dost thy seven - fold gifts im - part.
pet - ual light the dull - ness of our blind - ed sight.
peace at home: where thou art guide, no ill can come.

7. Teach us to know the Fa - ther, Son, and thee, of

both, to be but One, 8. that through the a - ges

all a - long, this may be our end - less song:

9. praise to thy e - ter - nal mer - it,

Fa - ther, Son, and Ho - ly Spi - rit.

Words: Latin, 9th cent.; tr. John Cosin (1594-1672); para. of *Veni Creator Spiritus*.
Music: *Veni Creator Spiritus*, plainsong, Mode 8

LM

The Holy Spirit

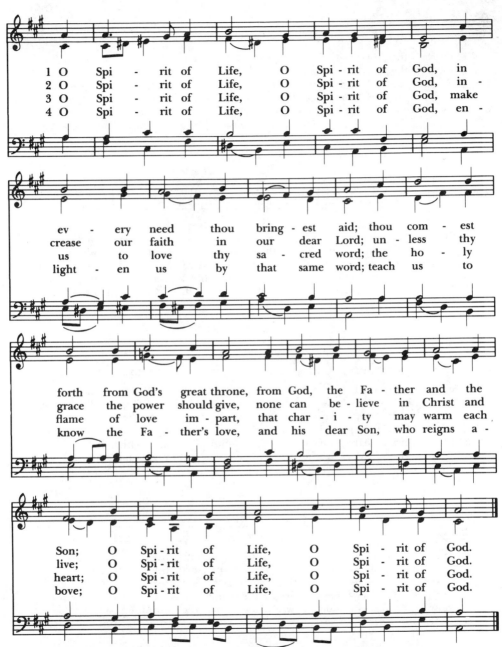

1 O Spi - rit of Life, O Spi - rit of God, in
2 O Spi - rit of Life, O Spi - rit of God, in -
3 O Spi - rit of Life, O Spi - rit of God, make
4 O Spi - rit of Life, O Spi - rit of God, en -

ev - ery need thou bring - est aid; thou com - est
crease our faith in our dear Lord; un - less thy
us to love thy sa - cred word; the ho - ly
light - en us by that same word; teach us to

forth from God's great throne, from God, the Fa - ther and the
grace the power should give, none can be - lieve in Christ and
flame of love im - part, that char - i - ty may warm each
know the Fa - ther's love, and his dear Son, who reigns a -

Son; O Spi - rit of Life, O Spi - rit of God.
live; O Spi - rit of Life, O Spi - rit of God.
heart; O Spi - rit of Life, O Spi - rit of God.
bove; O Spi - rit of Life, O Spi - rit of God.

Words: Johann Niedling (1602-1668); tr. John Caspar Mattes (1876-1948), alt.
Music: *O heiliger Geist*, melody from *Geistliche Kirchengesang*, 1623;
        harm. Johann Sebastian Bach (1685-1750); arr. Alastair Cassels-Brown (b. 1927)

10 8. 88. 10

506

1 Praise the Spi - rit in cre - a - tion, breath of God, life's
2 Praise the Spi - rit, close com - pan - ion of our in - most
3 Praise the Spi - rit, who en - light - ened priests and pro - phets
4 Tell of how the a - scend - ed Je - sus armed a peo - ple
5 Pray we then, O Lord the Spi - rit, on our lives de -
6 Praise, O praise the Ho - ly Spi - rit, praise the Fa - ther,

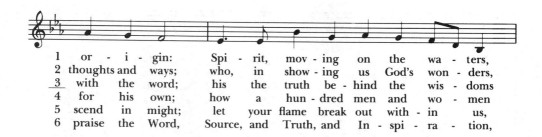

1 or - i - gin: Spi - rit, mov - ing on the wa - ters,
2 thoughts and ways; who, in show - ing us God's won - ders,
3 with the word; his the truth be - hind the wis - doms
4 for his own; how a hun - dred men and wo - men
5 scend in might; let your flame break out with - in us,
6 praise the Word, Source, and Truth, and In - spi - ra - tion,

1 quick - ening worlds to life with - in, source of breath to
2 is him - self the power to gaze; and God's will, to
3 which as yet know not our Lord; by whose love and
4 turned the known world up - side down, to its dark and
5 fire our hearts and clear our sight, till, white - hot in
6 Trin - i - ty in deep ac - cord: through your voice which

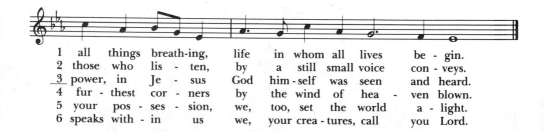

1 all things breath-ing, life in whom all lives be - gin.
2 those who lis - ten, by a still small voice con - veys.
3 power, in Je - sus God him - self was seen and heard.
4 fur - thest cor - ners by the wind of hea - ven blown.
5 your pos - ses - sion, we, too, set the world a - light.
6 speaks with - in us we, your crea - tures, call you Lord.

Words: Michael Hewlett (b. 1916), alt.
Music: *Finnian*, Christopher Dearnley (b. 1930)

87. 87. 87

The Holy Spirit

1 Praise the Spirit in cre - a - tion, breath of God, life's or - i -
2 Praise the Spirit, close com - pan - ion of our in - most thoughts and
3 Praise the Spirit, who en - light-ened priests and pro - phets with the
4 Tell of how the a-scend - ed Je - sus armed a peo - ple for his
5 Pray we then, O Lord the Spi - rit, on our lives de - scend in
6 Praise, O praise the Ho - ly Spi - rit, praise the Fa - ther, praise the

1 gin: Spi - rit, mov - ing on the wa - ters, quick-ening
2 ways; who, in show - ing us God's won - ders, is him -
3 word; his the truth be - hind the wis - doms which as
4 own; how a hun - dred men and wo - men turned the
5 might; let your flame break out with - in us, fire our
6 Word, Source, and Truth, and In - spi - ra - tion, Trin - i -

1 worlds to life with - in, source of breath to all things
2 self the power to gaze; and God's will, to those who
3 yet know not our Lord; by whose love and power, in
4 known world up - side down, to its dark and fur - thest
5 hearts and clear our sight, till, white - hot in your pos -
6 ty in deep ac - cord: through your voice which speaks with -

Interlude/Conclusion

1 breath - ing, life in whom all lives be - gin.
2 lis - ten, by a still small voice con - veys.
3 Je - sus God him - self was seen and heard.
4 cor - ners by the wind of hea - ven blown.
5 ses - sion, we, too, set the world a - light.
6 in us we, your crea - tures, call you Lord.

Words: Michael Hewlett (b. 1916), alt.
Music: *Julion*, David Hurd (b. 1950)

87. 87. 87

1 Breathe on me, Breath of God, fill me with life a - new,
2 Breathe on me, Breath of God, un - til my heart is pure,
3 Breathe on me, Breath of God, till I am whol - ly thine,
4 Breathe on me, Breath of God, so shall I nev - er die;

that I may love what thou dost love, and do what thou wouldst do.
un - til with thee I will one will, to do or to en - dure.
till all this earth - ly part of me glows with thy fire di - vine.
but live with thee the per - fect life of thine e - ter - ni - ty.

Words: Edwin Hatch (1835-1889), alt.
Music: *Nova Vita*, Lister R. Peace (1885-1969)

SM

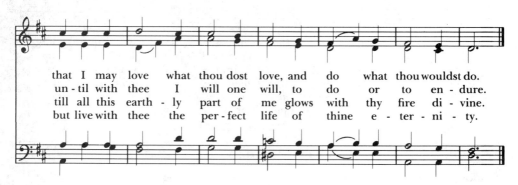

1 Spi - rit di - vine, at - tend our prayers, and make this house thy home;
2 Come as the light; to us re - veal our emp - ti - ness and woe,
3 Come as the fire, and purge our hearts like sac - ri - fi - cial flame;
4 Come as the dove, and spread thy wings, the wings of peace - ful love;
5 Spi - rit di - vine, at - tend our prayers; make a lost world thy home;

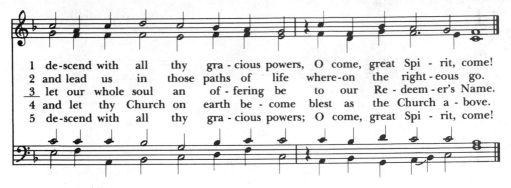

1 de-scend with all thy gra-cious powers, O come, great Spi - rit, come!
2 and lead us in those paths of life where-on the right-eous go.
3 let our whole soul an of - fering be to our Re - deem - er's Name.
4 and let thy Church on earth be - come blest as the Church a - bove.
5 de-scend with all thy gra-cious powers; O come, great Spi - rit, come!

Words: Andrew Reed (1787-1862)
Music: *Nun danket all und bringet Ehr,* melody att. Johann Cruger (1598-1662)

CM

The Holy Spirit

510

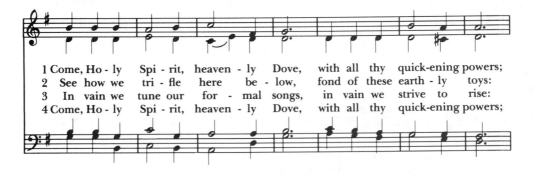

1 Come, Ho - ly Spi - rit, heaven - ly Dove, with all thy quick-ening powers;
2 See how we tri - fle here be - low, fond of these earth - ly toys:
3 In vain we tune our for - mal songs, in vain we strive to rise:
4 Come, Ho - ly Spi - rit, heaven - ly Dove, with all thy quick-ening powers;

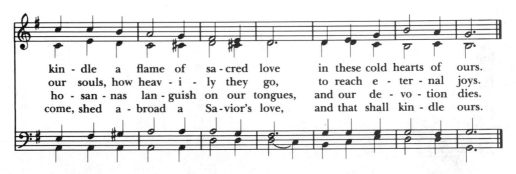

kin - dle a flame of sa - cred love, in these cold hearts of ours.
our souls, how heav - i - ly they go, to reach e - ter - nal joys.
ho - san - nas lan - guish on our tongues, and our de - vo - tion dies.
come, shed a - broad a Sa-vior's love, and that shall kin - dle ours.

Words: Isaac Watts (1674-1748), alt.
Music: *Saint Agnes,* John Bacchus Dykes (1823-1876)

CM

1 Holy Spirit, ever living as the Church's very life; Holy Spirit, ever striving through her in a ceaseless strife; Holy Spirit, ever forming in the Church the mind of Christ; thee we praise with

2 Holy Spirit, ever working through the Church's ministry; quickening, strengthening and absolving, setting captive sinners free; Holy Spirit, ever binding age to age, and soul to soul, in a fellow-

end - less wor-ship   for   thy   fruits   and   gifts   un - priced.
ship   un - end-ing   thee   we   wor - ship   and   ex - tol.

Words: Timothy Rees (1874-1939), alt.
Music: *Abbot's Leigh*, Cyril Vincent Taylor (b. 1907)

87. 87. D

The Holy Spirit

512

1 Come, gra - cious   Spi - rit,   heaven - ly   Dove,   with light and
2 The light of   truth   to   us   dis - play,   and make us
3 Lead us   to   Christ,   the   liv - ing   way,   nor let us
4 Lead us   to   heaven,   that we may   share   full - ness of

com - fort   from   a - bove;   be thou our   guard - ian,
know and   choose thy   way;   plant ho - ly   fear   in
from his   pre - cepts stray; lead us to   ho - li -
joy   for   ev - er   there;   lead us to   God,   our

thou   our   guide   o'er ev - ery thought and   step   pre - side.
ev - ery heart, that we from thee may   ne'er de - part.
ness, the   road   that we must take to   dwell with God.
fin - al   rest,   to be with him   for   ev - er   blest.

Words: Simon Browne (1680-1732), alt.
Music: *Mendon*, melody from *Methodist Harmonist*, 1821; adapt. and harm. Lowell Mason (1792-1872)

LM

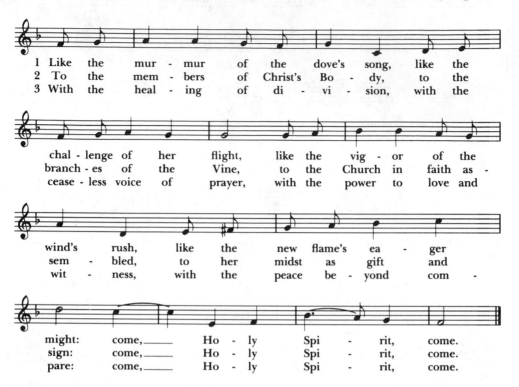

1 Like the mur - mur of the dove's song, like the
2 To the mem - bers of Christ's Bo - dy, to the
3 With the heal - ing of di - vi - sion, with the

chal - lenge of her flight, like the vig - or of the
branch - es of the Vine, to the Church in faith as -
cease - less voice of prayer, with the power to love and

wind's rush, like the new flame's ea - ger
sem - bled, to her midst as gift and
wit - ness, with the peace be - yond com -

might: come,_____ Ho - ly Spi - rit, come.
sign: come,_____ Ho - ly Spi - rit, come.
pare: come,_____ Ho - ly Spi - rit, come.

Phrase 1 of each stanza may be sung by one group, with a contrasted group singing phrase 2, and all joining for the final phrase.

Words: Carl P. Daw, Jr. (b. 1944)
Music: *Bridegroom*, Peter Cutts (b. 1937)

87. 87. 6

1 To thee, O Com - fort - er di - vine,
2 To thee, whose faith - ful love had place
3 To thee, whose faith - ful power doth heal,
4 To thee, by Je - sus Christ sent down,

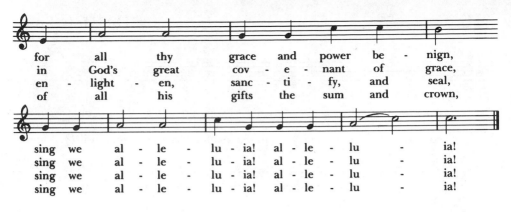

for all thy grace and power be - nign,
in God's great cov - e - nant of grace,
en - light - en, sanc - ti - fy, and seal,
of all his gifts the sum and crown,

sing we al - le - lu - ia! al - le - lu - ia!
sing we al - le - lu - ia! al - le - lu - ia!
sing we al - le - lu - ia! al - le - lu - ia!
sing we al - le - lu - ia! al - le - lu - ia!

Words: Frances Ridley Havergal (1836-1879)
Music: *St. Bartholomew's*, David McKinley Williams (1887-1978)

88. 10

The Holy Spirit

515

1 Ho - ly Ghost, dis - pel our sad - ness; pierce the clouds of
2 Au - thor of the new cre - a - tion, come with unc - tion

na - ture's night; come, thou source of joy and glad - ness,
and with power. Make our hearts thy ha - bi - ta - tion;

breathe thy life, and spread thy light. From the height which
with thy grace our spi - rits shower. Hear, oh, hear our

knows no mea - sure, as a gra - cious shower de - scend,
sup - pli - ca - tion, bless - ed Spi - rit, God of peace!

bring - ing down the rich - est trea - sure we can wish, or God can send.
Rest up - on this con - gre - ga - tion, with the full - ness of thy grace.

Words Paul Gerhardt (1607-1676); tr. John Christian Jacobi (1670-1750), alt.
Music: *Geneva*, George Henry Day (1883-1966)

87. 87. D

1 Come down, O Love di - vine, seek thou this soul of mine,
2 O let it free - ly burn, till earth - ly pas - sions turn
3 And so the yearn - ing strong, with which the soul will long,

and vis - it it with thine own ar - dor glow - ing;
to dust and ash - es in its heat con - sum - ing;
shall far out - pass the power of hu - man tell - ing;

O Com - fort - er, draw near, with - in my heart ap - pear,
and let thy glo - rious light shine ev - er on my sight,
for none can guess its grace, till Love cre - ate a place

and kin - dle it, thy ho - ly flame be - stow - ing.
and clothe me round, the while my path il - lum - ing.
where - in the Ho - ly Spi - rit makes a dwell - ing.

Words: Bianco da Siena (d. 1434?); tr. Richard Frederick Littledale (1833-1890), alt.
Music: *Down Ampney*, Ralph Vaughan Williams (1872-1958)

66. 11. D

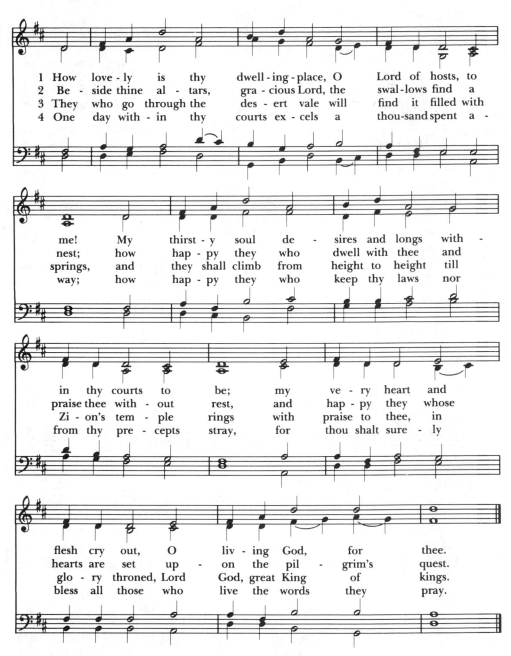

1 How love-ly is thy dwell-ing-place, O Lord of hosts, to
2 Be-side thine al-tars, gra-cious Lord, the swal-lows find a
3 They who go through the des-ert vale will find it filled with
4 One day with-in thy courts ex-cels a thou-sand spent a-

me! My thirst-y soul de-sires and longs with-
nest; how hap-py they who dwell with thee and
springs, and they shall climb from height to height till
way; how hap-py they who keep thy laws nor

in thy courts to be; my ve-ry heart and
praise thee with-out rest, and hap-py they whose
Zi-on's tem-ple rings with praise to thee, in
from thy pre-cepts stray, for thou shalt sure-ly

flesh cry out, O liv-ing God, for thee.
hearts are set up-on the pil-grim's quest.
glo-ry throned, Lord God, great King of kings.
bless all those who live the words they pray.

Words: Para. of Psalm 84; sts. 1-2, *The Psalms of David in Meeter*, 1650; sts. 3-4, Carl P. Daw, Jr. (b. 1944)
Music: *Brother James' Air*, J. L. Macbeth Bain (1840?-1925)   86. 86. 86

518 — The Church

Descant

4 Here vouch-safe to all thy serv-ants what they ask of

1 Christ is made the sure foun-da-tion, Christ the head and
2 All that ded-i-cat-ed ci-ty, dear-ly loved of
3 To this tem-ple, where we call thee, come, O Lord of
4 Here vouch-safe to all thy serv-ants what they ask of

thee to gain; what they gain from thee, for ev-er

cor-ner-stone, cho-sen of the Lord, and pre-cious,
God on high, in ex-ult-ant ju-bi-la-tion
Hosts, to-day; with thy wont-ed lov-ing-kind-ness
thee to gain; what they gain from thee, for ev-er

with the bless-ed to re-tain, and here-af-ter

bind-ing all the Church in one; ho-ly Zi-on's
pours per-pet-ual mel-o-dy; God the One in
hear thy serv-ants as they pray, and thy full-est
with the bless-ed to re-tain, and here-af-ter

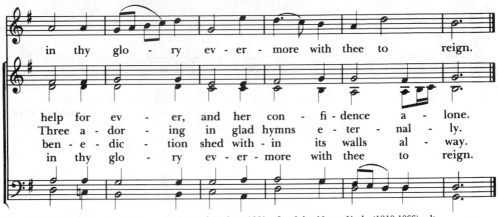

in thy glo - ry ev - er - more with thee to reign.

help for ev - er, and her con - fi - dence a - lone.
Three a - dor - ing in glad hymns e - ter - nal - ly.
ben - e - dic - tion shed with - in its walls al - way.
in thy glo - ry ev - er - more with thee to reign.

Words: Latin, ca. 7th cent.; tr. *Hymns Ancient and Modern*, 1861, after John Mason Neale (1818-1866), alt.
Music: *Westminster Abbey*, Henry Purcell (1659-1695), adapt.; desc. James Gillespie (b. 1929)　　87. 87. 87

The Church

519

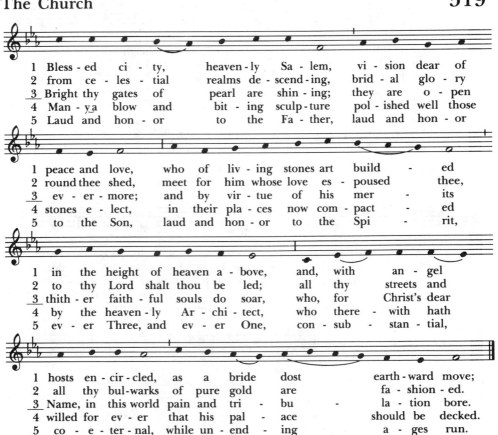

1 Bless - ed ci - ty, heaven - ly Sa - lem, vi - sion dear of
2 from ce - les - tial realms de - scend - ing, brid - al glo - ry
3 Bright thy gates of pearl are shin - ing; they are o - pen
4 Man - y a blow and bit - ing sculp - ture pol - ished well those
5 Laud and hon - or to the Fa - ther, laud and hon - or

1 peace and love, who of liv - ing stones art build - ed
2 round thee shed, meet for him whose love es - poused thee,
3 ev - er - more; and by vir - tue of his mer - its
4 stones e - lect, in their pla - ces now com - pact - ed
5 to the Son, laud and hon - or to the Spi - rit,

1 in the height of heaven a - bove, and, with an - gel
2 to thy Lord shalt thou be led; all thy streets and
3 thith - er faith - ful souls do soar, who, for Christ's dear
4 by the heaven - ly Ar - chi - tect, who there - with hath
5 ev - er Three, and ev - er One, con - sub - stan - tial,

1 hosts en - cir - cled, as a bride dost earth - ward move;
2 all thy bul - warks of pure gold are fa - shion - ed.
3 Name, in this world pain and tri - bu - la - tion bore.
4 willed for ev - er that his pal - ace should be decked.
5 co - e - ter - nal, while un - end - ing a - ges run.

Words: Latin, ca. 7th cent.; tr. *Hymns Ancient and Modern*, 1861, after John Mason Neale (1818-1866), alt.
Music: *Urbs beata Jerusalem*, plainsong, Mode 2, Nevers MS., 13th cent.　　87. 87. 87

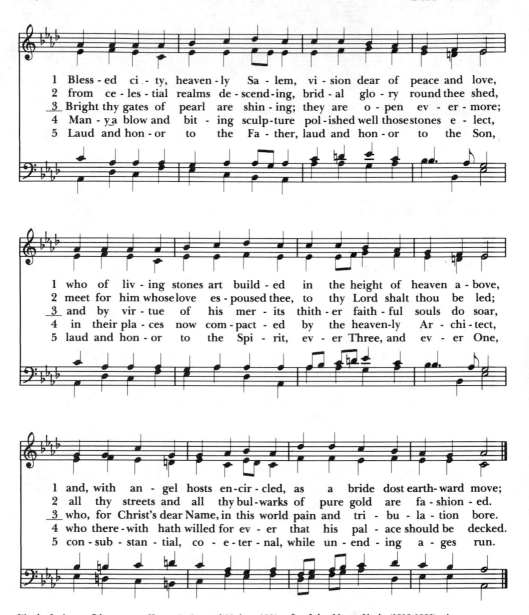

1 Bless - ed ci - ty, heaven - ly Sa - lem, vi - sion dear of peace and love,
2 from ce - les - tial realms de - scend - ing, brid - al glo - ry round thee shed,
3 Bright thy gates of pearl are shin - ing; they are o - pen ev - er - more;
4 Man - y a blow and bit - ing sculp - ture pol - ished well those stones e - lect,
5 Laud and hon - or to the Fa - ther, laud and hon - or to the Son,

1 who of liv - ing stones art build - ed in the height of heaven a - bove,
2 meet for him whose love es - poused thee, to thy Lord shalt thou be led;
3 and by vir - tue of his mer - its thith - er faith - ful souls do soar,
4 in their pla - ces now com - pact - ed by the heaven - ly Ar - chi - tect,
5 laud and hon - or to the Spi - rit, ev - er Three, and ev - er One,

1 and, with an - gel hosts en - cir - cled, as a bride dost earth - ward move;
2 all thy streets and all thy bul - warks of pure gold are fa - shion - ed.
3 who, for Christ's dear Name, in this world pain and tri - bu - la - tion bore.
4 who there - with hath willed for ev - er that his pal - ace should be decked.
5 con - sub - stan - tial, co - e - ter - nal, while un - end - ing a - ges run.

Words: Latin, ca. 7th cent.; tr. *Hymns Ancient and Modern*, 1861, after John Mason Neale (1818-1866), alt.
Music: *Oriel*, Caspar Ett (1788-1847)

87. 87. 87

The Church

521

Words: Howard Chandler Robbins (1876-1952)
Music: *Chelsea Square*, Howard Chandler Robbins (1876-1952);
　　　harm. Ray Francis Brown (1897-1964); desc. Lois Fyfe (b. 1927)

CM

Descant

4 Blest in-hab-it-ants of Zi-on, washed in the Re-

1 Glo-rious things of thee are spo-ken, Zi-on, ci-ty
2 See! the streams of liv-ing wa-ters, spring-ing from e-
3 Round each ha-bi-ta-tion hov-ering, see the cloud and
4 Blest in-hab-it-ants of Zi-on, washed in the Re-

deem-er's blood! Whom their souls re-

of our God; he whose word can-not be
ter-nal love, well sup-ply thy sons and
fire ap-pear for a glo-ry and a
deem-er's blood! Je-sus, whom their souls re-

ly on, makes them kings and priests to God.

bro-ken formed thee for his own a-bode;
daugh-ters and all fear of want re-move.
cov-ering, show-ing that the Lord is near.
ly on, makes them kings and priests to God.

'Tis his love his peo-ple raise o-ver

on the Rock of A-ges found-ed, what can shake thy
Who can faint, when such a riv-er ev-er will their
Thus de-riv-ing from their ban-ner, light by night, and
'Tis his love his peo-ple rais-es o-ver self to

self to reign: and as priests, his

sure re-pose? With sal-va-tion's walls sur-
thirst as-suage? Grace which, like the Lord, the
shade by day, safe they feed up-on the
reign as kings: and as priests, his sol-emn

sol-emn prais-es each an of-fering brings.

round-ed, thou may'st smile at all thy foes.
giv-er, nev-er fails from age to age.
man-na which he gives them when they pray.
prais-es each for a thank-of-fering brings.

Words: John Newton (1725-1807), alt.
Music: *Austria*, Franz Joseph Haydn (1732-1809); desc. Michael E. Young (b. 1939)

87. 87. D

1 Glo - rious things of thee are spo - ken, Zi - on, ci - ty
2 See! the streams of liv - ing wa - ters, spring - ing from e -
3 Round each ha - bi - ta - tion hov-ering, see the cloud and
4 Blest in - hab - it - ants of Zi - on, washed in the Re -

of our God; he whose word can - not be bro - ken
ter - nal love, well sup - ply thy sons and daugh-ters
fire ap - pear for a glo - ry and a cov - ering,
deem - er's blood! Je - sus, whom their souls re - ly on,

formed thee for his own a - bode; on the Rock of A - ges
and all fear of want re - move. Who can faint, when such a
show - ing that the Lord is near. Thus de - riv - ing from their
makes them kings and priests to God. 'Tis his love his peo - ple

found - ed, what can shake thy sure re - pose? With sal -
riv - er ev - er will their thirst as - suage? Grace which,
ban - ner, light by night, and shade by day, safe they
rais - es o - ver self to reign as kings: and as

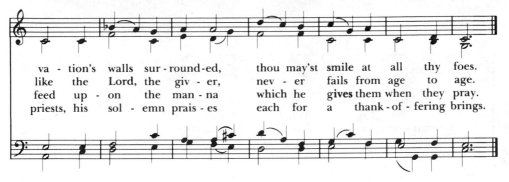

va - tion's walls sur - round - ed, thou may'st smile at all thy foes.
like the Lord, the giv - er, nev - er fails from age to age.
feed up - on the man - na which he gives them when they pray.
priests, his sol - emn prais - es each for a thank - of - fering brings.

Words: John Newton (1725-1807), alt.
Music: *Abbot's Leigh*, Cyril Vincent Taylor (b. 1907)

87. 87. D

The Church

524

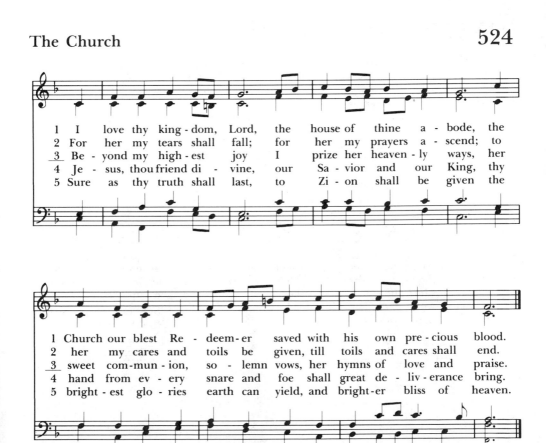

1 I love thy king - dom, Lord, the house of thine a - bode, the
2 For her my tears shall fall; for her my prayers a - scend; to
3 Be - yond my high - est joy I prize her heaven - ly ways, her
4 Je - sus, thou friend di - vine, our Sa - vior and our King, thy
5 Sure as thy truth shall last, to Zi - on shall be given the

1 Church our blest Re - deem - er saved with his own pre - cious blood.
2 her my cares and toils be given, till toils and cares shall end.
3 sweet com - mun - ion, so - lemn vows, her hymns of love and praise.
4 hand from ev - ery snare and foe shall great de - liv - erance bring.
5 bright - est glo - ries earth can yield, and bright - er bliss of heaven.

Words: Timothy Dwight (1725-1817)
Music: *St. Thomas (Williams)*, melody Aaron Williams (1731-1776); harm. Lowell Mason (1792-1872)

SM

1 The Church's one foun-da-tion is Je-sus Christ her Lord;
2 E-lect from ev-ery na-tion, yet one o'er all the earth,
3 Though with a scorn-ful won-der men see her sore op-pressed,
4 Mid toil and tri-bu-la-tion, and tu-mult of her war
5 Yet she on earth hath un-ion with God, the Three in One,

1 she is his new cre-a-tion by wa-ter and the word:
2 her char-ter of sal-va-tion, one Lord, one faith, one birth;
3 by schi-sms rent a-sun-der, by her-e-sies dis-tressed;
4 she waits the con-sum-ma-tion of peace for ev-er-more;
5 and mys-tic sweet com-mun-ion with those whose rest is won.

1 from heaven he came and sought her to be his ho-ly bride;
2 one ho-ly Name she bless-es, par-takes one ho-ly food,
3 yet saints their watch are keep-ing, their cry goes up, "How long?"
4 till with the vi-sion glo-rious her long-ing eyes are blessed,
5 O hap-py ones and ho-ly! Lord, give us grace that we

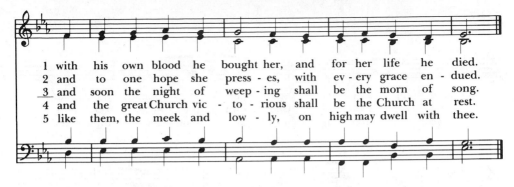

1 with his own blood he bought her, and for her life he died.
2 and to one hope she press - es, with ev - ery grace en - dued.
3 and soon the night of weep - ing shall be the morn of song.
4 and the great Church vic - to - rious shall be the Church at rest.
5 like them, the meek and low - ly, on high may dwell with thee.

Words: Samuel John Stone (1839-1900)
Music: *Aurelia*, Samuel Sebastian Wesley (1810-1876)

76. 76. D

The Church

526

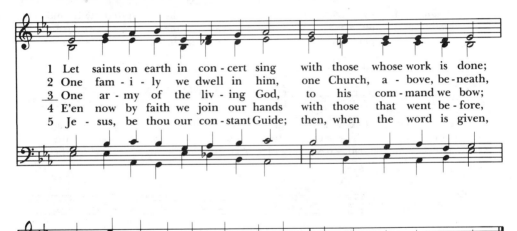

1 Let saints on earth in con - cert sing with those whose work is done;
2 One fam - i - ly we dwell in him, one Church, a - bove, be - neath,
3 One ar - my of the liv - ing God, to his com - mand we bow;
4 E'en now by faith we join our hands with those that went be - fore,
5 Je - sus, be thou our con - stant Guide; then, when the word is given,

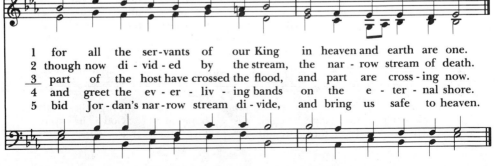

1 for all the ser - vants of our King in heaven and earth are one.
2 though now di - vid - ed by the stream, the nar - row stream of death.
3 part of the host have crossed the flood, and part are cross - ing now.
4 and greet the ev - er - liv - ing bands on the e - ter - nal shore.
5 bid Jor - dan's nar - row stream di - vide, and bring us safe to heaven.

Words: Charles Wesley (1707-1788), alt.
Music: *Dundee*, melody from *The CL Psalmes of David*, 1615; harm. Thomas Ravenscroft (1592?-1635?), alt.

CM

1 Sing - ing songs of ex - pec - ta - tion, on - ward
2 One the light of God's own pres - ence, o'er his
3 One the strain the lips of thou - sands lift as

goes the pil - grim band, through the night of
ran - somed peo - ple shed, chas - ing far the
from the heart of one; one the con - flict,

doubt and sor - row, march - ing to the prom - ised land.
gloom and ter - ror, bright - ening all the path we tread:
one the per - il, one the march in God be - gun:

Clear be - fore us through the dark - ness gleams and
one the ob - ject of our jour - ney, one the
one the glad - ness of re - joic - ing on the

burns the guid - ing light: trust - ing God we
faith which nev - er tires, one the ear - nest
far e - ter - nal shore, where the one al -

march to - geth - er step - ping fear - less through the night.
look - ing for - ward, one the hope our God in - spires.
might - y Fa - ther reigns in love for ev - er - more.

Words: Bernard Severin Ingemann (1789-1862); tr. Sabine Baring-Gould (1834-1924), alt.
Music: *Ton-y-Botel*, Thomas John Williams (1869-1944)

87. 87. D

The Church's Mission

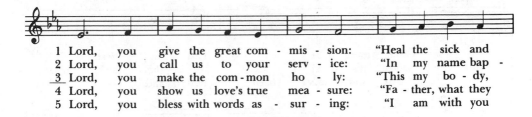

1 Lord, you give the great com - mis - sion: "Heal the sick and
2 Lord, you call us to your serv - ice: "In my name bap -
3 Lord, you make the com - mon ho - ly: "This my bo - dy,
4 Lord, you show us love's true mea - sure: "Fa - ther, what they
5 Lord, you bless with words as - sur - ing: "I am with you

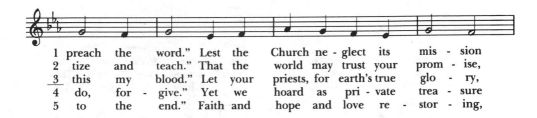

1 preach the word." Lest the Church ne - glect its mis - sion
2 tize and teach." That the world may trust your prom - ise,
3 this my blood." Let your priests, for earth's true glo - ry,
4 do, for - give." Yet we hoard as pri - vate trea - sure
5 to the end." Faith and hope and love re - stor - ing,

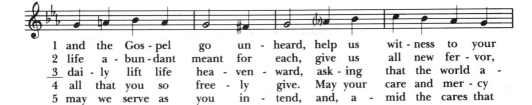

1 and the Gos - pel go un - heard, help us wit - ness to your
2 life a - bun - dant meant for each, give us all new fer - vor,
3 dai - ly lift life hea - ven - ward, ask - ing that the world a -
4 all that you so free - ly give. May your care and mer - cy
5 may we serve as you in - tend, and, a - mid the cares that

Refrain

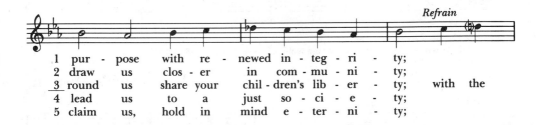

1 pur - pose with re - newed in - teg - ri - ty;
2 draw us clos - er in com - mu - ni - ty;
3 round us share your chil - dren's lib - er - ty;   with the
4 lead us to a just so - ci - e - ty;
5 claim us, hold in mind e - ter - ni - ty;

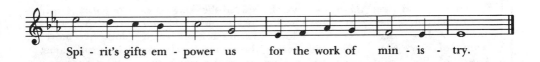

Spi - rit's gifts em - power us   for the work of min - is - try.

Words: Jeffery Rowthorn (b. 1934)
Music: *Rowthorn*, Alec Wyton (b. 1921)

87. 87. 87 with Refrain

Unison or harmony

1 In Christ there is no East or West, in
2 Join hands, dis - ci - ples of the faith, what -
3 In Christ now meet both East and West, in

him no South or North, but one great fel - low -
e'er your race may be! Who serves my Fa - ther
him meet South and North, all Christ - ly souls are

ship of love through - out the whole wide earth.
as his child is sure - ly kin to me.
one in him, through - out the whole wide earth.

Words: John Oxenham (1852-1941), alt.
Music: *McKee*, Afro-American spiritual; adapt. and harm. Harry T. Burleigh (1866-1949)   CM

530   The Church's Mission

1 Spread, O spread, thou might - y word, spread the king - dom of the Lord,
2 word of how the Fa - ther's will made the world, and keeps it, still;
3 word of how the Sa - vior's love earth's sore bur - den doth re - move;
4 word of how the Spi - rit came bring - ing peace in Je - sus' name;
5 Word of life, most pure and strong, word for which the na - tions long,

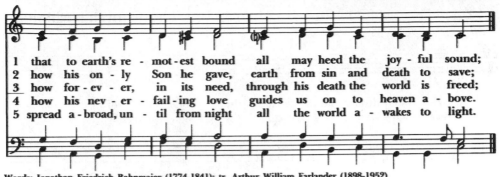

Words: Jonathan Friedrich Bahnmaier (1774-1841); tr. Arthur William Farlander (1898-1952)
and Charles Winfred Douglas (1867-1944), alt. St. 4, F. Bland Tucker (1895-1984)
Music: *Gott sei Dank*, melody from *Geistreiches Gesangbuch*, 1704;
adapt. and harm. William Henry Havergal (1793-1870)

77. 77

The Church's Mission 531

Words: James Montgomery (1771-1854), alt.
Music: *Melcombe*, Samuel Webbe (1740-1816)

LM

1 How won-drous and great thy works, God of praise!
How just, King of saints, and true are thy ways!
O who shall not fear thee, and hon - or thy Name?
Thou on - ly art ho - ly, thou on - ly su - preme.

2 To na - tions of earth thy light shall be shown;
their wor - ship and vows shall come to thy throne:
thy truth and thy judg - ments shall spread all a - broad,
till earth's ev - ery peo - ple con - fess thee their God.

Words: Henry Ustick Onderdonk (1759-1858), alt.; para. *The Song of the Redeemed*
Music: *Old 104th*, melody from *The Whole Booke of Psalmes*, 1621; har. *Hymnal 1982*

10 10. 11 11

1 How won-drous and great thy works, God of praise!
2 To na-tions of earth thy light shall be shown;

How just, King of saints, and true are thy ways!
their wor-ship and vows shall come to thy throne:

O who shall not fear thee, and hon-or thy Name?
thy truth and thy judg-ments shall spread all a-broad,

Thou on-ly art ho-ly, thou on-ly su-preme.
till earth's ev-ery peo-ple con-fess thee their God.

Words: Henry Ustick Onderdonk (1759-1858), alt.; para. *The Song of the Redeemed*
Music: *Lyons*, att. Johann Michael Haydn (1737-1806)

10 10. 11 11

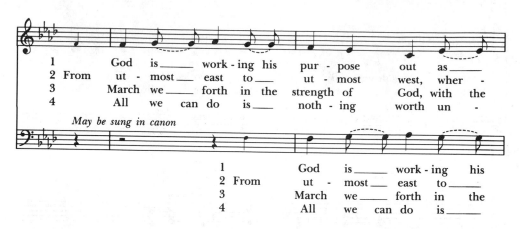

1. God is ___ work-ing his pur - pose out as ___
2. From ut - most ___ east to ___ ut - most west, wher -
3. March we ___ forth in the strength of God, with the
4. All we can do is ___ noth - ing worth un -

May be sung in canon

1. God is ___ work - ing his
2. From ut - most ___ east to ___
3. March we ___ forth in the
4. All we can do is ___

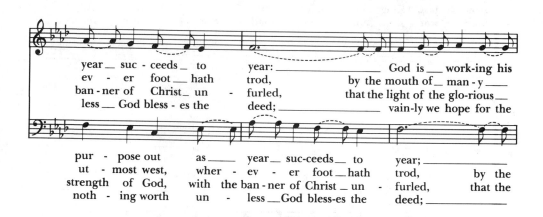

year ___ suc - ceeds ___ to year: ___ God is ___ work-ing his
ev - er foot ___ hath trod, by the mouth of ___ man - y ___
ban - ner of Christ ___ un - furled, that the light of the glo-rious ___
less ___ God bless - es the deed; ___ vain-ly we hope for the

pur - pose out as ___ year ___ suc-ceeds ___ to year; ___
ut - most west, wher - ev - er foot ___ hath trod, by the
strength of God, with the ban - ner of Christ ___ un - furled, that the
noth - ing worth un - less ___ God bless-es the deed; ___

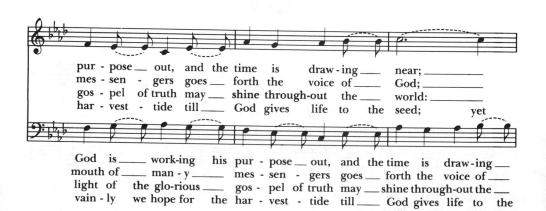

pur - pose ___ out, and the time is draw-ing ___ near; ___
mes - sen - gers goes ___ forth the voice of ___ God; ___
gos - pel of truth may ___ shine through-out the ___ world: ___
har - vest - tide till ___ God gives life to the seed; yet

God is ___ work-ing his pur - pose ___ out, and the time is draw-ing ___
mouth of ___ man - y ___ mes - sen - gers goes ___ forth the voice of ___
light of the glo-rious ___ gos - pel of truth may ___ shine through-out the ___
vain - ly we hope for the har - vest - tide till ___ God gives life to the

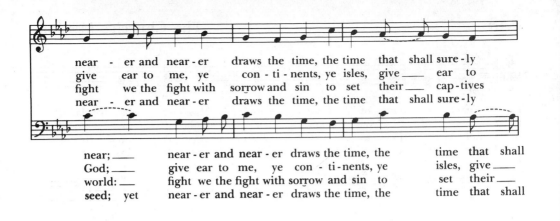

near - er and near - er draws the time, the time that shall sure - ly
give ear to me, ye con - ti - nents, ye isles, give ___ ear to
fight we the fight with sorrow and sin to set their ___ cap - tives
near - er and near - er draws the time, the time that shall sure - ly

near; ___ near - er and near - er draws the time, the time that shall
God; ___ give ear to me, ye con - ti - nents, ye isles, give ___
world: ___ fight we the fight with sorrow and sin to set their ___
seed; yet near - er and near - er draws the time, the time that shall

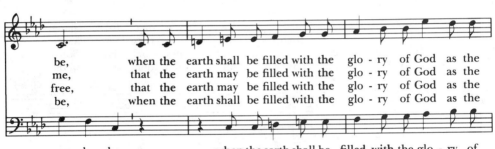

be, when the earth shall be filled with the glo - ry of God as the
me, that the earth may be filled with the glo - ry of God as the
free, that the earth may be filled with the glo - ry of God as the
be, when the earth shall be filled with the glo - ry of God as the

sure - ly be, when the earth shall be filled with the glo - ry of
ear to me, that the earth may be filled with the glo - ry of
cap - tives free, that the earth may be filled with the glo - ry of
sure - ly be, when the earth shall be filled with the glo - ry of

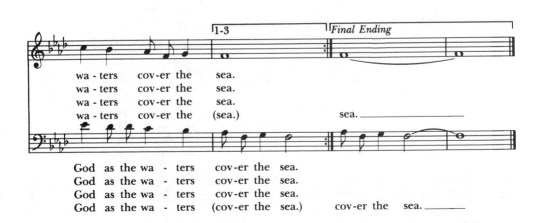

1-3 **Final Ending**

wa - ters cov - er the sea.
wa - ters cov - er the sea.
wa - ters cov - er the sea.
wa - ters cov - er the (sea.) sea. ___

God as the wa - ters cov - er the sea.
God as the wa - ters cov - er the sea.
God as the wa - ters cov - er the sea.
God as the wa - ters (cov - er the sea.) cov - er the sea. ___

Words: Arthur Campbell Ainger (1841-1919), alt.
Music: *Purpose*, Martin Fallas Shaw (1875-1958)

Irr.

535

1 Ye ser-vants of God, your Mas-ter pro-claim,
2 God rul-eth on high, al-might-y to save;
3 Sal-va-tion to God who sits on the throne!
4 Then let us a-dore, and give him his right:

and pub-lish a-broad his won-der-ful Name;
and still he is nigh: his pres-ence we have.
Let all cry a-loud, and hon-or the Son.
All glo-ry and power, all wis-dom and might,

the Name all-vic-to-rious of Je-sus ex-tol:
The great con-gre-ga-tion his tri-umph shall sing,
The prais-es of Je-sus the an-gels pro-claim,
and hon-or and bless-ing, with an-gels a-bove,

his king-dom is glo-rious; he rules o-ver all.
as-crib-ing sal-va-tion to Je-sus our King.
fall down on their fa-ces, and wor-ship the Lamb.
and thanks nev-er-ceas-ing and in-fi-nite love.

Words: Charles Wesley (1707-1788), alt.
Music: *Paderborn*, melody from *Catolisch-Paderbornisches Gesang-buch*, 1765;
    harm. Sydney Hugo Nicholson (1875-1947)

10 10. 11 11

"Torah ora" is Hebrew for, "The Law is our Light."

Words: Willard F. Jabusch (b. 1930), alt.
Music: *Torah Song [Yisrael V'oraita]*, Hasidic melody; arr. Richard Proulx, (b. 1937)

98. 95 with Refrain

1 Christ for the world we sing! The world to
2 Christ for the world we sing! The world to
3 Christ for the world we sing! The world to
4 Christ for the world we sing! The world to

Christ we bring with lov - ing zeal; the poor, and
Christ we bring with fer - vent prayer; the way - ward
Christ we bring with one ac - cord; with us the
Christ we bring with joy - ful song; the new - born

them that mourn, the faint and o - ver - borne,
and the lost, by rest - less pas - sions tossed,
work to share, with us re - proach to dare,
souls, whose days, re - claimed from er - ror's ways,

sin - sick and sor - row-worn, whom Christ doth heal.
re - deemed at count - less cost from dark de - spair.
with us the cross to bear, for Christ our Lord.
in - spired with hope and praise, to Christ be - long.

Words: Samuel Wolcott (1813-1886)
Music: *Moscow*, melody Felice de Giardini (1716-1796); harm. *The New Hymnal*, 1916,
    based on *Hymns Ancient and Modern*, 1875, and Lowell Mason (1792-1872)

664. 6664

1 God of mer - cy, God of grace, show the bright - ness of thy
2 Let thy peo - ple praise thee, Lord; be by all that live a -

face. Shine up - on us, Sa - vior, shine, fill thy
dored. Let the na - tions shout and sing glo - ry

Church with light di - vine, and thy sav - ing health ex -
to their Sa - vior King; let all be, be - low, a -

tend un - to earth's re - mot - est end.
bove, one in joy, and light, and love.

Words: Henry Francis Lyte (1793-1847), alt.
Music: *Lucerna Laudoniae*, David Evans (1874-1948)

77. 77. 77

1 O Zi - on, haste, thy mis - sion high ful - fill - ing,
2 Pro - claim to ev - ery peo - ple, tongue, and na - tion
3 Send her - alds forth to bear the mes - sage glo - rious;
4 He comes a - gain! O Zi - on, ere thou meet him,

to tell to all the world that God is Light;
that God, in whom they live and move, is Love;
give of thy wealth to speed them on their way;
make known to ev - ery heart his sav - ing grace;

that he who made all na - tions is not will - ing
tell how he stooped to save his lost cre - a - tion,
pour out thy soul for them in prayer vic - to - rious
let none whom he hath ran - somed fail to greet him,

one soul should fail to know his love and might.
and died on earth that all might live a - bove.
till God shall bring his king - dom's joy - ful day.
through thy ne - glect, un - fit to see his face.

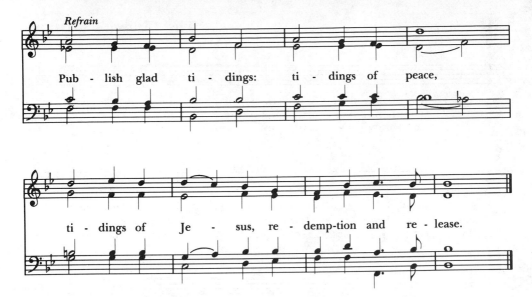

Refrain

Pub - lish glad ti - dings: ti - dings of peace, ti - dings of Je - sus, re - demp-tion and re - lease.

Words: Mary Ann Thomson (1834-1923), alt.
Music: *Tidings*, James Walch (1837-1901)

11 10. 11 10 with Refrain

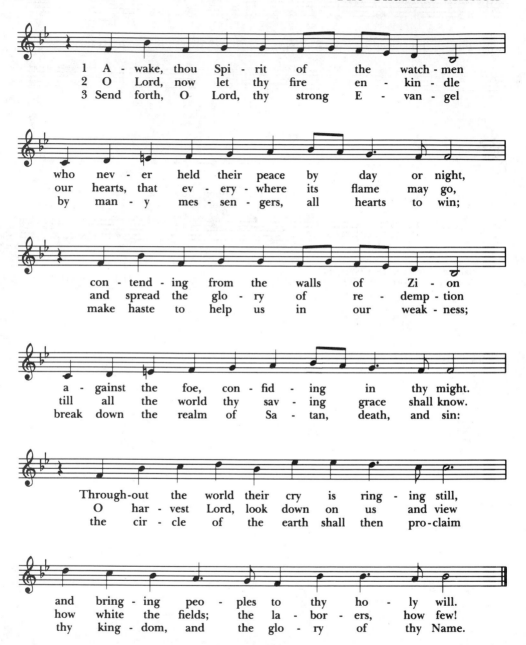

1 Awake, thou Spirit of the watch-men
who never held their peace by day or night,
con-tend-ing from the walls of Zi-on
a-gainst the foe, con-fid-ing in thy might.
Through-out the world their cry is ring-ing still,
and bring-ing peo-ples to thy ho-ly will.

2 O Lord, now let thy fire en-kin-dle
our hearts, that ev-ery-where its flame may go,
and spread the glo-ry of re-demp-tion
till all the world thy sav-ing grace shall know.
O har-vest Lord, look down on us and view
how white the fields; the la-bor-ers, how few!

3 Send forth, O Lord, thy strong E-van-gel
by man-y mes-sen-gers, all hearts to win;
make haste to help us in our weak-ness;
break down the realm of Sa-tan, death, and sin:
the cir-cle of the earth shall then pro-claim
thy king-dom, and the glo-ry of thy Name.

Words: Karl Heinrich von Bogatzky (1690-1774); tr. Arthur William Farlander (1898-1952)
       and Charles Winfred Douglas (1867-1944)
Music: *Dir, dir, Jehovah*, melody from *Hamburger Musikalisches handbuch*, 1690   9 10. 9 10. 10 10

The Church's Mission

1 Come, la-bor on. Who dares stand i-dle
2 Come, la-bor on. The en-e-my is
3 Come, la-bor on. A-way with gloom-y
4 Come, la-bor on. Claim the high call-ing
5 Come, la-bor on. No time for rest, till

1 on the har-vest plain, while all a-round us
2 watch-ing night and day, to sow the tares, to
3 doubts and faith-less fear! No arm so weak but
4 an-gels can-not share— to young and old the
5 glows the west-ern sky, till the long sha-dows

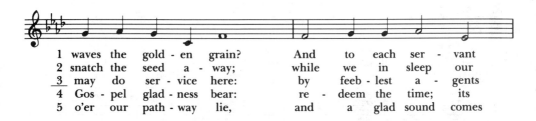

1 waves the gold-en grain? And to each ser-vant
2 snatch the seed a-way; while we in sleep our
3 may do ser-vice here: by feeb-lest a-gents
4 Gos-pel glad-ness bear: re-deem the time; its
5 o'er our path-way lie, and a glad sound comes

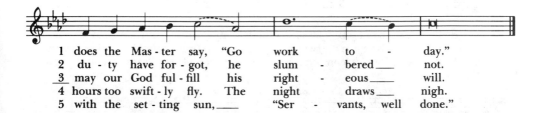

1 does the Mas-ter say, "Go work to-day."
2 du-ty have for-got, he slum-bered not.
3 may our God ful-fill his right-eous will.
4 hours too swift-ly fly. The night draws nigh.
5 with the set-ting sun, "Ser-vants, well done."

Words: Jane Laurie Borthwick (1813-1897), alt.
Music: *Ora Labora*, Thomas Tertius Noble (1867-1953)

4. 10 10. 10 4

1 Christ is the world's true Light, its Cap-tain of sal-va - tion,
2 In Christ all rac-es meet, their an-cient feuds for-get - ting,
3 One Lord, in one great Name u-nite us all who own thee;

the Day-star clear and bright of ev-ery race and na - tion;
the whole round world com-plete, from sun-rise to its set - ting:
cast out our pride and shame that hin-der to en-throne thee;

new life, new hope a - wakes, for all who own his sway:
when Christ is throned as Lord all shall for-sake their fear,
the world has wait - ed long, has tra-vailed long in pain;

free - dom her bond-age breaks, and night is turned to day.
to plough-share beat the sword, to prun-ing-hook the spear.
to heal its an-cient wrong, come, Prince of Peace, and reign.

Words George Wallace Briggs (1875-1959), alt.
Music: *St. Joan*, Percy E. B. Coller (b. 1895)

67. 67. 66. 66

1 O Zi-on, tune thy voice, and raise thy hands on
2 He gilds thy morn-ing face with beams that can-not
3 In hon-or to his Name re-flect that sa-cred
4 There on his ho-ly hill a bright-er sun shall

high; tell all the earth thy joys, and boast sal-
fade; his all-re-splen-dent grace he pours a-
light; and loud that grace pro-claim, which makes thy
rise, and with his ra-diance fill those fair-er

va-tion nigh. Cheer-ful in God, a-
round thy head; the na-tions round thy
dark-ness bright; pur-sue his praise, till
pur-er skies; while round his throne ten

rise and shine, while rays di-vine stream all a-broad.
form shall view, with lus-ter new di-vine-ly crowned.
sov-ereign love in worlds a-bove the glo-ry raise.
thou-sand stars in no-bler spheres his in-fluence own.

Words: Philip Doddridge (1702-1751) alt.; based on *The Third Song of Isaiah*
Music: *Eastview*, J. V. Lee (1892-1959)

66. 66 88

544

1 Je - sus shall reign wher - e'er the sun doth his suc -
2 To him shall end - less prayer be made, and prais - es
3 Peo - ple and realms of ev - ery tongue dwell on his
4 Bless - ings a - bound where - e'er he reigns: the pris - oners
5 Let ev - ery crea - ture rise and bring pe - cu - liar

1 ces - sive jour - neys run; his king - dom stretch from
2 throng to crown his head; his Name like sweet per -
3 love with sweet - est song; and in - fant voic - es
4 leap to lose their chains, the wea - ry find e -
5 hon - ors to our King; an - gels de - scend with

1 shore to shore, till moons shall wax and wane no more.
2 fume shall rise with ev - ery morn - ing sac - ri - fice.
3 shall pro - claim their ear - ly bless - ings on his Name.
4 ter - nal rest, and all who suf - fer want are blest.
5 songs a - gain, and earth re - peat the loud a - men.

Words: Isaac Watts (1674-1748), alt.
Music: *Duke Street*, John Hatton (d. 1793)

LM

1 Lo! what a cloud of wit - ness - es en -
2 Let us, with zeal like theirs in - spired, strive
3 Be - hold a Wit - ness no - bler still, who
4 He, for the joy be - fore him set, and
5 Thith - er, for - get - ting things be - hind, press

1 com - pass us a - round! They, once like us with
2 in the Chris - tian race; and, freed from ev - ery
3 trod af - flic - tion's path: Je - sus, the au - thor,
4 moved by pit - ying love, en - dured the cross, de -
5 we to God's right hand; there, with the Sa - vior

1 suf - fering tried, are now with glo - ry crowned.
2 weight of sin, their ho - ly foot - steps trace.
3 fi - nish - er, re - ward - er of our faith.
4 spised the shame, and now he reigns a - bove.
5 and his saints, tri - um - phant - ly to stand.

Words: *Translations and Paraphrases*, 1745, alt.; para. of Hebrews 12:1-3
Music: *St. Fulbert*, Henry John Gauntlett (1805-1876)

CM

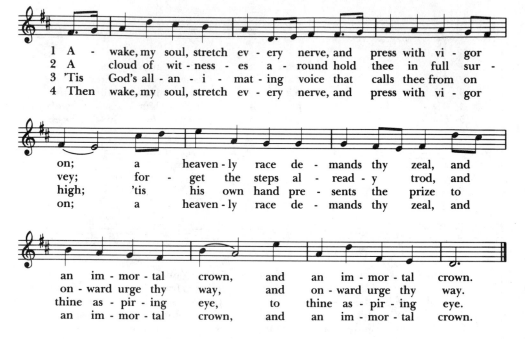

1　A - wake, my soul, stretch ev - ery nerve, and press with vi - gor
2　A cloud of wit - ness - es a - round hold thee in full sur -
3　'Tis God's all - an - i - mat - ing voice that calls thee from on
4　Then wake, my soul, stretch ev - ery nerve, and press with vi - gor

on;　a heaven - ly race de - mands thy zeal, and
vey;　for - get the steps al - read - y trod, and
high;　'tis his own hand pre - sents the prize to
on;　a heaven - ly race de - mands thy zeal, and

an im - mor - tal crown, and an im - mor - tal crown.
on - ward urge thy way, and on - ward urge thy way.
thine as - pir - ing eye, to thine as - pir - ing eye.
an im - mor - tal crown, and an im - mor - tal crown.

Words: Philip Doddridge (1702-1751)
Music: *Siroë*, George Frideric Handel (1685-1759); adapt. *Melodia Sacra*, 1815

86. 866

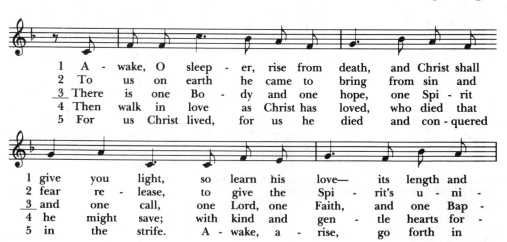

1　A - wake, O sleep - er, rise from death, and Christ shall
2　To us on earth he came to bring from sin and
3　There is one Bo - dy and one hope, one Spi - rit
4　Then walk in love as Christ has loved, who died that
5　For us Christ lived, for us he died and con - quered

1　give you light, so learn his love— its length and
2　fear re - lease, to give the Spi - rit's u - ni -
3　and one call, one Lord, one Faith, and one Bap -
4　he might save; with kind and gen - tle hearts for -
5　in the strife. A - wake, a - rise, go forth in

1 breadth, its full - ness, depth, and height.
2 ty, the ve - ry bond of peace.
3 tism, one Fa - ther of us all.
4 give as God in Christ for - gave.
5 faith, and Christ shall give you life.

Words: F. Bland Tucker (1895-1984)
Music: *Marsh Chapel*, Max Miller (b. 1927)

CM

Christian Vocation and Pilgrimage

548

1 Sol - diers of Christ, a - rise, and put your
2 strong in the Lord of hosts, and in his
3 Stand then in his great might, with all his
4 From strength to strength go on, wres - tle, and
5 That, hav - ing all things done, and all your

1 ar - mor on, strong in the strength which
2 might - y power: who in the strength of
3 strength en - dued, and take, to arm you
4 fight, and pray: tread all the powers of
5 con - flicts past, ye may o'er - come, through

1 God sup - plies through his e - ter - nal Son;
2 Je - sus trusts is more than con - quer - or.
3 for the fight, the pan - o - ply of God.
4 dark - ness down, and win the well - fought day.
5 Christ a - lone, and stand com - plete at last.

Words: Charles Wesley (1707-1788)
Music: *Silver Street*, Isaac Smith (1734?-1805)

SM

1 Je - sus calls us; o'er the tu - mult of our
2 as, of old, Saint An - drew heard it by the
3 Je - sus calls us from the wor - ship of the
4 In our joys and in our sor - rows, days of
5 Je - sus calls us! By thy mer - cies, Sa - vior,

1 life's wild, rest - less sea, day by day his clear voice
2 Gal - i - le - an lake, turned from home and toil and
3 vain world's gold - en store; from each i - dol that would
4 toil and hours of ease, still he calls, in cares and
5 may we hear thy call, give our hearts to thine o -

1 sound - eth, say - ing, "Chris - tian, fol - low me;" say - ing
2 kin - dred, leav - ing all for his dear sake. leav - ing
3 keep us, say - ing, "Chris - tian, love me more." say - ing
4 plea - sures, "Chris-tian, love me more than these." "Chris-tian,
5 be - dience, serve and love thee best of all. serve and

Final Ending

1 "Chris - tian, fol - low me;"
2 all for his dear sake.
3 "Chris - tian, love me more."
4 love me more than these."
5 love thee best of all.

Words: Cecil Frances Alexander (1818-1895), alt.
Music: *St. Andrew*, David Hurd (b. 1950)

87. 877

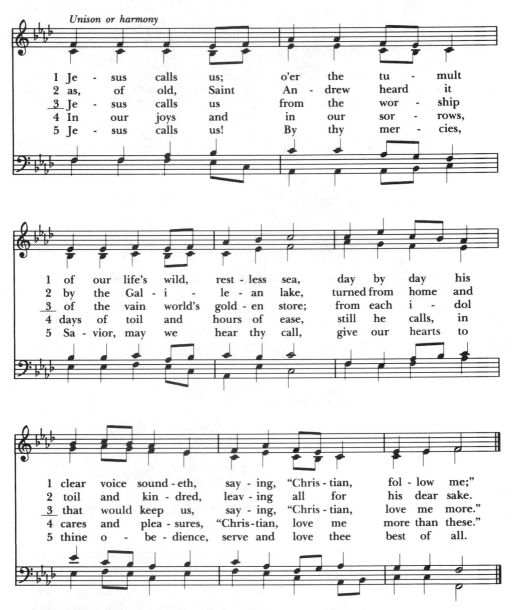

Unison or harmony

1 Je - sus calls us; o'er the tu - mult
2 as, of old, Saint An - drew heard it
3 Je - sus calls us from the wor - ship
4 In our joys and in our sor - rows,
5 Je - sus calls us! By thy mer - cies,

1 of our life's wild, rest - less sea, day by day his
2 by the Gal - i - le - an lake, turned from home and
3 of the vain world's gold - en store; from each i - dol
4 days of toil and hours of ease, still he calls, in
5 Sa - vior, may we hear thy call, give our hearts to

1 clear voice sound - eth, say - ing, "Chris - tian, fol - low me;"
2 toil and kin - dred, leav - ing all for his dear sake.
3 that would keep us, say - ing, "Chris - tian, love me more."
4 cares and plea - sures, "Chris - tian, love me more than these."
5 thine o - be - dience, serve and love thee best of all.

Words: Cecil Frances Alexander (1818-1895), alt.
Music: *Restoration*, melody from *The Southern Harmony*, 1835; harm. *Hymnal 1982*,
    after *The Southern Harmony*, 1835

87. 87

1 Rise up, ye saints of God! Have done with less-er things, give
2 Rise up, ye saints of God! His king-dom tar-ries long: Lord,
3 Lift high the cross of Christ! Tread where his feet have trod; and

heart and soul and mind and strength to serve the King of kings.
bring the day of truth and love and end the night of wrong.
quick-ened by the Spi - rit's power, rise up, ye saints of God!

Words: William Pierson Merrill (1867-1954), alt.
Music: *Festal Song*, William H. Walter (1825-1893)

SM

1 Fight the good fight with all thy might, Christ is thy
2 Run the straight race through God's good grace, lift up thine
*3 Cast care a - side, lean on thy Guide; his bound-less
*4 Faint not nor fear, his arms are near; he chan-geth

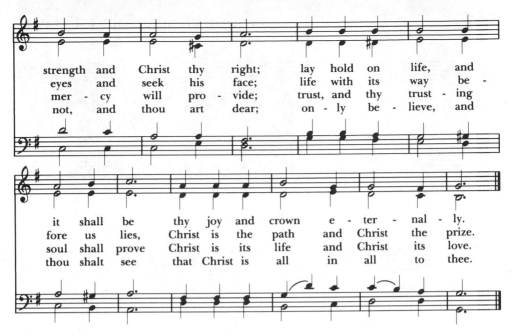

strength and Christ thy right; lay hold on life, and
eyes and seek his face; life with its way be -
mer - cy will pro - vide; trust, and thy trust - ing
not, and thou art dear; on - ly be - lieve, and

it shall be thy joy and crown e - ter - nal - ly.
fore us lies, Christ is the path and Christ the prize.
soul shall prove Christ is its life and Christ its love.
thou shalt see that Christ is all in all to thee.

Words: John Samuel Bewley Monsell (1811-1875), alt
Music: *Pentecost*, William Boyd (1847-1928)

LM

Christian Vocation and Pilgrimage

553

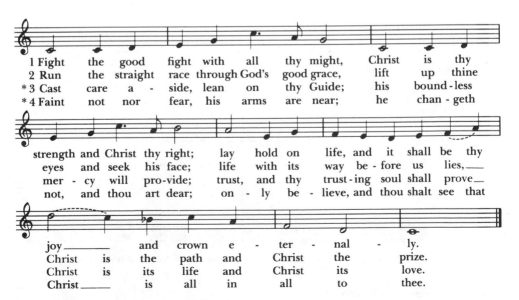

1 Fight the good fight with all thy might, Christ is thy
2 Run the straight race through God's good grace, lift up thine
*3 Cast care a - side, lean on thy Guide; his bound - less
*4 Faint not nor fear, his arms are near; he chan - geth

strength and Christ thy right; lay hold on life, and it shall be thy
eyes and seek his face; life with its way be - fore us lies,___
mer - cy will pro - vide; trust, and thy trust - ing soul shall prove___
not, and thou art dear; on - ly be - lieve, and thou shalt see that

joy___ and crown e - ter - nal - ly.
Christ is the path and Christ the prize.
Christ is its life and Christ its love.
Christ___ is all in all to thee.

Words: John Samuel Bewley Monsell (1811-1875), alt.
Music: *Rushford*, Henry G. Ley (1887-1962)

LM

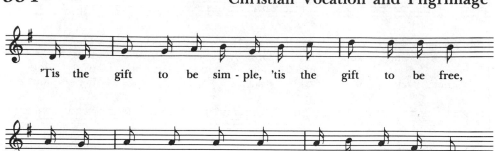

'Tis the gift to be sim - ple, 'tis the gift to be free,

'tis the gift to come down where we ought to be,

and when we find our - selves in the place just right,

'twill be in the val - ley of love and de - light.

When true sim - plic - i - ty is gained to

bow and to bend we shan't be a - shamed, to turn, turn, will

be our de - light till by turn - ing, turn - ing we come round right.

Words: Joseph Brackett, Jr. (1797-1882)
Music: *Simple Gifts*, Joseph Brackett, Jr. (1797-1882)

Irr. with Refrain

1 Lead on, O King e - ter - nal, the day of march has come;
hence - forth in fields of con - quest thy tents shall be our home:
through days of prep - a - ra - tion thy grace has made us strong,
and now, O King e - ter - nal, we lift our bat - tle song.

2 Lead on, O King e - ter - nal, till sin's fierce war shall cease,
and ho - li - ness shall whis - per the sweet a - men of peace;
for not with swords loud clash - ing, nor roll of stir - ring drums,
but deeds of love and mer - cy, the heaven - ly king - dom comes.

3 Lead on, O King e - ter - nal: we fol - low, not with fears;
for glad - ness breaks like morn - ing wher - e'er thy face ap - pears.
Thy cross is lift - ed o'er us; we jour - ney in its light:
the crown a - waits the con - quest; lead on, O God of might!

Words: Ernest Warburton Shurtleff (1862-1917)
Music: *Lancashire*, Henry Thomas Smart (1813-1879)

76. 76 D

1 Re - joice, ye pure in heart! Re - joice, give thanks, and sing! Your
2 With all the an - gel choirs, with all the saints of earth, pour
3 Your clear ho - san - nas raise, and al - le - lu - ias loud; while
4 Yes, on through life's long path, still chant-ing as ye go, from
5 Still lift your stand-ard high, still march in firm ar - ray, as

1 glo - rious ban - ner wave on high, the cross of Christ your King.
2 out the strains of joy and bliss, true rap - ture, no - blest mirth.
3 an - swering ech - oes up - ward float, like wreaths of in - cense cloud.
4 youth to age, by night and day, in glad - ness and in woe.
5 war - riors through the dark - ness toil, till dawns the gold - en day.

Refrain

Re - joice, re - joice, re - joice, give thanks, and sing.

re - joice, re - joice,

*6 At last the march shall end;
    the wearied ones shall rest;
the pilgrims find their Father's house,
    Jerusalem the blest.

        Refrain

*7 Then on, ye pure in heart!
    Rejoice, give thanks, and sing!
Your glorious banner wave on high
    the cross of Christ your King.

        Refrain

Words: Edward Hayes Plumptre (1821-1891)
Music: *Marion*, Arthur Henry Messiter (1834-1916)

SM with Refrain

Christian Vocation and Pilgrimage

1. Re - joice, ye pure in heart! Re - joice, give thanks, and
2. With all the an - gel choirs, with all the saints of
3. Your clear ho - san - nas raise, and al - le - lu - ias
4. Yes, on through life's long path, still chant-ing as ye
5. Still lift your stand - ard high, still march in firm ar -
*6. At last the march shall end; the wea - ried ones shall
*7. Then on, ye pure in heart! Re - joice, give thanks, and

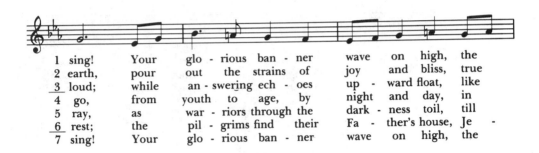

1. sing! Your glo - rious ban - ner wave on high, the
2. earth, pour out the strains of joy and bliss, true
3. loud; while an - swering ech - oes up - ward float, like
4. go, from youth to age, by night and day, in
5. ray, as war - riors through the dark - ness toil, till
6. rest; the pil - grims find their Fa - ther's house, Je -
7. sing! Your glo - rious ban - ner wave on high, the

Refrain

1. cross of Christ your King.
2. rap - ture, no - blest mirth.
3. wreaths of in - cense cloud.
4. glad - ness and in woe. Ho - san - na, ho -
5. dawns the gold - en day.
6. ru - sa - lem the blest.
7. cross of Christ your King.

san - na! Re - joice, give thanks, and sing.

Words: Edward Hayes Plumptre (1821-1891)
Music: *Vineyard Haven*, Richard Wayne Dirksen (b. 1921)

SM with Refrain

1 Faith of our fa - thers! liv - ing still in spite of dun - geon,
2 Faith of our fa - thers! faith and prayer shall win all na - tions
3 Faith of our fa - thers! we will love both friend and foe in

fire, and sword: O how our hearts beat high with joy,
un - to thee; and through the truth that comes from God,
all our strife: and preach thee, too, as love knows how,

Refrain

when-e'er we hear that glo - rious word:
man - kind shall then in - deed be free. Faith of our fa - thers,
by kind - ly deeds and vir - tuous life.

ho - ly faith! We will be true to thee till death.

Words: Frederick William Faber (1814-1863), alt.
Music: *St. Catherine*, Henri Frédéric Hemy (1818-1888); adapt. and arr. James G. Walton (1821-1905)   88. 88. 88

1 Lead us, heaven-ly Fa - ther, lead us o'er the world's tem -
pes - tuous sea; guard us, guide us, keep us, feed us,
for we have no help but thee, yet pos - ses - sing
ev - ery bless - ing, if our God our Fa - ther be.

2 Sa - vior, breathe for - give - ness o'er us; all our weak - ness
thou dost know; thou didst tread this earth be - fore us;
thou didst feel its keen - est woe; yet un - fear - ing,
per - se - ver - ing, to thy pas - sion thou didst go.

3 Spi - rit of our God, de - scend - ing, fill our hearts with
heaven - ly joy; love with ev - ery pas - sion blend - ing
plea - sure that can nev - er cloy; thus pro - vid - ed,
par - doned, guid - ed, noth - ing can our peace des - troy.

Words: James Edmeston (1791-1867), alt.
Music: *Dulce carmen*, melody from *An Essay on the Church Plain Chant*, 1782;
adapt. *Collection of Motetts or Antiphons*, ca. 1840; harm. William Henry Monk (1823-1889)

87. 87. 87

Antiphon

Re-mem-ber your ser-vants, Lord,   when you come in your kingly pow - er.

1. Bless-ed   are the poor in spi - rit;   for theirs is the kingdom of hea - ven.

2. Bless - ed   are those who mourn;   for they shall be com - fort - ed.

3. Bless - ed   are   the meek;   for they shall in - her - it the earth.

4. Bless - ed   are   those who hunger and thirst af - ter right - eous-ness;

for theirs is the kingdom of hea - - ven.

9. Bless - ed are you when the world re - viles you and per - se - cutes you;

and utters all manner of evil against you false - ly for my sake:

Re - joice and be ex - ceed - ing glad; for great is your reward in hea - ven.

Antiphon

Re - mem - ber your ser - vants, Lord, when you come in your kingly pow - er.

The second bass part is optional.

Words: Russian Orthodox liturgy; Matthew 5:3-12
Music: *Beatitudes*, Russian Orthodox hymn; arr. Richard Proulx (b. 1937)

Irr. with Refrain

1 Stand up, stand up, for Je - sus, ye sold-iers of the cross;
2 Stand up, stand up, for Je - sus; the trum-pet call o - bey;
3 Stand up, stand up, for Je - sus; stand in his strength a - lone;
4 Stand up, stand up, for Je - sus: the strife will not be long:

lift high his roy - al ban - ner, it must not suf - fer loss:
forth to the might - y con - flict in this his glo-rious day:
the arm of flesh will fail you, ye dare not trust your own:
this day, the noise of bat - tle; the next, the vic - tor's song.

from vic - tory un - to vic - tory his ar - my shall he lead,
ye that are his now serve him a - gainst un-num-bered foes;
put on the Gos - pel ar - mor, and watch-ing un - to prayer,
To val - iant hearts tri - um - phant, a crown of life shall be;

till ev - ery foe is van - quished and Christ is Lord in - deed.
let cour-age rise with dan - ger, and strength to strength op - pose.
when du - ty calls, or dan - ger, be nev - er want-ing there.
they with the King of glo - ry shall reign e - ter - nal - ly.

Words: George Duffield, Jr. (1818-1888), alt.
Music: *Morning Light*, George James Webb (1803-1887)

76. 76. D

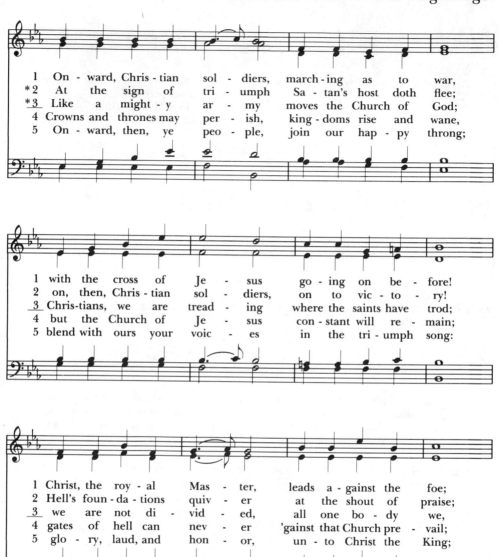

1 On - ward, Chris - tian sol - diers, march - ing as to war,
*2 At the sign of tri - umph Sa - tan's host doth flee;
*3 Like a might - y ar - my moves the Church of God;
4 Crowns and thrones may per - ish, king - doms rise and wane,
5 On - ward, then, ye peo - ple, join our hap - py throng;

1 with the cross of Je - sus go - ing on be - fore!
2 on, then, Chris - tian sol - diers, on to vic - to - ry!
3 Chris - tians, we are tread - ing where the saints have trod;
4 but the Church of Je - sus con - stant will re - main;
5 blend with ours your voic - es in the tri - umph song:

1 Christ, the roy - al Mas - ter, leads a - gainst the foe;
2 Hell's foun - da - tions quiv - er at the shout of praise;
3 we are not di - vid - ed, all one bo - dy we,
4 gates of hell can nev - er 'gainst that Church pre - vail;
5 glo - ry, laud, and hon - or, un - to Christ the King;

1 for - ward in - to bat - tle, see, his ban - ners go.
2 Chris - tians, lift your voic - es, loud your an - thems raise.
3 one in hope and doc - trine, one in char - i - ty.
4 we have Christ's own prom - ise, and that can - not fail.
5 this through count - less a - ges we with an - gels sing.

Refrain

On - ward, Chris - tian sol - diers, march - ing as to war,

with the cross of Je - sus go - ing on be - fore!

Words: Sabine Baring-Gould (1834-1924), alt.
Music: *St. Gertrude*, Arthur Seymour Sullivan (1842-1900)

65. 65. D with Refrain

1 Go for-ward, Chris-tian sol - dier, be - neath his ban - ner true:
2 Go for-ward, Chris-tian sol - dier, fear not the se - cret foe;
3 Go for-ward, Chris-tian sol - dier, nor dream of peace - ful rest,
4 Go for-ward, Chris-tian sol - dier, fear not the gath - ering night:

the Lord him-self, thy Lead - er, shall all thy foes sub - due.
far more o'er thee are watch - ing than hu - man eyes can know:
till Sa - tan's host is van - quished and heaven is all pos - sessed;
the Lord has been thy shel - ter; the Lord will be thy light.

His love fore-tells thy tri - als; he knows thine hour - ly need;
trust on - ly Christ, thy Cap-tain; cease not to watch and pray;
till Christ him-self shall call thee to lay thine ar - mor by,
When morn his face re - veal - eth thy dan - gers all are past:

he can with bread of hea - ven thy faint - ing spi - rit feed.
heed not the treach-erous voic - es that lure thy soul a - stray.
and wear in end - less glo - ry the crown of vic - to - ry.
O pray that faith and vir - tue may keep thee to the last!

Words: Laurence Tuttiett (1825-1895)
Music: *Lancashire*, Henry Thomas Smart (1813-1879)

76. 76. D

1 He who would val - iant be 'gainst all dis - as - ter,
2 Who so be - set him round with dis - mal sto - ries,
3 Since, Lord, thou dost de - fend us with thy Spi - rit,

let him in con - stan - cy fol - low the Mas - ter.
do but them - selves con-found, his strength the more is.
we know we at the end shall life in - her - it.

There's no dis - cour - age-ment shall make him once re - lent
No foes shall stay his might, though he with gi - ants fight;
Then fan - cies flee a - way; I'll fear not what men say,

his first a - vowed in - tent to be a pil - grim.
he will make good his right to be a pil - grim.
I'll la - bor night and day to be a pil - grim.

Words: Percy Dearmer (1867-1936), after John Bunyan (1628-1688)
Music: *St. Dunstan's,* Charles Winfred Douglas (1867-1944)

65. 65. 6665

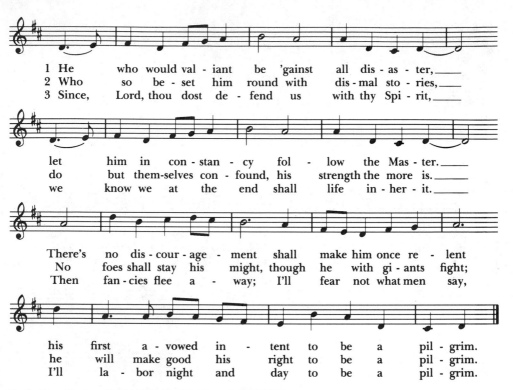

1 He who would val - iant be 'gainst all dis - as - ter,____
2 Who so be - set him round with dis - mal sto - ries,____
3 Since, Lord, thou dost de - fend us with thy Spi - rit,____

let him in con - stan - cy fol - low the Mas - ter.____
do but them-selves con - found, his strength the more is.____
we know we at the end shall life in - her - it.____

There's no dis - cour - age - ment shall make him once re - lent
No foes shall stay his might, though he with gi - ants fight;
Then fan - cies flee a - way; I'll fear not what men say,

his first a - vowed in - tent to be a pil - grim.
he will make good his right to be a pil - grim.
I'll la - bor night and day to be a pil - grim.

Words: Percy Dearmer (1868-1936), after John Bunyan (1628-1688)
Music: *Monk's Gate,* Sussex folk melody; adapt and arr. Ralph Vaughan Williams (1872-1958)   11 11. 12 11

Christian Responsibility

1 From thee all skill and sci-ence flow, all pi-ty, care, and love,
2 And has-ten, Lord, that per-fect day when pain and death shall cease,

all calm and cour-age, faith and hope: O pour them from a-bove!
and thy just rule shall fill the earth with health and light and peace;

Im - part them, Lord, to each and all, as each and all shall need,
when ev - er-blue the sky shall gleam, and ev - er-green the sod,

to rise, like in - cense, each to thee, in no - ble thought and deed.
and our rude work de - face no more the hand - i - work of God.

Words: Charles Kingsley (1819-1875), alt.
Music: *The Church's Desolation*, traditional melody; harm. J. T. White (19th cent.);
adapt. C. H. Cayce (19th-20th cent.)

CMD

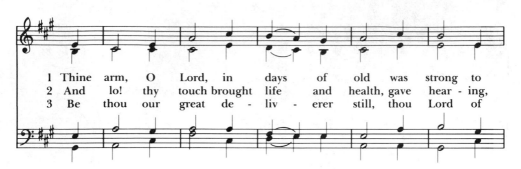

1 Thine arm, O Lord, in days of old was strong to
2 And lo! thy touch brought life and health, gave hear - ing,
3 Be thou our great de - liv - erer still, thou Lord of

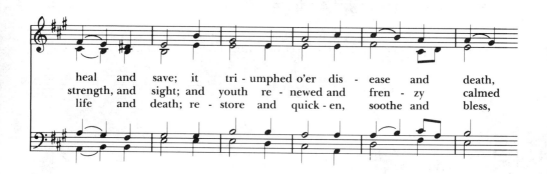

heal and save; it tri - umphed o'er dis - ease and death,
strength, and sight; and youth re - newed and fren - zy calmed
life and death; re - store and quick - en, soothe and bless,

o'er dark - ness and the grave. To thee they went, the
owned thee, the Lord of light: and now, O Lord, be
with thine al - might - y breath: to hands that work and

blind, the deaf, the pal - sied, and the lame, the lep - er
near to bless, al - might - y as of yore, in crowd - ed
eyes that see, give wis - dom's heaven - ly lore, that whole and

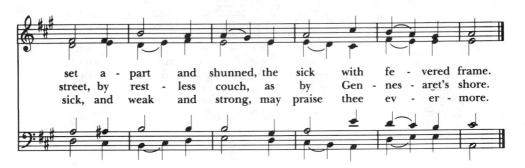

set a - part and shunned, the sick with fe - vered frame.
street, by rest - less couch, as by Gen - nes - aret's shore.
sick, and weak and strong, may praise thee ev - er - more.

Words: Edward Hayes Plumptre (1821-1891), alt.
Music: *St. Matthew*, from *Supplement to the New Version of Psalms by Dr. Brady and Mr. Tate*, 1708

CMD

1 Fa - ther all lov - ing, who rul - est in ma - jes - ty,
2 Bless - ed Lord Je - sus, who cam - est in pov - er - ty,
3 Come, Ho - ly Spi - rit, cre - ate in us ho - li - ness,
4 Ho - li - est Trin - i - ty, per - fect in u - ni - ty,

judg - ment is thine, and con - demn - eth our pride;
shar - ing a sta - ble with beasts at thy birth,
lift up our lives to thy stand - ard of right;
bind in thy love ev - ery na - tion and race;

stir up our lead - ers and peo - ples to pen - i - tence,
stir us to work for thy jus - tice and char - i - ty,
stir ev - ery will to new ven - tures of faith - ful - ness,
may we a - dore thee for time and e - ter - ni - ty,

sor - row for sins that for ven - geance have cried.
tru - ly to care for the poor of the earth.
flood the whole Church with thy glo - ri - ous light.
Fa - ther, Re - deem - er, and Spi - rit of grace.

Words: Patrick Robert Norman Appleford (b. 1925), alt.
Music: *Was lebet,* melody from *Choral-Buch vor Johann Heinrich Reinhardt,* 1754;
    harm. Ralph Vaughan Williams (1872-1958)

12 10. 12 10

Christian Responsibility

1 God the Om - ni - po - tent! King, who or - dain - est
2 God the All - mer - ci - ful! earth hath for - sak - en
3 God, the All - right - eous One! earth hath de - fied thee;
4 God the All - prov - i - dent! earth by thy chas - tening

thun - der thy clar - ion, the light - ning thy sword;
thy ways all ho - ly, and slight - ed thy word;
yet to e - ter - ni - ty stand - eth thy word,
yet shall to free - dom and truth be re - stored;

show forth thy pi - ty on high where thou reign - est:
bid not thy wrath in its ter - rors a - wak - en:
false - hood and wrong shall not tar - ry be - side thee:
through the thick dark - ness thy king - dom is haste - ning:

give to us peace in our time, O Lord.
give to us peace in our time, O Lord.
give to us peace in our time, O Lord.
thou wilt give peace in thy time, O Lord.

Words: Sts. 1-2, Henry Fothergill Chorley (1808-1872), alt.; sts. 3-4, John Ellerton (1826-1893), alt.
Music: *Russia*, Alexis Lvov (1799-1870)

11 10. 11 9

570

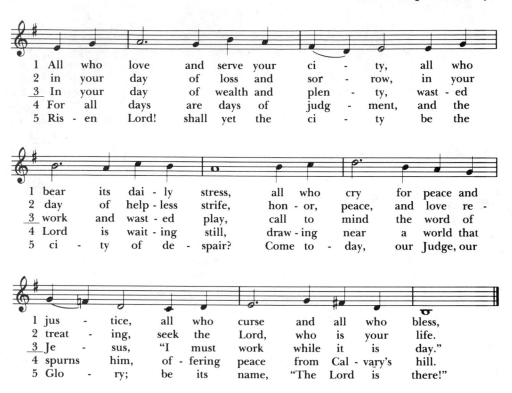

1 All who love and serve your ci - ty, all who
2 in your day of loss and sor - row, in your
3 In your day of wealth and plen - ty, wast - ed
4 For all days are days of judg - ment, and the
5 Ris - en Lord! shall yet the ci - ty be the

1 bear its dai - ly stress, all who cry for peace and
2 day of help - less strife, hon - or, peace, and love re -
3 work and wast - ed play, call to mind the word of
4 Lord is wait - ing still, draw - ing near a world that
5 ci - ty of de - spair? Come to - day, our Judge, our

1 jus - tice, all who curse and all who bless,
2 treat - ing, seek the Lord, who is your life.
3 Je - sus, "I must work while it is day."
4 spurns him, of - fering peace from Cal - vary's hill.
5 Glo - ry; be its name, "The Lord is there!"

Words: Erik Routley (1917-1982), rev.
Music: *Birabus*, Peter Cutts (b. 1937)

87. 87

Music: Copyright © 1969 by Hope Publishing Company. All Rights Reserved. Used by Permission.

571

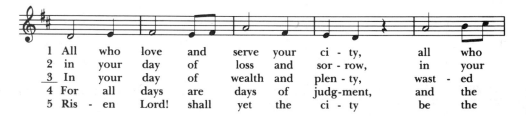

1 All who love and serve your ci - ty, all who
2 in your day of loss and sor - row, in your
3 In your day of wealth and plen - ty, wast - ed
4 For all days are days of judg-ment, and the
5 Ris - en Lord! shall yet the ci - ty be the

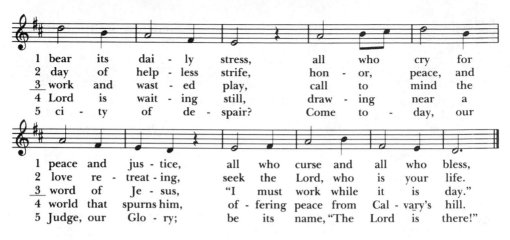

1 bear its dai - ly stress, all who cry for
2 day of help - less strife, hon - or, peace, and
3 work and wast - ed play, call to mind the
4 Lord is wait - ing still, draw - ing near a
5 ci - ty of de - spair? Come to - day, our

1 peace and jus - tice, all who curse and all who bless,
2 love re - treat - ing, seek the Lord, who is your life.
3 word of Je - sus, "I must work while it is day."
4 world that spurns him, of - fering peace from Cal - vary's hill.
5 Judge, our Glo - ry; be its name, "The Lord is there!"

Words: Erik Routley (1917-1982), rev.
Music: *Charlestown*, melody from *The Southern Harmony*, 1835

87. 87

Christian Responsibility   572

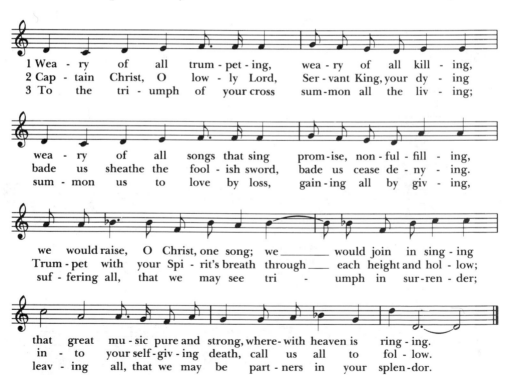

1 Wea - ry of all trum - pet - ing, wea - ry of all kill - ing,
2 Cap - tain Christ, O low - ly Lord, Ser - vant King, your dy - ing
3 To the tri - umph of your cross sum - mon all the liv - ing;

wea - ry of all songs that sing prom - ise, non - ful - fill - ing,
bade us sheathe the fool - ish sword, bade us cease de - ny - ing.
sum - mon us to love by loss, gain - ing all by giv - ing,

we would raise, O Christ, one song; we_____ would join in sing - ing,
Trum - pet with your Spi - rit's breath through___ each height and hol - low;
suf - fering all, that we may see tri - umph in sur - ren - der;

that great mu - sic pure and strong, where - with heaven is ring - ing.
in - to your self - giv - ing death, call us all to fol - low.
leav - ing all, that we may be part - ners in your splen - dor.

Words: Martin H. Franzmann (1907-1976), alt.
Music: *Distler*, Hugo Distler (1908-1942)

76. 76. D

1 Fa - ther e - ter - nal,   Ru - ler of cre - a - tion,
2 Rac - es and peo - ples,   lo, we stand di - vid - ed,
3 En - vious of heart, blind - eyed, with tongues con - found - ed,
4 Lust of pos - ses - sion work - eth des - o - la - tions;
5 How shall we love thee, ho - ly hid - den Be - ing,

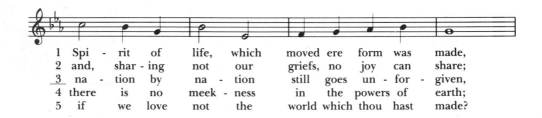

1 Spi - rit of life, which moved ere form was made,
2 and, shar - ing not our griefs, no joy can share;
3 na - tion by na - tion still goes un - for - given,
4 there is no meek - ness in the powers of earth;
5 if we love not the world which thou hast made?

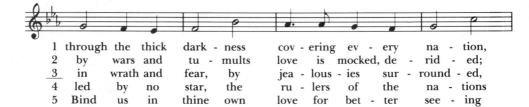

1 through the thick dark - ness cov - ering ev - ery na - tion,
2 by wars and tu - mults love is mocked, de - rid - ed;
3 in wrath and fear, by jea - lous - ies sur - round - ed,
4 led by no star, the ru - lers of the na - tions
5 Bind us in thine own love for bet - ter see - ing

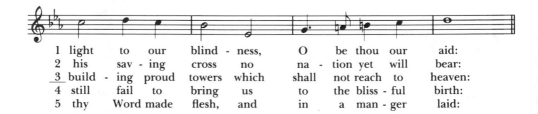

1 light to our blind - ness, O be thou our aid:
2 his sav - ing cross no na - tion yet will bear:
3 build - ing proud towers which shall not reach to heaven:
4 still fail to bring us to the bliss - ful birth:
5 thy Word made flesh, and in a man - ger laid:

Refrain

thy king - dom come, O Lord, thy will be done.

Words: Laurence Housman (1865-1959), alt.
Music: *Langham*, Geoffrey Turton Shaw (1879-1943)

11 10. 11 10. 10

1 Be - fore thy throne, O God, we kneel: give us a con - science
2 Search out our hearts and make us true; help us to give to
3 For sins of heed - less word and deed, for pride am - bi - tious
4 Let the fierce fires which burn and try, our in - most spi - rits

quick to feel, a rea - dy mind to un - der - stand the
all their due. From love of plea - sure, lust of gold, from
to suc - ceed, for craft - y trade and sub - tle snare to
pu - ri - fy: con - sume the ill; purge out the shame; O

mean - ing of thy chas - tening hand; what - e'er the pain and
sins which make the heart grow cold, wean us and train us
catch the sim - ple un - a - ware, for lives be - reft of
God, be with us in the flame; a new - born peo - ple

shame may be, bring us, O Fa - ther, near - er thee.
with thy rod; teach us to know our faults, O God.
pur - pose high, for - give, for - give, O Lord, we cry.
may we rise, more pure, more true, more no - bly wise.

Words: William Boyd Carpenter (1841-1918), alt.
Music: *St. Petersburg*, Dimitri S. Bortniansky (1751-1825)

88. 88. 88

1 Be-fore thy throne, O God, we kneel: give us a con-science quick to feel, a rea-dy mind to un-der-stand the mean-ing of thy chas-tening hand; what-e'er the pain and shame may be, bring us, O Fa-ther, near-er thee.

2 Search out our hearts and make us true; help us to give to all their due. From love of plea-sure, lust of gold, from sins which make the heart grow cold, wean us and train us with thy rod; teach us to know our faults, O God.

3 For sins of heed-less word and deed, for pride am-bi-tious to suc-ceed, for craft-y trade and sub-tle snare to catch the sim-ple un-a-ware, for lives be-reft of pur-pose high, for-give, for-give, O Lord, we cry.

4 Let the fierce fires which burn and try, our in-most spi-rits pu-ri-fy: con-sume the ill; purge out the shame; O God, be with us in the flame; a new-born peo-ple may we rise, more pure, more true, more no-bly wise.

Words: William Boyd Carpenter (1841-1918), alt.
Music: *Vater unser im Himmelreich*, melody from *Geistliche lieder auffs new gebessert und gemehrt*, 1539;
adapt. Martin Luther (1483-1546); harm. Hans Leo Hassler (1564-1612)

88. 88. 88

Christian Responsibility

Descant (after stanzas 2 and 3)

God   is   love,   God   is   love,

Refrain

God   is   love,   and   where true   love   is

1-3   *Final Ending*

God him - self   is   there.   there. _____

God him - self   is   there.   there. _____

1 Here in Christ we gath - er,   love of Christ our call - ing.
2 When we Chris-tians gath - er, mem-bers of one Bo - dy,
3 Grant us love's ful - fill - ment, joy with all the bless - ed,

Christ, our love, is with us,   glad - ness be his greet - ing.
let there be in us no   dis - cord but one spi - rit.
when we see your face, O   Sa - vior, in its glo - ry.

Let us fear and love him,   ho - ly God e - ter - nal.
Ban - ished now be an - ger, strife and ev - ery quar - rel.
Shine on us, O pur - est Light of all cre - a - tion,

Repeat Refrain

Lov - ing him, let each love Christ in one an - oth - er.
Christ, our God, be al - ways pres - ent here a - mong us.
be our bliss while end - less a - ges sing your prais - es.

Words: Latin; tr. James Quinn (b. 1919), alt.
Music: *Mandatum*, Richard Proulx (b. 1937)

12. 12. 12. 12 with Refrain

Refrain

God is love, and where true love is God him-self is there.

1 Here in Christ we gath - er, love of Christ our call - ing.
2 When we Chris-tians gath - er, mem-bers of one Bo - dy,
3 Grant us love's ful - fill - ment, joy with all the bless - ed,

Christ, our love, is with us, glad-ness be his greet - ing.
let there be in us no dis - cord but one spi - rit.
when we see your face, O Sa - vior, in its glo - ry.

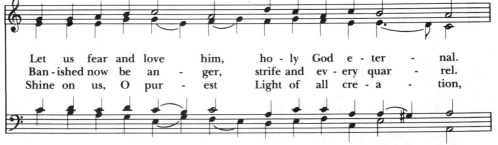

Let us fear and love him, ho - ly God e - ter - nal.
Ban - ished now be an - ger, strife and ev - ery quar - rel.
Shine on us, O pur - est Light of all cre - a - tion,

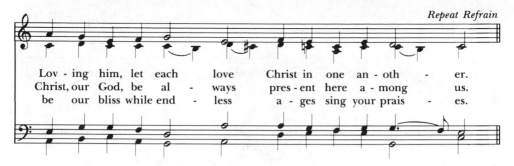

Lov - ing him, let each love Christ in one an - oth - er.
Christ, our God, be al - ways pres - ent here a - mong us.
be our bliss while end - less a - ges sing your prais - es.

Words: Latin; tr. James Quinn (b. 1919), alt.
Music: *Ubi caritas (Murray)*, A. Gregory Murray (b. 1905)

12. 12. 12. 12 with Refrain

Christian Responsibility

578

Unison or harmony

1 O God of love, O King of peace, make wars through-
2 Re - mem - ber, Lord, thy works of old, the won - ders
3 Whom shall we trust but thee, O Lord? Where rest but

out the world to cease; the wrath of na - tions now re -
that thy peo - ple told; re - mem - ber not our sin's dark
on thy faith - ful word? None ev - er called on thee in

strain, give peace, O God, give peace a - gain!
stain, give peace, O God, give peace a - gain!
vain, give peace, O God, give peace a - gain!

Words: Henry Williams Baker (1821-1877), alt.
Music: *Eltham*, melody Nathaniel Gawthorn (18th cent.); harm. Samuel Sebastian Wesley (1810-1876)

LM

1 Almighty Father, strong to save, whose arm hath bound the
restless wave, who bidd'st the mighty ocean deep its
own appointed limits keep: O hear us when we
cry to thee for those in peril on the sea.

2 O Christ, the Lord of hill and plain o'er which our traffic
runs amain by mountain pass or valley low; wher-
ever, Lord, thy people go, protect them by thy
guarding hand from every peril on the land.

3 O Spirit, whom the Father sent to spread abroad the
firmament; O Wind of heaven, by thy might save
all who dare the eagle's flight, and keep them by thy
watchful care from every peril in the air.

4 O Trinity of love and power, our people shield in
danger's hour; from rock and tempest, fire and foe, protect them wheresoe'er they go; thus evermore shall
rise to thee glad praise from space, air, land, and sea.

Words: Sts. 1 and 4, William Whiting (1825-1878), alt.; sts. 2-3, Robert Nelson Spencer
(1877-1961), alt.
Music: *Melita*, John Bacchus Dykes (1823-1876)

88. 88. 88

Christian Responsibility

Unison

1 God, who stretched the span-gled hea-vens in-fi-nite in
*2 Proud-ly rise our mod-ern ci - ties, state-ly build-ings,
3 We have ven - tured worlds un - dreamed of since the child-hood
4 As each far ho - ri - zon beck - ons, may it chal -lenge

time and place, flung the suns in burn-ing ra - diance
row on row; yet their win-dows, blank, un - feel - ing,
of our race; known the ec - sta - sy of wing - ing
us a - new, chil - dren of cre - a - tive pur - pose,

through the si - lent fields of space: we, your chil - dren
stare on can - yoned streets be - low, where the lone - ly
through un - trav - eled realms of space; probed the se - crets
serv - ing o - thers, hon - oring you. May our dreams prove

in your like - ness, share in - ven - tive powers with you;
drift un - no - ticed in the ci - ty's ebb and flow,
of the at - om, yield - ing un - im - ag - ined power,
rich with prom - ise, each en - deav - or well be - gun:

Great Cre - a - tor, still cre - at - ing,
lost to pur - pose and to mean - ing,
fac - ing us with life's de - struc - tion
Great Cre - a - tor, give us guid - ance

show us what we yet may do.
scarce - ly car - ing where they go.
or our most tri - um - phant hour.
till our goals and yours are one.

Words: Catherine Cameron (b. 1927), alt.
Music: *Holy Manna*, from *The Southern Harmony*, 1835

Harmony (the melody is in the tenor).

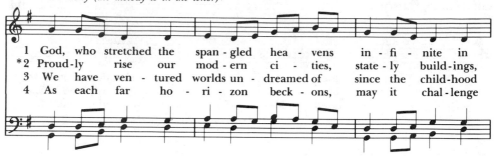

1 God, who stretched the span - gled hea - vens in - fi - nite in
*2 Proud-ly rise our mod - ern ci - ties, state - ly build-ings,
3 We have ven - tured worlds un - dreamed of since the child-hood
4 As each far ho - ri - zon beck - ons, may it chal - lenge

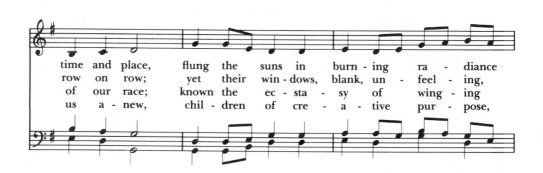

time and place, flung the suns in burn - ing ra - diance
row on row; yet their win - dows, blank, un - feel - ing,
of our race; known the ec - sta - sy of wing - ing
us a - new, chil - dren of cre - a - tive pur - pose,

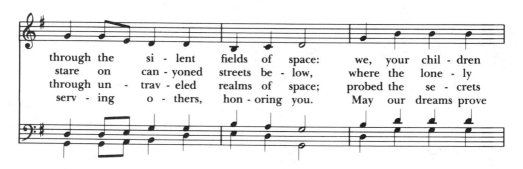

through the si - lent fields of space: we, your chil - dren
stare on can - yoned streets be - low, where the lone - ly
through un - trav - eled realms of space; probed the se - crets
serv - ing o - thers, hon - oring you. May our dreams prove

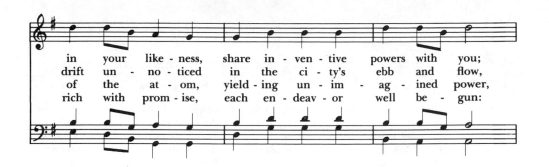

in   your   like - ness,   share   in - ven - tive   powers   with   you;
drift   un - no - ticed   in   the   ci - ty's   ebb   and   flow,
of   the   at - om,   yield - ing   un - im - ag - ined   power,
rich   with   prom - ise,   each   en - deav - or   well   be - gun:

Great   Cre - a - tor,   still   cre - at - ing,
lost   to   pur - pose   and   to   mean - ing,
fac - ing   us   with   life's   de - struc - tion
Great   Cre - a - tor,   give   us   guid - ance

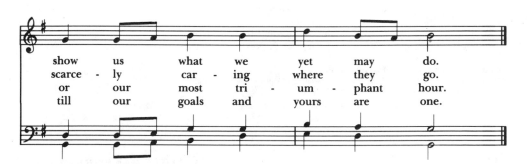

show   us   what   we   yet   may   do.
scarce - ly   car - ing   where   they   go.
or   our   most   tri - um - phant   hour.
till   our   goals   and   yours   are   one.

Words: Catherine Cameron (b. 1927), alt.
Music: *Holy Manna*, from *The Southern Harmony*, 1835

87. 87. D

1 Where char - i - ty and love pre - vail there God is ev - er found;
2 With grate-ful joy and ho - ly fear his char - i - ty we learn;
3 For - give we now each o - ther's faults as we our faults con - fess;
4 Let strife a-mong us be un - known, let all con - ten - tion cease;
5 Let us re-call that in our midst dwells God's be - got - ten Son;

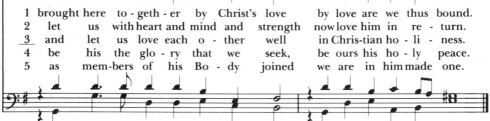

1 brought here to-geth-er by Christ's love by love are we thus bound.
2 let us with heart and mind and strength now love him in re - turn.
3 and let us love each o - ther well in Chris-tian ho - li - ness.
4 be his the glo - ry that we seek, be ours his ho - ly peace.
5 as mem-bers of his Bo - dy joined we are in him made one.

6 Love can exclude no race or creed
if honored be God's Name;
our common life embraces all
whose Father is the same.

Words: Latin; tr. J. Clifford Evers (b. 1916)
Music: *Cheshire*, melody and bass from *The Whole Booke of Psalmes*, 1592, alt.;
harm. *Hymns III*, 1979   LM

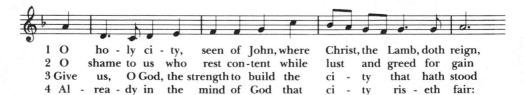

1 O ho - ly ci - ty, seen of John, where Christ, the Lamb, doth reign,
2 O shame to us who rest con-tent while lust and greed for gain
3 Give us, O God, the strength to build the ci - ty that hath stood
4 Al - rea - dy in the mind of God that ci - ty ris - eth fair:

with - in whose four-square walls shall come no night, nor need, nor pain,
in street and shop and ten - e - ment wring gold from hu - man pain,
too long a dream, whose laws are love, whose crown is ser - vant - hood,
lo, how its splen-dor chal - leng - es the souls that great - ly dare—

and where the tears are wiped from eyes that shall not weep a - gain!
and bit - ter lips in blind de - spair cry, "Christ hath died in vain!"
and where the sun that shin - eth is God's grace for hu - man good.
yea, bids us seize the whole of life and build its glo - ry there.

Words: Walter Russell Bowie (1882-1969), alt.
Music: *Sancta Civitas*, Herbert Howells (1892-1983)

86. 86. 86

Christian Responsibility

583

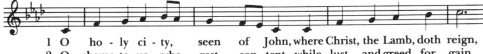

1 O ho - ly ci - ty, seen of John, where Christ, the Lamb, doth reign,
2 O shame to us who rest con - tent while lust and greed for gain
3 Give us, O God, the strength to build the ci - ty that hath stood
4 Al - rea - dy in the mind of God that ci - ty ris - eth fair:

with - in whose four-square walls shall come no night, nor need, nor pain,
in street and shop and ten - e - ment wring gold from hu - man pain,
too long a dream, whose laws are love, whose crown is ser - vant - hood,
lo, how its splen - dor chal - leng - es the souls that great - ly dare—

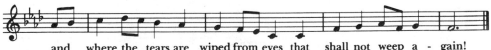

and where the tears are wiped from eyes that shall not weep a - gain!
and bit - ter lips in blind de - spair cry, "Christ hath died in vain!"
and where the sun that shin - eth is God's grace for hu - man good.
yea, bids us seize the whole of life and built its glo - ry there.

Words: Walter Russell Bowie (1882-1969), alt.
Music: *Morning Song*, melody att. Elkanah Kelsay Dare (1782-1826)

86. 86. 86

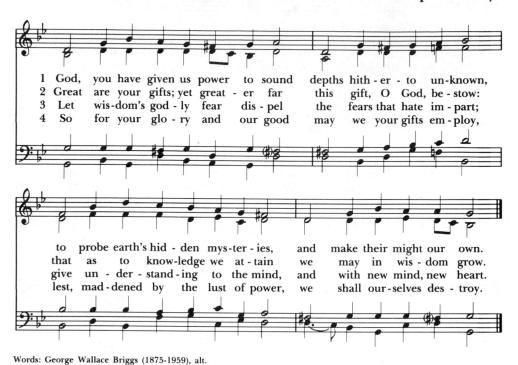

1 God, you have given us power to sound depths hith - er - to un-known,
2 Great are your gifts; yet great - er far this gift, O God, be - stow:
3 Let wis-dom's god - ly fear dis - pel the fears that hate im - part;
4 So for your glo - ry and our good may we your gifts em - ploy,

to probe earth's hid - den mys-ter - ies, and make their might our own.
that as to know-ledge we at - tain we may in wis - dom grow.
give un - der - stand - ing to the mind, and with new mind, new heart.
lest, mad - dened by the lust of power, we shall our-selves des - troy.

Words: George Wallace Briggs (1875-1959), alt.
Music: *Culross*, melody from *The Psalmes of David in Prose and Meeter*, 1635

CM

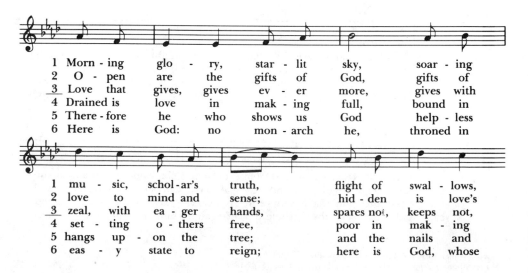

1 Morn - ing glo - ry, star - lit sky, soar - ing
2 O - pen are the gifts of God, gifts of
3 Love that gives, gives ev - er more, gives with
4 Drained is love in mak - ing full, bound in
5 There-fore he who shows us God help - less
6 Here is God: no mon - arch he, throned in

1 mu - sic, schol-ar's truth, flight of swal - lows,
2 love to mind and sense; hid - den is love's
3 zeal, with ea - ger hands, spares not, keeps not,
4 set - ting o - thers free, poor in mak - ing
5 hangs up - on the tree; and the nails and
6 eas - y state to reign; here is God, whose

1 au - tumn   leaves,   mem-ory's   trea - sure, grace of   youth:
2 a - go - ny,   love's en - deav - or, love's ex - pense.
3 all out - pours,   ven - tures   all, its   all ex - pends.
4 man - y rich,   weak in   giv - ing power to   be.
5 crown of   thorns   tell of   what God's love must   be.
6 arms of   love   ach - ing, spent, the   world sus - tain.

Words: W. H. Vanstone (b. 1923)
Music: *Bingham*, Dorothy Howell Sheets (b. 1915)

77. 77

Christian Responsibility

586

1 Je - sus, thou di - vine Com - pan - ion,   by   thy low - ly
2 Where the   man - y   toil to - geth - er,   there art   thou a -
3 Ev - ery   task, how - ev - er sim - ple,   sets the   soul that

hu - man birth   thou hast   come to   join the work - ers,
mong thine own;   where the   sol - i - tar - y   la - bor,
does it   free;   ev - ery   deed of   hu - man kind - ness

bur - den - bear - ers   of the earth. Thou, the   car - pen - ter   of
thou art there with   them a - lone;   thou, the peace that   pass - eth
done in   love is   done to thee. Je - sus, thou di - vine Com -

Naz - areth, toil - ing for thy   dai - ly   food,   by   thy pa - tience
know-ledge, dwell - est in the   dai - ly   strife;   thou, the Bread of
pan - ion, help us   all to   work our best;   bless us   in our

and thy cour - age, thou hast taught us   toil is good.
heaven, art bro - ken in the   sac - ra - ment of life.
dai - ly la - bor, lead us to our   Sab - bath rest.

Words: Henry Van Dyke (1852-1933), alt.
Music: *Pleading Savior*, melody from *The Christian Lyre*, 1830

87. 87. D

1 Our Father, by whose Name all fa-ther-hood is known,
2 O Christ, thy-self a child with-in an earth-ly home,
3 O Spi-rit, who dost bind our hearts in u-ni-ty,

who dost in love pro-claim each fam-i-ly thine own,
with heart still un-de-filed, thou didst to man-hood come;
who teach-est us to find the love from self set free,

bless thou all par-ents, guard-ing well, with con-stant love as
our chil-dren bless, in ev-ery place, that they may all be-
in all our hearts such love in-crease, that ev-ery home, by

sen-ti-nel, the homes in which thy peo-ple dwell.
hold thy face, and know-ing thee may grow in grace.
this re-lease, may be the dwell-ing place of peace.

Words: F. Bland Tucker (1895-1984)
Music: *Rhosymedre*, John Edwards (1806-1885)

66. 66. 888

1 Al-might-y God, your word is
2 Let not our self - ish-ness and
3 Let not the world's de - ceit-ful

cast like seed up - on the ground, now let the dew of heaven de -
hate this ho - ly seed re - move, but give it root in ev - ery
cares the ris - ing plant des - troy, but let it yield a hun-dred -

1-2

scend and right-eous fruits a - bound.
heart to bring forth fruits of love.
fold the fruits of peace and (joy.)

Final Ending

joy.

Words: John Cawood (1775-1852), alt.
Music: *Call Street,* Roy Henry Johnson (b. 1933)

CM

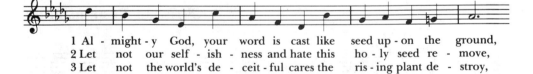

1 Al - might-y God, your word is cast like seed up - on the ground,
2 Let not our self - ish - ness and hate this ho - ly seed re - move,
3 Let not the world's de - ceit - ful cares the ris - ing plant de - stroy,

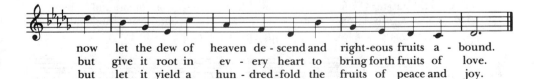

now let the dew of heaven de - scend and right-eous fruits a - bound.
but give it root in ev - ery heart to bring forth fruits of love.
but let it yield a hun - dred-fold the fruits of peace and joy.

Words: John Cawood (1775-1852), alt.
Music: *Walden,* Jane Manton Marshall (b. 1924)

CM

1 O Je - sus Christ, may grate - ful hymns be ris - ing,____
2 Grant us new cour - age, sac - ri - fi - cial, hum - ble,____
3 Show us your Spi - rit, brood-ing o'er each ci - ty,____

in ev - ery ci - ty for your love and care;____
strong in your strength to ven - ture and to dare;____
as you once wept a - bove Je - ru - sa - lem,____

in - spire our wor - ship, grant the glad sur - pris - ing____
to lift the fall - en, guide the feet that stum - ble,____
seek - ing to gath - er all in love and pi - ty,____

that your blest Spi - rit rous - es ev - ery - where.
seek out the lone - ly and God's mer - cy share.
and heal - ing those who touch your gar - ment's hem.

Words: Bradford Gray Webster (b. 1898), alt.
Music: *Charterhouse*, David Evans (1874-1948)

11 10. 11 10

Words: Copyright © 1954 Renewal 1982 by The Hymn Society of America. All rights reserved. Used by permission.

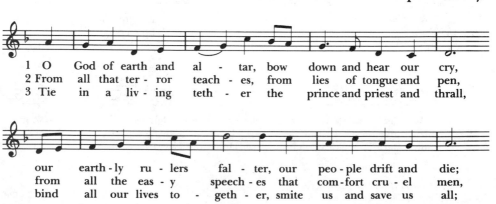

1 O God of earth and al - tar, bow down and hear our cry,
2 From all that ter - ror teach - es, from lies of tongue and pen,
3 Tie in a liv - ing teth - er the prince and priest and thrall,

our earth - ly ru - lers fal - ter, our peo - ple drift and die;
from all the eas - y speech - es that com - fort cru - el men,
bind all our lives to - geth - er, smite us and save us all;

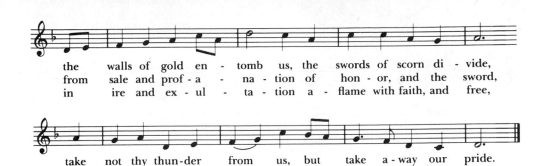

the walls of gold en - tomb us, the swords of scorn di - vide,
from sale and prof - a - na - tion of hon - or, and the sword,
in ire and ex - ul - ta - tion a - flame with faith, and free,

take not thy thun-der from us, but take a - way our pride.
from sleep and from dam - na - tion, de - liv - er us, good Lord!
lift up a liv - ing na - tion, a sin - gle sword to thee.

Words: Gilbert Keith Chesterton (1874-1936)
Music: *King's Lynn*, English melody; adapt. Ralph Vaughan Williams (1872-1958)

76. 76. D

Christian Responsibility

592

1 Teach me, my God and King, in all things thee to see, and
2 All may of thee par - take; noth - ing can be so mean, which
3 A ser - vant with this clause makes drudg - er - y di - vine: who
4 This is the fa - mous stone that turn - eth all to gold; for

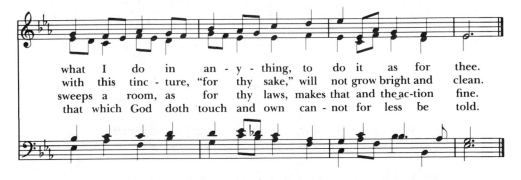

what I do in an - y - thing, to do it as for thee.
with this tinc - ture, "for thy sake," will not grow bright and clean.
sweeps a room, as for thy laws, makes that and the ac-tion fine.
that which God doth touch and own can - not for less be told.

Words: George Herbert (1593-1633)
Music: *Carlisle*, Charles Lockhart (1745-1815)

SM

1 Lord, make us ser - vants of your peace: where there is
2 Where all is doubt, may we sow faith; where all is
3 Je - sus, our Lord, may we not seek to be con -
4 May we not look for love's re - turn, but seek to
5 Dy - ing, we live, and are re - born through death's dark

1 hate, may we sow love; where there is hurt, may we for -
2 gloom, may we sow hope; where all is night, may we sow
3 soled, but to con - sole, nor look to un - der - stand - ing
4 love un - self - ish - ly, for in our giv - ing we re -
5 night to end - less day: Lord, make us ser - vants of your

1 give; where there is strife, may we make one.
2 light; where all is tears, may we sow joy.
3 hearts, but look for hearts to un - der - stand.
4 ceive, and in for - giv - ing are for - given.
5 peace, to wake at last in hea - ven's light.

Words: James Quinn (b. 1919), based on prayer att. Francis of Assisi (1182-1226)
Music: *Dickinson College*, Lee Hastings Bristol, Jr. (1923-1979)

LM

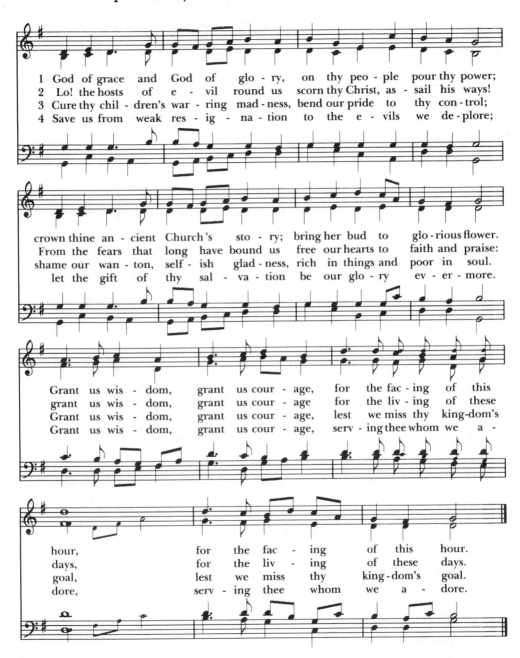

1 God of grace and God of glo - ry, on thy peo - ple pour thy power;
2 Lo! the hosts of e - vil round us scorn thy Christ, as - sail his ways!
3 Cure thy chil - dren's war - ring mad - ness, bend our pride to thy con - trol;
4 Save us from weak res - ig - na - tion to the e - vils we de - plore;

crown thine an - cient Church's sto - ry; bring her bud to glo - rious flower.
From the fears that long have bound us free our hearts to faith and praise:
shame our wan - ton, self - ish glad - ness, rich in things and poor in soul.
let the gift of thy sal - va - tion be our glo - ry ev - er - more.

Grant us wis - dom, grant us cour - age, for the fac - ing of this
grant us wis - dom, grant us cour - age for the liv - ing of these
Grant us wis - dom, grant us cour - age, lest we miss thy king - dom's
Grant us wis - dom, grant us cour - age, serv - ing thee whom we a -

hour, for the fac - ing of this hour.
days, for the liv - ing of these days.
goal, lest we miss thy king - dom's goal.
dore, serv - ing thee whom we a - dore.

Words: Harry Emerson Fosdick (1878-1969), alt.
Music: *Cwm Rhondda*, John Hughes (1873-1932)

87. 87. 877

595

1 God of grace and God of glo - ry, on thy peo - ple
2 Lo! the hosts of e - vil round us scorn thy Christ, as -
3 Cure thy chil - dren's war - ring mad - ness, bend our pride to
4 Save us from weak res - ig - na - tion to the e - vils

pour thy power; crown thine an - cient Church's sto - ry;
sail his ways! From the fears that long have bound us
thy con - trol; shame our wan - ton, self - ish glad - ness,
we de - plore; let the gift of thy sal - va - tion

bring her bud to glo - rious flower. Grant us wis - dom,
free our hearts to faith and praise: grant us wis - dom,
rich in things and poor in soul. Grant us wis - dom,
be our glo - ry ev - er - more. Grant us wis - dom,

grant us cour - age, for the fac - ing of this hour.
grant us cour - age, for the liv - ing of these days.
grant us cour - age, lest we miss thy king - dom's goal.
grant us cour - age, serv - ing thee whom we a - dore.

Words: Harry Emerson Fosdick (1878-1969), alt.
Music: *Mannheim*, melody from *Vierstimmiges Choralbuch*, 1847; harm. Lowell Mason (1792-1872)   87. 87. 87

Christian Responsibility

1 Judge e - ter - nal, throned in splen - dor, Lord of lords and
2 Still the wea - ry folk are pin - ing for the hour that
3 Crown, O God, thine own en - deav - or; cleave our dark - ness

King of kings, with thy liv - ing fire of judg - ment
brings re - lease, and the ci - ty's crowd - ed clang - or
with thy sword; feed all those who do not know thee

purge this land of bit - ter things; sol - ace all its
cries a - loud for sin to cease; and the home - steads
with the rich - ness of thy word; cleanse the bo - dy

wide do - min - ion with the heal - ing of thy wings.
and the wood - lands plead in si - lence for their peace.
of this na - tion through the glo - ry of the Lord.

Words: Henry Scott Holland (1847-1918), alt.
Music: *Komm, o komm, du Geist des Lebens*, melody from *Neu-vermehrtes und zu Ubung Christl.*
Gottseligkeit eingerichtetes Meiningisches Gesangbuch, 1693

87. 87. 87

1 O day of peace that dim-ly shines through all our
2 Then shall the wolf dwell with the lamb, nor shall the

hopes and prayers and dreams, guide us to jus - tice, truth, and
fierce de - vour the small; as beasts and cat - tle calm - ly

love, de - liv - ered from our self - ish schemes. May swords of
graze, a lit - tle child shall lead them all. Then en - e -

hate fall from our hands, our hearts from en - vy find re -
mies shall learn to love, all crea - tures find their true ac -

lease, till by God's grace our war - ring world shall see Christ's
cord; the hope of peace shall be ful - filled, for all the

Interlude

prom-ised reign of peace.
earth shall know the (Lord.)

Final Ending

Lord._____

Words: Carl P. Daw, Jr. (b. 1944)
Music: *Jerusalem*, Charles Hubert Hastings Parry (1848-1918)

LMD

Christian Responsibility

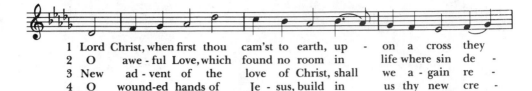

1 Lord Christ, when first thou cam'st to earth, up - on a cross they
2 O awe - ful Love, which found no room in life where sin de -
3 New ad - vent of the love of Christ, shall we a - gain re -
4 O wound-ed hands of Je - sus, build in us thy new cre -

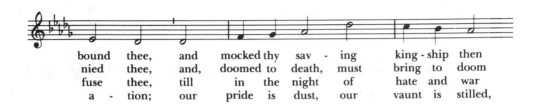

bound thee, and mocked thy sav - ing king - ship then
nied thee, and, doomed to death, must bring to doom
fuse thee, till in the night of hate and war
a - tion; our pride is dust, our vaunt is stilled,

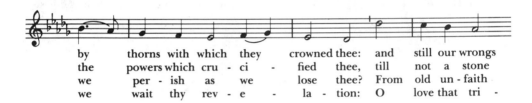

by thorns with which they crowned thee: and still our wrongs
the powers which cru - ci - fied thee, till not a stone
we per - ish as we lose thee? From old un - faith
we wait thy rev - e - la - tion: O love that tri -

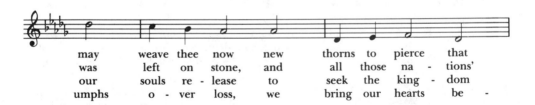

may weave thee now new thorns to pierce that
was left on stone, and all those na - tions'
our souls re - lease to seek the king - dom
umphs o - ver loss, we bring our hearts be -

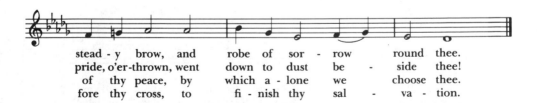

stead - y brow, and robe of sor - row round thee.
pride, o'er-thrown, went down to dust be - side thee!
of thy peace, by which a - lone we choose thee.
fore thy cross, to fi - nish thy sal - va - tion.

Words: Walter Russell Bowie (1882-1969), alt.

Music: *Mit Freuden zart*, melody from "Une pastourelle gentille," 1529; adapt. *Pseaumes cinquante de David*, 1547, and *Kirchengeseng darinnen die Heubtartickel des Christlichen Glaubens gefasset*, 1566

87. 87. 887

1 Lift ev-ery voice and sing till earth and hea - ven ring, ring with the
2 Ston-y the road we trod, bit - ter the chas-tening rod, felt in the
3 God of our wea - ry years, God of our si - lent tears, thou who hast

har - mon - ies of lib - er - ty. Let our re - joic-ing rise
days when hope un - born had died; yet, with a stead - y beat,
brought us thus far on the way; thou who hast by thy might

high as the lis - tening skies; let it re - sound loud as the
have not our wea - ry feet come to the place for which our
led us in - to the light; keep us for ev - er in the

roll - ing sea. Sing a song full of the faith that the dark past has
par - ents sighed? We have come o - ver a way that with tears has been
path, we pray. Lest our feet stray from the pla - ces, our God, where we

taught us; sing a song full of the hope that the pres-ent has
wa - tered; we have come, tread-ing our path through the blood of the
met thee; lest, our hearts drunk with the wine of the world, we for -

brought us; fac - ing the ris - ing sun of our new
slaugh - tered, out from the gloom - y past, till now we
get thee; sha-dowed be - neath thy hand may we for

day be - gun, let us march on, till vic - to - ry is won.
stand at last where the white gleam of our bright star is cast.
ev - er stand, true to our God, true to our na - tive land.

Words: James Weldon Johnson (1871-1938)
Music: *Lift Every Voice*, J. Rosamond Johnson (1873-1954)   66 10. 66 10. 14. 66 10

600

1 O day of God, draw nigh in beau-ty and in power, come
2 Bring to our trou-bled minds, un - cer-tain and a - fraid, the
3 Bring jus-tice to our land, that all may dwell se - cure, and
4 Bring to our world of strife thy sov-ereign word of peace, that
5 O day of God, draw nigh as at cre - a - tion's birth, let

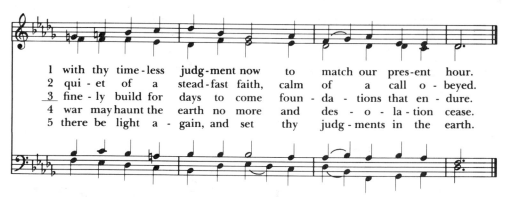

1 with thy time-less judg-ment now to match our pres-ent hour.
2 qui - et of a stead-fast faith, calm of a call o - beyed.
3 fine - ly build for days to come foun - da - tions that en - dure.
4 war may haunt the earth no more and des - o - la-tion cease.
5 there be light a - gain, and set thy judg - ments in the earth.

Words: Robert Balgarnie Young Scott (b. 1899)
Music: *Bellwoods*, James Hopkirk (1908-1972)

SM

601

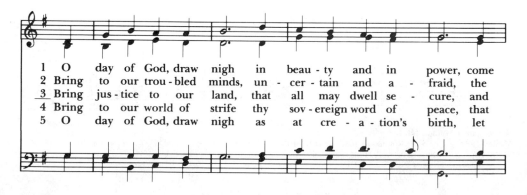

1 O day of God, draw nigh in beau-ty and in power, come
2 Bring to our trou-bled minds, un - cer-tain and a - fraid, the
3 Bring jus-tice to our land, that all may dwell se - cure, and
4 Bring to our world of strife thy sov-ereign word of peace, that
5 O day of God, draw nigh as at cre - a - tion's birth, let

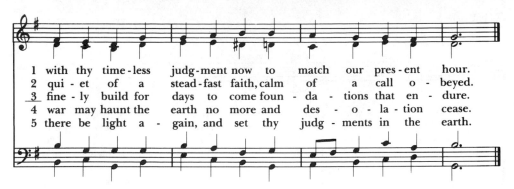

1 with thy time-less judg-ment now to match our pres-ent hour.
2 qui-et of a stead-fast faith, calm of a call o - beyed.
3 fine-ly build for days to come foun - da - tions that en - dure.
4 war may haunt the earth no more and des - o - la - tion cease.
5 there be light a - gain, and set thy judg - ments in the earth.

Words: Robert Balgarnie Young Scott (b. 1899)
Music: *St. Michael*, Louis Bourgeois (1510?-1561?); harm. William Henry Monk (1823-1889)

SM

Christian Responsibility

602

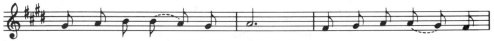

Chorus

Je - su, Je - su, fill us with your love, show

us how to serve the neigh-bors we have from you.

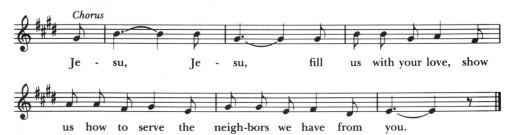

1 Kneels at the feet of his friends, si - lent - ly wash - es their
2 Neigh-bors are rich__ and poor, neigh-bors are black__ and
3 These are the ones we should serve, these are the ones we should
4 Lov - ing puts us on our knees, serv - ing as though we were

Repeat Chorus

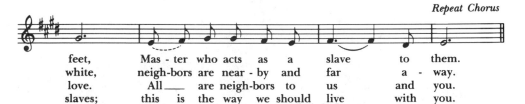

feet, Mas - ter who acts as a slave to them.
white, neigh-bors are near - by and far a - way.
love. All__ are neigh-bors to us and you.
slaves; this is the way we should live with you.

Words: Ghanaian; tr. Thomas Stevenson Colvin (b. 1925), alt.
Music: *Chereponi [Jesu, Jesu]*, Ghanaian folk song; adapt. Thomas Stevenson Colvin (b. 1925)

Irr.

1 When Christ was lift - ed from the earth, his arms stretched out a - bove through ev - ery cul - ture, ev - ery birth, to draw an an - swering love.
2 Still east and west his love ex - tends and al - ways, near or far, he calls and claims us as his friends and loves us as we are.
3 Where gen - er - a - tion, class, or race di - vide us to our shame, he sees not la - bels but a face, a per - son, and a name.
4 Thus free - ly loved, though ful - ly known, may I in Christ be free to wel - come and ac - cept his own as Christ ac - cept - ed me.

Words: Brian A. Wren (b. 1936)
Music: *St. Botolph*, Gordon Slater (1896-1979)

CM

604 Christian Responsibility

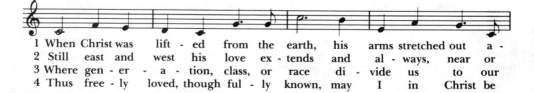

1 When Christ was lift - ed from the earth, his arms stretched out a -
2 Still east and west his love ex - tends and al - ways, near or
3 Where gen - er - a - tion, class, or race di - vide us to our
4 Thus free - ly loved, though ful - ly known, may I in Christ be

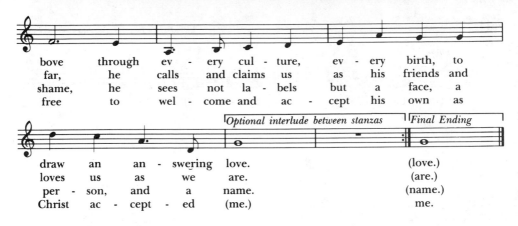

bove through ev - ery cul - ture, ev - ery birth, to
far, he calls and claims us as his friends and
shame, he sees not la - bels but a face, a
free to wel - come and ac - cept his own as

Optional interlude between stanzas | *Final Ending*

draw an an - swering love. (love.)
loves us as we are. (are.)
per - son, and a name. (name.)
Christ ac - cept - ed (me.) me.

Words: Brian A. Wren (b. 1936)
Music: *San Rocco*, Derek Williams (b. 1945)

CM

Words: Copyright © 1980 by Hope Publishing Company. All Rights Reserved. Used by Permission.

Christian Responsibility

605

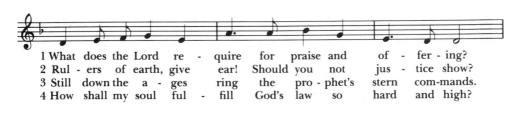

1 What does the Lord re - quire for praise and of - fer - ing?
2 Rul - ers of earth, give ear! Should you not jus - tice show?
3 Still down the a - ges ring the pro - phet's stern com-mands.
4 How shall my soul ful - fill God's law so hard and high?

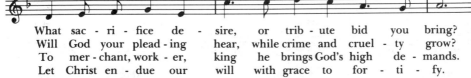

What sac - ri - fice de - sire, or trib - ute bid you bring?
Will God your plead - ing hear, while crime and cruel - ty grow?
To mer - chant, work - er, king he brings God's high de - mands.
Let Christ en - due our will with grace to for - ti - fy.

1-3

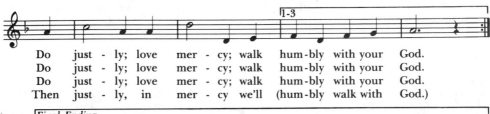

Do just - ly; love mer - cy; walk hum-bly with your God.
Do just - ly; love mer - cy; walk hum-bly with your God.
Do just - ly; love mer - cy; walk hum-bly with your God.
Then just - ly, in mer - cy we'll (hum-bly walk with God.)

Final Ending

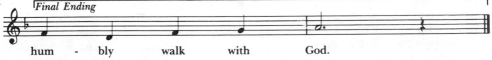

hum - bly walk with God.

Words: Albert F. Bayly (1901-1984), alt.
Music: *Sharpthorne*, Erik Routley (1917-1982)

66. 66. 33. 6

Music: Copyright © 1969 by Hope Publishing Company. All Rights Reserved. Used by Permission.

Antiphon

Where true char - i - ty and love dwell, God him-self is there.

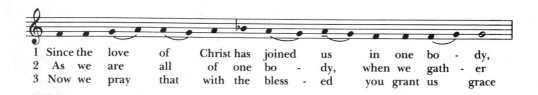

1 Since the love of Christ has joined us in one bo - dy,
2 As we are all of one bo - dy, when we gath - er
3 Now we pray that with the bless - ed you grant us grace

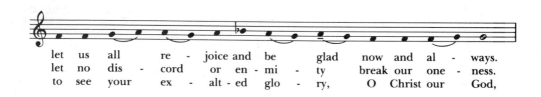

let us all re - joice and be glad now and al - ways.
let no dis - cord or en - mi - ty break our one - ness.
to see your ex - alt - ed glo - ry, O Christ our God,

And as we hear and love our Lord, the liv - ing God,
May all our pet - ty jeal - ous - ies and ha - tred cease
our bound-less source of joy and truth, of peace and love,

so let us in sin-cer - i - ty love all peo - ple. [Ant.]
that Christ the Lord may be with us through all our days. [Ant.]
for ev - er and for ev - er - more, world with - out end. [Ant.]

Words: Latin; tr. Joyce MacDonald Glover (b. 1923)
Music: *Ubi caritas*, plainsong, Mode 6

12. 12. 12. 12 with Refrain

1 O God of ev-ery na-tion, of ev-ery race and land,
2 From search for wealth and pow-er and scorn of truth and right,
3 Lord, strength-en all who la-bor that we may find re-lease
4 Keep bright in us the vi-sion of days when war shall cease,

re-deem the whole cre-a-tion with your al-might-y hand;
from trust in bombs that show-er de-struc-tion through the night,
from fear of rat-tling sa-ber, from dread of war's in-crease;
when ha-tred and di-vi-sion give way to love and peace,

where hate and fear di-vide us and bit-ter threats are hurled,
from pride of race and na-tion and blind-ness to your way,
when hope and cour-age fal-ter, your still small voice be heard;
till dawns the morn-ing glo-rious when truth and jus-tice reign

in love and mer-cy guide us and heal our strife-torn world.
de-liv-er ev-ery na-tion, e-ter-nal God, we pray!
with faith that none can al-ter, your ser-vants un-der-gird.
and Christ shall rule vic-to-rious o'er all the world's do-main.

Words: William Watkins Reid, Jr. (b. 1923), alt.
Music: *Llangloffan*, melody from *Hymnau a Thonau er Gwasanaeth yr Eglwys yng Nghymru*, 1865;
harm. *The English Hymnal*, 1906

76. 76. D

1 E - ter - nal Fa - ther, strong to save, whose arm hath bound the
2 O Christ, whose voice the wa - ters heard and hushed their ra - ging
3 Most Ho - ly Spi - rit, who didst brood up - on the cha - os
4 O Trin - i - ty of love and power, thy chil - dren shield in

rest - less wave, who bidd'st the might - y o - cean deep its
at thy word, who walk - edst on the foam - ing deep, and
dark and rude, and bid its an - gry tu - mult cease, and
dan - ger's hour; from rock and tem - pest, fire and foe, pro -

own ap - point - ed lim - its keep: O hear us when we
calm a - mid its rage didst sleep: O hear us when we
give, for wild con - fu - sion, peace: O hear us when we
tect them where - so - e'er they go; thus ev - er - more shall

cry to thee for those in per - il on the sea.
cry to thee for those in per - il on the sea.
cry to thee for those in per - il on the sea.
rise to thee glad hymns of praise from land and sea.

Words: William Whiting (1825-1878), alt.
Music: *Melita*, John Bacchus Dykes (1823-1876)

88. 88. 88

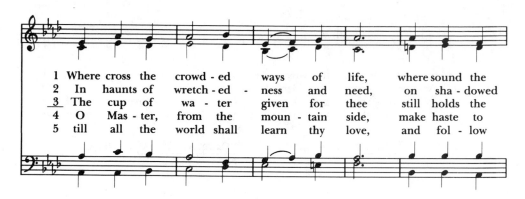

1 Where cross the crowd-ed ways of life, where sound the
2 In haunts of wretch-ed - ness and need, on sha-dowed
3 The cup of wa - ter given for thee still holds the
4 O Mas-ter, from the moun - tain side, make haste to
5 till all the world shall learn thy love, and fol - low

1 cries of race and clan, a - bove the noise of
2 thresh-olds dark with fears, from paths where hide the
3 fresh-ness of thy grace; yet long these mul - ti -
4 heal these hearts of pain; a - mong these rest - less
5 where thy feet have trod; till glo - rious from thy

1 self - ish strife, we hear thy voice, O Son of Man.
2 lures of greed, we catch the vi - sion of thy tears.
3 tudes to see the true com - pas - sion of thy face.
4 throngs a - bide, O tread the ci - ty's streets a - gain;
5 heaven a - bove, shall come the ci - ty of our God.

Words: Frank Mason North (1850-1935), alt.
Music: *Gardiner*, from *Sacred Melodies*, 1815; arr. William Gardiner (1770-1853)

LM

1 Lord, whose love through hum - ble ser - vice bore the weight of hu - man
2 Still your chil - dren wan - der home-less; still the hun - gry cry for
3 As we wor - ship, grant us vi - sion, till your love's re - veal - ing
4 Called by wor - ship to your ser - vice, forth in your dear name we

need, who up - on the cross, for - sak - en, of - fered mer - cy's
bread; still the cap - tives long for free - dom; still in grief we
light, in its height and depth and great - ness, dawns up - on our
go, to the child, the youth, the a - ged, love in liv - ing

per - fect deed, we, your ser - vants, bring the wor - ship
mourn our dead. As, O Lord, your deep com - pas - sion
quick-ened sight, mak - ing known the needs and bur - dens
deeds to show; hope and health, good will and com - fort,

not of voice a - lone, but heart, con - se - crat - ing
healed the sick and freed the soul, use the love your
your com - pas - sion bids us bear, stir - ring us to
coun - sel, aid, and peace we give, that your ser - vants,

to your pur - pose ev - ery gift that you im - part.
Spi - rit kin - dles still to save and make us whole.
tire - less striv - ing, your a - bun - dant life to share.
Lord, in free - dom may your mer - cy know and live.

Words: Albert F. Bayly (1901-1984), alt.
Music: *Blaenhafren*, Welsh melody

87. 87. D

Christian Responsibility

611

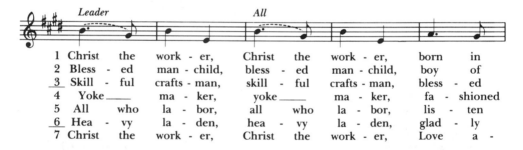

1 Christ the work - er, Christ the work - er, born in
2 Bless - ed man - child, bless - ed man - child, boy of
3 Skill - ful crafts - man, skill - ful crafts - man, bless - ed
4 Yoke___ ma - ker, yoke___ ma - ker, fa - shioned
5 All who la - bor, all who la - bor, lis - ten
6 Hea - vy la - den, hea - vy la - den, glad - ly
7 Christ the work - er, Christ the work - er, Love a -

1 Beth - le - hem, born to work and die for ev - ery one.
2 Naz - a - reth, grew in wis - dom as he grew in skill.
3 car - pen - ter, prais - ing God by la - bor at his bench.
4 by his hands, eas - y yokes that made the la - bor less.
5 to his call, he will make that hea - vy bur - den light.
6 come to him, he will ease your load and give you rest.
7 live for us, teach us how to do all work for God.

*The leader may begin successive stanzas here.

Words: Ghanaian work song; tr. Thomas Stevenson Colvin (b. 1925), alt.
Music: *African Work Song*, African work song; adapt. Thomas Stevenson Colvin (b. 1925)
Words, Music: Copyright © 1969 by Hope Publishing Company. International Copyright Secured. All Rights Reserved.
    Used by Permission.

444. 9

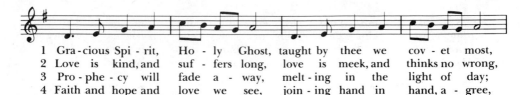

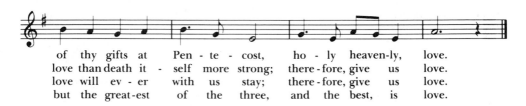

1. Gra-cious Spi-rit, Ho-ly Ghost, taught by thee we cov-et most,
2. Love is kind, and suf-fers long, love is meek, and thinks no wrong,
3. Pro-phe-cy will fade a-way, melt-ing in the light of day;
4. Faith and hope and love we see, join-ing hand in hand, a-gree,

of thy gifts at Pen-te-cost, ho-ly heaven-ly, love.
love than death it-self more strong; there-fore, give us love.
love will ev-er with us stay; there-fore, give us love.
but the great-est of the three, and the best, is love.

Words: Christopher Wordsworth (1807-1885)
Music: *Troen*, Daniel Moe (b. 1926)

777. 5

613   The Kingdom of God

1. Thy king-dom come, O God! Thy rule, O Christ, be-gin!
2. Where is thy reign of peace, and pu-ri-ty, and love?
3. When comes the prom-ised time that war shall be no more,
4. We pray thee, Lord, a-rise, and come in thy great might;
5. Wher-ev-er near or far thick dark-ness brood-eth yet:

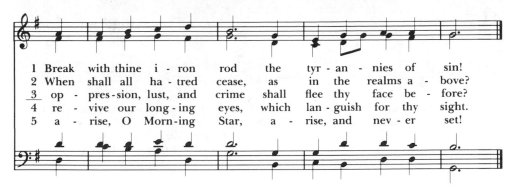

1 Break with thine i-ron rod the tyr-an-nies of sin!
2 When shall all ha-tred cease, as in the realms a-bove?
3 op-pres-sion, lust, and crime shall flee thy face be-fore?
4 re-vive our long-ing eyes, which lan-guish for thy sight.
5 a-rise, O Morn-ing Star, a-rise, and nev-er set!

Words: Lewis Hensley (1824-1905), alt.
Music: *St. Cecilia*, Leighton George Hayne (1836-1883)

66. 66

The Kingdom of God 614

1 Christ is the King! O friends up-raise an-thems of
2 O Chris-tian wo-men, Chris-tian men, all the world
3 Let Love's un-con-quer-a-ble might your scat-tered

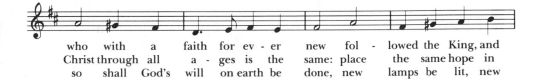

joy and ho-ly praise for his brave saints of an-cient days,
o-ver, seek a-gain the Way dis-ci-ples fol-lowed then.
com-pa-nies u-nite in ser-vice to the Lord of light:

who with a faith for ev-er new fol-lowed the King, and
Christ through all a-ges is the same: place the same hope in
so shall God's will on earth be done, new lamps be lit, new

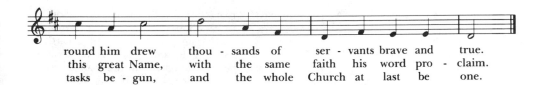

round him drew thou-sands of ser-vants brave and true.
this great Name, with the same faith his word pro-claim.
tasks be-gun, and the whole Church at last be one.

Words: George Kennedy Allen Bell (1883-1958)
Music: *Christus Rex*, David McKinley Williams (1887-1978)

888. 888

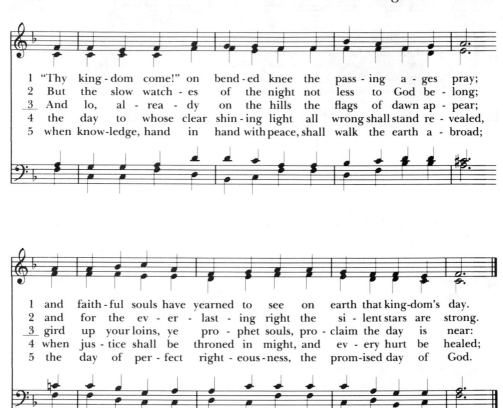

1 "Thy king - dom come!" on bend - ed knee the pass - ing a - ges pray;
2 But the slow watch - es of the night not less to God be - long;
3 And lo, al - rea - dy on the hills the flags of dawn ap - pear;
4 the day to whose clear shin - ing light all wrong shall stand re - vealed,
5 when know - ledge, hand in hand with peace, shall walk the earth a - broad;

1 and faith - ful souls have yearned to see on earth that king - dom's day.
2 and for the ev - er - last - ing right the si - lent stars are strong.
3 gird up your loins, ye pro - phet souls, pro - claim the day is near:
4 when jus - tice shall be throned in might, and ev - ery hurt be healed;
5 the day of per - fect right - eous - ness, the prom - ised day of God.

Words: Frederick Lucian Hosmer (1840-1929)
Music: *St. Flavian*, melody from *Day's Psalter*, 1562; adapt. and harm. Richard Redhead (1820-1901)   CM

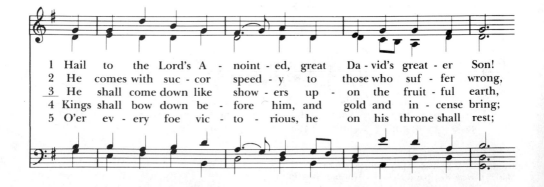

1 Hail to the Lord's A - noint - ed, great Da - vid's great - er Son!
2 He comes with suc - cor speed - y to those who suf - fer wrong,
3 He shall come down like show - ers up - on the fruit - ful earth,
4 Kings shall bow down be - fore him, and gold and in - cense bring;
5 O'er ev - ery foe vic - to - rious, he on his throne shall rest;

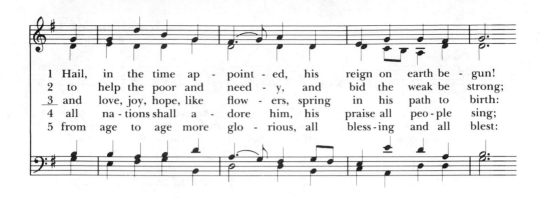

1 Hail, in the time ap - point - ed, his reign on earth be - gun!
2 to help the poor and need - y, and bid the weak be strong;
3 and love, joy, hope, like flow - ers, spring in his path to birth:
4 all na - tions shall a - dore him, his praise all peo - ple sing;
5 from age to age more glo - rious, all bless - ing and all blest:

1 He comes to break op - pres - sion, to set the cap - tive free;
2 to give them songs for sigh - ing, their dark - ness turn to light,
3 be - fore him on the moun - tains shall peace, the her - ald, go;
4 to him shall prayer un - ceas - ing and dai - ly vows a - scend;
5 the tide of time shall nev - er his cov - e - nant re - move;

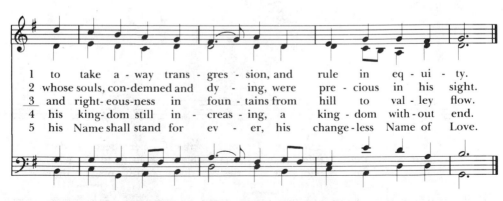

1 to take a - way trans - gres - sion, and rule in eq - ui - ty.
2 whose souls, con - demned and dy - ing, were pre - cious in his sight.
3 and right - eous - ness in foun - tains from hill to val - ley flow.
4 his king - dom still in - creas - ing, a king - dom with - out end.
5 his Name shall stand for ev - er, his change - less Name of Love.

Words: James Montgomery (1771-1854); para. of Psalm 72
Music: *Es flog ein kleins Waldvögelein*, German folk song; adapt. and harm.
    A Student's Hymnal, 1923, after Henry Walford Davies (1869-1941)

76. 76. D

Unison or harmony

1 E - ter - nal Ru - ler of the cease - less round
2 We would be one in ha - tred of all wrong,
3 Oh, clothe us with thy heaven - ly ar - mor, Lord,

of cir - cling plan - ets sing - ing on their way,
one in the love of all things sweet and fair,
thy trust - y shield, thy sword of love di - vine;

guide of the na - tions from the night pro - found
one with the joy that break - eth in - to song,
our in - spi - ra - tion be thy con - stant word,

in - to the glo - ry of the per - fect day;
one with the grief that trem - bleth in - to prayer;
we ask no vic - to - ries that are not thine;

rule	in	our	hearts,	that	we	may	ev - er	be
one	in	the	power	that	makes	thy	chil - dren	free
give	or	with - hold,		let	pain	or	plea - sure	be;

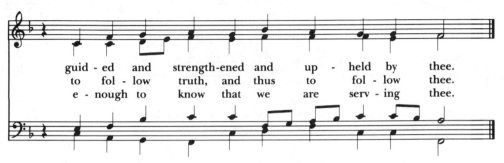

guid - ed	and	strength-ened	and	up - held	by	thee.
to	fol - low	truth,	and	thus	to	fol - low	thee.
e - nough	to	know	that	we	are	serv - ing	thee.

Words: John White Chadwick (1840-1904), alt.
Music: *Song 1*, melody and bass Orlando Gibbons (1583-1625);
    harm. *Hymns for Church and School*, 1964

10 10. 10 10. 10 10

1 Ye watch-ers and ye ho-ly ones, bright ser-aphs, cher-u-
2 O high-er than the cher-u-bim, more glo-rious than the
3 Re-spond, ye souls in end-less rest, ye pa-tri-archs and
4 O friends, in glad-ness let us sing, su-per-nal an-thems

bim, and thrones, raise the glad strain, Al-le-lu-ia! Cry
ser-a-phim, lead their prais-es, Al-le-lu-ia! Thou
pro-phets blest, Al-le-lu-ia, al-le-lu-ia! Ye
ech-o-ing, Al-le-lu-ia, al-le-lu-ia! To

out, do-min-ions, prince-doms, powers, vir-tues, arch-an-gels, an-gels'
bear-er of the e-ter-nal Word, most gra-cious, mag-ni-fy the
ho-ly twelve, ye mar-tyrs strong, all saints tri-um-phant raise the
God the Fa-ther, God the Son, and God the Spi-rit, Three in

choirs, Al-le-lu-ia, al-le-lu-ia, al-le-
Lord, Al-le-lu-ia, al-le-lu-ia, al-le-
song, Al-le-lu-ia, al-le-lu-ia, al-le-
One, Al-le-lu-ia, al-le-lu-ia, al-le-

Words: John Athelstan Laurie Riley (1858-1945)
Music: *Lasst uns erfreuen,* melody from *Auserlesene Catholische Geistliche Kirchengeseng,* 1623;
adapt. and harm. Ralph Vaughan Williams (1872-1958)

88. 44. 88 with Refrain

The Church Triumphant

619

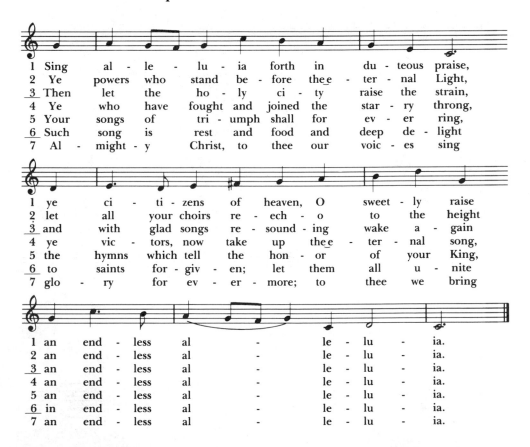

1 Sing al - le - lu - ia forth in du - teous praise,
2 Ye powers who stand be - fore the e - ter - nal Light,
3 Then let the ho - ly ci - ty raise the strain,
4 Ye who have fought and joined the star - ry throng,
5 Your songs of tri - umph shall for ev - er ring,
6 Such song is rest and food and deep de - light,
7 Al - might - y Christ, to thee our voic - es sing

1 ye ci - ti - zens of heaven, O sweet - ly raise
2 let all your choirs re - ech - o to the height
3 and with glad songs re - sound - ing wake a - gain
4 ye vic - tors, now take up the e - ter - nal song,
5 the hymns which tell the hon - or of your King,
6 to saints for - giv - en; let them all u - nite
7 glo - ry for ev - er - more; to thee we bring

1 an end - less al - le - lu - ia.
2 an end - less al - le - lu - ia.
3 an end - less al - le - lu - ia.
4 an end - less al - le - lu - ia.
5 an end - less al - le - lu - ia.
6 in end - less al - le - lu - ia.
7 an end - less al - le - lu - ia.

Words: Latin, 5th-8th cent.; ver. *Hymnal 1940*
Music: *Martins,* Percy Carter Buck (1871-1947)

10 10. 7

1. Je - ru - sa - lem,   my hap - py home, when
2. Thy saints are crowned with glo - ry great; they
3. There Da - vid stands with harp in hand as
4. Our La - dy sings Mag - ni - fi - cat with
5. Je - ru - sa - lem, Je - ru - sa - lem, God

1. shall   I come to thee? When shall   my sor - rows
2. see God face to face; they tri - umph still, they
3. mas - ter of the choir: ten thou - sand times would
4. tune sur - pass - ing sweet, and bless - ed mar - tyrs'
5. grant that I may see thine end - less joy, and

1. have   an end? Thy joys when shall   I see?
2. still re - joice in that most hap - py place.
3. one be blest who might this mu - sic hear.
4. har - mo - ny doth ring in ev - ery street.
5. of the same par - ta - ker ev - er be!

Words: F. B. P. (ca. 16th cent.), alt.
Music: *Land of Rest*, American folk hymn; adapt. and harm. Annabel Morris Buchanan (1889-1983)   CM

The Church Triumphant

1 Light's a-bode, ce - les - tial Sa - lem, vi - sion whence true peace doth spring,
2 There for ev - er and for ev - er al - le - lu - ia is out-poured;
3 There no cloud nor pass-ing va - por dims the bright-ness of the air;
*4 O how glo-rious and re-splen-dent, fra - gile bo - dy, shalt thou be,
5 Now with glad-ness, now with cour-age, bear the bur-den on thee laid,

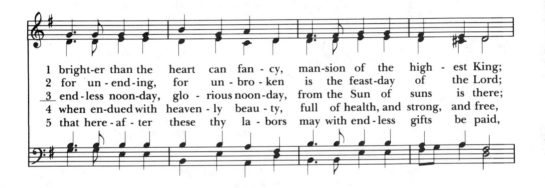

1 bright-er than the heart can fan - cy, man-sion of the high - est King;
2 for un - end - ing, for un - bro - ken is the feast-day of the Lord;
3 end - less noon-day, glo - rious noon-day, from the Sun of suns is there;
4 when en-dued with heaven - ly beau - ty, full of health, and strong, and free,
5 that here - af - ter these thy la - bors may with end - less gifts be paid,

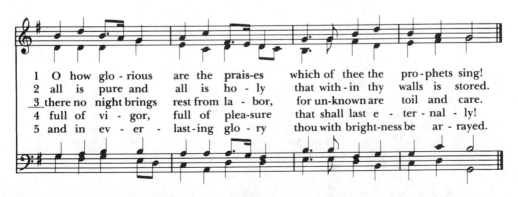

1 O how glo - rious are the prais - es which of thee the pro - phets sing!
2 all is pure and all is ho - ly that with - in thy walls is stored.
3 there no night brings rest from la - bor, for un-known are toil and care.
4 full of vi - gor, full of plea-sure that shall last e - ter - nal - ly!
5 and in ev - er - last-ing glo - ry thou with bright-ness be ar - rayed.

Words: Latin, 15th cent.; tr. John Mason Neale (1818-1866), alt.
Music: *Rhuddlan*, Welsh melody

87. 87. 87

1 Light's a - bode, ce - les - tial Sa - lem, vi-sion whence true peace doth spring,
2 There for ev - er and for ev - er al - le - lu - ia is out-poured;
3 There no cloud nor pass-ing va - por dims the bright-ness of the air;
*4 O how glo - rious and re-splend-ent, frag - ile bo - dy, shalt thou be,
5 Now with glad - ness, now with cour-age, bear the bur - den on thee laid,

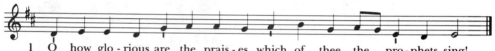

1 bright-er than the heart can fan - cy, man-sion of the high-est King;
2 for un-end - ing, for un-bro - ken is the feast-day of the Lord;
3 end - less noon-day, glo - rious noon-day, from the Sun of suns is there;
4 when en - dued with heaven-ly beau - ty, full of health, and strong, and free,
5 that here-af - ter these thy la - bors may with end-less gifts be paid,

1 O how glo - rious are the prais - es which of thee the pro-phets sing!
2 all is pure and all is ho - ly that with - in thy walls is stored.
3 there no night brings rest from la - bor, for un-known are toil and care.
4 full of vi - gor, full of plea-sure that shall last e - ter - nal - ly!
5 and in ev - er - last-ing glo - ry thou with bright-ness be ar - rayed.

Words: Latin, 15th cent.; tr. John Mason Neale (1818-1866), alt.
Music: *Urbs beata Jerusalem*, plainsong, Mode 2; Nevers Ms., 13th cent.; ver. Schola Antiqua, 1983   87. 87. 87
Music: Melody rhythmic version © 1984, Schola Antiqua Inc. Used by permission.

1 O what their joy and their glo - ry must be,
2 Tru - ly, "Je - ru - sa - lem" name we that shore,
3 There, where no trou - bles dis - trac - tion can bring,
4 Now, in the mean - while, with hearts raised on high,
5 Low be - fore him with our prais - es we fall,

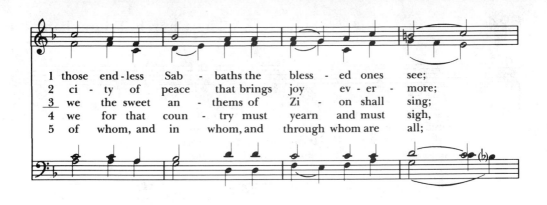

1 those end-less Sab - baths the bless - ed ones see;
2 ci - ty of peace that brings joy ev - er - more;
3 we the sweet an - thems of Zi - on shall sing;
4 we for that coun - try must yearn and must sigh,
5 of whom, and in whom, and through whom are all;

1 crown for the val - iant, to wea - ry ones rest:
2 wish and ful - fill - ment are not sev - ered there,
3 while for thy grace, Lord, their voic - es of praise
4 seek - ing Je - ru - sa - lem, dear na - tive land,
5 of whom, the Fa - ther; and in whom, the Son;

1 God shall be all, and in all ev - er blest.
2 nor do things prayed for come short of the prayer.
3 thy bless - ed peo - ple e - ter - nal - ly raise.
4 through our long ex - ile on Bab - y - lon's strand.
5 through whom, the Spi - rit, with them ev - er One.

Words: Peter Abelard (1079-1142); tr. John Mason Neale (1818-1866), alt.
Music: *O quanta qualia*, melody from *Antiphoner*, 1681;
    harm. John Bacchus Dykes (1823-1876)

10 10. 10 10

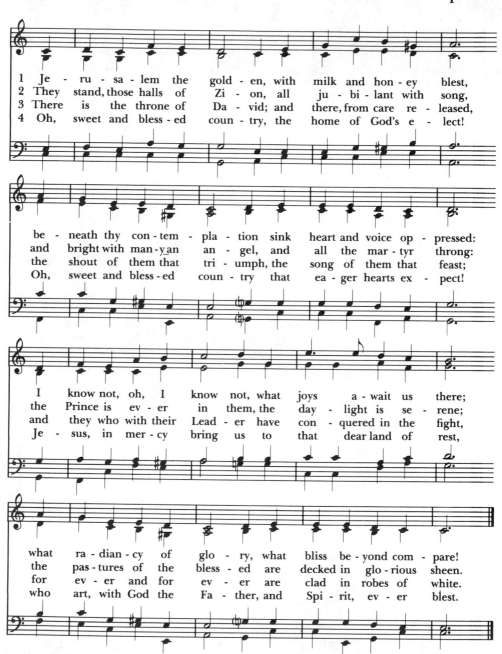

1 Jerusalem the golden, with milk and honey blest,
beneath thy contemplation sink heart and voice oppressed:
I know not, oh, I know not, what joys await us there;
what radiancy of glory, what bliss beyond compare!

2 They stand, those halls of Zion, all jubilant with song,
and bright with many an angel, and all the martyr throng:
the Prince is ever in them, the daylight is serene;
the pastures of the blessed are decked in glorious sheen.

3 There is the throne of David; and there, from care released,
the shout of them that triumph, the song of them that feast;
and they who with their Leader have conquered in the fight,
for ever and for ever are clad in robes of white.

4 Oh, sweet and blessed country, the home of God's elect!
Oh, sweet and blessed country that eager hearts expect!
Jesus, in mercy bring us to that dear land of rest,
who art, with God the Father, and Spirit, ever blest.

Words: Bernard of Cluny (12th cent.); tr. John Mason Neale (1818-1866), alt.
    St. 4, *Hymns Ancient and Modern*, 1861
Music: *Ewing*, Alexander Ewing (1830-1895)

76. 76. D

The Church Triumphant

Words: Richard Baxter (1615-1691); rev. John Hampden Gurney (1802-1862)
Music: *Darwall's 148th*, melody and bass John Darwall (1731-1789);
    harm. William Henry Monk (1823-1889), alt.; desc. Sydney Hugo Nicholson (1875-1947)

66. 66. 44. 44

1 Lord, be thy word my rule; in it may I re- joice;
2 thy prom-is-es my hope; thy prov-i-dence my guard;

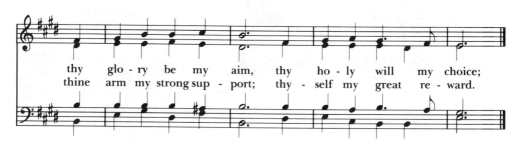

thy glo-ry be my aim, thy ho-ly will my choice;
thine arm my strong sup-port; thy-self my great re-ward.

Words: Christopher Wordsworth (1807-1885)
Music: *Quam dilecta*, Henry Lascelles Jenner (1820-1898)

66. 66

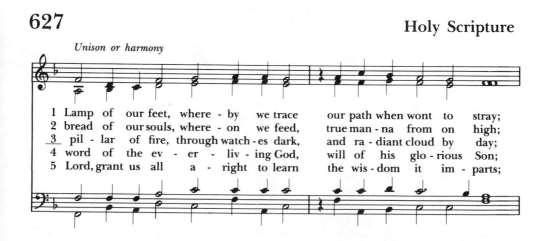

Unison or harmony

1 Lamp of our feet, where-by we trace   our path when wont to stray;
2 bread of our souls, where-on we feed, true man-na from on high;
3 pil-lar of fire, through watch-es dark, and ra-diant cloud by day;
4 word of the ev-er-liv-ing God,   will of his glo-rious Son;
5 Lord, grant us all a-right to learn   the wis-dom it im-parts;

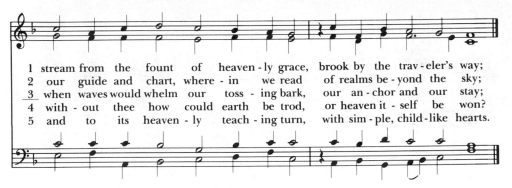

1	stream from the	fount	of	heaven - ly grace,	brook by the trav - eler's	way;
2	our guide and	chart, where - in	we read	of realms be - yond the	sky;
3	when waves would whelm our	toss - ing bark,	our an - chor and our	stay;
4	with - out thee how	could earth	be trod,	or heaven it - self be	won?
5	and to its	heaven - ly	teach - ing turn,	with sim - ple, child - like	hearts.

Words: Bernard Barton (1784-1849)
Music: *Nun danket all und bringet Ehr*, melody att. Johann Cruger (1598-1662), alt.

CM

Holy Scripture

628

1 Help us, O Lord, to learn the truths your word im - parts: to
2 Help us, O Lord, to live the faith which we pro - claim, that
3 Help us, O Lord, to teach the beau - ty of your ways, that

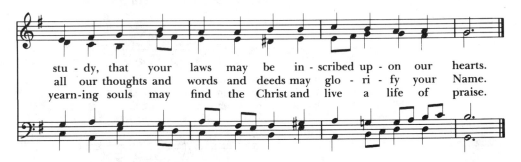

stu - dy, that your laws may be in - scribed up - on our hearts.
all our thoughts and words and deeds may glo - ri - fy your Name.
yearn - ing souls may find the Christ and live a life of praise.

Words: William Watkins Reid, Jr. (b. 1923), alt.
Music: *St. Ethelwald*, William Henry Monk (1823-1889)

SM

Introduction

1 We limit not the
2 Who dares to bind to
3 O Fa - ther, Son, and

truth of God to our poor reach of mind, to
one's own sense the or - a - cles of heaven, for
Spi - rit, send us in - crease from a - bove; en -

no - tions of our day and place, crude, par - tial, and con -
all the na - tions, tongues, and climes and all the a - ges
large, ex - pand all liv - ing souls to com - pre - hend your

fined; no, let a new and bet - ter hope with -
given? That u - ni - verse, how much un - known! The
love; and make us all go on to know with

in our hearts be stirred; the Lord has yet more
o - cean un - ex - plored! the Lord has yet more
no - bler powers con - ferred— the Lord has yet more

Interlude/Conclusion

light and truth to break forth from his word.
light and truth to break forth from his word.
light and truth to break forth from his word.

Words: George Rawson (1807-1889), alt.
Music: *Halifax*, George Frideric Handel (1685-1759); adapt. and arr. David Hurd (b. 1950)

CMD

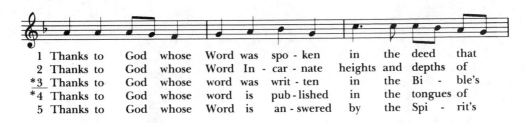

1 Thanks to God whose Word was spo-ken in the deed that
2 Thanks to God whose Word In-car-nate heights and depths of
*3 Thanks to God whose word was writ-ten in the Bi-ble's
*4 Thanks to God whose word is pub-lished in the tongues of
5 Thanks to God whose Word is an-swered by the Spi-rit's

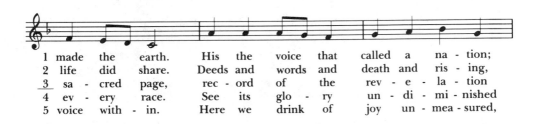

1 made the earth. His the voice that called a na-tion;
2 life did share. Deeds and words and death and ris-ing,
3 sa-cred page, rec-ord of the rev-e-la-tion
4 ev-ery race. See its glo-ry un-di-mi-nished
5 voice with-in. Here we drink of joy un-mea-sured,

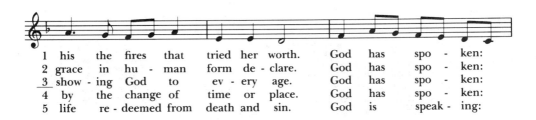

1 his the fires that tried her worth. God has spo-ken:
2 grace in hu-man form de-clare. God has spo-ken:
3 show-ing God to ev-ery age. God has spo-ken:
4 by the change of time or place. God has spo-ken:
5 life re-deemed from death and sin. God is speak-ing:

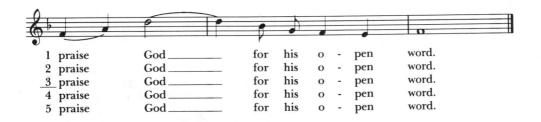

1 praise God_____ for his o-pen word.
2 praise God_____ for his o-pen word.
3 praise God_____ for his o-pen word.
4 praise God_____ for his o-pen word.
5 praise God_____ for his o-pen word.

Words: R. T. Brooks (b. 1918), alt.
Music: *Wylde Green*, Peter Cutts (b. 1937)

87. 87 with Refrain

631

1 Book of books, our peo-ple's strength, states-man's, teach-er's, he - ro's
2 Thank we those who toiled in thought, man - y di - verse scrolls com -
3 Praise we God, who hath in - spired those whose wis - dom still di -

trea - sure, bring - ing free - dom, spread - ing truth,
plet - ing, po - ets, pro - phets, schol - ars, saints,
rects us; praise him for the Word made flesh,

shed-ding light that none can mea - sure: wis - dom comes to
each a word from God re - peat - ing; till they came, who
for the Spi - rit which pro - tects us. Light of know - ledge,

those who know thee, all the best we have we owe thee.
told the sto - ry of the Word, and showed his glo - ry.
ev - er burn - ing, shed on us thy death-less learn - ing.

Words: Percy Dearmer (1867-1936)
Music: *Liebster Jesu*, melody Johann Rudolph Ahle (1625-1673); alt. *Das grosse Cantional oder
Kirchen-Gesangbuch*, 1687; harm. George Herbert Palmer (1846-1926)

78. 78. 88

1 O Christ, the Word In-car-nate, O Wis-dom from on high,
2 The Church from our dear Mas-ter re-ceived the word di-vine,
3 O make thy Church, dear Sa-vior, a lamp of pur-est gold,

O Truth, un-changed, un-chang-ing, O Light of our dark sky;
and still that light is lift-ed o'er all the earth to shine.
to bear be-fore the na-tions thy true light as of old;

we praise thee for the ra-diance that from the scrip-ture's page,
It is the chart and com-pass that o'er life's surg-ing sea,
O teach thy wan-dering pil-grims by this their path to trace,

a lan-tern to our foot-steps, shines on from age to age.
mid mists and rocks and quick-sands, still guides, O Christ, to thee.
till, clouds and dark-ness end-ed, they see thee face to face.

Words: William Walsham How (1823-1897), alt.
Music: *Munich*, melody from *Neu-vermehrtes und zu Übung Christl. Gottseligkeit eingerichtetes
Meiningisches Gesangbuch*, 1693; adapt. and harm. Felix Mendelssohn (1809-1847)

76. 76. D

633

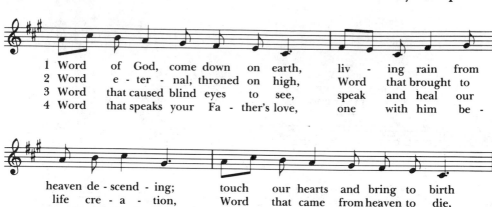

1 Word of God, come down on earth, liv - ing rain from
2 Word e - ter - nal, throned on high, Word that brought to
3 Word that caused blind eyes to see, speak and heal our
4 Word that speaks your Fa - ther's love, one with him be -

heaven de - scend - ing; touch our hearts and bring to birth
life cre - a - tion, Word that came from heaven to die,
mor - tal blind - ness; deaf we are: our heal - er be;
yond all tell - ing, Word that sends us from a - bove

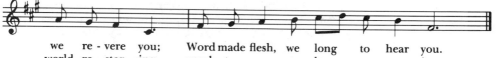

faith and hope and love un - end - ing. Word al - might - y,
cru - ci - fied for our sal - va - tion, sav - ing Word, the
loose our tongues to tell your kind - ness. Be our Word in
God the Spi - rit, with us dwell - ing, Word of truth, to

we re - vere you; Word made flesh, we long to hear you.
world re - stor - ing, speak to us, your love out - pour - ing.
pi - ty spo - ken; heal the world, by our sin brok - en.
all truth lead us, Word of life, with one Bread feed us.

Words: James Quinn (b. 1919)
Music: *Mt. St. Alban NCA*, Richard Wayne Dirksen (b. 1921)

78. 78. 88

Holy Scripture

Unison or harmony

I call on thee, Lord Je-sus Christ, I have none o-ther help but thee. My heart is nev-er set at rest till thy sweet word have com-fort-ed me. And stead-fast faith grant me there-fore, to hold by thy word ev-er-more, a-bove all thing, nev-er re-sist-ing but to in-crease in faith more and more.

Words: Miles Coverdale (1487-1568)
Music: *Ich ruf zu dir*, melody from *Geistliche Lieder*, 1533;
   harm. *Thuringer Evangelisches Gesangbuch*, 1928

Irr.

Unison or harmony

1 If thou but trust in God to guide thee, and hope in him through
2 Sing, pray, and keep his ways un - swerv-ing; so do thine own part

all thy ways, he'll give thee strength what - e'er be - tide thee,
faith - ful - ly, and trust his word, though un - de - serv-ing;

and bear thee through the e - vil days. Who trusts in God's un -
thou yet shalt find it true for thee; God nev - er yet for -

chang - ing love builds on a rock that nought can move.
sook in need the soul that trust - ed him in - deed.

Words: Georg Neumark (1621-1681); tr. Catherine Winkworth (1827-1878), alt.
Music: *Wer nur den lieben Gott*, Georg Neumark (1621-1681)

98. 98. 88

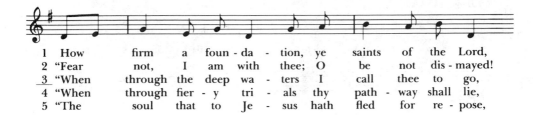

1 How firm a foun-da-tion, ye saints of the Lord,
2 "Fear not, I am with thee; O be not dis-mayed!
3 "When through the deep wa-ters I call thee to go,
4 "When through fier-y tri-als thy path-way shall lie,
5 "The soul that to Je-sus hath fled for re-pose,

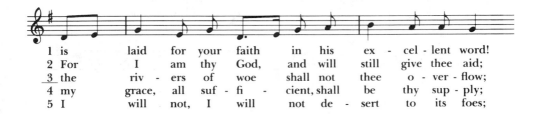

1 is laid for your faith in his ex-cel-lent word!
2 For I am thy God, and will still give thee aid;
3 the riv-ers of woe shall not thee o-ver-flow;
4 my grace, all suf-fi-cient, shall be thy sup-ply;
5 I will not, I will not de-sert to its foes;

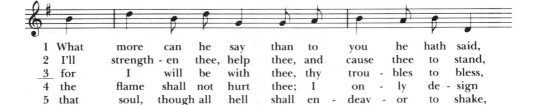

1 What more can he say than to you he hath said,
2 I'll strength-en thee, help thee, and cause thee to stand,
3 for I will be with thee, thy trou-bles to bless,
4 the flame shall not hurt thee; I on-ly de-sign
5 that soul, though all hell shall en-deav-or to shake,

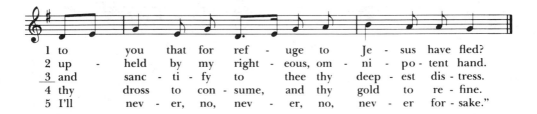

1 to you that for ref-uge to Je-sus have fled?
2 up-held by my right-eous, om-ni-po-tent hand.
3 and sanc-ti-fy to thee thy deep-est dis-tress.
4 thy dross to con-sume, and thy gold to re-fine.
5 I'll nev-er, no, nev-er, no, nev-er for-sake."

Optional Interlude

Words: K. in John Rippon's *Selection*, 1787, alt.
Words: *Foundation*, melody from *The Sacred Harp*, 1844

11 11. 11 11

Descant

5 "The soul that to Je - sus hath fled for re - pose,

1 How firm a foun - da - tion, ye saints of the Lord,
2 "Fear not, I am with thee; O be not dis - mayed!
3 "When through the deep wa - ters I call thee to go,
4 "When through fier - y tri - als thy path - way shall lie,
5 "The soul that to Je - sus hath fled for re - pose,

5 I will not, I will not de - sert to its foes;

1 is laid for your faith in his ex - cel - lent word!
2 For I am thy God, and will still give thee aid;
3 the riv - ers of woe shall not thee o - ver - flow;
4 my grace, all suf - fi - cient, shall be thy sup - ply;
5 I will not, I will not de - sert to its foes;

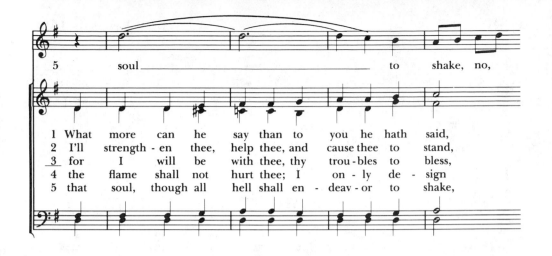

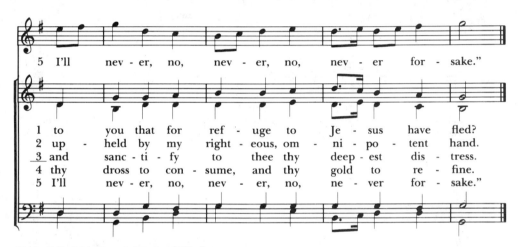

5 soul _____ to shake, no,

1 What more can he say than to you he hath said,
2 I'll strength - en thee, help thee, and cause thee to stand,
3 for I will be with thee, thy trou - bles to bless,
4 the flame shall not hurt thee; I on - ly de - sign
5 that soul, though all hell shall en - deav - or to shake,

5 I'll nev - er, no, nev - er, no, nev - er for - sake."

1 to you that for ref - uge to Je - sus have fled?
2 up - held by my right - eous, om - ni - po - tent hand.
3 and sanc - ti - fy to thee thy deep - est dis - tress.
4 thy dross to con - sume, and thy gold to re - fine.
5 I'll nev - er, no, nev - er, no, ne - ver for - sake."

Words: K. in John Rippon's *Selection*, 1787, alt.
Music: *Lyons*, att. Johann Michael Haydn (1737-1806); desc. Lois Fyfe (b. 1927)

11 11. 11 11

1 Come, O thou Trav - el - er un - known, whom
2 I need not tell thee who I am, my
3 Yield to me now, for I am weak but
4 'Tis Love, 'tis Love! Thou diedst for me! I

still I hold, but can - not see; my com - pa -
mis - er - y or sin de - clare; thy - self hast
con - fi - dent in self - de - spair; speak to my
hear thy whis - per in my heart: the morn - ing

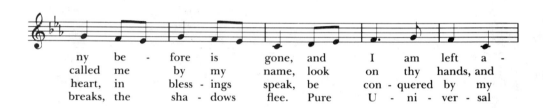

ny be - fore is gone, and I am left a -
called me by my name, look on thy hands, and
heart, in bless - ings speak, be con - quered by my
breaks, the sha - dows flee. Pure U - ni - ver - sal

lone with thee. With thee all night I mean to
read it there. But who, I ask thee, who art
in - stant prayer. Speak, or thou nev - er hence shalt
Love thou art; thy mer - cies nev - er shall re -

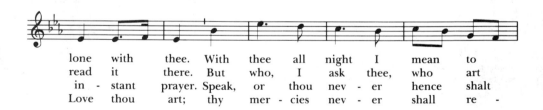

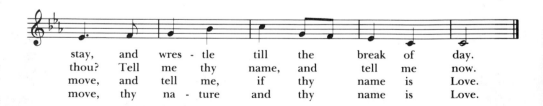

stay, and wres - tle till the break of day.
thou? Tell me thy name, and tell me now.
move, and tell me, if thy name is Love.
move, thy na - ture and thy name is Love.

Words: Charles Wesley (1707-1788), alt.
Music: *Vernon*, traditional melody

88. 88. 88

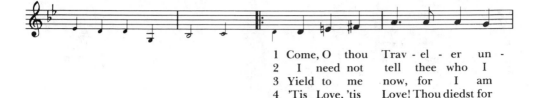

1 Come, O thou Trav - el - er un -
2 I need not tell thee who I
3 Yield to me now, for I am
4 'Tis Love, 'tis Love! Thou diedst for

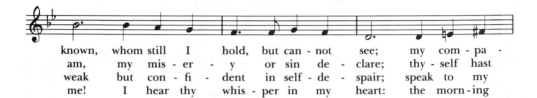

known, whom still I hold, but can - not see; my com - pa -
am, my mis - er - y or sin de - clare; thy - self hast
weak but con - fi - dent in self - de - spair; speak to my
me! I hear thy whis - per in my heart: the morn - ing

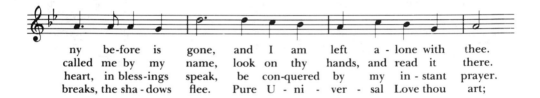

ny be - fore is gone, and I am left a - lone with thee.
called me by my name, look on thy hands, and read it there.
heart, in bless - ings speak, be con - quered by my in - stant prayer.
breaks, the sha - dows flee. Pure U - ni - ver - sal Love thou art;

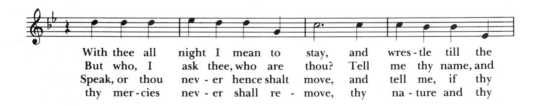

With thee all night I mean to stay, and wres - tle till the
But who, I ask thee, who are thou? Tell me thy name, and
Speak, or thou nev - er hence shalt move, and tell me, if thy
thy mer - cies nev - er shall re - move, thy na - ture and thy

1-3

break of day. _____
tell me now. _____
name is Love. _____
name is (Love.)

Final Ending

Love. _____

Words: Charles Wesley (1707-1788), alt.
Music: *Woodbury*, Eric Routley (1917-1982)

88. 88. 88

brings the day, prom - ised day of Is - ra - el.
are its own; see, it bursts o'er all the earth.
Prince of Peace, lo! the Son of God is come!

Two groups may sing antiphonally, alternating by sentences.

Words: John Bowring (1792-1872)
Music: *Aberystwyth*, Joseph Parry (1841-1903)

77. 77. D

The Christian Life

641

1 Lord Je - sus, think on me, and purge a - way my sin;
2 Lord Je - sus, think on me, with care and woe op - pressed;
3 Lord Je - sus, think on me, nor let me go a - stray;
4 Lord Je - sus, think on me, that, when the flood is passed,

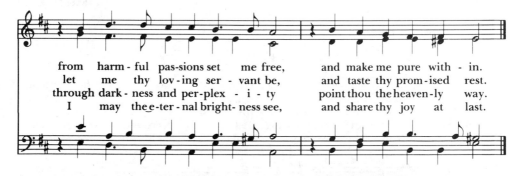

from harm - ful pas-sions set me free, and make me pure with - in.
let me thy lov-ing ser - vant be, and taste thy prom-ised rest.
through dark - ness and per-plex - i - ty point thou the heaven-ly way.
I may the e-ter - nal bright- ness see, and share thy joy at last.

Words: Synesius of Cyrene (375?-414?); tr. Allen William Chatfield (1808-1896), alt.
Music: *Southwell*, from *Daman's Psalter*, 1579; adapt. *Hymnal 1982*

SM

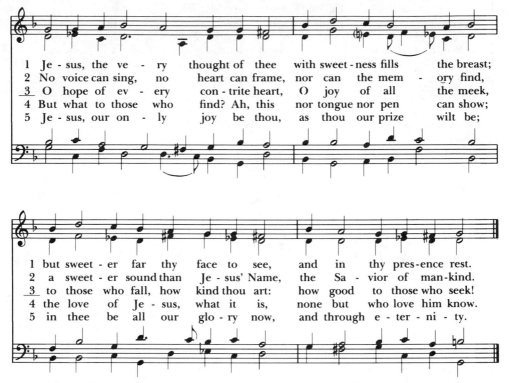

1 Je - sus, the ve - ry thought of thee with sweet - ness fills the breast;
2 No voice can sing, no heart can frame, nor can the mem - ory find,
3 O hope of ev - ery con - trite heart, O joy of all the meek,
4 But what to those who find? Ah, this nor tongue nor pen can show;
5 Je - sus, our on - ly joy be thou, as thou our prize wilt be;

1 but sweet - er far thy face to see, and in thy pres - ence rest.
2 a sweet - er sound than Je - sus' Name, the Sa - vior of man - kind.
3 to those who fall, how kind thou art: how good to those who seek!
4 the love of Je - sus, what it is, none but who love him know.
5 in thee be all our glo - ry now, and through e - ter - ni - ty.

Words: Latin, 12th cent.; st. 5, Latin, 15th cent.; tr. Edward Caswall (1814-1878), alt.
Music: *Windsor*, melody William Damon (1540?-1591?); harm. Thomas Este (1540?-1608?)   CM

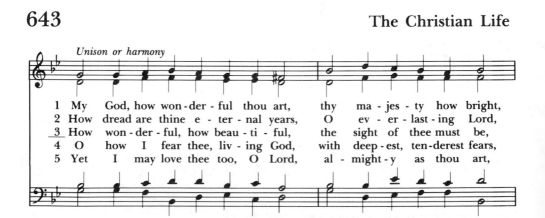

Unison or harmony

1 My God, how won - der - ful thou art, thy ma - jes - ty how bright,
2 How dread are thine e - ter - nal years, O ev - er - last - ing Lord,
3 How won - der - ful, how beau - ti - ful, the sight of thee must be,
4 O how I fear thee, liv - ing God, with deep - est, ten - derest fears,
5 Yet I may love thee too, O Lord, al - might - y as thou art,

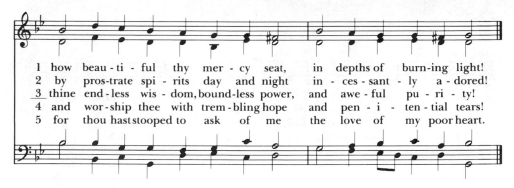

1 how beau-ti-ful thy mer-cy seat, in depths of burn-ing light!
2 by pros-trate spi-rits day and night in-ces-sant-ly a-dored!
3 thine end-less wis-dom, bound-less power, and awe-ful pu-ri-ty!
4 and wor-ship thee with trem-bling hope and pen-i-ten-tial tears!
5 for thou hast stooped to ask of me the love of my poor heart.

Words: Frederick William Faber (1814-1863)
Music: *Windsor*, melody William Damon (1540?-1591?), alt.; harm. *Booke of Musicke*, 1591   CM

The Christian Life   644

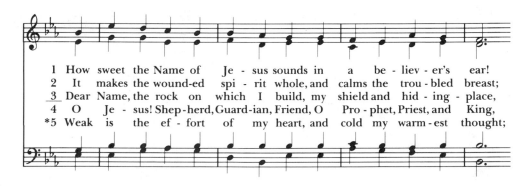

1 How sweet the Name of Je-sus sounds in a be-liev-er's ear!
2 It makes the wound-ed spi-rit whole, and calms the trou-bled breast;
3 Dear Name, the rock on which I build, my shield and hid-ing-place,
4 O Je-sus! Shep-herd, Guard-ian, Friend, O Pro-phet, Priest, and King,
*5 Weak is the ef-fort of my heart, and cold my warm-est thought;

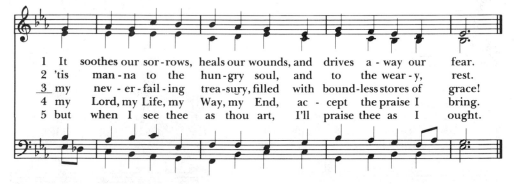

1 It soothes our sor-rows, heals our wounds, and drives a-way our fear.
2 'tis man-na to the hun-gry soul, and to the wear-y, rest.
3 my nev-er-fail-ing trea-sury, filled with bound-less stores of grace!
4 my Lord, my Life, my Way, my End, ac-cept the praise I bring.
5 but when I see thee as thou art, I'll praise thee as I ought.

Words: John Newton (1725-1807), alt.
Music: *St. Peter*, Alexander Robert Reinagle (1799-1877)   CM

645

1 The King of love my shep-herd is, whose good-ness
2 Where streams of liv - ing wa - ter flow, my ran - somed
*3 Per - verse and fool - ish oft I strayed, but yet in
*4 In death's dark vale I fear no ill with thee, dear
5 Thou spread'st a ta - ble in my sight; thy unc - tion
6 And so through all the length of days thy good - ness

1 fail - eth nev - er; I noth - ing lack if
2 soul he lead - eth, and where the ver - dant
3 love he sought me, and on his shoul - der
4 Lord, be - side me; thy rod and staff my
5 grace be - stow - eth; and oh, what trans - port
6 fail - eth nev - er: Good Shep - herd, may I

1 I am his, and he is mine for ev - er.
2 pas - tures grow, with food ce - les - tial feed - eth.
3 gent - ly laid, and home, re - joic - ing, brought me.
4 com - fort still, thy cross be - fore to guide me.
5 of de - light from thy pure chal - ice flow - eth!
6 sing thy praise with - in thy house for ev - er.

Words: Henry Williams Baker (1821-1877); para. of Psalm 23
Music: *St. Columba,* Irish melody

87. 87

646

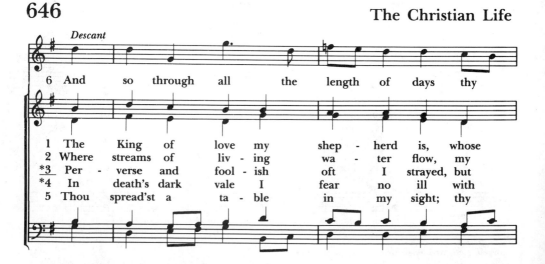

Descant

6 And so through all the length of days thy

1 The King of love my shep - herd is, whose
2 Where streams of liv - ing wa - ter flow, my
*3 Per - verse and fool - ish oft I strayed, but
*4 In death's dark vale I fear no ill with
5 Thou spread'st a ta - ble in my sight; thy

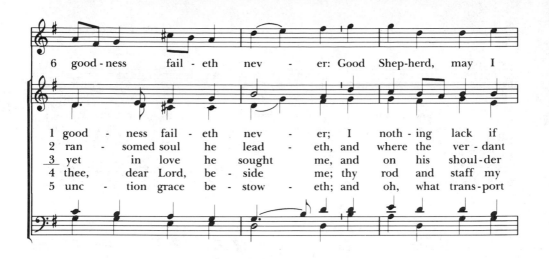

6 good - ness fail - eth nev - er: Good Shep-herd, may I

1 good - ness fail - eth nev - er; I noth - ing lack if
2 ran - somed soul he lead - eth, and where the ver - dant
3 yet in love he sought me, and on his shoul - der
4 thee, dear Lord, be - side me; thy rod and staff my
5 unc - tion grace be - stow - eth; and oh, what trans-port

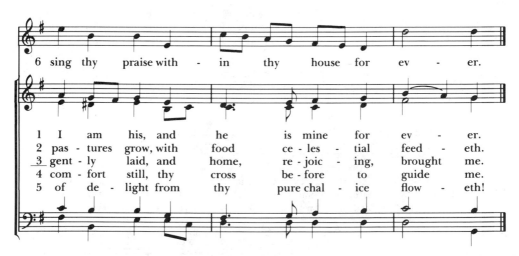

6 sing thy praise with - in thy house for ev - er.

1 I am his, and he is mine for ev - er.
2 pas - tures grow, with food ce - les - tial feed - eth.
3 gent - ly laid, and home, re - joic - ing, brought me.
4 com - fort still, thy cross be - fore to guide me.
5 of de - light from thy pure chal - ice flow - eth!

6 And so through all the length of days
thy goodness faileth never:
Good shepherd, may I sing thy praise
within thy house for ever.

Words: Henry Williams Baker (1821-1877); para. of Psalm 23
Music: *Dominus regit me*, John Bacchus Dykes (1823-1876); desc. David Willcocks (b. 1919)   87. 87

1 I know not where the road will lead I fol-low day by day,
2 And some I love have reached the end, but some with me may stay,
3 The count-less hosts lead on be-fore, I must not fear nor stray;

or where it ends: I on-ly know I walk the King's high-way.
their faith and hope still guid-ing me: I walk the King's high-way.
with them, the pil-grims of the faith, I walk the King's high-way.

I know not if the way is long, and no one else can say;
The way is truth, the way is love, for light and strength I pray,
Through light and dark the road leads on till dawns the end-less day,

but rough or smooth, up hill or down, I walk the King's high-way.
and through the years of life, to God I walk the King's high-way.
when I shall know why in this life I walk the King's high-way.

Words: Evelyn Atwater Cummins (1891-1971)
Music: *Laramie*, Arnold George Henry Bode (1866-1952)   CMD

1 When Is - rael was in E - gypt's land, let my peo-ple go;
2 The Lord told Mo - ses what to do, let my peo-ple go;
3 They jour-neyed on at his com-mand, let my peo-ple go;
4 Oh, let us all from bond-age flee, let my peo-ple go;

op - pressed so hard they___ could not stand, let my peo-ple go.
to lead the chil-dren of Is - rael through, let my peo-ple go.
and came at length to___ Ca - naan's land, let my peo-ple go.
and let us all in___ Christ be free, let my peo-ple go.

Refrain

Go down, Mo - ses, way down in E - gypt's land;

tell old Pha - raoh to let my peo-ple go.

Words: Afro-American spiritual
Music: *Go Down, Moses,* Afro-American spiritual; arr. Horace Clarence Boyer (b. 1935)   85. 85 with Refrain

1 O Je - sus, joy of lov - ing hearts, the fount of
2 We taste in you our liv - ing bread, and long to
3 For you our rest - less spi - rits yearn wher - e'er our
4 O Je - sus, ev - er with us stay; make all our

life and our true light, we seek the peace your love im -
feast up - on you still; we drink of you, the foun - tain -
chang - ing lot is cast; glad, when your pres - ence we dis -
mo - ments calm and bright; oh, chase the night of sin a -

parts, and stand re - joic - ing in your sight.
head, our thirst - ing souls to quench and fill.
cern, blest, when our faith can hold you fast.
way, shed o'er the world your ho - ly light.

Words: Att. Bernard of Clairvaux (1091-1153); tr. and para. Ray Palmer (1808-1887), alt.
Music: *Dickinson College*, Lee Hastings Bristol, Jr. (1923-1979)

LM

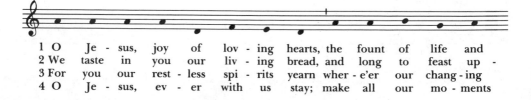

1 O Je - sus, joy of lov - ing hearts, the fount of life and
2 We taste in you our liv - ing bread, and long to feast up -
3 For you our rest - less spi - rits yearn wher - e'er our chang - ing
4 O Je - sus, ev - er with us stay; make all our mo - ments

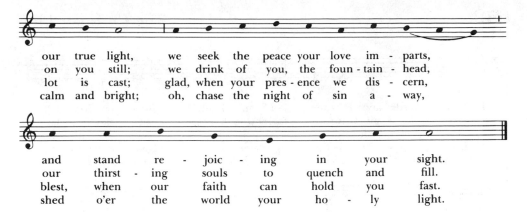

our	true	light,	we	seek	the	peace your love im - parts,
on	you	still;	we	drink	of	you,	the	foun - tain - head,
lot	is	cast;	glad,	when	your	pres - ence	we	dis - cern,
calm	and	bright;	oh,	chase	the	night of	sin	a - way,

and	stand	re - joic - ing	in	your	sight.
our	thirst - ing	souls	to	quench	and	fill.
blest,	when	our	faith	can	hold	you	fast.
shed	o'er	the	world	your	ho - ly	light.

Words: Att. Bernard of Clairvaux (1091-1153); tr. and para. Ray Palmer (1808-1887), alt.
Music: *Jesu dulcis memoria*, plainsong, Mode 2
LM

The Christian Life   651

1 This is my Fa - ther's world,   and to my lis - tening ears
2 This is our Fa - ther's world,   oh, let us not for - get

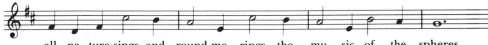

all na - ture sings and round me rings the mu - sic of the spheres.
that though the wrong is great and strong, God is our Fa - ther yet.

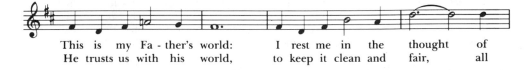

This is my Fa - ther's world: I rest me in the thought of
He trusts us with his world,   to keep it clean and fair, all

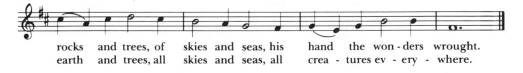

rocks and trees, of skies and seas, his hand the won - ders wrought.
earth and trees, all skies and seas, all crea - tures ev - ery - where.

Words: St. 1, Maltbie D. Babcock (1858-1901); st. 2, Mary Babcock Crawford (b. 1909)
Music: *Mercer Street*, Malcolm Williamson (b. 1931)
SMD

1 Dear Lord and Fa-ther of man-kind, for-give our fool-ish
2 In sim-ple trust like theirs who heard, be-side the Syr-ian
3 O Sab-bath rest by Gal-i-lee! O calm of hills a-
4 Drop thy still dews of qui-et-ness, till all our striv-ings
5 Breathe through the heats of our de-sire thy cool-ness and thy

1 ways! Re-clothe us in our right-ful mind, in
2 sea, the gra-cious call-ing of the Lord, let
3 bove, where Je-sus knelt to share with thee the
4 cease; take from our souls the strain and stress, and
5 balm; let sense be dumb, let flesh re-tire; speak

1 pur-er lives thy ser-vice find, in deep-er rev-erence, praise.
2 us, like them, with-out a word, rise up and fol-low thee.
3 si-lence of e-ter-ni-ty in-ter-pret-ed by love!
4 let our or-dered lives con-fess the beau-ty of thy peace.
5 through the earth-quake, wind, and fire, O still, small voice of calm.

Words: John Greenleaf Whittier (1807-1892), alt.
Music: *Rest,* Frederick Charles Maker (1844-1927)

86. 886

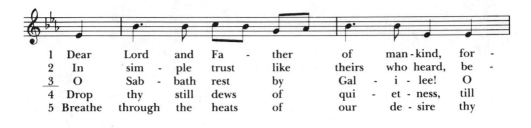

1 Dear Lord and Fa - ther of man - kind, for -
2 In sim - ple trust like theirs who heard, be -
3 O Sab - bath rest by Gal - i - lee! O
4 Drop thy still dews of qui - et - ness, till
5 Breathe through the heats of our de - sire thy

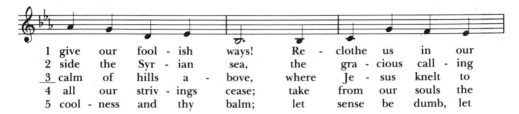

1 give our fool - ish ways! Re - clothe us in our
2 side the Syr - ian sea, the gra - cious call - ing
3 calm of hills a - bove, where Je - sus knelt to
4 all our striv - ings cease; take from our souls the
5 cool - ness and thy balm; let sense be dumb, let

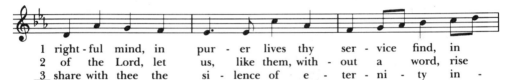

1 right - ful mind, in pur - er lives thy ser - vice find, in
2 of the Lord, let us, like them, with - out a word, rise
3 share with thee the si - lence of e - ter - ni - ty in -
4 strain and stress, and let our or - dered lives con - fess the
5 flesh re - tire; speak through the earth - quake, wind, and fire, O

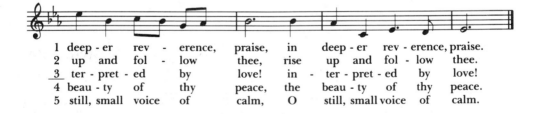

1 deep - er rev - erence, praise, in deep - er rev - erence, praise.
2 up and fol - low thee, rise up and fol - low thee.
3 ter - pret - ed by love! in - ter - pret - ed by love!
4 beau - ty of thy peace, the beau - ty of thy peace.
5 still, small voice of calm, O still, small voice of calm.

Words: John Greenleaf Whittier (1807-1892), alt.
Music: *Repton*, Charles Hubert Hastings Parry (1848-1918), alt.

86. 886

Day by day, dear Lord, of thee three things I pray:
to see thee more clear - ly, love thee more dear - ly,
fol - low thee more near - ly, day by day.

Words: Att. Richard of Chichester (1197-1253)
Music: *Sumner*, Arthur Henry Biggs (1906-1954)

Irr.

1 O Je - sus, I have prom - ised to serve thee to the end:
2 O let me hear thee speak - ing in ac - cents clear and still,
3 O Je - sus, thou hast prom - ised to all who fol - low thee,

be thou for ev - er near me, my Mas - ter and my friend;
a - bove the storms of pas - sion, the mur - murs of self - will;
that where thou art in glo - ry there shall thy ser - vant be;

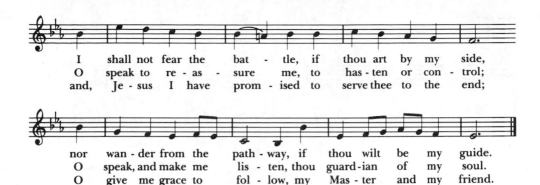

I	shall not fear the	bat - tle, if	thou art by my	side,
O	speak to re - as -	sure me, to	has - ten or con -	trol;
and,	Je - sus I have	prom - ised to	serve thee to the	end;

nor	wan - der from the	path - way, if	thou wilt be my	guide.
O	speak, and make me	lis - ten, thou	guard-ian of my	soul.
O	give me grace to	fol - low, my	Mas - ter and my	friend.

Words: John Ernest Bode (1816-1874), alt.
Music: *Nyland*, Finnish folk melody; adapt. David Evans (1874-1948)

76. 76. D

The Christian Life

656

1 Blest	are the pure in	heart, for	they shall see our	God; the
2 The	Lord, who left the	heavens our	life and peace to	bring, to
3 he	to the low - ly	soul will	still him - self im -	part and
4 Lord,	we thy pres-ence	seek; may	ours this bless-ing	be; give

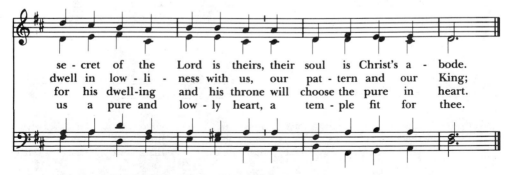

se - cret of the	Lord is theirs, their	soul is Christ's a -	bode.
dwell in low - li -	ness with us, our	pat - tern and our	King;
for his dwell-ing	and his throne will	choose the pure in	heart.
us a pure and	low - ly heart, a	tem - ple fit for	thee.

Words: Sts. 1 and 3, John Keble (1792-1866), alt.; sts. 2 and 4, William John Hall (1793-1861), alt.
Music: *Franconia*, melody Johann Balthasar König (1691-1758):
  adapt. and harm. William Henry Havergal (1793-1870)

SM

657

1 Love di - vine, all loves ex - cell - ing, joy of heaven, to
2 Come, al - might - y to de - liv - er, let us all thy
3 Fi - nish then thy new cre - a - tion; pure and spot - less

earth come down, fix in us thy hum - ble dwell - ing, all thy
life re - ceive; sud - den - ly re - turn, and nev - er, nev - er -
let us be; let us see thy great sal - va - tion per - fect -

faith - ful mer - cies crown. Je - sus, thou art all com - pas - sion,
more thy tem - ples leave. Thee we would be al - way bless - ing,
ly re - stored in thee: changed from glo - ry in - to glo - ry,

pure, un - bound - ed love thou art; vis - it us with
serve thee as thy hosts a - bove, pray, and praise thee
till in heaven we take our place, till we cast our

thy sal - va - tion, en - ter ev - ery trem-bling heart.
with - out ceas - ing, glo - ry in thy per - fect love.
crowns be - fore thee, lost in won - der, love, and praise.

Words: Charles Wesley (1707-1788)
Music: *Hyfrydol*, Rowland Hugh Prichard (1811-1887)

87. 87. D

The Christian Life

658

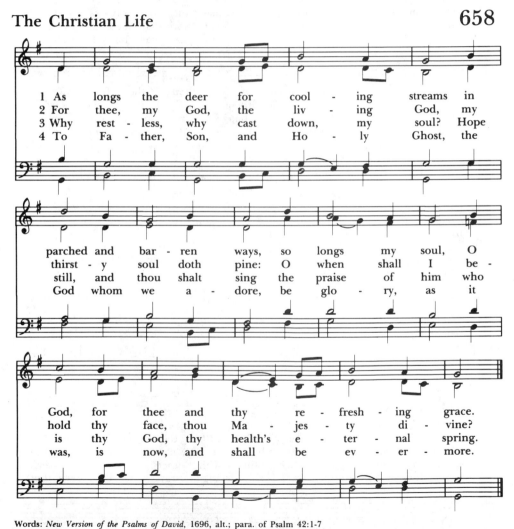

1 As longs the deer for cool - ing streams in
2 For thee, my God, the liv - ing God, my
3 Why rest - less, why cast down, my soul? Hope
4 To Fa - ther, Son, and Ho - ly Ghost, the

parched and bar - ren ways, so longs my soul, O
thirst - y soul doth pine: O when shall I be -
still, and thou shalt sing the praise of him who
God whom we a - dore, be glo - ry, as it

God, for thee and thy re - fresh - ing grace.
hold thy face, thou Ma - jes - ty di - vine?
is thy God, thy health's e - ter - nal spring.
was, is now, and shall be ev - er - more.

Words: *New Version of the Psalms of David*, 1696, alt.; para. of Psalm 42:1-7
Music: *Martyrdom*, melody and bass Hugh Wilson (1764-1824); adapt. and harm. Robert Smith (1780-1829)

CM

1 O Mas - ter, let me walk with thee　in low - ly
2 (Help me the slow of heart to) move　by some clear,
3 (Teach me thy pa - tience; still with) thee　in clos - er,
4 (in hope that sends a shin - ing) ray　far down the

paths of ser - vice free;　tell me thy se - cret; help me
win - ning word of love;　teach me the way - ward feet to
dear - er com - pa - ny,　in work that keeps faith sweet and
fu - ture's broad - ening way,　in peace that on - ly thou canst

bear　the strain of　toil, the fret of
stay,　and guide them in　the home - ward
strong,　in trust that　tri - umphs o - ver
give,　with thee, O　Mas - ter, let me

[1-3]　　　　　　　　　　Final Ending

care.　2 Help me the slow of heart to
way.　3 Teach me thy pa - tience; still with
wrong,　4 in hope that sends a shin - ing
live.

Words: Washington Gladden (1836-1918)
Music: *de Tar*, Calvin Hampton (1938-1984)

LM

1 O Mas - ter, let me walk with thee in low - ly
2 Help me the slow of heart to move by some clear,
3 Teach me thy pa - tience; still with thee in clos - er,
4 in hope that sends a shin - ing ray far down the

paths of ser - vice free; tell me thy se - cret;
win - ning word of love; teach me the way - ward
dear - er com - pa - ny, in work that keeps faith
fu - ture's broad - ening way, in peace that on - ly

help me bear the strain of toil, the fret of care.
feet to stay, and guide them in the home - ward way.
sweet and strong, in trust that tri - umphs o - ver wrong,
thou canst give, with thee, O Mas - ter, let me live.

Words: Washington Gladden (1836-1918)
Music: *Maryton*, Henry Percy Smith (1825-1898)

. LM

The Christian Life

661

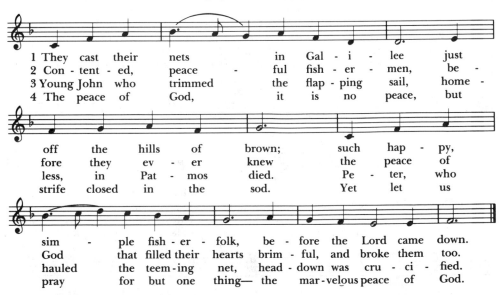

1 They cast their nets in Gal - i - lee just
2 Con - tent - ed, peace - ful fish - er - men, be -
3 Young John who trimmed the flap - ping sail, home -
4 The peace of God, it is no peace, but

off the hills of brown; such hap - py,
fore they ev - er knew the peace of
less, in Pat - mos died. Pe - ter, who
strife closed in the sod. Yet let us

sim - ple fish - er - folk, be - fore the Lord came down.
God that filled their hearts brim - ful, and broke them too.
hauled the teem - ing net, head - down was cru - ci - fied.
pray for but one thing— the mar - velous peace of God.

Words: William Alexander Percy (1885-1942), alt.
Music: *Georgetown*, David McKinley Williams (1887-1978)

CM

1 A - bide with me: fast falls the e - ven - tide;
2 I need thy pres - ence ev - ery pass - ing hour;
3 I fear no foe, with thee at hand to bless;
4 Hold thou thy cross be - fore my clos - ing eyes;

the dark - ness deep - ens; Lord, with me a - bide:
what but thy grace can foil the tempt-er's power?
ills have no weight, and tears no bit - ter - ness.
shine through the gloom, and point me to the skies;

when o - ther help - ers fail and com-forts flee,
Who, like thy - self, my guide and stay can be?
Where is death's sting? where, grave, thy vic - to - ry?
heaven's morn - ing breaks, and earth's vain sha-dows flee;

help of the help - less, O a - bide with me.
Through cloud and sun - shine, Lord, a - bide with me.
I tri - umph still, if thou a - bide with me.
in life, in death, O Lord, a - bide with me.

Words: Henry Francis Lyte (1793-1847)
Music: *Eventide*, William Henry Monk (1823-1889)

10 10. 10 10

The Christian Life

1 The Lord my God my shep - herd is; how
2 To whole - ness he re - stores my soul and
3 Yea, e - ven when I must pass through the
4 Thou hast in grace my ta - ble spread se -
5 Then sure - ly I can trust thy love for

1 could I want or need? In pas - tures green, by
2 doth in mer - cy bless, and helps me take for
3 val - ley of death's shade, I will not fear, for
4 cure in all a - larms, and filled my cup, and
5 all the days to come, that I may tell thy

1 streams se - rene, he safe - ly doth me lead.
2 his Name's sake the paths of right - eous - ness.
3 thou art here, to com - fort and to aid.
4 borne me up in ev - er - last - ing arms.
5 praise, and dwell for ev - er in thy home.

Words: F. Bland Tucker (1895-1984); para. of Psalm 23
Music: *Crimond*, melody Jesse Seymour Irvine (1836-1887); harm. *Hymnal 1982*

CM

1 My Shep-herd will sup-ply my need, Je-ho-vah
2 When I walk through the shades of death, thy pres-ence
3 The sure pro-vi-sions of my God at-tend me

is his Name; in pas-tures fresh he
is my stay; one word of thy sup-
all my days; oh, may thy house be

makes me feed be-side the liv-ing stream.
port-ing breath drives all my fears a-way.
mine a-bode and all my work be praise.

He brings my wan-dering spi-rit back when I for-
Thy hand, in sight of all my foes, doth still my
There would I find a set-tled rest, while o-thers

sake his ways, and leads me, for his
ta-ble spread; my cup with bless-ings
go and come; no more a stran-ger

mer-cy's sake, in paths of truth and grace.
o-ver-flows, thy oil a-noints my head.
or a guest, but like a child at home.

Words: Isaac Watts (1674-1748); para. of Psalm 23
Music: *Resignation*, American folk melody

CMD

1 All my hope on God is found - ed; he doth still my
2 Mor - tal pride and earth - ly glo - ry, sword and crown be -
3 God's great good-ness e'er en - dur - eth, deep his wis - dom
*4 Dai - ly doth the al - might - y Giv - er boun - teous gifts on
5 Still from earth to God e - ter - nal sac - ri - fice of

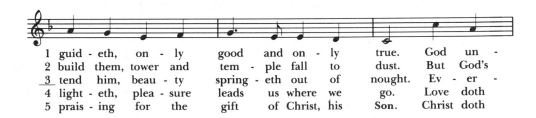

1 trust re - new, me through change and chance he
2 tray our trust; though with care and toil we
3 pass - ing thought: splen - dor, light, and life at -
4 us be - stow; his de - sire our soul de -
5 praise be done, high a - bove all prais - es

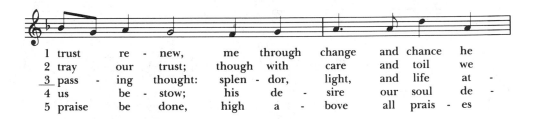

1 guid - eth, on - ly good and on - ly true. God un -
2 build them, tower and tem - ple fall to dust. But God's
3 tend him, beau - ty spring - eth out of nought. Ev - er -
4 light - eth, plea - sure leads us where we go. Love doth
5 prais - ing for the gift of Christ, his Son. Christ doth

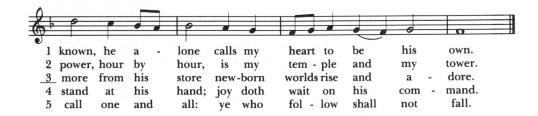

1 known, he a - lone calls my heart to be his own.
2 power, hour by hour, is my tem - ple and my tower.
3 more from his store new-born worlds rise and a - dore.
4 stand at his hand; joy doth wait on his com - mand.
5 call one and all: ye who fol - low shall not fall.

Words: Robert Seymour Bridges (1844-1930), alt., after Joachim Neander (1650-1680)
Music: *Michael*, Herbert Howells (1892-1983)

87. 87. 337

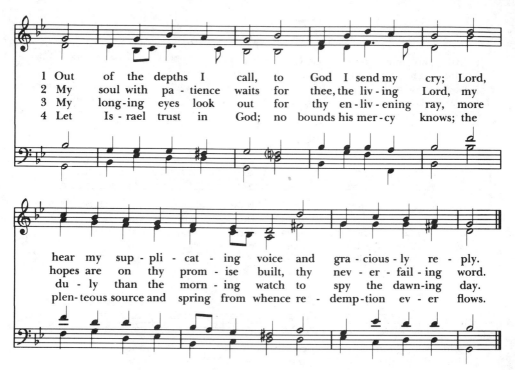

1 Out of the depths I call, to God I send my cry; Lord,
2 My soul with pa-tience waits for thee, the liv-ing Lord, my
3 My long-ing eyes look out for thy en-liv-ening ray, more
4 Let Is-rael trust in God; no bounds his mer-cy knows; the

hear my sup-pli-cat-ing voice and gra-cious-ly re-ply.
hopes are on thy prom-ise built, thy nev-er-fail-ing word.
du-ly than the morn-ing watch to spy the dawn-ing day.
plen-teous source and spring from whence re-demp-tion ev-er flows.

Words: Tate and Brady, *New Version of the Psalms*, 1698, alt.; para. of Pslam 130
Music: *St. Bride*, Samuel Howard (1710-1782)

SM

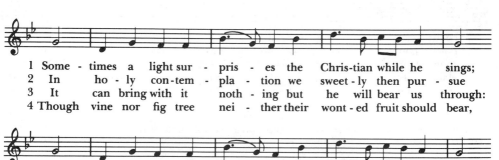

1 Some-times a light sur-pris-es the Chris-tian while he sings;
2 In ho-ly con-tem-pla-tion we sweet-ly then pur-sue
3 It can bring with it noth-ing but he will bear us through:
4 Though vine nor fig tree nei-ther their wont-ed fruit should bear,

it is the Lord who ris-es with heal-ing in his wings:
the theme of God's sal-va-tion, and find it ev-er new;
who gives the lil-ies cloth-ing will clothe his peo-ple, too:
though all the fields should with-er, nor flocks nor herds be there;

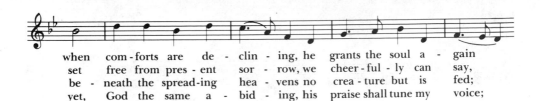

when com-forts are de - clin - ing, he grants the soul a - gain
set free from pres - ent sor - row, we cheer-ful - ly can say,
be - neath the spread-ing hea - vens no crea - ture but is fed;
yet, God the same a - bid - ing, his praise shall tune my voice;

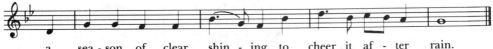

a sea - son of clear shin - ing, to cheer it af - ter rain.
let the un-known to - mor - row bring with it what it may.
and he who feeds the rav - ens will give his chil - dren bread.
for, while in him con - fid - ing, I can - not but re - joice.

Words: William Cowper (1731-1800)
Music: *Light*, melody from *The Christian Lyre*, 1830

76. 76. D

The Christian Life

668

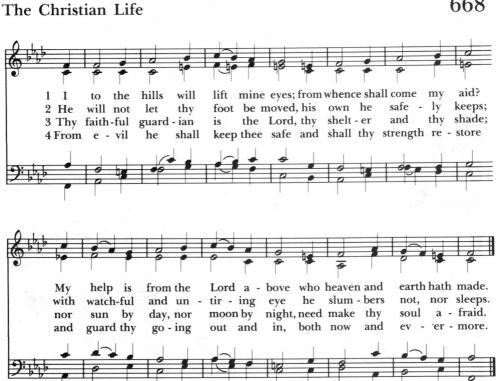

1 I to the hills will lift mine eyes; from whence shall come my aid?
2 He will not let thy foot be moved, his own he safe - ly keeps;
3 Thy faith-ful guard - ian is the Lord, thy shelt - er and thy shade;
4 From e - vil he shall keep thee safe and shall thy strength re - store

My help is from the Lord a - bove who heaven and earth hath made.
with watch-ful and un - tir - ing eye he slum - bers not, nor sleeps.
nor sun by day, nor moon by night, need make thy soul a - fraid.
and guard thy go - ing out and in, both now and ev - er - more.

Words: *The Psalms of David in Meeter*, 1650, alt.; st. 4, F. Bland Tucker (1895-1984); para. of Psalm 121
Music: *Burford*, from *A Book of Psalmody*, 1718

CM

1 Com - mit thou all that grieves thee and fills thy heart with
2 O trust the Lord then whol - ly, if thou wouldst be se -
3 Thy last - ing truth and mer - cy, O Fa - ther, see a -
4 Hope on, then, bro - ken spi - rit; hope on, be not a -

care to him whose faith - ful mer - cy the
cure; his work must thou con - sid - er for
right the needs of all thy chil - dren, their
fraid: fear not the griefs that plague thee and

skies a - bove de - clare, who gives the winds their
thy work to en - dure. What prof - it doth it
an - guish or de - light: what lov - ing wis - dom
keep thy heart dis - mayed: thy God, in his great

cours - es, who points the clouds their way; 'tis
bring thee to pine in grief and care? God
choos - eth, re - deem - ing might will do, and
mer - cy, will save thee, hold thee fast, and

he will guide thy foot - steps and be thy staff and stay.
ev - er sends his bless - ing in an - swer to thy prayer.
bring to sure ful - fill - ment thy coun - sel good and true.
in his own time grant thee the sun of joy at last.

Words: Paul Gerhardt (1607-1676); tr. Arthur William Farlander (1898-1952)
and Charles Winfred Douglas (1867-1944), alt.
Music: *Herzlich tut mich verlangen [Passion Chorale]*, Hans Leo Hassler (1564-1612);
adapt. and harm. Johann Sebastian Bach (1685-1750)

76. 76. D

The Christian Life

670

Unison or harmony

1 Lord, for ev - er at thy side let my place and por - tion be,
2 When I come be - fore thy Word, qui - et my anx - i - e - ty;
3 What thy Spi - rit doth re - veal, that may I in faith re - ceive;
4 Is - rael, now and ev - er - more in the Lord Al - might - y trust;

strip me of the robe of pride, clothe me with hu - mil - i - ty.
teach me thou a - lone art Lord, let my heart find rest in thee.
though my doubts I sore - ly feel, thy sure prom - ise I be - lieve.
him, in all his ways, a - dore, wise, and won - der - ful, and just.

Words: Sts. 1 and 4, James Montgomery (1771-1854), alt.; sts. 2-3, Charles P. Price (b. 1920)
Music: *Song 13*, melody and bass Orlando Gibbons (1583-1625); harm. *More Hymns for Today*, 1980

77. 77

1 A - maz - ing grace! how sweet the sound, that
2 'Twas grace that taught my heart to fear, and
3 The Lord has prom - ised good to me, his
4 Through man - y dan - gers, toils, and snares, I
*5 When we've been there ten thou - sand years, bright

1 saved a wretch like me! I once was lost but
2 grace my fears re - lieved; how pre - cious did that
3 word my hope se - cures; he will my shield and
4 have al - rea - dy come; 'tis grace that brought me
5 shin - ing as the sun, we've no less days to

1 now am found, was blind but now I see.
2 grace ap - pear the hour I first be - lieved!
3 por - tion be as long as life en - dures.
4 safe thus far, and grace will lead me home.
5 sing God's praise than when we'd first be - gun.

The melody may be sung in canon at distances of either two or three beats.

Words: John Newton (1725-1807), alt.; st. 5, from *A Collection of Sacred Ballads*, 1790; compiled by
Richard Broaddus and Andrew Broaddus
Music: *New Britain*, from *Virginia Harmony*, 1831; adapt. att. Edwin Othello Excell (1851-1921);   CM
harm. Austin Cole Lovelace (b. 1919)

1 O very God of very God, and
2 Our hopes are weak, our fears are strong, thick
3 And even now, though dull and gray, the
4 O guide us till our path is done, and
5 We wait in faith, and turn our face to

1 very Light of Light, whose feet this earth's dark
2 darkness blinds our eyes; cold is the night; thy
3 east is brightening fast, and kindling to the
4 we have reached the shore where thou, our ever -
5 where the daylight springs, till thou shalt come our

1 valley trod that so it might be bright:
2 people long that thou, their Sun, wouldst rise.
3 perfect day that never shall be past.
4 lasting Sun, art shining evermore!
5 gloom to chase, with healing in thy wings.

Words: John Mason Neale (1818-1866)
Music: *Bangor*, from *A Compleat Melody or Harmony of Zion*, 1734

CM

1 The first one ev-er, oh, ev-er to know of the
2 The first one ev-er, oh, ev-er to know of Me-
3 The first ones ev-er, oh, ev-er to know of the

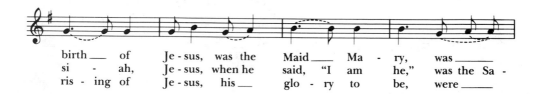

birth __ of Je-sus, was the Maid __ Ma-ry, was __
si-ah, Je-sus, when he said, "I am he," was the Sa-
ris-ing of Je-sus, his __ glo-ry to be, were __

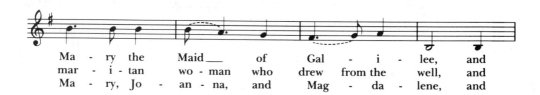

Ma-ry the Maid __ of Gal-i-lee, and
mar-i-tan wo-man who drew from the well, and
Ma-ry, Jo-an-na, and Mag-da-lene, and

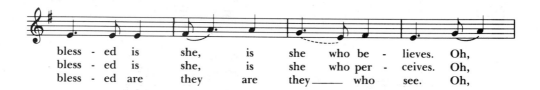

bless-ed is she, is she who be-lieves. Oh,
bless-ed is she, is she who per-ceives. Oh,
bless-ed are they are they __ who see. Oh,

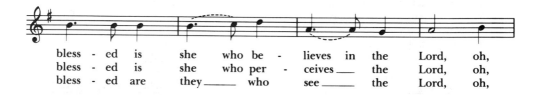

bless-ed is she who be-lieves in the Lord, oh,
bless-ed is she who per-ceives __ the Lord, oh,
bless-ed are they __ who see __ the Lord, oh,

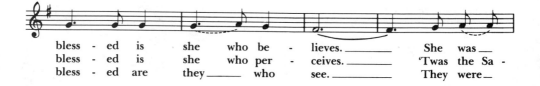

bless-ed is she who be-lieves. __ She was __
bless-ed is she who per-ceives. __ 'Twas the Sa-
bless-ed are they __ who see. __ They were __

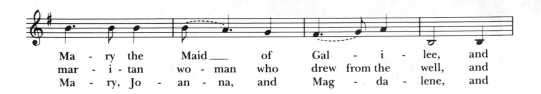

Ma - ry the Maid___ of Gal - i - lee, and
mar - i - tan wo - man who drew from the well, and
Ma - ry, Jo - an - na, and Mag - da - lene, and

bless - ed is she, is she who be - lieves.
bless - ed is she, is she who per - ceives.
bless - ed are they, are they ___ who see.

Words: Linda Wilberger Egan (b. 1946), alt.
Music: *Ballad*, Linda Wilberger Egan (b. 1946)

Irr.

The Christian Life

674

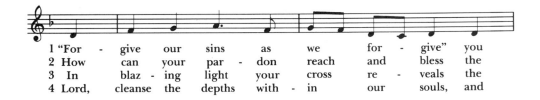

1 "For - give our sins as we for - give" you
2 How can your par - don reach and bless the
3 In blaz - ing light your cross re - veals the
4 Lord, cleanse the depths with - in our souls, and

taught us, Lord, to pray; but you a - lone can
un - for - giv - ing heart that broods on wrongs and
truth we dim - ly knew, how small the debts men
bid re - sent - ment cease; then, rec - on - ciled to

grant us grace to live the words we say.
will not let old bit - ter - ness de - part?
owe to us, how great our debt to you.
God and man, our lives will spread your peace.

Words: Rosamond E. Herklots (b. 1905)
Music: *Detroit*, from *Supplement to Kentucky Harmony*, 1820

CM

675

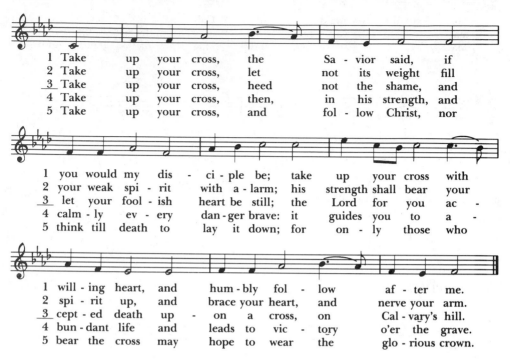

1 Take up your cross, the Sa - vior said, if
2 Take up your cross, let not its weight fill
3 Take up your cross, heed not the shame, and
4 Take up your cross, then, in his strength, and
5 Take up your cross, and fol - low Christ, nor

1 you would my dis - ci - ple be; take up your cross with
2 your weak spi - rit with a - larm; his strength shall bear your
3 let your fool - ish heart be still; the Lord for you ac -
4 calm - ly ev - ery dan - ger brave: it guides you to a -
5 think till death to lay it down; for on - ly those who

1 will - ing heart, and hum - bly fol - low af - ter me.
2 spi - rit up, and brace your heart, and nerve your arm.
3 cept - ed death up - on a cross, on Cal - vary's hill.
4 bun - dant life and leads to vic - tory o'er the grave.
5 bear the cross may hope to wear the glo - rious crown.

Words: Charles William Everest (1814-1877), alt.
Music: *Bourbon*, melody att. Freeman Lewis (1780-1859)

LM

676

Refrain

There is a balm in Gil - e - ad, to make the wound-ed

whole, there is a balm in Gil - e - ad, to

heal the sin - sick soul. soul.

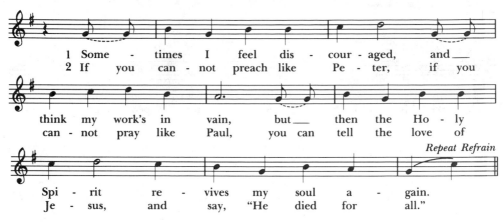

1 Some - times I feel dis - cour - aged, and ___
2 If you can - not preach like Pe - ter, if you

think my work's in vain, but ___ then the Ho - ly
can - not pray like Paul, you can tell the love of

Repeat Refrain

Spi - rit re - vives my soul a - gain.
Je - sus, and say, "He died for all."

Words: Afro-American spiritual
Music: *Balm in Gilead,* Afro-American spiritual

Irr. with Refrain

The Christian Life

677

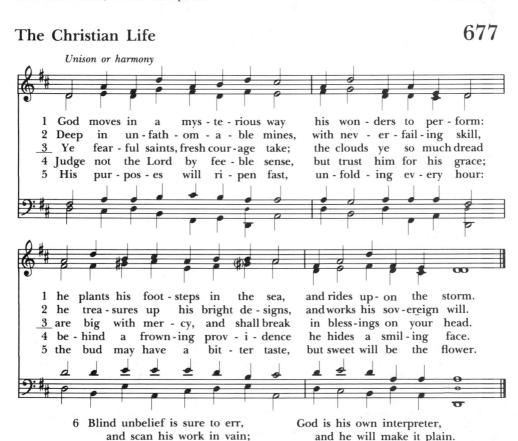

Unison or harmony

1 God moves in a mys - te - rious way   his won - ders to per - form:
2 Deep in un - fath - om - a - ble mines,   with nev - er - fail - ing skill,
3 Ye fear - ful saints, fresh cour - age take;   the clouds ye so much dread
4 Judge not the Lord by fee - ble sense,   but trust him for his grace;
5 His pur - pos - es will ri - pen fast,   un - fold - ing ev - ery hour:

1 he plants his foot - steps in the sea,   and rides up - on the storm.
2 he trea - sures up his bright de - signs,   and works his sov - ereign will.
3 are big with mer - cy, and shall break   in bless - ings on your head.
4 be - hind a frown - ing prov - i - dence   he hides a smil - ing face.
5 the bud may have a bit - ter taste,   but sweet will be the flower.

6 Blind unbelief is sure to err,   God is his own interpreter,
  and scan his work in vain;   and he will make it plain.

Words: William Cowper (1731-1800)
Music: *London New,* melody from *The Psalmes of David in Prose and Meeter,* 1635, alt.;
harm. John Playford (1623-1686)

CM

1 Sure - ly   it   is   God_____ who   saves   me;
2 Make   his   deeds__ known   to   the   peo - ples;

trust - ing him, I shall not   fear.   For   the   Lord   de - fends and
tell   out his ex - alt - ed   Name. Praise the   Lord,   who has   done

shields me   and his   sav - ing help is   near.   So re - joice   as
great things; all his   works his   might pro - claim.   Zi - on,   lift   your

you draw wa - ter   from sal - va - tion's liv - ing spring;   in the
voice in   sing - ing; for   with you   has come to   dwell,   in your

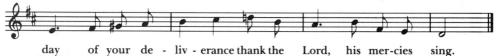

day   of your de - liv - erance thank the   Lord,   his mer - cies   sing.
ve - ry midst, the   great and   Ho - ly   One   of Is - ra - el.

Words: Carl P. Daw, Jr. (b. 1944); para. of *The First Song of Isaiah*
Music: *College of Preachers*, Arthur Rhea (b. 1919)

87. 87. D

1 Sure - ly   it   is   God_ who saves me;   trust - ing   him,   I   shall   not
2 Make his deeds__ known to the   peo - ples;   tell out   his   ex - alt - ed

fear.   For the   Lord de - fends and shields me   and his   sav - ing
Name.   Praise the   Lord, who has   done great things;   all his   works his

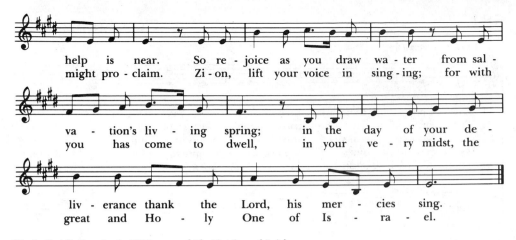

help is near. So re-joice as you draw wa-ter from sal-
might pro-claim. Zi-on, lift your voice in sing-ing; for with

va-tion's liv-ing spring; in the day of your de-
you has come to dwell, in your ve-ry midst, the

liv-erance thank the Lord, his mer-cies sing.
great and Ho-ly One of Is-ra-el.

Words: Carl P. Daw, Jr. (b. 1944); para. of *The First Song of Isaiah*
Music: *Thomas Merton*, Ray W. Urwin (b. 1950)

87. 87. D

The Christian Life

680

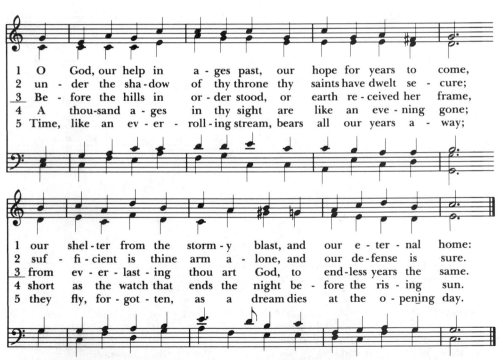

1 O God, our help in a-ges past, our hope for years to come,
2 un-der the sha-dow of thy throne thy saints have dwelt se-cure;
3 Be-fore the hills in or-der stood, or earth re-ceived her frame,
4 A thou-sand a-ges in thy sight are like an eve-ning gone;
5 Time, like an ev-er-roll-ing stream, bears all our years a-way;

1 our shel-ter from the storm-y blast, and our e-ter-nal home:
2 suf-fi-cient is thine arm a-lone, and our de-fense is sure.
3 from ev-er-last-ing thou art God, to end-less years the same.
4 short as the watch that ends the night be-fore the ris-ing sun.
5 they fly, for-got-ten, as a dream dies at the o-pening day.

6 O God, our help in ages past,   be thou our guide while life shall last,
our hope for years to come,   and our eternal home.

Words: Issac Watts (1674-1748), alt.; para. of Psalm 90:1-5
Music: *St. Anne*, melody att. William Croft (1678-1727), alt., harm. William Henry Monk (1823-1889), alt.

CM

Unison or harmony

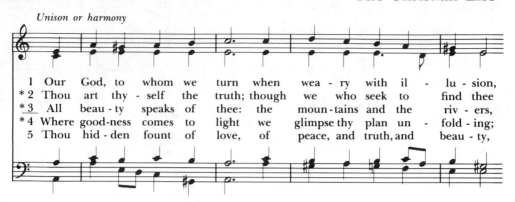

1 Our God, to whom we turn when wea - ry with il - lu - sion,
*2 Thou art thy - self the truth; though we who seek to find thee
*3 All beau - ty speaks of thee: the moun - tains and the riv - ers,
*4 Where good-ness comes to light we glimpse thy plan un - fold - ing;
5 Thou hid - den fount of love, of peace, and truth, and beau - ty,

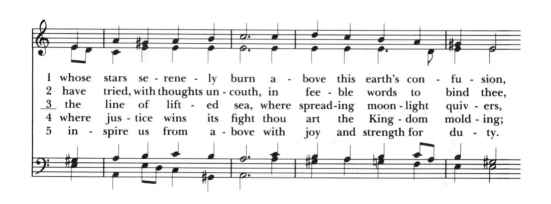

1 whose stars se - rene - ly burn a - bove this earth's con - fu - sion,
2 have tried, with thoughts un - couth, in fee - ble words to bind thee,
3 the line of lift - ed sea, where spread-ing moon - light quiv - ers,
4 where jus - tice wins its fight thou art the King - dom mold - ing;
5 in - spire us from a - bove with joy and strength for du - ty.

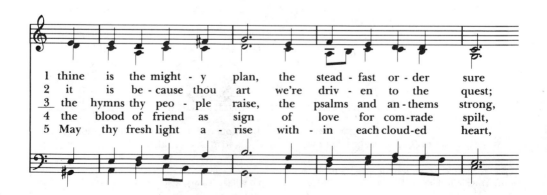

1 thine is the might - y plan, the stead - fast or - der sure
2 it is be - cause thou art we're driv - en to the quest;
3 the hymns thy peo - ple raise, the psalms and an - thems strong,
4 the blood of friend as sign of love for com-rade spilt,
5 May thy fresh light a - rise with - in each cloud-ed heart,

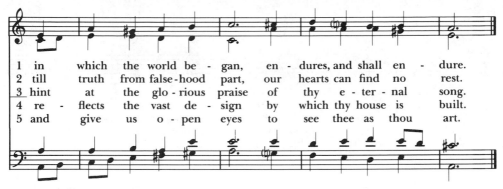

1 in which the world be - gan, en - dures, and shall en - dure.
2 till truth from false - hood part, our hearts can find no rest.
3 hint at the glo - rious praise of thy e - ter - nal song.
4 re - flects the vast de - sign by which thy house is built.
5 and give us o - pen eyes to see thee as thou art.

Words: Edward Grubb (1854-1939), alt.
Music: *O Gott, du frommer Gott*, melody from *Neu ordentlich Gesangbuch*, 1646;
　　harm. Johann Sebastian Bach (1685-1750), alt.

67. 67. 66. 66

The Christian Life

682

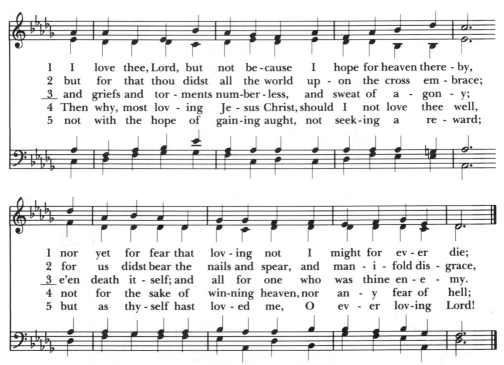

1 I love thee, Lord, but not be - cause I hope for heaven there - by,
2 but for that thou didst all the world up - on the cross em - brace;
3 and griefs and tor - ments num - ber - less, and sweat of a - gon - y;
4 Then why, most lov - ing Je - sus Christ, should I not love thee well,
5 not with the hope of gain - ing aught, not seek - ing a re - ward;

1 nor yet for fear that lov - ing not I might for ev - er die;
2 for us didst bear the nails and spear, and man - i - fold dis - grace,
3 e'en death it - self; and all for one who was thine en - e - my.
4 not for the sake of win - ning heaven, nor an - y fear of hell;
5 but as thy - self hast lov - ed me, O ev - er lov - ing Lord!

6 E'en so I love thee, and will love,
　　and in thy praise will sing,
　　solely because thou art my God
　　and my eternal King.

Words: Spanish, 17th cent.; tr. Edward Caswall (1814-1878); adapt. Percy Dearmer (1867-1936), alt.
Music: *St. Fulbert*, Henry John Gauntlett (1805-1876)

CM

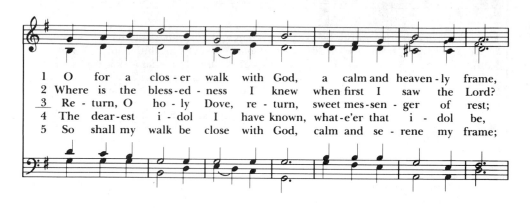

1 O for a clos-er walk with God, a calm and heaven-ly frame,
2 Where is the bless-ed-ness I knew when first I saw the Lord?
3 Re-turn, O ho-ly Dove, re-turn, sweet mes-sen-ger of rest;
4 The dear-est i-dol I have known, what-e'er that i-dol be,
5 So shall my walk be close with God, calm and se-rene my frame;

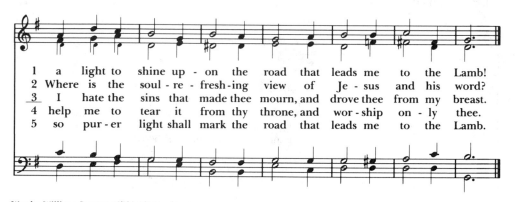

1 a light to shine up-on the road that leads me to the Lamb!
2 Where is the soul-re-fresh-ing view of Je-sus and his word?
3 I hate the sins that made thee mourn, and drove thee from my breast.
4 help me to tear it from thy throne, and wor-ship on-ly thee.
5 so pur-er light shall mark the road that leads me to the Lamb.

Words: William Cowper (1731-1800), alt.
Music: *Beatitudo*, John Bacchus Dykes (1823-1876)

CM

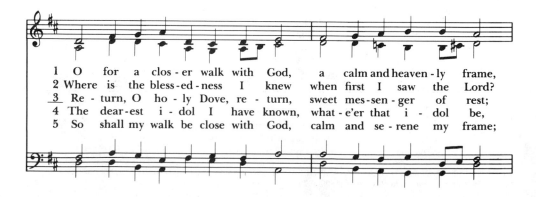

1 O for a clos-er walk with God, a calm and heaven-ly frame,
2 Where is the bless-ed-ness I knew when first I saw the Lord?
3 Re-turn, O ho-ly Dove, re-turn, sweet mes-sen-ger of rest;
4 The dear-est i-dol I have known, what-e'er that i-dol be,
5 So shall my walk be close with God, calm and se-rene my frame;

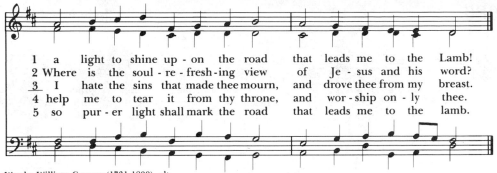

1 a light to shine up-on the road that leads me to the Lamb!
2 Where is the soul-re-fresh-ing view of Je-sus and his word?
3 I hate the sins that made thee mourn, and drove thee from my breast.
4 help me to tear it from thy throne, and wor-ship on-ly thee.
5 so pur-er light shall mark the road that leads me to the lamb.

Words: William Cowper (1731-1800), alt.
Music: *Caithness*, from *The Psalmes of David in Prose and Meeter*, 1635; harm. *The English Hymnal*, 1906   CM

The Christian Life   685

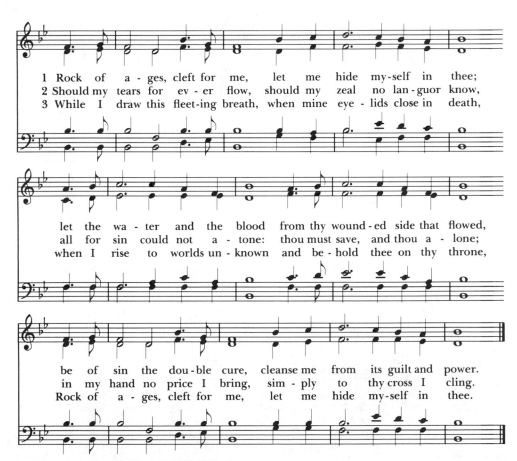

1 Rock of a-ges, cleft for me, let me hide my-self in thee;
2 Should my tears for ev-er flow, should my zeal no lan-guor know,
3 While I draw this fleet-ing breath, when mine eye-lids close in death,

let the wa-ter and the blood from thy wound-ed side that flowed,
all for sin could not a-tone: thou must save, and thou a-lone;
when I rise to worlds un-known and be-hold thee on thy throne,

be of sin the dou-ble cure, cleanse me from its guilt and power.
in my hand no price I bring, sim-ply to thy cross I cling.
Rock of a-ges, cleft for me, let me hide my-self in thee.

Words: Augustus Montague Toplady (1740-1778), alt.
Music: *Toplady*, Thomas Hastings (1784-1872)   77. 77. 77

1 Come, thou fount of ev-ery bless-ing, tune my
2 Here I find my great-est trea-sure; hith-er,
3 Oh, to grace how great a debt-or dai-ly

heart to sing thy grace! Streams of mer-cy nev-er
by thy help, I've come; and I hope, by thy good
I'm con-strained to be! Let thy good-ness, like a

ceas-ing, call for songs of loud-est praise.
plea-sure, safe-ly to ar-rive at home.
fet-ter, bind my wan-dering heart to thee:

Teach me some me-lo-dious son-net, sung by
Je-sus sought me when a stran-ger wan-dering
prone to wan-der, Lord, I feel it, prone to

flam-ing tongues a-bove. Praise the mount! Oh, fix me
from the fold of God; he, to res-cue me from
leave the God I love; here's my heart, oh, take and

on it, mount of God's un-chang-ing love.
dan-ger, in-ter-posed his pre-cious blood.
seal it, seal it for thy courts a-bove.

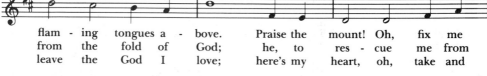

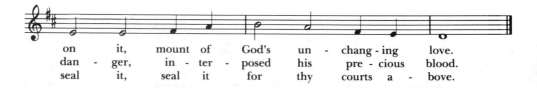

Words: Robert Robinson (1735-1790), alt.
Music: *Nettleton*, melody from *A Repository of Sacred Music, Part II*, 1813

87. 87. D

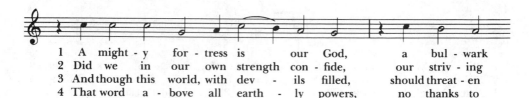

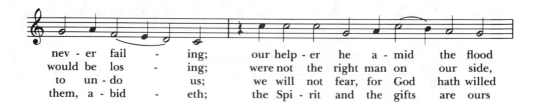

1 A might-y for-tress is our God, a bul-wark
2 Did we in our own strength con-fide, our striv-ing
3 And though this world, with dev-ils filled, should threat-en
4 That word a-bove all earth-ly powers, no thanks to

nev-er fail-ing; our help-er he a-mid the flood
would be los-ing; were not the right man on our side,
to un-do us; we will not fear, for God hath willed
them, a-bid-eth; the Spi-rit and the gifts are ours

of mor-tal ills pre-vail-ing: for still our an-cient foe
the man of God's own choos-ing: dost ask who that may be?
his truth to tri-umph through us; the prince of dark-ness grim,
through him who with us sid-eth: let goods and kin-dred go,

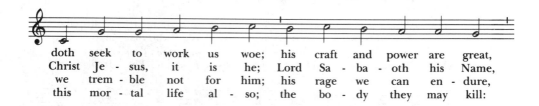

doth seek to work us woe; his craft and power are great,
Christ Je-sus, it is he; Lord Sa-ba-oth his Name,
we trem-ble not for him; his rage we can en-dure,
this mor-tal life al-so; the bo-dy they may kill:

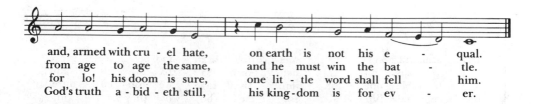

and, armed with cru-el hate, on earth is not his e-qual.
from age to age the same, and he must win the bat-tle.
for lo! his doom is sure, one lit-tle word shall fell him.
God's truth a-bid-eth still, his king-dom is for ev-er.

Words: Martin Luther (1483-1546); tr. Frederic Henry Hedge (1805-1890); based on Psalm 46
Music: *Ein feste Burg*, Martin Luther (1483-1546)

87. 87. 66. 66. 7

1 A might-y for-tress is our God, a bul-wark nev-er
2 Did we in our own strength con-fide, our striv-ing would be
3 And though this world, with dev-ils filled, should threat-en to un-
4 That word a-bove all earth-ly powers, no thanks to them, a -

fail - ing; our help-er he a - mid the flood
los - ing; were not the right man on our side,
do us; we will not fear, for God hath willed
bid - eth; the Spi - rit and the gifts are ours

of mor-tal ills pre-vail - ing: for still our an-cient foe
the man of God's own choos - ing: dost ask who that may be?
his truth to tri-umph through us; the prince of dark-ness grim,
through him who with us sid - eth: let goods and kin-dred go,

doth seek to work us woe; his craft and power are great,
Christ Je - sus, it is he; Lord Sa - ba-oth his Name,
we trem-ble not for him; his rage we can en - dure,
this mor-tal life al - so; the bo - dy they may kill:

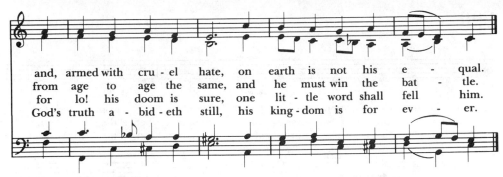

and, armed with cru - el hate, on earth is not his e - qual.
from age to age the same, and he must win the bat - tle.
for lo! his doom is sure, one lit - tle word shall fell him.
God's truth a - bid - eth still, his king - dom is for ev - er.

Words: Martin Luther (1483-1546); tr. Frederick Henry Hedge (1805-1890); based on Psalm 46
Music: *Ein feste Burg*, melody Martin Luther (1483-1546);
harm. Johann Sebastian Bach (1685-1750)

87. 87. 66. 66. 7

The Christian Life

689

1 I sought the Lord, and af - ter - ward I knew he
2 Thou didst reach forth thy hand and mine en - fold; I
3 I find, I walk, I love, but oh, the whole of

moved my soul to seek him, seek - ing me; it was not
walked and sank not on the storm-vexed sea; 'twas not so
love is but my an - swer, Lord, to thee; for thou wert

I that found, O Sa - vior true; no, I was found of thee.
much that I on thee took hold, as thou, dear Lord, on me.
long be - fore - hand with my soul, al - ways thou lov - edst me.

Words: Anon., *Pilgrim Hymnal*, 1904
Music: *Faith*, J. Harold Moyer (b. 1927)

10. 10. 10. 6

1 Guide me, O thou great Je - ho - vah, pil - grim through this
2 O - pen now the crys - tal foun - tain, whence the heal - ing
3 When I tread the verge of Jor - dan, bid my anx - ious

bar - ren land; I am weak, but thou art might - y;
stream doth flow; let the fire and cloud - y pil - lar
fears sub - side; death of death, and hell's de - struc - tion,

hold me with thy power - ful hand; bread of hea - ven,
lead me all my jour - ney through; strong de - liv - erer,
land me safe on Ca - naan's side; songs of prais - es,

bread of hea - ven, feed me now and ev - er -
strong de - liv - erer, be thou still my strength and
songs of prais - es, I will ev - er give to

more,　　　　　feed　me　now　and　　ev - er - more.
shield,　　　　be　thou　still　my　strength and　shield.
thee,　　　　　I　will　ev - er　　give　to　thee.

Words: William Williams (1717-1791); tr. Peter Williams (1722-1796), alt.
Music: *Cwm Rhondda*, John Hughes (1873-1932)

87. 87. 877

The Christian Life

691

1 My　faith looks　up　to thee,　thou　Lamb of　Cal - va - ry,
2 May　thy　rich　grace im-part　strength to　my　faint - ing heart,
3 While　life's dark　maze　I tread,　and　griefs a - round me spread,

Sa - vior di - vine!　Now　hear me　while　I pray,　take　all　my
my　zeal in - spire;　as　thou hast　died for me,　O　may my
be　thou my　guide;　bid　dark-ness　turn to day;　wipe　sor-row's

guilt a - way;　O　let　me　from this day　be　whol - ly　thine.
love to thee　pure,　warm, and　change-less be,　a　liv - ing　fire.
tears a - way,　nor　let　me　ev - er stray from thee a - side.

Words: Ray Palmer (1808-1887)
Music: *Olivet*, Lowell Mason (1792-1872)

664. 6664

692

The Christian Life

1 I heard the voice of Je-sus say, "Come un - to me and rest;
2 I heard the voice of Je-sus say, "Be-hold, I free-ly give
3 I heard the voice of Je-sus say, "I am this dark world's light;

and in your wea - ri-ness lay down your head up-on my breast."
the liv-ing wa - ter; thirst-y one, stoop down and drink, and live."
look un - to me, your morn shall rise, and all your day be bright."

I came to Je - sus as I was, so wea - ry, worn, and sad;
I came to Je - sus, and I drank of that life - giv - ing stream;
I looked to Je - sus, and I found in him my Star, my Sun;

I found in him a rest - ing place, and he has made me glad.
my thirst was quenched, my soul re - vived, and now I live in him.
and in that light of life I'll walk till pil-grim days are done.

*The bracketed notes are to be treated as triplet groups.

Words: Horatius Bonar (1808-1889), alt.
Music: *The Third Tune*, Thomas Tallis (1505?-1585); ed. John Wilson (b. 1905)

CMD

The Christian Life

1 Just as I am, with-out one plea, but that thy
2 Just as I am, though tossed a-bout with man-y a
*3 Just as I am, poor, wretch-ed, blind; sight, rich-es,
4 Just as I am: thou wilt re-ceive; wilt wel-come,
5 Just as I am, thy love un-known has bro-ken

1 blood was shed for me, and that thou bidd'st me
2 con-flict, man-y a doubt; fight-ings and fears with-
3 heal-ing of the mind, yea, all I need, in
4 par-don, cleanse, re-lieve, be-cause thy prom-ise
5 ev-ery bar-rier down; now to be thine, yea,

1 come to thee, O Lamb of God, I come, I come.
2 in, with-out, O Lamb of God, I come, I come.
3 thee to find, O Lamb of God, I come, I come.
4 I be-lieve, O Lamb of God, I come, I come.
5 thine a-lone, O Lamb of God, I come, I come.

6 Just as I am, of thy great love
   the breadth, length, depth, and height to prove,
   here for a season, then above:
   O Lamb of God, I come, I come.

Words: Charlotte Elliott (1789-1871)
Music: *Woodworth*, William Batchelder Bradbury (1816-1868)

LM

God be in my head, and in my un-der-stand-ing;

God be in mine eyes, and in my look-ing;

God be in my mouth, and in my speak-ing;

God be in my heart, and in my think-ing;

God be at mine end, and at my de-part-ing.

Words: *Sarum Primer,* 1514
Music: *Lytlington,* Sydney Hugo Nicholson (1875-1947)

Irr.

The Christian Life

1 By gra - cious powers so won - der - ful - ly shel - tered,
2 Yet is this heart by its old foe tor - ment - ed,
3 And when this cup you give is filled to brim - ming
4 Yet when a - gain in this same world you give us

and con - fi - dent - ly wait - ing come what may,
still e - vil days bring bur - dens hard to bear;
with bit - ter suf - fering, hard to un - der - stand,
the joy we had, the bright - ness of your Sun,

we know that God is with us night and morn - ing,
O give our fright - ened souls the sure sal - va - tion,
we take it thank - ful - ly and with - out trem - bling,
we shall re - mem - ber all the days we lived through,

and nev - er fails to greet us each new day.
for which, O Lord, you taught us to pre - pare.
out of so good and so be - loved a hand.
and our whole life shall then be yours a - lone.

Words: F. Pratt Green (b. 1903), after Dietrich Bonhoeffer (1906-1945)
Music: *Intercessor*, Charles Hubert Hastings Parry (1848-1918)

11 10. 11 10

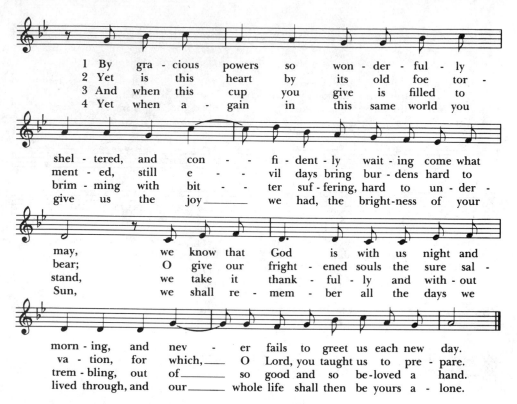

1 By gra - cious powers so won - der - ful - ly
2 Yet is this heart by its old foe tor -
3 And when this cup you give is filled to
4 Yet when a - gain in this same world you

shel - tered, and con - - - fi - dent - ly wait - ing come what
ment - ed, still e - - - vil days bring bur - dens hard to
brim - ming with bit - - - ter suf - fering, hard to un - der -
give us the joy_____ we had, the bright-ness of your

may, we know that God is with us night and
bear; O give our fright - ened souls the sure sal -
stand, we take it thank - ful - ly and with - out
Sun, we shall re - mem - ber all the days we

morn - ing, and nev - er fails to greet us each new day.
va - tion, for which,____ O Lord, you taught us to pre - pare.
trem - bling, out of____ so good and so be-loved a hand.
lived through, and our____ whole life shall then be yours a - lone.

Words: F. Pratt Green (b. 1903), after Dietrich Bonhoeffer (1906-1945)
Music: *Le Cénacle*, Joseph Gelineau (b. 1920)

11 10. 11 10

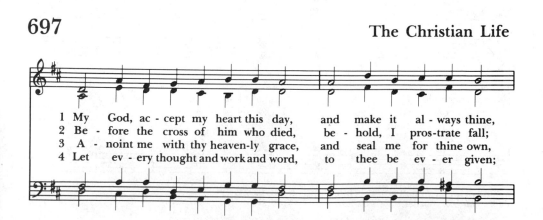

1 My God, ac - cept my heart this day, and make it al - ways thine,
2 Be - fore the cross of him who died, be - hold, I pros-trate fall;
3 A - noint me with thy heaven-ly grace, and seal me for thine own,
4 Let ev - ery thought and work and word, to thee be ev - er given;

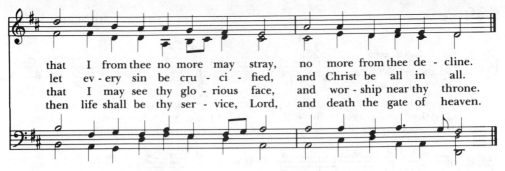

that I from thee no more may stray, no more from thee de - cline.
let ev - ery sin be cru - ci - fied, and Christ be all in all.
that I may see thy glo - rious face, and wor - ship near thy throne.
then life shall be thy ser - vice, Lord, and death the gate of heaven.

Words: Matthew Bridges (1800-1894), alt.
Music: *Song 67*, melody from *Llyfr y Psalmau*, 1621; bass perhaps by Orlando Gibbons (1583-1625);
other harmony *The Hymnal*, 1940

CM

The Christian Life 698

1 E - ter - nal Spi - rit of the liv - ing Christ,
2 Come, pray in me the prayer I need this day;
3 Come with the vi - sion and the strength I need

I know not how to ask or what to say;
help me to see your pur - pose and your will—
to serve my God, and all hu - man - i - ty;

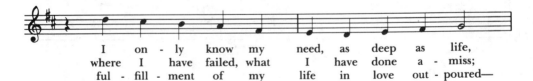

I on - ly know my need, as deep as life,
where I have failed, what I have done a - miss;
ful - fill - ment of my life in love out - poured—

and on - ly you can teach me how to pray.
held in for - giv - ing love, let me be still.
my life in you, O Christ, your love in me.

Words: Frank von Christierson (b. 1900), rev.
Music: *Flentge*, Carl Flentge Schalk (b. 1929)

10 10. 10 10

1 Je - sus, Lov - er of my soul, let me to thy bos - om
2 O - ther ref - uge have I none, hangs my help - less soul on
3 Plen - teous grace with thee is found, grace to cleanse from ev - ery

fly, while the near - er wa - ters roll, while the tem - pest
thee; leave, ah! leave me not a - lone, still sup - port and
sin; let the heal - ing streams a - bound, make and keep me

still is high: hide me, O my Sa - vior, hide,
com - fort me! All my trust on thee is stayed;
pure with - in. Thou of life the foun - tain art,

till the storm of life be past; safe in - to the
all my help from thee I bring; cov - er my de -
free - ly let me take of thee: spring thou up with -

ha - ven guide, O re - ceive my soul at last.
fense - less head with the sha - dow of thy wing.
in my heart, rise to all e - ter - ni - ty.

Words: Charles Wesley (1707-1788), alt.
Music: *Aberystwyth*, Joseph Parry (1841-1903)

77. 77. D

The Christian Life

700

1 O love that casts out fear, O love that casts out sin,
2 True sun-light of the soul, sur-round us as we go;
3 Great love of God, come in! Well-spring of heaven-ly peace;
4 Love of the liv-ing God, of Fa-ther and of Son;

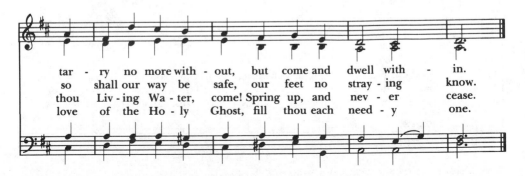

tar - ry no more with - out, but come and dwell with - in.
so shall our way be safe, our feet no stray-ing know.
thou Liv-ing Wa-ter, come! Spring up, and nev-er cease.
love of the Ho-ly Ghost, fill thou each need-y one.

Words: Horatius Bonar (1808-1889)
Music: *Moseley*, Henry Thomas Smart (1813-1879)

66. 66

701

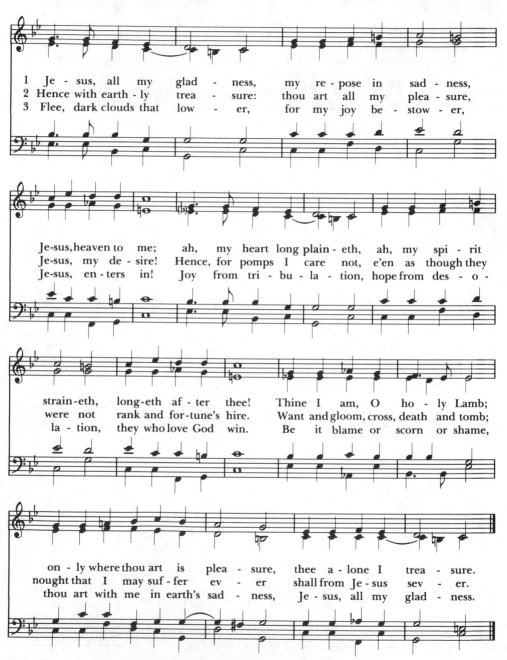

1 Je - sus, all my glad - ness, my re - pose in sad - ness,
2 Hence with earth - ly trea - sure: thou art all my plea - sure,
3 Flee, dark clouds that low - er, for my joy be - stow - er,

Je-sus, heaven to me; ah, my heart long plain - eth, ah, my spi - rit
Je-sus, my de - sire! Hence, for pomps I care not, e'en as though they
Je-sus, en - ters in! Joy from tri - bu - la - tion, hope from des - o -

strain-eth, long-eth af - ter thee! Thine I am, O ho - ly Lamb;
were not rank and for-tune's hire. Want and gloom, cross, death and tomb;
la - tion, they who love God win. Be it blame or scorn or shame,

on - ly where thou art is plea - sure, thee a - lone I trea - sure.
nought that I may suf - fer ev - er shall from Je - sus sev - er.
thou art with me in earth's sad - ness, Je - sus, all my glad - ness.

Words: Johann Franck (1618-1677); tr. Arthur Wellesley Wotherspoon (1853-1936), alt.
Music: *Jesu, meine Freude*, Johann Cruger (1598-1662), alt.

665. 665. 786

The Christian Life

Unison or harmony

1 Lord, thou hast searched me and dost know wher-
2 My words from thee I can-not hide; I
3 Where can I go a-part from thee, or
4 If I the wings of morn-ing take, and
5 If deep-est dark-ness cov-er me, the

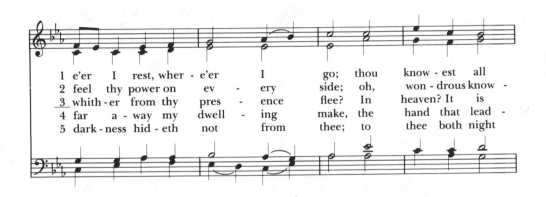

1 e'er I rest, wher-e'er I go; thou know-est all
2 feel thy power on ev-ery side; oh, won-drous know-
3 whith-er from thy pres-ence flee? In heaven? It is
4 far a-way my dwell-ing make, the hand that lead-
5 dark-ness hid-eth not from thee; to thee both night

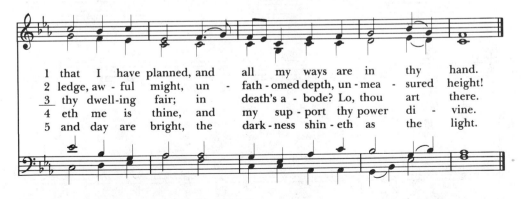

1 that I have planned, and all my ways are in thy hand.
2 ledge, aw-ful might, un-fath-omed depth, un-mea-sured height!
3 thy dwell-ing fair; in death's a-bode? Lo, thou art there.
4 eth me is thine, and my sup-port thy power di-vine.
5 and day are bright, the dark-ness shin-eth as the light.

Words: *The Psalter Hymnal*, 1927; para. of Psalm 139:1-11
Music: *Tender Thought*, from *Kentucky Harmony*, 1816

LM

Unison or harmony

1 Lead us, O Fa - ther, in the paths of peace;
2 Lead us, O Fa - ther, in the paths of right;
3 Lead us, O Fa - ther, to thy heaven-ly rest,

With - out thy guid - ing hand we go a - stray,
blind - ly we stum - ble when we walk a - lone,
how - ev - er rough and steep the path may be;

and doubts ap - pall, and sor - rows still in - crease;
in - volved in sha - dows of a dark - some night;
through joy or sor - row, as thou deem - est best,

lead us through Christ, the true and liv - ing Way.
on - ly with thee we jour - ney safe - ly on.
un - til our lives are per - fect - ed in thee.

Words: William Henry Burleigh (1812-1871), alt.
Music: *Song 22*, melody and bass Orlando Gibbons (1583-1625)

10 10. 10 10

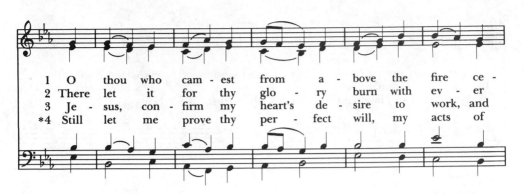

1 O thou who cam-est from a-bove the fire ce-
2 There let it for thy glo-ry burn with ev-er
3 Je-sus, con-firm my heart's de-sire to work, and
*4 Still let me prove thy per-fect will, my acts of

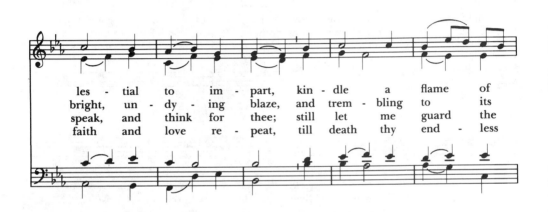

les-tial to im-part, kin-dle a flame of
bright, un-dy-ing blaze, and trem-bling to its
speak, and think for thee; still let me guard the
faith and love re-peat, till death thy end-less

sa-cred love up-on the al-tar of my heart.
source re-turn in hum-ble prayer and fer-vent praise.
ho-ly fire and still stir up the gift in me.
mer-cies seal, and make the sac-ri-fice com-plete.

Words: Charles Wesley (1707-1788), alt.
Music: *Hereford*, Samuel Sebastian Wesley (1810-1876)

LM

Unison or harmony

1 As those of old their first fruits brought of vine - yard, flock, and
*2 A world in need now sum - mons us to la - bor, love, and
3 With grat - i - tude and hum - ble trust we bring our best to

field to God, the giv - er of all good, the
give; to make our life an of - fer - ing to
thee to serve thy cause and share thy love with

source of boun - teous yield; so we to - day our
God that all may live; the Church of Christ is
all hu - man - i - ty. O thou who gav - est

first fruits bring, the wealth of this good land, of
call - ing us to make the dream come true: a
us thy - self in Je - sus Christ thy Son, help

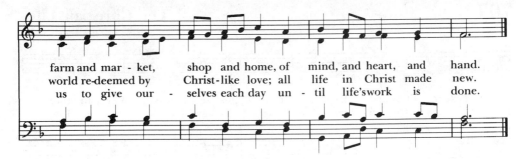

farm and mar - ket, shop and home, of mind, and heart, and hand.
world re-deemed by Christ-like love; all life in Christ made new.
us to give our - selves each day un - til life's work is done.

Words: Frank von Christierson (b. 1900), alt.
Music: *Forest Green,* English melody; adapt. and harm. Ralph Vaughan Williams (1872-1958)

CMD

The Christian Life

706

1 In your mer - cy, Lord, you called me, taught my
2 Lord, I did not free - ly choose you till by
3 Now my heart sets none a - bove you, for your

sin - filled heart and mind, else this world had
grace you set me free; for my heart would
grace a - lone I thirst, know - ing well, that

still en - thralled me, and to glo - ry kept me blind.
still re - fuse you had your love not cho - sen me.
if I love you, you, O Lord, have loved me first.

Words: Josiah Conder (1789-1855); alt. Charles P. Price (b. 1920)
Music: *Halton Holgate,* William Boyce (1711-1779)

87. 87

1 Take my life, and let it be con-se-crat-ed, Lord, to thee;
2 Take my voice, and let me sing al-ways, on-ly, for my King;

take my mo-ments and my days, let them flow in cease-less praise.
take my in-tel-lect, and use ev-ery power as thou shalt choose.

Take my hands, and let them move at the im-pulse of thy love;
Take my will, and make it thine; it shall be no long-er mine.

take my heart, it is thine own; it shall be thy roy-al throne.
Take my-self, and I will be ev-er, on-ly, all for thee.

Words: Frances Ridley Havergal (1836-1879), alt.
Music: *Hollingside*, John Bacchus Dykes (1823-1876)

77. 77. D

1 Sa - vior, like a shep-herd lead us; much we need thy
2 Ear - ly let us seek thy fa - vor, ear - ly let us

ten - der care; in thy pleas - ant pas - tures feed us;
learn thy will; do thou, Lord, our on - ly Sa - vior,

for our use thy folds pre - pare. Bless - ed Je - sus!
with thy love our bos - oms fill. Bless - ed Je - sus!

Bless - ed Je - sus! Thou hast bought us, thine we are.
Bless - ed Je - sus! Thou hast loved us: love us still.

Words: *Hymns for the Young*, ca. 1830, alt.
Music: *Sicilian Mariners*, Sicilian melody, from *The European Magazine and London Review*, 1792   87. 87. 87

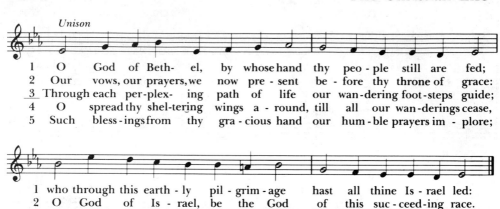

1   O   God of Beth- el,   by whose hand   thy peo - ple still are   fed;
2   Our   vows, our prayers, we   now pre - sent   be - fore thy throne of   grace:
3   Through each per-plex- ing   path of life   our wan-dering foot-steps guide;
4   O   spread thy shel-tering   wings a - round, till   all our wan-derings cease,
5   Such   bless-ings from thy   gra - cious hand our   hum - ble prayers im - plore;

1   who through this earth - ly   pil - grim - age   hast   all thine Is - rael led:
2   O   God   of   Is - rael, be   the   God   of   this suc - ceed-ing race.
3   give   us   each day   our   dai - ly bread,   and   rai - ment fit pro - vide.
4   and   at   our   Fa - ther's loved a - bode   our   souls ar - rive in peace!
5   and   thou   shalt be   our   cov - enant God   and   por - tion ev - er - more.

Words: Philip Doddridge (1702-1751), alt.
Music: *Dundee*, melody from *The CL Psalmes of David*, 1615;
      fauxbourdon *The Psalmes of David in Prose and Meeter*, 1635   CM

Harmony (the melody is in the tenor)

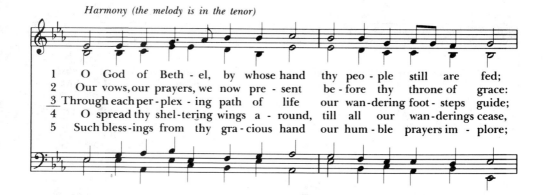

1   O   God of Beth - el,   by whose hand   thy peo - ple still are   fed;
2   Our vows, our prayers, we   now pre - sent   be - fore thy throne of   grace:
3   Through each per-plex - ing   path of life   our wan-dering foot - steps guide;
4   O   spread thy shel-tering wings a - round, till   all our   wan-derings cease,
5   Such bless-ings from thy   gra - cious hand   our hum - ble   prayers im - plore;

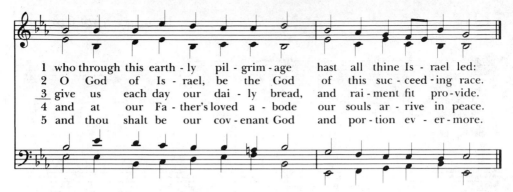

1 who through this earth-ly pil-grim-age hast all thine Is-rael led:
2 O God of Is-rael, be the God of this suc-ceed-ing race.
3 give us each day our dai-ly bread, and rai-ment fit pro-vide.
4 and at our Fa-ther's loved a-bode our souls ar-rive in peace.
5 and thou shalt be our cov-enant God and por-tion ev-er-more.

Words: Philip Doddridge (1702-1751), alt.
Music: *Dundee*, melody from *The CL Psalmes of David*, 1615;
fauxbourdon *The Psalmes of David in Prose and Meeter*, 1635

CM

Rounds and Canons

710

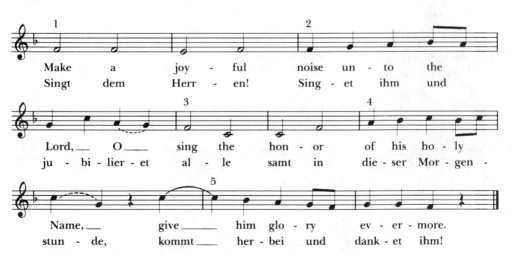

Make a joy-ful noise un-to the
Singt dem Herr-en! Sing-et ihm und

Lord,__ O__ sing the hon-or of his ho-ly
ju-bi-lier-et al-le samt in die-ser Mor-gen-

Name,__ give_____ him glo-ry ev-er-more.
stun-de, kommt__ her-bei und dank-et ihm!

Words: German; adapt. Ann M. Gilman (b. 1932) and Lawrence Gilman (b. 1930)
Music: *Singt dem Herren*, Michael Praetorius (1571-1621)

Irr.

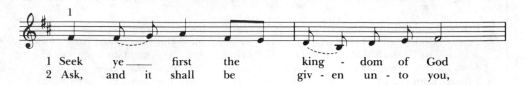

1 Seek ye___ first the king - dom of God
2 Ask, and it shall be giv - en un - to you,

and its right - eous - ness, and all these things shall be
seek, and ye shall find, knock, and the door shall be

add - ed un - to you; Al - le - lu, al - le - lu - ia!
o - pened un - to you; Al - le - lu, al - le - lu - ia!

Refrain

Al - le - lu - ia, al - le -

lu - ia, al - le - lu - ia!

Al - le - lu, al - le - lu - ia!

Words: St. 1, Matthew 6:33; adapt. Karen Lafferty (20th cent.). St. 2, Matthew 7:7.
Stanza 2 is not part of the hymn as originally written.
Music: *Seek Ye First*, Karen Lafferty (20th cent.)

13. 11. 7 with Alleluias

Do - na no - bis pa - cem, pa - cem. Do - na no - bis pa - cem. Do - na no - bis pa - cem. Do - na no - bis pa - cem. Do - na no - bis pa - cem. Do - na no - bis pa - cem.

Words: Traditional Latin
Music: *Dona nobis pacem,* traditional canon

Irr.

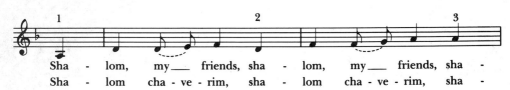

Words: German, ca. 1529, adapt.
Music: *Christ is arisen*, Richard Rudolf Klein (b. 1921); based on the chorale *Christ ist erstanden*

Irr.

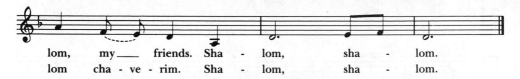

lom, my___ friends. Sha - lom, sha - lom.
lom cha - ve - rim. Sha - lom, sha - lom.

Words: Israeli round
Music: *Shalom chaverim*, Hebrew melody

Irr.

Rounds and Canons

715

When Je - sus wept, the fall - ing tear in

mer - cy flowed be - yond all bound; when Je - sus groaned, a

trem - bling fear seized all the guilt - y world a - round.

Words: *The New England Psalm Singer*, 1770
Music: *When Jesus Wept*, William Billings (1746-1800)

LM

1 God bless our na-tive land; firm may she
2 For her our prayers shall rise to God, a-

ev-er stand through storm and night: when the wild
bove the skies; on him we wait; thou who art

tem - pests rave, ru - ler of wind and wave,
ev - er nigh, guard - ing with watch - ful eye,

do thou our coun - try save by thy great might.
to thee a - loud we cry, God save the state!

Words: Siegfried August Mahlmann (1771-1826); tr. Charles Timothy Brooks (1813-1883) and
John Sullivan Dwight (1812-1893), alt.
Music: *America*, from *Thesaurus Musicus*, 1745

664. 6664

1 My country, 'tis of thee, sweet land of
2 My native country, thee, land of the
3 Let music swell the breeze, and ring from
4 Our fathers' God, to thee, author of

lib - er - ty, of thee I sing; land where my
no - ble free, thy name I love; I love thy
all the trees sweet free - dom's song; let mor - tal
lib - er - ty, to thee we sing; long may our

fa - thers died, land of the pil - grim's pride,
rocks and rills, thy woods and tem - pled hills;
tongues a - wake, let all that breathe par - take,
land be bright with free - dom's ho - ly light;

from ev - ery moun - tain - side let free - dom ring.
my heart with rap - ture thrills like that a - bove.
let rocks their si - lence break, the sound pro - long.
pro - tect us by thy might, great God, our King.

Words: Samuel Francis Smith (1808-1895)
Music: *America*, from *Thesaurus Musicus*, 1745

664. 6664

1 God of our fa - thers, whose al - might - y
2 Thy love di - vine hath led us in the
3 From war's a - larms, from dead - ly pes - ti -
4 Re - fresh thy peo - ple on their toil - some

hand leads forth in beau - ty all the star - ry band
past, in this free land by thee our lot is cast;
lence, be thy strong arm our ev - er sure de - fense;
way, lead us from night to nev - er - end - ing day;

of shin - ing worlds in splen - dor through the skies,
be thou our ru - ler, guard - ian, guide, and stay,
thy true re - li - gion in our hearts in - crease,
fill all our lives with love and grace di - vine,

our grate - ful songs be - fore thy throne a - rise.
thy word our law, thy paths our cho - sen way.
thy boun - teous good - ness nour - ish us in peace.
and glo - ry, laud, and praise be ev - er thine.

Words: Daniel Crane Roberts (1841-1907)
Music: *National Hymn*, George William Warren (1828-1902)

10 10. 10 10

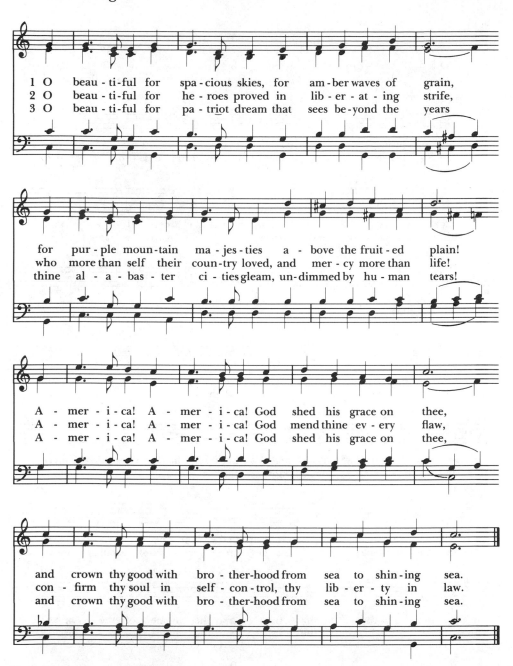

1 O beau-ti-ful for spa-cious skies, for am-ber waves of grain,
2 O beau-ti-ful for he-roes proved in lib-er-at-ing strife,
3 O beau-ti-ful for pa-triot dream that sees be-yond the years

for pur-ple moun-tain ma-jes-ties a-bove the fruit-ed plain!
who more than self their coun-try loved, and mer-cy more than life!
thine al-a-bas-ter ci-ties gleam, un-dimmed by hu-man tears!

A - mer - i - ca! A - mer - i - ca! God shed his grace on thee,
A - mer - i - ca! A - mer - i - ca! God mend thine ev - er - y flaw,
A - mer - i - ca! A - mer - i - ca! God shed his grace on thee,

and crown thy good with bro - ther-hood from sea to shin-ing sea.
con - firm thy soul in self - con - trol, thy lib - er - ty in law.
and crown thy good with bro - ther-hood from sea to shin-ing sea.

Words: Katherine Lee Bates (1859-1929), alt.
Music: *Materna*, Samuel Augustus Ward (1848-1903)

CMD

1 O say can you see, by the dawn's ear-ly light,
2 O thus be it ev-er, when free-men shall stand

what so proud-ly we hailed at the twi-light's last gleam-ing,
be-tween their loved homes and the war's des-o-lat-tion!

whose broad stripes and bright stars, through the per-il-lous fight,
Blest with vic-to-ry and peace, may the heaven-re-scued land

o'er the ram-parts we watched, were so gal-lant-ly stream-ing?
praise the Power that hath made and pre-served us a na-tion!

And the rock-ets' red glare, the bombs burst-ing in air,
Then___ con-quer we must, when our cause it is just,

gave proof through the night that our flag was still there.
and this be our mot-to, "In God is our trust."

O___ say does that star-span-gled ban-ner yet wave
And the star-span-gled ban-ner in tri-umph shall wave

o'er the land of the free and the home of the brave?
o'er the land of the free and the home of the brave!

Words: Francis Scott Key (1779-1843)
Music: *National Anthem*, source unknown, ca. 18th cent.

Irr.

Indexes

Copyright Acknowledgments for Service Music

The following settings are copyrighted by The Church Pension Fund:

S-1, S-3, S-8, S-21, S-22, S-23, S-24, S-25, S-26, S-28, S-30, S-31, S-32, S-33, S-51, S-52, S-53, S-54, S-55, S-56, S-57, S-58, S-60, S-62, S-64, S-65, S-66, S-68, S-69, S-70, S-73, S-74, S-75, S-80, S-82, S-92, S-102, S-103, S-106, S-110, S-112, S-115, S-118, S-119, S-120, S-129, S-142, S-159, S-163, S-173, S-174, S-177, S-203, S-205, S-210, S-212, S-217, S-222, S-223, S-228, S-231, S-235, S-250, S-253, S-263, S-265, S-272, S-280, S-287.

The following melodies are copyrighted by The Church Pension Fund:

S-46, S-90, S-113, S-157, S-201, S-237

Individual copyright acknowledgments are as follows:

S-2   Melody © 1985, Bruce E. Ford.
S-11   Melody © 1985, Bruce E. Ford.
S-16   Melody © 1985, Bruce E. Ford.
S-27   Melody © by Estate of Victor Judson Schramm.
S-29   © 1971 by Mason Martens.
S-34   Melody © 1985, Bruce E. Ford.
S-35   © 1971, Walton Music Corporation. Used by permission.
S-41   Melody © 1985, Bruce E. Ford.
S-42   Used by permission of Peter Hurford.
S-45   By permission of Collins Liturgical Press.
S-50   © 1982, David Hurd.
S-59   Melody © 1985, Bruce E. Ford.
S-61   Copyright © 1964, Theodore Presser Co. Used by permission of the publisher.
S-63   © 1971 by Mason Martens.
S-67   © 1927 by Wallace Goodrich, Secretary for the Joint Commission on Church Music.
S-71   © 1971 by Mason Martens.
S-72   © 1971 by Mason Martens.
S-76   © 1971 by Mason Martens.
S-77   Copyright © 1979, G.I.A. Publications, Inc.
S-78   © 1971 by Mason Martens.
S-79   Copyright © 1979, G.I.A. Publications, Inc.
S-81   Copyright © 1979, G.I.A. Publications, Inc.
S-83   Copyright © 1979, G.I.A. Publications, Inc.
S-84   Copyright © 1979, G.I.A. Publications, Inc.
S-85   Rhythmic reconstruction © 1983, Schola Antiqua Inc. Used by permission.
S-86   Copyright © 1981, G.I.A. Publications, Inc.
S-87   © 1978, Jackson Hill.
S-88   From: *Music For The Lord's Supper* © 1984, Theodore Presser Company. Used by permission.
S-89   © 1976, James McGregor.
S-91   By permission of Oxford University Press.
S-93   © 1937 by the H.W. Gray Co., a division of Belwin-Mills Pub. Corp. Copyright renewed. Used with permission. All rights reserved.
S-94   © 1984 by Mason Martens.
S-95   Copyright © 1985, G.I.A. Publications, Inc.
S-96   Copyright © 1985, G.I.A. Publications, Inc.
S-97   © by E. C. Schirmer Music Company, Boston, Mass. Reprinted by permission.
S-98   © 1976, Oxford University Press, Inc.
S-99   Melody © 1985, Bruce E. Ford.
S-100 Copyright © 1981, G.I.A. Publications, Inc.
S-101 © 1982, Oxford University Press, Inc.
S-104 © 1984 by Mason Martens.
S-105 Copyright © 1975, G.I.A. Publications, Inc.
S-107 © 1985, Bruce E. Ford.
S-108 © 1982, David Hurd. Used by permission.
S-109 © 1971 by Mason Martens.
S-111 © 1971 by Mason Martens.
S-114 By permission of Oxford University Press.
S-116 Melody copyright © 1915, by Charles Winfred Douglas.
S-117 © 1976, James McGregor.
S-121 © 1983, James McGregor.
S-122 © 1983 by Mason Martens.
S-123 © 1985, Howard E. Galley, Jr.
S-124 Copyright © 1981, G.I.A. Publications, Inc.
S-125 Copyright © 1971, 1977, G.I.A. Publications, Inc.
S-126 © by E.C. Schirmer Music Company, Boston, Mass. Reprinted by permission.
S-127 Copyright © Inter-Lutheran Commission on Worship. Used by permission of Augsburg Publishing House.
S-128 © 1976, Oxford University Press, Inc.
S-130 Adaptation copyright © 1985, G.I.A. Publications, Inc.
S-131 © 1985 by Aureole Editions, Dallas, Texas.
S-132 © 1985, Bruce E. Ford.
S-133 © 1971 by Mason Martens.
S-134 Copyright © 1985, G.I.A. Publications, Inc.
S-135 © 1974, Jackson Hill.
S-136 © 1971 by Mason Martens.

S-137 © 1983 by Mason Martens.
S-138 Copyright © 1984, Theodore Presser Co. Used by permission of the publisher.
S-139 © 1983 by Mason Martens.
S-140 Copyright © 1985, G.I.A. Publications, Inc.
S-141 © 1984, Theodore Presser Company. Used by permission.
S-143 © 1983 by Mason Martens.
S-144 © 1983 by Mason Martens.
S-145 © 1983 by Mason Martens.
S-146 © 1984, Theodore Presser Company. Used by permission.
S-147 © 1984, Theodore Presser Company. Used by permission.
S-148 © 1971 by Mason Martens.
S-149 From: *Music For The Lord's Supper* © 1984, Theodore Presser Company. Used by permission.
S-150 Copyright © 1979, 1982, G.I.A. Publications, Inc.
S-151 Copyright © 1979, G.I.A. Publications, Inc.
S-152 © 1971 by Mason Martens.
S-153 © 1971 by Mason Martens.
S-154 Copyright © 1981, G.I.A. Publications, Inc.
S-155 © 1985 by Aureole Editions, Dallas, Texas.
S-156 © 1985 by Aureole Editions, Dallas, Texas.
S-158 By permission of Oxford University Press.
S-160 © 1984 by Mason Martens.
S-161 Copyright © 1981, G.I.A. Publications, Inc.
S-162 © by E.C. Schirmer Music Company, Boston, Mass. Reprinted by permission.
S-164 Adaptation copyright © 1985, G.I.A. Publications, Inc.
S-165 © 1976, Oxford University Press, Inc.
S-166 © 1985 by Aureole Editions, Dallas, Texas.
S-167 © 1971 by Mason Martens.
S-168 © 1971 by Mason Martens.
S-169 © 1984 by Ray W. Urwin. Used by permission.
S-170 © 1983 by Mason Martens.
S-171 © 1971 by Mason Martens.
S-172 © 1971 by Mason Martens.
S-176 Copyright © 1979, G.I.A. Publications, Inc.
S-180 © 1985, Bruce E. Ford.
S-185 Antiphon © 1985, Bruce E. Ford. Canticle setting © The Church Pension Fund.
S-188 By permission of Oxford University Press.
S-189 © 1985, Benjamin Hutto.
S-190 Melody © 1985, Bruce E. Ford.
S-194 By permission of Richard Lloyd.
S-196 Antiphon © 1985, Bruce E. Ford.
S-202 By permission of Oxford University Press.
S-208 Antiphon melody © 1985, Bruce E. Ford. Canticle setting © 1979, The Church Pension Fund.
S-213 Melody © 1985, Bruce E. Ford.
S-214 From *The Oxford American Psalter* by Ray F. Brown. Copyright © 1949 by Ray F. Brown, 1976 by Stuart Brown. Reprinted by permission of Oxford University Press, Inc.
S-216 © 1970, David Hurd.
S-220 © Ned Rorem. Used by permission of Ned Rorem and Boosey and Hawkes.
S-227 © 1976, J. Marcus Ritchie.
S-236 © 1985, Oxford University Press, Inc.
S-237 Adaptation © 1985, Bruce E. Ford.
S-240 © Ned Rorem. Used by permission of Ned Rorem and Boosey and Hawkes.
S-242 Melody © 1985, Bruce E. Ford.
S-245 © 1985, Benjamin Hutto.
S-247 Copyright © 1978, Celebration. P.O. Box 309, Aliquippa, PA 15001, USA. All rights reserved. Used by permission.
S-248 Melody © 1985, Bruce E. Ford.
S-254 Melody © 1985, Bruce E. Ford.
S-257 © The Royal School of Church Music. Used by permission.
S-259 © 1985, The Estate of Charles B. Fisk.
S-260 © 1984, Ronald Arnatt.
S-261 Melody © 1985, Bruce E. Ford.
S-263 By permission of Oxford University Press.
S-266 © 1984, M. Pambrun.
S-267 Melody © 1985, Bruce E. Ford.

Copyright Acknowledgments for Hymns

The following texts are copyrighted by The Church Pension Fund:

16(Sts.1-3), 17(1-3), 18, 19(1-2), 20(1-2), 25, 26, 38(1-4), 39(1-4), 40(1-4), 41(1-4), 44(1-3), 45(1-3), 48(4), 56, 60, 63, 64, 81(3), 91, 121, 135(4), 139, 152, 153, 159, 162, 164, 166, 173(1,4), 176(3), 177(3), 193, 220, 221, 231, 232, 233, 234, 261, 262, 268(4), 269(4), 282, 283, 302, 303, 314(1-3), 319, 320, 322(1), 329, 330, 331, 353, 356, 364(6-8), 366, 375, 390, 421, 428, 443, 475(1,2,4), 477, 478, 489, 499, 530, 540, 579(2,3), 587, 619, 647, 663, 668(4), 669.

The following musical settings are copyrighted by The Church Pension Fund:

9, 37, 107, 153, 157, 163, 185, 187, 312, 316, 403, 454, 514, 515, 532, 542, 564, 614, 647, 654, 661.

The following harmonizations and accompaniments are copyrighted by The Church Pension Fund:

8, 149, 172, 173, 203, 359, 364, 366, 404, 505, 697.

Individual copyright acknowledgments are as follows:

1 Words: By permission of Oxford University Press.
2 Words: By permission of Oxford University Press. Music: Melody rhythmic version © 1984, Schola Antiqua Inc. Used by permission.
3 Words: Sts.2-4 Copyright © 1972, Peter J. Scagnelli. From *Catholic Liturgy Book*. Used by permission.
4 Words: Sts.2-4 Copyright © 1972, Peter J. Scagnelli. From *Catholic Liturgy Book*. Used by permission.
6 Music: Copyright by Edward B. Marks Music Company, New York, NY. International Copyright Secured. ALL RIGHTS RESERVED. Used by permission.
8 Words: By permission of David Higham Associates Limited, London.
9 Words: By permission of Hodder and Stoughton Limited.
12 Words: © 1982, Charles P. Price.
13 Words: © 1982, Charles P. Price.
14 Words: St.3 © 1982, James Waring McCrady.
15 Words: St.3 © 1982, James Waring McCrady.
16 Words: St.4 © 1982, Anne LeCroy.
17 Words: St.4 © 1982, Anne LeCroy. Music: By permission of Oxford University Press.
19 Words: St.3 © 1982, James Waring McCrady.
20 Words: St.3 © 1982, James Waring McCrady.
21 Words: St.3 © 1982, James Waring McCrady.
22 Words: St.3 © 1982, James Waring McCrady.
23 Words: © 1982, Charles P. Price.
27 Words: © 1982, Anne LeCroy.
28 Words: © 1982, Anne LeCroy.
31 Words: © 1982, Anne LeCroy. Music: Reprinted from the *New Catholic Hymnal* by permission of the publishers, Faber Music Ltd., London.
32 Words: © 1982, Anne LeCroy. Music: Melody rhythmic version © 1984, Schola Antiqua Inc. Used by permission.
33 Words: © 1982, Anne LeCroy.
34 Words: © 1982, Anne LeCroy. Music: © 1984, Richard W. Dirksen.
35 Words: © 1982, Anne LeCroy. Music: Copyright © 1985, G.I.A. Publications, Inc.
38 Words: St.5 © 1982, Anne LeCroy.
39 Words: St.5 © 1982, Anne LeCroy. Music: By permission of Oxford University Press.
40 Words: St.5 © 1982, Charles P. Price.
41 Words: St.5 © 1982, Charles P. Price. Music: Copyright © 1985, G.I.A. Publications, Inc.
44 Words: St.4 © 1982, James Waring McCrady.
45 Words: St.4 © 1972, James Waring McCrady.
48 Words: St.3 © 1982, Charles P. Price.
49 Words: Copyright © 1977 by Hinshaw Music, Inc. Used by permission.
51 Words: By permission of John E. Bowers. Music: © 1984, Richard W. Dirksen.
52 Music: Copyright © 1936 Ascherberg, Hopwood and Crew Limited, Chappell Music Limited London. Reproduced by permission.
54 Words: Sts.3-4 © 1982, James Waring McCrady.
55 Words: © 1982, Charles P. Price.
59 Music: Descant used by permission of Cambridge University Press.
61 Words: © 1982, Carl P. Daw, Jr.
62 Words: © 1982, Carl P. Daw, Jr.
65 Words: © 1982, Charles P. Price.
69 Words: © 1971, Carol C. Stone.
70 Words: By permission of Margaret Waters. Music: © 1983, Robert J. Powell.
72 Music: Desc. by permission of Novello and Co. Ltd.
74 Words: Copyright © 1974 by Hope Publishing Company, Carol Stream, IL 60188. All Rights Reserved. Used by Permission. Music: Harmonization © 1984, Ronald Arnatt.
75 Music: © 1938, H. Hugh Bancroft.

78 Music: By permission of Oxford University Press.
80 Words: Translation copyright © 1978, LUTHERAN BOOK OF WORSHIP. Used by permission of Augsburg Publishing House.
84 Music: By permission of Oxford University Press.
85 Words: Copyright © 1978, Lutheran Book of Worship. Used by permission.
86 Words: Copyright © 1978, Lutheran Book of Worship. Used by permission. Music: By permission of Oxford University Press.
88 Music: By permission of Oxford University Press.
92 Words: Copyright by G. Schirmer, Inc. Reprinted by permission. Music: Used by arrangement with G. Schirmer, Inc.
94 Music: Descant by permission of Novello and Company Limited.
95 Music: Copyright © 1985, Theodore Presser Co. Used by permission of the publisher.
96 Words: By permission of Fleming H. Revell Company.
98 Words: From The Oxford Book of Carols © 1964, Oxford University Press. Music: By permission of Oxford University Press.
99 Music: Arrangement © 1984, Horace Clarence Boyer.
102 Words: St.3 © 1982, James Waring McCrady. Music: Copyright © 1957, Novello and Company Limited. Used by permission.
103 Words: Copyright © 1964, G.I.A. Publications, Inc.
104 Words: Copyright © 1961 by Richard Wilbur. Reprinted from his volume, *Advice to a Prophet and other Poems* by permission of Harcourt Brace Jovanovich, Inc. Music: Copyright © 1984, G.I.A. Publications, Inc.
105 Words: By permission of Fleming H. Revell Company.
109 Music: Alternative setting with descant © 1926; by permission of Oxford University Press, Inc.
113 Words, Music: Copyright © 1954, University of New Mexico Press. Used by permission.
114 Words: English text by J. E. Middleton. Used by permission of The Frederick Harris Music Co., Limited. Music: Setting Copyright © 1978, LUTHERAN BOOK OF WORSHIP. Used by permission of Augsburg Publishing House.
116 Music: By permission of Oxford University Press.
120 Words: From *English Praise*. By permission of Oxford University Press. Music: By permission of Oxford University Press.
123 Music: Melody rhythmic version © 1984, Schola Antiqua Inc. Used by permission.
125 Music: Music Copyright © 1964 by Abingdon Press. Used by permission.
127 Music: Harmonization by permission of K. D. Smith.
129 Words: Copyright © 1977 by Hope Publishing Company, Carol Stream, IL 60188. All Rights Reserved. Used by Permission. Music: Copyright © 1985 by Hope Publishing Company, Carol Stream, IL 60188. All Rights Reserved. Used by Permission.
130 Words, Music: Copyright © 1977 by Hope Publishing Company, Carol Stream, IL 60188. All Rights Reserved. Used by Permission.
131 Words: Reprinted from *The Hymn Book of the Anglican Church of Canada and the United Church of Canada*. Used by permission.
132 Words: Reprinted from *The Hymn Book of the Anglican Church of Canada and the United Church of Canada*. Used by permission.
133 Music: © 1982, Cary Ratcliff.
137 Music: Descant by permission of Royal School of Church Music.
143 Words: By permission of Oxford University Press.
144 Words: © 1982, Anne LeCroy. Music: By permission of Oxford University Press.

492 Music: By permission of Oxford University Press.
494 Music: Descant copyright © 1970, Augsburg Publishing House. Used by permission.
499 Music: From *Hymns for Church and School*, 1964.
501 Words: © 1971, John Webster Grant.
502 Words: © 1971, John Webster Grant.
503 Music: Harmonization © 1985, David Hurd.
505 Words: Reprinted by permission from *The Common Service Book of the Lutheran Church*, copyright 1917 and 1918 by The United Lutheran Church of America, a predecessor of the Lutheran Church in America.
506 Words, Music: By permission of Oxford University Press.
507 Words: By permission of Oxford University Press. Music: Copyright © 1983, G.I.A. Publications, Inc.
511 Words: Copyright held by A. R. Mowbray & Co. Ltd. Music: Copyright © 1942, Renewal 1970 by Hope Publishing Company, Carol Stream, IL 60188. All Rights Reserved. Used by Permission.
513 Words: © 1982, Carl P. Daw, Jr. Music: Copyright © 1969 by Hope Publishing Company, Carol Stream, IL 60188. All Rights Reserved. Used by Permission.
516 Music: By permission of Oxford University Press.
517 Words: Sts.3–4 © 1982, Carl P. Daw, Jr. Music: By permission of Oxford University Press.
518 Music: Descant by permission of Church Society, London.
521 Music: Melody by permission of the Estate of Howard C. Robbins. Harmonization copyright © 1940, Estate of Ray F. Brown. Used by permission. Descant © 1944, The Cumberland Press. All Rights Reserved. Used by Permission.
522 Music: Descant copyright © 1979, G.I.A. Publications, Inc.
523 Music: Copyright © 1942. Renewal 1970 by Hope Publishing Company, Carol Stream, IL 60188. All Rights Reserved. Used by Permission.
528 Words: © 1978, Jeffery W. Rowthorn. Music: Copyright © 1985 by Hope Publishing Company, Carol Stream, IL 60188. All Rights Reserved. Used by Permission.
529 Words: Reprinted by permission of The American Tract Society, Garland, Texas. Music: Copyright © 1940, Henry T. Burleigh. Used by permission of the Estate of Henry T. Burleigh.
534 Music: By permission of Oxford University Press.
536 Words: © 1966, 1984 by Willard F. Jabusch. Music: Arrangement copyright © 1985, G.I.A. Publications, Inc.
538 Music: By permission of Oxford University Press.
542 Words: By permission of Oxford University Press.
543 Music: By permission of the United Reformed Church in the United Kingdom.
547 Words: Copyright © 1980, Augsburg Publishing House. Used by permission. Music: © 1984, Max Miller.
549 Music: Copyright © 1983, G.I.A. Publications, Inc.
551 Words: Used by permission of The Presbyterian Outlook, Richmond, VA.
553 Music: Copyright © 1936 Ascherberg, Hopwood and Crew Limited, Chappell Music Limited London. Reproduced by Permission.
557 Music: Copyright © 1974, Harold Flammer, Inc., Delaware Water Gap, PA 18327. All Rights Reserved. Used with permission.
560 Music: Copyright © 1985, G.I.A. Publications, Inc.
564 Words: By permission of Oxford University Press.
565 Words, Music: By permission of Oxford University Press.
568 Words: By permission of The United Society for the Propagation of the Gospel.
570 Words: Copyright © 1969 by Galliard Ltd. All Rights Reserved. Used by permission. Music: Copyright © 1969 by Hope Publishing Company, Carol Stream, IL 60188. All Rights Reserved. Used by Permission.
571 Words: Copyright © 1969 by Galliard Ltd. All Rights Reserved. Used by permission.
572 Words: By permission of Inter-Lutheran Commission on Worship. Music: Melody copyright © 1972 by Chantry Music Press, Inc. Used by permission.
573 Words: By permission of Oxford University Press. Music: Used by permission of the United Nations Association.
576 Words: © 1969, James Quinn, SJ, printed by permission of Geoffrey Chapman, a division of Cassell Ltd. Music: Copyright © 1985, G.I.A. Publications, Inc.
577 Words: © 1969, James Quinn, SJ, printed by permission of Geoffrey Chapman, a division of Cassell Ltd. Music: By permission of A. Gregory Murray.
580 Words: Copyright © 1967 Copyright by Hope Publishing Company, Carol Stream, IL 60188. All Rights Reserved. Used by Permission.
581 Words: Copyright © 1961–62, World Library Publications, 3815 N. Willow Rd. Schiller Park, IL 60176. ALL RIGHTS RESERVED. USED BY PERMISSION.
582 Words: From HYMNS OF THE CHRISTIAN LIFE, edited by Milton S. Littlefield. Copyright 1910 by Harper & Row, Publishers, Inc. Courtesy of the publishers. Music: Copyright © 1968, Novello & Company Limited. Used by permission.

583 Words: From HYMNS OF THE CHRISTIAN LIFE, edited by Milton S. Littlefield. Copyright 1910 by Harper & Row, Publishers, Inc. Courtesy of the publishers.
584 Words: By permission of Oxford University Press.
585 Words: By permission of J. W. Shore. Music: © 1984, Dorothy Howell Sheets.
586 Words: Copyright © 1909, 1911 by Charles Scribner's Sons. © Renewed. Reprinted by permission of Charles Scribner's Sons.
588 Music: © 1984, Roy Johnson.
589 Music: © 1983, Jane M. Marshall.
590 Words: Copyright © 1954. Renewal 1982 by The Hymn Society of America, Texas Christian University, Fort Worth, TX 76129. All rights reserved. Used by permission. Music: By permission of Oxford University Press.
591 Words, Music: By permission of Oxford University Press.
593 Words: Copyright ©, James Quinn, SJ, printed by permission of Geoffrey Chapman, a division of Cassell Ltd. Music: Copyright © 1962, Theodore Presser Co. Used by permission of the publisher.
594 Words: By permission of the author.
595 Words: By permission of the author.
597 Words: © 1982, Carl P. Daw, Jr. Music: Copyright © 1916, 1944, 1977, Robertson Publications. Used by permission.
598 Words: By permission of the family of Walter Russell Bowie.
599 Words, Music: Copyright © 1921 by Edward B. Marks Music Company. Copyright Renewed. International Copyright Secured. ALL RIGHTS RESERVED. Used by permission.
600 Words: Copyright © Emmanuel College, Toronto. Used by permission. Music: Copyright © 1938, Estate of James Hopkirk.
601 Words: Copyright © Emmanuel College, Toronto. Used by permission.
602 Words, Music: Copyright © 1969 by Hope Publishing Company, Carol Stream, IL 60188. International Copyright Secured. All Rights Reserved. Used by Permission.
603 Words: Copyright © 1980 by Hope Publishing Company, Carol Stream, IL 60188. All Rights Reserved. Used by Permission. Music: By permission of Oxford University Press.
604 Words: Copyright © 1980 by Hope Publishing Company, Carol Stream, IL 60188. All Rights Reserved. Used by Permission. Music: © 1968, Derek Williams.
605 Words: © 1949, Albert F. Bayly. Used by permission of Oxford University Press. Music: Copyright © 1969 by Hope Publishing Company, Carol Stream, IL 60188. All Rights Reserved. Used by Permission.
606 Words: © 1982, Joyce M. Glover.
607 Words: Copyright © 1958 by The Hymn Society of America, Texas Christian University, Fort Worth, TX 76129. All rights reserved. Used by permission.
610 Words: Copyright © 1961, Albert F. Bayly. Used by permission of Oxford University Press.
611 Words, Music: Copyright © 1969 by Hope Publishing Company, Carol Stream, IL 60188. International Copyright Secured. All Rights Reserved. Used by Permission.
612 Music: © 1984, Daniel Moe.
614 Words: By permission of Oxford University Press.
617 Music: From *Hymns for Church and School*, 1964.
618 Words, Music: By permission of Oxford University Press.
620 Music: Copyright © 1938 by J. Fischer & Bro., a division of Belwin-Mills Publishing Corp. Copyright renewed. Used with permission. All rights reserved.
622 Music: Melody rhythmic version © 1984, Schola Antiqua Inc. Used by permission.
625 Music: Descant by permission of Hymns Ancient & Modern Limited.
628 Words: Copyright © 1959 by The Hymn Society of America, Texas Christian University, Fort Worth, TX 76129. All rights reserved. Used by permission.
629 Music: Arrangement copyright © 1985, David Hurd.
630 Words: Copyright © 1954. Renewal 1982 by Hope Publishing Company. Music: Copyright © 1966 by Hope Publishing Company, Carol Stream, IL 60188. International Copyright Secured. Used by Permission.
631 Words: By permission of Oxford University Press.
633 Words: © 1969, James Quinn, SJ, printed by permission of Geoffrey Chapman, a division of Cassell Ltd. Music: © 1984, Richard W. Dirksen.
637 Music: Descant copyright © 1974, The Cumberland Press. All Rights Reserved. Used by Permission.
639 Music: Copyright © 1971 by Carl Fischer, Inc., New York. All Rights Reserved. Used by Permission.
646 Music: Descant by permission of Oxford University Press.
648 Music: Arrangement © 1984, Horace Clarence Boyer.
649 Words: Adapted text from *ICEL Resource Collection of Hymns and Service Music for the Liturgy* © 1981, International Committee on English in the Liturgy, Inc. All rights reserved. Music: Copyright © 1962, Theodore Presser Co. Used by permission of the Publisher.

Authors, Translators, and Sources

Bridges, Robert Seymour (1844–1930) 5, 36, 46, 158, 168, 169, 427, 665
Briggs, George Wallace (1875–1959) 289, 305, 306, 542, 584
Bright, William (1824–1901) 242, 281, 337
Brokering, Herbert F. (b. 1926) 412
Brooks, Charles Timothy (1813–1883) 716
Brooks, Phillips (1835–1893) 78, 79
Brooks, R. T. (b. 1918) 630
Browne, Simon (1680–1732) 512
Brownlie, John (1859–1925) 73, 313
Bunyan, John (1628–1688) 564, 565
Burleigh, William Henry (1812–1871) 703
Byrne, Mary Elizabeth (1880–1931) 488
Byrom, John (1692–1763) 106

Cain, Thomas H. (b. 1931) 149
Caird, George B. (1917–1984) 422
Cameron, Catherine (b. 1927) 580
Campbell, Jane Montgomery (1817–1878) 291
Campbell, Robert (1814–1868) 174, 223, 224, 244
Carpenter, William Boyd (1841–1918) 574, 575
Casanate, Hieronimo (d. 1700) 261, 262
Caswall, Edward (1814–1878) 257, 310, 311, 479, 642, 682
Cawood, John (1775–1852) 588, 589
Chadwick, James (1813–1882) 96
Chadwick, John White (1840–1904) 617
Chandler, John (1806–1876) 3, 4, 29, 30, 76, 124
Charles, Elizabeth Rundle (1828–1896) 97, 190, 217, 218
Chatfield, Allen William (1808–1896) 641
Chesterton, Gilbert Keith (1874–1936) 591
Chorley, Henry Fothergill (1808–1872) 569
Christian Hymnbook, 1865 116
Claudius, Matthias (1740–1815) 291
Clausnitzer, Tobias (1619–1684) 440
Clement of Alexandria (170?–220?) 163, 478
Clephane, Elizabeth Cecilia (1830–1869) 498
Coffin, Charles (1676–1749) 3, 4, 29, 30, 76, 124
Coffin, Henry Sloane (1877–1954) 475
Coles, Vincent Stucky Stratton (1845–1929) 268, 269
Colvin, Thomas Stevenson (b. 1925) 602, 611
Conder, Josiah (1789–1855) 323, 706
Cosin, John (1594–1672) 503, 504
Cosnett, Elizabeth (b. 1936) 476
Coventry carol, 15th cent. 247
Coverdale, Miles (1487–1568) 634
Cowper, William (1731–1800) 667, 677, 683, 684
Cox, Frances Elizabeth (1812–1897) 194, 195, 286, 408
Crawford, Mary Babcock (b. 1909) 651
Crossman, Samuel (1624–1683) 458
Crum, John Macleod Campbell (1872–1958) 204

Cummins, Evelyn Atwater (1891–1971) 647

Daw, Carl P., Jr. (b. 1944) 18, 61, 62, 266, 358, 359, 513, 517, 597, 678, 679
Dearmer, Percy (1867–1936) 1, 2, 98, 145, 211, 312, 564, 565, 631, 682
Decius, Nikolaus (1490?–1541) 421
de Santeüil, Jean Baptiste (1630–1697) 257
Dix, William Chatterton (1837–1898) 115, 119, 460, 461
Doan, Gilbert E. (b. 1930) 85, 86
Doane, George Washington (1799–1859) 457
Doane, William Croswell (1832–1913) 363
Doddridge, Philip (1702–1751) 71, 72, 284, 321, 543, 546, 709
Donne, John (1573–1631) 140, 141, 322
Douglas, Charles Winfred (1867–1944) 76, 173, 375, 530, 540, 669
Drake, Carol Christopher (b. 1933) 69
Draper, William H. (1855–1933) 400
Dryden, John (1631–1700) 500
Dudley-Smith, Timothy (b. 1926) 431, 437, 438
Duffield, George, Jr. (1818–1888) 561
Dwight, John Sullivan (1812–1893) 716
Dwight, Timothy (1725–1817) 524

Eastern Orthodox Memorial Service 355
Eddis, Edward W. (1825–1905) 37
Edmeston, James (1791–1867) 559
Egan, Linda Wilberger (b. 1943) 673
Ellerton, John (1826–1893) 24, 77, 179, 255, 259, 280, 345, 492, 569
Elliott, Charlotte (1789–1871) 693
English carol, 18th cent. 109
English carol, ca. 18th cent. 453
English Hymnal, The, 1906 175, 216, 225
English Praise, 1975 347
Ephrem of Edessa (4th cent.) 443
Epistle to Diognetus, ca. 150 489
Evans, Mark (b. 1916) 295
Everest, Charles William (1814–1877) 675
Evers, J. Clifford (b. 1916) 581
Exodus 15:1–2 425

Faber, Frederick William (1814–1863) 469, 470, 558, 643
Farjeon, Eleanor (1881–1965) 8
Farlander, Arthur William (1898–1952) 375, 530, 540, 669
Fawcett, John (1739/40–1817) 344
F.B.P. (ca. 16th cent.) 620
Feith, Rhijnvis (1753–1824) 484, 485
Findlater, Sarah B. (1823–1907) 68
First Song of Isaiah, The 678, 679
Fishel, Donald (b. 1950) 178
Fortunatus, Venantius Honorius (540?–600?) 161, 162, 165, 166, 175, 179, 216, 225
Fosdick, Harry Emerson (1878–1969) 594, 595
Foundling Hospital Psalms and Hymns, 1797 373

Francis of Assisi (1182–1226)   400, 406, 407, 593

Franck, Johann (1618–1677)   399, 701

Franz, Ignaz (1719–1790)   366

Franzen, Frans Mikael (1772–1847)   65

Franzmann, Martin H. (1907–1976)   381, 572

Frazier, Philip (1892–1964)   385

French carol   96

Gaunt, Howard Charles Adie (b. 1902)   334

Gellert, Christian Furchtegott (1715–1769) 194, 195

Gerhardt, Paul (1607–1676)   46, 168, 169, 515, 669

German   319, 383, 384, 710

German, 15th cent.   81

German, ca. 1529   713

German, ca. 1800   427

Geyer, John Brownlow (b. 1932)   296

Ghanaian   602, 611

Gilman, Ann M. (b. 1932)   710

Gilman, Lawrence (b. 1930)   710

Gladden, Washington (1836–1918)   659, 660

Gloria in excelsis   421

Glover, Joyce MacDonald (b. 1923)   606

Grant, John Webster (b. 1919)   161, 228, 236, 501, 502

Grant, Robert (1779–1838)   388

Greek   73

Greek, ca. 110   302, 303

Greek, 3rd cent.   25, 26, 36, 37

Green, F. Pratt (b. 1903)   74, 170, 348, 420, 424, 452, 695, 696

Gregory the Great (540–604)   146, 147, 152

Grieve, J. Nichol   404

Grindal, Gracia (b. 1943)   256

Griswold, Alexander Viets (1766–1843)   368

Grubb, Edward (1854–1939)   681

Gurney, John Hampden (1802–1862)   625

Hall, William John (1793–1861)   656

Hammond, William (1719–1783)   181

Harkness, Georgia (1891–1974)   472

Hatch, Edwin (1835–1889)   508

Havergal, Frances Ridley (1836–1879)   514, 707

Hay, Granton Douglas (b. 1943)   447

Heber, Reginald (1783–1826)   117, 118, 258, 301, 362, 486

Hebrews 12:1–3   545

Hedge, Frederic Henry (1805–1890)   687, 688

Heermann, Johann (1585–1647)   158

Hensley, Lewis (1824–1905)   613

Herbert, George (1593–1633)   382, 402, 403, 487, 592

Herklots, Rosamond E. (b. 1905)   246, 674

Herman, Nikolaus (1480?–1561)   201

Hernaman, Claudia Frances (1838–1898)   142

Hewlett, Michael (b. 1916)   506, 507

Hilary of Poitiers (4th cent.)   223, 224

Hispanic folk song   113

Holland, Henry Scott (1847–1918)   596

Holmes, Oliver Wendell (1809–1894)   419

Hopkins, John Henry, Jr. (1820–1891)   128, 336

Hosmer, Frederick Lucian (1840–1929)   615

Housman, Laurence (1865–1959)   133, 134, 573

How, William Walsham (1823–1897)   52, 252, 254, 287, 632

Hughes, Donald W. (1911–1967)   148

Hull, Eleanor H. (1860–1935)   488

Hume, Ruth Fox (1922–1980)   103

Humphreys, Charles William (1840–1921)   312, 326

Hunterian MS. 83, 15th cent.   266

Hymnal 1940   56, 60, 81, 152, 193, 233, 234, 282, 283, 314, 320, 329, 330, 331, 390, 475, 619

Hymnal 1982   16, 17, 19, 20, 38, 39, 40, 41, 44, 45, 48, 63, 64, 91, 159, 162, 165, 166, 176, 177, 231, 232, 261, 262, 314, 320, 364

Hymn Book of the Anglican Church of Canada and the United church of Canada, The, 1971   131, 132

Hymns Ancient and Modern, 1861   59, 124, 127, 136, 137, 244, 248, 249, 263, 264, 518, 519, 520, 624

Hymns for the Festivals and Saints' Days of the Church of England, 1846   267

Hymns for the Young, ca. 1830   708

Idle, Christopher (b. 1938)   465, 466

Ingemann, Bernard Severin (1789–1862)   527

Irish, ca. 700   488

Isaiah 9:2–7   125, 126

Israeli round   714

Italian, 18th cent.   479

Jabusch, Willard F. (b. 1930)   536

Jacobi, John Christian (1670–1750)   515

Janzow, F. Samuel (b. 1913)   245

Jenkins, William Vaughan (1868–1920)   350

Jervois, William Henry Hammond (1852–1905) 338

Jewish liturgy, Medieval   372

John of Damascus (8th cent.)   198, 199, 200, 210

John 6   335

Johnson, James Weldon (1871–1938)   599

Joseph, Jane M. (1894–1929)   92

Joseph the Hymnographer (9th cent.)   237

K.   636, 637

Keble, John (1792–1866)   10, 656

Kelly, Thomas (1769–1855)   471, 483

Ken, Thomas (1637–1711)   11, 43, 380

Kethe, William (d. 1608?)   377, 378

Key, Francis Scott (1779–1843)   720

Kingo, Thomas Hansen (1634–1703)   298

Kingsley, Charles (1819–1875)   566

Kitchin, George William (1827–1912)   473

Knox, Ronald A. (1888–1957)   187

Composers, Arrangers, and Sources for Service Music

Elvey, Stephen (1805–1860)   S-37, S-178, S-206

Farrant, Richard (1525?–1580)   S-206
Felciano, Richard (b. 1930)   S-97, S-126, S-162, S-281
Fenstermaker, John, Jr. (b. 1942)   S-250
Fisk, Charles (1925–1983)   S-259
Flintoff, Luke (1678–1727)   S-239
Ford, Bruce E. (b. 1947)   S-2, S-11, S-16, S-34, S-41, S-59, S-99, S-107, S-115, S-132, S-180, S-185, S-190, S-196, S-208, S-213, S-237, S-242, S-248, S-254, S-261, S-267, S-282

Galley, Howard E. (b. 1929)   S-123
Garrett, George Mursell (1834–1897)   S-193, S-244
Gibbons, Christopher (1615–1676)   S-15
Goodson, R. (1655–1719)   S-229
Goss, John (1800–1880)   S-184, S-218, S-230, S-269
Greene, Maurice (1695–1755)   S-10, S-271

Hampton, Calvin (1938–1984)   S-105, S-127, S-266
Harrison, J. (1808–1871)   S-275
Hassler, Hans Leo (1564–1612)   S-89, S-117
Havergal, William Henry (1793–1870)   S-207, S-243
Hill, Jackson (b. 1941)   S-87, S-135
Hindle, John (1761–1796)   S-49
Hodges, Edward (1796–1867)   S-276
Hopkins, Edward John (1818–1901)   S-12, S-191
Hurd, David (b. 1950)   S-50, S-77, S-79, S-81, S-83, S-84, S-86, S-100, S-108, S-124, S-150, S-151, S-154, S-161, S-176, S-216, S-277
Hurford, Peter (b. 1930)   S-42
Hutto, Benjamin (b. 1947)   S-189, S-245, S-285
Hymnal 1982   S-74, S-102, S-157, S-201

Imperial Tune, The, 1630?   S-233
Intercession Mass   S-150
Irregular Tone, *see:*
  Plainsong, Irregular Tone

Jones, John (1728–1796)   S-182

Kelway, Thomas (1695–1749)   S-14
Koehring, David (b. 1940)   S-235

Lawes, W. (1596–1662)   S-246
Ley, Henry G. (1887–1962)   S-257
Litany of the Saints   S-30, S-64, S-95
Lloyd, Richard (b. 1933)   S-194
Longhurst, W. H. (1819–1904)   S-226
Luther, Martin (1483–1546)   S-283

MacFarren, George A. (1813–1887)   S-36, S-181
Martens, Mason (b. 1933)   S-29, S-30, S-56, S-63, S-64, S-71, S-72, S-73, S-76, S-78, S-80, S-82, S-94, S-104, S-109, S-111, S-122, S-133, S-136, S-137, S-139, S-143, S-144, S-145, S-148, S-152, S-153, S-160, S-167, S-168, S-170, S-171, S-172, S-273, S-288
Mass 8   S-116
Mass 9   S-92, S-115, S-159, S-203
Mass 11   S-84
Mass 13   S-273
Mass 15   S-274
Mass 16   S-85
Mass 18   S-94, S-122, S-160
Mathias, William (b. 1934)   S-98, S-128, S-165, S-278
McGregor, James (b. 1930)   S-59, S-89, S-117, S-121
Mealy, Norman (b. 1923)   S-46, S-208, S-222
Merbecke, John (1510?–1585?)   S-67, S-90, S-113, S-157, S-201
Missa de Angelis   S-116, S-143
Missa de Sancta Maria Magdalena   S-91, S-114, S-158, S-202
Missa Marialis   S-92, S-115, S-159, S-203
Missa orbis factor   S-77, S-79, S-81, S-83, S-84, S-151, S-176
Mode 1 antiphons   S-208
Mode 1 melody   S-170
Mode 2 melody   S-59
Mode 3 antiphon   S-237
Mode 6 melody   S-167, S-171
Mode 7 antiphon   S-196
Mode 8 antiphon   S-185
Monk, Edwin George (1819–1909)   S-4, S-230
Morley, William (1680–1731)   S-195
Mozarabic chant   S-123, S-140, S-272

Nares, James (1715–1783)   S-20, S-44
Naylor, John (1838–1897)   S-5, S-197
Near, Gerald R. (b. 1942)   S-131, S-155, S-156, S-166, S-279
New Plainsong   S-86, S-100, S-124, S-154, S-161, S-277
Noble, Thomas Tertius (1867–1953)   S-38
Norris, T. (1741–1790)   S-207

Oakley, Herbert S. (1830–1903)   S-225
Old Scottish Chant   S-204
Ouseley, Frederick A. Gore (1825–1909)   S-198
Oxford Chant   S-48

Pinkham, Daniel (b. 1923)   S-212, S-265
Plainsong   S-119, S-122
Plainsong, Irregular Tone   S-237, S-253
Plainsong, Mode 1   S-84, S-92, S-99
Plainsong, Mode 3   S-85
Plainsong, Mode 4   S-94, S-103, S-104, S-274
Plainsong, Mode 5   S-115, S-116, S-159
Plainsong, Mode 6   S-143
Plainsong, Mode 7   S-273
Plainsong, Mode 8   S-203
Plainsong, Te Deum Tone   S-121, S-134, S-137, S-139

Plainsong, Te Deum (Solemn) Tone S-282
Plainsong, Tone 1 S-177, S-208, S-228, S-267
Plainsong, Tone 1 Introit Form S-46
Plainsong, Tone 2 S-3, S-8, S-217
Plainsong, Tone 3 S-213, S-237
Plainsong, Tone 4 S-34, S-41, S-228, S-254
Plainsong, Tone 5 S-223
Plainsong, Tone 7 S-2, S-11, S-16, S-196, S-228
Plainsong, Tone 8 S-180, S-185, S-205, S-228, S-231, S-248, S-261
Plainsong, Tone 8 (Solemn) S-185
Plainsong, Tonus Peregrinus S-151, S-176, S-177, S-190, S-208, S-228, S-242
Powell, Robert (b. 1932) S-129, S-163, S-280
Proulx, Richard (b. 1937) S-95, S-96, S-125, S-130, S-134, S-140, S-164
Pulkingham, Betty Carr (b. 1928) S-247
Purcell, Henry (1659–1695) S-221
Purcell, Thomas (d. 1682?) S-255, S-268

Ritchie, J. Marcus (b. 1946) S-227
Robinson, John (1682–1762) S-178
Robinson, McNeil, II (b. 1943) S-61, S-88, S-138, S-141, S-146, S-147, S-149
Roper, E. Stanley (1878–1953) S-263
Rorem, Ned (b. 1923) S-220, S-240
Rutter, John (b. 1945) S-101, S-236

Schola Antiqua S-85, S-274
Schramm, Victor Judson (1944–1984) S-27
Schubert, Franz Peter (1797–1828) S-96, S-130, S-164
Slavonic Chant S-288
Smart, Henry (1813–1879) S-270

Soaper, J. (1743–1794) S-183
Sowerby, Leo (1895–1968) S-93
Stainer, John (1840–1901) S-18
Standing Commission on Church Music, The, 1979 S-3, S-8, S-177, S-196, S-217, S-223, S-228, S-231, S-237, S-253
Stanford, Charles Villiers (1852–1924) S-39
Steel, David Warren (b. 1947) S-272
Stewart, C. Hylton (1884–1932) S-262

Talbot, George S. (1875–1918) S-9, S-40
Te Deum Tone, see:
   Plainsong, Te Deum Tone
Teesdale, C. (1782–1855) S-6
Tomlinson, R. (fl. 1724) S-19, S-232
Tonus Peregrinus, see:
   Plainsong, Tonus Peregrinus
Turle, James (1802–1882) S-178, S-209, S-221

Urwin, Ray W. (b. 1950) S-169

Verbum caro factum est S-89, S-117

Walmisley, Thomas Attwood (1814–1856) S-7, S-249
Walter, William Henry (1825–1893) S-47
Wesley, Samuel Sebastian (1810–1876) S-251
Wesley, Samuel (1766–1837) S-187, S-241
White, Jack Noble (b. 1938) S-35
Willan, Healey (1880–1968) S-91, S-114, S-158, S-202
Wise, Michael (1648?–1687) S-200
Woodward, Richard (1744–1777) S-17, S-43, S-264

Composers, Arrangers, and Sources for Hymns

African work song 611
Afro-American spiritual 172, 325, 468, 529, 648, 676
Afro-American spiritual, 19th cent. 99
Ahle, Johann Rudolph (1625–1673) 440, 631
Airs sur les hymnes sacrez, odes et noëls, 1623 203, 206
Albright, William (b. 1944) 196, 227, 303
Allison, Richard (16th cent.) 259
Alte Catholische Geistliche Kirchengesäng, 1599 81
American folk melody 304, 620, 664
Antes, John (1740–1811) 389
Antiphonale Sarisburiense, Vol. II 15, 44
Antiphoner, 1681 1, 348, 623
Antiphoner, 1728 282
Antiphoner, 1753 285, 448
Arnatt, Ronald (b. 1930) 74, 443
Arne, Augustine (1710–1778) 57
Auserlesene Catholische Geistliche Kirchengeseng, 1623 400, 618

Bach, Johann Sebastian (1685–1750) 46, 61, 91, 108, 135, 141, 168, 174, 186, 244, 309, 310, 334, 336, 484, 497, 505, 669, 681, 688
Bain, J. L. Macbeth (1840?–1925) 517
Bancroft, Henry Hugh (b. 1904) 75
Barnby, Joseph (1838–1896) 42, 427
Barnes, Edward Shippen (1887–1958) 96
Barthélémon, François Hippolyte (1741–1808) 11
Basque carol 265
Beebe, Hank (b. 1926) 177, 262
Beethoven, Ludwig van (1770–1872) 376
Benedictine Processional, 14th cent. 103
Biggs, Arthur Henry (1906–1954) 654
Billings, William (1746–1800) 715
Bode, Arnold George Henry (1866–1952) 647
Bohemian Brethren, Kirchengeseng, 1566 224, 430
Book of Psalmody, A, 1718 668
Booke of Musicke, 1591 643
Bortniansky, Dimitri S. (1751–1825) 574

Fedak, Alfred V. (b. 1953)   250
Ferguson, William Harold (1874–1950)   289
Filitz, Friedrich (1804–1860)   479
Finnish folk melody   232, 655
Fischel, Donald (b. 1950)   178
Fleur des noëls, 1535   152
Foster, Thomas (b. 1938)   190
Freiburg MS., 14th cent.   33
French carol   96, 145
French carol, 17th cent.   324
French church melody, Mode 5   314, 357
French folk melody, 16th cent.   114
Freylinghausen, 1704   389
Freylinghausen, Johann Anastasius
   (1670–1739)   375
Fritsch, Ahasuerus (1629–1701)   108
Fyfe, Lois (b. 1927)   521, 637

Gaelic melody   8
Galley, Howard E. (b. 1929)   157
Gallican chant   157
Gardiner, William (1770–1853)   609
Gauntlet, Henry John (1805–1876)   102, 194,
   267, 279, 545, 682
Gawthorn, Nathaniel (18th cent.)   434, 578
Geist und Lehr-reiches Kirchen und Haus Buch,
   1694   141
Geistliche Gesangbüchlein, 1524   319
Geistliche Kirchengesang, 1623   505
Geistliche lieder auffs new gebessert und gemehrt,
   1539   80, 575
Geistliche Lieder, 1533   184, 634
Geistliche Lieder, 1543   132, 143, 297
Geistreiches Gesang-buch, 1698   286
Geistreiches Gesangbuch, 1704   47, 530
Gelineau, Joseph (b. 1920)   696
George, Graham (b. 1912)   156
German carol, 14th cent.   107
German folk song   48, 616
Gerovitch, Eliezer (1844–1914)   425
*Gesangbuch…der Herzogl. Wirtembergischen
   katholischen Hofkapelle* 1784   210
Geystliche gesangk Buchleyn, 1524   7, 139, 185,
   186
Ghanaian folk song   602
Gibbons, Orlando (1583–1625)   21, 264, 315,
   328, 346, 499, 617, 670, 697, 703
Gillespie, James (b. 1929)   518
Gläser, Carl Gotthilf (1784–1829)   493
Goss, John (1800–1880)   410
Goudimel, Claude (1514–1572)   36, 67, 258
Graduale, 1685   17, 120
Graduale Romanum, 1974   354
Gray, Alan (1855–1935)   59
Greatorex, Walter (1877–1949)   438
Griffiths, Vernon (b. 1894)   31, 455
Gross Catolisch Gesangbuch, 1631   341
Gruber, Franz Xaver (1787–1863)   111

Hallock, Peter R. (b. 1923)   418
Hamburger Musikalisches handbuch, 1690   540
Hampton, Calvin (1938–1984)   403, 407, 456,
   469, 659
Hancock, Gerre (b. 1934)   350
Handel, George Frideric (1685–1759)   100, 459,
   481, 546, 629
Harding, James Proctor (1850–1911)   117
Harmonia Sacra, ca. 1760   188, 257
Harwood, Basil (1859–1949)   444
Hasidic melody   536
Hassler, Hans Leo (1564–1612)   168, 169, 298,
   575, 669
Hastings, Thomas (1784–1872)   685
Hatton, John (d. 1793)   544
Havergal, William Henry (1793–1870)   7, 47,
   66, 127, 414, 530, 656
Haweis, Thomas (1734–1820)   72, 212
Haydn, Franz Joseph (1732–1809)   28, 29, 409,
   522
Haydn, Johann Michael (1737–1809)   533, 637
Hayes, William (1706–1777)   387
Hayne, Leighton George (1836–1883)   613
Hebrew melody   372, 393, 401, 714
Heinlein, Paul (1626–1686)   323
Held, Wilbur (b. 1914)   246
Helmore, Thomas (1811–1890)   56
Hemy, Henri Frédéric (1818–1888)   558
Herbst, Martin (1654–1681)   150
Hermann, Nikolaus (1480?–1561)   201
Hill, Jackson (b. 1941)   122, 123, 329
Hillert, Richard (b. 1923)   417
Hilton, John (1599–1657)   140
Himlischer Lieder, 1641   173
Hintze, Jakob (1622–1702)   135, 174
Hispanic folk melody   113
Hodges, Edward (1796–1867)   376
Holden, Oliver (1765–1844)   450
Holst, Gustav Theodore (1874–1934)   112
Hopkins, Edward John (1818–1901)   345
Hopkins, John Henry (1861–1945)   293
Hopkins, John Henry, Jr. (1820–1891)   128, 503
Hopkirk, James (1908–1972)   600
Horsley, William (1774–1858)   167
Howard, Samuel (1710–1782)   666
Howells, Herbert (1892–1983)   582, 665
Hughes, John (1873–1932)   594, 690
Hullah, John Pyke (19th cent.)   447, 483
Hundert Arien, 1694   187, 269
Hunterian MS., 15th cent.   266
Hurd, David (b. 1950)   35, 41, 104, 268, 322,
   325, 395, 459, 463, 503, 507, 549, 629
Hymnal 1940   299, 697
Hymnal 1982   173, 203, 364, 532, 550, 641, 663
*Hymnau a Thonau er Gwasanaeth yr Eglwys yng
   Nghymru,* 1865   68, 607
Hymns Ancient and Modern, 1875   20, 137, 353,
   365, 371, 372, 401, 537

Oude en Nieuwe Hollantse Boerenlities en
Contradanseu, 1710   215, 495
Owen, William (1813–1893)   307

Pageant of the Shearmen and Tailors, 15th
cent.   247
Palestrina, Giovanni Pierluigi da (1525–1594)
208
Palmer, George Herbert (1846–1926)   440, 631
Paris MS., 12th cent.   202
Parker, Horatio (1864–1919)   222
Parratt, Walter (1841–1924)   355
Parry, Charles Hubert Hastings (1848–1918)
278, 367, 432, 597, 653, 695
Parry, Joseph (1841–1903)   349, 640, 699
Peace, Lister R. (1885–1969)   508
Pelz, Walter (b. 1926)   49
Petrie Collection of Irish Melodies, Part II, 1902   84
Pettman, Edgar (1865–1943)   265
Piae Cantiones, 1582   82, 92, 97, 98, 270
Pilgrim Hymnal, 1958   610
Plainsong, Mode 1   5, 22, 32, 55, 56, 85, 103,
136, 155, 161, 162, 165, 183, 217, 220, 223, 226,
261, 283, 361
Plainsong, Mode 2   4, 18, 40, 63, 122, 123, 134,
146, 263, 271, 311, 519, 622, 650
Plainsong, Mode 3   2, 166, 329
Plainsong, Mode 4   26, 60, 273
Plainsong, Mode 5   16, 19, 330
Plainsong, Mode 6   606
Plainsong, Mode 7   33, 354
Plainsong, Mode 7, 12th cent.   320
Plainsong, Mode 8   13, 15, 27, 30, 38, 44, 45,
202, 233, 236, 354, 502, 504
Playford, John (1623–1686)   50, 251, 677
Powell, Robert (b. 1932)   70
Praetorius, Michael (1571–1621)   81, 124, 193,
219, 235, 710
Prichard, Rowland Hugh (1811–1887)   460, 657
Processionale, 15th cent.   56
Processionale, 1697   314, 357
Proulx, Richard (b. 1937)   343, 399, 405, 431,
473, 477, 494, 536, 560, 576
Psalm and Choralbuch, 1719   475
Psalmen, 1685   192
Psalmes of David in Prose and Meeter, The, 1635
50, 121, 251, 352, 584, 677, 684, 709
Psalmodia Evangelica, Part II, 1789   182, 436
Psalmodia Sacra, oder Andächtige und Schöne
Gesange, 1715   66, 127, 414
Pseaumes cinquante de David, 1547   408, 598
Pseaumes octante trois de David, 1551   149, 359,
377, 378, 380, 404
Pulkingham, Betty (b. 1928)   178, 335
Purcell, Henry (1659–1695)   518

Ratcliff, Cary (b. 1953)   133
Ravenscroft, Thomas (1592?–1635?)   126, 259,
364, 415, 526

Redhead, Richard (1820–1901)   142, 171, 241,
615
Redner, Lewis H. (1831–1908)   79
Reinagle, Alexander Robert (1799–1877)   644
Reinecke, Carl H. (1824–1910)   111
Repository of Sacred Music, A, Part II, 1813   437,
686
Rhea, Arthur (b. 1919)   678
Rheinfelsisches Deutsches Catholisches Gesangbuch,
1666   14, 64
Robb, John Donald (b. 1892)   113
Robbins, Howard Chandler (1876–1952)   521
Roberts, John (1822–1877)   423
Robinson, McNeil, II (b. 1943)   95
Rockstro, William Smith (1823–1895)   341
Rome MS., 12th cent.   161, 162
Roth, Robert (b. 1928)   176
Routley, Erik (1917–1982)   347, 402, 605, 639
Russian Orthodox hymn   560

Sachs, Hans (1494–1576)   61, 62, 484, 485
Sacred Harp, The, 1844   636
Sacred Melodies, 1815   609
Sanctus trope, 11th cent.   82
Sarum Melody   166
Schalk, Carl Flentge (b. 1929)   333, 698
Scheidt, Samuel (1587–1654)   465
Schein, Johann Hermann (1586–1630)   198
Schlesische Volkslieder, 1842   383
Schola Antiqua, 1983   2, 32, 123, 155, 161, 165,
261, 283, 361, 622
Scholefield, Clement Cottevill (1839–1904)   24
Schop, Johann (d. 1665?)   91, 336
Schulz, Johann Abraham Peter (1747–1800)
291
Schütz, Heinrich (1585–1672)   452
Second Supplement to Psalmody in Miniature, ca.
1780   321, 474
Shaw, Geoffrey Turton (1879–1943)   88, 573
Shaw, Martin Fallas (1875–1958)   145, 247, 405,
476, 534
Sheets, Dorothy Howell (b. 1915)   585
Shrubsole, William (1760–1806)   451
Sicilian melody   344, 708
Slater, Gordon (1896–1979)   209, 603
Smart, Henry Thomas (1813–1879)   93, 368,
555, 563, 700
Smith, Alfred Morton (1879–1971)   306, 406
Smith, Henry Percy (1825–1898)   660
Smith, Isaac (1734?–1805)   548
Smith, K. D. (b. 1928)   127
Smith, Robert (1780–1829)   658
Sohren, Peter (1630?–1692?)   375
Solesmes,   271
Songs and Games of American Children,
1884–1911   468
Songs of Praise, 1925   249, 331, 437
Source Unknown   77, 131

Index of Tune Names

Deo gracias   218, 449
Detroit   674
Deus tuorum militum   285, 448
Diademata   494
Dicamus laudes Domino   16
Dickinson College   593, 649
Dies est laetitiae   97
Dir, dir, Jehovah   540
Distler   572
Divinum mysterium   82
Dix   119, 288
Dominus regit me   646
Dona nobis pacem   712
Donne   140
Donne secours   472
Down Ampney   516
Du Lebensbrot, Herr Jesu
   Christ   375
Du meiner Seelen   23
Duke Street   544
Dulce carmen   559
Dundee   126, 526, 709
Dunedin   31, 455
Dunlap's Creek   276
Durham   415

Earth and All Stars   412
East Acklam   424
Easter Hymn   207
Eastview   543
Ebenezer, see:
   Ton-y-Botel
Edmonton   257
Ein feste Burg (isometric)   688
Ein feste Burg (rhythmic)   687
Eisenach, see:
   Mach's mit mir, Gott
Elbing, see:
   Du Lebensbrot, Herr Jesu
   Christ
Ellacombe   210
Ellers   345
Elmhurst   133
Eltham   434, 578
Ely, see:
   Manchester
Engelberg   296, 420, 477
England's Lane   88
Epworth   476
Erhalt uns, Herr (isometric)
   143, 297
Erhalt uns, Herr (rhythmic)
   132
Ermuntre dich   91
Erschienen ist der herrlich Tag
   201
Es flog ein kleins
   Waldvögelein   48, 616
Es ist das Heil   298

Es ist ein Ros   81
Evening Hymn   37
Eventide   662
Ewing   624
Ex more docti mystico   146

Faciem ejus videtis   240
Fairest Lord Jesus, see:
   Schönster Herr Jesu
Faith   689
Festal Song   551
Festival Canticle   417
Finnian   492, 506
Fisk of Gloucester   190
Flentge   698
Forest Green   78, 398, 705
Fortunatus   179
Foundation   636
Franconia   656
Frankfort, see:
   Wie schön leuchtet
   (isometric)
Frohlockt mit Freud   452
From heaven high, see:
   Vom Himmel hoch

Gabriel's Message   265
Gardiner   609
Gartan   84
Gaudeamus pariter   200, 237
Gelobt sei Gott   205
General Seminary   382
Geneva   515
Georgetown   661
Gerontius   445
Gloria   96
Gloria, laus, et honor   155
Go Down, Moses   648
Go Tell It on the Moutain   99
God Rest You Merry   105
Gonfalon Royal   86, 221, 234
Gopsal   481
Got sei Dank   47, 530
Gott sei gelobet   319
Gottes Sohn ist kommen   53
Gräfenberg, see:
   Nun danket all und
   bringet Ehr
Grafton   249, 331
Grand Isle   293
Grand Prairie   197
Greensleeves   115
Grosser Gott   366

Halifax   459, 629
Hall   463
Halton Holgate   280, 351, 706
Hampton   95
Hanover   388

Heinlein, see:
   Aus der Tiefe rufe ich
Helmsley   57
Herald, Sound   70
Hereford   704
Herr Jesu Christ (isometric)
   310
Herr Jesu Christ (rhythmic)   3
Herr Jesu Christ, meins Lebens
   Licht, see: Breslau
Herzlich tut mich verlangen
   (rhythmic)   169
Herzlich tut mich verlangen
   [Passion Chorale] (isometric)
   168, 669
Herzliebster Jesu   158
Hilariter   211
Hollingside   707
Holy Manna   238, 580
Holy Name, see:
   Louez Dieu
Horsley   167
Hosanna   486
Houston   490
Hyfrydol   460, 657
Hymn to Joy   376

I Am the Bread of Life   335
Ich ruf zu dir   634
Immense caeli Conditor   32
In Babilone   215, 495
In Bethlehem   246
In dulci jubilo   107
In paradisum   354
Innisfree Farm   34
Innsbruck, see:
   O Welt, ich muss dich lassen
Intercessor   695
Irby   102
Irish   428

Jacob   242, 466
Jacob's Ladder   453
Jam lucis orto sidere   217
Jerusalem   597
Jesu dulcis memoria   18, 134,
   650
Jesu, Jesu, du mein Hirt   323
Jesu, Joy, see:
   Werde munter
Jesu, meine Freude   701
Jesu, nostra redemptio
   (equalist rhythm)   38, 236
Jesu, nostra redemptio
   (syllabic rhythm)   233
Jesus, all my gladness, see:
   Jesu, meine Freude
Jesus, meine Zuversicht   313
Julion   268, 507

Index of First Lines

Lo! what a cloud of witnesses   545
Look there! the Christ, our Brother, comes
   196, 197
Lord, be thy word my rule   626
Lord Christ, when first thou cam'st to
   earth   598
Lord, dismiss us with thy blessing   344
Lord, enthroned in heavenly splendor   307
Lord, for ever at thy side   670
Lord God, you now have set your servant
   free   499
Lord Jesus, Sun of Righteousness   144
Lord Jesus, think on me   641
Lord, make us servants of your peace   593
Lord of all being, throned afar   419
Lord of all hopefulness, Lord of all joy   482
Lord, thou hast searched me and dost
   know   702
Lord, we have come at your own invitation   348
Lord, who throughout these forty days   142
Lord, whose love through humble service   610
Lord, you give the great commission   528
Love came down at Christmas   84
Love divine, all loves excelling   657
Love's redeeming work is done   188, 189
Lully, lullay, thou little tiny child   247

Make a joyful noise unto the Lord
   (Singt dem Herren!)   710
Many and great, O God, are thy works   385
Master of eager youth, *see:*
   Jesus, our mighty Lord
May choirs of angels lead you   356
May the grace of Christ our Savior   351
Morning glory, starlit sky   585
Morning has broken   8
Most High, omnipotent, good Lord   406, 407
Most Holy God, the Lord of heaven   31, 32
My country, 'tis of thee   717
My faith looks up to thee   691
My God, accept my heart this day   697
My God, how wonderful thou art   643
My God, I love thee; not because, *see:*
   I love thee, Lord, but not because
My God, thy table now is spread   321
My Shepherd will supply my need   664
My song is love unknown   458

Nature with open volume stands   434
New every morning is the love   10
New songs of celebration render   413
Not far beyond the sea, nor high   422
Not here for high and holy things   9
Nova, nova   266
Now greet the swiftly changing year   250
Now Holy Spirit, ever One   19, 20
Now let us all right merry be, *see:*
   From heaven above to earth I come
Now let us all with one accord   146, 147
Now let us sing our praise to God   16, 17

Now, my tongue, the mystery telling
   329, 330, 331
Now quit your care   145
Now thank we all our God   396, 397
Now that the daylight fills the sky   3, 4
Now the day is over   42
Now the green blade riseth from the buried
   grain   204
Now the silence   333
Now yield we thanks and praise   108

O all ye works of God, now come   428
O beautiful for spacious skies   719
O bless the Lord, my soul!   411
O blest Creator of the light, *see:*
   O blest Creator, source of light
O blest Creator, source of light   27, 28
O Bread of life, for sinners broken   342
O brightness of the immortal Father's face   37
O Christ, the Word Incarnate   632
O Christ, you are both light and day   40, 41
O come, all ye faithful   83
O come, O come, Emmanuel   56
O day of God, draw nigh   600, 601
O day of peace that dimly shines   597
O day of radiant gladness   48
O day of rest and gladness, *see:*
   O day of radiant gladness
O Food to pilgrims given   308, 309
O Food of men wayfaring, *see:*
   O Food to pilgrims given
O for a closer walk with God   683, 684
O for a thousand tongues to sing   493
O gladsome Light, O grace   36
O God, creation's secret force   14, 15
O God of Bethel, by whose hand   709
O God of earth and altar   591
O God of every nation   607
O God of love, O King of peace   578
O God of love, to thee we bow   350
O God of truth, O Lord of might   21, 22
O God, our help in ages past   680
O God, to those who here profess   352
O God, unseen yet ever near   332
O God, we praise thee, and confess   364
O God, whom neither time nor space   251
O gracious Light, Lord Jesus Christ   25, 26
O heavenly Word, eternal Light   63, 64
O holy city, seen of John   582, 583
O Holy Spirit, by whose breath   501, 502
O Jesus Christ, may grateful hymns be
   rising   590
O Jesus, crowned with all renown   292
O Jesus, I have promised   655
O Jesus, joy of loving hearts   649, 650
O Light of Light, Love given birth   133, 134
O little town of Bethlehem   78, 79
O Lord Most High, eternal King   220, 221
O love, how deep, how broad, how high
   448, 449

When Christ's appearing was made known
131, 132
When I survey the wondrous cross   474
When in our music God is glorified   420
When Israel was in Egypt's land   648
When Jesus died to save us   322
When Jesus left his Father's throne   480
When Jesus went to Jordan's stream   139
When Jesus wept, the falling tear   715
When morning gilds the skies   427
When Stephen, full of power and grace   243
Where charity and love prevail   581
Where cross the crowded ways of life   609
Where is this stupendous stranger?   491
Where true charity and love dwell   606
Wherefore, O Father, we thy humble
servants   338

While shepherds watched their flocks by
night   94, 95
Who are these like stars appearing   286
Wilt thou forgive that sin, where I begun
140, 141
Word of God, come down on earth   633

Ye holy angels bright   625
Ye servants of God, your Master proclaim   535
Ye watchers and ye holy ones   618
Ye who claim the faith of Jesus   268, 269
You are the Christ, O Lord   254
You, Lord, we praise in songs of
celebration   319
Your love, O God, has called us here   353

Zion, praise thy Savior, singing   320